PENGUIN BOOKS

The Ultimate Trivia Quiz Game B

The Ultimate Trivia Quiz Game Book

Edited by Maureen Hiron

Penguin Books

Penguin Books Ltd, Harmondsworth, Middlesex, England
Viking Penguin Inc., 40 West 23rd Street, New York, New York 10010, U.S.A.
Penguin Books Australia Ltd, Ringwood, Victoria, Australia
Penguin Books Canada Limited, 2801 John Street, Markham, Ontario, Canada L3R 1B4
Penguin Books (N.Z.) Ltd, 182–190 Wairau Road, Auckland 10, New Zealand

First published 1984
Reprinted 1985 (three times), 1986 (three times)

Typeset by CCC, printed and bound in Great Britain by
William Clowes Limited, Beccles and London

Typeset in Century

Contents

Introduction vii

- How to Play the Book viii
- Onwards, Ever Onwards x
- Quizwrangle xii
- Tic Tac Trivia xiv
- Count-up xv
- Trivel Travia xv
- Get Out of That xvi

THE ULTIMATE TRIVIA QUIZ 1

Introduction

'What have Dr Benjamin Spock, Errol Flynn and the Emperor Nero got in common?' It is a funny question and it has a funny answer. It is not that they were all two-legged or left-handed. The intriguing thing about this unlikely trio is that they all competed in the Olympic Games (at rowing, boxing and chariot-racing respectively)!

Don't worry if you didn't get that one right. To date, no one we have tested has guessed the answer. But you must admit that it is rather fun to know it; and – here's the odd thing – once you have heard it you can hardly forget it. You could even add Princess Anne and General 'Blood and Guts' Patton to the list if you liked.

Try one more. You must have seen *Casablanca* at least once. Try to remember – how many times did Humphrey Bogart say, 'Play it again, Sam'? Once, twice, three times ...? Wrong, he never actually used those words. But 'Here's looking at you, kid' came in four times. It is not earthshaking – you couldn't write a thesis about it – but it is good trivia!

Unlike some quiz books, the questions in *The Ultimate Trivia Quiz Game Book* have not been graded into easy, fairly easy, difficult, really tricky and impossible. After all, you *could* regard every question as coming under one of two headings: (a) Easy – you know the answer; or (b) Difficult – you don't. Perhaps a better way is to consider the questions as ranging from 'What you do know', through 'What you do know but can't think of at the spur of the moment' and 'What you didn't know but are now pleased to know', right up to 'What you are amused to know and intend bringing up in conversation at the earliest possible opportunity!'

Quiz games have been around for a long time. They started by relying purely and simply on the knowledge of the competitors and proved excellent and popular listening and viewing on radio and TV. But don't you wince a little when you hear that a contestant will answer questions on 'The Italian influence on Persian art from 1907 to 1911'?

Well, here's how this book is different. Together with over 10,000 questions covering a very wide range of knowledge, we suggest a number of games that you may like to try out in conjunction with them. Some need a board (diagrams are provided), some don't. *Of course you can play an absolutely straight quiz game with no trimmings or you can even test yourself.* What is more, you can invent your own games: you are not likely to run out of questions! Just suppose that there are two of you and you are both keen chess players. Can you see the possibilities? Get a question right and you can make a move; get it wrong and you forfeit your turn. It will lead to a wild game, but it will be fun. Invent your own game – here are all the questions you will need for some while.

By the way, if you are asking a competitor a question, try not to be too pedantic about their answer. If you are asking how much each of the 2,300,000 limestone blocks of the Great Pyramid weighs (answer, about $2\frac{1}{2}$ tons), accept anything from 2 to 3 tons. But if you ask 'How many legs has a spider?' (eight), don't accept 'About nine'!

With over 10,000 questions it is just possible that there may be an occasional inaccuracy. We call them 'deliberate mistakes' in order to keep you on your toes. If, when answering a question, you can prove beyond reasonable doubt that our answer is wrong or out of date, then don't call us, we'll call you. In the mean time, score double marks at whatever game you are playing. We have tried to avoid questions like 'What is the world high-jump record?' which can obviously change before publication, but if we have asked for the date of the earliest known something or other, it is just possible that a new archaeological discovery may be made next month . . .

Above all, enjoy the games. Remember that although general knowledge helps, the best games also contain elements of luck and strategy as well.

How to Play the Book

All answers are on the following left-hand page, overleaf, so that there is no need to grub around the back of the book. Nor is there any need to turn back, unless your questionee has forgotten the question. Keep going through the book in numerical order. Even if only one question is answered from each quiz, ask the next contestant a question from the following quiz. This eliminates cheating. Only when you have reached Quiz 371 do you return to the beginning of the book, to start again with the middle section (372–742), and again for Quizzes 743–1113. In the fullness of time, you may be lucky enough to be asked a question that you or someone else has had before – and you might even remember the answer!

All the Trivia Quizzes contain nine questions. They are roughly grouped into the following categories, which remain the same throughout the book:

1. Ragbag
2. Mainly historical
3. Mainly geographical
4. Literature, mythology and the Bible
5. Sport
6. Entertainment
7. Leisure, people and art
8. Music, in all its manifestations
9. Loosely, science and natural history

So, if you choose or are given question 5, be prepared for sport.

Following are some of the games that you can play competitively, between individuals or teams. Game charts are provided.

Some hints on equipment

If you haven't got any dice or, for Quizwrangle, the rather special ten-sided dice which are not readily available in the shops, then you can easily find an alternative way of selecting question numbers. For Quizwrangle, take a pack of cards and remove the Kings, Queens and Jacks. Shuffle the remaining forty cards and simply turn up the top three for the first player (10 counts as zero in Quizwrangle). Any rejects are put in a discard pile and new cards taken from the top of the pack (this is the equivalent of rerolling dice). Only when the stockpile is finished are the cards reshuffled and used again.

Similarly, if you are playing a game such as 'Onwards, Ever Onwards' that needs only six categories, you can sort out the appropriate twenty-four cards and use them in the same way. Use two packs if you like; not everyone has dice in the house, but a pack of cards is usually within range.

Onwards, Ever Onwards

Equipment needed This book; 1 standard six-sided die; a distinguishing marker for each player.

All players place their marker on the *Start* square. Decide the order of play. Then each player throws the die and moves his or her marker the number of squares shown on the die, following the direction of the arrows. If you land on a zero your turn is over, and the die passes to the next contestant. Land on any other number, and an opponent asks you the question appropriate to that number from the next quiz. If you answer correctly you retain the die and throw again, and continue to do so until you answer incorrectly or land on a zero, when your turn ends.

To win You *must* answer a question that takes you on to or past the *Finish* square. You *cannot* win just by throwing the dice and galloping past the post.

Note In theory, you could win without your opponents ever getting their paws on the die; but it won't happen – well, it hasn't yet.

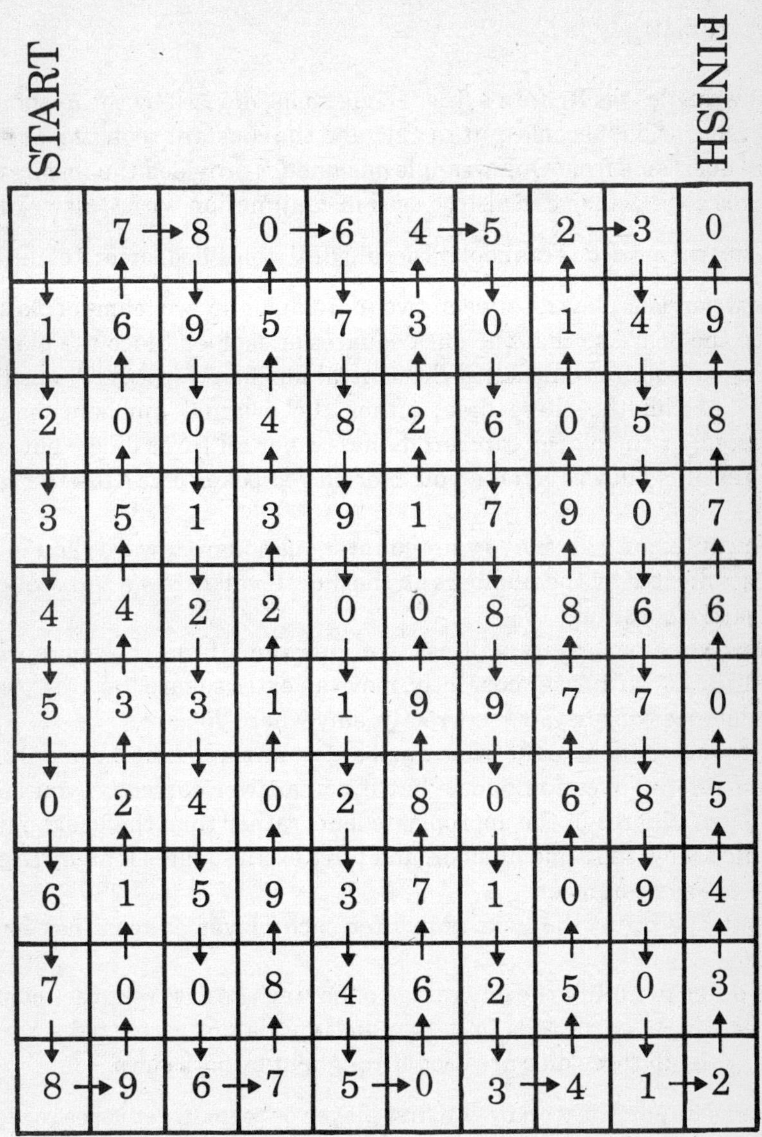

ONWARDS, EVER ONWARDS

Quizwrangle

Quizwrangle was Britain's first Trivia game, devised by the authors of this tome. It has become quite a cult, and the constant requests for even more questions from Quizwrangle *aficionados* provided the inspiration for this book, which can also be used in conjunction with Quizwrangle.

Equipment needed This book; 3 decahedral (ten-sided) dice; 9 counters.

Quizwrangle is played between two individuals or two teams of players. Place the board so that the dark squares at each end face the players. Place one counter on each of the central numbered spaces. Teams take turns to roll the three dice: either the original numbers may be accepted, or the player can reroll one, two or all three dice – but only one reroll is allowed. (Have you ever played poker dice? It's the same idea.)

You automatically move your counter one square towards you in the lanes indicated by the numbers on the dice. If you throw a zero, tough – you miss a question!

Now your opponents will ask you questions from the appropriate numbers. If you answer correctly, move an extra square towards you in that lane; if you answer incorrectly, stay where you are.

If your dice include the same number two or three times, you only get to answer the question once – but if you answer correctly, you move *two* extra squares in the appropriate lane, rather than the usual one, if *two* dice show the same number, and *three* extra squares if all *three* dice show the same number.

Continue on to the next quiz after each player or team has had a turn.

In order to nullify the advantage of having the first roll, the team or player which starts rolls only two dice and is not permitted a reroll. After this, all three dice are used throughout by both sides.

To win The game is won by the first player or team to get three (or four – decide *before* play begins) counters into the dark squares nearest to them. It's rather like nine simultaneous tugs-of-war.

QUIZWRANGLE BOARD

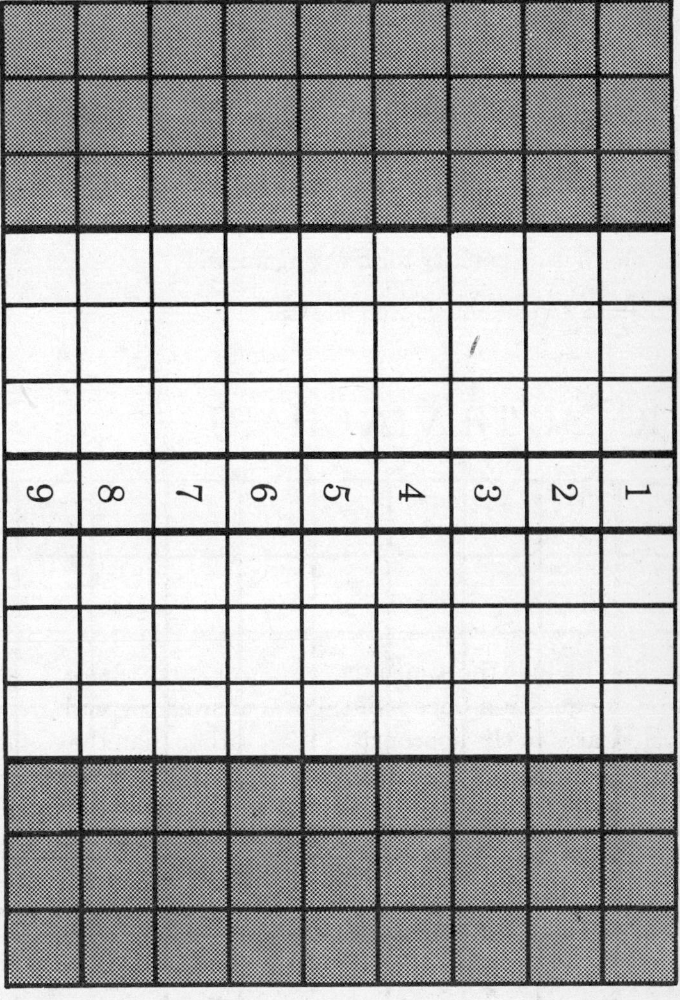

Tic Tac Trivia

For two or more players or teams.

How to win Get your initials, or other distinguishing feature, in a consecutive row of three, horizontally, vertically or diagonally.

How to play Choose any section. Another player asks the question, and if you answer correctly, place your mark in any space along the line of that section only. One question per turn, and play passes in rotation. There is no penalty for a wrong answer.

Note It can pay to defend as well as attack!

TIC TAC TRIVIA CHART

T I C T A C T R I V I A

1									
2									
3									
4									
5									
6									
7									
8									
9									

Count-up

For any number of players.

Equipment needed A pack of cards with Kings, Queens, Jacks and 10s removed; scorepad.

First decide the order of play. Then shuffle the cards and place them face down. Each player turns up the top card and is asked the question relating to the number on that card from the next quiz. Score 1 point for each correct answer. The first player to reach 10 points wins (or any other number of points that you agree upon *before* play starts).

Trivel Travia

You can play a very simple game to while away the time spent in travelling by car, train, coach or plane.

In turn, each player has the option of selecting a category of his choice – for which he scores *1* point if he gets the answer right – or allowing the opposition (the player on his left, if there are more than two contestants) to choose the category. If the player gets this one right, he scores *2* points. The winner is the first player to collect 15 points (or any other tally that you choose).

Get Out of That

Equipment needed This book; a small distinguishing marker for each player.

For any number of players.

All players place their markers in the centre circle. Each player is asked question 1 in turn – not question 1 from the same quiz: plough on through the book. (There is an advantage to being quizzed early, so we suggest that you cut a pack of cards to determine the order of play.)

If you answer correctly, move your marker one space outwards on the circle to any number, even if there is already someone else's marker on it. If you answer incorrectly, stay put, and have another go at category 1 when it is your turn again.

The procedure for the next round is as follows. If you have moved, you must now correctly answer a question from the category whose number you are occupying, so that you can continue your journey outwards. You may choose which of the two adjoining numbers to move on to, but once you've moved, you cannot change your mind. That is the category on which you will next be quizzed in the next round. If you answer incorrectly, you remain where you are until your next turn, when you will be asked another question from the same category.

The first player to reach the *Winner's Enclosure* is the winner.

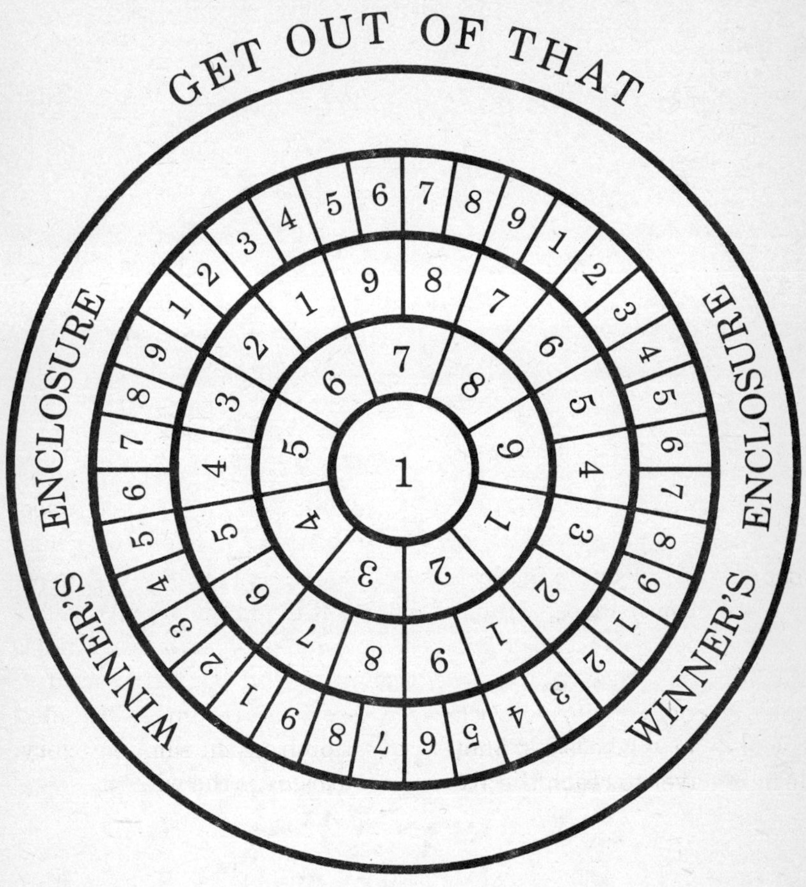
GET OUT OF THAT
WINNER'S ENCLOSURE
WINNER'S ENCLOSURE

Q

1

1. From what material are millefiori ornaments made?
2. In which war did the Battle of Isandwlana take place?
3. Which sea lies between Korea and Shanghai?
4. Who or what was the Empress of Blandings?
5. In which sport is the MacRobertson International Shield contested?
6. Who directed the films *Bugsy Malone* and *Midnight Express*?
7. What was curious about the Danish astronomer Tycho Brahe's nose?
8. Whose life is featured in the musical *Song of Norway*?
9. To what age have sea anemones been known to live?

372

1. On which day are Hot Cross buns traditionally eaten?
2. In which century did the pagan Midwinter Feast become the Christian Christmas?
3. Where was William I of Prussia crowned German Emperor?
4. John Creasey wrote 560 books; under how many pseudonyms?
5. With which sport was the late Aga Khan connected?
6. Which British prime minister also wrote film scripts?
7. Who said, 'Drink no longer water, but use a little wine for thy stomach's sake'?
8. Which great composer was once a butcher's boy?
9. What colour is iridium?

743

1. Which body founded the anti-smoking organization ASH in 1971?
2. Which French king was succeeded by his great-grandson?
3. Which European country's flag is red and gold and incorporates an eagle in its crest?
4. Who are the authors of the Fighting Fantasy Gamebooks?
5. What is baseball's equivalent of the Cup Final?
6. Why don't actors whistle in the dressing-room?
7. Which South African prime minister visited Britain in 1984?
8. What was given on the seventh day of Christmas?
9. Which planet lies between Venus and Mars?

1

1. Glass.
2. The Zulu War.
3. The Yellow Sea.
4. A pig (in the novel by P. G. Wodehouse).
5. Croquet.
6. Alan Parker.
7. It was made of gold.
8. Grieg.
9. 100 years.

372

1. Good Friday.
2. The ninth century.
3. At Versailles.
4. Twenty-eight.
5. Horse racing.
6. Winston Churchill.
7. St Paul.
8. Dvorak.
9. Steel grey.

743

1. The Royal College of Physicians.
2. Louis XIV (le Roi Soleil) by Louis XV.
3. Spain.
4. Steve Jackson and Ian Livingstone.
5. The World Series.
6. It means that one of the cast will soon be out of work.
7. P. W. Botha.
8. Seven swans a-swimming.
9. The earth.

2

1. What is the exact translation of 'pot-pourri'?
2. Which Saudi Arabian king was assassinated in 1975?
3. Who are the world's greatest cheese-eaters?
4. Of the nine muses, who is the muse of history?
5. Whose CB handle is Big Bopper?
6. Who did James Bond marry?
7. Who was Clyde Barrow's partner in crime?
8. What was Fats Waller's theme song?
9. How many moons has the planet Mercury?

373

1. From whom did John F. Kennedy accept his dog Pushinka?
2. Who was Julius Caesar's third wife?
3. Where can the largest cannon in the world be seen?
4. In which of Shakespeare's plays does Puck appear?
5. What nationality is tennis player Neale Fraser?
6. What is the alias of Hannibal Heyes?
7. Who did Sitting Bull call 'Little Sure Shot'?
8. In *Alice in Wonderland*, who sings of 'Soup of the evening, beautiful soup'?
9. Of what is widgeon a wild variety?

744

1. Which wedding anniversary is paper?
2. In which century were the Wars of the Roses fought?
3. Which Italian cathedral has 4,440 statues?
4. What was Louisa May Alcott's most famous book?
5. In which year did Ian Botham achieve his first cap?
6. Who both directed and produced the film *Citizen Kane*?
7. Which war reporter did Louis Botha capture during the Boer War?
8. Who was the 1958 Cha Cha Champ of Hong Kong?
9. Which is the nearest galaxy to our own?

A

2

1. Putrid pot.
2. King Faisal.
3. The French.
4. Clio.
5. Muhammad Ali's.
6. Teresa Draco.
7. Bonnie Parker.
8. 'Ain't Misbehavin''.
9. None.

373

1. Nikita Khrushchev.
2. Calpurnia.
3. The Kremlin.
4. *A Midsummer Night's Dream.*
5. Australian.
6. Joshua Smith.
7. Annie Oakley.
8. The Mock Turtle.
9. Duck.

744

1. The first.
2. The fifteenth century.
3. Milan.
4. *Little Women.*
5. 1977.
6. Orson Welles.
7. Winston Churchill.
8. The late Bruce Lee, of Kung Fu fame.
9. Andromeda.

3

1. Out of every ten women in Scotland, how many were pregnant on their wedding day, according to a Royal Commission of 1868?
2. When was the 'anarchy' when 'Christ and his angels slept'?
3. Where is the lost city of the Incas to be found?
4. Who created the detective Auguste C. Dupin?
5. If you entered a Canadian pairs race, what would you be doing?
6. Name the American comedy series starring Bob Newhart.
7. Which famous fighter plane did R. J. Mitchell design in 1936?
8. Whose first opera was *Oberto, Conte di San Bonifacio*?
9. What is studied in the science of somatology?

374

1. How many fluid ounces make up an American pint?
2. Who was John Wycliffe's patron?
3. Which sea has no coast?
4. Who wrote *Finnegans Wake*?
5. Where was the first three-day event held in this country?
6. What is the name of the Ewing ranch?
7. The largest stamp produced by Britain was issued to commemorate the International Stamp Exhibition in London. In what year was it held?
8. How many operas are in Wagner's *Ring* cycle?
9. An epidemic caused forty-three deaths in Croydon in the winter of 1937; of what disease?

745

1. What was the name of Jason's ship?
2. In 1783 the Peace Treaty with the thirteen colonies of America gave Florida to Spain in compensation for failing to recover – what?
3. In 1700 BC there was one great city in Africa outside Egypt. What was it?
4. Who created *The Cisco Kid*?
5. Who was the first professional cricketer to captain England?
6. Who starred in *The Man with the Golden Arm*?
7. How old was Major Yuri Gagarin on his first space flight?
8. How many Paris Symphonies did Haydn compose?
9. What is the principal food of reindeer and caribou?

3

1. Nine.
2. The civil war following the accession of Matilda in 1135.
3. In the Peruvian Andes.
4. Edgar Allan Poe.
5. Canoeing.
6. *Newhart.*
7. The Spitfire.
8. Verdi.
9. The body.

374

1. Sixteen.
2. John of Gaunt.
3. The Sargasso Sea.
4. James Joyce.
5. Badminton.
6. Southfork.
7. 1980.
8. Four.
9. Typhoid.

745

1. *Argo.*
2. Gibraltar.
3. Carthage.
4. O. Henry (William Sydney Porter).
5. Len Hutton.
6. Frank Sinatra.
7. Twenty-seven.
8. Six.
9. Reindeer moss.

4

1. What is the name of Hugh Hefner's super-jet?
2. In the Middle Ages, what was lichen scraped from crucifixes supposed to cure?
3. Which sea is really the world's largest lake?
4. Of which bird did Sindbad the Sailor discover the eggs?
5. If you were standing in a diamond, what would you be playing?
6. Who played Lord Beaverbrook in the 1952 film *The Magic Box*?
7. How many points are there on a Nine Men's Morris board?
8. Who composed the Goldberg Variations?
9. What is particularly prominent in the proboscis monkey?

375

1. Who invented braille?
2. The Fabian Society was named after the Roman General, Quintus Fabius Maximus. Why?
3. Tarom Airlines belong to which country?
4. Who wrote the novel *Brighton Rock*?
5. Which is Britain's longest cycling race?
6. Who won the Oscar for best actor in 1955 for his part in *Marty*?
7. Who beat the English at Stirling and was disembowelled at Smithfield?
8. Which was the first complete symphony ever to be recorded?
9. What does an armadillo's flesh taste like?

746

1. From which district in France do the majority of fine clarets come?
2. In which decade was the law under which witches could be burnt abolished?
3. How many of the world's population are Chinese?
4. Who wrote under the pseudonym Kyle Hunt?
5. In which country is Benfica FC?
6. Who are Mary Campbell's two sons from her first marriage?
7. Who created the famous willow pattern ware?
8. What did Handel originally study?
9. How many miles of arteries, veins and capillaries does the human body contain?

4

1. *Big Bunny.*
2. Nightmares.
3. The Caspian Sea.
4. The roc.
5. Baseball.
6. Robert Beatty.
7. Twenty-four.
8. J. S. Bach.
9. Its nose.

375

1. Louis Braille.
2. Fabius saved Rome by delaying; the Fabians similarly seek slow change.
3. Romania.
4. Graham Greene.
5. The Milk Race.
6. Ernest Borgnine.
7. Sir William Wallace.
8. Beethoven's Fifth.
9. Pork.

746

1. Médoc.
2. 1730s (1736).
3. 800,000,000.
4. John Creasey.
5. Portugal.
6. Danny and Jodie Dallas.
7. Thomas Minton, the English potter, at Stoke-on-Trent in 1789.
8. The law.
9. Approximately 60,000.

5

1. Which air force rank is the equivalent of an army major?
2. Which European nation was the first to drink tea?
3. What is the world's longest rail journey that can be made without changing trains?
4. Who was Sherlock Holmes's housekeeper and landlady?
5. In which sport can you be held in a half-nelson?
6. Which film ends, 'After all, tomorrow is another day'?
7. In which opera does Lily the Strawberry Woman feature?
8. Name Johann Sebastian Bach's youngest son.
9. What were the first vehicles to take people into the air?

376

1. After which saint is a revolving firework named?
2. During the fourteenth century in Spain, what was strange about the vogue for wearing beards?
3. In which ocean was the *Mary Celeste* found abandoned and adrift?
4. Who was Becky Thatcher's boyfriend?
5. To what did Thomas Lord give his name?
6. Who plays Del-boy in 'Only Fools and Horses'?
7. Who was the head of the Gestapo?
8. Who wrote *The King's Hunt*?
9. After whom was the drug morphine named?

747

1. Who flew for over forty years without a licence?
2. What was first erected on the Place de Grève in 1792?
3. What are French police called?
4. In which book did Humpty Dumpty first appear?
5. In showjumping, what is the penalty for three refusals?
6. Which famous actress won acclaim for playing the lead role in a French production of *Hamlet* in 1900?
7. Which writer cabled to the United States from Europe, 'The report of my death was an exaggeration'?
8. Who composed the opera *Albert Herring*?
9. Of what is smuck a group?

5

1. Squadron-Leader.
2. The Dutch.
3. The Moscow to Peking run on the Trans-Siberian Railway.
4. Mrs Hudson.
5. Wrestling.
6. *Gone with the Wind.*
7. *Porgy and Bess.*
8. Johann Christian Bach.
9. Hot-air balloons.

376

1. St Catherine.
2. Most of them were false.
3. The Atlantic.
4. Tom Sawyer.
5. Lord's Cricket Ground.
6. David Jason.
7. Heinrich Himmler.
8. John Bull.
9. Morpheus, the Greek God of Dreams.

747

1. Orville Wright.
2. The original French guillotine.
3. Police. (*Gendarmes* are soldiers acting as policemen.)
4. *Through the Looking Glass* by Lewis Carroll.
5. Elimination.
6. Sarah Bernhardt.
7. Mark Twain (Samuel Clemens).
8. Benjamin Britten.
9. Jellyfish.

6

1. How many signs of the zodiac are there?
2. Who was the Man of Destiny?
3. Which city is nicknamed the City of Light?
4. Which Canadian city used to be called Bytown?
5. Which Frenchman dominated downhill skiing between 1966 and 1968?
6. Who played boxer Jake La Motta in the 1980 film *Raging Bull*?
7. Who was the man responsible for the 'big bang' theory?
8. Who was the guest conductor at the opening of Carnegie Hall in 1891?
9. How long does it take the moon to complete a full revolution of the earth?

377

1. In Nottingham, an owl was stolen from an exhibition. What was the exhibition called?
2. Which of Henry VIII's wives survived him?
3. In a New York crying contest, what volume of tears did the winner produce in three hours?
4. Against whom did both Samson and David fight?
5. On which day are the John Player League matches played?
6. What are Olive Oyl's vital statistics?
7. In which castle was Princess Margaret born?
8. Who composed the song 'I've Got You Under My Skin'?
9. How many hairs does an average healthy scalp shed in twenty-four hours?

748

1. What is London's Central Criminal Court called?
2. Who killed Abel?
3. Of which island group is Viti Levu the largest?
4. In mythology, which flower sprang from the blood of a young man killed by Apollo?
5. Who was the only female competitor in the 1976 Olympics not to be given a sex test?
6. Who starred in *Easy Street*?
7. Was Giovanni Bellini a cubist, Renaissance or impressionist painter?
8. Which modern instrument does the shawa most resemble?
9. Which admiral gave his name to a wind force scale?

6

1. Twelve.
2. Napoleon.
3. Paris.
4. Ottawa.
5. Jean Claude Killy.
6. Robert De Niro.
7. Georges Lemaître.
8. Tchaikovsky.
9. 27·3 days.

377

1. 'Vanishing Village'.
2. Catherine Parr.
3. One-third of a pint.
4. The Philistines.
5. Sunday (cricket).
6. 19–19–19.
7. Glamis.
8. Cole Porter.
9. About sixty-five.

748

1. The Old Bailey.
2. Cain.
3. Fiji.
4. The hyacinth.
5. Princess Anne.
6. Charlie Chaplin.
7. Renaissance.
8. The oboe.
9. Admiral Beaufort.

Q

7

1. What bird is the symbol of Penguin Books' children's section?
2. What was Admiral Raeder's sentence at Nuremberg?
3. In which sea is the Dogger Bank?
4. Whose court was at Camelot?
5. What was Diane Leather's athletic first?
6. From which planet does Mork come?
7. With what did the first artists draw?
8. What was Glenn Miller's intended destination when he disappeared while flying over the North Sea in 1944?
9. In view of the sun's great distance from the earth, how long has it been up at dawn before we can actually see it?

378

1. In Muslim countries, what is the equivalent of the Red Cross?
2. Who was the French criminal who founded the Service de Sûreté?
3. Which country owns the Queen Elizabeth Islands in the Arctic?
4. Who wrote *The Mill on the Floss*?
5. Which was the first English soccer club to achieve the FA Cup and League double?
6. Which type of TV programme is best for your health?
7. For what event were Britain's first commemorative postage stamps issued?
8. Who were the first king and queen of England to make a record?
9. Which heavenly bodies did the Greeks call 'wandering stars'?

749

1. Who or what is a 'carpet-bagger'?
2. At what battle did Miltiades, heavily outnumbered, lead the Athenians to victory?
3. Which is North America's highest mountain?
4. Who wrote of the Golden Road to Samarkand?
5. Who ran with Roger Bannister when he broke the 4-minute mile?
6. In which 1935 film did Errol Flynn star as a physician turned pirate?
7. How did Danish astronomer Tycho Brahe lose his nose?
8. Who composed the overtures *Egmont* and *Coriolan*?
9. What is the chemical symbol for iodine?

7

1. The puffin.
2. Life imprisonment.
3. The North Sea.
4. King Arthur's.
5. She was the first woman to better the 5-minute mile.
6. Ork.
7. Rocks.
8. Paris.
9. 8 minutes.

378

1. The Red Crescent.
2. Vidocq.
3. Canada.
4. George Eliot.
5. Preston North End.
6. The comedy, as laughing tones up the system.
7. The British Empire Exhibition, 1924–5.
8. King George V and Queen Mary.
9. The planets.

749

1. This is an American political term for an entrepreneur who began business in the devastated southern states with no more than could be carried in a carpet-bag.
2. Marathon.
3. Mount McKinley.
4. James Elroy Flecker, in *Hassan*.
5. Christopher Brasher.
6. *Captain Blood*.
7. In a duel.
8. Beethoven.
9. I.

8

1. Of what are 'Dorothy Perkins', 'Grandpa Dickson' and 'Iceberg' varieties?
2. Until 1942, what metal was used to make Victoria Crosses?
3. After the end of the Vietnam war, to what was Saigon's name changed?
4. What is M's name?
5. How many players are there in an ice hockey team?
6. Who wrote the comedy *French Without Tears*?
7. Jon Magnusson was prime minister of which country from 1924 to 1926?
8. In which Italian town were the greatest violins made?
9. What was the Wright brothers' plane called?

379

1. What are English, Orator and Elite?
2. Who was Cleopatra's husband?
3. Which Scottish city boasts an underground system?
4. Who in the Bible was taken up to heaven in a fiery chariot?
5. Which teams play for the Ashes?
6. Which film was based on L. P. Davies's novel *The Alien*?
7. What is the technique of painting directly on to wet plaster on walls called?
8. From which opera came Caruso's earliest known recording?
9. What did the largest hailstone on record weigh?

750

1. In which trade are composing frames and sticks used?
2. Who, according to Herodotus, led an army of a million men?
3. Which British duke's stately home is at Stratford Saye?
4. What do the initials E. M. stand for in Forster's name?
5. In which year was Moorhouse the sprint Racehorse of the Year?
6. Which historical character has been portrayed on screen more often than any other?
7. How many squares in a Rubik's cube never alter their position?
8. Who wrote the music for Flecker's *Hassan*?
9. What is an emmet?

8

1. Roses.
2. Metal from guns captured at Sebastopol (1855).
3. Ho Chi Minh City.
4. Admiral Sir Miles Messervy.
5. Six.
6. Terence Rattigan.
7. Iceland.
8. Cremona.
9. *Flyer*.

379

1. Type-faces.
2. Her brother, Ptolemy Dionysius.
3. Glasgow.
4. The prophet Elijah, or Elias.
5. England and Australia.
6. *The Groundstar Conspiracy* (1972).
7. Fresco.
8. Puccini's *Tosca*.
9. $1\frac{1}{2}$ lb.

750

1. Printing.
2. Xerxes.
3. The Duke of Wellington.
4. Edward Morgan.
5. 1980.
6. Napoleon Bonaparte.
7. Six – the centre squares on each side.
8. Delius.
9. An ant.

Q

9

1. Approximately how many known human illnesses are there?
2. Which act was called 'Dora'?
3. In which range of English hills lies the village of Broadway?
4. Which early poet was once Controller of Customs on wools, skins and hides?
5. Which football club has the nickname 'The Blades'?
6. Who does Katherine Helmond play in 'Soap'?
7. Which famous author and editor was born in Lichfield in 1709?
8. Which orchestral wind instrument has a reedy tone?
9. From which country does the chihuahua originate?

380

1. The annual marking of Thames swans – 'swan-upping' – takes place each summer. When?
2. Of which kingdom was Offa the king?
3. Which city does Speke airport serve?
4. What was John Dawkins's nickname in *Oliver Twist*?
5. Who won the 1981 Calcutta Cup match?
6. What was odd about the Shakespeare Jubilee of 1769?
7. Which explorer accompanied Sir Ranulph Fiennes on the Transglobe Expedition?
8. Who composed what is usually called Haydn's Toy Symphony?
9. About how far away from a 1-megaton nuclear explosion would you have to be to escape immediate burns?

751

1. How many new human illnesses are identified each year?
2. Who was Henry VII's eldest son?
3. By what name do we know the country Chosun Minchu-Chui Inmin Konghwa-Guk?
4. What is the nature of the central relationship in Ford's *'Tis Pity She's a Whore*?
5. Who plays at Stamford Bridge?
6. What made *The Terror of Tiny Town* an unusual film?
7. Who preceded Richard Nixon as president of the United States?
8. In which year did Toscanini make his first recording?
9. What colour are peridots (semi-precious stones)?

9

1. About 33,000.
2. Defence of the Realm Act (1914).
3. In the Cotswolds.
4. Chaucer.
5. Sheffield United.
6. Jessica Tate.
7. Dr Samuel Johnson.
8. The oboe, or cor anglais.
9. Mexico.

380

1. During the third week of July.
2. Mercia.
3. Liverpool.
4. The Artful Dodger.
5. England.
6. It was late. (The bi-centenary of Shakespeare's birth was in 1764.)
7. Charles Burton.
8. Leopold Mozart, Mozart's father, as part of a longer work.
9. About 20 miles.

751

1. About 500.
2. Prince Arthur, Catherine of Aragon's first husband.
3. Korea.
4. Incest between brother and sister.
5. Chelsea.
6. It had an all-midget cast.
7. Lyndon Johnson.
8. 1920.
9. Green.

Q

10

1. In Scotland, what is the third alternative to the verdicts 'Guilty' and 'Not Guilty'?
2. Who died at Rouen after being thrown against his horse's pommel?
3. What is the unit of currency in Poland?
4. Who wrote *The School for Scandal*?
5. What is Carnoustie famous for?
6. Which film star has his statue in Leicester Square?
7. Who won the 1979 Nobel Prize for Peace?
8. How many operas did Gilbert and Sullivan write?
9. What is the lifespan of a turkey who evades the cooking pot?

381

1. How often approximately does the human race double its number?
2. For what crime was the Protestant reformer Latimer burned at the stake in 1555?
3. How many 4-inch sausages would be needed to circle the earth at the equator?
4. Who wrote the poem *Maud*?
5. What is skeet?
6. Whose girlfriend is Olive Oyl?
7. Who sculpted 'The Thinker'?
8. Who composed the opera *Billy Budd*?
9. Quarantine is isolation because of sickness. What else can it be?

752

1. Which letter is at the far left of the bottom row of a typewriter keyboard?
2. What was Henri Sanson, France's chief executioner, sacked for pawning?
3. How many rivers are there in Saudi Arabia?
4. What is Lord Peter Wimsey's favourite drink?
5. What is Kendo?
6. By what name was Virginia McMath better known?
7. Which United States president achieved the highest grade in the Boy Scouts?
8. Who orchestrated Bach's famous Toccata and Fugue in D Minor under the pseudonym Paul Klenovsky?
9. Which element has the symbol Ag?

10

1. 'Not proven'.
2. William the Conqueror.
3. The zloty.
4. Richard Brinsley Sheridan.
5. Golf.
6. Charlie Chaplin.
7. Mother Teresa of Calcutta.
8. Fourteen.
9. 12 years.

381

1. Every 35 years.
2. Heresy.
3. 394,444,512.
4. Tennyson.
5. A form of clay pigeon shooting.
6. Popeye's.
7. Rodin.
8. Benjamin Britten.
9. A sort of red apple (also called a Quarrender).

752

1. Z.
2. His guillotine.
3. None.
4. Napoleon brandy.
5. The Japanese art of sword fighting.
6. Ginger Rogers.
7. Gerald Ford.
8. Henry Wood.
9. Silver.

11

1. What was Ethel Cain the first to record?
2. Who were the Rochdale Pioneers?
3. Where were glass mirrors first made in Europe?
4. Which author created the detective Nick Charles?
5. Who was the world record holder for the long jump before Ralph Boston took it in 1960?
6. Which French comedian created Monsieur Hulot?
7. Which of the Mexican muralists could be called a Trotskyist?
8. What was the first Dylan album to be recorded in Nashville?
9. How many lines to a picture were there in the first television sets in widespread use in Britain?

382

1. What is blennophobia?
2. Which queen of England had eleven fingers?
3. Where was the capital of the Assyrian Empire?
4. What did James Macpherson pass off as translations until rumbled by Dr Johnson and others?
5. Name the British heavyweight who beat Berndt August for the European championship.
6. Name the two families in 'Soap'.
7. Who did Cicero describe as 'the father of history'?
8. Where was composer Thea Musgrave born?
9. Some elements exist in two or more different forms with different molecular arrangements. What is the name given to these variant forms?

753

1. What are the six main vitamins?
2. Which eighteenth-century monarch was vaccinated?
3. What had Marylebone, Ranelagh and Vauxhall in common in the eighteenth century?
4. What is the name of the ship in which Captain Ahab seeks Moby Dick?
5. What is Hashim Khan's sport?
6. Which character did Harrison Ford play in *Star Wars*?
7. The British philanthropist Jonas Hanway (1712–86) was scorned for years for being among the first notables to use a recent invention. What?
8. What question did the Small Faces ask in 1965?
9. Which is the most distant planet just visible to the naked eye?

11

1. The talking clock.
2. Founders of the first Cooperative store (in Toad Lane, Rochdale).
3. Venice, in about 1300.
4. Dashiell Hammett.
5. Jesse Owens.
6. Jacques Tati.
7. Diego Rivera. Trotsky lived in his house during his Mexican exile.
8. *Blonde on Blonde.*
9. 405.

382

1. A fear of slime.
2. Anne Boleyn.
3. Nineveh.
4. The poems of Ossian.
5. Richard Dunn.
6. The Tates and the Campbells.
7. Herodotus.
8. Edinburgh.
9. Allotropes.

753

1. A, B, C, D, E and K.
2. Catherine the Great of Russia.
3. They were all pleasure gardens.
4. *Pequod.*
5. Squash.
6. Han Solo.
7. An umbrella.
8. 'Watcha Gonna Do About It?'
9. Uranus.

Q

12

1. What is the Feast of First Fruits on 1 August?
2. Which English king reigned for ten years but only spent about six months of this time in England?
3. What mistake was made when installing the new prisoners' waiting-rooms in Reading gaol?
4. Which poet married a mathematician and was father-in-law of Charles Babbage, the inventor of the adding machine?
5. How many people play in a polo team?
6. Who played Roxie Hart on film?
7. Who was defeated by Roosevelt in the presidential election of 1932?
8. On which instrument would you find a gemshorn?
9. What gives the sea its blue colour?

383

1. What is the Trial of the Pyx?
2. How did a small animal please the Jacobites in 1702?
3. When did India go metric?
4. Who wrote, 'Man's inhumanity to man/Makes countless thousands mourn'?
5. What is the name of the area at Old Trafford where the Manchester United fans congregate?
6. What name was Bela Blasko better known by?
7. Who wrote twenty-five plays in seven years, was a JP and is remembered as a novelist?
8. Who composed the choral suite 'Five Tudor Portraits'?
9. What is the smallest unit of length measurement?

754

1. What is 1970 in Roman numerals?
2. The rarest stamp in the world is generally accepted to be the 1856 one-cent black. Which country issued it?
3. Who is the American state of Virginia named after?
4. Who succeeded Shakespeare as principal writer to the King's Men?
5. Over which course is the Stewards' Cup run?
6. In which film did Woody Allen and Diane Keaton win Oscars in 1977?
7. Which Speaker of the House of Commons was canonized?
8. Which dance was introduced to Paris in 1843 and went one-two-three-hop?
9. Border, Leicester and Corriedale are all breeds of what?

12

1. Lammas.
2. Richard I.
3. The door locks were on the inside only!
4. Lord Byron.
5. Four.
6. Ginger Rogers.
7. President Hoover.
8. An organ.
9. Sunlight; pure sea water is colourless, but the surface water absorbs all but blue rays of the sun.

383

1. A yearly examination of coins from the Mint.
2. William III's horse stumbled on a molehill, killing him.
3. In 1958.
4. Robert Burns ('Man was Made to Mourn').
5. Stretford End.
6. Bela Lugosi.
7. Henry Fielding.
8. Ralph Vaughan Williams.
9. The femtometre.

754

1. MCMLXX.
2. British Guiana.
3. Queen Elizabeth I.
4. John Fletcher.
5. Goodwood.
6. *Annie Hall.*
7. St Thomas More.
8. The polka.
9. Sheep.

13

1. How is it known that a new Pope has been elected?
2. What nationality were the thousands of people killed in the Sicilian Vespers massacre of 1282?
3. In which harbour did the *Mary Rose* sink in 1545?
4. Which poet wrote *The Borderers* and *The Prelude*?
5. What is the lightest weight category in boxing?
6. Which famous American TV presenter lost $500,000 in the De Lorean car venture?
7. What is Harold Macmillan's first name?
8. Where did the polka originate?
9. How much food does the average person eat in a lifetime?

384

1. What make-up is French for 'red'?
2. Which murdered Roman emperor was succeeded by his uncle Claudius?
3. Which country's kings used to be crowned on Tara Hill?
4. Name the image set up by Aaron while Moses was on Mount Sinai.
5. What do the Philadelphia Flyers and Boston Bruins play?
6. Which Indian actor had his first film part in *Elephant Boy*?
7. What is Alex Higgins's nickname?
8. After whom was the Music Hall, New York, renamed?
9. What is the most radiation-sensitive part of the body?

755

1. What French name is given to clear meat soup or broth?
2. Which tsar met Charles II and was a keen carpenter and barber?
3. Near which city is Lulsgate airport?
4. Who wrote *The History of Mr Polly*?
5. How many strokes below par is an albatross?
6. Who chairs BBC TV's 'Question Time'?
7. Which Australian outlaw made himself a suit of armour from stolen ploughshares?
8. When was the first LP released commercially in England?
9. By what name is the flower convallaria better known?

13

1. Smoke rises from a chimney in the Vatican.
2. French; Sicily was under French rule.
3. Portsmouth.
4. William Wordsworth.
5. Light flyweight.
6. Johnny Carson.
7. Maurice.
8. Poland.
9. 50 tons.

384

1. Rouge.
2. Caligula.
3. Ireland's.
4. The Golden Calf.
5. Ice hockey.
6. Sabu.
7. Hurricane.
8. Andrew Carnegie.
9. The blood.

755

1. Consommé.
2. Peter the Great.
3. Bristol.
4. H. G. Wells.
5. Three; it is a golfing term.
6. Sir Robin Day.
7. Ned Kelly.
8. 1950.
9. Lily of the valley.

Q

14

1. When is the next partial eclipse of the sun visible in the UK due?
2. Who fought the Punic Wars? How many were there?
3. The Bay of Pigs is the name given to the unsuccessful invasion of an island in the early 1960s. Which island?
4. Shakespeare wrote a play about two gentlemen. Which city did they come from?
5. In which country was Sir Donald Bradman born?
6. Who said, 'Thirteen at a table is unlucky when the hostess only has twelve chops'?
7. If I roll a four on a dice, what is the sum of the other four visible faces?
8. What was Gay's sequel to *The Beggar's Opera*?
9. Where in your body would you find the atrium?

385

1. What is St Nicholas the patron saint of?
2. What is the name given to the years 1810–20 in English history?
3. Which is the second largest town in Zimbabwe?
4. In which Jane Austen novel do Miss Bates and Jane Fairfax appear?
5. Which country do the All Blacks represent?
6. Which film has been remade fifty-eight times, including cartoon, ballet, operatic, pornographic and parody versions?
7. Who was the Greek mathematician who claimed the earth was a sphere rotating on its own axis?
8. Which singer is known as 'La Stupenda'?
9. What is the deficiency which causes anaemia?

756

1. What do we call the first day of Lent?
2. Who was Queen Victoria's royal grandfather?
3. Which European state did George I rule before he became King of England?
4. Who wrote *The Time Machine*?
5. What game did Sir Donald Bradman play?
6. Which American president wrote the original scenario for *The President's Mystery*?
7. Who was the prime minister of the first majority Labour government?
8. How was Louis Barraud connected with HMV?
9. What was Apollo II's landing module called?

14

1. 1995.
2. Carthage and Rome; there were two.
3. Cuba.
4. Verona.
5. Australia.
6. Groucho Marx.
7. Fourteen.
8. *Polly*.
9. The heart.

385

1. Children.
2. The Regency.
3. Bulawayo.
4. *Emma*.
5. New Zealand.
6. *Cinderella*.
7. Pythagoras.
8. Joan Sutherland.
9. Iron.

756

1. Ash Wednesday.
2. George III.
3. Hanover.
4. H. G. Wells.
5. Cricket.
6. President Roosevelt.
7. Clement Attlee, Prime Minister from 1945 to 1951.
8. His painting of a dog with a trumpet inspired their logo.
9. 'Eagle'.

15

1. What does 'infra dignitatem' mean?
2. Under the Emperor Charlemagne, which two knights fought for five days, without any advantage being gained by either?
3. Which country was formerly East Pakistan?
4. At which school did Mr Chips teach Latin?
5. What is a luge?
6. How many Oscars did the film *Gigi* win?
7. What are burnt sienna and cadmium red?
8. Which opera singer and film star was killed in an air crash in 1947?
9. What is measured by an interferometer?

386

1. Where can you earn a doctorate in hamburgerology?
2. Who reigned in England from 1558 to 1603?
3. What is orology?
4. Who wrote the boys' stories *Stalky and Co.*?
5. What is Gilliam Gilks's game?
6. What was Gary Cooper's last film?
7. If four regular dice are placed on top of each other with a six on top what do the seven concealed numbers add up to?
8. What does a belly-man do?
9. What was the middle name of John Baird, of television pioneering fame?

757

1. Which mammal lives longest?
2. Which king of England ordered all paper to be made with the royal arms as a watermark?
3. In which country is a pig brought into the house for good luck on New Year's Eve?
4. Who wrote the poem 'To a Louse'?
5. What is Evonne Cawley's maiden name?
6. Who did actress Jean Peters marry in 1957?
7. Who invented the rocking chair?
8. How old was Duke Ellington when he composed his first song 'Soda Fountain Rag'?
9. Which planet is surrounded by rings?

15

1. Beneath one's dignity.
2. Roland and Oliver.
3. Bangladesh.
4. Brookfield.
5. A small toboggan.
6. Eight.
7. Colours used in painting.
8. Grace Moore.
9. The wavelength of light.

386

1. Hamburger College, Chicago.
2. Queen Elizabeth I.
3. The scientific study of mountains.
4. Rudyard Kipling.
5. Badminton.
6. *The Naked Edge.*
7. Twenty-two.
8. Assembles and adjusts soundboards of pianos.
9. Logie.

757

1. Man.
2. Charles I.
3. Yugoslavia.
4. Robert Burns.
5. Evonne Goolagong.
6. Howard Hughes.
7. Benjamin Franklin.
8. Fourteen.
9. Saturn.

Q

16

1. What sort of bottom has a scow?
2. Who was James I's eldest son?
3. Where in Roman times was the Saxon shore?
4. Who wrote *The Agony and the Ecstasy*?
5. For whom did Eusebio play?
6. Who stood trial for attempting to kill JR?
7. Who died before a firing squad saying, 'Patriotism is not enough. I must have no hatred or bitterness to anyone'?
8. Which composer did Alan Badel play in the film *Magic Fire*?
9. Scientists were working on the Manhattan Project in 1942. What was it?

387

1. If you were born on 2 April what would your sign of the zodiac be?
2. How did drunken seamen cause the civil war between Matilda and Stephen?
3. What powers the London Underground system?
4. Who was Nehemiah a cup-bearer to?
5. What would you use a sand wedge for?
6. In which film did Howard Hughes launch Jane Russell?
7. How was Matthew Hopkins hoist with his own petard?
8. What did Berlioz originally study?
9. What was the communal module of Apollo 11 called?

758

1. Which vegetable comes in globe and Jerusalem varieties?
2. How many times have the Olympic Games been cancelled due to war?
3. Where in London are the Crown Jewels kept?
4. Who was David Copperfield's nurse?
5. Who was the first cricketer to score a century in the final of the Benson & Hedges Cup (in 1979)?
6. Who, on a telegram, said, 'Please accept my resignation. I don't want to belong to any club that will accept me as a member'?
7. Who invented the telegraph?
8. Who was Poland's prime minister from 1919 to 1921?
9. Which creatures accompany sharks and ships?

16

1. Flat – it's a type of boat.
2. Prince Henry, who died in suspicious circumstances in 1612; some said he had been poisoned by his father.
3. From the Wash to the Solent.
4. Irving Stone.
5. Portugal and Benfica.
6. Sue Ellen.
7. Nurse Edith Cavell.
8. Richard Wagner.
9. The atomic bomb.

387

1. Aries.
2. Their carelessness contributed to the drowning of Prince William, who would have been Henry I's successor.
3. Electricity.
4. King Artaxerxes.
5. Getting out of a bunker in golf.
6. *The Outlaw*.
7. He was a notorious witch-finder and was himself hanged as a wizard in 1647.
8. Medicine.
9. Columbia.

758

1. The artichoke.
2. Three – in 1916, 1940 and 1944.
3. The Tower of London.
4. Clara Peggotty.
5. Graham Gooch.
6. Groucho Marx.
7. Samuel Morse.
8. The concert pianist Ignace Jan Paderewski.
9. Pilot fish.

17

1. What form does a kelpie take?
2. What were the Casket Letters?
3. Which ocean is not recognized by the International Hydrographic Bureau?
4. What are Inspector Teal's Christian names?
5. What was cricketer Bishan Bedi famous for?
6. How are Jessica Tate and Mary Campbell related?
7. One British stamp issue carries the heads of two monarchs. In which year was this set issued and what does it commemorate?
8. For which opera did Beethoven write three overtures called 'Leonora'?
9. In 1937, the earth missed a major disaster by less than three seconds when it nearly collided with a minor planet. Which?

388

1. What is the main ingredient of cheese?
2. The names of two articles of clothing originated in the Crimean War; what are they?
3. Which is the commonest surname in Spain?
4. Who buried the treasure on Treasure Island?
5. Who beat Bobby Riggs in three straight sets at Houston Astrodome in 1973?
6. By what name is Dino Crocetti Isetto known?
7. Who was the first to reach the North Pole?
8. *The Slave of Duty* is the sub-title of an opera. Which?
9. Which poison is obtained from wolf's-bane?

759

1. Name the type of government formed by a small group after a *coup d'état*.
2. Which Roman emperor was called the Apostate because he forsook Christianity for paganism?
3. Which country produces Gruyère cheese?
4. Who was '*mom ami*' to Hercule Poirot?
5. In the game of fives, what do the players hit the ball with?
6. By what name is Sofia Scicolone better known?
7. Who was the 'Forces' Sweetheart'?
8. Who composed the forty-part motet *Spem in Alium*?
9. How much does the level of the sea drop each spring?

17

1. A horse; it is a spirit of water in Scottish folk-lore.
2. Letters supposedly exchanged by Mary Queen of Scots and Bothwell, proving Mary's complicity in Darnley's murder.
3. The Antarctic Ocean.
4. Claud Eustace.
5. Spin bowling.
6. They are sisters.
7. 1940; the centenary of the issue of 'the first adhesive postage stamp'.
8. *Fidelio.*
9. Hermes.

388

1. Milk.
2. Balaclava and cardigan.
3. Garcia.
4. Captain Flint.
5. Billie Jean King.
6. Dean Martin.
7. The American admiral Robert E. Peary on 6 April 1909.
8. *The Pirates of Penzance.*
9. Aconite.

759

1. Junta.
2. Julian, Emperor from 361 to 363 AD.
3. Switzerland.
4. Captain Hastings.
5. The hand.
6. Sophia Loren.
7. Vera Lynn.
8. Thomas Tallis.
9. 8 inches (approximately).

18

1. What Australian city was named after the wife of King William IV?
2. Who styled himself Richard IV and was imprisoned by Henry VII?
3. Which country was Mrs Jeanne Sauvé appointed the first woman Governor-General of?
4. Who wrote *Man and Superman*?
5. Which month is the Ascot Gold Cup run in?
6. In 'Soap', what is Chuck's dummy's name?
7. Who was President Lyndon Johnson's vice-president from 1964 to 1966?
8. What was the claim to fame of the twelve-year-old pianist Josef Hofmann?
9. What is studied by an oologist?

389

1. What is 'Jewish penicillin'?
2. According to legend, what did Hubert do to Arthur on behalf of John?
3. Which group of islands does Fair Isle belong to?
4. What did Foxe write in Strasbourg?
5. What was the UEFA Cup competition called between 1958 and 1971?
6. Which Greek actress became the Greek minister of culture?
7. Which king of Great Britain won world-wide recognition as a stamp collector?
8. In which year did Caruso make his last recording?
9. How many square metres are in a hectare?

760

1. If you were born on 10 July what would your sign of the zodiac be?
2. What did Ignatius Loyola found?
3. Of which country was Solon one of the seven sages?
4. Name the little elephant in books by Jean de Brunhoff.
5. When is the Henley Regatta?
6. In which Sheridan play do Sir Peter Teazle and Lady Sneerwell appear?
7. Which politician was nicknamed 'Sunny Jim'?
8. Which collaborators wrote the music and lyrics for *South Pacific*?
9. Which stimulant is found in coffee, tea and cocoa?

18

1. Adelaide.
2. Perkin Warbeck.
3. Canada.
4. George Bernard Shaw.
5. June.
6. Bob.
7. Hubert Humphrey.
8. He was the first classical artist to be recorded on gramophone.
9. Birds' eggs.

389

1. Chicken soup.
2. He put his eyes out. Prince Arthur had a superior claim to the throne; he died in grisly circumstances.
3. The Shetlands.
4. His *Book of Martyrs*.
5. The European Fairs Cup.
6. Melina Mercouri.
7. George V.
8. 1920.
9. 10,000.

760

1. Cancer.
2. The Jesuits.
3. Greece.
4. Babar.
5. The first week in July.
6. *The School for Scandal.*
7. James Callaghan.
8. Rodgers and Hammerstein.
9. Caffeine.

Q

19

1. What is Walpurgis Night?
2. In whose reign was a £5 postage stamp first issued?
3. In which country was Auschwitz?
4. 'That which we call a rose, by any other name would smell as sweet' – who said it and who wrote the play?
5. What is the name of the dog that found the missing World Cup in 1966?
6. Which colour did Peter Sellers dislike anyone wearing on stage?
7. In philately, what is a 'Maltese Cross'?
8. Who founded the London Philharmonic Orchestra?
9. Who invented the first astronomical telescope?

390

1. What is the most common language used in home computing?
2. From which culture did the custom of wearing paper hats and pulling crackers at Christmas come?
3. Which is the largest town in Zimbabwe?
4. Which mythological sisters had snakes instead of hair?
5. What is the ABA?
6. Who did Bernard Hill portray in the 1983 film *Squaring the Circle*?
7. How many backgammon pieces does each player start with?
8. Who wrote the 'Surprise Symphony'?
9. Why is a polyanthus so called?

761

1. What is belonephobia?
2. Who was king of England at the time of the Battle of Bannockburn?
3. In which city are the parliamentary constituencies of Itchen and Test?
4. Who created Dr Fu Manchu?
5. Which football team plays at Highbury?
6. Who was the Tates' original butler?
7. Which famous fantasy novel has become the subject of a highly successful computer adventure game?
8. Who wrote the music for the popular ballet *Giselle*?
9. Who invented the lightning rod?

19

1. The night when witches were supposed to be free to roam about.
2. Queen Victoria's.
3. Poland.
4. Juliet in Shakespeare's play *Romeo and Juliet*.
5. Pickles.
6. Purple.
7. An early Victorian postal cancellation mark.
8. Sir Thomas Beecham – in 1932.
9. Galileo – in 1609.

390

1. Basic.
2. Ancient Roman.
3. Salisbury.
4. The Gorgons.
5. Amateur Boxing Association.
6. Lech Walesa.
7. Fifteen.
8. Haydn.
9. Because it has many flowers on a single stem.

761

1. Fear of pins and needles.
2. Edward II.
3. Southampton.
4. Sax Rohmer.
5. Arsenal.
6. Benson.
7. *The Hobbit*.
8. Adolphe Adam.
9. Benjamin Franklin.

20

1. What is a funicular?
2. What was the penalty in 1810 for forging a birth certificate, stealing a pocket handkerchief or impersonating a Chelsea pensioner?
3. How many standard time divisions are there in the USA?
4. What is Christian's ultimate destination in *Pilgrim's Progress*?
5. What differentiates Alpine from Nordic skiing?
6. What was the title of Polanski's horror spoof?
7. Who was the first man to climb the Matterhorn?
8. Who sang about Lady d'Arbanville?
9. In 1959 Frank Drake initiated the project Ozma. What was it?

391

1. What is the name of Dennis the Menace's dog?
2. What action by Gavrilo Princip started the First World War?
3. Name two of the three most common surnames in China.
4. In which novel is Rebecca rejected for Rowena?
5. What do Jack Dempsey, Rocky Marciano and Sonny Liston have in common?
6. Which TV series is based on the novel *Poor, Poor Ophelia*?
7. Which artist painted the well-known 'Bubbles'?
8. Which was the first British instrumental recording to top the US charts?
9. Why are black clothes warmer than similar white ones?

762

1. The most devastating motorway pile-up in Britain due to fog occurred on 13 September 1971. How many vehicles collided?
2. Whose funeral was upset by flooding of the Bath Road, Maidenhead, in 1852?
3. Roman London has sunk. By how many feet?
4. Where does Stephen Blackpool appear?
5. Which famous racehorse was kidnapped in Ireland?
6. Who played Ilya Kuryakin in 'The Man From UNCLE'?
7. In sailing, what is a warp?
8. Where would you find the vox humana and vox angelica together?
9. What is sericulture?

20

1. A cable railway.
2. Hanging.
3. Four.
4. Celestial City.
5. Alpine is downhill; Nordic is cross-country.
6. *Dance of the Vampires.*
7. Edward Whymper, English mountaineer, in 1865.
8. Cat Stevens.
9. The object was to look for extraterrestial radio signals.

391

1. Gnasher.
2. He assassinated the Austrian Archduke Franz Ferdinand.
3. Chang, Wang, Li.
4. *Ivanhoe.*
5. They were all heavyweight boxing champions of the world.
6. 'The Streets of San Francisco'.
7. Millais.
8. 'Telstar', by the Tornados.
9. Because black surfaces absorb heat and white ones reflect it.

762

1. 200.
2. The Duke of Wellington's.
3. 15 feet.
4. In Dickens's *Hard Times.*
5. Shergar.
6. David McCallum.
7. Rope used for mooring or anchoring.
8. On an organ. They are stops.
9. Breeding silk-worms.

21

1. What are military policemen called?
2. What 'science of heathen devilry' did Cromwell indulge in at his daughter's wedding in 1657?
3. On which national flag is there an eagle and a snake?
4. In which play does Dame Pliant appear?
5. Within Britain, who was the first player to be transferred for £200,000?
6. Who plays George Cowley in 'The Professionals'?
7. Who started Biba?
8. Whose music was featured in *The Exorcist*?
9. How many kingdoms are there in the modern system of classification of living things?

392

1. What word is derived from the Arab word *mawsim*, meaning 'season'?
2. How many paces (of five feet each) made up the Roman mile?
3. Where is the Valley of Ten Thousand Smokes?
4. Which D. H. Lawrence book figured in a famous court case?
5. When was Tony Jacklin the English Open champion?
6. In which Billy Wilder comedy do Jack Lemmon and Tony Curtis play jazz musicians and appear in drag?
7. How long is a full-sized billiards table?
8. Who wrote the words to the hymn 'Jerusalem'?
9. Insects have one inefficient physiological function which prevents them from reaching any size bigger than a mouse. What is it?

763

1. Which measurement did Henry III define by laying down three barleycorns in a continuous line?
2. Where was the Young Pretender defeated by the Duke of Cumberland in 1746?
3. For what was the Eiffel Tower built?
4. For how many months was Noah's Ark afloat?
5. Which horse first won the King George VI and Queen Elizabeth Stakes twice?
6. Who was the most famous Dracula?
7. What is the major hot colour?
8. How many ways did Paul Simon have of leaving his lover?
9. What is a group of cats called?

21

1. Redcaps.
2. Dancing.
3. Mexico's (from Aztec legend).
4. Ben Jonson's *The Alchemist.*
5. Martin Peters, from West Ham to Tottenham, in 1970.
6. Gordon Jackson.
7. Barbara Hulanicki.
8. Mike Oldfield's *Tubular Bells.*
9. Five.

392

1. Monsoon.
2. 1,000.
3. Alaska.
4. *Lady Chatterley's Lover.*
5. 1969.
6. *Some Like It Hot.*
7. Twelve feet.
8. William Blake.
9. Breathing.

763

1. The inch.
2. Culloden.
3. The Paris Exhibition of 1889.
4. Seven.
5. Dahlia, in 1973 and 1974.
6. Bela Lugosi.
7. Red.
8. Fifty.
9. A clowder.

Q

22

1. Which saint's 11,000 maidens were slain by Huns?
2. At which battle did William Prescott say, 'Don't fire until you see the whites of their eyes'?
3. Which annual contest is associated with Olney?
4. Whose diary did the Reverend John Smith decipher in the nineteenth century?
5. How long is a badminton court?
6. From where was the first British television service broadcast?
7. Who introduced 'Panorama' for many years, and now has an annual lecture delivered in his honour?
8. Who is the Divine Miss M?
9. What was Edison's first practical invention?

393

1. Describe a 'Sam Browne'?
2. Who founded the Order of Merit?
3. Out of over 58,000 Americans who died in Vietnam, only one has not been what?
4. Who wrote *The Foundation Trilogy*?
5. Name Sir Gordon Richards's only Derby winner.
6. Who directed, produced, co-wrote and starred in the film based on John Reed's book *Ten Days That Shook the World*?
7. What famous colony-builder of America was expelled from Oxford University after his conversion to the views of the Society of Friends?
8. Who sang 'Sealed with a Kiss'?
9. What is the chemical symbol for Tungsten?

764

1. What are lines from the centre of a circle to its circumference called?
2. What is Epidaurus famous for?
3. Which mountain range contains thirteen of the world's twenty highest mountains?
4. To which city did the Wooden Horse gain entrance?
5. In which Olympics were butterfly-stroke races first held?
6. Who starred in the film *Better Late than Never*?
7. What was the French writer Arouet's better-known name?
8. Which festival links the cities of Hereford, Worcester and Gloucester?
9. What colour is a female blackbird?

22

1. Ursula.
2. Bunker Hill, in 1775.
3. The pancake race.
4. Samuel Pepys's.
5. 44 feet.
6. Alexandra Palace.
7. Richard Dimbleby.
8. Bette Midler.
9. The ticker-tape for stock market information.

393

1. A military officer's belt adjoining a shoulder strap.
2. King Edward VII, in 1902.
3. Properly identified.
4. Isaac Asimov.
5. Pinza, in 1953.
6. Warren Beatty, in *Reds*.
7. William Penn.
8. Brian Hyland.
9. W.

764

1. Radii.
2. Its Greek theatre, built in 350 BC.
3. The Himalayas.
4. Troy.
5. 1956.
6. Harold Gould.
7. Voltaire.
8. The Three Choirs Festival.
9. Brown.

23

1. Which famous poet's wife created Frankenstein?
2. Which forces occupied the hill called Spion Kop?
3. In which country is the port of Alexandria?
4. Who are the two most translated English writers (dead or alive)?
5. What number did Roger Bannister wear on his vest when he broke the four-minute mile?
6. At what age did Raquel Welch win her first beauty contest?
7. What made A. L. Sawyer unique among newspaper editors?
8. Which Sibelius composition is used as the theme of the 1934 film *Death Takes a Holiday*?
9. The earth weighs about 5,882 million million million tons. What percentage of that is taken up by the oceans?

394

1. Of which god is the Egyptian Sphinx a statue?
2. Under which South African statesman's will were scholarships founded at Oxford?
3. Where is Fregate?
4. How many ages of man are there, according to Shakespeare's *As You Like It*?
5. For what is 'Citius, Altius, Fortius' the motto?
6. What did Al Jolson use to blacken his face?
7. Which artist animated Pink Floyd's *The Wall*?
8. Franz Liszt was the father-in-law of which famous composer?
9. What is the centre of our solar system?

765

1. How many Nobel Prizes are awarded annually?
2. Where and in what year was the first fire insurance in the world organized?
3. Bartholomew Diaz called it the Cape of Storms. How is it known now?
4. How long does Puck say it will take him to put a girdle round the earth in *A Midsummer Night's Dream*?
5. Which skater is married to Alexander Zaitsev?
6. Who spent much of her screen career in the water?
7. In which town was Leonardo da Vinci born?
8. Which 1961 Acker Bilk record remained in the charts for fifty-five weeks?
9. What measures horizontal and vertical angles in surveying?

23

1. Percy Bysshe Shelley.
2. The Boers.
3. Egypt.
4. Shakespeare and Agatha Christie.
5. Forty-one.
6. Fourteen.
7. He was only 2 foot 6 inches tall.
8. 'Valse Triste'.
9. 0·022 per cent (accept less than 1 per cent as an answer).

394

1. Harmachis.
2. Cecil Rhodes.
3. The Seychelles (it's an island).
4. Seven.
5. The Olympic Games.
6. Burnt cork.
7. Gerald Scarfe.
8. Richard Wagner.
9. The sun.

765

1. Six.
2. In London in 1680, by the Phoenix Fire Office.
3. The Cape of Good Hope.
4. 40 minutes.
5. Irina Rodnina.
6. Esther Williams, 'Hollywood's Mermaid'.
7. Vinci.
8. 'Stranger on the Shore'.
9. A theodolite.

24

1. Where is the keystone of an arch located?
2. Which building in Rome used to be the arena where people were thrown to the lions?
3. Which is Britain's most visited stately home?
4. Who wrote *Private Angelo*?
5. Which racecourse, now closed, was nicknamed 'The Frying Pan'?
6. Which television programme used a detail of *The Creation of Adam* by Michelangelo in its introduction?
7. Which nationality was Matthias Grünewald?
8. How many semi-quavers are there in a semi-breve?
9. In which season does the earth move fastest round the sun?

395

1. In the Royal Navy, badges of rank are worn on the jacket cuffs. What rank is indicated by a single stripe surmounted by a small hoop?
2. How many children did the average married couple have in the 1850s?
3. Which Channel Island is nearest to France?
4. Who is John Osborne's 'angry young man'?
5. In 1973, who broke Muhammad Ali's jaw?
6. Who played Fleur in BBC TV's 'Forsyte Saga'?
7. What were D. H. Lawrence's first two names?
8. By what name were Cam and the Passions better known?
9. How many times would the earth fit inside the sun?

766

1. An organization of business and professional men was founded in 1905 in Chicago out of a weekly luncheon club. What is it called?
2. What was the last word of Charles I on the scaffold?
3. Who said, and where, 'Great God! This is an awful place!'?
4. With whom did Middleton collaborate in writing *The Changeling*?
5. Who was the first Welshman to win an Olympic gold medal?
6. Who played Pink in the movie *The Wall*?
7. Which French writer had an affair with Alfred de Musset?
8. Who claimed that the sun wasn't 'gonna shine anymore'?
9. The British Interplanetary Society completed designs for an interstellar craft in 1978. What was the project called?

24

1. The top.
2. The Colosseum.
3. Woburn Abbey.
4. Eric Linklater.
5. Alexandra Park.
6. 'The South Bank Show'.
7. German.
8. Sixteen.
9. Summer.

395

1. Commodore.
2. Six.
3. Alderney.
4. Jimmy Porter, in *Look Back in Anger*.
5. Ken Norton.
6. Susan Hampshire.
7. David Herbert.
8. The Beach Boys.
9. 109.

766

1. The Rotary Club.
2. 'Remember' (said to Bishop Juxon).
3. Captain Scott at the South Pole.
4. William Rowley.
5. Lynn Davies.
6. Bob Geldorf.
7. George Sand.
8. The Walker Brothers.
9. Daedalus.

25

1. Of what is the Fourth Sea Lord in charge?
2. What were last seen in naval action at the Battle of Navarino in 1827?
3. Les Baux in France gave its name to the ore of what metal?
4. Which play revolves around the relationship of Martha and George?
5. What distance is the competitive biathlon?
6. Who starred in television's *Kung Fu*?
7. Where was El Greco born?
8. Which musical featured 'the oldest established permanent floating crap game in New York'?
9. In computer jargon what does the acronym ROM mean?

396

1. The 'Querty' typewriter key board was introduced specifically to do what?
2. Who beat whom at the Battle of Sedan in 1870?
3. In which year did a huge earthquake hit San Francisco?
4. Of where was Pericles prince, according to Shakespeare?
5. Which events make up the heptathlon?
6. Who played Inspector Clouseau's deranged superior officer in the Pink Panther movies?
7. Which evangelist was chiefly responsible for bringing the Protestant faith to Scotland?
8. Which socialist song is sung to the tune of 'Der Tannenbaum'?
9. In computer jargon what does the acronym RAM mean?

767

1. What are scout rallies called?
2. Of which battle fought in 1805 is 21 October the anniversary?
3. From where in Eire do they take the water to make Guinness?
4. How many Bond novels did Ian Fleming write?
5. Name two teams for which Danny Blanchflower played.
6. Who starred as a security agent in *The Groundstar Conspiracy*?
7. Which English poet did Lady Caroline Lamb call, 'Mad, bad, and dangerous to know'?
8. By what name is John Lydon better known?
9. *Troglodytes troglodytes* is the scientific name of which bird?

25

1. Naval supplies and transport.
2. Wooden ships (the majority of the Turkish and Egyptian fleet was destroyed by a British, French and Russian fleet).
3. Aluminium, which is obtained from bauxite.
4. *Who's Afraid of Virginia Woolf?*, by Edward Albee.
5. Twenty kilometres.
6. David Carradine.
7. Crete.
8. *Guys and Dolls.*
9. Read Only Memory.

396

1. Slow down the typist's speed.
2. William I of Prussia beat Napoleon III of France.
3. 1906.
4. Tyre.
5. 100-metre hurdles, shot put, high jump, long jump, 200 metres, javelin and 800 metres.
6. Herbert Lom.
7. John Knox.
8. 'The Red Flag'.
9. Random Access Memory.

767

1. Jamborees.
2. Trafalgar.
3. The River Liffey.
4. Twelve.
5. Northern Ireland, Glentoran, Barnsley, Aston Villa, Tottenham Hotspur.
6. George Peppard.
7. Lord Byron.
8. Johnny Rotten.
9. The wren.

26

1. What is the chief ingredient of *sauce lyonnaise*?
2. Who was the last king to be crowned in Scotland?
3. Originally, Rhodes Scholars were selected from students of the United States, the Commonwealth and which other country?
4. By what name is the author Charles Hamilton better known?
5. Which Olympic ice-skater went on to become a Hollywood film star in the 1930s and 1940s?
6. Who played Miss Marple in six films?
7. What is the name of the colour used to describe old brown-and-white photographs?
8. Which Hoagy Carmichael song gave Ray Charles a big hit in 1960?
9. What metal impurity gives ruby its red colour and emerald its green colour?

397

1. To the nearest 50,000, how many cars are stolen in Britain each year?
2. How many blows did Mary Queen of Scots' executioner use to cut off her head?
3. What is the capital of Australia?
4. Who created Jane Marple?
5. What soccer position does Joe Corrigan play?
6. In which film did Edward G. Robinson play Lancy Howard?
7. Who was the US president during the First World War?
8. Pibroch is a form of music for which instrument?
9. What was a macaroni box?

768

1. What was the original trade of William Morris the car manufacturer?
2. Complete Carlyle's view of history: 'The history of the world is but . . .'
3. Which is the smallest county in the British Isles?
4. Which poet wrote *The Borderers* and *The Prelude*?
5. Which world heavyweight champion was nicknamed 'Cinderella Man'?
6. Who played the central character in Fritz Lang's *M*?
7. What do we call in English that type of painting known in French as *nature morte* and in Spanish as *bodegón*?
8. By what name was Mark Field better known?
9. What was George Stevenson's first successful railway engine called?

26

1. Onions.
2. Charles II, at Scone, 1 January 1651.
3. Germany.
4. Frank Richards, creator of Billy Bunter.
5. Sonja Henie.
6. Margaret Rutherford.
7. Sepia.
8. 'Georgia on My Mind'.
9. Chromium.

397

1. 550,000, of which about 500,000 are eventually recovered.
2. Fifteen.
3. Canberra.
4. Agatha Christie.
5. Goalkeeper.
6. *The Cincinnati Kid.*
7. Woodrow Wilson.
8. The bagpipes.
9. A primitive calculator.

768

1. Bicycle repairer.
2. '. . . the biography of great men.'
3. The Isle of Wight.
4. William Wordsworth.
5. Jimmy Braddock.
6. Peter Lorre.
7. Still life.
8. Marc Bolan.
9. Locomotion No. 1.

27

1. What type of pastry is used to make éclairs?
2. What did VE Day signify?
3. When does Bermuda's lease to the US run out?
4. Who wrote *Watership Down*?
5. How many lanes are there in an Olympic swimming pool?
6. What is the name of the ranch home of the Cartwright family in 'Bonanza'?
7. Who invented the board game Cavendish?
8. By what name was the soprano Helen Mitchell better known?
9. For how many months in each year does a dormouse hibernate?

398

1. Which biscuit is named after Queen Victoria's holiday home in the Isle of Wight?
2. Which king licensed actresses to play women's parts on stage?
3. Which country produces Parmesan cheese?
4. Who wrote *The Deserted Village*?
5. What do the Los Angeles Lakers play?
6. Who stars in the vintage crime series 'Highway Patrol'?
7. Who sailed single-handed round the world in 1967?
8. What was Sinding's most famous piano composition?
9. Who discovered penicillin in 1928?

769

1. Which festival did the first popular greetings card celebrate?
2. How many of Queen Anne's children survived infancy?
3. Where did Arthur Thistlewood meet his co-conspirators to plot the murder of the Cabinet?
4. In Arthurian legend who found the Holy Grail?
5. How many players are on each side at one time in American basketball?
6. Who produced the film *Hell's Angels*?
7. Who by his digging proved ancient Troy to be no myth?
8. The famous British scientist Sir Charles Wheatstone is said to be the inventor not only of the concertina but also of another popular instrument. Which one?
9. What is the chemical symbol for silver?

27

1. Choux.
2. The end of the Second World War in Europe.
3. 2 September 2039.
4. Richard Adams.
5. Eight.
6. The Ponderosa.
7. Maureen and Alan Hiron.
8. Nellie Melba.
9. Six.

398

1. Osborne.
2. Charles II, in 1662.
3. Italy.
4. Oliver Goldsmith.
5. Basketball.
6. Broderick Crawford.
7. Sir Francis Chichester.
8. 'Rustle of Spring'.
9. Sir Alexander Fleming.

769

1. St Valentine's Day.
2. One – William of Gloucester, who died when he was nine.
3. Cato Street, London.
4. Sir Galahad.
5. Five.
6. Howard Hughes.
7. Heinrich Schliemann.
8. The harmonica.
9. Ag.

28

1. What was a recusant?
2. What were built along the south coast to guard against French invasions in 1805–6?
3. Where is Britain's tallest nave?
4. Which author created the detective Piet van der Valk?
5. Who was the first pole-vaulter to clear 19 feet?
6. Who played Dracula in the New-York-set spoof *Love At First Bite*?
7. Who did a series of paintings of young men and light reflecting in water?
8. Who tied a yellow ribbon round an old oak tree?
9. What was extracted from the bark of the cinchona tree?

399

1. What is written defamation called?
2. Who were the parents of the first Plantagenet king?
3. What is the name of the tiny Pyrenean nation between France and Spain?
4. Which author's Christian names are John Ronald Reuel?
5. Who makes the rules for flat horse-racing in England?
6. Who was Humphrey Bogart's female co-star in *Casablanca*?
7. Which English novelist didn't learn English till he was twenty?
8. How many overtures did Beethoven write to his opera *Fidelio*?
9. What instrument measures the intensity of earthquakes?

770

1. What did hospital social workers used to be called?
2. Which pistol, also favoured by John Steed and James Bond, did Adolf Hitler use to commit suicide?
3. From which language does the word 'alphabet' come?
4. Who killed Blunderbore?
5. What colour jerseys are worn by England in international Rugby matches?
6. What part does Billy Welles play in J. Arthur Rank films?
7. What is aqueous paint?
8. Who composed 'Brigg Fair'?
9. Which unit is used to express the purity of gold?

28

1. One who refused to attend Church of England services from the time of Elizabeth I.
2. Martello towers.
3. Westminster Abbey.
4. Nicholas Freeling.
5. Thierry Vigneron of France in 1981.
6. George Hamilton.
7. David Hockney.
8. Tony Orlando and Dawn.
9. Quinine.

399

1. Libel.
2. Queen Matilda and Geoffrey of Anjou, parents of Henry II.
3. Andorra.
4. J. R. R. Tolkien.
5. The Jockey Club.
6. Ingrid Bergman.
7. Joseph Conrad.
8. Four.
9. The seismograph.

770

1. Almoners.
2. Walther 7·65.
3. Greek, the first two letters being alpha and beta.
4. Jack the Giant Killer.
5. White.
6. He strikes the gong at the beginning of each film.
7. Any paint that may be diluted with water.
8. Delius.
9. Carat.

29

1. What does the acronym SHAPE stand for?
2. What was a Fleet marriage?
3. In which river did the Pied Piper drown the rats of Hamelin?
4. Who first wrote about haggis?
5. Which great Russian gymnast is married to a great Russian sprinter?
6. Who were Hedda Hopper and Louella Parsons?
7. Where is the finest collection of Leonardo da Vinci's drawings kept?
8. Which artist did Don McLean sing about in 'Starry Starry Night'?
9. Robert Whitehead invented which weapon in 1866?

400

1. Who launched the *Daily Mail*?
2. What was the Stars and Bars?
3. What are Grimes' Graves?
4. Who is Archie Rice?
5. Who was England's youngest-ever test cricketer?
6. Mark Hamill played which character in *Star Wars*?
7. Who wrote a poem about Vasari and another about painting the Sistine Chapel?
8. Which ex-Beatle was the first to have a Number One hit after the break-up?
9. Zymase is a natural catalyst which acts on glucose to create what drug?

771

1. What was the speed limit fixed by the Motor Car Act of 1903?
2. Who was nicknamed Old Rowley?
3. On which river in Portugal is Oporto?
4. Who is Ngaio Marsh's detective?
5. Which boxer had the nickname the 'Boston Strong Boy'?
6. Which part, written for a man, was first played by one 80 years later in spite of many intervening productions?
7. What London art gallery is named after a manufacturer of artificial silk?
8. Who is the Big Yin?
9. For hundreds of years Sicily was the traditional source of which element?

29

1. Supreme Headquarters, Allied Powers, Europe.
2. One performed by an imprisoned clergyman in the Fleet Prison without banns or licence (abolished in 1753).
3. The Weser.
4. Aristophanes.
5. Lyudmila Tourischeva to Valery Borzov.
6. Hollywood gossip columnists.
7. Royal Library, Windsor Castle.
8. Vincent Van Gogh.
9. The torpedo.

400

1. Alfred Harmsworth, Viscount Northcliffe, in 1896.
2. The flag of the eleven confederate states in the American Civil War.
3. Neolithic flint quarries near Thetford, Norfolk.
4. 'The Entertainer' in John Osborne's play of that name.
5. Brian Close, who first played when he was eighteen.
6. Luke Skywalker.
7. Michelangelo.
8. George Harrison.
9. Alcohol.

771

1. Twenty miles per hour.
2. Charles II, after his horse.
3. The Duoro.
4. Chief Detective Inspector Alleyn.
5. John L. Sullivan.
6. Peter Pan, played by Miles Anderson for the RSC in 1982.
7. The Courtauld Institute.
8. Billy Connolly.
9. Sulphur.

30

1. What is spoken defamation called?
2. What in Greek history was the March of the Ten Thousand?
3. Which bridge collapsed in 1879, causing a train to fall into the river, killing seventy-eight people?
4. Where is the poet Robert Browning buried?
5. What is the oldest Rugby football club in existence?
6. In which film did José Ferrer star as Alfred Dreyfus?
7. Who is the present Queen of Spain?
8. What was Rimsky-Korsakov's original job?
9. What makes the rattlesnake rattle?

401

1. The sorceress Circe changed what into what?
2. In which year did the Seminole Indian tribe sign a peace treaty with the United States?
3. Which European country produces the most wine?
4. Name the principal horse in George Orwell's *Animal Farm*.
5. Which cricketer played in seventy-eight test matches and also played football for Arsenal?
6. Who is Jaime Summer?
7. What colours make a scene appear to recede on a picture?
8. What is Canada's national anthem called?
9. How do frogs breathe underwater?

772

1. What is Friday's child?
2. Who praised English women for their kisses and was a leading light of the Reformation?
3. Troops of which foreign country set fire to the White House in the nineteenth century?
4. Who wrote *The Day of the Jackal*?
5. Which Italian team were tragically killed in a plane crash in 1949?
6. Which was the first film to be made in Cinemascope?
7. Who was the architect of the Queen's House at Greenwich?
8. Whose tenth hit was 'I Feel Like Buddy Holly'?
9. By what name is an arbutus colloquially known?

30

1. Slander.
2. The march of Greek mercenaries from Babylon to the Black Sea through a hostile Persian Empire in 401 BC.
3. The Tay Bridge.
4. Westminster Abbey.
5. Guy's Hospital RFC.
6. *J'accuse.*
7. Sophia.
8. A sailor.
9. The remnants of old skin at the end of its tail.

401

1. Humans into animals.
2. 1975.
3. Italy.
4. Boxer.
5. Denis Compton.
6. Television's first bionic woman.
7. Blues and violets.
8. 'O Canada'.
9. Through their skins.

772

1. Loving and giving.
2. Erasmus.
3. Great Britain, in 1814.
4. Frederick Forsyth.
5. Torino.
6. *The Robe.*
7. Inigo Jones.
8. Alvin Stardust.
9. A strawberry tree.

31

1. What does the prefix 'tele-' actually mean?
2. Who was the Pope during the Second World War?
3. For which city was Jorvik the Viking name?
4. What were the names of the Magi?
5. Which is the Canon Football League's oldest club?
6. In what year did the BBC inaugurate the Third Programme, 'devoted entirely to broadcasts of a cultural nature'?
7. Who said, 'I do not seek, I find'?
8. In which Puccini opera does the poet Rodolfo appear?
9. The earth actually takes less than 24 hours of mean solar time to spin once on its axis. How much less?

402

1. From which language does the word 'gymnasium' come?
2. At what age did William Pitt (the Younger) become prime minister of England?
3. Which country's flag consists of a red background with a white crescent moon and star?
4. Name Shakespeare's Moor of Venice.
5. What was James J. Corbett's nickname?
6. Who was Abbott's comedy partner?
7. Who tried Jesus and sentenced him to be executed?
8. Who fittingly starred in the 1938 film *Moonlight Sonata*?
9. About how long will an overdose of cyanide take to kill an average person?

773

1. How many fathoms are there to a cable?
2. Name one of the two kings of England who were never crowned.
3. It can be said that France's extravagant support (£50,000,000) of which revolution led to her bankruptcy and her own revolution?
4. Who was received into the Catholic church by the priest on whom he modelled his most famous character?
5. Which country has won Badminton's Thomas Cup most often?
6. Who invented custard pies?
7. Who wrote, 'All art constantly aspires towards the condition of music'?
8. Who wrote, 'This land is your land'?
9. Originally gelatine came from what?

31

1. Far.
2. Pope Pius XII.
3. York.
4. Melchior, Balthasar and Kaspar.
5. Notts County (founded 1862).
6. 1946.
7. Picasso.
8. *La Bohème*.
9. 3 minutes 56 seconds.

402

1. Greek.
2. Twenty-four.
3. Turkey.
4. Othello.
5. Gentleman Jim.
6. Costello.
7. Pontius Pilate.
8. The concert pianist and ex Polish PM Jan Paderewski.
9. 15 minutes.

773

1. About 100.
2. Edward V and Edward VIII.
3. The American War of Independence.
4. G. K. Chesterton.
5. Indonesia.
6. Mable Normand, at the Keystone studios in California.
7. Walter Pater.
8. Woody Guthrie.
9. Animal bones and tissue.

32

1. What is the Hawaiian word of greeting?
2. After the Restoration the bodies of three regicides were disinterred, dismembered and put on show. Name two of them.
3. Where was the Battle of Hastings fought?
4. Where did the Hellfire Club meet?
5. Which wicketkeeper scored a century in the 1977 Centenary Test?
6. What was Yosser's catchword?
7. What is an icon?
8. What was the Supremes' first UK hit?
9. The axis of the earth is moving and in 12,000 years the Pole Star will be replaced by which other star?

403

1. What does IQ stand for?
2. Who was the last direct Stuart claimant to the throne?
3. Under what circumstances is duelling legal in Uruguay?
4. Of which sea-captain did Galsworthy say, 'I had never before seen a man so masculinely keen, yet so femininely sensitive'?
5. What is the maximum number of clubs allowed in a competition in golf?
6. By what name is Allen Stewart Konigsberg better known?
7. Who was known as 'the Warrior Queen'?
8. Which composer did Richard Tauber play in *Blossom Time*?
9. The fleas of which animal carried the plague known as the Black Death?

774

1. What have *gazpacho* and *vichyssoise* got in common?
2. How did Jane Seymour, wife of Henry VIII, die?
3. Which is the only European country in which a wife does not take the name of her husband upon marriage?
4. Who loved Sarah Hutchinson and wrote 'Dejection: An Ode'?
5. What is Jochen Maas's sport?
6. How old is Lily Munsto?
7. Who said of which battle, 'I don't think it would have done if I had not been there'?
8. Who wrote the sonata given the title 'Les Adieux'?
9. The gear which enables the drive wheels of a car to turn a corner while on the same axle is called what?

32

1. Aloha.
2. Cromwell, Ireton and Bradshaw.
3. Senlac Hill (north of what is now Battle village).
4. Medmenham Abbey.
5. Rodney Marsh of Australia.
6. 'Gizzajob'.
7. A painting, mosaic or enamel of Christ, the Virgin Mary or a saint thought to be a sacred object.
8. 'Where Did Our Love Go', 1964.
9. Vega.

403

1. Intelligence quotient.
2. Cardinal Henry Stuart, brother of the Young Pretender. He died in 1807.
3. If both protagonists are registered blood donors.
4. Joseph Conrad.
5. Fourteen.
6. Woody Allen.
7. Boadicea.
8. Franz Schubert.
9. The black rat.

774

1. They are both soups served chilled.
2. Of septicaemia, within days of giving birth to the future Edward VI.
3. Spain.
4. Coleridge.
5. Motor racing.
6. 157.
7. Wellington, of Waterloo.
8. Beethoven.
9. The differential gear.

33

1. The most frequent letters in English are E, T, O, A, N. Which language has the letter frequency E, S, A, N, T?
2. Why was Barnaby Fitzpatrick eager that Edward VI should behave?
3. Which city does Tempelhof airport serve?
4. Name the Greek goddess of retribution.
5. What is a golf ball made of?
6. Who was Peter Sellers's co-star in *The Millionairess*?
7. In what medium did a twelfth-century emperor of Japan, Sukoku, copy out a Buddhist religious work?
8. Which composer did Carl Boehm play in the film *The Magnificent Rebel*?
9. Of which fruit is 'Pearmain' a variety?

404

1. What percentage of people in the US and Europe have four or more colds a year?
2. What, within half a million, was the population of England in 1086 (the year of the Domesday Book)?
3. What is the capital of Tunisia?
4. Who gets the black spot from Blind Pew?
5. When did Sir Francis Chichester sail around the world?
6. Who wrote *Arms and the Man*?
7. In which city is the world's largest indoor games convention held annually?
8. Which of Beethoven's symphonies is known as the 'Eroica'?
9. When coke burns, what dangerous gas is given off?

775

1. What is the most expensive pâté you can buy?
2. Who were the Angevin kings of England?
3. Which is considered to be the oldest of the English cheeses?
4. Homer's *Iliad* tells of the siege of which city?
5. Who was the first woman to win an individual medal in the Olympic Games showjumping event?
6. Who starred in the 1972 film *Pete 'n' Tillie*?
7. By what name was Vladimir I. Ulyanov better known?
8. Ginette Neveu was killed in an air crash in 1949. Which instrument did she play?
9. What is your tarsus?

33

1. French.
2. He was the royal whipping boy, whipped in place of the prince when the prince deserved punishment.
3. Berlin.
4. Nemesis.
5. Elastic thread wound under tension around a central core surrounded by plastic.
6. Sophia Loren.
7. His own blood.
8. Beethoven.
9. The apple.

404

1. 25 per cent.
2. 2 million.
3. Tunis.
4. Billy Bones (in R. L. Stevenson's *Treasure Island*).
5. 1966–7.
6. George Bernard Shaw.
7. London.
8. The third.
9. Carbon monoxide.

775

1. Pâté de foie gras.
2. Early Plantagenet kings from Henry II to John (who lost Anjou in 1204).
3. Cheshire.
4. Troy.
5. Marion Mould.
6. Carol Burnett and Walter Matthau.
7. Lenin.
8. Violin.
9. Your ankle.

34

1. What is currently the most popular aphrodisiac?
2. What was 'the Harrowing of the North'?
3. Flowers in modern gardens have one attribute which the native flowers of Australia lack. What is it?
4. Who was Christopher Robin's nurse?
5. What are Gleneagles and Sandwich?
6. Name Jock and Ellie's three sons in 'Dallas'.
7. Who is the most eminent living British sculptor?
8. Who did Fernand Gravet play in the film *The Great Waltz*?
9. About what percentage of white people have rhesus-positive blood?

405

1. Strabismus is another name for which affliction of the eyes?
2. Why was everybody buried 'in woollen' after 1666?
3. Which language appears on the Rosetta stone?
4. Who was Tamora's lover in *Titus Andronicus*?
5. Who competes for the Stanley Cup?
6. Who won the Oscar for best actor in 1957 for his part in *The Bridge on the River Kwai*?
7. What colour is the bull on an archery target?
8. For which instrument did the composer Widor write his best-known works?
9. What are ceps, morels and chanterelles?

776

1. What is 'mordanting'?
2. In which civilization do the first examples of (cuneiform) writing appear?
3. From which London railway station do trains depart for the West of England?
4. Whose son was Absalom?
5. Where did Muhammad Ali fight Henry Cooper for the world heavyweight title in 1966?
6. In which play by Shaw does Nurse Ftatateeta feature?
7. Who used the pseudonym 'Ellis Bell'?
8. What was the first Rolling Stones No. 1 hit?
9. What is the chemical symbol for phosphorus?

34

1. Asparagus, according to *The New York Times*.
2. William I's campaign of devastation after the Saxon uprising of 1069.
3. Perfume.
4. Alice.
5. Golf clubs.
6. J.R., Gary and Bobby.
7. Henry Moore.
8. Johann Strauss (the younger).
9. 84 per cent.

405

1. A squint.
2. An Act of that year prohibited shrouds of other material in order to encourage the wool industry.
3. Egyptian and Greek (found at Rosetta by a French army officer in 1799).
4. Aaron.
5. Ice hockey teams.
6. Alec Guinness.
7. Gold or yellow.
8. The organ.
9. Edible fungi.

776

1. Fixing a dye into cloth.
2. Sumerian.
3. Paddington.
4. David, King of Judah.
5. Highbury Stadium (Arsenal FC).
6. *Caesar and Cleopatra*.
7. Emily Brontë.
8. 'It's All Over Now'.
9. P.

35

1. What do gypsies call non-gypsies?
2. Who was taken ill at a banquet in Babylon and died?
3. What are the Caelian, Esquiline, Quirinal, Viminal, Aventine, Capitoline and Palatine?
4. Name the five books of Moses.
5. From which country do Juventus FC hail?
6. Who was that man?
7. Of the fifteen children of a tallow-chandler, one became 'America's versatile sage'. Who was he?
8. B.B. King's most famous album is called: *Live at* — —?
9. The Roman Emperor Marcus Aurelius was one of which famous physician's patients?

406

1. How many kittens lost their mittens?
2. What was the surname of the second and the sixth presidents of the USA?
3. How many characters are there in the Russian alphabet?
4. Who was the Roman equivalent of Demeter?
5. Which soccer team is nicknamed the 'Filberts'?
6. What happened to vests when Clark Gable took off his shirt in *It Happened One Night*?
7. Under whose patronage was the Royal Academy of Arts founded?
8. What was Dusty Springfield's first No. 1 hit?
9. Which prince contributed to the development of the Quantum Theory?

777

1. The new Gregorian calendar demands the leap day every four years but how many times every 400 years doesn't this happen?
2. What did 'Unready' mean when first attributed to Ethelred?
3. After which French town is the textile cambric named?
4. Where is Shakespeare's *As You Like It* set?
5. Who first put the shot over 70 feet?
6. How many words of dialogue were there in Mel Brooks's *Silent Movie*?
7. Which Irish painter paints grotesquely deformed human figures and images?
8. Name the two rival gangs in the musical *West Side Story*.
9. How many legs has a daddy-long-legs?

35

1. Gajos.
2. Alexander the Great.
3. The Seven Hills of Rome.
4. Genesis, Exodus, Leviticus, Numbers and Deuteronomy.
5. Italy.
6. Tommy Handley, star of radio's 'ITMA'.
7. Benjamin Franklin.
8. *The Regal.*
9. Galen.

406

1. Three.
2. Adams.
3. Thirty-one.
4. Ceres.
5. Leicester City.
6. Sales of men's vests in the US fell by 40 per cent – Gable *wasn't* wearing one.
7. George III in 1768.
8. 'You Don't Have To Say You Love Me'.
9. Prince de Broglie.

777

1. Three.
2. Deficient in counsel ('redeless').
3. Cambrai.
4. In the Ardennes in France.
5. Randy Matson.
6. One – spoken by Marcel Marceau, the French mime virtuoso.
7. Francis Bacon.
8. Jets and Sharks.
9. Eight.

36

1. Which language does Flemish most closely resemble?
2. In Mussolini's Italy what was the *Balilla*?
3. Which country's flag comprises three equal vertical stripes, in green, white and red?
4. Where does this quotation originate, 'This above all: to thine own self be true'?
5. In which year did Ayala win the Grand National?
6. 'You're never alone with . . .' what?
7. Which great British Field Marshal was the son of an Ulster clergyman?
8. Whose first manager was Andrew Loog Oldham?
9. How do you tell the age of a horse?

407

1. What is the origin of the word 'brandy'?
2. Which king once owned the *Kensington and Chelsea Post*?
3. What is Uruguay's chief port?
4. Which writer was recognized on a surgeon's slab, the victim of body snatchers?
5. Which athlete was killed in a car accident a year after winning the Olympic 3,000 metres steeplechase?
6. What was the name of Diana Dors's actor husband?
7. Who was mortally wounded in the heel by an arrow from Paris?
8. Who wrote, 'If I were a carpenter'?
9. What kind of animal is a snow-shoe rabbit?

778

1. The derrick crane was named after Dick Derrick. What was his occupation?
2. Who did the Emperors Tiberius and Caligula both murder?
3. Of which country is Mombasa the chief port?
4. Which is the longest part written by Shakespeare?
5. Which dog first won the Greyhound Derby in consecutive years?
6. Which Noel Coward play features Elyot and Amanda?
7. Who was Henry Cooper's manager, nicknamed 'The Bishop'?
8. Dalcroze, Professor of Harmony at the Geneva Conservatoire, conceived of which form of exercise?
9. In all tests on drugs and poisons there is a dose called the LD–50 dose. What is it?

36

1. Dutch.
2. The Junior Military organization for boys of six and upwards.
3. Italy.
4. Shakespeare's *Hamlet.*
5. 1963.
6. '... a Strand', from the legendary cigarette ad.
7. Field Marshal Montgomery.
8. The Rolling Stones.
9. By the growth of its teeth.

407

1. From the Dutch *brandewijn* (burnt wine).
2. King Zog of Albania, who died in 1961, in London, where he had lived since 1938.
3. Montevideo.
4. Laurence Sterne.
5. Bronislaw Malinowski.
6. Alan Lake.
7. Achilles.
8. Tim Hardin.
9. A hare.

778

1. A seventeenth-century hangman.
2. Their respective wives.
3. Kenya.
4. Hamlet (11,610 words).
5. Mick the Miller (1929–30).
6. *Private Lives.*
7. Jim Wicks.
8. Eurhythmics.
9. The dose at which 50 per cent (or half) the subjects die.

37

1. Who believe that the 'City of God' will be founded in the USA?
2. What was given the code name 'Mulberry' in the Second World War?
3. What was built on the site of the old Waldorf Astoria hotel in New York?
4. Who was Serjeant Buzfuz?
5. In golf, what is the American name for an albatross?
6. Who wrote the play *The Entertainer*?
7. Who was the son of Eric the Red?
8. Which pop singer has compiled a book of equine anecdotes?
9. What is the antimatter equivalent of the electron?

408

1. Whose portrait appears on the reverse of the £50 note?
2. Who did Achilles kill and drag three times round the walls of Troy?
3. What is the state capital of Texas?
4. Who, in prison, wrote of Arthur?
5. Who won the men's shot put at the 1974 Commonwealth Games?
6. In which year did James Dean die?
7. Who was the headmaster of Rugby School who reformed English public school education?
8. Name one of the actresses who portrayed the Little Ladies in 'Rock Follies'.
9. What is a group of hounds called?

779

1. In which year was the old-age pension introduced?
2. Alaric, King of the Goths, besieged Rome in AD 408 and demanded a ransom of gold, silver and 3,000 lb of what?
3. Where is Darwin buried?
4. Who was Helen of Troy's husband?
5. Who play home soccer at Goodison Park?
6. What are Rhett Butler's last words in *Gone with the Wind*?
7. Which famous Indian is buried at Gravesend, Kent?
8. An organ built in the tenth century was so powerful that seventy men were needed to pump the bellows. Where was it?
9. What are fingerlings?

37

1. The Mormons.
2. The construction of floating harbours for D-Day.
3. The Empire State Building.
4. A barrister in Dickens's *Pickwick Papers* (counsel for Mrs Bardell in the breach-of-promise trial).
5. A double eagle.
6. John Osborne.
7. Leif Ericsson.
8. Alvin Stardust.
9. The positron.

408

1. Sir Christopher Wren's.
2. Hector.
3. Austin.
4. Sir Thomas Malory (*Le Morte D'Arthur*).
5. Geoff Capes.
6. 1955 (30 September).
7. Thomas Arnold.
8. Rula Lenska, Charlotte Cornwell, Julie Covington.
9. A mute of hounds.

779

1. 1909.
2. Pepper.
3. Westminster Abbey.
4. Menelaus.
5. Everton.
6. 'My dear, I don't give a damn.'
7. Pocahontas (d. 1617).
8. At Winchester Cathedral.
9. Baby salmon about to leave for the sea.

38

1. What is French for 'honey'?
2. Which emperor had St Peter crucified?
3. The first three Eddystone lighthouses were lit by what?
4. The first printed Bible, the Mazarin Bible, was also named after the number of lines on each page. How many lines were there?
5. From which bridge does the Boat Race start?
6. Which famous American novelist co-wrote, with Raymond Chandler, the screenplay for *The Big Sleep*?
7. Which one-time 'Fauve' decorated the interior of a chapel in Venice?
8. What was first performed as 'Count Walsegg's Requiem'?
9. By what common name is acetyl-salicylic acid known?

409

1. Who opened the world's first full-scale atomic generating plant?
2. Which revolt took place in 1381?
3. Which French town is noted for glove-making?
4. Around which event does *Barnaby Rudge* centre?
5. In which weight category did John Conteh fight?
6. Who produced the original film of *Scarface*?
7. Who were the 'Mormon Mafia' hired to protect from outside contamination?
8. To whom were the 'Abegg Variations' dedicated?
9. Counting outwards from the sun, which is the third planet in our solar system?

780

1. What is mocha?
2. During the eighteenth century, Kitty Fisher was London's most highly paid – what?
3. Which canal links the Mediterranean with the Red Sea?
4. Who is the fourth musketeer?
5. Which country did Johann Cruyff play for?
6. Who played Marco Polo in the 1962 film?
7. By what name did Dr Richard Raskind become known after his sex change operation?
8. Who wrote the 'Hungarian Rhapsody'?
9. If a rabbit's front teeth were never worn down by eating, to what length could they grow?

38

1. *Le miel.*
2. Nero (AD 68).
3. Candles.
4. Forty-two lines. (It was known as the 42-line version.)
5. Putney.
6. William Faulkner.
7. Matisse.
8. Mozart's 'Requiem'.
9. Aspirin.

409

1. Queen Elizabeth II (Calder Hall, 1956).
2. The Peasants' Revolt.
3. Grenoble.
4. The Gordon Riots of 1780.
5. Light heavyweight.
6. Howard Hughes.
7. Howard Hughes.
8. Countess Abegg.
9. The earth.

780

1. A fine arabica coffee or blend of chocolate and coffee.
2. Prostitute.
3. The Suez Canal.
4. D'Artagnan.
5. The Netherlands.
6. Gary Cooper.
7. Renee Richards.
8. Liszt.
9. 10 feet.

39

1. Where would you find a juttock plate?
2. In 1933 Mrs Klarius Mikkelson was the first women to set foot where?
3. In which country does bribery run most rife?
4. Who is the hero of Captain W. E. John's best-known stories?
5. Which English footballer joined Hamburg FC in 1977?
6. In which year was Lynda Carter (Wonder Woman) Miss USA?
7. On which number at roulette did Sean Connery bet if it came up three consecutive times?
8. Which was Tchaikovsky's first ballet?
9. Which animal is sometimes called the river horse?

410

1. What is the French for Saturday?
2. Who did Louis XVI give the Hope Diamond to?
3. Where was Voltaire buried, though he is not there now?
4. How tall is Tom Thumb according to the Brothers Grimm?
5. How many Olympic gold medals has Mark Spitz won?
6. What is the interval between performances of the Passion Play at Oberammergau?
7. Father Gourier of Paris killed a number of people but was never convicted. How did they die?
8. Who wrote the music 'Tubular Bells' used as the theme to *The Exorcist*?
9. How many feet are there in a chain?

781

1. What stands under the spreading chestnut tree?
2. What did the followers of Captain Swing do?
3. In 1867 the United States paid £1,450,000 for what?
4. Name H. G. Wells's first major publication.
5. Which Test cricketer was the first president of the English Bowling Association?
6. Who directed the film version of *Jesus Christ Superstar*?
7. Which writer 'married' Annabel Lee and died of alcohol?
8. Who sang 'Falling in Love Again' in *The Blue Angel*?
9. The largest known eyes in the animal kingdom belonged to a squid washed up in 1933 in New Zealand. How big were they?

39

1. On a ship's mast.
2. The Antarctic.
3. The USSR.
4. Biggles.
5. Kevin Keegan.
6. 1974.
7. Seventeen.
8. *Swan Lake*.
9. The hippopotamus.

410

1. Samedi.
2. Marie Antoinette.
3. The Pantheon, Paris, but his remains were found to be missing in 1864.
4. 5½ inches.
5. Nine (two in 1968 and seven in 1972).
6. 10 years.
7. Happily, of over-eating. He took them to the best Paris restaurant twice daily.
8. Mike Oldfield.
9. Sixty-six.

781

1. The village smithy.
2. They smashed farm machinery in the 1830s.
3. Alaska.
4. A textbook of biology.
5. W. G. Grace.
6. Norman Jewison.
7. Edgar Allan Poe.
8. Marlene Dietrich, in about 1930.
9. 15¾ inches across.

40

1. What is another name for the alligator pear?
2. What was a wapentake?
3. From where did the banana first come?
4. Coleridge said, 'How well we seem to know Chaucer! How absolutely nothing do we know of —.' Who?
5. Which TV golf commentator won the Whyte and Mackay PGA Championships in 1957, 1962 and 1965?
6. Who is the heroine of Shakespeare's *As You Like It*?
7. Which poet was Sir Thomas More's great-great nephew?
8. Which great jazz clarinetist recorded Mozart's Clarinet Concerto with the Boston Symphony Orchestra?
9. What is alopecia?

411

1. What is $\frac{1}{2} \times \frac{1}{2}$?
2. Who allegedly ordered the slaughter of all the infants in Bethlehem?
3. Which major country has the slowest population growth rate?
4. In the Bible, who were Isaac's two sons?
5. In golf, what is a gimmie?
6. Who are Blake Carrington's two children?
7. Most stamps carry watermarks. Two common Commonwealth ones are 'CC' and 'CA'. What do these letters stand for?
8. What is a 'tail piece' rounding off a musical composition called?
9. What is mimulus colloquially called?

782

1. When is St Swithin's Day?
2. Which king converted Leeds Castle into a Royal Palace?
3. Which was the only European country before the Second World War where more than half the inhabitants were Muslim?
4. Who wrote *Self-Help: With Illustrations of Character and Conduct*, the Victorian best-seller?
5. This century, which club won the FA Cup in successive years?
6. Which part of his body did Charlie Chaplin insure?
7. Which Russian poet had African blood and died in a duel?
8. Which member of The Who switched to literature?
9. What is the more popular name for crane flies?

40

1. The avocado.
2. A sub-division of a county once under Danish influence (especially Yorkshire).
3. Southern Asia.
4. Shakespeare.
5. Peter Alliss.
6. Rosalind.
7. John Donne.
8. Benny Goodman.
9. Loss of hair.

411

1. $\frac{1}{4}$.
2. Herod the Great.
3. West Germany.
4. Jacob and Esau.
5. A putt short enough to be conceded.
6. Fallon and Stephen.
7. CC = Crown Colonies; CA = Crown Agents.
8. A coda.
9. The monkey-flower.

782

1. 15 July.
2. Henry VIII.
3. Albania.
4. Dr Samuel Smiles.
5. Newcastle United (1951 and 1952).
6. His feet, for 150,000 dollars.
7. Pushkin.
8. Pete Townshend.
9. Daddy-long-legs.

Q

41

1. Who invented the pneumatic tyre in 1888?
2. Which Irishmen wore blue shirts?
3. Of which Australian state is Adelaide the capital?
4. How long did it take Gray to write his 'Elegy in a Country Churchyard'?
5. In golf, what would you put in your shag bag?
6. In which film did Larry Hagman make a cameo appearance in 1978?
7. In judo, if the referee shouts 'Sono-mama', what should the players do?
8. By what name is Vera Welch better known?
9. What is a group of salmon called?

412

1. If you were born on 5 September, what would be your star sign?
2. What was hippocras?
3. Which language is spoken in Brazil?
4. Who could not 'write a serious romance under any other motive than to save my life'?
5. Who was the first West Indian cricketer to be knighted?
6. What type of car did Emma Peel drive in 'The Avengers'?
7. In 1983 Britain issued stamps depicting four British river fishes. Name two.
8. Which Damon Runyon story inspired *Guys and Dolls*?
9. Catching bream can be a very awkward task. Which predominant characteristic of this fish makes it so difficult?

783

1. In Britain, how many lbs are there in a hundredweight?
2. Where was the 'Battle Above the Clouds' fought in 1863?
3. On which lake was Donald Campbell killed in *Bluebird*?
4. Who created Gideon, the Baron and the Toff?
5. If a hole in golf is 249 yards long, what par is it?
6. Which BBC TV comedy series involves an army concert party?
7. Where was Marco Polo born?
8. Which of Mahler's symphonies did he leave unfinished?
9. Where are the largest crabs in the world to be found?

41

1. John Dunlop.
2. The men of the Irish Brigade, who fought on Franco's side in the Spanish Civil War.
3. Southern Australia.
4. 8 years.
5. Practice balls.
6. *Superman*.
7. Freeze.
8. Vera Lynn.
9. A bind.

412

1. Virgo.
2. A medieval spiced wine, often served warm.
3. Portuguese.
4. Jane Austen.
5. Sir Learie Constantine.
6. A Lotus Elan.
7. Pike, perch, salmon, and trout.
8. 'The Idylls of Sarah Brown'.
9. It is incredibly slimy.

783

1. 112.
2. Chattanooga – more particularly at Lookout Mountain.
3. Coniston Water in the Lake District.
4. John Creasey.
5. Three.
6. 'It Ain't Half Hot, Mum'.
7. Venice.
8. His tenth.
9. Off the coast of Japan. Some stand 3 feet high and weigh 30 lb.

42

1. What were known as Nürnberg (Nuremberg) ware?
2. Whose reign saw the end of the occasional tax of Danegeld, started by Ethelred the Unready?
3. Which mountain stands at the entrance to Rio de Janeiro harbour?
4. Which Apostle replaced Judas Iscariot?
5. Which county won the very first John Player League?
6. Who played Wicked Uncle Ernie in the film *Tommy*?
7. After which First World War heroine was a peak in the Rockies named?
8. What did Musical Youth want you to pass?
9. What is a pangolin?

413

1. If you park at a road junction at night, how far away from it should you be?
2. At which battle did Thomas 'Stonewall' Jackson get his nickname?
3. Which sea is sometimes called the Euxine Sea?
4. Who wrote the first essays in English?
5. Which Briton won the silver medal in the 50,000-metre walk at the 1964 Olympics?
6. Who was The Prisoner?
7. The works of Mrs Darrell Waters have been translated into 128 languages. Who was she?
8. Which Country and Western star sings with Dylan on the album *Nashville Skyline*?
9. What is the axolotl also called?

784

1. In CB slang, what is a water hole?
2. In the Middle Ages, what was a pavis?
3. The Pillars of Hercules stand on either side of which stretch of water?
4. Who created Dr Fu Manchu?
5. What is the English equivalent of the Australian cricketing term, a bosie?
6. Who operates Orville?
7. Which writer was condemned to death, reprieved at the last minute, and sent to Siberia for 10 years?
8. Who is said to have fiddled while Rome burned?
9. Which is the most prevalent infectious disease threatening man?

42

1. Toys.
2. Henry II (1163).
3. Sugar Loaf Mountain.
4. St Matthias.
5. Lancashire.
6. Keith Moon, drummer in The Who.
7. Edith Cavell.
8. The Dutchie.
9. An ant-eater.

413

1. 15 yards.
2. The Battle of Bull Run.
3. The Black Sea.
4. Francis Bacon.
5. Paul Nihill.
6. Patrick McGoohan.
7. Enid Blyton.
8. Johnny Cash.
9. The salamander.

784

1. A pub.
2. A large shield.
3. The Straits of Gibraltar.
4. Sax Rohmer.
5. A googly.
6. Keith Harris.
7. Dostoyevsky.
8. Nero.
9. Malaria.

43

1. What is deer meat called?
2. Who was the first person known to own a billiards table?
3. The Alps extend into more than one country. Name three.
4. A favourite role for actor-managers was Sir Giles Overreach. In which play does he appear?
5. Who won both the PFA Player *and* Young Player of the Year awards in 1977?
6. Who has 'short, fat, hairy legs'?
7. How many points would you score in cribbage if you had three nines and one six in your hand?
8. Who got his 'Uptown Girl'?
9. What is a smaller form of kangaroo usually called?

414

1. What are the Fesse, Bend, Per Bend, Saltire and Cross?
2. What was the exact date of Rhodesian UDI?
3. Which town is said to have taken its name from a number of trees on the Tonbridge road?
4. Who wrote the poem 'Sea Fever'?
5. Who succeeded Lasse Viren as 10,000 metre world record holder in 1973?
6. Which well-muscled young stud-about-town displayed most of his many charms in several Warhol movies?
7. What fish can you catch between 20 March and 30 September?
8. Which group first recorded 'Do You Believe in Magic'?
9. What breed of dog would you use to hunt hares on foot?

785

1. What is Romaic?
2. When was the first 10-yearly census?
3. Where did Drake's memorable game of bowls take place?
4. Who said of the novel, 'As I am the founder of a new province in writing so I am at liberty to make what laws I please therein'?
5. Which woman first put the shot over 60 feet?
6. Who played the pawnbroker in the film of that name?
7. Which chessman usually has a slit in its head?
8. He recorded '18 with a Bullet', which reached that slot in the US charts. What was his name?
9. What constituent in cheese gives it its flavour?

43

1. Venison. (Do *not* accept 'expensive'!)
2. Mary, Queen of Scots.
3. Austria, Italy, France, Germany, Switzerland and Liechtenstein.
4. *A New Way to Pay Old Debts* by Philip Massinger.
5. Andy Gray.
6. Ernie Wise.
7. 12 points.
8. Billy Joel.
9. A wallaby.

414

1. Simple charges (designs) in heraldry.
2. 11 November 1965.
3. Sevenoaks.
4. John Masefield.
5. David Bedford.
6. Joe Dalessandro.
7. Trout.
8. The Lovin' Spoonful.
9. The Beagle.

785

1. The modern Greek language.
2. 1801, when it recorded the population of Britain as 10,472,048.
3. Plymouth Hoe.
4. Henry Fielding.
5. Tamara Press.
6. Rod Steiger.
7. The bishop.
8. Pete Wingfield.
9. Strains of bacteria.

44

1. What are the four Quarter Days in England and Wales?
2. Who were the Shakers?
3. Ailsa Craig, an island in the Firth of Clyde, is composed of a greyish granite found hardly anywhere else in Britain. What sport is this connected with?
4. Of which town was Michael Henchard mayor?
5. Which England cricket captain once held the world long-jump record?
6. Who plays TV's Invisible Man?
7. What are crampons used for?
8. Which actress wanted to wash that man right out of her hair in *South Pacific*?
9. On average, how many times does a human heart beat in a day?

415

1. How many Law Sittings are there in a year?
2. Who was the last monarch to be canonized?
3. How many cities of over 1,000,000 inhabitants were there in the USA in 1983?
4. Who walked from Lichfield to London together?
5. For which Scottish football team is Ibrox Park the home ground?
6. One of BBC radio's first serials featured a special agent. What was his name?
7. Which famous Italian painter, born some 500 years ago in Urbino, specialized in painting pictures of the Madonna and Child?
8. Which Beach Boy died in 1983?
9. About how many red corpuscles of the blood stacked upon each other would make an inch?

786

1. How did the tank get its name?
2. Where and by whom was the original 'Draconian measure' introduced?
3. Where are the remains of a Roman lighthouse to be seen in Britain?
4. Whose name in Czech means 'jackdaw'?
5. In golf, what is a forecaddie?
6. What kind of business venture is Falcon Crest?
7. Who was the artist of a self-portrait with bandaged ear?
8. Who wrote the song 'Smoke Gets in Your Eyes'?
9. In the ancient world, approximately how long was a cubit?

44

1. 25 March (Lady Day), 24 June (Midsummer Day), 29 September (Michaelmas Day), 25 December (Christmas Day).
2. A breakaway Quaker sect, so called because of their excited behaviour at meetings.
3. Curling. The granite is used for curling stones.
4. Casterbridge.
5. C.B.Fry.
6. David McCallum.
7. Climbing mountains or telegraph poles.
8. Mitzi Gaynor.
9. 100,000.

415

1. Four.
2. Louis IX of France (1226–70).
3. Twenty-seven.
4. Samuel Johnson and David Garrick.
5. Glasgow Rangers.
6. Dick Barton.
7. Raphael.
8. Dennis Wilson.
9. About 11,500.

786

1. For security reasons they were sent to France in crates labelled WATER TANKS.
2. In Athens by Draco (seventh century BC).
3. Dover (Dubris).
4. Kafka.
5. A ball-spotter at blind holes.
6. Wine-growing.
7. Van Gogh.
8. Jerome Kern.
9. About 18 inches, the length of a man's forearm.

45

1. What name is given to a word or sentence that reads the same forwards and backwards?
2. Who expelled the Jews in 1290 and confiscated their property?
3. What English county has the motto: *Invicta* – 'unconquered'?
4. Which actor in Sir Henry Irving's company wrote *Trelawny of the Wells*?
5. What is Rudy Hartono's sport?
6. Who played Wolf J. Flywheel?
7. Which politician was known as RAB?
8. Which great composer became a monk and was given quarters in the Vatican?
9. When was the first US satellite, Explorer I, launched?

416

1. If you were born on 6 May, what would be your star sign?
2. Who were the Brownists?
3. Who came to Iona in AD 563?
4. Where did Noah's Ark come to rest?
5. Who has held the mile world record for the longest period since the 4-minute barrier was broken?
6. Who played Spartacus in the film of that name?
7. Which Russian wrote under a pseudonym and has a town named after him?
8. Name one of the two singer-songwriters credited with composing Sinatra's 'My Way'?
9. An Australian parakeet is known as what?

787

1. How many roods in an acre?
2. To which society did Charles II grant a royal charter in 1662 'to promote natural knowledge'?
3. How many cities with over 1,000,000 inhabitants are there in the UK?
4. What was unusual about the giants called Cyclopes?
5. Which country won all five titles in the 1976 World Bowls Championships?
6. Whose former wife is now Bobby Ewing's girlfriend?
7. Which London art gallery is associated with a famous brew?
8. Who is the lead singer in Duran Duran?
9. Obsession with the numbers 23 and 28 led Wilhelm Fliess to the notion of what?

45

1. A palindrome.
2. Edward I.
3. Kent.
4. Sir Arthur Wing Pinero.
5. Badminton.
6. Groucho Marx.
7. R. A. Butler – afterwards Lord Butler.
8. Liszt.
9. February 1958.

416

1. Taurus.
2. Early Congregationalists named after their minister, Robert Browne of Norwich (*c.* 1580).
3. St Columba.
4. Mount Ararat.
5. Jim Ryun, who held the record from 1966 to 1975.
6. Kirk Douglas.
7. Maxim Gorky.
8. Claude François and Paul Anka.
9. A budgerigar.

787

1. Four.
2. The Royal Society.
3. Seven.
4. They had only one eye, set in the middle of their foreheads.
5. South Africa.
6. Elvis Presley's. Priscilla Beaulieu Presley plays the part in 'Dallas'.
7. Kenwood House. One of the owners was a member of the Guinness family.
8. Simon Le Bon.
9. Biorhythms.

Q

46

1. What is the colloquial name for lignite?
2. In which year did the bubonic plague reach London?
3. What was the Anschluss?
4. On which town did Thomas Hardy base his Casterbridge?
5. Who was the first PFA Player of the Year?
6. Why is Nicholas Parsons in *The Guinness Book of Records*?
7. Where did St Simon Stylites live for 30 years?
8. What tune follows 'This is London' on the BBC World Service and was much whistled by Uncle Toby in *Tristram Shandy*?
9. What experiment did Sir Isaac Newton set up in a corridor of Trinity College, Cambridge?

417

1. What phrase in Irish politics means 'ourselves alone'?
2. Which French emperor died in Kent?
3. Which town in the Lake District is famous for its mint cake?
4. Which novel by William Golding is set in fourteenth-century Salisbury?
5. Who was the first coloured boxer to win a British title?
6. In which TV series do Bodie and Doyle appear?
7. Who married the visionary William Godwin's granddaughter, Mary Wollstonecraft Godwin?
8. If a note is preceded by a 'flat' sign, by how much is it lowered?
9. What is the diameter of an average stroke of lightning?

788

1. What type of plane was a Lancaster?
2. Who was responsible for the calendar we now use?
3. Where is the seat of government in the Netherlands?
4. How old, within 3 years, was Defoe in 1665 – the year of his *Journal of the Plague Year*?
5. Who succeeded Jim Ryun as 1,500 metre world record holder in 1974?
6. How long was the mission on which the Star Ship *Enterprise* was engaged?
7. Who was first proclaimed Emperor of All Russia?
8. Schumann's wife was a talented musician. What was her name?
9. What is a localization of pus called?

46

1. Brown coal.
2. 1665.
3. The union of Austria and Germany in 1938.
4. Dorchester.
5. Norman Hunter.
6. He is the joint holder of the record for the longest after-dinner speech (11 hours).
7. On top of a pillar.
8. Lillibullero.
9. He used an echo to calculate the speed of sound.

417

1. Sinn Fein.
2. Napoleon III.
3. Kendal.
4. *The Spire.*
5. Dick Turpin in 1948.
6. 'The Professionals'.
7. Shelley.
8. A semitone.
9. 6 inches.

788

1. A bomber.
2. Pope Gregory XIII. He introduced it into Catholic Europe in 1582 and it came to Britain in 1752.
3. The Hague.
4. Five.
5. Filbert Bayi.
6. 5 years.
7. Peter the Great in 1721.
8. Clara Schumann.
9. An abscess.

47

1. Which was the first manufactured item to be sold on hire-purchase?
2. Who was George IV's consort?
3. Name Senegal's chief port.
4. Who wrote of the schoolmaster Ichabod Crane?
5. Which Briton won the hammer event at the 1962, 1966 and 1970 Commonwealth Games?
6. Who played Merrick in 'The Jewel in the Crown'?
7. Who led the British and German troops at the Battle of Alamein?
8. In Mozart's opera, how many lovers did Don Giovanni have in Spain?
9. Which type of winged insect has existed the longest?

418

1. Who was the god of wine?
2. When was the name United Kingdom first used?
3. Which is the oldest theatre still in use in Britain?
4. Which work was produced by a committee of forty-seven?
5. Which athlete first won gold medals at the Olympic, European *and* Commonwealth Games?
6. Which was the first British full-length feature cartoon?
7. Whose estate was named Yasnaya Polyana?
8. He was known as 'The Bird'. Who was he?
9. *Elements* has been in use as a standard textbook for over 2,000 years. Who wrote it and what was its subject?

789

1. What is an American tramp called?
2. What did Harriette Wilson cause Wellington to say?
3. Which region of France do the wines Sauterne and Médoc come from?
4. What did Robert Burton anatomize?
5. Who immediately preceded Henry Rono as 3,000 metre world record holder?
6. Who played the insurance rep. in Truffaut's *Day for Night*?
7. How many cards are dealt to each player in German Whist?
8. Which song was George Harrison accused of plagiarizing in 'My Sweet Lord'?
9. To which family does the adjutant bird belong?

47

1. The sewing-machine. The Singer Co. initiated this system of payment in the 1850s.
2. Queen Caroline.
3. Dakar.
4. Washington Irving.
5. Howard Payne.
6. Tim Pigott-Smith.
7. General Montgomery and Field Marshal Rommel.
8. 1,003.
9. A dragonfly.

418

1. Bacchus.
2. After 1 January 1801, when Great Britain and Ireland were united.
3. Bristol's Theatre Royal, built in 1766.
4. The Authorized Version of the Bible.
5. Lynn Davies.
6. Hala and Batchelor's 1954 version of *Animal Farm.*
7. Leo Tolstoy's.
8. Charlie Parker, king of bebop.
9. Euclid; geometry.

789

1. A hobo.
2. 'Publish and be damned.' She was his mistress.
3. Bordeaux.
4. Melancholy. He wrote *An Anatomy of Melancholy.*
5. Brendan Foster.
6. The novelist Graham Greene.
7. Thirteen.
8. The Chiffons' hit 'He's So Fine'.
9. The stork family.

Q

48

1. What is *esprit d'escalier*?
2. Which great pre-Roman emperor died, defeated, in an ox-cart?
3. Which Cornish castle is associated with Arthurian legends?
4. Where, in *Pilgrim's Progress*, are all forms of worldly pleasure sold?
5. Which Finnish athlete was accused of 'blood-boosting'?
6. In which European city is *The Third Man* set?
7. What would separate Adam from a group of naked men?
8. Which opera-writer wrote his own epitaph: 'Life is a jest and all things show it: / I thought so once and now I know it'?
9. In what way is a camel's movement peculiar?

419

1. In what year was the leap day last omitted in the Gregorian calendar?
2. Edwin Drake sank the first of them in 1859. What were they?
3. In which ship did Amundsen reach Antarctica?
4. Finish the Kipling quote, 'You're a better man than I am, — —!'
5. The Greeks dated everything from the year in which a list was begun (generally reckoned to be in 776 BC). What was its name?
6. Did Garbo *really* laugh in *Ninotchka*?
7. Arlington is the advanced form of what card game?
8. Where is the House of the Rising Sun?
9. The polemoscope was invented in 1687. What is it?

790

1. English people prefer eggs of what colour?
2. Which famous battle was fought near the town of Drogheda?
3. Which continent has the most continuous coastline?
4. Who wrote of God as a travelling salesman in *Mr Weston's Good Wine*?
5. Who won the highboard diving event at three successive Olympics?
6. Which radio programme in the early 1950s starred a ventriloquist's dummy?
7. Who said to Parliament, 'This I count the glory of my crown that I have reigned with your loves'?
8. Who wrote 'Blue Suede Shoes'?
9. How many bones are there in the human skull (excluding the ears)?

48

1. Tardy wit, i.e. a rejoinder which comes to mind too late.
2. Darius the Persian.
3. Tintagel.
4. Vanity Fair.
5. Lasse Viren.
6. Vienna.
7. He would not have a navel.
8. John Gay.
9. It lifts both feet on one side at the same time.

419

1. 1900.
2. Oil wells.
3. The *Fram*.
4. Gunga Din.
5. The Olympic Register – a list of winners of the Olympic Games.
6. No. She was *seen* to laugh, but the laugh itself was dubbed.
7. Rummy.
8. New Orleans.
9. A simple periscope.

790

1. Brown.
2. The Battle of the Boyne.
3. Africa.
4. T.F. Powys.
5. Klaus Dibiasi in 1968, 1972 and 1976.
6. 'Educating Archie'.
7. Elizabeth I.
8. Carl Perkins.
9. Twenty-two.

Q

49

1. Which letters denote 'Jesus of Nazareth, King of the Jews'?
2. Who said, on being told she was Queen, 'The Crown is not my right, and pleaseth me not'?
3. A tidal bore occurs on two English rivers. Which ones?
4. Who is the wife and sister of Osiris?
5. In 1978 which girl won badminton's All England Championship?
6. Name two of Hancock's familiars in 'Hancock's Half Hour'.
7. Great Britain has produced only one 'charity' stamp. In which year was it issued?
8. Cynthia Loper claims that girls just want to have what?
9. Since the birth of Christ, what is the longest time between solar eclipses visible from London?

420

1. What would you eat at a traditional Swiss fondue?
2. What, in French history, was the Fronde?
3. Which is the northernmost island of the Channel Islands?
4. How did Phaethon, the son of the Greek sun god, come to grief?
5. Who took charge of QPR for the second time in 1979?
6. When did ITV start broadcasting?
7. Name the commoner twice honoured by being portrayed on two separate issues of British stamps.
8. Who sang about toothbrushes?
9. The constellation of Gemini has a pair of bright stars named after which two brothers?

791

1. The Greek for a 'circle of animals' gave its name to what?
2. Which assassins were defeated by Antony at Philippi?
3. Where did calico originate?
4. Who wrote the play *Uncle Vanya*?
5. Who cost Arsenal £220,000, at that time their record fee?
6. Who starred in the radio programme 'Have a Go'?
7. Who designed the major part of the Great Western Railway?
8. Whose bells were tubular?
9. Which planet was going to be named George by its discoverer Herschel?

49

1. INRI.
2. Lady Jane Grey.
3. Severn and Trent.
4. Isis.
5. Gillian Gilks.
6. Bill Kerr, Sid James, Kenneth Williams and Hattie Jacques – take your pick.
7. 1975.
8. Fun.
9. 575 years – from 1140 to 1715.

420

1. Melted cheese and wine, with cubes of bread.
2. Opposition to Cardinal Mazarin during the minority of Louis XIV.
3. Alderney.
4. Driving the horses of his father, Helios, he got out of control and was struck by Zeus's thunderbolt.
5. Tommy Docherty.
6. 1955.
7. Sir Winston Churchill.
8. Max Bygraves: 'You're a pink toothbrush, I'm a blue toothbrush . . .'
9. Castor and Pollux.

791

1. The Zodiac.
2. Brutus and Cassius (42 BC).
3. India.
4. Chekhov.
5. Alan Ball.
6. Wilfred Pickles (and Mabel).
7. Isambard Kingdom Brunel.
8. Mike Oldfield's.
9. Uranus.

50

1. The pedestrian curricle first appeared in Paris in 1816. What was it?
2. Whom did Scipio Africanus defeat at Zama when all others had failed?
3. Which famous ruined abbey is near Chepstow?
4. Who was the Roman god of agriculture?
5. Who succeeded Ron Clarke as 5,000 metre world record holder in 1965?
6. Under what title did 'The Goon Show' start?
7. Bone porcelain contains bone ash. It was invented at the end of the eighteenth century by whom?
8. Who was the lead singer and guitarist for The Jam?
9. Which variety of pigeons has spreading tail-feathers?

421

1. Pogonophobia is a fear of what?
2. Who used to count in groups of sixty?
3. Antimony, a metal, was used by Egyptian women for what?
4. Complete the following: 'The clever men at Oxford / Know all that there is to be knowed. / But they none of them know one half as much / As . . .'?
5. Which Yorkshire team first won the F A Cup?
6. Who played Archie's tutor in the radio programme 'Educating Archie'?
7. A famous diarist 'sat for half an hour afraid to pass a cow'. Who was she?
8. Who was 'still crazy after all these years'?
9. What is the 'woolly rock'?

792

1. What is dittology?
2. What was 'Curtana' to Edward the Confessor?
3. With what sort of lace is the Belgian city of Malines associated?
4. Who traditionally said, 'Dr Donne's verses are like the peace of God: they pass all understanding'?
5. Where was the world's first bobsleigh run built?
6. Who played Bluebottle in 'The Goon Show'?
7. How many players take part in a game of Solo?
8. From which musical does 'Hey Big Spender' come?
9. What is the maximum number of eclipses of the sun possible in one year?

50

1. A primitive bicycle without pedals.
2. Hannibal, in 202 BC.
3. Tintern Abbey.
4. Saturn.
5. Kip Keino.
6. 'Crazy People'.
7. Josiah Spode.
8. Paul Weller.
9. The fantail.

421

1. Beards.
2. The Sumerians.
3. Eye shadow.
4. '. . . intelligent Mr Toad' (Kenneth Grahame's *The Wind in the Willows*).
5. Sheffield Wednesday in 1896.
6. Tony Hancock.
7. Dorothy Wordsworth.
8. Paul Simon.
9. Asbestos.

792

1. Double meaning.
2. His sword.
3. Mechlin.
4. James I.
5. St Moritz in 1902.
6. Peter Sellers.
7. Four.
8. *Sweet Charity*.
9. Five.

Q

51

1. What is ikebana?
2. Whose marriage gave rise to the Tudor rose?
3. A thin netlike silk is named after which town in France?
4. What is the concluding novel in Powell's fictional cycle *A Dance to the Music of Time*?
5. The Radcliffe Road end is at which cricket ground?
6. Who played Lorelei Lee in the film *Gentlemen Prefer Blondes*?
7. Who was the Sea-Green Incorruptible?
8. Who sang with Martha in the 1963 hit 'Heat Wave'?
9. The group of insects which includes cicadas, grasshoppers and crickets employ sound as their signalling medium. Why is this so unusual?

422

1. The most frequently used letters in English are E, T, O, A, N. In what language are the letters E, N, I, R, S most frequently used?
2. Who placed the sword of Damocles over Damocles' head?
3. The flag of which country is split horizontally, bottom half red, top half white?
4. Which flying island did Gulliver visit?
5. How many AAA sprint titles did McDonald Bailey win between 1946 and 1953?
6. *Krakatoa, East of Java* is misleading. Why?
7. What was the nationality of the code inventor, Morse?
8. What was the theme tune for ITV's 'Ready Steady Go'?
9. Which planet is fourth from the sun?

793

1. What are the names of the two legendary City of London giants whose effigies stand in the Guildhall?
2. During whose reign were accents introduced into written French?
3. Where was the treaty establishing the EEC signed?
4. Who wrote *The Thin Man*?
5. Who was the first woman to long jump over 22 feet?
6. Who originally played the lead role in the show *No Sex Please, We're British*?
7. Who wrote children's books in the Lake District?
8. In which Cuban dance is the leader followed in single file?
9. Your external ones are auricles. What are they?

51

1. The Japanese art of flower arranging.
2. Henry VII (of Lancaster) and Elizabeth of York in 1486.
3. Tulle.
4. *Hearing Secret Harmonies.*
5. Trent Bridge.
6. Marilyn Monroe.
7. Robespierre, according to Carlyle.
8. The Vandellas.
9. Most insects are deaf.

422

1. German.
2. Dionysius, tyrant of Syracuse.
3. Poland.
4. Laputa.
5. Fourteen.
6. Krakatoa is 200 miles *west* of Java.
7. American.
8. Manfred Mann's '5–4–3–2–1'.
9. Mars.

793

1. Gog and Magog.
2. Louis XIII's (1601–43).
3. Rome.
4. Dashiell Hammett.
5. Mary Rand.
6. Michael Crawford.
7. Beatrix Potter.
8. The Conga.
9. Ears.

52

1. What would you do with absinthe?
2. Whose arms bore a white heart with a gold chain?
3. Which German line lay opposite the Maginot Line?
4. Freud published his most influential book in 1900. What was it called?
5. What game do the Boston Red Socks and the Chicago White Socks play?
6. What is Automan?
7. Which famous Quaker kept his hat on when he met Charles II?
8. How often did Tchaikovsky meet his patron, Madam von Meck?
9. What is your scapula?

423

1. Who were the first thugs?
2. To whom did Alexander the Great bequeath his empire?
3. Which was the first hotel to be built on the famous Las Vegas strip?
4. Who is the lazy, supine hero of the nineteenth-century Russian novel that bears his name?
5. In 1950–51, the Football League was extended to ninety-two clubs. How many were there before?
6. Which small sheep starred in BBC radio's 'Toytown'?
7. In which year did Thomas Edison win a Nobel prize?
8. Who 'Ain't Misbehavin''?
9. How old does a horse have to be before it is classed as 'aged'?

794

1. Who were the Red Shirts?
2. Who commanded the royalist troops at the Battle of Naseby?
3. Of which country is Goa a former colony?
4. In which of the gospels does a boy bring five loaves and two fishes to Jesus?
5. What are the four major international golf championships?
6. In which city does the Carrington family live?
7. How many moves does it take White to achieve Fool's Mate if Black does not defend against it?
8. Where did reggae originate?
9. What is the range of the Beaufort scale?

52

1. Drink it.
2. Richard II.
3. The Siegfried Line.
4. *The Interpretation of Dreams.*
5. Baseball.
6. A holograph.
7. William Penn.
8. Never.
9. Your shoulder blade.

423

1. The Thuggee of northern India, who strangled victims in the name of Kali.
2. 'The strongest'.
3. The Flamingo.
4. Oblomov, in the novel by Goncharov.
5. Eighty-eight.
6. Larry the Lamb.
7. 1915.
8. Fats Waller.
9. Seven years.

794

1. Followers of Garibaldi.
2. Charles I.
3. Portugal.
4. St John.
5. The British Open, the United States Open, the Masters, the United States PGA.
6. Denver.
7. Four.
8. Jamaica.
9. Force 0 to force 12.

53

1. For which church did Wren design his tallest steeple?
2. At which battle did the tank make its first appearance?
3. Which city is at the mouth of the Menam river?
4. Which designer wrote a Utopian vision which opens in Hammersmith?
5. Which pre-war British heavyweight champion hailed from Tonypandy?
6. Who, before Robin Day, presented 'The World At One' and 'PM' on BBC radio?
7. What colour is produced by dyeing wool with redcurrants and alum?
8. What was the name of Junior Walker's backing band?
9. Matter is thought to consist essentially of two classes of particles. One class is called hadrons; what is the other?

424

1. What does a galactophagist drink?
2. Which religious order became known as the Black Friars?
3. In which state was Australia's gold rush?
4. Victor Hugo, wanting to know how *Les Misérables* was selling, wrote to his publisher '?'. What was the reply?
5. What is the golfer's cry of warning?
6. Who does Joan Collins play in 'Dynasty'?
7. Which writer was a military champion, a convicted murderer and in receipt of a royal pension?
8. What, non-musically, are 'Lincolnshire Bagpipes'?
9. Which forces on the Beaufort scale represent a full gale?

795

1. What does a Union Jack flying upside down signify?
2. Who said, 'I never see any home cooking. All I get is the fancy stuff'?
3. Legend has it that one European city got its name from the great number of bears killed there on the day it was founded. Which city?
4. Who wrote the *Essays of Elia*?
5. Which club did Malcolm McDonald go to from Newcastle?
6. What part does Jamie Farr play in 'MASH'?
7. Where did the card game of canasta originate?
8. Which was the Muse of dance, and the dramatic chorus?
9. There are three types of nuclear radiation. What are they?

53

1. St Bride's, Fleet Street.
2. The Battle of the Somme, 1916.
3. Bangkok.
4. William Morris, in *News from Nowhere.*
5. Tommy Farr.
6. William Hardcastle.
7. Dark brown.
8. The All Stars.
9. Leptons.

424

1. Milk.
2. The Dominicans.
3. Victoria.
4. '!'
5. Fore!
6. Alexis Carrington.
7. Ben Jonson.
8. Croaking frogs.
9. Forces 10 and 11.

795

1. Distress.
2. Prince Philip.
3. Berne, Switzerland.
4. Charles Lamb.
5. Arsenal.
6. Corporal Klinger.
7. South America.
8. Terpsichore.
9. Alpha, beta and gamma.

54

1. What do philatelists collect?
2. How, traditionally, did Alfred the Great get his first book?
3. Simon Bolivar was, in 1928, the president of three countries. Which ones?
4. Which is Britain's oldest publisher?
5. Which Briton won medals in the ladies' 100 metres and 200 metres at the 1960 Olympics?
6. What nationality is the film star Raf Vallone?
7. What nationality was the murderer Dr Crippen?
8. Who lost his money in the South Sea Bubble and wrote a prison pastoral for Swift?
9. How many legs has a slow-worm?

425

1. Which is the oldest part of the Tower of London?
2. What saved Rome when the Gauls attacked in 390 BC?
3. Ermine Street runs from where to where?
4. Which Bristol poet produced some notorious forgeries and died in a garret?
5. What is a putter called when used off the green?
6. How much is Larry Hagman said to be paid per episode of 'Dallas'?
7. How did the first Duchess of Marlborough save ink?
8. How much recording tape moves past the heads of a cassette recorder each second?
9. What is a group of foxes called?

796

1. In which professions are members of the disciplinary committee called benchers?
2. Who committed suicide after the Battle of Actium?
3. In which county is Tiverton?
4. Which writer and actor died on stage playing his own invalid?
5. Which team replaced Gateshead in the Football League?
6. Who presents 'Police Five' on TV?
7. Who was called the Scourge of God?
8. The Comets were whose backing band?
9. Which American engineer was the first to put steam engines in boats and built the first steam warship for the USA?

54

1. Stamps.
2. His mother promised it to him if he learned to read it. He did.
3. Columbia, Peru, Bolivia.
4. Oxford University Press, whose first publication is dated 1469.
5. Dorothy Hyman.
6. Italian.
7. American.
8. John Gay.
9. None.

425

1. The White Tower.
2. The honking of the sacred geese.
3. London to Lincoln.
4. Thomas Chatterton.
5. A Texas Wedge.
6. $100,000.
7. By not dotting her *i*'s or using full stops.
8. $1\frac{7}{8}$ inches.
9. A skulk.

796

1. The legal profession.
2. Anthony, and then Cleopatra.
3. Devon.
4. Molière. He was playing *Le Malade Imaginaire.*
5. Peterborough United.
6. Shaw Taylor.
7. Attila the Hun.
8. Bill Haley's.
9. Robert Fulton.

55

1. Introduced in 1835 to replace a less reliable product, what were 'congreves'?
2. Protestant Britain did not adopt the Gregorian calendar until 1752. How many days were lost in order to do so?
3. Burma has what sort of government?
4. What did God create on the fifth day?
5. At which sport was Victor Barna world champion five times?
6. Which self-confessed alcoholic played W. C. Fields in the film biography?
7. The coarse fishing season in Britain runs from 16 March to when?
8. Where was Bob Dylan born?
9. What is a geodesic?

426

1. What is a runcible spoon?
2. One of the most precious cloths in the ancient world was a bolt of cloth Alexander took from Persia. What colour was it?
3. Which famous school is at Godalming?
4. From what sort of wood was Noah's Ark built?
5. What did Babe Ruth play?
6. Who wrote the play *The Winslow Boy*?
7. Which statesman was often called 'el Caudillo'?
8. Which French singer is associated with a straw hat and *Gigi*?
9. What does an osteologist study?

797

1. What was put under central control in 1832 in London, having previously been carried out by insurance companies?
2. What is the *Entente Cordiale*?
3. In the Yugoslav language, Belgrade is called *Beograd*. What does *Beograd* mean?
4. Which fictional character tilted at windmills?
5. A duelling sword, which has a triangular blade and large bell-like guard but is heavier than a foil, is called a what?
6. Who played Mr Rigby in 'Rising Damp'?
7. Who sculpted the Elgin Marbles?
8. Who was satirized by Gilbert and Sullivan as Bunthorne?
9. What do dates grow on?

55

1. Matches.
2. Eleven.
3. Socialist.
4. Sea creatures and birds.
5. Table tennis.
6. Rod Steiger.
7. 16 June.
8. Duluth, Minnesota.
9. The shortest distance between two points on a spherical surface, usually the earth.

426

1. A broad-pronged pickle fork.
2. Purple.
3. Charterhouse.
4. Gopher wood.
5. Baseball.
6. Terence Rattigan.
7. Franco.
8. Maurice Chevalier.
9. Bones.

797

1. Fire fighting.
2. The friendly relations between France and Britain, formally established in 1904.
3. White city.
4. Don Quixote.
5. An épée.
6. Leonard Rossiter.
7. Pheidias.
8. Oscar Wilde, in *Patience*.
9. Palm trees.

56

1. A term was coined in 1846 to take the place of the expression 'popular antiquities'. What is it?
2. Which Roman writer was killed in a litter?
3. Which Malaysian port is associated with a walking cane?
4. Who is Prospero's treacherous brother in *The Tempest*?
5. Who scored Southampton's goal in the 1976 Cup Final, and to which pop star is he related?
6. Which family was featured in the radio programme 'Take It From Here'?
7. What is the difference between post and ante-post betting?
8. What does jazzman Stephane Grappelli play?
9. Why do sunspots appear dark?

427

1. What would 'pencil' have meant in the eighteenth century?
2. Agrippina poisoned her husband/uncle. Who was he?
3. In which country would you find the Heights of Abraham?
4. Name the hypnotic Hungarian in *Trilby*.
5. Who lit the flame at the 1956 Olympics and went on to break eight different world records?
6. What is Doyle's number in 'The Professionals'?
7. Which explorer discovered the Niger river?
8. In which year did Sadler's Wells hold its first Gilbert and Sullivan festival?
9. What is a group of rooks called?

798

1. What is a homonym?
2. Who led the Greek and Persian armies at the battles of Issus and Gaugamela?
3. Which country did Texas belong to until 1821?
4. Who was the last of Job's comforters?
5. Who succeeded John Akii-Bua as 400-metre hurdles world record holder in 1976?
6. Who wrote the novel *Gigi*?
7. What or who was Tutankhamen?
8. Which song is heard at the end of *Dr Strangelove*?
9. The first public supply was obtained from the River Wey at Godalming, Surrey in 1881. What is it?

56

1. Folk-lore, coined by W. J. Thoms.
2. Cicero.
3. Malacca.
4. Antonio.
5. Roy Dwight. His nephew is Elton John.
6. The Glums – Mr Glum, his son Ron, and Eth, Ron's fiancée.
7. Post betting does not begin until the numbers of the runners are up on the board; ante-post betting opens any time before the event.
8. Violin.
9. They are cooler than the sun's surface.

427

1. Brush.
2. Claudius.
3. Canada.
4. Svengali.
5. Ron Clarke.
6. 45.
7. Mungo Park.
8. 1984.
9. A building or clamour.

798

1. A word with more than one sense (e.g. bat).
2. Alexander the Great led the Greeks and Darius led the Persians.
3. Spain.
4. Elihu.
5. Ed Moses.
6. Colette.
7. An Egyptian king.
8. 'We'll Meet Again'.
9. Electricity.

57

1. What is a catachresis?
2. What was a hypocaust?
3. Who was responsible for the building of the Flamingo hotel in Las Vegas?
4. Which of Shaw's plays did he describe as 'a fantasia in the Russian manner on English themes'?
5. Who was the first cricketer to receive a benefit of over £100,000?
6. Where did Tony Hancock claim to live?
7. Who did Ian Smith meet on board the *Tiger* and then the *Fearless*?
8. Who used to be lead singer with Japan, and was once voted the most beautiful man in the world?
9. Which is the hottest part of a rainbow?

428

1. What is the third letter of the Greek alphabet?
2. What, to the nearest half million, was the population of England at the beginning of Elizabeth I's reign?
3. What is the largest town in Alaska?
4. Which of Chekhov's plays was a flop at first but was hailed as a success within a year?
5. Who were the winners of the 1980 Gillette Cup?
6. Which comedy film starring Chevy Chase shows a typical day at Bushwood Country Club?
7. In solo, what is an undertaking to take zero tricks called?
8. Who chairs 'My Music'?
9. How long is a newly born crocodile?

799

1. What is enamel?
2. How many years after Waterloo did Napoleon die?
3. Where, according to Burke, was the toyshop of Europe?
4. Who were Abel's father and mother?
5. If you were playing in a Stableford golf competition, how many points would you score for a par?
6. Which novelist created the Mallens, in a one-time popular TV series?
7. Who is the hereditary spiritual leader of the Ismaili sect of Islam?
8. What does *pizzicato* mean?
9. What is the anatomical name for the gullet?

57

1. A misused word (e.g. 'exalt' for 'exult').
2. Roman under-floor heating.
3. The gangster Bugsy Siegel.
4. *Heartbreak House.*
5. Jack Simmons of Lancashire, in 1980.
6. 23 Railway Cuttings, East Cheam.
7. Harold Wilson, in 1966 and 1968 respectively.
8. David Sylvian.
9. The blue side.

428

1. Gamma.
2. Four million.
3. Anchorage.
4. *The Seagull.*
5. Middlesex.
6. *Caddyshack.*
7. Misère.
8. Steve Race.
9. About 8 inches.

799

1. A fine layer of glass on metal.
2. Six.
3. Birmingham.
4. Adam and Eve.
5. 2 points.
6. Catherine Cookson.
7. The Aga Khan.
8. That notes on a stringed instrument should be plucked, not bowed.
9. The oesophagus.

58

1. The actual crowning of an English sovereign is done with which crown?
2. Alexander the Great said, 'If I were not Alexander, I would be —'?
3. In which Welsh county is Aberystwyth?
4. Who wrote *The Ballad of Peckham Rye*?
5. What is the longest distance over which official greyhound races are run in England?
6. Who punched Russell Harty on his TV chat show?
7. Who was known as the Railway King?
8. Whose nickname is Slowhand?
9. What are the three primary colours of light?

429

1. If you were born on 1 October, what would your star sign be?
2. Who were sent to Lazar houses?
3. In 1764 Louis Bougainville sailed south to found a French colony. Where?
4. Who is Uncle Toby's companion from the other ranks in *Tristram Shandy*?
5. Who was the first PFA Young Player of the Year?
6. Which two broadcasters presided over 'Much Binding in the Marsh'?
7. Henry Vincent Yorke wrote five novels with one-word titles ending in – ing. What was his pseudonym?
8. In the film *Gigi* what did Maurice Chevalier claim, in song, to be able to do?
9. What does a hygrometer measure?

800

1. Which out of 1800, 1850, 1900, 1950 and 2000 are leap years?
2. Who was the first person to wear a wristwatch?
3. Name a country which has the dragon as its symbol.
4. In *Tarka the Otter* who or what was Old Nog?
5. In which sport is the Palma Match contested?
6. In legal stories, what is the actual name of She Who Must Be Obeyed?
7. Who sculpted the Victoria Memorial outside Buckingham Palace?
8. In which musical does the Russian village of Anatevka feature?
9. Of what vitamin does rose-hip syrup have a plentiful supply?

58

1. St Edward's crown.
2. Diogenes.
3. Cardiganshire.
4. Muriel Spark.
5. 1,200 yards.
6. Grace Jones.
7. George Hudson.
8. Eric Clapton.
9. Red, blue, green.

429

1. Libra.
2. Lepers (the first such house was built during King Stephen's reign at Burton-Lazars in Leicestershire).
3. The Falkland Islands.
4. Corporal Trim.
5. Kevin Beattie.
6. Richard Murdoch and Kenneth Horne.
7. Henry Green.
8. To 'remember it well'.
9. Humidity.

800

1. Only 2000. A leap year is one divisible by 4, except the year of the century which is a leap year only when divisable by 400.
2. Queen Elizabeth I.
3. China, Wales.
4. A heron.
5. Shooting.
6. Hilda Rumpole.
7. Sir Thomas Brock.
8. *Fiddler on the Roof.*
9. Vitamin C.

59

1. What small cakes and biscuits would you serve at the end of a formal meal?
2. Who were the signatories of the Atlantic Charter in 1941?
3. Which are the two principal Dutch cheeses?
4. Which town did the Pied Piper rid of rats?
5. What is the cricketing term for a ball that turns to leg on pitching?
6. By what name is Ruby Stevens better known?
7. Who managed the 1984 European Cup winners?
8. What is the leading female role in Puccini's *La Bohème*?
9. How long after birth does it take a baby guppy to double its length?

430

1. What was the donjon of a castle?
2. In which decade was the lawn-mower invented?
3. The first commercial air transport route was begun in 1911 by the British Post Office as an air mail link between Hendon and where?
4. Who in *Candide* is modelled on Leibnitz?
5. How many feathers are on a standard badminton shuttlecock?
6. What was the last Goon Show called?
7. What did George Fox found after having a vision on Pendle Hill?
8. Who did Maddy Prior sing with?
9. Orange-red 'pixie-cups' are types of what?

801

1. What colour is the wax covering Edam cheese?
2. What relation was James I to Henry VIII?
3. The manufacture of Dresden china was transferred to where?
4. Tom Traddles was a close friend of whom?
5. For which two league clubs did Stanley Matthews play?
6. Who invented a special cantilevered bra to show off Jane Russell's bust to its best advantage?
7. Which famous furniture maker was born in 1718?
8. What does LTCL stand for?
9. From which country does the Doberman Pinscher originate?

59

1. Petits fours.
2. Franklin D. Roosevelt and Winston Churchill.
3. Edam and Gouda.
4. Hamelin.
5. Off-break.
6. Barbara Stanwyck.
7. Joe Fagan, manager of Liverpool.
8. Mimi.
9. One week.

430

1. The great tower, or keep.
2. In the 1830s, by Edwin Budding of Stroud.
3. Windsor (it lasted one week).
4. Pangloss.
5. Sixteen.
6. 'The Last Smoking Seagoon', broadcast on 28 January 1960.
7. The Society of Friends.
8. Steeleye Span.
9. Lichen.

801

1. Red.
2. Great-great-nephew (his great-grandmother Margaret was Henry's sister).
3. Meissen.
4. David Copperfield.
5. Blackpool and Stoke.
6. Howard Hughes.
7. Thomas Chippendale.
8. Licentiate of Trinity College, London.
9. Germany.

60

1. What happens to the atmospheric pressure on the approach of a cold front?
2. How were Mary Queen of Scots and Elizabeth I related?
3. What are aeolian deposits?
4. Who wrote *Room at the Top*?
5. In which sport is the Eisenhower Trophy contested?
6. Who were the Blue Meanies?
7. Which decorator/architect's name is the same as that of an English county?
8. Brian de Palma directed a rock version of *Phantom of the Opera*. What was it called?
9. What does the Mercalli Scale measure?

431

1. How many quires make a ream?
2. The date of what was fixed as a result of the deliberations of the Council of Nicaea in 325?
3. What is the longest river in north-east Africa?
4. Who wrote *Riceyman Steps*?
5. Name the two boxing Baers – both world champions.
6. When did Channel 4 start?
7. Which modern painter has published several books of his watercolour pictures of nature, particularly birds, including *A Sketchbook of Birds*?
8. Who sang about 'My Boy Lollipop' in 1964?
9. What did Leo Baekeland invent in 1909?

802

1. What name was given to short-barrelled rifles formerly used by cavalry?
2. What was the Missouri Compromise?
3. Which mountain range runs from the Arctic to the Caspian Sea?
4. In *The Forsyte Saga*, what was Irene's original surname?
5. Who was the first man to high jump 7 feet?
6. How much did a colour TV licence cost in 1974?
7. Which famous Victorian writer lived at 24 Cheyne Walk, Chelsea?
8. Who asked, 'Where do you go to, my lovely'?
9. In July 1885, a nine-year-old boy was said to be the first person to survive rabies infection. Who treated him?

60

1. It falls.
2. They were cousins.
3. Geographical features formed by the wind (e.g. sand dunes).
4. John Braine.
5. Golf. It's the world amateur team championship.
6. The villains in *Yellow Submarine.*
7. William Kent.
8. *Phantom of the Paradise.*
9. Earthquakes.

431

1. Twenty.
2. Easter.
3. The Nile.
4. Arnold Bennett.
5. Max and Buddy.
6. November 1982.
7. C.F. Tunnicliffe.
8. Millie Small.
9. Bakelite.

802

1. Carbines.
2. In 1820, Missouri was admitted to the Union provided there was no slavery in the north of the state.
3. The Urals.
4. Heron.
5. Charles Dumas.
6. £12.
7. Thomas Carlyle.
8. Peter Sarstedt.
9. Louis Pasteur.

61

1. Whose law states that work will always last as long as the time available for it?
2. By whom was Poppaea kicked to death?
3. A French commander of the First World War has his statue in Grosvenor Gardens. Who is he?
4. Which masque of Milton's was performed at Ludlow Castle in 1634?
5. When was Matt Busby knighted?
6. When did Radio 1 start?
7. Between them, mother and daughter received three Nobel prizes. Who were they?
8. Who sang 'American Pie'?
9. Which famous scientist started out as a bookbinder's apprentice?

432

1. In a reference book what would the abbreviation 'op. cit.' mean?
2. At what stage in his career was the Emperor Constantine, who 'christianized' the Roman Empire, baptized?
3. Which race invented the mariner's compass?
4. Which lame American wrote about New England sin?
5. In which year were the Olympic Games first held in London?
6. Who is the producer of 'That's Life'?
7. What nationality was Renaissance philosopher Erasmus?
8. What instrument does Osian Ellis play?
9. What does the Achilles tendon join?

803

1. Dr Johnson considered claret to be the drink for boys, port for men, and what for heroes?
2. Which was the first daily newspaper in England?
3. In which USA state is 'Hell' a tourist resort?
4. Which brothers, a singer and an actor, together wrote a novel first serialized in *Punch*?
5. For which country did John Akii-Bua win his Olympic 400-metre hurdles gold medal?
6. Who had a *succès de scandale* in *Pink Flamingoes*?
7. What colour is produced by dyeing wool in dandelion?
8. Who sang 'Walk Right In' in 1963?
9. What is the average number of hairs per square inch of scalp?

61

1. Parkinson's Law.
2. Nero.
3. Marshal Foch.
4. *Comus*.
5. 1968.
6. 1967.
7. Marie Curie and Irène Joliot-Curie.
8. Don McLean.
9. Michael Faraday.

432

1. The book or work previously mentioned.
2. Just before his death, after a reign lasting 24 years.
3. The Chinese.
4. Nathaniel Hawthorne, in *The Scarlet Letter*.
5. 1908.
6. Esther Rantzen.
7. Dutch.
8. The harp.
9. The calf muscle to the heel.

803

1. Brandy.
2. The *Daily Courant*, started in March 1702.
3. Michigan.
4. George and Weedon Grossmith (*Diary of a Nobody*).
5. Uganda.
6. Divine, a grossly overweight transvestite.
7. Magenta.
8. The Rooftop Singers.
9. 1,200.

62

1. What is the albumen of an egg?
2. Which king founded the Order of the Garter in 1350?
3. What is the name of the port which used to be the capital of Egypt?
4. What was ambrosia?
5. In which sport would you expect to find a night watchman?
6. Which Peter Gibbs play won the 1983 Radio Times Play Competition?
7. Where was the 1984 World Poker Championship held?
8. Which singer was born Marie McDonald McLaughlin Lawrie?
9. How does the possum try to avoid capture?

433

1. Friday was named after Frigga. Who was she?
2. Who was Henry VIII's first Queen?
3. Which country's flag has three equal vertical stripes of green, white and orange?
4. Who in Shakespeare says: 'He hath put all my substance into that fat belly of his'?
5. Who was Britain's most successful swimmer in the 1976 Olympics?
6. What was the famous closing line of the original BBC 'Tonight' programme?
7. Who became Secretary of State for Employment in 1974?
8. Whose rags were used in the film *The Sting*?
9. To what family of sea-birds does the guillemot belong?

804

1. 'What is the use of a W.C. without a seat?' This was a telegram. To whom was it sent?
2. Which year does the Union Jack date from?
3. Where did Covent Garden move to?
4. How many of Shakespeare's signatures survive?
5. In which event did Dave Wottle win an Olympic gold medal?
6. Who was Walt Disney's first real cartoon character?
7. Who wrote in her diary: 'I shall do my utmost to fulfil my duty towards my country. I am very young'?
8. Which musical uses tunes by Borodin?
9. Where does a fish have its dorsal fin?

62

1. The white.
2. Edward III.
3. Alexandria.
4. The food of the gods.
5. Cricket.
6. *Benefit of the Doubt.*
7. Las Vegas.
8. Lulu.
9. By pretending to be dead.

433

1. Frigga was Odin's wife.
2. Catherine of Aragon.
3. The Republic of Ireland.
4. Mistress Quickly, in *Henry IV*.
5. David Wilkie.
6. 'The next "Tonight" will be tomorrow night.'
7. Michael Foot.
8. Scott Joplin's.
9. The auk family.

804

1. To Winston Churchill when he lost an election in Manchester.
2. 1801.
3. Nine Elms.
4. Six.
5. The 800 metres.
6. Oswald the Rabbit.
7. Queen Victoria on her accession.
8. *Kismet.*
9. On its back.

63

1. What were maverick cattle in the US?
2. To which king's birthday does Oak-apple Day correspond?
3. Name the famous beauty spot near Eastbourne.
4. In which village does Miss Marple live?
5. Who succeeded John Walker as world record holder in the 1-mile event in 1979?
6. What is the English title of 'Jeux Sans Frontières'?
7. Which writer was the son of an archbishop and became mayor of Rye?
8. What was actor–singer John Leyton's first hit?
9. New Zealand and Ireland may be the only countries in the world to lack these. What?

434

1. When a cold front has passed you what usually happens to the atmospheric pressure?
2. How long did Queen Victoria reign?
3. Which is the world's shortest frontier?
4. Who wrote *Where Eagles Dare*?
5. What are toxophilites?
6. 'Not only . . . but also.' Who?
7. Who debated pornography with Peter Webb at Hornsey College of Art in 1971?
8. Who sang 'When a Man loves a Woman' in 1966?
9. It is thought that dogs are descended from wolves. Yet wolves cannot do one thing that dogs do. What?

805

1. The original Egyptian hieroglyph for our letter 'N' represented what?
2. When was NATO formed?
3. What river is so powerful that the surface sea is still composed of fresh water 50 miles from its mouth?
4. Which tavern did Falstaff frequent?
5. In cricket, how many times does a full toss bounce before reaching the batsman?
6. Who played Cleever Loophole?
7. Who cried on his death: 'What an artist dies in me'?
8. Who was 'Helpless'?
9. How many more bones in the human arm are there than in a human leg?

63

1. Animals found without an owner's brand.
2. Charles II's.
3. Beachy Head.
4. St Mary Mead (in Agatha Christie's novels).
5. Sebastian Coe.
6. 'It's a Knockout'.
7. E.F. Benson.
8. 'Johnny Remember Me'.
9. Snakes.

434

1. It rises.
2. 64 years.
3. Gibraltar's (1,672 yards).
4. Alistair MacLean.
5. Archers.
6. Peter Cook and Dudley Moore, in their TV series.
7. Lord Longford.
8. Percy Sledge.
9. Bark.

805

1. Waves.
2. 4 April 1949.
3. The Amazon.
4. The Boar's Head.
5. None.
6. Groucho Marx.
7. The Emperor Nero.
8. Neil Young.
9. One.

64

1. In what did Wynken, Blynken and Nod sail off?
2. Who was Hecuba's husband and father of fifty children?
3. Where would you have found Vendémiaire, Ventôse, Germinal, etc.?
4. Who was Lady Chatterley's lover?
5. Which track stages the Greyhound Derby each year?
6. What were Radios 1, 2, 3 and 4 originally called?
7. How many 'genuine' Mona Lisas are there in existence?
8. For what does MC5 stand?
9. NASA has given the US National Air and Space Museum an object that is still on the surface of another planet. What is it?

435

1. Castor and Pollux are the names of two stars in the constellation of Gemini. In legend they were twin brothers to which famous woman?
2. Which Russian ruler imposed a beard tax?
3. From where to where did William Kemp dance in 1600?
4. Who wrote *Under the Volcano*?
5. Who scored a century in the 1979 Prudential World Cup Final?
6. What was the name of Lulu's first film?
7. Sepia originally came from which creature?
8. Where does 'There's No Business Like Show Business' come from?
9. The huanaco and the vicuña are types of what?

806

1. What are men's full-length underpants commonly called?
2. Who coined the phrase 'a whiff of grapeshot' referring to Napoleon's dispersal of the 1795 Paris insurrection?
3. Where did the massacre of the Macdonald clan take place?
4. Who wrote the children's classic *Black Beauty*?
5. When a right-handed golfer draws a shot what happens to the ball?
6. The first active telecommunications satellite was called what?
7. Who was the famous action painter who simply poured paint on the canvas?
8. Whose autobiography is called *A Knight At the Opera*?
9. The Chevalier de Méré approached Pascal over a specific problem and the result was what?

64

1. A wooden shoe.
2. Priam.
3. They were months in the French Revolutionary Calendar 1792–1805.
4. Mellors, the gamekeeper.
5. White City.
6. The Home Service, the Light Programme and the Third Programme. There wasn't a fourth.
7. Four.
8. Motor City Five.
9. Viking Lander I, on Mars.

435

1. Helen of Troy.
2. Peter the Great.
3. London to Norwich.
4. Malcolm Lowry.
5. Viv Richards.
6. *Gonks Go Beat.*
7. The cuttlefish.
8. The musical *Annie Get Your Gun.*
9. Llama.

806

1. Long-johns.
2. Carlyle.
3. Glencoe.
4. Anna Sewell.
5. It travels from right to left.
6. Telstar.
7. Jackson Pollock.
8. Sir Geraint Evans's.
9. The Theory of Probability.

65

1. What are the snaffle, the pelham and the weymouth?
2. Jack Cade led the men of which county in a rebellion?
3. Ernest Shackleton's ship was crushed in the Antarctic. What was its name?
4. Who wrote the play *Chips with Everything*?
5. Which cricketer has scored the most runs for England in test matches?
6. Name the Steptoes, father and son.
7. Where did the word 'impressionism' come from?
8. What is a flourish of trumpets called?
9. Name Clive Sinclair's revolutionary machine that brought home computing to the masses.

436

1. What is Indian corn otherwise called?
2. What destroyed Nagasaki in the Second World War?
3. Which mountains form the 'backbone' of Italy?
4. Who 'sighed as a lover' but 'obeyed as a son' and didn't marry but wrote history instead?
5. Who created World Series cricket in Australia?
6. What are bison called in America?
7. What would you be playing if you said 'and one for his nob'?
8. Who wrote the symphonic poem *Les Préludes*?
9. The first self-contained home computer was manufactured by Commodore. What was its name?

807

1. What is the Latin for 'wood'?
2. Who died at Longwood on 5 May 1821 and might have been poisoned with arsenic?
3. For which town was Camulodunum the Roman name?
4. Which novel has achieved the highest worldwide sales?
5. Which Briton before Coe last held the world mile record?
6. What part is played by Walter Koenig in 'Star Trek'?
7. Who devised the terms 'introvert' and 'extrovert'?
8. What was the first album of husband-and-wife singing duo Womack and Womack?
9. How does an ice-skater acquire a friction-free surface on which to glide?

65

1. Types of horse bit.
2. Kent.
3. *Endurance.*
4. Arnold Wesker.
5. Geoff Boycott (8,114 in 108 tests).
6. Albert and Harold.
7. From a painting by Monet called 'Impression, Sunrise'.
8. A fanfare.
9. The ZX80.

436

1. Maize.
2. An atom bomb.
3. The Apennines.
4. Edward Gibbon.
5. Kerry Packer.
6. Buffalo.
7. Cribbage.
8. Liszt.
9. Pet.

807

1. *Lignum.*
2. Napoleon, on the island of St Helena. Traces of arsenic were found in his hair but it seems he had been using increasingly large doses for medicinal purposes.
3. Colchester.
4. *Valley of the Dolls* by Jacqueline Susann (26.5 million copies in April 1983).
5. Derek Ibbotson.
6. That of Ensign Chekov.
7. Carl Jung.
8. *Love Wars.*
9. Intense pressure exerted by the blade melts the ice under it.

66

1. Of what is the drink posset made?
2. What exploded in 1720?
3. Where is it that the remains of earliest man were found?
4. Who was the prolific English writer who created a famous schoolboy?
5. From which country does speedway star Ole Olsen come?
6. Who plays Miss Jones in 'Rising Damp'?
7. Who was the leading British Romantic painter of the twentieth century?
8. Who had a hit with 'Tonight's the Night'?
9. What sort of creature was a diplodocus?

437

1. In what form did Galileo publish his astronomical views (1616) in order to disguise their revolutionary content?
2. How many soldiers did a Roman centurion command?
3. Between which towns did the Great Western Railway originally run?
4. Name Bram Stoker's vampire.
5. What are the uprights of cricket wickets called?
6. Which part did Telly Savalas play in *On Her Majesty's Secret Service*?
7. Name the most famous French underwater explorer.
8. Who had a hit with 'Devil Woman'?
9. To which planet did Viking One go?

808

1. What were the first false teeth made of?
2. Who named a city after his horse?
3. From which country does Vichy water come?
4. Who had 'promises to keep / And miles to go before I sleep'?
5. At what age did Ian Botham first play for Somerset?
6. Name Jane Wyman's daughter.
7. The statesman Neville Chamberlain came from which English city?
8. Which of Beethoven's symphonies is the Choral?
9. What did Foucault's pendulum prove?

66

1. Hot spiced milk curdled with ale or wine.
2. The South Sea Bubble.
3. Kenya.
4. Frank Richards, Billy Bunter's creator.
5. Denmark.
6. Frances de la Tour.
7. Graham Sutherland.
8. Rod Stewart.
9. A dinosaur.

437

1. As a dialogue between the two opposed views.
2. 100.
3. London and Bristol.
4. Dracula.
5. Stumps.
6. That of Ernst Stavro Blofeld.
7. Jacques Cousteau.
8. Cliff Richard.
9. Mars.

808

1. Ivory.
2. Alexander the Great so named Bucephala in India, which was to be a mausoleum for his horse Bucephalus, 30 years old when it died.
3. France.
4. Robert Frost.
5. 17 years.
6. Maureen Reagan.
7. Birmingham.
8. The Ninth.
9. That the earth rotates.

Q

67

1. What colour is an amethyst?
2. Who was nicknamed Beauclerc?
3. In which country did the most destructive earthquake ever recorded occur?
4. Where are Swift's Lilliput and Brobdingnag?
5. Who were the finalists who lost on penalties in the 1984 European Cup?
6. On which school is the TV series 'Fame' based?
7. Which artist, sister of another famous artist, became Rodin's mistress?
8. Which singer lived at 'Graceland'?
9. What does an ammeter measure?

438

1. What is pyrophobia?
2. What were the Janissaries?
3. Which port is the capital of Trinidad and Tobago?
4. Name T.S. Eliot's mystery cat.
5. For which county did Wally Hammond play cricket?
6. Who played TV's Hadleigh?
7. Who held the World Professional Billiards title from 1928–33?
8. Which English composer was the leading musical figure of the Restoration?
9. How far away from a 100-kiloton nuclear explosion would you have to be not to be knocked off your feet by the first blast wave?

809

1. Which two letters are the newest in the English alphabet?
2. Who was the first MP to take his seat without swearing an oath on the Bible?
3. Of which island state is Bridgetown the capital?
4. Name Miss Marple's writer-nephew.
5. Which was the first British club to win the Fairs Cup in 1968?
6. Who played the Boston Strangler in the film?
7. Who was the second president of the USA?
8. What was the title of Bob Dylan's book?
9. If they are not fruits what are an Apple and an Apricot?

67

1. Purple or violet.
2. Henry I.
3. In China, where it killed at least 830,000 people in 1556.
4. In the South Seas.
5. A C Roma.
6. The New York School of Performing Arts.
7. Gwen John.
8. Elvis Presley.
9. Electric current.

438

1. Fear of fire.
2. An elite Turkish corps of mainly Christian troops serving the Ottoman Empire. Founded in 1330, it was abolished after rebelling in 1826.
3. Port of Spain.
4. Macavity.
5. Gloucestershire.
6. Gerald Harper.
7. Joe Davis.
8. Henry Purcell.
9. About $2\frac{1}{2}$ miles.

809

1. J and V, which came into use around 1630.
2. Charles Bradlaugh, in 1886.
3. Barbados.
4. Raymond West, in Agatha Christie's novels.
5. Leeds United.
6. Tony Curtis.
7. John Adams.
8. *Tarantula*.
9. Computers.

68

1. What was the name of the girl who wove so beautifully that the jealous goddess Athene turned her into a spider?
2. Who was the Maid of Norway?
3. Where would you find Kirkstone Pass?
4. Which English newspaper first reached one million daily sales?
5. Who first broke 3 minutes 50 seconds in the mile?
6. Who is the head of CI5 in 'The Professionals'?
7. Who won the World Professional Billiards Championship for the first time in 1980?
8. To whom is Alvin Stardust married?
9. In cryosurgery surgeons cool the body by 10° or 15°. This allows them to operate on a bloodless heart for how long?

439

1. What was the name of the last British battleship to be built and which survived both world wars?
2. Which English king was on the throne throughout the Napoleonic Wars?
3. On which island in New York is Brooklyn?
4. Who was the treacherous knight of the Round Table?
5. What is the height of a badminton net, measured at the centre?
6. Who or what was James Stewart talking to in *Harvey*?
7. Who won the first World Bowls title in 1956?
8. Which film star did Madness sing about?
9. Who capitalized on the chance remark: 'I cannot take smallpox for I have had cowpox'?

810

1. What do Americans call 'maths'?
2. Which king was known as Silly Billy?
3. Which chapel in Westminster Abbey is used as the Chapel of the Order of the Bath?
4. Which wealthy Norfolk family wrote famous medieval letters?
5. Who was the first woman to finish in the Grand National?
6. Who was the poor little rich girl, discovered by Andy Warhol, who died of drug abuse?
7. Who wrote: 'Art seeks to disengage itself from its own medium'?
8. Who did Sam the Sham play with?
9. A fossil of the great fish-like dinosaur known as the ichthyosaurus was first found by Mary Anning in 1811. How old was she at the time?

68

1. Arachne.
2. Margaret (*c.* 1283–90), daughter of King Eric II of Norway. Acknowledged Queen of Scotland on the death of Alexander III, she died on her voyage to Scotland.
3. In the Lake District.
4. The *Daily Mail*, on 2 March 1900.
5. John Walker.
6. George Cowley.
7. Fred Davis.
8. Liza Goddard.
9. About 14 minutes.

439

1. HMS *Renown*, built in 1916.
2. George III.
3. Long Island.
4. Sir Mordred.
5. 5 feet.
6. His companion, a 6-foot-high invisible rabbit of that name.
7. David Bryant.
8. Michael Cane.
9. Edward Jenner, who discovered vaccination.

810

1. Math.
2. William IV.
3. Henry VII's Chapel.
4. The Pastons.
5. Geraldine Rees, in 1982.
6. Edie Sedgwick.
7. Aristotle.
8. The Pharaohs.
9. 12 years old.

69

1. When is Maundy money given away, relative to Good Friday?
2. Who is said to have invited the Saxons Hengist and Horsa to Kent?
3. Where would you hope to find an abominable snowman?
4. Who, according to Boswell, said: 'To speak English one must place the tongue between the teeth and I have lost my teeth'?
5. Who first ran the 10,000 metres in under 28 minutes?
6. For which actress did Arthur Miller write *The Misfits*?
7. In which city would you find Michelangelo's 'David'?
8. From which opera does the 'Anvil Chorus' come?
9. Where is the tarsal joint?

440

1. What does the name Jesus mean?
2. What relation was Julius Caesar to the Emperor Augustus?
3. Where was the wartime seat of the Pétain government in France?
4. Who wrote the tragedy in blank verse *Samson Agonistes*?
5. What is the maximum number of greyhounds that can run in one race?
6. Which cartoon character is associated with Peter Sellers?
7. Apart from England, six other regions of the United Kingdom are legally allowed to issue postage stamps. Name four of these.
8. Who wrote the 'Maple Leaf Rag'?
9. When were the last wild boars seen in England?

811

1. How many pints of milk are needed to make 1 lb of cheddar cheese?
2. Who was the son of Duke Robert the Devil and Arlette?
3. On which Japanese island is the port of Osaka?
4. In mythology, how did Actaeon die?
5. What position did Stanley Matthews play?
6. By what name is Natasha Gurdin better known?
7. Whom do most Frenchmen consider to be their greatest novelist, born in 1799?
8. Who was nicknamed 'The Last of the Red-Hot Mamas'?
9. What do pangolins eat?

69

1. The day before.
2. Vortigern.
3. In the Himalayas.
4. Voltaire.
5. Ron Clarke.
6. Marilyn Monroe.
7. Florence.
8. *Il Trovatore.*
9. In the ankle.

440

1. Saviour.
2. Great-uncle.
3. Vichy.
4. Milton.
5. Eight.
6. The Pink Panther.
7. Jersey, Guernsey, the Isle of Man, Scotland, Northern Ireland and Wales.
8. Scott Joplin.
9. In the 1680s (a more precise date is 1683, in Chartlet Forest, Staffordshire).

811

1. Eight.
2. William the Conqueror.
3. Honshu Island.
4. Artemis turned him into a stag and he was torn to pieces by his own hounds.
5. Outside right.
6. Natalie Wood.
7. Honoré de Balzac.
8. Sophie Tucker.
9. Ants, chiefly.

70

1. What is the 'Senior Service'?
2. Which was the only City of London church not destroyed in the Great Fire of 1666?
3. Where did the gigantic moa bird live?
4. Who wrote *A Room with a View*?
5. How many Grand National winners did Fred Rimell train between 1956 and 1976?
6. Who played the Scarecrow in *The Wiz* – the all-black version of *The Wizard of Oz*?
7. What nationality was Alfred Nobel?
8. Which Beatle was not one of the original four?
9. Who first studied hydraulics?

441

1. In politics, by what name were the forerunners of the Liberals known?
2. Who was arguably Persia's most famous astronomer?
3. In the USA the Beaufort scale has been extended to what wind force?
4. Who was Laura's sonneteer?
5. Who succeeded Alberto Juantorena as 800-metre world record holder in 1979?
6. Which European country has a patron saint of cinema?
7. Who was the captain of HMS *Beagle*?
8. Who wrote the Monkees hit 'I'm a believer'?
9. Apart from dye, ink for ball-point pens contains which nutritious substance?

812

1. The term 'cab' comes from what word?
2. For which king was the Coronation Chair in Westminster Abbey originally made?
3. Which is the highest mountain in the Isle of Man?
4. Which printer and businessman wrote his first novel as a series of letters?
5. Who won the 1980 New York City marathon?
6. Which rock star starred in David Cronenbourg's 1982 movie *Videodrome*?
7. Who was the slave-owner who drafted most of the American Declaration of Independence?
8. Which song from *Evita* became a hit before the show opened?
9. What does a sphygmomanometer measure?

70

1. The Royal Navy.
2. St Bartholomew-the-Great.
3. New Zealand.
4. E.M. Forster.
5. Four.
6. Michael Jackson.
7. Swedish.
8. Ringo Starr.
9. Pascal.

441

1. Whigs.
2. Omar Khayyam.
3. Force 13 to 17.
4. Petrarch.
5. Sebastian Coe.
6. Spain – St John Bosco.
7. Fitzroy.
8. Neil Diamond.
9. Castor oil.

812

1. Cabriolet, meaning a small coach.
2. Edward I.
3. Snaefell.
4. Samuel Richardson, the novel being *Pamela*.
5. Alberto Salazar.
6. Debbie Harry.
7. Thomas Jefferson.
8. 'Don't Cry for Me, Argentina'.
9. Blood pressure.

71

1. To what is the nursery rhyme 'Ring a Ring o' Roses' referring?
2. What was the sacred beetle of the ancient Egyptians?
3. What are the Pawnees?
4. Who wrote *How Green Was My Valley*?
5. Which fast test-bowler suffered stress fractures of the lower spine early in his career?
6. Which film began the *Carry On* series?
7. Which oil is commonly used in oil-painting?
8. Which of Grieg's works does Anitra's Dance come from?
9. Hans Lippershey produced the first practical version of what?

442

1. Which is the system of Hindu philosophy whose name means 'union'?
2. Which queen ordered Ascot racecourse to be laid out?
3. By what name is Abyssinia now known?
4. Where was King Arthur's legendary capital?
5. Which world heavyweight champion won the 1952 Olympic middleweight gold medal at the age of seventeen?
6. Who starred in *Sutherland's Law*?
7. Who said of the French: 'Do they run already? Then I die happy'?
8. What is Kenny Baker's instrument?
9. What are felines?

813

1. What is heraldic black called?
2. What was the nickname of George Villiers, James I's favourite?
3. Which London district was associated with artists?
4. Which poet was encouraged by Siegfried Sassoon and killed a week before the First World War armistice?
5. Which writer rode Devon Loch in the 1956 Grand National?
6. In which film did George Lazenby play James Bond?
7. Who wrote: 'It is only shallow people who do not judge by appearances. The mystery of the world is the visible, not the invisible'?
8. Who wrote to his parents from Camp Grenada?
9. Who proved the organized circulation of the blood?

71

1. The Great Plague.
2. The scarab.
3. A North American Indian tribe.
4. Richard Llewellyn.
5. Dennis Lillee.
6. *Carry On Sergeant.*
7. Linseed.
8. *Peer Gynt.*
9. The microscope.

442

1. Yoga.
2. Queen Anne.
3. Ethiopia.
4. Camelot.
5. Floyd Patterson.
6. Ian Cuthbertson.
7. General Wolfe.
8. The trumpet.
9. Cats.

813

1. Sable.
2. Steenie.
3. Chelsea.
4. Wilfred Owen.
5. Dick Francis.
6. *On Her Majesty's Secret Service.*
7. Oscar Wilde.
8. Allan Sherman in 'Hello Muddah, Hello Fadduh'.
9. William Harvey.

Q

72

1. In which year were family allowances introduced?
2. Which British university first permitted women to take its degrees?
3. In 1971, how many inhabitants did the Pitcairn Islands have?
4. In which John Osborne play does Archie Rice appear?
5. David Acfield played cricket for Essex. In which sport did he represent Britain at the Olympic Games?
6. What happened in complete silence in *Rififi*?
7. Who promoted 'the greatest happiness of the greatest number'?
8. By what name is Stuart Goddard better known?
9. Anders Celsius published an idea in 1742 which at the time did not catch on. What was it?

443

1. What is French for 'king'?
2. What war was ended by the Treaty of Westphalia?
3. What was the eldest son of the king of France called?
4. Which poet was solicitor to the Woolwich Equitable Building Society?
5. Who first ran 200 metres in under 20 seconds?
6. Who starred in the film *Zorba the Greek*?
7. Which thriller writer's first name means 'flowering tree' in Maori?
8. How many hours away from Tulsa was Gene Pitney?
9. The moa, hunted to extinction in addition to being flightless, had the distinction of being what?

814

1. A Frenchman, Adolphe Pégoud, was the first pilot to do what in 1913?
2. At which battle did Nelson turn his blind eye to a signal?
3. A route over the curved surface of the earth that is the minimum distance between two points is called what?
4. Who wrote *The Lion, the Witch and the Wardrobe*?
5. Who was the first woman to finish in the 1981 London Marathon?
6. Who was the voice of Eccles?
7. Which prince planned the Great Exhibition of 1851?
8. Who recorded the album *Zenyatta Mondata*?
9. Which tree is also called the Scots mahogany?

72

1. 1945.
2. London University, in 1878.
3. Ninety-two.
4. *The Entertainer.*
5. Fencing.
6. A robbery – a cinema first.
7. Jeremy Bentham.
8. Adam Ant.
9. Nominating 0°C for the freezing point of water and 100°C for the boiling point.

443

1. *Roi.*
2. The Thirty Years War.
3. The Dauphin.
4. Roy Fuller.
5. Tommie Smith.
6. Anthony Quinn.
7. Ngaio Marsh.
8. Twenty-four.
9. The tallest bird.

814

1. Loop-the-Loop.
2. Copenhagen.
3. Great Circle Route.
4. C.S. Lewis.
5. Joyce Smith.
6. Spike Milligan.
7. Prince Albert.
8. Police.
9. The alder.

73

1. In American universities, what is a second-year student called?
2. When was the Court of Criminal Appeal set up?
3. Which 102-storey skyscraper was finished in 1931?
4. What did the Ark of the Covenant contain?
5. In golf, if a right-handed player cuts a shot, what will happen to the ball?
6. Who played Ensign Pulver in the 1955 film *Mister Roberts* and won an Oscar as best supporting actor?
7. Of whom did his steward say, 'A larger soul, I think, hath seldom dwelt in a house of clay than his was'?
8. By how much does a sharp raise a note?
9. Where was the explosive lyddite first tested?

444

1. Which Chancellor of the Exchequer introduced Premium Bonds?
2. Which body was founded in the reign of Henry VII for the protection of the royal person?
3. Where was the German fleet scuttled in 1919?
4. Which writer used the pseudonym Diedrich Knickerbocker?
5. Which jockey was the first to win over five million dollars in prize money in a season?
6. Born in Stockholm, who first became internationally acclaimed in the 1924 Swedish film *The Atonement of Gosta Berling*?
7. Who was Britain's first Minister of Technology?
8. Who founded the Ballet Russe?
9. How do male moths find female moths in the dark?

815

1. Which British bird was depicted on the farthing?
2. During which war was the Mills grenade designed?
3. Which palace is the official residence of the Queen when in Scotland?
4. Who wrote *Barchester Towers*?
5. What type of competition is the Benson and Hedges Cup?
6. In how many films has Peter Cushing played Doctor Who?
7. Who was the founder of Judaism?
8. By what name was Paul Klenovsky generally known?
9. What is the most common name for the vegetable Brassica oleracea?

73

1. A sophomore.
2. 1907.
3. The Empire State Building.
4. The tablets of the Ten Commandments.
5. It will travel from left to right.
6. Jack Lemmon.
7. Oliver Cromwell.
8. A semitone.
9. Lydd.

444

1. Harold Macmillan.
2. The Yeomen of the Guard.
3. Scapa Flow.
4. Washington Irving.
5. Steve Cauthen.
6. Greta Garbo.
7. Frank Cousins (1964).
8. Diaghilev.
9. By smell.

815

1. The wren. Appropriate as it was so small.
2. World War I.
3. Holyrood Palace.
4. Anthony Trollope.
5. One-day cricket.
6. Two.
7. Abraham.
8. Henry Wood.
9. Cabbage.

74

1. Which female name means 'bee'?
2. Which travel agent first organized continental holidays in 1855?
3. What connects Kabul with Peshawar?
4. Who died in Dublin in 1889, 30 years before the publication of his poems?
5. In golf, what is a bandit?
6. Of what is St Clare patron saint?
7. Whose middle name is McLane and is a child-care expert?
8. Which four periods are represented by Vivaldi's concertos Op. 8 Nos. 1–4?
9. What kind of waves are eliminated by the ozone layer in our atmosphere?

445

1. If you were born on 30 May what would your star sign be?
2. Who called whom the 'Flanders mare'?
3. In which country is Agadir?
4. Who achieved fame for his *Confessions of an English Opium Eater*?
5. Which was the last club before Wigan to join the Football League?
6. What is 'an everyday story of country folk'?
7. In which game might you collect a 'pung' of East Winds?
8. Who recorded the album *Heartbreak and Vine*?
9. Which insect stage comes between larva and imago?

816

1. For what speed is 'ton' slang?
2. To whom was Queen Anne married?
3. An 'oozie' in Burma is called what in India?
4. Who, in fact, lived at Shandy Hall?
5. At least how many banked turns must there be on a championship bob-sleigh course?
6. Who was the first British TV announcer?
7. Who published *The Gentleman and Cabinet-Maker's Director* in 1754 and made himself famous?
8. Which famous musical is by Dorothy Reynolds and Julian Slade?
9. What is a Lampyris noctiluca?

74

1. Melissa.
2. Thomas Cook.
3. The Khyber pass.
4. Gerard Manley Hopkins.
5. A golfer considered by others to play regularly below his current handicap.
6. Television.
7. Dr Benjamin Spock.
8. The seasons.
9. Ultra-violet rays.

445

1. Gemini.
2. Henry VIII his fourth wife, Anne of Cleves.
3. Morocco.
4. Thomas De Quincey.
5. Wimbledon.
6. 'The Archers'.
7. Mah-jong.
8. Tom Waits.
9. Pupa.

816

1. 100 m.p.h.
2. Prince George of Denmark.
3. A mahout.
4. Laurence Sterne. He called his own house this after the success of his book.
5. Fifteen.
6. Leslie Mitchell.
7. Thomas Chippendale.
8. *Salad Days*.
9. A glow-worm (European).

75

1. In a ship's routine, the first watch runs from when?
2. What was a unite?
3. The Tyrrhenian Sea is bounded by what land masses?
4. With whom did Shakespeare collaborate on *Henry VIII*?
5. Robin Dixon and Tony Nash won the gold medal for which event at the 1964 Winter Olympics?
6. Who starred in *The Untouchables*?
7. Which famous artist was responsible for a series of anatomical drawings?
8. What is the English name for the opera *Die Verkaufte Braut*?
9. At the equator a pendulum 39 inches in length oscillates within what period?

446

1. Which letter in Morse code is represented by three dots?
2. Troops of which country stormed Vimy Ridge in 1917?
3. Which language is spoken in Liechtenstein?
4. What was Thomas Hardy's first profession?
5. On which racecourse is the Rowley mile?
6. Which British actress was one of the regulars on 'Laugh In'?
7. Who captained England's inaugural international ladies' darts team in 1977?
8. How many of Rossini's operas have the same overture?
9. Which bird is known for its booming call and lives in reed-beds?

817

1. What was moved from Paris to Brussels in 1966 after France went on her own?
2. Which monarch called the longest-serving parliament?
3. What is the third largest island in the Mediterranean?
4. Who wrote *Love in a Cold Climate*?
5. How many are in an Olympic biathlon relay team?
6. What was the film called that was adapted from Noel Coward's play *Still Life*?
7. Who was the first Minister of Munitions in 1915?
8. In which city was Handel's *Messiah* first publicly performed?
9. Southey, Wordsworth and Coleridge were famous enjoyers of something Humphrey Davy discovered in 1800. What was it?

75

1. 8 p.m.
2. A gold coin (value 20 shillings) minted in 1604 to commemorate the union of England and Scotland. It was replaced in 1663.
3. Sardinia, Italy, Sicily.
4. John Fletcher.
5. Two-man bob-sleigh.
6. Robert Stack.
7. Leonardo da Vinci.
8. *The Bartered Bride*.
9. 1 second.

446

1. S.
2. Canada.
3. German.
4. Architecture.
5. Newmarket.
6. Judy Carne.
7. Maureen Flowers.
8. Three.
9. The bittern.

817

1. NATO headquarters.
2. Charles II. The 'Pensioners' Parliament' summoned in 1661 lasted for 17 years and 9 months.
3. Cyprus.
4. Nancy Mitford.
5. Four.
6. *Brief Encounter*.
7. David Lloyd George.
8. Dublin.
9. Laughing gas.

Q

76

1. What is the derivation of the word posh?
2. Why was the division of an English shire called a hundred?
3. The North Sea has an average depth of 300 feet. What is the average depth of the Persian Gulf?
4. Clotho spun the thread, Lachesis measured the length, Atropos cut it. What was the thread?
5. What nationality is tennis ace Guillermo Vilas?
6. In which film does Fred Astaire fall for Salvation Army lass Vera Ellen?
7. To which islands was Archbishop Makarios exiled?
8. Buck's Fizz won the Eurovision Song Contest with what song?
9. Which is Britain's smallest native bird?

447

1. What is the date of Walpurgis Night?
2. To which king of England was Eleanor of Aquitaine married?
3. Which Irish county shares its name with a type of fine glass?
4. Of what was Morpheus the Roman god?
5. In which sport did Jane Bridge win a gold medal in the first ever ladies' World Championships in 1980?
6. Who does Peter Sallis play in 'The Last of the Summer Wine'?
7. Who is arguably the most famous of sherpas?
8. Sid Vicious recorded what must be regarded as the definitive version of which hoary old chestnut?
9. What is produced by a Bessemer converter?

818

1. Name two of the three terms at Oxford.
2. What was the Hanseatic league?
3. Adam's Bridge is a chain of islands linking which two eastern states?
4. Who wrote *The First Blast of the Trumpet against the Monstrous Regiment of Women*?
5. How many teams played in the Minor Counties cricket championship?
6. Which 'real royal' inspired Coward's film *In Which We Serve*?
7. Paul Cézanne was very friendly with which famous French author of the late nineteenth century?
8. What did the Average White Band 'cut' in 1975?
9. An incredible gambling mania began in Holland in 1634 centred on which flower?

76

1. P O S H was the abbreviation used for cabin bookings on ships to the East. Wealthy passengers travelled 'Port Out, Starboard Home' – i.e. on the cooler side of the ship.
2. It consisted of 100 'hides' (one hide of land being a variable amount needed to support a family).
3. 80 feet.
4. In Greek mythology, a man's life.
5. Argentinian.
6. *The Belle of New York.*
7. The Seychelles.
8. 'Making Your Mind Up'.
9. The goldcrest.

447

1. 30 April.
2. Henry II.
3. Waterford.
4. Sleep.
5. Judo.
6. Clegg.
7. Sherpa Tensing who first scaled Everest with Sir Edmund Hillary.
8. 'My Way'.
9. Steel.

818

1. Trinity, Michaelmas, Hilary.
2. An organization of North European merchants headed by those of Lübeck; it monopolized Baltic trade in particular.
3. Sri Lanka and India.
4. John Knox (1558).
5. Twenty-one.
6. Lord Mountbatten.
7. Émile Zola.
8. 'The Cake'.
9. The tulip.

Q

77

1. What were eighteenth-century macaronis?
2. Which country according to its rulers needed 'a small victorious war to stem the tide of revolution' and got a costly defeat?
3. What lies 15 miles north of Quito?
4. Which Australian won the 1973 Nobel Prize for Literature?
5. Which racecourse is called the Rooddee?
6. On which musical instrument was the theme to *The Third Man* played?
7. Who was the world's first woman prime minister?
8. Which Scottish rocker described himself as 'Sensational'?
9. The word 'walrus' is the contraction of which whimsical name?

448

1. Where was Interpol founded in 1923?
2. How many judges sit in the International Court of Justice?
3. Which is Scotland's longest river?
4. Euphuism stands for a rich, self-consciously elaborate style. Where does it come from?
5. Where were the Winter Olympics of 1960 held?
6. What, in the theatre, is 'papering the house'?
7. Which darts player is nicknamed 'The Man in Black'?
8. Who was the leader of the band called the Crypt Kickers?
9. A leaf of the crown that Caesar wore might well be used in a meat stew. Laurus nobilis is also called what?

819

1. What is the Fahrenheit equivalent of Gas Regulo 7?
2. Why was verse 1 of Psalm 51 called 'the neck verse'?
3. Which was the last English town to be made into a city?
4. By what name is the *New English Dictionary on Historical Principles* now known?
5. Which sport uses the terms bonspiel, crampit, kiggle-kaggle, rink, house, stone and besom?
6. Which TV series starred Adam Faith?
7. If you stick various materials on to a canvas to make a picture, what would it be called?
8. Who composed the theme tune for 'Crossroads'?
9. What is the Latin name of the North American bison?

77

1. Dandies. Young men about town who had adopted continental fashions.
2. Russia in the 1904–5 war with Japan.
3. The equator.
4. Patrick White.
5. Chester.
6. A zither (by Anton Karas).
7. Mrs Bandaranaike of Ceylon (now Sri Lanka), in 1960.
8. Alex Harvey.
9. Whale-horse.

448

1. Vienna.
2. 15 (quorum of 9).
3. The Tay.
4. *Euphues* (1579–80) by John Lyly.
5. Squaw Valley.
6. Filling the house with invited guests with free tickets.
7. Alan Glazier.
8. Bobby 'Boris' Pickett.
9. The bay leaf or sweet bay.

819

1. 425°F.
2. Ability to read it could save your neck. From the fourteenth century it meant you could claim 'benefit of clergy'.
3. Derby.
4. The *Oxford English Dictionary* (as from 1933).
5. Curling.
6. 'Budgie'.
7. A collage.
8. Tony Hatch.
9. Bison Bison.

78

1. For what are Pulitzer prizes awarded?
2. Where was Acadia?
3. What is the name of the island lying off the southern end of the Isle of Man?
4. In *Gulliver's Travels*, from what do scientists seek to get sunshine?
5. Who rode Tap on Wood to victory in the 1979 Two Thousand Guineas?
6. What does a TV licence cost in the USA?
7. Of whom did Margot Asquith say, 'He could not see a belt without hitting below it'?
8. Name Donovan's first two singles.
9. Name the two satellites of Mars.

449

1. The average European uses how much domestic water a day?
2. Which European monarch ruled over the most territory in Europe?
3. What is the capital city of Nevada?
4. Who was the Greek equivalent of Venus?
5. How high is a tennis court net in the centre?
6. Who is 'Her Indoors'?
7. At which musical instrument was the composer Liszt a virtuoso?
8. Who had a hit about 'Baker Street'?
9. What has been in use for centuries and was known all over the world except in Peru by AD 1500?

820

1. What is Mariolatry?
2. To which monastic order did Tintern Abbey belong?
3. In which town is the National Library of Wales?
4. Who wrote, 'One short sleep past, we wake eternally,/And Death shall be no more; Death, thou shalt die'?
5. What nationality is speedway's Ole Olsen?
6. Which actor and actress starred in *Brief Encounter*?
7. In which style of architecture is Reims Cathedral?
8. Who sang about 'Your Cheatin' Heart'?
9. The custodians of the Vatican Library were shocked to discover in 1949 that many manuscripts had been destroyed by what?

78

1. Journalism and literature.
2. Nova Scotia (the first settlers were French and gave it this name).
3. The Calf of Man.
4. Cucumbers.
5. Steve Cauthen.
6. Nothing. They don't have TV licences over there.
7. David Lloyd George.
8. 'Catch the Wind' and 'Colours'.
9. Phobos and Deimos.

449

1. 40 gallons.
2. Charles V, the Habsburg Emperor.
3. Carson City.
4. Aphrodite.
5. 3 feet.
6. Arthur Daley's wife, in 'Minder'.
7. The piano.
8. Gerry Rafferty.
9. The wheel.

820

1. Idolatrous worship of the Virgin Mary as conceived by opponents of Roman Catholicism.
2. The Cistercians.
3. Aberystwyth.
4. John Donne (Holy Sonnet XVII).
5. Danish.
6. Trevor Howard and Celia Johnson.
7. Gothic.
8. Hank Williams.
9. Termites.

Q

79

1. Which letter in Morse code is represented by three dashes?
2. Who was the last queen of England to be tried for adultery?
3. The greatest what occurs at the Bay of Fundy, Canada?
4. Shakespeare wrote of them that they 'come before the swallow dares and take/The winds of March with beauty'. To what was he referring?
5. Who won the Olympic Games marathon in both 1976 and 1980?
6. What musical instrument did Kay Kendall play in *Genevieve*?
7. Which artist and poet's colour-printed drawings include 'Elijah in the Chariot of Fire'?
8. Who skipped the light fandango with sixteen vestal virgins?
9. A doctor specializing in myology studies what?

450

1. If you suffer from musophobia of what are you afraid?
2. Who were the European 'Mohocks'?
3. The Tibetan 'Sacred Mother of the Waters' is what?
4. Which Waugh's first novel was *The Loom of Youth*?
5. In men's fencing competitions, how many hits are needed to win?
6. Who sang the 'I-Feel-Like-I'm-Fixin'-To-Die-Rag' in the *Woodstock* movie?
7. As what was M. Escoffier renowned?
8. Who were the first British group to top the American charts?
9. A horse is measured in hands. How many hands is a pony at most?

821

1. Who was the man, Lord of a Neolithic monument, who introduced Bank Holidays?
2. Who said in 1888, 'We are part of the community of Europe, and we must do our duty as such'?
3. What are the Dodecanese?
4. A craving for what exposed the Duchess of Malfi's pregnancy?
5. What nationality was Adolf Wiklund, the first biathlon world champion?
6. What was the name of the film in which Sting had his first acting role?
7. Who was the first Secretary of State for Wales?
8. On whose play was the opera *Boris Godunov* based?
9. What is a dzo?

79

1. O.
2. Caroline of Brunswick (in 1820).
3. Range of tide (as much as 50 feet).
4. Daffodils.
5. Waldemar Cierponski.
6. The trumpet.
7. William Blake.
8. Procul Harum in 'A Whiter Shade of Pale'.
9. Muscles.

450

1. Mice.
2. Eighteenth-century muggers and ruffians in London.
3. Mount Everest.
4. Alec (Evelyn's brother).
5. Five.
6. Country Joe McDonald.
7. A chef.
8. The Tornados.
9. 14.2.

821

1. Lord Avebury (Sir John Lubbock).
2. W. E. Gladstone (in a speech at Caernarvon).
3. Islands off Turkey belonging to Greece.
4. Apricots.
5. Swedish.
6. *Quadrophenia*.
7. Jim Griffiths.
8. Alexander Pushkin's.
9. A cross between a cow and a yak.

80

1. If you were hypermetropic, what would you have?
2. In whose reigns did the Hundred Years War with France begin and end?
3. In which city is the Heriot-Watt university?
4. Whose first novel was withdrawn on the advice of George Meredith and never published?
5. For which rugby club did Gareth Edwards play?
6. Who starred in the 1968 film *Green Shoes*?
7. Which artist collaborated with Luis Buñuel to make the film *Un Chien andalou*?
8. Who asked Rhonda for help?
9. What is pasteurization?

451

1. In heraldry, a bar sinister means that the bearer is what?
2. Which monarch is associated with Weymouth?
3. What is unusual about the Cinque Port of Rye?
4. Different guilds were responsible for different parts of the miracle plays. Which guilds traditionally presented the Crucifixion?
5. In which sport does the World Championship have three classes called open, standard and 15 metres?
6. *Carve Her Name With Pride* was based on whose life story?
7. Who said, '... the materials for city planning are: sky, space, trees, steel and cement in this order and in this hierarchy'?
8. Who 'Set the Controls for the Heart of the Sun'?
9. What are the four small bones at the base of the spine called?

822

1. What was awarded to Dag Hammarskjöld a month after he died?
2. Where did the main battle of the 1916 Easter Rising in Dublin take place?
3. What is the nearest part of England to Ireland?
4. What is Alfred Lord Tennyson's longest poetic work?
5. For which sport would you practise on nursery slopes?
6. Who starred in the film *Grey Lady Down*?
7. Who was a bricklayer at the building of Lincoln's Inn and was buried at Westminster Abbey in 1637?
8. Which canal was opened with a specially commissioned opera?
9. What is the primeval land mass called from which all the world's continents sprang?

80

1. Long sight.
2. Those of Edward III and Henry VI.
3. Edinburgh.
4. Thomas Hardy's.
5. Cardiff.
6. George Cole.
7. Salvador Dali.
8. The Beach Boys.
9. Heat-treating milk to about 150°F.

451

1. Illegitimate.
2. George III who holidayed there.
3. It is now a mile or more from the sea.
4. Nailmakers and ironmongers.
5. Gliding.
6. Violette Szabo.
7. Le Corbusier.
8. Pink Floyd.
9. The coccyx.

822

1. The Nobel Peace Prize.
2. In the General Post Office in O'Connell Street.
3. St Bees Head.
4. *Idylls of the King.*
5. Skiing.
6. Charlton Heston.
7. Ben Jonson.
8. Suez, in 1869. The opera was *Aïda.*
9. Pangea.

81

1. As apple juice makes cider, what does pear juice make?
2. During the D-Day invasion for what did PLUTO stand?
3. Where do Vectians live?
4. How many lines are there in a Spenserian stanza?
5. How many times did Muhammad Ali fight Joe Bugner?
6. Who were the Beach Boy and the singer-songwriter who starred in *Two-Lane Blacktop*?
7. Who was the Astronomer Royal who retired at the end of 1971?
8. Who had 'Breakfast in America'?
9. About what proportion of a man's body weight is the weight of his blood?

452

1. What colour ribbon does the Victoria Cross have?
2. In ancient Greece, what was a hoplite?
3. Tuvalu is the name of which former UK protectorate?
4. Who in reality was the grand old man of letters in Maugham's *Cakes and Ale*?
5. Why did the very first Oxford and Cambridge Boat Race have to be restarted?
6. Which British actor won a British Academy award for the part of Claudius in the TV series 'I, Claudius'?
7. Whose piece of sculpture was called 'Lobster Telephone'?
8. What was The Band's first album called?
9. Swallows, martins and swifts have two distinct characteristics. What are they?

823

1. What is tahina made from?
2. Charles V said he spoke 'Spanish to God, Italian to women, French to men, and German . . .' to what or whom?
3. What was the Potola?
4. Whose first play was *Catalina*?
5. What nationality is speedway's Barry Briggs?
6. Two of James Hilton's novels have been filmed – twice. Name one.
7. Watson, Crick and Wilkins received the Nobel Prize for Medicine in 1962. For what discovery?
8. What is Toyah's surname?
9. How many incisors should a human adult have?

81

1. Perry.
2. Pipe Line Under The Ocean.
3. On the Isle of Wight. Vectis was the old Roman name for the island.
4. Nine.
5. Twice.
6. Denis Wilson and James Taylor.
7. Sir Richard Woolley.
8. Supertramp.
9. About one-thirteenth, or nearly 8 per cent.

452

1. Purple.
2. A soldier.
3. Ellice Islands.
4. Thomas Hardy.
5. Because the boats collided.
6. Derek Jacobi.
7. Salvador Dali.
8. *Music from Big Pink.*
9. Pointed wings and forked tails.

823

1. Sesame seeds.
2. '. . . my horse.'
3. The palace of the Dalai Lama in Lhasa, Tibet.
4. Henrik Ibsen's.
5. A New Zealander.
6. *Lost Horizon, Goodbye Mr Chips.*
7. DNA.
8. Wilcox.
9. 8 (4 in each jaw).

82

1. What is a marron glacé?
2. Of what order, established in Jerusalem, did an offshoot found the St John's Ambulance Association?
3. What did America adopt on 14 June 1777?
4. Who were Oedipus's parents?
5. Which jockey won his first English classic on Polygamy (1974 Oaks)?
6. Whose first play was *The Room*?
7. What is the Princess of Wales's middle name?
8. Covent Garden opera house was built on the site of what?
9. Davy Crockett is said to have worn an early pioneer style of hat made from the fur of which animal?

453

1. What percentage of French wines are labelled Appellation Contrôlée?
2. Which civilization preceded that of the Aztecs in Mexico?
3. When did the last British troops leave Suez?
4. Who wrote *Cranford*?
5. How many times was Bobby Charlton capped?
6. On which tale is the musical *Chu Chin Chow* based?
7. What adjective describes Ben Jonson on his tombstone in Westminster Abbey?
8. Who composed the song 'Camptown Races'?
9. The Dragoon, the Antwerp, the Pouter, the Tumbler and the Horseman are all types of what?

824

1. Sayonara is 'goodbye' in which language?
2. Who was the last king of Israel?
3. How many hours ahead of GMT is Moscow?
4. Who wrote the science fiction book *Hothouse*?
5. Which Peruvian won the Wimbledon tennis singles in 1959?
6. How many records are castaways allowed on 'Desert Island Discs'?
7. Which artist used Mae West's face to portray a surrealist apartment?
8. Who composed *The Dream of Gerontius*?
9. The cross of Christ's crucifixion was said to be made of this, which is now a semi-parasitic dwarf plant. What is it?

82

1. A chestnut preserved in sugar.
2. The Knights Hospitallers.
3. The Stars and Stripes as its banner.
4. King Laius of Thebes and Queen Jocasta.
5. Pat Eddery.
6. Harold Pinter's.
7. Frances.
8. A convent garden (it was a produce garden of Westminster Abbey).
9. The raccoon.

453

1. 15 per cent.
2. The Toltecs.
3. 1956.
4. Mrs Elizabeth Gaskell.
5. 106.
6. *Ali Baba and the Forty Thieves.*
7. Rare.
8. Stephen Foster.
9. Pigeon.

824

1. Japanese.
2. Hoshea.
3. Three.
4. Brian Aldiss.
5. Alex Olmedo.
6. Eight.
7. Salvador Dali.
8. Edward Elgar.
9. Mistletoe.

83

1. What is a bouquet garni?
2. Which foreign monarch appeared on some English coins in the sixteenth century?
3. Which country has the largest number of airlines?
4. Who is Sir George Etherege's *Man of Mode*?
5. Who plays cricket at Edgbaston?
6. By what name is Malden Sukilovich better known?
7. Who said, 'The executioner is, I believe, very expert and my neck is very slender'?
8. Who was the subject of the film *Lonely Boy*?
9. What breed of dog is obtained by crossing a collie with a greyhound?

454

1. Where would you find a parlour, a scriptorium, a dorter and a cellarium?
2. In what sense is the October Revolution of 1917 misnamed?
3. For where is 0792 the dialling code?
4. What crime is the subject of *Memoirs and Confessions of a Justified Sinner*?
5. The US lawn tennis championships moved from where to where?
6. What was the canine star of the *Thin Man* films called?
7. Which discoverer found a man clothed in goatskins who looked wilder than the first owner of them?
8. Who had a hit with 'I Know a Place' in 1965?
9. Where would you find Volans?

825

1. What is 'tomorrow' in Spanish?
2. Who married Henry VIII in 1533?
3. What is the capital of Hong Kong?
4. What is the subject-matter of the Book of Kells?
5. If you went orienteering what equipment would you take with you?
6. By which name is Joseph Levitch better known?
7. Which Irish writer of comedies gave up acting on wounding a colleague in a stage fight and died in penury?
8. What national anthem is sung to the theme of a drinking song?
9. Which variety of cheese is also a breed of long-haired sheep?

83

1. A small bunch of herbs tied together in muslin.
2. Philip of Spain (with Mary I, his wife, in 1555).
3. The USA.
4. Sir Fopling Flutter.
5. Warwickshire County Cricket Club.
6. Karl Malden.
7. Anne Boleyn.
8. Paul Anka.
9. A lurcher.

454

1. In a monastery.
2. It took place in November (the Gregorian calendar was adopted in Russia in 1918).
3. Swansea.
4. Fratricide.
5. Forest Hills to Flushing Meadows.
6. Asta.
7. Alexander Selkirk.
8. Petula Clark.
9. The southern sky (constellation Flying Fish).

825

1. Mañana.
2. Anne Boleyn.
3. Victoria.
4. The four gospels in Latin.
5. A map and compass.
6. Jerry Lewis.
7. George Farquhar.
8. 'The Star-spangled Banner'.
9. Wensleydale.

84

1. What is a jacuzzi?
2. In ancient Egypt the standard length was a cubit (the length of a forearm from elbow to fingertip). How many palms made a cubit?
3. In Welsh, what does cwm mean?
4. When did Charles Dickens die? 1830, 1840, 1850, 1860 or 1870?
5. What is the name of London's principal fencing centre?
6. Which BBC 'soaper' of the 1960s was about life on a women's magazine?
7. How many numbers are on a British roulette wheel?
8. From which opera does Handel's famous 'Largo' come?
9. What is scotopic vision?

455

1. What have the words 'apron,' 'adder' and 'umpire' in common?
2. In which year did the 'Jack the Ripper' murders occur?
3. In which city was the first public telephone kiosk set up in 1908?
4. Who was the nymph who loved Narcissus and pined away?
5. Which Yorkshire racecourse never stages flat racing?
6. Who were Sandy and Julian?
7. Which English novelist invented pillar-boxes while working as a civil servant?
8. Who composed the opera *Boris Godunov*?
9. Of what are barbastelle and pipistrelle varieties?

826

1. What is the female equivalent of a warlock?
2. Which prime minister led the first Liberal government?
3. What was once named New Albion by Francis Drake?
4. In which Shakespeare play does the word 'honorificabilitudinitatibus' appear?
5. How many bases are there in softball?
6. Which American film star made a memorable German film called *Pandora's Box*?
7. By what name is the eighteenth-century dice game of hazard now known?
8. Who composed the opera *Oedipus Rex*?
9. Pencil lead is mostly made from what substance?

84

1. A whirlpool bath.
2. Seven.
3. Valley.
4. 1870.
5. The de Beaumont centre.
6. 'Compact'.
7. 37 (1 to 36 + zero).
8. *Xerxes.*
9. Seeing in the dark.

455

1. They've lost their initial 'n' (being originally 'napron,' 'nadder' and 'numpire').
2. 1888.
3. Nottingham.
4. Echo.
5. Wetherby.
6. Two unmistakably gay characters played by Kenneth Williams and Hugh Paddick in 'Round the Horne'.
7. Anthony Trollope.
8. Mussorgsky.
9. Bats.

826

1. A witch.
2. Gladstone (1868–74).
3. Oregon, USA.
4. *Love's Labour's Lost.*
5. Three.
6. Louise Brooks.
7. Craps.
8. Stravinsky.
9. Graphite.

85

1. What name is given to the Usher of the Upper Chamber?
2. In which year did the Thames dry up for 9 miles from its source?
3. What is a sand devil?
4. Complete the clerihew 'Sir Christopher Wren/ Said "I'm going to dine with some men/ . . ."'
5. Who followed Ron Saunders as manager of Manchester City?
6. In which film did Elvis play a double role?
7. If you planted a banderilla what would you be doing?
8. What was the first Pink Floyd album?
9. What was the real name of Paracelsus?

456

1. What was the first frozen food available in Britain?
2. Within how many years of each other did the Buddha and Confucius die?
3. The Lapps are among Europe's last surviving what?
4. Where did the *Pickwick Papers* parliamentary election take place?
5. Who took Maurice Hope's world title?
6. Who played the skipper of the charter boat in the 1944 film *To Have and Have Not*?
7. What was Sir Walter Scott's original profession?
8. In which city was the first public opera house opened?
9. The adhesive on postage stamps was originally what substance?

827

1. What is a lazy Susan?
2. Who sang 'Hallelujah, I'm a bum' and campaigned for American revolution?
3. To where did Concorde make its first commercial flight in 1976?
4. Who first wrote, 'All hell broke loose'?
5. Which sport uses the terms upshoot, knuckler, roundhouse, sacrifice bunt?
6. What was John Huston's first *British* film?
7. Who became Lord Warden of the Cinque Ports in 1978?
8. Who were 'On the Road Again'?
9. Which fish-eating bird of prey has recently returned to Scotland?

85

1. Black Rod.
2. 1976.
3. A local whirlwind, usually in the desert.
4. '"... If anyone calls/ Say I am designing St Paul's."'
5. Tony Book.
6. *Kissin' Cousins.*
7. Bullfighting.
8. *Piper at the Gates of Dawn.*
9. Theophrastus Bombartus von Hohenheim.

456

1. Asparagus (in 1937).
2. 3 to 4 years (the Buddha died in 483 BC, Confucius in 480 or 479 BC).
3. Nomads.
4. Eatanswill.
5. Wilfred Benitez.
6. Humphrey Bogart.
7. The law.
8. Venice.
9. Gum arabic.

827

1. A tray which revolves on a central bearing.
2. The Wobblies (Industrial Workers of the World).
3. Bahrain.
4. Milton (in *Paradise Lost*).
5. Baseball.
6. *The African Queen,* believe it or not.
7. The Queen Mother.
8. Canned Heat.
9. The osprey.

86

1. Which sense does a dying person tend to lose last?
2. Against which country did England fight the war of Jenkins's Ear in 1739?
3. Who destroyed the Czech mining village of Lidice?
4. Who is Hagar the Horrible's wife?
5. Where were the first Winter Olympics held?
6. Which part did Charlton Heston play in the 1956 film *The Ten Commandments*?
7. Which artist painted sixty-two self-portraits?
8. Which composer's life is the basis for the musical *Lilac Time*?
9. For how long has the cockroach, in its modern form, existed on earth?

457

1. To the nearest million, how many other people share your birthday?
2. Which country's merchant ships fly the flag often called the 'Red Duster'?
3. Where are the Heights of Abraham?
4. Which author's first novel was *Battle Cry*?
5. In which sport is the Walker Cup contested?
6. Who played Princess Dala in the 1964 film *The Pink Panther*?
7. Whose autobiography is entitled *Day by Day*?
8. Which famous jazz clarinettist usually sports a bowler?
9. How many eyes has an earthworm?

828

1. Name the place of detention for prisoners in the US navy.
2. Whose horse, ridden during the Crusades, was called Fauvel?
3. Where is Henry VIII buried?
4. Who wrote *The Spy Who Came in from the Cold*?
5. Al Oerter of the USA is the only Olympian to win four gold medals in the same event in consecutive Olympics. In which event?
6. Who played St Peter in the film *The Robe*?
7. Which philosopher is said to have lived in a tub?
8. Where is the festival staged by the Dolmetsch family held?
9. What name is given to ploughed land that has remained untilled or unsown for at least a year?

86

1. Hearing.
2. Spain.
3. The Nazis.
4. Helga.
5. Chamonix, France.
6. Moses.
7. Rembrandt.
8. Schubert.
9. 250 million years.

457

1. 9 million.
2. Britain's.
3. Quebec, Canada.
4. Leon Uris.
5. Golf (amateur).
6. Claudia Cardinale.
7. Robin Day.
8. Acker Bilk.
9. None.

828

1. The brig.
2. King Richard the Lionheart.
3. St George's Chapel, Windsor.
4. John Le Carré.
5. Discus.
6. Michael Rennie.
7. Diogenes.
8. Haslemere, Surrey.
9. Fallow.

87

1. What is the lowest-value postal order available?
2. Which ministers did Hitler sentence to death from his bunker in April 1945?
3. What was the colonial name for Ghana?
4. Who invented the Three Laws of Robotics in his books?
5. Which rugby club plays home matches at Old Deer Park?
6. Who played the private detectives in the 1972 film *Hickey and Boggs*?
7. On which holiday was Isaac Newton born?
8. What was Gene Vincent's biggest hit?
9. Which element's name is derived from the Greek word meaning 'lazy'?

458

1. Which country has the lowest suicide rate?
2. Which king married for the first time in 1509?
3. Which major Western country refused to participate in the League of Nations?
4. What was Glubbdubdrib?
5. Who rode Doublet to an individual gold medal at the 1971 European Championships?
6. Who wrote the play *Chicken Soup With Barley* as part of a trilogy?
7. In which town were snooker's Joe and Fred Davis born?
8. Who was known in Germany as 'der Bingle'?
9. Which animal family does the ibex belong to?

829

1. Who won the Nobel Prize for Peace in 1944?
2. For how long was Mary Queen of Scots a prisoner in England?
3. Where is the oldest university in the world?
4. What did the Allies call what the Germans called the Siegfried Line?
5. Which Rugby Union team won the 1983 Welsh Cup?
6. Who sang – if that's the word – 'Wanderin' Star' in the film *Paint Your Wagon*?
7. The Aphrodite of Melos is generally known as what?
8. Who composed the opera *The Rake's Progress*?
9. What was the Moho Project?

87

1. 25p.
2. Himmler and Goering.
3. The Gold Coast Colony.
4. Isaac Asimov.
5. London Welsh.
6. Bill Cosby and Robert Culp.
7. Christmas Day.
8. 'Be Bop A Lula'.
9. Argon.

458

1. Jordan (0.04 per 100,000).
2. Henry VIII.
3. USA.
4. The land of sorcerers and magicians in *Gulliver's Travels.*
5. Princess Anne.
6. Arnold Wesker.
7. Chesterfield.
8. Bing Crosby.
9. Wild goats.

829

1. The International Red Cross (awarded 1945).
2. 19 years (1568–87).
3. Fez, Morocco (founded 859).
4. The Hindenburg Line.
5. Pontypool.
6. Lee Marvin.
7. The Venus de Milo.
8. Stravinsky.
9. To drill down to molten magna beneath the earth's crust.

88

1. Who is depicted on horseback on the 1977 Jubilee crown?
2. What was a carronade?
3. What gave Poland access to the Baltic after the First World War?
4. Who wrote of a new Eden and a new Temptation on Venus in *Perelandra*, part of a science-fiction trilogy?
5. How many 'holes in one' were there during the British Open Golf Championships in 1981?
6. Who took the male lead in *Saturday Night and Sunday Morning*?
7. Of which political party was Michael Collins the leader in 1916–21?
8. Who sang about 'My Chérie Amour'?
9. Name Saturn's largest moon.

459

1. What is the former *Daily Worker* now called?
2. How were Charles II, Nell Gwyn and the Duke of St Albans related?
3. Which English island is separated from the mainland by the Swale?
4. Which prophet came from the village of Anathoth?
5. Which famous annual race first took place in 1829?
6. Which cars were the real stars of the movie *The Italian Job*?
7. Who described assassination as the 'extreme form of censorship'?
8. For which instrument was Bach's Italian Concerto written?
9. From the failure of which gland does the condition known as cretinism arise?

830

1. What does 'decimate' mean?
2. Which writer was held to ransom in Algiers and later helped to organize the Armada?
3. Which cathedral is dedicated to St Saviour?
4. Name Shylock's wife.
5. For which event did Brian Phelps win a bronze medal at the 1960 Olympics?
6. Which abominable doctor–organist was played to great effect by Vincent Price?
7. Whom did Jennie Lee marry?
8. From which country did the dance the gavotte originate?
9. What does BMEWS stand for?

88

1. The Queen.
2. A short gun of large calibre with a chamber for powder like a mortar.
3. The Polish Corridor.
4. C.S.Lewis.
5. Three.
6. Albert Finney.
7. Sinn Féin.
8. Stevie Wonder.
9. Titan.

459

1. The *Morning Star*.
2. The last was the son of the first two.
3. The Isle of Sheppey.
4. Jeremiah.
5. The Oxford and Cambridge Boat Race.
6. Mini-Coopers.
7. George Bernard Shaw.
8. The harpsichord.
9. The thyroid.

830

1. To reduce by one-tenth.
2. Cervantes.
3. Southwark.
4. Leah.
5. High-board diving.
6. Doctor Phibes (in the film *The Abominable Dr Phibes*).
7. Aneurin Bevan.
8. France.
9. Ballistic Missile Early Warning System.

89

1. If you suffer from cynanthropy, what do you think you are?
2. When was the last sea-battle between galleys fought?
3. With which country did Tanganyika unite in 1964 to become Tanzania?
4. Name one of Lord Peter Wimsey's clubs.
5. In the 1949 British Open, Harry Bradshaw played a memorable golf stroke. Where was the ball lying?
6. Who played Little Joe in 'Bonanza'?
7. Who was the first woman to hold ministerial office in the UK?
8. Which R and B star died during a concert interval while playing Russian roulette?
9. Who cried the word 'photon'?

460

1. You may legally ride a moped with a car driver's licence if the engine does not exceed what capacity?
2. During which war was the term 'concentration camp' coined?
3. How many Spanish Steps are there in Rome?
4. Name one of the parents of John the Baptist.
5. How often are bob-sleighing world championships held?
6. Who played the photographer in *Blow-Up*?
7. Which gardener built the Crystal Palace?
8. You've heard of platinum albums, but who was the first artiste to win a rhodium record?
9. What is a lepton?

831

1. What is inscribed on the reverse of the Military Medal?
2. How did William Paterson help William III's foreign wars?
3. Where did the Investiture of the Prince of Wales take place in 1969?
4. Of which work does the novel known in translation as *The Cities of the Plain* form part?
5. Who pipped Allan Wells at the Moscow Olympics in the 200 metres finals?
6. Name the first St Trinian's film.
7. How many dots are there on a set of standard dominoes?
8. Who sang about Finchley Central?
9. What are the two poles of the celestial horizon?

89

1. A dog.
2. 1571 (the Battle of Lepanto).
3. Zanzibar.
4. The Egotists, according to his *Who's Who* entry.
5. In a broken bottle.
6. Michael Landon.
7. The Duchess of Atholl.
8. Johnny Ace, in 1954.
9. Einstein, in 1905.

460

1. 50cc.
2. The Boer War.
3. 138.
4. Zacharias or Elisabeth.
5. Annually.
6. David Hemmings.
7. Sir Joseph Paxton (gardener to the Duke of Devonshire at Chatsworth).
8. Paul McCartney.
9. A light elementary particle.

831

1. 'For bravery in the field'.
2. He was instrumental in founding the Bank of England in 1695.
3. Caernarvon Castle.
4. Proust's *Remembrance of Things Past.*
5. Pietro Mennea of Italy.
6. *The Belles of St Trinians.*
7. 168.
8. The New Vaudeville Band.
9. Nadir and zenith.

90

1. To what curious meteorological phenomenon did King Arthur's sister give her name?
2. Who was the first British king since 1743 to join his army in the field?
3. What lies between Nepal and Bhutan?
4. Who wrote *No Highway*?
5. Who did Virginia Wade beat in the 1977 Wimbledon Final?
6. Who played 'Mother' in 'The Avengers'?
7. How did Van Gogh die?
8. Where were Ziggy Stardust's spiders from?
9. A working model of the planets and their motions was built by Rowley in 1715. What was it called?

461

1. What is the upper age limit for MPs?
2. About 50,000 were killed in France in one day in 1572 at the instigation of the king's mother. Who was she?
3. In which country does the river Niger rise?
4. Which was the first European town evangelized by Paul according to the New Testament?
5. Which Briton lost his world boxing title to Carlos Palomino?
6. Which BBC film, commissioned but never shown, has become the most famous anti-nuclear protest movie?
7. Who was born at Glamis Castle on 21 August 1930?
8. Who did the Funky Chicken?
9. Which common foot disease is a form of ringworm?

832

1. At which British university can you take a degree in brewing?
2. When was the last time the English crown changed hands on the field of battle?
3. Of which Canadian province is Regina the capital?
4. Who changed Sultan Shahriyar's outlook on women?
5. Zimbabwe won its first ever gold medal at the 1980 Olympics. In which event?
6. Who played Joe Lampton in Jack Clayton's film *Room At the Top*?
7. How many legal opening chess moves for White are there?
8. By which name is the Hall of Arts and Sciences now called?
9. A valuable plant for feeding cattle is a member of the pea, bean and clover family. What is it?

90

1. Fata Morgana, a type of mirage.
2. George V in the First World War.
3. Sikkim.
4. Nevil Shute.
5. Betty Stove.
6. Patrick Newell.
7. He shot himself.
8. Mars.
9. An orrery (after the Earl of Orrery, who commissioned it).

461

1. There is none.
2. Catherine de Medici.
3. Guinea.
4. Philippi.
5. John H. Stracey.
6. Peter Watkins's *The War Game.*
7. Princess Margaret.
8. Rufus Thomas.
9. Athlete's foot.

832

1. Heriot-Watt, in Edinburgh.
2. In 1485 at Bosworth Field, when it passed from Richard III to Henry VII.
3. Saskatchewan.
4. Scheherazade.
5. Women's hockey.
6. Laurence Harvey.
7. Twenty.
8. The Royal Albert Hall.
9. Alfalfa.

Q

91

1. Singing before breakfast, seeing an owl by day, seeing three butterflies: what kind of omen are all these supposed to be?
2. Where did the Great Fire of London end?
3. What country's Dominion Day is 1 July?
4. Where was the case of Jarndyce v. Jarndyce heard?
5. Where did ice hockey originate?
6. In which TV series did Elvis Costello make his acting debut?
7. Which game featured in the BBC TV series 'The Master Game'?
8. Whose commercial jingle became a hit in 1976?
9. What is the giraffe's only living relative?

462

1. Which is the most precious stone nowadays?
2. What type of clothing was banned by statute in 1746?
3. To which island did Sir Ernest Shackleton's ill-fated Antarctic expedition escape from their trapped ship in 1915?
4. Which famous English novelist died writing in Lisbon?
5. Who won the Milk Cup for football in 1984?
6. In which comedy series does Molly Sugden play a doctor's other mother?
7. Who lived in Russia, England and the USA and founded the Kuomintang party in China?
8. What are lieder?
9. For how long can a bed-bug exist without eating?

833

1. What is another name for chiromancy?
2. Of whom did George II say, 'Mad is he? Then I wish he would bite some other of my generals'?
3. What is the area of the Isle of Wight in square miles?
4. Who created Sergeant Cuff?
5. Which Scottish football club plays home matches at Pittodrie Stadium?
6. In which film did Greta Garbo say 'I want to be alone'?
7. Which celebrated doctor was the first woman to be a mayor?
8. Which number-one hit was inspired by a homicidal rampage?
9. Which bird were ancient mariners said to take with them on long voyages because it imitated many other birdsongs?

91

1. Bad omens.
2. Pie Corner, where houses were blown up to arrest its course.
3. Canada's.
4. In the Court of Chancery in *Bleak House*.
5. Canada.
6. 'Scully', by Alan Bleasdale, screened in 1984.
7. Chess.
8. David Dundas's 'Jeans On'.
9. The okapi.

462

1. The ruby.
2. Highland dress.
3. Elephant Island.
4. Henry Fielding.
5. Liverpool.
6. 'That's My Boy'.
7. Sun Yat-Sen.
8. Songs.
9. 1 year.

833

1. Palmistry.
2. General Wolfe.
3. 147 square miles.
4. Wilkie Collins in *The Moonstone*.
5. Aberdeen.
6. In the film *Grand Hotel*.
7. Elizabeth Garrett Anderson (Mayor of Aldeburgh in 1908).
8. The Boomtown Rats' 'I don't like Mondays'.
9. The starling.

92

1. Why did the Queen miss the Derby at Epsom for the first time ever in 1984?
2. Who said of the House of Lords debating a divorce bill that it was 'better than a play'?
3. From where does the Serpent's Mouth separate Venezuela?
4. Who wrote *The Ingoldsby Legends*?
5. Where were the 1982 Commonwealth Games held?
6. John Huston scored a hit with his first film. What was it?
7. Who was the first reigning British monarch to visit a communist country?
8. Who sang 'All I Want for Christmas is a Beatle'?
9. How deep was the first oil well?

463

1. From which political party did the Liberal Party develop?
2. Who, on 7 September 1838, saved nine people from the *Forfarshire*?
3. There are fifty-eight cities in Britain defined as such. Name all those beginning with the letter T.
4. Name two sons of Noah.
5. Who won $1,000,000 by completing the tennis Grand Slam with her victory in the French Open?
6. Which film began, 'Most of what follows is true...'?
7. Who said, 'Is man an ape or an angel? I am on the side of the angels'?
8. Whose pig floated away?
9. What is mogadon?

834

1. Where did the word 'robot' originate?
2. Who reigned in Britain in 1936?
3. By which states is Kuwait surrounded?
4. Who first wrote, 'For fools rush in where angels fear to tread'?
5. What is another name for trotting?
6. Which French film director played a scientist in *Close Encounters of the Third Kind*?
7. The Empire State Building is typical of the Art Deco style of architecture. In which decade was it built?
8. Which Rolling Stones song was a hit for Chris Farlowe?
9. What is the stamen of a flower?

92

1. She was in France attending the D-Day celebrations.
2. Charles II.
3. Trinidad.
4. Richard Barham.
5. Brisbane.
6. *The Maltese Falcon* (1941).
7. Elizabeth II in 1972 when she went to Yugoslavia.
8. Dora Bryan.
9. 69½ feet, which took nearly a year to drill.

463

1. The Whigs.
2. Grace Darling.
3. Truro.
4. Shem, Ham, Japheth.
5. Martina Navratilova.
6. *Butch Cassidy and the Sundance Kid.*
7. Disraeli.
8. The Pink Floyd's giant inflatable pig, tethered by Battersea power station, broke its moorings during a promotional stunt and floated towards France.
9. A sleeping pill.

834

1. It is a Slav word meaning 'work'. *RUR* (Rossum's Universal Robots) was a play by the Czech Karel Čapek.
2. George V, Edward VIII and George VI successively.
3. Iraq and Saudi Arabia.
4. Pope.
5. Harness-racing.
6. François Truffaut.
7. The 1930s.
8. 'Out of Time'.
9. The pollen-producing part.

93

1. What is Samian ware?
2. Who made the first tipping-bucket rain gauge in 1662?
3. In Cape Town, what is fog over Table Mountain called?
4. Complete Auden's verse: 'To the man-in-the street, who, I'm sorry to say, / Is a keen observer of life, / The word "Intellectual" suggests straight away / A man who's . . .'
5. When were the first Winter Olympics held?
6. What did Deirdre do to upset Ken?
7. In which style did Canneloni paint?
8. Who was Crazy Diamond?
9. What was the name of the first space shuttle to fly in space?

464

1. What does a denier measure?
2. While watching what did Marshal Bosquet say (in French), 'It is magnificent, but it is not war'?
3. What is the current name of the town called by the Normans Beau Repair ('Beautiful Retreat')?
4. What is the name of the Fat Boy in *Pickwick Papers*?
5. Which British boxer has won two Olympic gold medals?
6. Of which other British film was *The Lavender Hill Mob* an affectionate spoof?
7. Which New Zealander married John Middleton Murry?
8. Which band replaced the Rolling Stones at the Crawdaddy, Richmond?
9. Which substance contained by most plants do fungi lack?

835

1. What word was declared unparliamentary by the Speaker in June 1984?
2. When was the last Frost Fair held on the frozen Thames?
3. In which country did the Cultural Revolution take place?
4. The various guilds enacted different biblical scenes in the Miracle Plays. What was the subject of the shipwrights' play?
5. What is Graham Noyce's sport?
6. Who plays Bet Lynch in 'Coronation Street'?
7. Which precious metal is used in photography?
8. Who sang about the Sultans of Swing?
9. What colour are laburnum flowers?

93

1. Fine pottery, originally made of clay from Samos, found on Roman sites.
2. Sir Christopher Wren.
3. The Table Cloth.
4. '. . . untrue to his wife'.
5. 1924.
6. She had an affair with another man in 'Coronation Street'.
7. Canneloni is a type of pasta, not an artist!
8. Syd Barrett, who left Pink Floyd after their first album.
9. Columbia.

464

1. It is a unit for measuring the thickness of silk, rayon or nylon yarn.
2. The Charge of the Light Brigade (Balaclava, 1854).
3. Belper.
4. Joe.
5. Harry Mallin.
6. *The Blue Lamp.*
7. Katherine Mansfield.
8. The Yardbirds.
9. Chlorophyll.

835

1. 'Fascist'.
2. January 1914.
3. China.
4. The story of Noah.
5. Motocross.
6. Julie Goodyear.
7. Silver.
8. Dire Straits.
9. Yellow.

94

1. For what phrase is Thomas Hobson, a Cambridge hirer of horses, remembered?
2. Who was the longest-reigning European monarch?
3. What extraordinary event in early 1968 was taken advantage of by polar bears?
4. What well-known play features the King of Navarre?
5. Who was the first athlete to win two gold medals in the Olympic decathlon?
6. Which artist was the documentary film *A Bigger Splash* about?
7. What is a 'spare' in ten-pin bowling?
8. What was Buddy Holly's current single at the time of his death?
9. How long do duck eggs take to hatch?

465

1. The artist Abbott Thayers spent his whole life studying the colour schemes of the animal world. What was he responsible for developing?
2. What was the first recorded 'dead language'?
3. Which river runs through Hamburg?
4. Who in *Journal to Stella* refers to himself as Dr Presto?
5. What is the former world champion Johnny Leach's game?
6. Where did Gary Cooper, the film star, get his first name?
7. Of what did Francis Bacon say, 'It is the purest of pleasures'?
8. Who recorded the album *Broken English*?
9. What does real chamois leather come from?

836

1. Which was the first stately home opened to the public?
2. Who was the last Aztec ruler of Mexico?
3. What are Royal Sovereign, Scilly, Valentia and Ronaldsway?
4. Who was fed by whom at the brook of Cherith?
5. Which British pair took the gold and silver Olympic medals in the 800 metres at the Moscow Olympics?
6. 'They're young . . . they're in love . . . and they kill people.' Who?
7. Who said, just before he was executed, 'So the heart be right, it matters little how the head lieth'?
8. Who had a posthumous hit with '(Sittin' on) the Dock of the Bay'?
9. In what state are kingfishers and swifts when they hatch out?

94

1. 'Hobson's choice'. He insisted that each customer should take the horse nearest the stable door.
2. Louis XIV of France, who reigned for 72 years and 110 days.
3. An ice-bridge formed between Greenland and Iceland.
4. *Love's Labour's Lost.*
5. Bob Mathias.
6. David Hockney.
7. Knocking down all the pins in two deliveries.
8. 'It Doesn't Matter Any More'.
9. 27 days.

465

1. Military camouflage.
2. Sumerian, which ceased to be spoken after the Amorites took over Ur.
3. The Elbe.
4. Swift.
5. Table tennis.
6. His home town of Gary, Indiana.
7. A garden.
8. Marianne Faithfull.
9. A small goat-like antelope.

836

1. Wilton House, near Salisbury, in 1776. Nearly 2,500 visited that year, not paying an entrance fee but tipping the housekeeper.
2. Montezuma II.
3. Coastal weather stations.
4. Elijah was fed by the ravens.
5. Steve Ovett and Sebastian Coe.
6. Bonnie and Clyde.
7. Sir Walter Raleigh.
8. Otis Redding.
9. Completely naked.

95

1. What is a 'sopha'?
2. Who set sail in HMS *Erebus* and HMS *Terror* in 1845 and never returned?
3. What was the unusual fate of Culbin, a village on the shores of the Moray Firth?
4. Who wrote 'a study of an absurd man in an absurd world' and died in a car accident in Algeria?
5. In American football, how many players does each team have on the field at one time?
6. Who wrote the book on which the play and film *Billy Liar* were based?
7. Where is Dr Livingstone buried?
8. Who chaired 'Juke Box Jury'?
9. What bird's egg is no bigger than a pea?

466

1. What is the source of the original colours used for tartan cloth?
2. 'Gaul is divided into three parts,' wrote Caesar. Name one.
3. What is the difference between GMT and the time in the Falkland Islands?
4. Who is represented by the Red Cross Knight in Spenser's *Faerie Queene*?
5. Lucinda Prior-Palmer, Richard Meade and Hugh Thomas were three of the four members of Britain's three-day event team in the 1976 Olympics. Name the fourth.
6. Who wrote the screenplay for *A Hard Day's Night*?
7. Whom did W.B. Yeats love but never marry?
8. What was the Searchers' biggest hit?
9. What is a Pacific sea wasp?

837

1. What is the Devil's Tattoo?
2. Which was the first spacecraft to land on another planet?
3. Which cape on the coast south of Brisbane is named after a famous poet?
4. Name one of the two authors of *Endymion.*
5. Where do Cardiff's Rugby League team play home matches?
6. Which film comic used the pseudonyms Mahatma Kane Jeeves and Otis Criblecoblis?
7. What have Svetlana Alliluyeva (Stalin's daughter), Elizabeth Barrett Browning and Martha ('the Mouth') Mitchell in common with regard to children?
8. **Which musical told us to 'keep talking happy talk'?**
9. What is an aphid?

95

1. It is the alternative spelling for 'sofa' (from the Arabic for 'bench' – *suffah*).
2. Sir John Franklin and his Arctic expedition.
3. It was buried by sandstorms in 1694.
4. Albert Camus (*L'Étranger*).
5. Eleven.
6. Keith Waterhouse.
7. Westminster Abbey.
8. David Jacobs.
9. The humming bird's.

466

1. Lichens.
2. Aquitania, Belgica, Lugdunensis.
3. Falkland Islands time is GMT minus 4 hours.
4. St George.
5. Princess Anne.
6. Alun Owen.
7. Maud Gonne.
8. 'Needles and Pins' (1964).
9. A jellyfish.

837

1. Drumming with fingers or feet as an unconscious habit or as a sign of impatience.
2. Venus III, the Russian craft which landed on Venus on 1 March 1966.
3. Cape Byron.
4. Keats (the poem) or Disraeli (the novel).
5. Ninian Park.
6. W.C.Fields.
7. They all gave birth to their first or only child at over 40 years old (45, 43 and 43 respectively).
8. *South Pacific.*
9. A greenfly.

96

1. How did worsted cloth get its name?
2. Who was the mother of three French kings, Francis II, Charles IX and Henry III?
3. What is the principal religion of the USA?
4. Who wrote *The Lyrical Ballads* with Coleridge?
5. Which horse won the English Triple Crown in 1970?
6. Who played the seedy detective in the TV series 'Private Eye'?
7. In which city is the Louvre?
8. Torvill and Dean used music from *Mack and Mabel* in one of their routines. Who was the original Mabel?
9. What is crucial to the preservation of banana cargoes carried long distances?

467

1. What are Arran Pilot, Homeguard and Ulster Chieftain?
2. For how long did the longest-serving parliament of the twentieth century sit?
3. Just 42 days after the bombing of Hiroshima, what further disaster occurred there?
4. Which playwright took part in the Armada expedition as well as writing over 600 plays?
5. Who captained England in the 1962 World Cup Final?
6. When was the first version of *Gentlemen Prefer Blondes* filmed?
7. In which game are spares and strikes scored?
8. Who was in a purple haze?
9. Approximately where is the visual centre of the brain?

838

1. Up to 180 years ago there was no such thing as a cotton reel. What was there instead?
2. What was the trade of Wolsey's father?
3. By what name is the Paris Stock Exchange known?
4. Whose autobiography is entitled *A Better Class of Person*?
5. Why was a Turkish goalkeeper given £50 bonus for letting in four goals?
6. Which former rock star played David Essex's manager in *Stardust*?
7. Who was the second American to go into space?
8. The composer of the music for Tommy Handley's 'ITMA' died in June 1984. Who was he?
9. Coal and oil are both fossil fuels. Why are they different from one another?

96

1. From Worstead in Norfolk, where many Flemish weavers settled.
2. Catherine de Medici.
3. The Roman Catholic, with 48 million adherents.
4. Wordsworth.
5. Nijinsky.
6. Alfred Burke.
7. Paris.
8. Mabel Normand, a Mack Sennett star.
9. That the temperature should not fall below 13° C (55° F).

467

1. Varieties of early potatoes.
2. 9 years and 6 months from 1935 to 1945.
3. A devastating typhoon which caused 4,500 casualties.
4. Lope de Vega.
5. Johnny Haynes.
6. 1928.
7. Ten-pin bowling.
8. Jimi Hendrix.
9. At the back.

838

1. Hanks of linen thread.
2. A butcher.
3. The Bourse.
4. John Osborne's.
5. The team had been expected to lose 8–0 at least.
6. Adam Faith.
7. 'Gus' Grissom.
8. Gordon Jacob.
9. Coal is produced from plant matter, oil from animal matter.

97

1. Who was Clio?
2. Who founded the Royal Mail?
3. The Caprivi Strip is a thin corridor between Botswana and Angola. To which country does it belong?
4. Who says, 'I'm Charley's aunt from Brazil, where the nuts come from'?
5. Which team did Arnold Muhren first play for when he came to England from Holland?
6. Who always wants the door shut?
7. Who said, 'Somebody left the cork out of my lunch'?
8. Who was the man with the golden trumpet?
9. In which year were all three Apollo 11 astronauts born?

468

1. On which day of the week does Pancake Day fall?
2. Who said, on acceding to the throne, 'I shall go back to bed. I have never slept with a queen before'?
3. Where is Tammany Hall?
4. Who said, 'If the law supposes that . . . the law is a ass – a idiot'?
5. Which Italian football team were relegated to Division Two in 1980–81 because of bribery scandals?
6. Which part did Donald Pleasance play in *You Only Live Twice*?
7. Who lived at Bateman's?
8. Name the original Shadows.
9. How many orbits did John Glen complete in his first space flight?

839

1. What was 'Big Willie'?
2. Which monarch was so drunk on his wedding night, according to his wife, that he lay on the floor?
3. Why is Muckle Flugga notable?
4. Which book consists of letters from a senior to a junior devil?
5. What position did Pope John Paul II play for the Polish amateur soccer team Woytyła?
6. Whose music features in *A Clockwork Orange*?
7. Which famous chef created Peach Melba?
8. Who wrote 'Smoke Gets in Your Eyes'?
9. Who first circled the earth in a satellite?

97

1. The Greek muse of history, or a pseudonym for Addison writing in the *Spectator*.
2. Charles I in 1635.
3. Namibia.
4. Lord Fancourt Baberley in *Charley's Aunt* by Brandon Thomas.
5. Ipswich.
6. Larry Grayson, whose catchphrase is 'Shut that door!'
7. W.C.Fields.
8. Eddie Calvert.
9. 1930.

468

1. Tuesday.
2. William IV.
3. New York.
4. Mr Bumble in *Oliver Twist.*
5. A C Milan.
6. Ernst Stavro Blofeld.
7. Rudyard Kipling.
8. Hank Marvin, Bruce Welch, Jet Harris and Tony Meehan.
9. Three.

839

1. One of the first military tanks.
2. George IV, according to Queen Caroline.
3. It is the most northerly point in the British Isles.
4. *The Screwtape Letters* by C.S.Lewis.
5. Goalkeeper.
6. Beethoven's.
7. Escoffier.
8. Jerome Kern.
9. Laika, a dog.

98

1. What is a Sally Lunn?
2. 'John Clarke' was once an English head of state. Who was he?
3. What do the Dardanelles separate?
4. What is defined by Johnson in his dictionary as a 'grain which in England is generally given to horses, but in Scotland supports the people'?
5. Who was the first non-Japanese to win a world judo title?
6. The studio report on his screen test read, 'Can't act; can't sing; can dance a little.' Who was he?
7. By what names is Frederick Rolfe, who fantasized about becoming Pope, also known?
8. What was the Troggs' most famous hit?
9. What is a well-known name for rolled, toasted, flavoured flakes of maize?

469

1. Which is the most popular eye shadow of all time?
2. Why did Charles II's wife, Catherine of Braganza, go to Bath?
3. Where does the river Tajo change to the river Tejo?
4. Who is the only Irishman in a Shakespeare play?
5. Who was twelve times champion skier of Norway, a great explorer, Professor of Zoology and Oceanography at Oslo and Ambassador to Britain, and received the Nobel Peace Prize?
6. Who played the senior doctor in 'Dr Kildare'?
7. In which city did Tintoretto do most of his painting?
8. What colour was mellow?
9. In the last 40 years strontium 90 has come to be detectable all over the world. What has caused this change?

840

1. Which fabric is named after Nîmes in France?
2. Who was known as Doctor Angelicus?
3. Which gun is named after a town in Czechoslovakia and an English rifle manufacturer?
4. Why were the Big- and Little-endians of Lilliput so called?
5. What are the two Olympic ski-jumping distances?
6. Who played a teacher in the TV series 'Welcome Back Kotter'?
7. Who sometimes gives a three-dimensional appearance to her paintings by using pieces of cardboard egg-boxes to make her figures' busts and bottoms?
8. When did Jim Morrison of The Doors die?
9. For what purpose did the astronomer Janssen make a daring escape by balloon from a besieged Paris in 1870?

98

1. A type of tea-cake.
2. Richard Cromwell, second Lord Protector, 1658–9. He lived under the alias of Clarke until 1712.
3. Europe and Asia.
4. Oats.
5. Anton Geesink in 1961.
6. Fred Astaire.
7. Baron Corvo and Hadrian the Seventh.
8. 'Wild Thing'.
9. Cornflakes.

469

1. Max Factor's 'powder blue'.
2. It was hoped that the waters would cure her apparent infertility.
3. On the Spanish–Portuguese border.
4. Captain Macmorris in *Henry V*.
5. Fritjof Nansen.
6. Raymond Massey, father of Anna and Daniel.
7. Venice.
8. Yellow (in Donovan's song).
9. Nuclear explosions.

840

1. Denim ('de Nîmes').
2. Thomas Aquinas.
3. The bren-gun (a combination of Brno and Enfield).
4. Because of their dispute over which end of an egg to open.
5. 70 metres and 90 metres.
6. John Travolta.
7. Beryl Cook.
8. 1971.
9. To view a solar eclipse.

99

1. What was the name of D.T.Barnum's giant elephant?
2. Who commanded the Confederate armies during the American Civil War?
3. Who discovered Jamaica?
4. Name the bear in *Reynard the Fox.*
5. In which year were women's track and field events introduced into the Olympic Games?
6. In which fictional town was the action in 'Z Cars' located?
7. What astonishingly unlikely occurrence was first reported in New Zealand on 8 July 1958?
8. Who composed the incidental music for the play *'Arlésienne*?
9. What piece of matter was discovered in the 1930s by Sir James Chadwick?

470

1. How old was the Queen when she married?
2. Whose body was cremated on the bank of the Ganges on 31 January 1948?
3. Which city was bombed on 6 August 1945?
4. How much money did Phileas Fogg wager that he would go 'around the world in eighty days'?
5. In tennis, how far are the service lines from the net?
6. Who gained an Oscar for her portrayal of Martha in *Who's Afraid of Virginia Woolf?*?
7. In bridge, which are the major suits?
8. How much did Sherlock Holmes's Stradivarius violin cost him?
9. From which plant is linen made?

841

1. To whom are Jews Gentiles?
2. Who was the first woman to make a solo flight from London to Australia?
3. In which country is Entebbe airport?
4. Who wrote the 1960 play *The Jeweller's Shop*?
5. How high is a soccer goal?
6. Which husband and wife played together in the 1958 film *The Long Hot Summer*?
7. Who is buried beneath the altar of St Peter's Basilica?
8. Who wrote 'I'm a Yankee Doodle Dandy' and 'Give My Regards to Broadway'?
9. In 1714 parliament offered a reward to anyone who could discover a method of finding longitude at sea. What was John Harrison's winning invention?

99

1. Jumbo.
2. Robert E. Lee.
3. Christopher Columbus.
4. Bruin.
5. 1928.
6. Newtown.
7. Four card players each being dealt a complete suit from a standard pack.
8. Bizet.
9. The neutron.

470

1. Twenty-one.
2. Mahatma Ghandi.
3. Hiroshima.
4. £20,000.
5. 21 feet.
6. Elizabeth Taylor.
7. Hearts and spades.
8. 55 shillings.
9. Flax.

841

1. Mormons.
2. Amy Johnson in 1930.
3. Uganda.
4. Pope John Paul II.
5. 8 feet.
6. Paul Newman and Joanne Woodward.
7. St Peter.
8. George M. Cohan.
9. The chronometer.

100

1. Which famous liner caught fire and sank in Hong Kong harbour?
2. In what container was Nelson's body returned to England?
3. In Japan, which colour car is reserved exclusively for the Japanese imperial family?
4. What is the name of the tame lioness in *Born Free*?
5. What is the maximum mark awarded by a single judge in international ice-dance competitions
6. Of which newspaper is Lou Grant city editor?
7. Why did J. Edgar Hoover never take a left turn, or allow his chauffeur to do so?
8. How many semitones are there in an octave?
9. Who is the cross-eyed lion?

471

1. What is 555 in Roman numerals?
2. By what name was William Bonney better known?
3. What did Cape Canaveral become in 1963, to become Cape Canaveral again in 1973?
4. Sophocles's greatest play was written when he was nearly ninety. What was it called?
5. How many stumps are used in a game of cricket?
6. What hardly ever happen in Hertford, Hereford and Hampshire?
7. Who said, 'Give me liberty or give me death'?
8. Which was Elvis Presley's first film?
9. From which continent do elephants with large flapping ears come?

842

1. What is the largest single gold object in the world?
2. Which railway terminus in Paris takes its name from one of Napoleon's victories?
3. Which city does Kagoshima airport serve?
4. In which Charles Dickens book does Bill Sykes appear?
5. Who was the last man before Bjorn Borg to win the Wimbledon men's title in successive years?
6. From which planet do the Daleks come?
7. What 'first' can Dame Mary Donaldson claim?
8. Whose theme music was 'Cuckoo Song'?
9. What percentage of an egg's weight is the shell?

100

1. The *Queen Elizabeth*.
2. A barrel of rum.
3. Maroon.
4. Elsa.
5. Six.
6. The *Los Angeles Tribune*.
7. Because of his total anti-communist commitment.
8. Twelve.
9. Clarence.

471

1. DLV.
2. Billy the Kid.
3. Cape Kennedy.
4. *Oedipus Rex*.
5. Six.
6. Hurricanes.
7. Patrick Henry.
8. *Love Me Tender*.
9. Africa.

842

1. Tutankhamen's coffin.
2. Austerlitz.
3. Tokyo.
4. *Oliver Twist*.
5. John Newcombe (1970 and 1971).
6. Skaro.
7. She became London's first ever lady Lord Mayor (in 1983).
8. Laurel and Hardy's.
9. About 12 per cent.

101

1. How many people were convicted for the murder of Aldo Moro?
2. Whose son did Bruno Richard Hauptmann kidnap and murder in 1932?
3. In which country was the bridge of San Luis Rey?
4. How many ghosts appeared to Scrooge?
5. How long does a fifteen-round boxing match take to complete?
6. Who was voted the most popular film performer in the USA in 1926?
7. What was gangster George Nelson's nickname?
8. How many calling birds were there?
9. How many teeth does a mature male horse have?

472

1. At what age does a Jewish boy traditionally celebrate his Bar Mitzvah?
2. Who was the religious member of Robin Hood's band?
3. Who was India's first female prime minister?
4. Which British newspaper was first called The *Daily Universal Register* (1785)?
5. Who beat the late Lillian Board in the 400 metres final at the 1968 Olympics?
6. Who plays John Steed in 'The Avengers'?
7. Whose first wife was Jane Wyman?
8. How did Buddy Holly die?
9. What is controlled by a rheostat?

843

1. Which country, per capita, uses the most umbrellas?
2. What happened to Catherine Eddowes on 30 September 1888?
3. In Muslim countries, what is the colour worn for mourning?
4. Under what name did Manfred B. Lee and Frederick Dannay jointly write?
5. Which athlete was nicknamed the Ebony Express?
6. By what name was Eric Stoner better known?
7. Who is the editor of *Private Eye*?
8. Who sings the theme song in the Bond film *Goldfinger*?
9. How many wisdom teeth does a person normally have?

101

1. Sixty-three.
2. Charles Lindbergh's.
3. Peru.
4. Four (Christmas past, Christmas present, Christmas to come and Marley's ghost).
5. 59 minutes (fifteen 3-minute rounds plus fourteen 1-minute breaks).
6. Rin Tin Tin.
7. Baby Face.
8. Four.
9. Forty.

472

1. Thirteen.
2. Friar Tuck.
3. Mrs Indira Gandhi.
4. *The Times*.
5. Colette Besson of France.
6. Patrick MacNee.
7. Ronald Reagan's.
8. He was killed in a plane crash.
9. Electric current.

843

1. England.
2. She was murdered by Jack the Ripper.
3. White.
4. Ellery Queen.
5. Jesse Owens.
6. The Cincinnati Kid.
7. Richard Ingrams.
8. Shirley Bassey.
9. Four.

102

1. Which organization places Bibles in hotel rooms?
2. Marie-Augustin, Marquis de Pelier, of Brittany spent 50 years in jail for whistling. At whom did he whistle?
3. Which famous harbour is on the island of Oahu?
4. In *Treasure Island*, what was the name of the inn owned by Jim Hawkins's mother?
5. What was the name of the 'Flying Finn' who won seven gold and three silver medals in the 1920, 1924 and 1928 Olympics?
6. What is 'Kid' Curry's alias?
7. What is the lowest hand to beat three of a kind in poker?
8. Which famous ballet dancer defected in 1961?
9. At what time of the day do ducks lay eggs?

473

1. What is the telephone area code for New York City?
2. So far, which has been the most popular name for European kings?
3. In which London thoroughfare is Claridge's situated?
4. '— : or, *The Modern Prometheus.*' What's missing?
5. What course did Douglas Bunn, the former showjumper, create?
6. In 'MASH', what is Radar's favourite drink?
7. Who used the pseudonym Dr A?
8. With which song are Bill Haley and his Comets most associated?
9. At what age does a filly become a mare?

844

1. Where were Prince Charles and Lady Diana Spencer married?
2. During the mid 1700s, what proportion of tea drunk was smuggled into England to avoid the high import tax?
3. Which is India's sacred river?
4. On which island was Ben Gunn marooned?
5. With which showjumper is Stroller associated?
6. In which town do the Flintstones live?
7. Madame Pauline de Vere was the first woman circus performer to do what?
8. Whose first number one record was 'The Candy Man'?
9. Why do you shiver when you are cold?

102

1. The Gideons.
2. Queen Marie Antoinette.
3. Pearl Harbour.
4. The Admiral Benbow.
5. Paavo Nurmi.
6. Thaddeus Jones.
7. A straight (or run).
8. Rudolf Nureyev.
9. In the morning.

473

1. 212.
2. Charles.
3. Brook Street.
4. *Frankenstein.*
5. The All England jumping course at Hickstead.
6. Grape Knee-high.
7. Isaac Asimov.
8. 'Rock Around the Clock'.
9. Five.

844

1. St Paul's Cathedral.
2. Two-thirds.
3. The Ganges.
4. Treasure Island.
5. Marion Mould.
6. Bedrock.
7. Put her head in a lion's mouth.
8. Sammy Davis Junior.
9. Because shivering increases muscular activity and so raises the body's temperature.

103

1. Which wedding anniversary is leather?
2. Whom did Robert Ford shoot dead on 3 April 1882?
3. What is the capital of Poland?
4. Whose first published book was *Down and Out in Paris and London*?
5. Name the horse from which 90 per cent of all thoroughbreds are descended.
6. Whom did Mia Farrow marry in 1966?
7. Of what are Aran, Fair Isle and cable types?
8. What is Bob Hope's theme song?
9. What is a young whale called?

474

1. To within 500, how many saffron-coloured crocuses are needed to make 1 ounce of saffron dye?
2. How was Alexander the Great's body preserved?
3. What are gauchos?
4. Who was Poet Laureate from 1843 to 1850?
5. With which showjumper is Mr Softee associated?
6. Who was the father of Luke Skywalker?
7. What, in April 1967, was Shirley Preston London's first?
8. Who was the best-known lead-singer with The Pips?
9. What phenomenon killed twenty-three people in Rostov, Russia, in July 1923?

845

1. Who writes the bridge column in the *Sunday Express*?
2. How did Hermann Goering escape execution?
3. A Californian law makes it illegal to shoot any game bird or animal from an automobile – except one. Which one?
4. Who wrote *Knock Down* and *Bonecrack*?
5. Which baseball player was married to Marilyn Monroe?
6. In which film did a Rolls Royce have the number plate AU 1?
7. How many spots are on a regular six-sided die?
8. Who hosts 'Desert Island Discs'?
9. Which well-known drink did Dr John S. Pemberton invent in 1886?

103

1. The third.
2. Jesse James.
3. Warsaw.
4. George Orwell's.
5. Eclipse.
6. Frank Sinatra.
7. Knitting.
8. 'Thanks for the Memory'.
9. A calf.

474

1. 4,500.
2. It was kept in a large jar of honey.
3. Cowboys (normally South American).
4. William Wordsworth.
5. David Broome.
6. Darth Vader.
7. Female taxi-cab driver.
8. Gladys Knight.
9. Giant hailstones, many of them weighing over 1 lb each.

845

1. Omar Sharif.
2. He committed suicide.
3. The whale!
4. Dick Francis.
5. Joe DiMaggio.
6. *Goldfinger* – it belonged to Auric Goldfinger himself.
7. Twenty-one.
8. Roy Plomley.
9. Coca-Cola.

104

1. To the nearest 2,000,000, how many people have been killed by earthquakes over the last 4,000 years?
2. Who was the first American president to resign?
3. In which country was Adolf Eichmann captured by the Israelis?
4. In which Ian Fleming book does Pussy Galore feature?
5. Who was the men's Olympic skating champion in 1976?
6. Who played Butch Cassidy in the 1969 film?
7. Who once shot a cigarette from Kaiser Wilhelm's mouth?
8. What is Vladimir Ashkenazy's instrument?
9. What is the commonest produce of insects eaten in the UK?

475

1. Which is the second most common international crime?
2. In which year did Hitler become Chancellor of Germany?
3. What protected London for the first time on 22 February 1983?
4. Which Gore Vidal character has a sex operation?
5. By what name was baseball star George Herman Ruth better known?
6. In which film did James Bond drive a white Lotus – PPW 306R – underwater?
7. Who painted 'Self Portrait with Bandaged Ear'?
8. Name the mythical Scottish town that appears for one day every 100 years in the musical by Lerner and Loewe.
9. With which organ does a snake hear?

846

1. When did the Chinese Year of the Rat most recently occur?
2. What was founded by William and Catherine Booth?
3. Which underground tube line goes to Heathrow Central?
4. Who wrote 'The Aunt and the Sluggard' and 'The Rummy Affair of Old Biffy'?
5. In which Australian city have the Olympic Games been held?
6. What is Dr Who's flying telephone box called?
7. On what is the Mona Lisa painted?
8. By what name was Ronald Wycherley better known?
9. How many times can you fold a pound note in half by hand?

104

1. 13,000,000.
2. Richard Nixon.
3. Argentina.
4. *Goldfinger*.
5. John Curry of Britain.
6. Paul Newman.
7. Annie Oakley.
8. The piano.
9. Honey.

475

1. Art theft.
2. 1933.
3. The Thames flood barrier.
4. Myra Breckinridge.
5. Babe Ruth.
6. *The Spy Who Loved Me.*
7. Vincent Van Gogh.
8. Brigadoon.
9. Its tongue.

846

1. 1984.
2. The Salvation Army.
3. Piccadilly.
4. P.G. Wodehouse. They are stories from *Carry On, Jeeves*.
5. Melbourne.
6. The Tardis.
7. Wood.
8. Billy Fury.
9. Six.

105

1. What was the only thing that remained in Pandora's box after she had opened it?
2. To which Royal House did Henry VIII belong?
3. In which American state is Disneyland?
4. Who won the 1983 Nobel Prize for Literature?
5. In which two sports does action take place on a piste?
6. Who are 'The Two Ronnies'?
7. How many points wins a game of cribbage?
8. Which was the Beatles' first hit record?
9. How long does an average-sized snowflake take to fall to earth from 1,000 feet?

476

1. Count de Grisley was the first magician to perform which trick in 1799?
2. To which gang did Kid Curry belong?
3. What are South Africa's two official languages?
4. Who wrote *The Tragedy of Pudd'nhead Wilson*?
5. Which South African tennis doubles player always wore a white cap on court?
6. Who played Harry Palmer in *The Ipcress File* (1965)?
7. Whose biography did Clifford Irving fake?
8. In German legend, who was Lohengrin's father?
9. How many brain cells does an average person lose per day from the age of about thirty?

847

1. What was a licensed vendor of papal indulgences called?
2. Who was assassinated while watching the play *Our American Cousin*?
3. By what name did Hitler intend calling Berlin when the new city was finished?
4. Who wrote *Les Misérables*?
5. In which event might you use the western roll technique?
6. To which MASH unit does Hawkeye Pierce belong?
7. How many dice are used to play Quadwrangle?
8. From which work does the cancan come?
9. Which bird turns its head upside down to eat?

105

1. Hope.
2. The House of Tudor.
3. California.
4. William Golding.
5. Skiing and fencing.
6. Ronnie Corbett and Ronnie Barker.
7. 121.
8. 'Love Me Do'.
9. 8–10 minutes.

476

1. Saw a woman in half.
2. The Hole-in-the-Wall gang.
3. Afrikaans and English.
4. Mark Twain (Samuel Clemens).
5. Frew McMillan.
6. Michael Caine.
7. Howard Hughes's.
8. Parsifal.
9. 100,000. (But don't worry, the human brain contains some ten trillion brain cells.)

847

1. A pardoner.
2. Abraham Lincoln.
3. Germania.
4. Victor Hugo.
5. The high-jump.
6. The 4077th.
7. Five.
8. *Orpheus in the Underworld*.
9. The flamingo.

106

1. How many attended the Last Supper?
2. Shakespeare was born in the year Michelangelo died. Which year?
3. What is the legislative assembly of Norway called?
4. Who are Dmitri, Ivan, Alyosha and Smerdyakov?
5. Where does the Tour de France cycle race finish?
6. Who played Fletcher Christian in *Mutiny on the Bounty* (1962)?
7. Which member of the royal family often uses the name Mr Perkins when travelling incognito?
8. What instrument does Sabine Meyer play?
9. Which is the largest planet in our solar system?

477

1. Why was 21 July 1983 in Antarctica memorable?
2. How did Sir John Popham, Chief Justice of England in 1592, become wealthy?
3. In which desert can the highest sand dunes be found?
4. Name King Arthur's sword.
5. Who trained the horses who took the first five places in the 1983 Cheltenham Gold Cup?
6. Who was first offered the TV role of Lieutenant Columbo?
7. What was the nickname of President Lyndon B. Johnson's first wife?
8. Who composed the opera *La Bohème*?
9. How many fluid ounces are there in a litre?

848

1. How many sides has a twenty-pence piece?
2. Which British battle cruiser was sunk by the *Bismarck* on 24 May 1941?
3. Over which building in India may no one fly?
4. Who is Edmond Dantès?
5. How many fences in the Grand National are jumped twice?
6. By what name is Bernard Schwartz better known?
7. What is named after Sir Benjamin Hall?
8. To which tune is 'The Battle Hymn of the Republic' sung?
9. How many times per second does a housefly beat its wings?

106

1. Thirteen.
2. 1564.
3. The storthing.
4. The brothers Karamazov.
5. Paris.
6. Marlon Brando.
7. Prince Charles.
8. The clarinet.
9. Jupiter.

477

1. Because the lowest temperature ever recorded on earth was registered there.
2. He was a burglar in his earlier days.
3. The Sahara.
4. Excalibur (also called Caliburn).
5. Michael Dickinson.
6. Bing Crosby.
7. Lady Bird.
8. Puccini.
9. 35.2.

848

1. Seven.
2. HMS *Hood*.
3. The Taj Mahal.
4. The Count of Monte Cristo.
5. Fourteen.
6. Tony Curtis.
7. Big Ben.
8. 'John Brown's Body'.
9. 190.

Q

107

1. Hugin and Munin are two ravens that sit on the shoulders of Odin. What do they represent?
2. On which date in 44 BC was Julius Caesar killed?
3. Where does the Chancellor of the Exchequer live?
4. Who did Jim, the Negro slave, accompany down the Mississippi on a raft?
5. In which sport is the Davis Cup awarded?
6. Which Marx brother had a moustache?
7. Who was nicknamed the Bard of Ayrshire?
8. Who was known as Gentleman Jim?
9. What was Donald Campbell's jet-powered motorboat called?

478

1. Which of the seven wonders of the world was a statue of Apollo?
2. Whose horse was Bucephalus?
3. Which is India's largest city?
4. Who is Winnie-the-Pooh's donkey friend who likes to eat thistles?
5. Which Englishman took four wickets in five balls in a test match in 1978?
6. In which film did Ingrid Bergman make her debut?
7. What was Al Capone's nickname?
8. Which twelve-tone composer wrote the opera *Wozzeck*?
9. What is special about Louise Brown?

849

1. Name Sebastian Flyte's teddy-bear (Evelyn Waugh's *Brideshead Revisited*).
2. What is the Jewish New Year called?
3. Which state in India is as large as France?
4. Who wrote *The Illustrated Man*?
5. In showjumping, how many faults are incurred by the rider falling off?
6. Who plays Lieutenant Columbo?
7. Who said, 'I am not prepared to stagger from compromise to compromise'?
8. What is Isaac Stern's instrument?
9. How many legs has a lobster?

107

1. Thought and memory.
2. 15 March (the ides of March).
3. 11 Downing Street.
4. Huckleberry Finn.
5. Tennis.
6. Groucho.
7. Robert Burns.
8. Jim Reeves.
9. *Bluebird*.

478

1. The Colossus of Rhodes.
2. Alexander the Great's.
3. Bombay.
4. Eeyore.
5. Chris Old.
6. *Intermezzo* (1938).
7. Scarface.
8. Alban Berg.
9. She was the first test-tube baby.

849

1. Aloysius.
2. Rosh ha-Shanah.
3. Uttar Pradesh.
4. Ray Bradbury.
5. Eight.
6. Peter Falk.
7. Margaret Thatcher.
8. The violin.
9. Eight.

108

1. If you are unlucky enough to have a serious accident, where is it most likely to occur?
2. How long did King Edward VIII's abdication broadcast last?
3. Which continent has the most people per square mile?
4. Who lived in the land of Brobdingnag?
5. Which sport is governed by the Queensberry rules?
6. Which martial arts champion and film star died in 1973 at the age of thirty-two?
7. Who did Sirhan Sirhan assassinate?
8. Who wrote the song 'Beautiful Dreamer'?
9. Which is generally the smallest breed of dog?

479

1. What was buried in the coffin with evangelist Aimée Semple McPherson in 1944?
2. Who or what killed Cleopatra?
3. Which is the largest island in Europe?
4. Who discovered the hiding place of the forty thieves?
5. Which famous old British motor-racing track was partly reopened in 1974?
6. Name the floorwalker in 'Are You Being Served?'
7. Who was nicknamed the Little Corporal?
8. Who was called the Waltz King?
9. Which is the brightest planet visible to the naked eye?

850

1. In weight, how much food and drink does an average person consume in a year?
2. To whom was Anne Hathaway married?
3. Over which ocean did Amelia Earhart disappear?
4. Which memorable book won the Pulitzer prize in 1937?
5. How many times were Britain's Diane Towler and Bernard Ford world ice-dance champions?
6. With whom did Bonzo the chimpanzee co-star in the 1951 film *Bedtime for Bonzo*?
7. What was Rommel's nickname?
8. Who pulled pussy out of the well?
9. In which year is Halley's comet next due to appear?

108

1. In your own home.
2. 1 minute.
3. Europe.
4. Giants (in *Gulliver's Travels*).
5. Boxing.
6. Bruce Lee.
7. Robert Kennedy.
8. Stephen Foster.
9. The chihuahua.

479

1. A telephone – but the line was discontinued in 1951.
2. An asp.
3. Great Britain.
4. Ali Baba.
5. Brooklands.
6. Captain Peacock.
7. Napoleon.
8. Johann Strauss Junior.
9. Venus.

850

1. 1 ton.
2. William Shakespeare.
3. The Pacific.
4. *Gone with the Wind.*
5. Four.
6. Ronald Reagan.
7. The Desert Fox.
8. Little Johnny Stout.
9. 1986.

109

1. Which pocket does a pickpocket find it easiest to pick?
2. How many prisoners were held in the Black Hole of Calcutta?
3. Which statue is at the centre of Piccadilly Circus?
4. To which club did Mycroft Holmes belong?
5. Who captained India to cricket World Cup victory in 1983?
6. Which famous film was based on the life of William Randolph Hearst?
7. What did William Addis invent while in Newgate prison?
8. Who had a hit in 1951 with 'Come On-a My House'?
9. What was the first recorded message, spoken by Thomas Edison?

480

1. For every ten attempted suicides, on average, how many are successful?
2. In the nineteenth century, what was the punishment for failed suicide attempts?
3. Where is Checkpoint Charlie?
4. Who wrote the *Iliad* and the *Odyssey*?
5. What is Sunil Gavaskar's sport?
6. What kind of animal is Godzilla?
7. Who succeeded Lenin?
8. Who had a hit in 1961 with 'Does Your Chewing Gum Lose Its Flavour on the Bedpost Overnight'?
9. Of what is glass chiefly composed?

851

1. Generally, how many teaspoonfuls equal a tablespoonful?
2. How many people died as a *direct* result of the great fire of London in 1666?
3. Which principality is ruled by the House of Grimaldi?
4. Whose three sons were Ham, Shem and Japheth?
5. What 'first' occurred in the Oxford and Cambridge Boat Race of 1981?
6. Which was Mae West's last film?
7. What was Sir Edwin Lutyens's profession?
8. What is performed at Glyndebourne?
9. How long does it take bacteria to reach danger level in cooked food left in a temperature of 70°F?

109

1. The breast pocket.
2. 146.
3. Eros.
4. The Diogenes Club.
5. Kapil Dev.
6. *Citizen Kane*.
7. The toothbrush.
8. Rosemary Clooney.
9. 'Mary had a little lamb.'

480

1. One.
2. Hanging (failsafe).
3. West Berlin.
4. Homer.
5. Cricket.
6. A Tyrannosaurus Rex.
7. Stalin.
8. Lonnie Donegan.
9. Sand.

851

1. Three.
2. Six.
3. Monaco.
4. Noah's.
5. A woman took part – as cox in the Oxford boat.
6. *Sextet*.
7. Architecture.
8. Opera.
9. Just 2 hours.

110

1. What does the acronym SNAFU stand for?
2. How old was Joan of Arc when she led the French army to victory against the English at Orléans?
3. In which abbey is Poets' Corner?
4. Of what did Dr Watson's first wife die?
5. Who wrote *Memoirs of a Foxhunting Man*?
6. Who played the village idiot in *Ryan's Daughter* and won an Oscar for it as best supporting actor?
7. By what name was William Frederick Cody better known?
8. What was Mario Lanza's theme song?
9. Which of the body's muscles can work for the longest time before getting tired?

481

1. What is the only duty of the Grachtenvissers, a branch of the Amsterdam police?
2. Who formally surrendered on HMS *Bellerophon* after Waterloo?
3. What are the colours of the Italian flag?
4. Which is the longest psalm in the Bible?
5. What is the golfer's cry of warning?
6. How many Oscars for best director has Alfred Hitchcock won?
7. Who is nicknamed the Iron Lady?
8. Who was the best-known lead singer with The Shadows?
9. How much perspiration does an average pair of feet give off daily?

852

1. Approximately how many pounds of earth must be mined and sifted to produce a half-carat diamond?
2. As what were Kleenex tissues originally manufactured?
3. What is the capital of Israel?
4. Who wrote, 'A little knowledge is a dang'rous thing'?
5. Who was the first footballer to score 100 goals for both a Scottish and an English football club?
6. In which play did Barbra Streisand first achieve fame?
7. About which game have the most books been written?
8. Which of his symphonies did Beethoven dedicate to Napoleon?
9. What makes the weight of the earth increase by about 100,000 lb each year?

110

1. Situation Normal All Fouled Up.
2. Seventeen.
3. Westminster Abbey.
4. Diphtheria.
5. Siegfried Sassoon.
6. John Mills.
7. Buffalo Bill.
8. 'Be My Love' – first sung in the 1950 film *The Toast of New Orleans*.
9. The jaw muscles!

481

1. To cope with motorists who drive into the canals!
2. Napoleon.
3. Green, white, red.
4. Psalm 119.
5. 'Fore.'
6. None.
7. Margaret Thatcher.
8. Cliff Richard.
9. Half a pint.

852

1. 46,000 (give or take 5,000).
2. As gas mask filters during the First World War.
3. Jerusalem.
4. The question-setter! But Pope wrote, 'A little *learning* is a dang'rous thing.'
5. Kenny Dalglish.
6. *Funny Girl.*
7. Chess.
8. His third (the 'Eroica').
9. Meteoric material, chiefly dust, falling from the sky.

111

1. What is curious about the words 'abstemiously' and 'facetiously'?
2. In medieval France, King Philip Augustus decreed that a person's rank should be immediately recognizable by a detail of dress. What was it?
3. Which are the three best-known colleges of the American Ivy League?
4. Who wrote the poem 'The Bride of Abydos'?
5. Which English team plays soccer in the Scottish League?
6. In which country is the film *The Bridge on the River Kwai* set?
7. Who was known as the Lady with the Lamp?
8. Who jumped off the Tallahatchee Bridge?
9. What live in apiaries?

482

1. What is a male witch called?
2. Who wrote to whom, 'Home in three days so don't wash'?
3. By what name is Danzig now known?
4. Which book contains the sentence, 'Works of charity negligently performed are of no worth'?
5. Who was nicknamed the Manassas Mauler?
6. What is the name of the book and film based on the life of King Mongut of Siam?
7. What was newspaper publisher William Maxwell Aitken's title?
8. Name the Magic Dragon, Jackie Paper's friend.
9. Which is the largest gland in the human body?

853

1. What don't orthodox Jews do on Yom Kippur?
2. Name the thief released by Pontius Pilate instead of Jesus.
3. In which country did the Mau Mau uprising take place?
4. Who wrote under the pseudonym Gordon Ashe?
5. Who followed Godfrey Evans as England's wicketkeeper?
6. Which was the only film in which Lionel, John and Ethel Barrymore played together?
7. Who was the first American world chess champion?
8. Which was the first keyboard instrument that could play both softly and loudly?
9. How many times thicker is blood than water?

111

1. They are the only two words in the English language in which all six vowels appear in their correct order.
2. The points on his shoes, which should be between 6 inches and 12 inches – the longer the point, the higher the rank.
3. Harvard, Princeton, Yale.
4. Byron.
5. Berwick Rangers.
6. Burma.
7. Florence Nightingale.
8. Billy Joe McAllister.
9. Bees.

482

1. A warlock.
2. Napoleon to Josephine.
3. Gdansk.
4. *Don Quixote.*
5. Jack Dempsey.
6. *The King and I.*
7. Lord Beaverbrook.
8. Puff.
9. The liver.

853

1. Eat, drink or work.
2. Barabbas.
3. Kenya.
4. John Creasey.
5. Roy Swetman.
6. *Rasputin and the Empress* (1932).
7. Bobby Fischer.
8. The pianoforte.
9. Six times (approximately).

112

1. Which people originated popcorn?
2. Which king married Wallis Warfield Simpson?
3. In which country is the ski resort of St Moritz?
4. Who is Earl Derr Biggers's best-known creation?
5. On which four pieces of apparatus do women compete in international gymnastics competitions?
6. Who was the first cartoon character to achieve worldwide fame?
7. By what name was Angelo Siciliano better known?
8. Which song did Rick ask Sam to play in *Casablanca*?
9. Name London zoo's giant panda.

483

1. How many letters are there in the Greek alphabet?
2. Of which battleship was Captain Lindemann in command when it was sunk in 1941?
3. What is the sacred language of the Buddhists of India?
4. Whose guardian was Daddy (Oliver) Warbucks?
5. In showjumping, how many faults are incurred for a refusal?
6. Who is the publisher of the *Los Angeles Tribune* in 'Lou Grant'?
7. Which playing card is known as the Curse of Scotland?
8. Who wrote the music for the film *Our Town*?
9. Why does hail rarely fall in winter?

854

1. Who slew the monster Grendel?
2. Which Irish adventurer was pardoned by Charles II after helping himself to some of the crown jewels?
3. In which country is the Algarve?
4. In Greek mythology, the sight of whom literally petrified mortals?
5. Which Rugby Union team has won the Hospitals Cup the most times?
6. Who played Fast Eddie Felson in *The Hustler*?
7. At what age did Mrs Beeton die?
8. How many operas make up Wagner's *Ring* cycle?
9. What is a marsupial?

112

1. The American Indians.
2. Edward VIII.
3. Switzerland.
4. Charlie Chan.
5. Beam, asymmetric bars, horse/box, floor/mat.
6. Mickey Mouse.
7. Charles Atlas.
8. 'As Time Goes By'.
9. Chi-Chi.

483

1. Twenty-four.
2. The *Bismarck*.
3. Pali.
4. Little Orphan Annie's.
5. Three.
6. Margaret Pynchon.
7. The nine of diamonds.
8. Aaron Copland.
9. Because ice balls will not fall when the ground temperature is below freezing.

854

1. Beowulf.
2. Colonel Blood.
3. Portugal.
4. Medusa, the gorgon.
5. Guy's.
6. Paul Newman.
7. Twenty-eight – surprisingly enough.
8. Four.
9. A mammal that carries its young in a natural pouch on its stomach.

113

1. What does Lloyd's Register categorize?
2. Who was King Solomon's mother?
3. What is the colour for mourning in Turkey?
4. What was the name of the steam launch in C. S. Forester's *The African Queen*?
5. Who won Britain's lone athletics track medal at the 1976 Olympics?
6. In which film did Clark Gable win the Oscar for best actor?
7. Who is Spandau jail's last and only prisoner?
8. Name the Everly Brothers.
9. What is the colloquial name for tetanus?

484

1. What does 'caveat actor' mean?
2. Who was the wife of Louis XVI of France?
3. By what name is St Petersburg now known?
4. Who slew Medusa, the gorgon?
5. How many players are there in an Australian football team?
6. Who in 'MASH' tries to get a discharge from the army by wearing women's clothes?
7. Of what did the novelist Arnold Bennett die in 1931?
8. *Lady Sings the Blues* is whose life story?
9. Which is the only marsupial native to North America?

855

1. Translate 'Veni, Vidi, Vici.'
2. What did Victor Lustig 'sell' in 1925?
3. Which country 'moved' from one continent to another?
4. In the Winnie-the-Pooh stories, what is Kanga's baby called?
5. What is thrown into the ring from a boxer's corner to stop a fight?
6. Which actor was numbered among both *The Magnificent Seven* and *The Dirty Dozen*?
7. What is the name of the novelist whose husband was deputy commander of the First Airborne Army at Arnhem?
8. How many geese were a-laying?
9. For what is spirits of salt another name?

113

1. Shipping.
2. Bathsheba.
3. Violet.
4. The *African Queen.*
5. Brendan Foster.
6. *It Happened One Night* (1934).
7. Rudolf Hess.
8. Don and Phil.
9. Lockjaw.

484

1. 'Let the doer beware.'
2. Marie Antoinette.
3. Leningrad.
4. Perseus.
5. Eighteen.
6. Corporal Maxwell Klinger.
7. Typhoid. Wanting to prove that water in Paris was safe to drink, he took a glass of it, contracted typhoid and died.
8. Billie Holliday's.
9. The opossum.

855

1. 'I came, I saw, I conquered.'
2. The Eiffel Tower.
3. Panama. After gaining independence from Colombia (South America) in 1903, it was considered to be part of Central America – which belongs to North America.
4. Roo.
5. A towel.
6. Charles Bronson.
7. Daphne du Maurier.
8. Six.
9. Hydrochloric acid.

114

1. In which month does pheasant shooting start?
2. Who was shot in front of the Biograph Theatre in Chicago on 22 July 1934?
3. Which is Scotland's longest freshwater lake?
4. Who saved Andromeda from a sea-monster?
5. In basketball, what distance is the free-throw line from the backboard?
6. What is the name of the captured African whose life story is told in *Roots*?
7. Who was America's first Roman Catholic president?
8. What is the special song of the US Navy?
9. At what speed is the earth revolving?

485

1. Name two of the Hindu Trinity.
2. Seventy-five-year-old Edmund Ruffin fired the first shot on Fort Sumter to start which war?
3. To which country do the Canary Islands belong?
4. Which car did Commander Caractacus Potts drive?
5. The initials of England test cricket captain J. W. H. T. Douglas gave him his familiar nickname. What was it?
6. In which year was the bridge over the river Kwai built?
7. How many points are there on a Kensington board?
8. Which Gilbert and Sullivan opera has the subtitle *The Lass that Loved a Sailor*?
9. Which planet in our solar system has the shortest day?

856

1. Where would you eat alfresco?
2. Whose horse was Black Bess?
3. In which country is the Costa del Sol?
4. Who lives with the coyotes in Needles?
5. What is the largest margin by which a tennis tie-breaker can be won?
6. By what name is Kal-el better known?
7. What were the Christian names of the brothers Grimm?
8. Name the Liverpool night club from which the Beatles sprang into prominence.
9. How long will an average man's face whisker grow in one year?

114

1. October – the first of the month, to be exact.
2. John Dillinger (Public Enemy Number One).
3. Loch Awe.
4. Perseus.
5. 15 feet.
6. Kunta Kinte.
7. John F. Kennedy.
8. 'Anchors Aweigh'.
9. About 1,000 m.p.h.

485

1. Brahma, Shiva, Vishnu.
2. The American Civil War.
3. Spain.
4. Chitty-Chitty-Bang-Bang.
5. 'Johnny Won't Hit Today'.
6. 1943.
7. Seventy-two.
8. HMS *Pinafore*.
9. Jupiter, which completely rotates on its axis in only 9 hours, 50 minutes.

856

1. In the open air.
2. Dick Turpin's.
3. Spain.
4. Spike, Snoopy's brother.
5. 7–0.
6. Superman.
7. Jakob and Wilhelm.
8. The Cavern.
9. 5½ inches.

115

1. Approximately how many words are there in the English language?
2. Incitatus was both a horse and a consul. To which mad Roman emperor did he belong?
3. Where can the Rosetta stone be seen?
4. Name Hercule Poirot's valet.
5. How many players are there in a water polo team?
6. Who reputedly first said, 'It's not the men in my life, it's the life in my men'?
7. By what infamous name was Albert De Salvo better known?
8. Who became known as the king of ragtime?
9. Approximately what percentage of the earth's surface is covered by glaciers?

486

1. Over what did the cow jump?
2. Between Stockton and what other town was the first proper railway opened in 1825?
3. In what ratio is the sheep population to the human in Australia?
4. What is the alternative title of *Peter Pan*?
5. What is the maximum mark awarded by a single judge in international gymnastics competitions?
6. Name the mummy in *The Mummy.*
7. Who succeeded U Thant as United Nations Secretary-General?
8. By what name is Reg Dwight better known?
9. How many fluid ounces make 1 litre?

857

1. How many sheets of paper are there in a ream?
2. Why were Yo-Yos banned in Damascus in 1933?
3. In which Italian city is the Bridge of Sighs?
4. Who are Anastasia and Drizella?
5. What is Wasim Bari's cricketing speciality?
6. Who plays Rumpole of the Bailey?
7. What was the nickname of Charles S. Stratton, who was employed by P. T. Barnum?
8. Which group founded Brother records?
9. How many chromosomes does a normal human being have?

115

1. 800,000.
2. Caligula.
3. In the British Museum.
4. George.
5. Seven.
6. Mae West.
7. The Boston Strangler.
8. Scott Joplin.
9. About 10 per cent.

486

1. The moon.
2. Darlington.
3. Ten to one.
4. *The Boy Who Would Not Grow Up.*
5. Ten.
6. Im-ho-tep.
7. Kurt Waldheim.
8. Elton John.
9. 35.2.

857

1. 500 (formerly 480).
2. The Holy Council believed that their up-and-down movement was causing the prevailing drought. (And it rained the following day!)
3. Venice.
4. Cinderella's ugly stepsisters.
5. Wicketkeeping.
6. Leo McKern.
7. General Tom Thumb.
8. The Beach Boys.
9. Forty-six.

116

1. Which is the longest palindromic English word?
2. In which year did Marconi make the first transatlantic radio transmission?
3. What is the holy city of Islam called?
4. Name Andy Capp's wife.
5. For which League football team did Ian Botham play centre forward?
6. In which film and series do Bill Owen, Peter Sallis and Brian Wilde star?
7. What, in darts, is the spider?
8. Which was the first film made by the Beatles?
9. What does the acronym RADAR stand for?

487

1. How many babies were involved in the largest multiple human birth in which all the children lived?
2. Why were productions of *King Lear* banned from 1788 to 1820?
3. Which London landmark now stands in Lake Havasu City, Arizona?
4. Which forbidden fruit did Adam and Eve eat, taken from the tree of knowledge of good and evil?
5. In archery, in what are arrows carried?
6. What is Peter Parker's other identity?
7. What, in snooker, is a spider?
8. Who composed the opera *Aïda*?
9. Which flower is the symbol of secrecy?

858

1. What is British Rail's hovercraft division called?
2. What curious commission was Queen Marie Antoinette said to have given to the famous Sèvres porcelain factory?
3. Which country's money is said to be the most difficult to counterfeit?
4. Who wrote *The Call of the Wild*?
5. In 1981, the Wimbledon mixed doubles champions had a combined age of seventy-five. Who were they?
6. In how many films did Grace Kelly appear?
7. What was Malcolm X's surname?
8. Who replaced Pete Best with the Beatles?
9. Which is the only mammal capable of true flight?

116

1. Redivider.
2. 1901.
3. Mecca.
4. Flo.
5. Scunthorpe United.
6. 'The Last of the Summer Wine'.
7. The wire scoring frame attached to the board.
8. *A Hard Day's Night.*
9. RAdio Detection And Ranging.

487

1. Six – born to Sue Rosenkowitz of South Africa on 11 January 1974.
2. In deference to King George III's acknowledged insanity.
3. The old London Bridge.
4. The Bible never states the type of fruit! It was just assumed that it was an apple.
5. A quiver.
6. Spiderman.
7. A type of cue rest.
8. Giuseppe Verdi.
9. The rose.

858

1. Seaspeed (*not* Sealink).
2. To model a cup to fit exactly her left breast.
3. Japan's.
4. Jack London.
5. Frew McMillan and Betty Stove.
6. Eleven.
7. Little.
8. Ringo Starr.
9. The bat.

117

1. What were originally called Hanways?
2. Who did Sheriff Pat Garrett shoot and kill on 14 July 1881?
3. What is Brussels' best-known statue?
4. Which monster, killed by Hercules, had nine heads?
5. What was Martina Navratilova's original nationality?
6. What was Jayne Mansfield's favourite colour, used both for her home and for her car?
7. What is the situation in chess when one player can make no legal move?
8. What was Mendelssohn's first name?
9. What is the outer layer of skin called?

488

1. In which language does God Jul mean Happy Christmas?
2. Of which ship was Edward J. Smith captain when he died in 1912?
3. What became Istanbul officially on 28 March 1930?
4. What was Ali Baba's female slave called?
5. What was Mickey Mantle's game?
6. Who is Inspector Clouseau's valet?
7. Who was called the Lone Eagle?
8. Which opera was written to commemorate the opening of the Suez Canal?
9. Which are the four most common blood types?

859

1. If the horse in a statue of a mounted man has two legs raised, how did the man die?
2. Who did Princess Marie Louise of Austria marry in 1810?
3. Representations of how many US presidents are carved on the face of Mount Rushmore?
4. Who is Ellery Queen's father?
5. Which game is the name of Derby County football club's ground?
6. To whom was Mike Todd married when he was killed in a plane crash in 1958?
7. How many pawns are used in a game of chess?
8. Who composed the opera *Peter Grimes*?
9. Through which organs do whales breathe?

117

1. Umbrellas.
2. Billy the Kid.
3. The 'Manneken Pis' – a figure of a boy responding to the call of nature.
4. The hydra.
5. Czechoslovakian.
6. Pink.
7. Stalemate.
8. Felix.
9. The epidermis.

488

1. Swedish.
2. The *Titanic.*
3. Constantinople.
4. Morgiana.
5. Baseball.
6. Kato.
7. Charles Lindbergh.
8. *Aïda.*
9. O, A, B, AB.

859

1. He was killed in action.
2. Napoleon Bonaparte.
3. Four.
4. Inspector Richard Queen.
5. Baseball.
6. Elizabeth Taylor.
7. Sixteen.
8. Benjamin Britten.
9. Lungs.

118

1. What is the creed of airline pilots?
2. Who was the first woman to receive the Order of Merit?
3. Which American state is the largest producer of potatoes?
4. From whom did Della Street take dictation?
5. What is the diameter of a basketball basket?
6. Name five of Snow White's seven dwarfs.
7. What is the alternative name for the castle in chess?
8. What is the favourite musical instrument of the Tinguian tribe of the Philippine Islands?
9. Of what is the white trail behind a jet plane composed?

489

1. How does a Muslim husband divorce his wife?
2. Whose heart did Dr Buckland, Dean of Westminster, reputedly swallow in 1905?
3. Which two countries border the Dead Sea?
4. Who wrote *Dr Zhivago*?
5. Who is Charlie Brown's favourite baseball player?
6. Whose voice was used for Lauren Bacall's song in *To Have and Have Not*?
7. What was Hopalong Cassidy's real first name?
8. Which song did Irving Berlin present to his wife as a wedding gift in 1926?
9. Which organ makes up about 2 per cent of the human body's weight, but uses about 25 per cent of its oxygen?

860

1. For which month is emerald the birth stone?
2. Which English king was so careless with royal funds that he once had to pawn his crown to make ends meet?
3. What is the capital of Switzerland?
4. Name the gipsy girl who befriended the hunchback of Notre Dame.
5. What is called 'The House that Ruth Built'?
6. What is Uncle Jesse's CB call sign in 'The Dukes of Hazzard'?
7. Whose yacht was called *Honey Fitz*?
8. Who wrote the song 'White Christmas'?
9. How far can a giant tortoise crawl in 1 minute?

118

1. 'In God we trust, everything else we check.'
2. Florence Nightingale (in 1907).
3. Idaho.
4. Perry Mason.
5. 18 inches.
6. Dopey, Grumpy, Sleepy, Happy, Bashful, Sneezy, Doc.
7. The rook.
8. The nose flute.
9. Ice crystals.

489

1. By saying 'I divorce you' three times.
2. Louis XIV's.
3. Israel and Jordan.
4. Boris Pasternak.
5. Joe Shlabotnik.
6. Andy Williams's.
7. William.
8. 'Always'.
9. The brain.

860

1. May.
2. Richard II.
3. Berne.
4. Esmeralda.
5. Yankee Stadium, New York.
6. Shepherd.
7. President John F. Kennedy's.
8. Irving Berlin.
9. About 5 yards.

119

1. What is MMM minus MD?
2. Which Italian habit did Thomas Coryat introduce to England in 1608?
3. What is the motto of the United States of America?
4. Who removed the thorn from the lion's foot?
5. In 1983, which was the only first division soccer team not to have a grass pitch?
6. Who hosts 'This is Your Life'?
7. Purl, fisherman's, cable are all examples of what?
8. In which film did Clint Eastwood sing 'I Talk to the Trees'?
9. Which class of creatures contains more than two-thirds of all known species?

490

1. Which drink comes in Jeroboams?
2. At which battle in 1314 did Robert the Bruce defeat the English forces?
3. Who discovered Virginia in the USA?
4. What is the flying island in *Gulliver's Travels* called?
5. Which nation holds the current Olympic polo championship?
6. Name the 1978 film based on *The Wizard of Oz* with an all-black cast.
7. For what game are Boris Schapiro and Terence Reese famous?
8. Who did Simple Simon meet on the way to the fair?
9. Approximately how many eggs can a mother cod lay at a single spawning?

861

1. What do philatelists collect?
2. Against which king was the Gunpowder Plot of 1605 directed?
3. By what name is Stalingrad now known?
4. How many plays by William Shakespeare exist?
5. Which type of club did Alan Shepard use to hit three golf balls on the moon in 1971?
6. Which dancer's legs were insured for 650,000 dollars?
7. What is Al short for in Al Capone?
8. Of which composer was the French authoress George Sand a close friend?
9. What is 21° Centigrade on the Fahrenheit scale?

119

1. MD. (Roman numerals: 3000 minus 1500 equals 1500.)
2. Eating with a fork instead of fingers.
3. 'In God we trust.'
4. Androcles.
5. Queen's Park Rangers.
6. Eamonn Andrews.
7. Knitting stitches.
8. *Paint Your Wagon.*
9. Insects.

490

1. Champagne.
2. Bannockburn.
3. Sir Walter Raleigh.
4. Laputa.
5. Argentina – but the event hasn't been held since 1936.
6. *The Wiz.*
7. Bridge.
8. A pieman.
9. 5 million – though only about half a dozen usually survive.

861

1. Stamps.
2. James I.
3. Volgograd.
4. Thirty-seven.
5. A number six iron.
6. Fred Astaire's.
7. Alphonse.
8. Chopin.
9. 70°.

120

1. What number does the Roman numeral M represent?
2. Why was Mary Mallon kept in permanent detention from 1915 until her death in 1938?
3. The ghost of which American president is supposed to haunt the White House?
4. Whose pet chimp is Chee Chee?
5. Where is the longest golf hole in the world?
6. Name Mrs Slocombe's junior in 'Are You Being Served?'
7. Where did Rolls and Royce first meet?
8. Which musical instrument did Sir Charles Wheatstone invent?
9. If you were indulging in vaccimulgence, what would you be doing?

491

1. Who ate Turkey Lurkey?
2. From whom did Winston Churchill take over as prime minister in the early stages of the Second World War?
3. By what name was Zaïre formerly known?
4. By which river does Hiawatha live?
5. In which year did David Hemery win the Olympic 400-metre hurdles?
6. Name one of the two films for which Marlon Brando has won Oscars.
7. Of which card game is Southern Cross a form?
8. Which company's trademark includes Nipper the dog?
9. Which is the only bird that can fly backwards and hover?

862

1. To the nearest 5 per cent, what percentage of the world's population go through the day without coming into contact with a newspaper, radio, TV or telephone?
2. Which was the last European nation to accept the potato?
3. What is the capital of Jamaica?
4. What covers the body of Ray Bradbury's Illustrated Man?
5. Which Swede was once world heavyweight boxing champion?
6. Who plays Serpico in the 1973 film?
7. Who was England's most famous diarist?
8. Who wrote the musical suite 'Façade'?
9. For what purpose was the chow-chow dog originally bred?

120

1. 1,000.
2. She was 'Typhoid Mary', the notorious typhoid carrier.
3. Abraham Lincoln's.
4. Doctor Dolittle's.
5. At the Black Mountain Golf Club in North Carolina, where the seventeenth hole measures 745 yards and is a par 6.
6. Miss Brahms.
7. The Midland Hotel, Manchester.
8. The concertina.
9. Milking a cow.

491

1. Foxy Loxy.
2. Neville Chamberlain.
3. The Belgian Congo.
4. The Gitchee Gumee.
5. 1968.
6. *On the Waterfront, The Godfather*.
7. Poker.
8. His Master's Voice.
9. The humming bird.

862

1. Sixty-five.
2. France.
3. Kingston.
4. Tattooing.
5. Ingemar Johansson.
6. Al Pacino.
7. Samuel Pepys.
8. William Walton.
9. For food.

121

1. What is *ignis fatuus*?
2. What experience did James Bartley survive in 1891?
3. In which city are the famous Tivoli gardens?
4. Who wrote *Goodbye, Mr Chips*?
5. Which American was the ladies' Olympic skating champion in 1976?
6. Who was Lauren Bacall's first husband?
7. What is James Callaghan's first name?
8. From which film did the song 'Raindrops Keep Fallin' on my Head' come?
9. What kind of a fruit is a kumquat?

492

1. What is 88 in Roman numerals?
2. Which two countries were separated by Hadrian's Wall?
3. Which is London's second airport?
4. What, in the book, is the name of George Orwell's *Animal Farm*?
5. Which country qualified for the 1978 soccer World Cup from the group that contained England?
6. What is the home town of the Flintstones?
7. Who was *Time* magazine's Man of the Year in 1979?
8. Who sang the theme song to 'Rawhide'?
9. Of what is trichology the scientific study?

863

1. What will happen if you eat the leaves of a cherry tree?
2. For approximately how long has the civilized world been at peace during the last 3,500 years?
3. Where is the Sea of Showers?
4. Who wrote *Heidi*?
5. Which Rugby Union team was founded by Percy Carpmael in Bradford in 1890?
6. Name Alfred Hitchcock's daughter, who appeared in *Psycho*.
7. How many times may a volleyball be touched by one team before it crosses the net?
8. What is Dean Martin's theme song?
9. Who is known as the father of geometry?

121

1. 'Will-o'-the-wisp', the phosphorescent glow sometimes seen in marshes.
2. He was swallowed by a whale and stayed inside its stomach for two days. He lived till 1926 to tell the tale.
3. Copenhagen.
4. James Hilton.
5. Dorothy Hamill.
6. Humphrey Bogart.
7. Leonard.
8. *Butch Cassidy and the Sundance Kid.*
9. A small orange.

492

1. LXXXVIII.
2. England and Scotland.
3. Gatwick.
4. Manor Farm.
5. Italy.
6. Bedrock.
7. Ayatollah Khomeini.
8. Frankie Laine.
9. Hair.

863

1. You will be poisoned.
2. 230 years.
3. On the moon.
4. Johanna Spyri.
5. The Barbarians.
6. Patricia Hitchcock.
7. Three.
8. 'Everybody Loves Somebody'.
9. Euclid.

122

1. Which alphabet is composed of just dots?
2. What were Admiral Horatio Nelson's last words?
3. Which ruined Egyptian city has a namesake in Tennessee?
4. Who wrote under the pseudonym J. J. Marric?
5. Who won the America's Cup for yachting in 1983?
6. Which star signed Hollywood's first million-dollar contract?
7. Who is the Galloping Gourmet?
8. What is the musical term for 'with'?
9. How many troy ounces are there in a pound?

493

1. How many cups of tea does the average Englishman drink per annum?
2. How many children did Queen Victoria have?
3. Through which town did Lady Godiva ride?
4. How many humans did Noah's ark carry?
5. What new Olympic event involves ribbons, balls and hoops?
6. What is Goldfinger's first name?
7. For what, chiefly, did Uri Geller become famous?
8. John Howard Payne, born 1791, achieved fame with one song. Which song?
9. What is the fastest bird on earth?

864

1. Who is the Greek goddess of love?
2. Name Tsar Nicholas II's youngest daughter – who may have survived the firing squad.
3. To which country were 75,000 convicts transported between 1790 and 1840?
4. Who wrote *Lord of the Flies*?
5. In which game are blue and black always partners against red and green?
6. For whom is Ilya Kuryakin an agent?
7. How many balls are used in billiards?
8. At what age did Mozart die?
9. What is named after Alessandro Volta?

122

1. Braille.
2. 'Thank God I have done my duty' (*not* 'Kiss me, Hardy').
3. Memphis.
4. John Creasey.
5. Australia.
6. Charles Chaplin.
7. Graham Kerr.
8. Con.
9. Twelve.

493

1. 2,000.
2. Nine.
3. Coventry.
4. Eight (Noah, his wife, and his three sons and their wives).
5. Rhythmic gymnastics.
6. Auric.
7. Spoon-bending.
8. 'Home, Sweet Home'.
9. The swift.

864

1. Aphrodite.
2. Anastasia.
3. Australia.
4. William Golding.
5. Croquet.
6. UNCLE.
7. Three.
8. Thirty-five.
9. The volt, unit of electromotor force.

123

1. What was the earliest form of shoe?
2. In which year did the first Pilgrims land in America?
3. Which city boasts the most canals?
4. In which army did G. B. Shaw's Major Barbara serve?
5. In which sport does Karl Schnabl compete internationally?
6. What value note did each of the Maverick brothers keep pinned inside his coat?
7. By what name was convict Robert Stroud better known?
8. Who had a hit in 1963 with 'Limbo Rock'?
9. Which planet was discovered by Percival Lovell?

494

1. Of the 250 known alphabets in the history of language, how many are alive today?
2. Where was Oceanus Hopkins born?
3. How many outside pockets do high officials have in China?
4. In which school were Tom Brown's schooldays spent?
5. On 6 February 1971, where was a golf ball hit for the first time?
6. Who are the stars of the film *Duck Soup*?
7. Which limbs of the Venus de Milo are missing?
8. Who became Master of the King's Musick in 1924?
9. What part of the body is affected by glaucoma?

865

1. What is the fate of the ship *The Flying Dutchman*?
2. What was the main cargo of HMS *Bounty* at the time of the mutiny?
3. What is the official residence of the President of France?
4. Who, in his nonsense verse, wrote of a runcible cat with crimson whiskers?
5. Who were the ice dance champions at the 1984 European figure skating championships?
6. Who directed the film *Spartacus*?
7. What is Harold Wilson's first name?
8. Who is Madame Butterfly's lover?
9. Which letter is top left on a typewriter?

123

1. The sandal.
2. 1620.
3. Birmingham.
4. The Salvation Army.
5. Ski-jumping.
6. 1,000 dollars.
7. The Birdman of Alcatraz.
8. Chubby Checker.
9. Pluto.

494

1. 50 – and half of these are in India.
2. On the *Mayflower* – the only child to be born on it (1620).
3. Four. Lesser men have only two.
4. Rugby.
5. On the moon.
6. The Marx brothers.
7. The arms.
8. Sir Edward Elgar.
9. The eye.

865

1. To sail for ever on the oceans of the world.
2. Breadfruit trees.
3. The Élysée Palace.
4. Edward Lear.
5. Jayne Torvill and Christopher Dean.
6. Stanley Kubrick.
7. James.
8. Lieutenant Pinkerton.
9. Q.

124

1. The first appeared in the *New York World* on 21 December 1913, and most newspapers now have one. What is it?
2. Who was known as the Serpent of the Nile?
3. Which is the largest building on the Acropolis in Athens?
4. What were the gifts of the Magi?
5. Which Olympic swimming multi-gold-medallist died on 21 January 1984?
6. Who plays Mr Moto in the majority of the Mr Moto films?
7. Which is the highest numbered segment on a dartboard?
8. Until 1984, which was the only million-selling record featuring bagpipes?
9. Approximately how long does sunlight take to reach the earth?

495

1. 'Red sky at night' is whose delight?
2. For how long did Prohibition last in the USA?
3. Baton Rouge is the capital of which US state?
4. In which Agatha Christie novel did Miss Marple first appear?
5. Name the horse on which Princess Anne competed in the Olympic Games.
6. What was captured in *The Taking of Pelham 123*?
7. Who reputedly first said, 'There's a sucker born every minute'?
8. Under what pseudonym did Philip Heseltine compose?
9. What is exceeded when a sonic boom is produced?

866

1. Who said, 'Genius is one per cent inspiration and ninety-nine per cent perspiration'?
2. What is the name given to a particularly intrepid group of Japanese Second World War pilots?
3. What is the most common surname in France?
4. Name Andy Capp's best friend.
5. At which sport was Boris Onishchenko found to be cheating at the Olympic games?
6. Who was Ernie Wise's comedy partner?
7. Who was the only US president to be elected for four terms?
8. Who sang 'The Ballad of Cat Ballou' in the 1965 film?
9. For how long are dogs pregnant?

124

1. The crossword puzzle.
2. Cleopatra.
3. The Parthenon.
4. Gold, frankincense and myrrh.
5. Johnny Weissmuller (Tarzan).
6. Peter Lorre.
7. Twenty.
8. 'Amazing Grace'.
9. 8 minutes.

495

1. Shepherds'.
2. 13 years.
3. Louisiana.
4. *Murder at the Vicarage* (1930).
5. Goodwill.
6. A New York subway train.
7. P. T. Barnum (of circus fame).
8. Peter Warlock.
9. The speed of sound.

866

1. Thomas Edison.
2. Kamikaze.
3. Martin.
4. Chalkie.
5. Fencing.
6. Eric Morecambe.
7. Franklin Delano Roosevelt (1932, 1936, 1940, 1944).
8. Nat King Cole.
9. Dogs tend not to become pregnant, but bitches carry for 9 weeks.

125

1. Which letter begins the fewest English words?
2. Which king signed the Magna Carta?
3. In 1978, which country lifted its ban on the works of Aristotle, Dickens and Shakespeare?
4. Which two birds did Noah send forth from the ark?
5. Which is the most popular sport in Spanish-speaking countries?
6. Who plays Harry Palmer?
7. What did Vincenzo Peruggia steal in 1911 and keep in a trunk for two years?
8. What are little girls made of?
9. Which day of the week is named after a planet?

496

1. Where in the world does each of our calendar days begin and end first?
2. What was the fire-and-brimstone preacher Cotton Mather responsible for instigating in 1692?
3. Which is the world's warmest sea?
4. To whom was Billy Bones first mate?
5. What was John Sholto Douglas's title?
6. Where was the setting for *Saturday Night Fever*?
7. For what is the Indian monarch Shah Jahan best known?
8. From which musical did the song 'How are Things in Glocca Morra' come?
9. For what is cete the collective name?

867

1. What is the world's most extensively used food?
2. Between which two cities was the first transatlantic telephone service inaugurated?
3. What are the colours of the French flag?
4. What was Ernest Hemingway's first novel?
5. Who was the first man to bowl 20,000 balls in test cricket?
6. Who played Beau Geste in the 1939 film?
7. Who was voted the most hated person in history in a poll conducted in England during the early 1970s?
8. Who composed the 'Christmas Oratorio'?
9. Approximately how many pints of air are inhaled in one normal breath by an adult?

125

1. X.
2. King John put his seal on it – he couldn't write!
3. China.
4. A raven and a dove.
5. Bullfighting.
6. Michael Caine.
7. The 'Mona Lisa'.
8. Sugar and spice and all things nice.
9. Saturday (Saturn).

496

1. Tonga.
2. The 'witch trials' in Salem, Massachusetts.
3. The Red Sea.
4. Captain Flint.
5. Marquis of Queensberry.
6. Brooklyn, New York.
7. Building the Taj Mahal.
8. *Finian's Rainbow.*
9. Badgers.

867

1. Rice.
2. London and New York (in 1927).
3. Red, white and blue.
4. *The Torrents of Spring.*
5. Lance Gibbs.
6. Gary Cooper.
7. Adolf Hitler.
8. J. S. Bach.
9. One.

126

1. What are the Star of Africa and the Hope?
2. How were King Charles II and King James II related?
3. Where are British monarchs crowned?
4. In which Ian Fleming novel did James Bond first appear?
5. Which British football club won nine successive League championships between 1966 and 1974?
6. Who won the Miss Hungary title for 1936 but had to give it up when it was discovered that she was not yet sixteen
7. What is the value of an outer bull in darts?
8. Which ballet by Delibes is subtitled *The Girl with the Enamel Eyes*?
9. Who wrote *Conditioned Reflexes*?

497

1. Who is the heir apparent to Britain's throne?
2. Who were the parents of Queen Elizabeth I?
3. Which country uses the most soap per capita?
4. Why was the Adulterer's Bible so called?
5. What is the open equivalent to the women's Federation Cup?
6. Whose best friend is Barney Rubble?
7. How many points are there on a backgammon board?
8. What was the Negro tapdancer Luther 'Bill' Robinson's nickname?
9. Relative to height and length, which creature is the world's champion jumper?

868

1. How many lines are there in a limerick?
2. What did the ancient Romans eat to prevent drunkenness?
3. Which country first used aircraft equipped with bombs for war?
4. What is the surname of Sir Roderick and his daughter Honoria (P. G. Wodehouse)?
5. Who captained Middlesex at cricket in 1982?
6. Who said, 'Beulah, peel me a grape'?
7. From what are the beds of snooker tables made?
8. Which composer was portrayed in the 1947 film *Song of Love*?
9. If a dog is a carnivore, what is a sheep?

126

1. Diamonds.
2. They were brothers.
3. In Westminster Abbey.
4. *Casino Royale*.
5. Glasgow Celtic.
6. Zsa Zsa Gabor.
7. Twenty-five.
8. *Coppélia*.
9. Ivan Pavlov.

497

1. Prince Charles.
2. Henry VIII and Anne Boleyn.
3. England.
4. Because of its famous misprint (Exodus 20:14), 'Thou shalt commit adultery.'
5. The Davis Cup (tennis).
6. Fred Flintstone's.
7. Twenty-four.
8. Mr Bojangles.
9. The flea, which can jump 80 times its own height and 150 times its own length.

868

1. Five.
2. Parsley – but it is not recorded whether it worked!
3. Italy, during the Italo-Turkish war of 1911–12 in North Africa.
4. Glossop.
5. Mike Brearley.
6. Mae West.
7. Slate.
8. Johannes Brahms.
9. A herbivore.

127

1. Which is the world's most popular green vegetable?
2. Which famous building is calculated to topple over in about 2015?
3. On which London tube line is Knightsbridge station?
4. At which school did Miss Jean Brodie teach?
5. Which object is usually thrown the furthest in field events?
6. Wilnelia Merced – Miss World 1975 – became whose third wife in 1983?
7. From which country does mah-jong originate?
8. Which honour did the Beatles receive in 1965?
9. For what is the mongoose chiefly famous?

498

1. What couldn't Jack Sprat eat?
2. In the nineteenth century, students at Cambridge University were not allowed to keep dogs in their rooms. What did Lord Byron keep instead?
3. Of which country is Bucharest the capital?
4. What nationality is Hercule Poirot?
5. For which county did J. B. Hobbs play cricket?
6. How many extras did the film *Quo Vadis* employ?
7. At what age did the poet Percy Bysshe Shelley die?
8. Who brought the bagpipes to the British Isles?
9. What is said to be the only man-made object visible without a telescope from the moon?

869

1. What is the original meaning of the word 'bride'?
2. What nationality was the pilot who fell 21,980 feet from his plane in 1942 – and lived?
3. What annual event takes place in May in the grounds of the Royal Hospital, Chelsea?
4. Who wrote *The Good Earth*?
5. Who ran the first Marathon?
6. Who does Miss Piggy love?
7. How many cards are in a tarot pack?
8. Who did Linda Eastman marry in 1969?
9. What is the only creature that can turn its stomach inside out?

127

1. The lettuce.
2. The leaning tower of Pisa.
3. Piccadilly.
4. Marcia Blaine School for Girls.
5. The javelin.
6. Bruce Forsyth's.
7. China.
8. The MBE.
9. Its ability to fight cobras.

498

1. Fat.
2. A bear.
3. Romania.
4. Belgian.
5. Surrey.
6. Around 30,000.
7. Twenty-nine.
8. The Romans.
9. The Great Wall of China.

869

1. 'To cook' – from an ancient Teutonic word.
2. Russian.
3. The Chelsea Flower Show.
4. Pearl Buck.
5. The Athenian, Pheidippides.
6. Kermit the frog.
7. Seventy-eight.
8. Paul McCartney.
9. The starfish.

128

1. Approximately how many loaves of bread does the average Briton eat in a week?
2. Which two mountain ranges did Hannibal and his elephants cross in 218 BC?
3. By what name do English-speakers know Shqipëria?
4. Who claimed to be able to recognize about 140 different forms of tobacco ash?
5. Which golfer has the nickname Golden Bear?
6. What is the home town of Batman and Robin?
7. Who is known as the father of poetry?
8. The Four Lovers changed their names to what?
9. What is curious about the raccoon's eating habits?

499

1. Which two airlines fly Concorde?
2. Only one dead language has been resurrected for everyday use. Which?
3. Where can a plane fly further below sea level than some submarines can dive?
4. By how many years is Mycroft Holmes older than Sherlock?
5. How many warm-up pitches is a relief pitcher allowed in baseball?
6. Who rode Hi Hat to victory in *A Day at the Races*?
7. How many squares and rectangles are there on a Quadwrangle board?
8. Which British composer died in 1628?
9. What are the four dimensions?

870

1. Approximately how many people per day commit suicide worldwide?
2. To which island was Napoleon first exiled?
3. Between which two cities did the Blue Train run?
4. Who created George Smiley?
5. In which sport do Mohawks and Choctaws figure?
6. On which British TV programme is the American series 'All in the Family' based?
7. Who was the only US president to be sworn in by a woman?
8. Who was the leader of the first black band to play at Carnegie Hall?
9. Which fruit contains the most calories?

128

1. 1 large one.
2. The Pyrenees and the Alps.
3. Albania.
4. Sherlock Holmes.
5. Jack Nicklaus.
6. Gotham City.
7. Homer.
8. The Four Seasons.
9. It first washes its food in water.

499

1. British Airways and Air France.
2. Hebrew – dead for 2,300 years until revived by the Jews in Israel as their common language.
3. Over the Dead Sea (which is 1,300 feet below sea level).
4. Seven.
5. Eight.
6. Harpo Marx.
7. 117 (the same as on a Quizwrangle board).
8. John Bull.
9. Length, width, depth and time.

870

1. 1,000.
2. Elba.
3. Paris and Monte Carlo.
4. John Le Carré.
5. Ice-skating.
6. 'Till Death Us Do Part'.
7. Lyndon B. Johnson – on the day John F. Kennedy was assassinated.
8. Count Basie.
9. The avocado pear.

129

1. For what does USSR stand?
2. King Mongut of Siam was probably the most married man in history. Approximately how many wives and concubines did he have?
3. On which plain is Stonehenge located?
4. Who wrote *Sex and the Single Girl*?
5. In which Olympic Games did Princess Anne compete?
6. Who is Mickey Mouse's girlfriend?
7. Who said, 'I will continue to be the essence of sweet reasonableness'?
8. Which famous nursery song did Sarah Josepha Hall write in 1830?
9. How many stars are in Orion's belt?

500

1. When did the Chinese Year of the Dog most recently occur?
2. Who was king of Sweden from 1907 to 1950?
3. By what name is East Pakistan now known?
4. Who is the local bobby of Market Blandings?
5. What footwear did Abebe Bikila favour when he won the 1960 Olympic marathon?
6. Who is Science Officer on the Starship *Enterprise*?
7. Which gangster used the pseudonym Al Brown?
8. What was the first opera Arthur Sullivan set to music?
9. What effect does alcohol have on your body temperature?

871

1. Approximately what percentage of the world's population customarily eats with a knife and fork?
2. Which country did Russia invade in 1956?
3. Which nation, on average, takes the longest time over its meals?
4. What is Sancho Panza's donkey called (in English)?
5. Over how many days is the decathlon held?
6. What is *Los Angeles Tribune* photographer Dennis Price's nickname in 'Lou Grant'?
7. What was William Tayton's claim to fame?
8. Name Milan's famous opera house.
9. What type of insect is a devil's coach-horse?

129

1. Union of Soviet Socialist Republics.
2. 9,000.
3. Salisbury Plain.
4. Helen Gurley Brown.
5. The Montreal Games of 1976.
6. Minnie Mouse.
7. Margaret Thatcher.
8. 'Mary Had a Little Lamb'.
9. Three.

500

1. 1982.
2. Gustav V.
3. Bangladesh.
4. Constable Evans in the stories by P. G. Wodehouse.
5. None – he ran in bare feet.
6. Mr Spock.
7. Alphonse Capone.
8. *Cox and Box.* (Libretto by F. C. Burnand – not Gilbert.)
9. It lowers it.

871

1. One-third.
2. Hungary.
3. The French.
4. Dapple.
5. Two.
6. Animal.
7. He was the first person ever to appear on TV – at J. L. Baird's demonstration.
8. La Scala.
9. A beetle.

130

1. Who cut off Samson's hair?
2. Which coin ceased to be legal tender on 30 June 1980?
3. From what does Monaco mainly derive its revenue?
4. Whose autobiography is entitled *Life on the Mississippi*?
5. In how many different ways can a batsman be out at cricket?
6. For which organization does Derek Flint work?
7. Who was the first American president to ride in an automobile?
8. What did Yankee Doodle name the feather he stuck in his cap?
9. In which mountain range is the Abominable Snowman said to live?

501

1. Which is the oldest and most widely used drug on earth?
2. Between which years was the Spanish Civil War fought?
3. Which country is by far the world's largest importer of herbs and spices?
4. Who did Henry Jekyll change into?
5. Which county has won the most championships at cricket?
6. Into whom was Professor Kelp transformed?
7. At what game have Maureen and Alan Hiron represented England and Britain?
8. Who composed the tune to 'Twinkle, Twinkle, Little Star'?
9. How many teeth do tortoises have?

872

1. What is the commonest item of international commerce?
2. Who was the first British monarch to visit America?
3. In which language does Store Christi mean Happy Birthday?
4. Who or what did Mark Antony call a 'bleeding piece of earth'?
5. How did Rocky Marciano die?
6. In which Frederick Forsyth novel and film does a German journalist hunt for a Nazi war criminal?
7. Whose fourth wife was Chiang Chin?
8. Who was known as the king of swing?
9. For what is nye the collective term?

130

1. A soldier ordered by Delilah to do so.
2. The sixpence.
3. Gambling.
4. Mark Twain's (Samuel Clemens).
5. Ten.
6. ZOWIE.
7. Theodore Roosevelt.
8. Macaroni.
9. The Himalayas.

501

1. Alcohol.
2. 1936 and 1939.
3. The USA.
4. Edward Hyde.
5. Yorkshire.
6. Mr Buddy Love (*The Nutty Professor* – Jerry Lewis).
7. Bridge.
8. Mozart.
9. None.

872

1. Petroleum and its by-products.
2. George VI (in 1939).
3. Norwegian.
4. Julius Caesar.
5. He was killed in a plane crash.
6. *The Odessa File.*
7. Mao Tse-tung's.
8. Benny Goodman.
9. Pheasants.

131

1. Why was a trireme so called?
2. Which queen's last speech to Parliament was known as 'The Golden Speech'?
3. Which Irish county shares its name with a type of five-line humorous verse?
4. What did Sir Richard Burton translate unexpurgated?
5. What is *ski évolutif*?
6. Who played Puck in the 1935 film of *A Midsummer Night's Dream*?
7. Who is the Lord High Admiral?
8. In which song do you pass Loch Tummel and Loch Rannock?
9. What type of creature is a fer de lance?

502

1. If you were anosmic what would be wrong with you?
2. How were the injuries from which George II reputedly died sustained?
3. Where does the Obelisk of Luxor stand?
4. What did the walrus and the carpenter feast on at the beach?
5. Who beat Scotland 7–0 in the 1954 Soccer World Cup?
6. Who said, 'I can't see who's ahead – it's either Oxford or Cambridge.'
7. Who won snooker's World Professional Championship in 1979?
8. What is B. B. King's guitar called?
9. What is so peculiar about an avocet's beak?

873

1. What is the German for Thursday?
2. What act of scientific curiosity resulted in Pliny the Elder's death in AD 79?
3. What country is Belmopan the capital of?
4. Where was the *Hesperus* wrecked?
5. How many play at one time in a Canadian football team?
6. What was D. W. Griffith's *The Birth of a Nation* originally called?
7. What American poet was imprisoned by the French in the First World War?
8. On which story by C. T. A. Hoffman did Tchaikovsky base his ballet *The Nutcracker*?
9. How many canines does a human adult have?

131

1. Because it was a vessel with three rows of oars.
2. Elizabeth I.
3. Limerick.
4. *The Arabian Nights.*
5. The French method of teaching skiing, starting with very short skis.
6. Mickey Rooney.
7. The Queen.
8. 'The Road to the Isles'.
9. A poisonous snake.

502

1. No sense of smell.
2. When he fell off the lavatory.
3. In the Place de la Concorde, Paris.
4. Oysters.
5. Uruguay.
6. John Snagge commentating for the BBC on the 1949 Boat Race.
7. Terry Griffiths.
8. Lucille.
9. It curves upwards at the end.

873

1. *Donnerstag.*
2. Observing too closely the eruption of Vesuvius.
3. Belize.
4. Massachusetts, at Norman's Woe near Gloucester.
5. Twelve.
6. *The Klansman.*
7. E. E. Cummings (described in his book *The Enormous Room*).
8. 'The Nutcracker and the Mouse King'.
9. Four; they are teeth.

132

1. Which is the largest prison in Great Britain?
2. What does the name Thermopylae, the site of a famous battle, actually mean?
3. Switzerland is a federal republic. What are the twenty-three constituent parts called?
4. For whom is the world in a 'state of chassis' according to Sean O'Casey?
5. Who took the world heavyweight boxing title from Max Schmelling and lost it to Primo Carnera?
6. Name two musicals based on plays by Shakespeare.
7. What is the three-dimensional image created by laser beams called?
8. Who composed the first opera ever performed?
9. What type of animal is a samoyed?

503

1. How much domestic water does the average American use in a day?
2. Who was the last king to lead his troops into battle?
3. What was Leningrad called immediately before it became Leningrad?
4. Who was the husband of Lucrezia for whom Browning wrote a monologue?
5. Who rode Mill Reef to victory in the 1971 Prix de L'Arc de Triomphe?
6. Who were the Blues Brothers?
7. Who reputedly died saying, 'Die, my dear doctor, that's the last thing I shall do'?
8. What is *opéra bouffe*?
9. What is a group of swine called?

874

1. What are you afraid of if you suffer from xenophobia?
2. From the eleventh to fifteenth centuries there were epidemics of hysteria called 'tarantism'. What form did these take?
3. Which city has the dialling code 0603?
4. Name T. S. Eliot's Railway Cat.
5. How long is the side line of a tennis court?
6. What is Godzilla?
7. Which artist professed a wish to eat his wife when she died?
8. Which song by Chuck Berry did Mary Whitehouse attack?
9. What colour is pure molten gold?

132

1. Wormwood Scrubs, London, with 1,208 cells.
2. 'Hot Gates'.
3. Cantons.
4. Captain Boyle in *Juno and the Paycock.*
5. Jack Sharkey.
6. *West Side Story* (*Romeo and Juliet*); *The Boys from Syracuse* (*A Comedy of Errors*); *Kiss me Kate* (*The Taming of the Shrew*).
7. A hologram.
8. Peri, *c.* 1600.
9. A dog.

503

1. 60 gallons.
2. George II at the Battle of Dettingen in 1743.
3. Petrograd.
4. Andrea del Sarto.
5. Geoff Lewis.
6. John Belushi and Dan Ackroyd, in the film of the same name.
7. Lord Palmerston in 1865.
8. Comic opera.
9. A sounder or a drift.

874

1. Foreigners.
2. Dancing mania.
3. Norwich.
4. Skimbleshanks.
5. 78 feet.
6. A Japanese film monster of cult status, seen to hilarious effect in *Godzilla Versus the Smog Monster.*
7. Salvador Dali.
8. 'My Ding-a-Ling'; her activities greatly enhanced sales.
9. Green.

133

1. How many different words does an educated English speaker use in speech on average?
2. What is the oldest British trade union?
3. What are the Tontons Macoute in Haiti?
4. Who wrote a puppet play featuring himself and Shakespeare?
5. When was Lester Piggott first champion jockey?
6. BBC TV features a Fleetwood Mac number as a title theme. Which programme?
7. Whose portrait is on the USA's $5 bill?
8. Who did Elsie marry in *The Yeoman of the Guard*?
9. Which is the brightest asteroid?

504

1. What was Mr Punch's famous advice to young men about to marry?
2. Where did Harold beat Harold?
3. How many King Leopolds of Belgium have there been?
4. On which day did God make the sun, the moon and stars?
5. On which course was the first ever English race meeting held in 1511?
6. Who is the only member of 'Dad's Army' to have had a chart-topping hit?
7. In which country did draughts originate?
8. Who is the heroine of Beethoven's opera *Fidelio*?
9. Which acid is HNO_3?

875

1. From which fruit is kirsch made?
2. Who was the son of Edward III, father of Henry IV and uncle to Richard II?
3. What is the national flower of Sweden?
4. Who created the detective Albert Campion?
5. Who rode Goodwill in the 1976 Olympics?
6. Which American film star's disastrous life was the subject of an equally disastrous musical?
7. At which game have Omar Sharif and the editors of this book represented their countries?
8. Who composed the song 'Hearts of Oak'?
9. What is the total capacity of the humnan lungs?

133

1. 5,000.
2. National Society of Brushmakers and General Workers, founded in 1747.
3. The secret police force.
4. G. B. Shaw.
5. 1960.
6. 'Grand Prix'.
7. Abraham Lincoln's.
8. Colonel Fairfax (Gilbert and Sullivan).
9. Vesta.

504

1. Don't.
2. Stamford Bridge (King Harold of Britain defeated Harold Haardraade of Norway).
3. Three.
4. The fourth day.
5. Chester.
6. Clive Dunn.
7. Egypt.
8. Leonora.
9. Nitric acid.

875

1. Cherries.
2. John of Gaunt.
3. Lily of the valley.
4. Margery Allingham.
5. Princess Anne.
6. Jean Seberg.
7. Bridge.
8. William Boyce.
9. Approximately 5 litres.

134

1. What is added to gin and vermouth to make the drink called a Gibson?
2. Which king was the first to use the royal 'we'?
3. Which country is Carrantual the highest peak of?
4. Which poet was a diplomat and the son of a wine merchant?
5. For which game is the Hitachi Cup awarded?
6. In which TV cops series do Sharon Gless and Tyne Daly star?
7. What is the craft of knotting and tying heavy string into patterns called?
8. Who composed *The Execution of Stepan Razin*?
9. At what speed is the earth orbiting the sun?

505

1. What do the initials DERV represent?
2. Who was the last king of Rome, expelled after his son's rape of Lucretia?
3. What city was called the 'Hundred-Gated'?
4. Which novel features Pinkie and Ida?
5. What is the longest hole in one ever recorded?
6. Which TV series do Bill Owen, Peter Sallis and Brian Wilde star in?
7. Who was Jean-Baptiste Poquelin?
8. What was Alvin Stardust's original stage name?
9. What is the greatest number of deaths due to lightning which has occurred in a single year this century in Britain?

876

1. Which bronze emblem is awarded to soldiers of the British Army who are mentioned in despatches?
2. Who was the first Prince of Wales?
3. On which coast of Australia is Perth?
4. Who guides Dante to paradise in the *Divine Comedy*?
5. What is the value of the gold spot in the centre of an archery target?
6. Whose 'Letter from America' is broadcast regularly?
7. How many cards are required to play bezique?
8. Christopher Seaman is the conductor of the BBC Scottish Symphony Orchestra. Which instrument did he play previously?
9. What weight was the largest carrot yet grown?

134

1. Onion.
2. Richard the Lionheart.
3. Ireland.
4. Geoffrey Chaucer.
5. Volleyball.
6. 'Cagney and Lacey'.
7. Macramé.
8. Shostakovitch.
9. 66,700 m.p.h.

505

1. Diesel Engined Road Vehicles.
2. Tarquinius Superbus.
3. Thebes, in Upper Egypt.
4. *Brighton Rock.*
5. 480 yards (fifth hole at Hope Country Club, Arkansas by L. Bruce in 1962, driving over a dog leg).
6. 'The Last of the Summer Wine'.
7. Molière.
8. Shane Fenton.
9. Thirty-one, in 1914.

876

1. An oak leaf.
2. Edward, later King Edward II.
3. West coast.
4. Beatrice.
5. Nine.
6. Alistair Cooke's.
7. Sixty-four.
8. Timpani (kettle-drums).
9. 11 lb, in 1967 in Australia.

135

1. What is a palimpsest?
2. Which principality did Victoria's Albert come from?
3. What is the capital of the Bahamas?
4. In which Dickens novel is Sissy Jupe adopted by Thomas Gradgrind?
5. What is the Devizes-to-Westminster Marathon?
6. What happened for the first time on screen in India in 1977?
7. What nationality was the author Franz Kafka?
8. What nationality was Gustav Mahler?
9. With which branch of medicine is Mesmer associated?

506

1. What was the code name of the Israeli raid on Entebbe airport to free the hostages?
2. Where did Washington and his army spend the winter of 1777–8?
3. Where is the Britannia Bridge built by Stevenson in 1850?
4. Who was Ruth's mother-in-law?
5. What country do the Springboks represent?
6. Which dramatist wrote *Death of a Salesman*?
7. Whose mistress was Eva Braun?
8. Which famous violin maker was born in 1644?
9. Which two reptiles have the loudest voices?

877

1. What is *raku*?
2. The world's population was estimated at 1,000 million in the mid nineteenth century. When did it reach 4,000 million?
3. On 13 February 1920 Jerusalem experienced something fairly exceptional. What?
4. Who did Lord Peter Wimsey marry?
5. In what type of riding would you find a coffin?
6. He starred in *Annie Get Your Gun, Showboat, Seven Brides for Seven Brothers,* but now has a very different role as Clayton Farlowe. Who is he?
7. What is a fresco?
8. Who asked where all the flowers had gone?
9. John Huxham in 1750 was the first to use a certain word. Which?

135

1. Twice-used writing material, where early writing can be seen below more recent writing.
2. Saxe-Coburg.
3. Nassau.
4. *Hard Times*.
5. A canoe race.
6. The first screen kiss seen in India.
7. Czech.
8. Austrian.
9. Hypnotism.

506

1. Thunderbolt.
2. Valley Forge.
3. The Menai Straits.
4. Naomi.
5. South Africa.
6. Arthur Miller.
7. Adolf Hitler's.
8. Antonius Stradivarius.
9. Crocodiles and alligators.

877

1. Japanese pottery; it is glazed and biscuit fired.
2. 1976.
3. 39 inches of snow.
4. Harriet Vane.
5. It is a fence in cross-country horse trials.
6. Howard Keel, now a 'Dallas' regular.
7. A painting on plaster, usually on walls or ceilings.
8. Pete Seeger.
9. Influenza.

136

1. What would you be if you had a certificate from the Worshipful Company of Farriers?
2. Who were the Princes in the Tower?
3. From which country is the airline TABSO?
4. What is the alternative title of Disraeli's *Sybil*?
5. Who won the last Soccer Home International Competition in 1984?
6. Who referees 'Call My Bluff'?
7. Who was King Zog?
8. Who wrote the comic opera *Robinson Crusoe*?
9. What are inflamed if you have acne?

507

1. Who or what is a palooka?
2. In 1392 Sir John Hawkwood wrote home from Florence. What is remarkable about his letter?
3. The guinea-pig is a native of which region?
4. In which book of the Old Testament are the Ten Commandments first written?
5. What distance is the soccer penalty spot from the goal mouth centre?
6. What happened on the first night of BBC 2?
7. Who moved from landscape in art through the nude to civilization?
8. Who did the painting on the cover of The Band's first album?
9. What was *Didus ineptus*?

878

1. When is St Martin's Day?
2. Which Chancellor of England lifted his daughter's nightdress to show her off to her future husband?
3. How deep is the Grand Canyon?
4. Why is Boccaccio's *Decameron* so called?
5. In golf, what was a baffy?
6. Which sport is featured in the 1980 film *Breaking Away*?
7. Which fish can you catch between 15 January and 14 October?
8. Which huntsman immortalized in song used to hunt in the Lake District?
9. What is the other name for the snow leopard – the same as a weight?

136

1. A blacksmith.
2. Edward V and Richard, Duke of York.
3. Bulgaria.
4. *The Two Nations.*
5. Northern Ireland.
6. Robert Robinson.
7. The last king of Albania.
8. Offenbach.
9. The sebaceous glands.

507

1. An incompetent games player.
2. It is the earliest known letter written in English.
3. South America.
4. Exodus.
5. 12 yards.
6. There was a power failure and the studio was blacked out.
7. Lord Clark (Kenneth Clark).
8. Bob Dylan.
9. The dodo.

878

1. 11 November.
2. Sir Thomas More.
3. 1 mile.
4. It is made up of ten tales; they are told by ten people over ten days during a plague in Florence in 1348.
5. An obsolete hickory-shafted club rather like a no. 4 wood.
6. Cycling.
7. Salmon.
8. John Peel.
9. Ounce.

137

1. Which political party takes its name from a band of Irish outlaws?
2. Roger Ascham found Greek easier to write than English. Which queen did he tutor?
3. Where would you find the Elgin Marbles?
4. Where is Samuel Butler's *Erewhon* set?
5. Who play home soccer at Gigg Lane?
6. Which film star was born Estelle O'Brien Thompson?
7. Who is famous for his Parisian posters?
8. Which city of West Virginia is also the name of a dance?
9. On what plant did Mendel base his experiments into heredity?

508

1. If you are eating something *en croûte* what would it be like?
2. Name one of the MPs Charles I tried to arrest in 1642.
3. Benares is the leading holy city of which religion?
4. How much did *Paradise Lost* earn Milton?
5. In which year did Chelsea win the Football League?
6. Who starred in *Von Ryan's Express*?
7. Which card game was 'Ambigu' the forerunner of?
8. Which minstrel was associated with Richard I?
9. What is the name of a cabbage in which the flower head remains for a long time in the bud stage, forms earlier and is larger than in an ordinary cabbage?

879

1. In computing, what is the unit of coded information?
2. Which political party took its name from Scottish cattle rustlers?
3. Where was the Barbary coast?
4. Which Ukrainian playwright said, 'I decided to collect everything evil in Russia . . . and laugh it off'?
5. Of what were golf balls originally made?
6. Who wrote *President Indicative* and *Future Indefinite*?
7. Which sea captain was hanged for piracy in 1701?
8. Which drink did Bach enjoy so much that he wrote a cantata for it?
9. What is another name for an aspidistra?

137

1. The Tories.
2. Elizabeth I.
3. The British Museum.
4. New Zealand.
5. Bury.
6. Merle Oberon.
7. Toulouse-Lautrec.
8. Charleston.
9. The garden pea.

508

1. Enveloped in pastry.
2. Pym, Hampden, Haselrig, Holles or Strode.
3. Hinduism.
4. £10.
5. 1955.
6. Frank Sinatra.
7. Poker.
8. Blondel.
9. A cauliflower.

879

1. A bit.
2. The Whigs.
3. Coast of Algeria.
4. Nicolai Gogol, in *The Government Inspector*.
5. A leather encasement around a lot of feathers.
6. Noel Coward.
7. Captain Kidd.
8. Coffee.
9. Cast-iron plant.

138

1. During which season is a criminal most likely to confess?
2. Which explorer was a servant to Kublai Khan and wrote his memoirs in a Genoese prison?
3. What does the name Tokyo mean?
4. Who wrote the novel *Northwest Passage*?
5. Which soccer team is nicknamed 'The Quakers'?
6. Who was Tarzan's girl friend?
7. How many points does a cannon score at billiards?
8. Who designed the covers for the group Yes's albums?
9. Which mathematician said, to stop a man beating a dog, 'That animal has the soul of a friend of mine, whom I recognized by his voice!'?

509

1. What does the legal phrase '*Volenti non fit injuria*' mean?
2. Which king wrote articles on farming under the name of Ralph Robinson?
3. Which European capital gives its name to a green vegetable?
4. What is cursive writing?
5. Which boxer was nicknamed the 'Brockton Blockbuster'?
6. His film, *Scorpio Rising*, is an underground cult. Who is he?
7. What is the most famous fantasy role-playing game?
8. What was the name of the blues club in Richmond made famous by the Rolling Stones?
9. What did Michael Begon, a French Superintendent of San Domingo in the seventeenth century, give his name to?

880

1. Who invented the first safety razor in 1895?
2. Which Prussian decoration was reinstated by Hitler in 1939?
3. Which county is Snowdon in?
4. Who wrote the play *The Second Mrs Tanqueray*?
5. Which Hollywood film star also captained England at cricket?
6. Who wrote the play *Romanoff and Juliet*?
7. Which writer wanted to act but became a parliamentary journalist?
8. What is an orchestral tam-tam?
9. If you had acromegaly, which parts of your body would be enlarged?

138

1. The winter.
2. Marco Polo.
3. Eastern City.
4. Kenneth Roberts.
5. Darlington.
6. Jane.
7. Two.
8. Roger Dean.
9. Pythagoras.

509

1. An injury cannot be done to a willing person.
2. George III.
3. Brussels (sprouts).
4. Writing done without lifting the pen, so the characters are joined.
5. Rocky Marciano.
6. Kenneth Anger.
7. Dungeons and Dragons.
8. The Crawdaddy.
9. Begonias.

880

1. King C. Gillette.
2. The Iron Cross.
3. Gwynedd.
4. Arthur Pinero.
5. C. Aubrey Smith.
6. Peter Ustinov.
7. Charles Dickens.
8. A large gong.
9. Hands, feet and jaw.

Q

139

1. On which part of the body are puttees worn?
2. The Romans built a wall between the Forth and the Clyde. What was it called?
3. What is the capital of the Ivory Coast?
4. Who wrote *Rebecca*?
5. If a boxer fails to make the weight at the official weigh-in, how much time does he have in which to try again before disqualification?
6. What is generally regarded as the most successful hoax on British TV?
7. Who preceded Sir John Betjeman as Poet Laureate?
8. Who was the Mad Monk?
9. What would you be lacking if you were acephalous?

510

1. What colour are survival dinghies?
2. Who was Alexander the Great's famous tutor?
3. Of which country is Alicante a seaport and a province?
4. Of which biblical region was Og king?
5. In golf, what is a putt called which falls into the hole from the far side?
6. Who starred with Michael Sarrazin in the 1974 film *For Pete's Sake*?
7. Which poet had himself drawn in his winding sheet?
8. With which group does Nick Beggs sing?
9. In which type of medicine would you find yin and yang, pulses and meridians mentioned?

881

1. What do 100 centimes make?
2. Who was the Citizen King?
3. Where is the Isle of Dogs?
4. Who is Quasimodo?
5. If you are playing golf, how long may you look for a ball before it is declared 'lost'?
6. In which state is the fictitious town of Knots Landing located?
7. Which British PM's wife rode her horse up a staircase in a house in Cavendish Street?
8. By what name is Mahler's Eighth Symphony often called?
9. How many sides has a dodecagon?

139

1. Legs.
2. The Antonine Wall.
3. Abidjan.
4. Daphne Du Maurier.
5. 1 hour.
6. The 'Panorama' report on the Swiss spaghetti harvest, 1 April 1957.
7. C. Day Lewis.
8. Thelonius Monk, jazz pianist.
9. A head.

510

1. Orange.
2. Aristotle.
3. Spain.
4. Bashan.
5. Entering by the 'tradesman's entrance'.
6. Barbra Streisand.
7. John Donne.
8. Kajagoogoo.
9. Acupuncture.

881

1. 1 franc.
2. Louis Philippe of France; he was elected, and ruled from 1830 to 1848.
3. London, Tower Hamlets.
4. The Hunchback of Notre Dame.
5. 5 minutes.
6. California.
7. Asquith's.
8. 'Symphony of a Thousand'.
9. Twelve.

140

1. What is the nautical term for 'stop'?
2. When was the George Cross instituted?
3. Which Scottish county is Aberdeen in?
4. Who, according to John Aubrey, was 'Swisser Swatter'?
5. Which great Irish soccer star once played for the Los Angeles Aztecs?
6. Who played Toulouse-Lautrec in the film *Moulin Rouge*?
7. Of whom did Whitman write, 'O the bleeding drops of red/Where on the deck my Captain lies/Fallen, cold and dead'?
8. Who composed the opera *La Gioconda*?
9. Where is your cornea?

511

1. Which saint, according to legend, nipped the Devil's nose with red-hot tongs?
2. What was Sir Henry Percy's nickname?
3. In which city was Martin Luther King assassinated?
4. Name one of the two poets who each began a poem with the line 'Come live with me and be my love'.
5. What is the width of a hockey goal?
6. Who twice won an Oscar and declined the award both times?
7. For which office was Victoria Woodhull the first woman candidate?
8. Who composed the 'Rasumovsky Quartets'?
9. Which planet is called the 'Horned Planet'?

882

1. Which mythological monster has a bull's head on a man's body?
2. How did Alexander III of Scotland die?
3. At which river's mouth does Sunderland lie?
4. Which 'harmless drudge' shared his house with the Negro Frank, blind Mrs Williams and Hodge the cat?
5. In golf, what is an ace?
6. Where is the Golden Rose television festival held annually?
7. What nationality is Thor Heyerdahl?
8. Who wrote the 'Hymn of Joy' sung in Beethoven's Choral Symphony?
9. Who designed the locomotive called *The Planet*?

140

1. Avast.
2. 1940.
3. Aberdeenshire.
4. Sir Walter Raleigh, so called in the height of passion by 'a wench he loved well'.
5. George Best.
6. José Ferrer.
7. Abraham Lincoln.
8. Ponchielli.
9. In your eye.

511

1. St Dunstan.
2. Hotspur.
3. Memphis, Tennessee.
4. Christopher Marlowe, John Donne.
5. 12 feet.
6. George C. Scott.
7. The Presidency of the USA.
8. Beethoven.
9. Venus.

882

1. The Minotaur.
2. His horse galloped over a cliff in the dark.
3. Wear.
4. Samuel Johnson.
5. A hole in one.
6. Montreux, Switzerland.
7. Norwegian.
8. Schiller.
9. Robert Stephenson.

Q

141

1. What are the ingredients of the 'Sidecar' cocktail?
2. Where was the first battle of the Wars of the Roses fought?
3. Luanda is the capital of which African country?
4. Who interrupted Coleridge in his Kubla Khan dream?
5. Where were the Olympic Games of 1900 held?
6. Who became director of the National Theatre in 1973?
7. On what subject did Uffa Fox chiefly write?
8. On which instrument is Gillian Weir a virtuoso?
9. What is the name of a star made of matter so dense that enough to go into a matchbox would weigh 10,000 million tons?

512

1. When, legally, is 'time immemorial'?
2. What was La Gironde?
3. What odd lake did Sir Walter Raleigh find in Trinidad?
4. To whom was Longfellow's Ojibway married?
5. What is the longest drive ever performed on a golf course?
6. Who directed the 1955 film *The Court Martial of Billy Mitchell*?
7. Who was Vice-President to Lyndon Johnson between 1964 and 1969, but was then beaten for the presidency by Richard Nixon?
8. What was the name of Kim Wilde's first hit single in 1981?
9. What does 1,013 millibars represent?

883

1. What is the highest rank in the RAF?
2. The Emperor Maximilian was put in power by French troops and later shot by a firing squad. Where was his Empire?
3. Where is the world's largest underground system?
4. In which Shakespearian play did the spirit Ariel appear?
5. In golf, where would you find a links course?
6. Name Jessica Tate's three children in 'Soap'.
7. Who said to a Roman soldier in Syracuse, 'Wait till I finish my problem', and was then killed by him?
8. What nationality is Sir Robert Helpmann the choreographer?
9. Why is celery considered to have 'negative' calories?

141

1. Brandy, cointreau and lemon juice.
2. St Albans, in 1455.
3. Angola.
4. A man from Porlock.
5. Paris.
6. Peter Hall.
7. Sailing.
8. The organ.
9. A black hole.

512

1. Before the reign of Richard I (1189–99).
2. A group of moderate republicans of the French Revolution.
3. A lake of asphalt.
4. Minnehaha.
5. 515 yards, by Michael Austin of Los Angeles in the US Seniors Open Championship at Las Vegas, Nevada.
6. Otto Preminger.
7. Hubert Humphrey.
8. 'Kids in America'.
9. The world's average barometric pressure.

883

1. Marshal.
2. Mexico.
3. London.
4. *The Tempest.*
5. The seaside.
6. Corrine, Eunice, Billy.
7. Archimedes.
8. Australian.
9. Because it burns up more calories than it contains.

142

1. What is Erse?
2. What was a tally?
3. Where are the Pentland Skerries?
4. About whom, traditionally, did Sir Thomas Wyatt write the poem that begins, 'They flee from me that sometime did me seek'?
5. Which Briton became world canoe slalom champion in 1977?
6. When did Radio Caroline start broadcasting?
7. Which impressionist is famous for his ballet paintings?
8. What group did Johnny Rotten form *after* the Sex Pistols?
9. *Sciuris carolinensis* was introduced into England from North America and ousted *Sciuris vulgaris*. What is it?

513

1. Which current UK coin has a diameter of 3 cm?
2. Which is the world's oldest extant treaty?
3. On which Hebridean island is the town of Tobermory?
4. Which Australian wrote the novels *Voss* and *Riders in the Chariot*?
5. What nationality is gymnast Nadia Comaneci?
6. Which Italian film star was sent to a German labour camp, escaped and spent the rest of the war hiding in a Venetian attic?
7. What colour is burnt umber?
8. Who composed the opera *A Village Romeo and Juliet*?
9. Deuterium oxide is used in atomic reactors. What is it?

884

1. The residual pulp of what is called bargasse?
2. Of which king of France was Marie Antoinette the wife?
3. In which city is Jan Smuts airport?
4. In the Bible which book precedes Leviticus?
5. Who won golf's Ryder Cup in 1969?
6. Which musical features Sky Masterson and Nathan Detroit?
7. In darts, what is the height from the floor to the centre of the bull?
8. Which Benjamin Britten opera is based on George Crabbe's poem *The Borough*?
9. Why are blackberries, raspberries and strawberries not strictly berries?

142

1. The Irish language or Irish Gaelic.
2. A length of wood scored across with notches representing details of a debt, etc., and split lengthwise. The two parties to the transaction kept one 'tally' each.
3. Pentland Firth, north of Duncansby Head.
4. Anne Boleyn.
5. Albert Kerr.
6. 1964.
7. Degas.
8. Public Image Ltd.
9. The grey squirrel.

513

1. The 50-pence piece.
2. That between England and Portugal signed in 1373.
3. Mull.
4. Patrick White.
5. Romanian.
6. Marcello Mastroianni.
7. Dark brown.
8. Delius.
9. Heavy water.

884

1. Sugar cane.
2. Louis XVI.
3. Johannesburg.
4. Exodus.
5. No one. It was a tie.
6. *Guys and Dolls*.
7. 5 feet, 8 inches.
8. *Peter Grimes*.
9. Because they have their seeds on the outside.

143

1. When pay was first introduced for MPs, how much was it?
2. How was the Roman Emperor Claudius summoned to Britain in AD 43?
3. What is the lake behind the Aswan Dam called?
4. Who created the detective Roderick Alleyn?
5. How many play in a softball team?
6. Which artist created the dream sequence for Hitchcock's film *Spellbound*?
7. In which country did chess originate?
8. Who brought 'his sisters and his cousins and his aunts' on board HMS *Pinafore*?
9. Which instrument measures birds' eggs?

514

1. Which sign of the Zodiac follows Libra?
2. Whose marriage united Spain?
3. Which is the largest island of the Inner Hebrides?
4. Whose best-known play is *The Second Mrs Tanqueray*?
5. At which cricket ground is the Radcliffe Road end?
6. Who plays the fictitious heir to the British throne in the 1976 film *Seven Nights in Japan*?
7. What was John Logie Baird's first successful invention?
8. For whom was Michael Jackson making a commercial when his hair caught fire?
9. What birds do Japanese fishermen use to help them catch fish?

885

1. What did John Paxton design for Prince Albert?
2. What was Benefit of Clergy?
3. Where are the headquarters of the World Health Organization?
4. Which playwright did Raphael Holinshed frequently provide with historical information?
5. In which sport is a contest called a shiai?
6. What form of transport was featured in the film *Grey Lady Down*?
7. Who won the first three World Indoor Bowls Championships?
8. By what name is Clementia Campbell better known?
9. What distinguishes gums from resins?

143

1. £400 per annum.
2. By a chain of beacons across Europe.
3. Lake Nasser.
4. Ngaio Marsh.
5. Nine.
6. Salvador Dali.
7. India.
8. Sir Joseph Porter.
9. An oometer.

514

1. Scorpio.
2. Isabella of Castile to Ferdinand of Aragon, in 1469.
3. Skye.
4. Arthur Wing Pinero's.
5. Trent Bridge.
6. Michael York.
7. Socks to prevent sweaty feet.
8. Pepsi-Cola.
9. Cormorants.

885

1. The Crystal Palace.
2. The right of 'criminous clerks' to be tried and punished by Church courts, established by the Constitution of Clarendon, 1164.
3. Geneva.
4. Shakespeare.
5. Judo.
6. Submarine.
7. David Bryant.
8. Cleo Laine.
9. Gums dissolve in water, resins do not.

144

1. After how many years of marriage is a crystal anniversary celebrated?
2. Which former prime minister died in the House of Lords within hours of pleading the American colonists' cause?
3. Of which African state is Freetown the capital?
4. Name two famous authors of *Fables*.
5. In which city is the Lansdowne Road rugby ground?
6. In which 1932 film does Marlene Dietrich play the prostitute Shanghai Lil?
7. Who introduced the willow-pattern plate?
8. Who claimed in 1962 that 'Big Girls Don't Cry'?
9. Which organ of the body might suffer from pericarditis?

515

1. In 1921 in the USA John Larsen constructed the first of which controversial instrument?
2. Name two stuttering monarchs.
3. Which London borough's pre-STD prefix was 'ROYal'?
4. Who was Hiawatha's father?
5. In how many consecutive world cups did Uwe Seeler play?
6. Who created the TV series 'It Takes a Worried Man'?
7. Who said, 'He who knows Nature, knows God'?
8. What school of architecture was founded in 1919 in Weimar and is now used by a modern rock group as a name?
9. What are the so-called 'white ants'?

886

1. What lies under the Arc de Triomphe de l'Étoile?
2. In which decade did Derby and Guildford become Anglican dioceses?
3. When was the Panama Canal opened?
4. Which one-time cowboy had the book of his sexual conquests banned?
5. What attaches ski-boots to skis?
6. Who created the TV comedy series 'Shelley'?
7. The French chemist Michel Eugène Chevreul is said to be the only first-class scientist who lived for how long?
8. The Stranglers named a record album after which species of rat?
9. Pneumonia is a disease of what?

144

1. Fifteen.
2. William Pitt, Earl of Chatham.
3. Sierra Leone.
4. Aesop, La Fontaine and Dryden.
5. Dublin.
6. *Shanghai Express.*
7. William Turner, *c.* 1780.
8. The Four Seasons.
9. The heart.

515

1. A lie-detector (polygraph).
2. William II, Charles I and George VI.
3. Tower Hamlets.
4. The West Wind (Mudjekeewis).
5. Four.
6. Peter Tinniswood.
7. Spinoza.
8. Bauhaus.
9. Termites.

886

1. The tomb of the French Unknown Warrior.
2. 1920s (1927).
3. 1914.
4. Frank Harris (*My Life and Loves*).
5. Bindings.
6. Peter Tinniswood.
7. Longer than 100 years: he died aged 103.
8. *Rattus norvegicus.*
9. The lungs.

145

1. In America what does a realtor sell?
2. Who did Wynkyn de Worde assist, then succeed?
3. Which city is at the mouth of the Loire?
4. Which play is generally accepted to be Shakespeare's last?
5. With what kind of ball was table tennis played before the current celluloid ball was introduced?
6. Who stars as the ex-detective in the 1949 film *A Dangerous Profession*?
7. What is marquetry?
8. What was Lulu's first hit?
9. What is a Charollais?

516

1. Die/dice, man/men are examples of irregular plurals in English. Just how many of them are there?
2. What was the 'King's Evil'?
3. What was called Rapa-nui by its inhabitants?
4. What does Shakespeare mean by a 'cockney'?
5. Where would you originally have found a penthouse?
6. Who starred as the politician in the 1953 film *A Lion is in the Street*?
7. What relation was Josiah Wedgwood to Charles Darwin?
8. Who composed the 'Fantasia' on a theme of Thomas Tallis?
9. What name is more commonly used for the disease variola?

887

1. Which is the next highest prime number after 23?
2. Who were the original EEC Six?
3. What is the capital of Yugoslavia?
4. Who, dying, said, 'Light, more light'?
5. At the 1976 Olympics who won the super-heavyweight class in weightlifting?
6. Who for one night only played the dead prince opposite Sarah Bernhardt in *Fedora* in Paris?
7. When did Mao Tse-tung die?
8. Bernie Taupin co-wrote songs with which rock singer in the earlier part of his career?
9. Trachoma is an infection of what?

145

1. Property, real estate.
2. The printer, William Caxton.
3. Nantes.
4. *The Tempest.*
5. Cork.
6. George Raft.
7. A design or picture consisting of a variety of wood veneers.
8. 'Shout'.
9. A breed of cattle.

516

1. Thirteen.
2. Scrofula (the practice of rulers touching to cure this disease was stopped by George I).
3. Easter Island.
4. An effeminate or foppish fellow (*Twelfth Night* and *King Lear*).
5. In a real-tennis court.
6. James Cagney.
7. Grandfather.
8. Ralph Vaughan Williams.
9. Smallpox.

887

1. 29.
2. Belgium, France, West Germany, Italy, Luxemburg, Netherlands.
3. Belgrade.
4. Goethe.
5. Vassily Alexeyev (USSR).
6. The Prince of Wales, the future Edward VII.
7. 1976.
8. Elton John.
9. The eye.

146

1. What did Otto Titzling invent?
2. Who was president of the Soviet Union from 1958 to 1964?
3. In which county is Leeds Castle?
4. Who wrote the play *An Inspector Calls*?
5. How many professional fights had Leon Spinks fought before winning the World Championship from Muhammad Ali?
6. Which character did Philip Wylie's 1930 science-fiction novel *Gladiator* inspire Jerry Siegel and Joe Shuster to create?
7. Who founded the DeBeers Mining Company?
8. Who was portrayed in the films *A Song to Remember* and *Song Without End*?
9. What is 100° Centigrade on the Fahrenheit scale?

517

1. Soho is a district of London. What else was it?
2. Name Germany's largest battleship in the Second World War.
3. Which state in the USA is known as the 'Yellowhammer State'?
4. Which novel by Jane Austen was originally called *Susan*?
5. What was Victor Barna's game?
6. Who played Major Donald Craig in the 1967 film *Tobruk*?
7. In which game is a whangdoodle a special pot?
8. Who is the present (1984) Master of the Queen's Music?
9. What was the original name for the butterfly?

888

1. Beside Isaac Newton's, whose picture appears on £1 notes?
2. When was D-Day?
3. Name Ireland's national airline.
4. Who is Don Vito Corleone?
5. Which is considered to be the fastest and most dangerous ball game in the world?
6. Whose car-radio call-sign is 7234?
7. Who originated the saying, 'Anyone seeing a psychiatrist should have his head examined'?
8. Who wrote 'This Land is Your Land'?
9. About how many species of bed-bug are there?

146

1. The bra.
2. Nikita Khrushchev.
3. Kent.
4. J. B. Priestley.
5. Seven.
6. Superman.
7. Cecil Rhodes.
8. Frédéric Chopin.
9. 212°.

517

1. An old hunting cry.
2. The *Bismarck*.
3. Alabama.
4. *Northanger Abbey*.
5. Table tennis.
6. Rock Hudson.
7. Poker.
8. Malcolm Williamson.
9. The flutterby.

888

1. The Queen's.
2. 6 June 1944.
3. Aer Lingus.
4. The Godfather, in the book of that name.
5. Jai alai (pelota).
6. Theo Kojak's.
7. Film producer Samuel Goldwyn.
8. Woody Guthrie.
9. Seventy-five.

147

1. Who are the publishers of this tome?
2. How many centuries before Columbus did the Vikings discover America?
3. Where was the Crystal Palace originally located?
4. Who had a favourite concubine called Abra?
5. Since the modern Olympics began, which country has won the most gold medals?
6. What is Diane Prince's other identity?
7. Which card game's name means 'discarded'?
8. Which North American city is considered to be the birthplace of jazz?
9. What did Georges Claude invent in 1911?

518

1. Who was the first graduate of the Royal Family?
2. Who was the inventor of the folding bed and the swivel chair?
3. On which day of the week are general elections always held in Russia?
4. According to Shakespeare, which quality is not strain'd?
5. What do the five Olympic rings represent?
6. For which 1965 film is *Or How I Flew from London to Paris in 25 Hours and 11 Minutes* the alternative title?
7. Where can the Venus de Milo be seen?
8. What was Count Basie's first name?
9. As dogs are canine, what are bears?

889

1. What is the international radio-telephonic distress signal used by aircraft and ships?
2. In which century were turnips first grown in England?
3. In which French city is Montmartre?
4. With which Lake District house is Jemima Puddleduck particularly associated?
5. In which month is the Le Mans 24-hour race held?
6. Who is half-Vulcan, half-human?
7. Whom did Fidel Castro overthrow?
8. To whom did Mendelssohn dedicate his third symphony, the Scottish?
9. What is a young hare called?

147

1. Penguin.
2. About four.
3. Hyde Park.
4. Solomon.
5. The USA.
6. Wonder Woman.
7. Écarté.
8. New Orleans.
9. Neon lights.

518

1. Prince Charles.
2. Thomas Jefferson, third President of the USA.
3. Sunday.
4. Mercy. 'The quality of mercy is not strain'd.'
5. The five continents.
6. *Those Magnificent Men in Their Flying Machines.*
7. The Louvre, Paris.
8. William.
9. Ursine.

889

1. Mayday.
2. Seventeenth.
3. Paris.
4. Hilltop Farm.
5. June.
6. Mr Spock.
7. Fulgencio Batista.
8. Queen Victoria.
9. A leveret.

148

1. What is stramonium?
2. What was Vasco da Gama the first to do?
3. What is the name of the Welsh nationalist party?
4. In which work did Lear and Cymbeline first appear?
5. In the 1968 Olympics Kip Keino won the gold medal in which event?
6. By what name was Arthur Jefferson better known?
7. Which famous coffee-drinker loved and married a Polish countess?
8. With whom did Jeanette MacDonald make a series of film musicals?
9. The poet Adam Lindsay Gordon is said to have started a myth about Australian birds. What is it?

519

1. What have a diesel, a boycott and a mackintosh in common?
2. Which is the oldest ruling family in the world?
3. Which is the largest island of the West Indies?
4. What, traditionally, was the name of the Roman who pierced Christ's side at the crucifixion?
5. In which Dutch city is Feijenoord Football Club based?
6. Who made the Dylan documentary, *Don't Look Back*?
7. Which keen angler wrote lives of Donne, Herbert, Sir Henry Wotton, Hooker and other friends?
8. Which rock band took their name from a Herman Hesse novel?
9. How many moons has the planet Mars?

890

1. Of what are Brussels, Wilton and Axminster types?
2. Who was the last king of England crowned in Paris?
3. Name the one European state without a single railway line.
4. There are in fact thirty-one pilgrims in *The Canterbury Tales.* How many does the Prologue claim there are?
5. Which sport uses the terms kitty, draw, tuck-in and firer?
6. Who was shot in Ford's Theater, Washington, DC, while watching *Our American Cousin*?
7. Whose artwork was often seen on the cover of the *Saturday Evening Post*?
8. Who took a ferry across the Mersey?
9. What are the destructive 'leather-jackets'?

148

1. The thorn-apple, or a drug obtained from it.
2. Round the Cape of Good Hope and continue to India.
3. Plaid Cymru.
4. Geoffrey of Monmouth's *Historia.*
5. 1,500 metres.
6. Stan Laurel.
7. Honoré de Balzac.
8. Nelson Eddy.
9. That they sing.

519

1. They are all eponymons (words taken from the names of people).
2. That of the Emperor Hirohito of Japan: he is 124th in line.
3. Cuba.
4. Longinus (or Longius).
5. Rotterdam.
6. D. A. Pennebaker.
7. Izaak Walton.
8. Steppenwolff.
9. Two.

890

1. Carpet.
2. Henry VI (1431).
3. San Marino.
4. Twenty-nine.
5. Bowls.
6. Abraham Lincoln.
7. Norman Rockwell's.
8. Gerry and the Pacemakers.
9. The grubs of the crane fly.

149

1. What grade of seaman comes between ordinary and leading seaman?
2. Which six were sentenced to transportation and pardoned two years later?
3. Which is the 'Cotton State'?
4. Who was the Greek goddess of chastity?
5. Who won the 1978 Wightman Cup for tennis?
6. Which great actor–manager lived from 1838 to 1905?
7. The composition of gunpowder was first written down (in code) by whom?
8. Which tune is called in German *Koteletten Walze*?
9. In what is a herpetologist interested?

520

1. Who was King Arthur's father?
2. Which king led the English at the Battle of Agincourt?
3. Lord Byron called it 'The Monarch of the Mountains'. What is it?
4. Whose private secretary was Nikki Porter?
5. If a hole in golf was 251 yards long, what par would it be?
6. Who was known to her fans as 'Our Gracie'?
7. In the game Hearts which card is the Black Lady?
8. What was Thin Lizzy's first hit?
9. Where in your body would you find your adenoids?

891

1. Where would you find a ram chasing a bull?
2. What have ginger, pepper, sugar and carpets in common?
3. In which American city is Harlem?
4. What relation is Sohrab to Rustum in Matthew Arnold's poem?
5. Which British woman was the beaten finalist in the 1956 and 1957 World Table Tennis Championships?
6. What song did Marilyn Monroe sing in the otherwise unmusical *Bus Stop*?
7. In what medium did Turner generally work?
8. Who was Lord High Everything Else?
9. From which general grouping of trees do soft woods come?

149

1. Able-bodied seaman.
2. The Tolpuddle Martyrs.
3. Alabama.
4. Artemis.
5. Great Britain.
6. Sir Henry Irving.
7. Roger Bacon.
8. Chopsticks.
9. Reptiles.

520

1. Uther Pendragon.
2. Henry V.
3. Mont Blanc.
4. Ellery Queen's.
5. Four.
6. Gracie Fields.
7. The Queen of Spades.
8. 'Whiskey in the Jar' (1973).
9. At the back of the nose and throat.

891

1. In the Zodiac.
2. These along with many other commodities were brought back after the Crusades.
3. New York.
4. Son.
5. Ann Haydon Jones.
6. 'That Old Black Magic'.
7. Water-colour.
8. Pooh Bah in *The Mikado*.
9. Conifers.

150

1. To which god did Valhalla belong?
2. Who were the Old Contemptibles?
3. After what is Fleet Street in London named?
4. Whose eighteenth-century translation of Homer was long accepted as the standard version?
5. Who refereed the 1896 world heavyweight fight between Tom Sharkey and Bob Fitzsimmons and pulled a gun during it?
6. In which Florida city does *Flamingo Road* take place?
7. Which Creole from Martinique became an empress?
8. Which composer was financed by Nadezda von Meck, a rich widow?
9. Turning an ordinary number into a power of 10 creates what?

521

1. From what did Florence Maybrick get the arsenic to poison her husband?
2. What happened in London on 'Evil May Day' 1517?
3. Where was Hitler's mountain hideout?
4. Whose first novel was *Desperate Remedies*?
5. How many individual gold medals did gymnast Boris Shaklin win at the 1960 Olympics?
6. Who wrote *Rookery Nook* and many other of the 'Aldwych Farces' in the 1920s?
7. Who invented the diesel engine?
8. Who composed *The Pearl Fishers*?
9. After which dog is a group of British moths named?

892

1. How frequently does a Hebdomadal Council meet?
2. Which battle, fought on 11 August 993, was commemorated in the Anglo-Saxon Chronicle in verse?
3. Which London tube line is usually red on maps?
4. Who created the sporting grocer Jorrocks?
5. Who was European Footballer of the Year in 1964?
6. In which play of 1608 did Webster dramatize the story of the Italian murderess Vittoria Corombona?
7. Whose work did Hans van Meegeren most fake?
8. For which film musical did Julie Andrews win an Oscar for best actress?
9. What does a viticulturist grow?

150

1. Odin (or Woden).
2. Members of the British Expeditionary Force under Sir John French in 1914.
3. The Fleet river.
4. Alexander Pope's.
5. Wyatt Earp.
6. Truro.
7. Napoleon's Josephine.
8. Tchaikovsky.
9. A logarithm.

521

1. Fly papers.
2. Apprentices rioted.
3. Berchtesgaden.
4. Thomas Hardy.
5. Four.
6. Ben Travers.
7. Rudolf Diesel.
8. Bizet.
9. Pug.

892

1. Weekly.
2. Battle of Maldon.
3. Central.
4. R. S. Surtees.
5. Denis Law.
6. *The White Devil.*
7. Vermeer.
8. *Mary Poppins.*
9. Grapevines.

151

1. What does *semper fidelis* mean?
2. In which year was the Berlin Wall erected?
3. Which Brazilian city is the centre of the coffee trade?
4. Whose first novel was *The Time Machine*?
5. How many rowing gold medals has John B. Kelly, Princess Grace of Monaco's father, won in the Olympics?
6. Who was driving a Porsche Spyder when he was killed on 30 September 1955?
7. At which card game did General Eisenhower and Ian McLeod excel?
8. What is a fandango?
9. To which fish family does the sprat belong?

522

1. Who was Pollux's twin brother?
2. Name the Spanish inquisitor said to have been responsible for the burning of 10,000 people.
3. In which country is the fishing port of Stavanger?
4. What work did the Seven Dwarfs do?
5. How many players are on court for one team in basketball?
6. Who does Humphrey Bogart play in *Casablanca*?
7. Whose husband was Nicky Arustein?
8. What is Bing Crosby's real first name?
9. What colour is chlorophyll?

893

1. Approximately how many right-handed people are there to each left-handed person?
2. What group did John Lilburne lead or inspire in the seventeenth century?
3. Which is Greece's second city?
4. What was Paul the apostle's real name?
5. Which club did Pelé join in 1975?
6. Who used to say that she was worried about Jim?
7. Where was V. S. Naipaul born?
8. How many strings does a cello have?
9. Which is the only type of duck found in Britain where the male and female both have the same colouring?

151

1. Always faithful.
2. 1961.
3. São Paulo.
4. H. G. Wells.
5. Three.
6. James Dean.
7. Bridge.
8. A Spanish dance.
9. Herring.

522

1. Castor.
2. Torquemada.
3. Norway.
4. Mining.
5. Five.
6. Rick Blaine.
7. Comedienne Fanny Brice's.
8. Harry.
9. Green.

893

1. Five.
2. The Levellers.
3. Salonika.
4. Saul.
5. New York Cosmos.
6. Mrs Dale in her diary.
7. Trinidad.
8. Four.
9. Shelduck.

152

1. What is a shoemaker's model of the human foot called?
2. Which British general helped to abolish slavery in China and the Sudan?
3. Where is the Eucumbene Dam?
4. Who was the first king of Israel?
5. In 1976, a Russian woman 7 feet 2 inches tall won a gold medal for what?
6. When is Superman's birthday?
7. Domenikos Theotocopoulos was born in Crete; when he died in Spain 73 years later, by what name was he known?
8. Who composed 'A Foggy Day in London Town'?
9. Richard Speck, who murdered eight nurses in Chicago, had an unusual defence. What was it?

523

1. Name the mark placed under the letter 'c' to indicate an 's' pronunciation in French.
2. For how long did Edward VIII reign?
3. How far is Dover from Calais?
4. Where was Goliath born?
5. After which famous Welshman was a Derby winner named?
6. Who portrayed Tony Rome in films?
7. What title did the poet Byron inherit?
8. Which of Elgar's Enigma Variations represents A. J. Jaeger?
9. Who ate the first hamburger in space?

894

1. Name three of the five permanent members of the United Nations Security Council.
2. Who ordered the execution of Mary, Queen of Scots?
3. Of which county is Portland Bill the southernmost tip?
4. Who wrote *Wuthering Heights*?
5. What is the diameter of a basketball ring?
6. Name the father and son who both won Oscars in the 1948 film *The Treasure of Sierra Madre*.
7. What is missing from this artist's name? Francisco José de . . . y Lucientes.
8. Who had a hit with 'Where a Child is Born'?
9. Being inside what geometrical pattern gives protection from demons?

152

1. A last.
2. General Charles Gordon.
3. New South Wales, Australia.
4. King Saul.
5. Women's basketball.
6. 29 February.
7. El Greco.
8. George Gershwin.
9. He claimed that he had an extra chromosome. In fact he hadn't, it later transpired.

523

1. Cedilla.
2. 325 days.
3. 22 miles.
4. Gath.
5. Owen Tudor.
6. Frank Sinatra.
7. Baron Byron of Rochdale.
8. Nimrod.
9. John Young in *Gemini 3*, in 1968.

894

1. Britain, China, France, USA, USSR.
2. Queen Elizabeth I.
3. Dorset.
4. Emily Brontë.
5. 18 inches.
6. John and Walter Huston.
7. Goya.
8. Johnny Mathis.
9. A pentagram or pentacle.

153

1. What is a cassoulet?
2. Who said, 'Ave, Imperator, morituri te salutant (Hail, Emperor, those about to die salute you)'?
3. Which countries regularly eat more beef per head of the population than the British? France, Belgium, Luxemburg, Italy or West Germany?
4. Who wrote *Thus Spake Zarathustra*?
5. What game does a tip-off start?
6. Who was the Vamp?
7. How tall was Queen Victoria?
8. How many movements does a concerto usually have?
9. What is the part of a fraction written below the numerator?

524

1. What colour is a cardinal's hat?
2. Clement C. Wragge began this christening custom in Australia between 1887 and 1902. What was it?
3. Near Ayers Rock there's a lake named after which composer?
4. Which Dickens character named a device for keeping off the rain?
5. Which sport features an Eskimo roll?
6. Paul Newman wore a knee-length toga in his screen début. What was the name of the film?
7. Who won the World Professional Snooker Championship in 1981?
8. Who was the lead singer in Wizzard?
9. The shape of a drop of water is due to what effect?

895

1. Bourbon whiskey is aged in new oak casks, the insides of which have been treated with what?
2. Who were the Decembrists?
3. Where is the Kremasta Dam?
4. Of whom did Hazlitt say, 'He talked on for ever; and you wished him to talk on for ever'?
5. Which country won Rugby Union's Grand Slam in 1977?
6. Which film producer said, 'I'll give you a definite maybe'?
7. Who said (as his epitaph), 'On the whole, I'd rather be in Philadelphia'?
8. What was the Sex Pistols' first single?
9. What is another name for Chinese gooseberries?

153

1. A French stew of beans, goose, mutton and other ingredients.
2. Gladiators and combatants in the Roman games.
3. They all do.
4. Nietzsche.
5. Basketball.
6. Theda Bara.
7. 5 feet.
8. Three.
9. The denominator.

524

1. Red.
2. Naming hurricanes.
3. Mozart (Lake Amadeus).
4. Mrs Gamp in *Martin Chuzzlewit.*
5. Canoeing.
6. *The Silver Chalice.*
7. Steve Davis.
8. Roy Wood.
9. Surface tension.

895

1. Fire (the insides are charred).
2. Russian army conspirators who tried to overthrow Nicholas I in December 1825.
3. Greece.
4. Coleridge.
5. France.
6. Sam Goldwyn.
7. W.C. Fields.
8. 'Anarchy in the UK'.
9. Kiwi fruits.

154

1. In radio communications, all letters of the alphabet have names. What is the name for 'S'?
2. How old was Alexander the Great's horse Bucephalus when he died?
3. What is Lac Léman?
4. Of what was the book *All The President's Men* an account?
5. Which football team plays at home at the Gay Meadow ground?
6. Which stage-musical star later played Mrs Dale on the radio?
7. Which American Confederate general was 'too much a gentleman for the ungentle business of war'?
8. Who composed the symphonic poem *Egdon Heath*?
9. Helm, purga and pampero are all types of what?

525

1. What is the Administration of the Roman Catholic Church called?
2. Who was a minister under the Republic, the Empire, and Louis XVIII?
3. On which continent is Queen Maud Land?
4. Complete Sir Henry Wotton's definition of an ambassador: 'An honest man sent to . . . abroad for the good of his country'.
5. Which country won the ladies' hockey gold medal at the Moscow Olympics?
6. Who starred in *Rancho Notorious*?
7. In sailing, what would you be doing if you were 'beating'?
8. What is Segovia's instrument?
9. What transport is needed to reach the Sea of Tranquillity?

896

1. Who were Clotho, Lachesis and Atropos?
2. What was the world's population at the time of Christ?
3. Which was the first country with women MPs?
4. What happens to the Green Knight after Sir Gawain cuts off his head at their first meeting?
5. Which country won the first World Cup for men's hockey?
6. Who played Princess Leia Organa in *Star Wars*?
7. What happened to Admiral Villeneuve after Trafalgar?
8. 'World Without Love' was a Beatles song. Who recorded it?
9. What is it called when a substance goes from solid to vapour without becoming liquid?

154

1. Sierra.
2. Thirty.
3. Lake Geneva.
4. The Watergate scandal.
5. Shrewsbury Town.
6. Jessie Matthews.
7. Robert E. Lee.
8. Gustav Holst.
9. Cold winds.

525

1. The Curia.
2. Talleyrand.
3. Antarctica.
4. 'Lie'.
5. Zimbabwe – its first ever gold medal.
6. Marlene Dietrich.
7. Sailing into the wind.
8. The guitar.
9. A spaceship: it's on the moon.

896

1. The Greek Fates.
2. An estimated 250 million.
3. Finland, with nineteen in March 1907.
4. He picks it up and rides away, reminding him of their meeting in a year's time.
5. Pakistan (1971).
6. Carrie Fisher.
7. He was captured, remained a prisoner till April 1806, was repatriated and stabbed himself to death.
8. Peter and Gordon.
9. Sublimation.

155

1. The flight recorder in aeroplanes goes by the name of which greedy king?
2. Who is responsible for the fact that there are almost no Crown Jewels predating Charles II?
3. Where was the Flaminian Way?
4. Of what quarterly was Aubrey Beardsley art editor?
5. Between 1928 and 1968, to which two countries did the Olympic men's hockey gold medal invariably go?
6. What was Hayley Mills's first film?
7. Formerly Lisa Halaby of Washington, DC, who is she now?
8. Who is the lead singer in the Pretenders?
9. For which insect is 'shiner' army slang?

526

1. In 1969 the Nobel Prize categories were expanded to include what?
2. In 1941 Germany had an ally in attacking Russia. Who?
3. Which lies furthest south: Casablanca, Houston, Tenerife or Miami?
4. Whose final words are 'The rest is silence'?
5. For what age horse is the Derby run?
6. Who plays Pam Ewing in 'Dallas'?
7. Who was famous for his series of water-lily paintings?
8. Which Shakespearian-based opera did Verdi always mean to write, but never quite get round to?
9. Who measured the strength of electricity used in his experiments by shocking himself?

897

1. In today's money, about how much would the original *Mayflower* expedition to the Americas cost?
2. Until when were mules part of the British army?
3. Where is the largest bell in the world situated?
4. Who said, 'Money is like a sixth sense and you can't make use of the other five without it'?
5. Name the Grand National course.
6. Where was Bob Hope born?
7. In 1974, Anders Svedlund of Sweden first rowed across which ocean?
8. How many symphonies did Haydn compose?
9. Where is your occiput?

155

1. Midas.
2. Charles I got his Queen Henrietta Maria to pawn them and buy military supplies on the Continent after the outbreak of the Civil War.
3. From Rome to Rimini.
4. *The Yellow Book.*
5. India and Pakistan.
6. *Tiger Bay.*
7. Queen Nor of Jordan.
8. Chrissie Hynde.
9. The cockroach.

526

1. Economics.
2. Finland.
3. Miami.
4. Hamlet's.
5. 3-year-olds.
6. Victoria Principal.
7. Claude Monet.
8. *King Lear.*
9. Henry Cavendish.

897

1. £18 million.
2. 1975.
3. The Kremlin.
4. W. Somerset Maugham.
5. Aintree.
6. London (Eltham).
7. The Pacific, in 118 days.
8. 104 (generally accepted).
9. At the back of your head.

156

1. What is the difference between lamb and mutton?
2. Who was introduced by his father as 'the last king of England'?
3. With which gulf does the Red Sea connect at its southern end?
4. Who were Adramelech, Ariel, Arioch and Asmadai?
5. How did the steeplechase originate?
6. Who was the 'King of Hollywood'?
7. As what did Herbert Austin work before he began to make cars?
8. Hoyt Axton's mother, Mae Boren Axton, wrote a song for Elvis. Name it.
9. Who designed the famous light plane, the D.H. Moth?

527

1. By what name is the International Criminal Police Organization generally known?
2. Who took part with the Earp brothers in the OK Corral shoot-out?
3. On the site of which prison does the Old Bailey stand?
4. What was Hamlet's father's name?
5. Why, in 1967, was Muhammad Ali stripped of his world heavyweight title and barred from professional boxing?
6. Which actress created a sensation by appearing nude in *Extase*?
7. Who was the first woman to fly across the Atlantic solo?
8. Who wrote 'The Star-spangled Banner'?
9. At what age does a baby first shed tears?

898

1. Soto and Rinzai are the two main branches of which religion?
2. Who commanded the English Fleet against the Spanish Armada in 1588?
3. At what age can you marry in France?
4. Who wrote the play *Widowers' Houses*?
5. In 1969, which players took part in the longest singles match ever played at Wimbledon?
6. Who is associated with the catch phrase, 'Can you hear me, mother?'?
7. Byron made one speech in the House of Lords: what was its subject?
8. Complete the song title: 'Je t'aime . . .'
9. If a flea were a man, how far could it jump?

156

1. Lamb refers to sheep less than twelve months old.
2. George V.
3. The Gulf of Aden.
4. Rebel angels in Milton's *Paradise Lost.*
5. It was originally a cross-country race towards a church steeple.
6. Clark Gable.
7. As an employee of Wolseley Sheep Shearing Machine Co. of Birmingham.
8. 'Heartbreak Hotel'.
9. Geoffrey de Havilland.

527

1. Interpol.
2. 'Doc' Holliday.
3. Newgate.
4. Hamlet.
5. Because he refused to be drafted into the US army.
6. Hedy Lamarr, then known as Hedy Kieslerova.
7. Amelia Ehrhart.
8. Francis Scott Key.
9. Not till about three months – earlier crying is tearless.

898

1. Zen Buddhism.
2. Admiral Charles Howard – *not* Drake.
3. Fifteen.
4. G. B. Shaw.
5. Pancho Gonzales beat Charlie Pasarell 22–24, 1–6, 16–14, 6–3, 11–9 in over 5 hours.
6. Sandy Powell.
7. Against the death penalty for Nottingham machine-breakers.
8. 'Moi non plus'.
9. 400 yards.

157

1. If you were born on 30 January what is your star sign?
2. Which war was fought over the loss of a part of a captain's anatomy?
3. What is the Italian name for Florence?
4. Which school does Charlie Brown attend?
5. What was Pigalle Wonder?
6. In which hotel was the play and film *Separate Tables* set?
7. What would you call someone who races pigeons?
8. What does animato mean?
9. How long does it take a healthy heart to pump a gallon of blood if a normal person is running for a bus?

528

1. What had E.E.Cummings, Walt Disney, Ernest Hemingway and Somerset Maugham in common with regard to war?
2. Who fought whom at Burford in 1649?
3. What is Great Smoo?
4. What relation was Lot to the mothers of his sons Moab and Ben-ammi?
5. What is the length of a hockey pitch?
6. Who recreated Elsa Lanchester's role in *Young Frankenstein*?
7. Who is the first European author said to have used a typewriter?
8. Which can play the lowest note: the tuba, the double bass, the double bassoon or the pianoforte?
9. About how many acres is a hectare?

899

1. What were known derisively in Victorian times as 'little bags of mystery'?
2. Which two Roman emperors were cousins and both born in Seville?
3. What is the capital of Guernsey?
4. Who is Molière's *L'Avare*?
5. What is Tessa Sanderson's main event?
6. Who played the scarecrow in *The Wizard of Oz*?
7. Of what was Charles Kingsley a Cambridge professor?
8. Who wrote the Crystals' smash hit 'He's a Rebel'?
9. The Archimedean Screw is mechanically limited to raise water to a maximum of how many feet?

157

1. Aquarius.
2. Jenkins's Ear War (1739).
3. Firenze.
4. Birchwood.
5. A greyhound.
6. Beauregard Hotel.
7. Pigeon fancier.
8. Lively.
9. 5 seconds.

528

1. They were all ambulance drivers in the First World War.
2. Forces under Cromwell defeated Levellers under Captain Thompson.
3. Scotland's largest cave.
4. Father.
5. 100 yards.
6. Madeline Kahn.
7. Leo Tolstoy.
8. Pianoforte.
9. About $2\frac{1}{2}$ acres.

899

1. Sausages.
2. Trajan and Hadrian.
3. St Peter Port.
4. Harpagon.
5. Javelin.
6. Ray Bolger.
7. Modern history.
8. Gene Pitney.
9. Three.

158

1. Which common sign was taken from the coat of arms of the Medici family?
2. Why did George I find it difficult to understand his subjects?
3. What is the capital of Belgium?
4. Name Dr Jekyll's butler.
5. What is the full title of Brighton FC?
6. Who was the first film star depicted on a postage stamp?
7. Which naturalist who created Slimbridge Wildfowl Trust is also noted for his wildlife art?
8. What is Antal Dorati's profession?
9. What did Sir David Brewster invent in 1816?

529

1. Whose private collection formed the foundation of the British Museum?
2. During which war were British troops first issued with hand grenades?
3. The old county of Radnor is represented in which new county?
4. Who captained Jules Verne's submarine *Nautilus*?
5. Who rode Woodcock to victory in the Newmarket Plate in 1671 and 1674?
6. In which film did Frank Sinatra play a drug addict?
7. At which game was William Steinitz world champion for 28 years?
8. Which Bach was known as the 'London' Bach?
9. Which chemical elements are found in all proteins?

900

1. What do you mix with sugar to make meringues?
2. Which king plunged his feet into the bowels of a dead stag to give himself strength?
3. What is Pinot Noir?
4. What were homilies?
5. What term is used to start an ice-hockey game?
6. Who sat opposite David Niven in *Separate Tables*?
7. The evil Blofeld in the James Bond stories used to hold audience with a cat on his knee. Which famous English statesman used to do likewise?
8. What pseudonym did Brian Jones use, early in his career?
9. In the study of sound what are 'woofs'?

158

1. The pawnbroker's sign – three golden balls.
2. He couldn't speak English.
3. Brussels.
4. Poole.
5. Brighton and Hove Albion Football Club.
6. Grace Kelly.
7. Sir Peter Scott.
8. Orchestral conductor.
9. The kaleidoscope.

529

1. Sir Hans Sloane.
2. The First World War.
3. Powys.
4. Captain Nemo.
5. King Charles II.
6. *Man With the Golden Arm.*
7. Chess.
8. Johann Christian Bach.
9. Nitrogen, oxygen, hydrogen and carbon.

900

1. Egg whites.
2. James I.
3. The world's best wine grape, from the Côte d'Or (Burgundy).
4. Sermons written for Elizabethan clergymen to read out in church.
5. Face-off.
6. Deborah Kerr.
7. Cardinal Wolsey.
8. Elmo Lewis.
9. Sounds below twenty cycles per second.

159

1. In nautical terms, what is 'whipping'?
2. When was the Victoria Cross instituted?
3. Which was the first town in England to have electric street lighting?
4. What is the Seventh Commandment?
5. Liverpool plays at Anfield, but who plays at Annfield?
6. Who is the most famous of the spaghetti western directors?
7. Who said of William Pitt, 'This is not a chip off the old block, it is the old block itself'?
8. What were 'sweeter than wine', according to the Beatles?
9. What is the circulation of winds around a central area of low pressure called?

530

1. Which is the smallest whole number which produces a total of over 200 when multiplied by itself?
2. The World War II German invasion of Russia was codenamed what?
3. Which is the westernmost region of France?
4. Name two of Arnold Bennett's fictitious five towns.
5. Who was women's British Open squash champion for 16 consecutive years?
6. Who supplied Mr Magoo's voice?
7. Some say he was born at Dumbarton, some at Boulogne, some in South Wales (*c.* 385). He became a patron saint. Who and of where?
8. Name any two of the Thompson Twins.
9. Which insect is called the 'Croton bug' in New York?

901

1. Which part of a vessel carries the ship's compass?
2. The only disastrous avalanche in Britain happened in 1836. Where?
3. In the gatehouse of which English castle is there a collection of ornamental dogcollars?
4. What is the title of Shaw's play about Napoleon?
5. Which sport takes place in a velodrome?
6. Which expensive TV series was made from an Irwin Shaw novel?
7. Whose painting of a Roman dictator for a Mantuan duke was later transferred to an English royal palace?
8. Which university gave Bob Dylan an honorary doctorate?
9. In geological terms, what are P and S waves?

159

1. Binding the ends of ropes to prevent them unravelling.
2. 1856.
3. Godalming.
4. Thou shalt not commit adultery.
5. Stirling Albion.
6. Sergio Leone.
7. Edmund Burke.
8. Kisses.
9. A cyclone.

530

1. 15.
2. Barbarossa.
3. Finistère.
4. Turnhill, Bursley, Hanbridge, Knype and Longshaw.
5. Heather Mackay.
6. Jim Backus.
7. St Patrick of Ireland.
8. Tom Bailey, Alannah Currie, Joe Leeway.
9. The cockroach.

901

1. Binnacle.
2. Lewes, Sussex.
3. Leeds Castle.
4. *The Man of Destiny*.
5. Cycling.
6. *Rich Man, Poor Man*.
7. Mantegna, whose 'Triumph of Caesar' hangs in Hampton Court.
8. Princeton.
9. Seismic waves.

160

1. Which stately home had the first bathroom with hot and cold running water?
2. Who speaks Quechua?
3. Which state lies between Guyana and French Guiana?
4. What is a dactyl?
5. Before Fulham, which was the last club to join the Rugby League?
6. Which 'Cockney Sparrer' carried on?
7. Who designed 'prefabs' with Brunel, was the first woman member of the Statistical Society and the first woman to receive the Order of Merit?
8. Which Rolling Stone got married in 1983?
9. What colour, generally, are cornflowers?

531

1. What are Franklin D. Roosevelt's four Freedoms of Democracy?
2. It was predicted that Henry IV would die in Jerusalem. Where did he die?
3. Which was the northernmost slave state of the American Civil War?
4. Who said, 'Whatever you really and seriously want, Gothic will do it for you'?
5. What does BASI stand for?
6. Which soldier wore female clothes in the hope of getting a discharge in 'MASH'?
7. Who won the 1983 World Professional Darts Championship?
8. When did Elvis Presley die?
9. About how many species of living fish are known?

902

1. 'In Utmost Good Faith' is the motto of which famous organization in the city?
2. What did the Romans mine at Dolaucothy (Carmarthen)?
3. In which county are the Dukeries?
4. Who was the brewer's wife with whom Johnson spent much time at Streatham?
5. Which football club's home ground is at Elland Road?
6. What does T.W.T.W.T.W. stand for?
7. How old was the artist Grandma Moses when she held her first exhibition?
8. Who produced the album *Let It Be* for the Beatles?
9. What is the larva of a moth or butterfly called?

160

1. Chatsworth, Derbyshire, in 1700.
2. Originally the Incas, but now Peruvian Indians.
3. Surinam.
4. In prosody, a metrical foot of three syllables – one long followed by two short.
5. Blackpool Borough in 1954.
6. Barbara Windsor.
7. Florence Nightingale.
8. Keith Richards.
9. Blue.

531

1. Freedom of Speech, of Worship, from Want, from Fear.
2. In the Jerusalem Chamber, Westminster Abbey.
3. Delaware.
4. John Ruskin.
5. British Association of Ski Instructors.
6. Corporal Klinger.
7. Keith Deller.
8. 16 August 1977.
9. 23,000.

902

1. Lloyd's of London.
2. Gold.
3. Nottinghamshire.
4. Mrs Thrale.
5. Leeds United.
6. *That Was The Week That Was.*
7. Seventy-eight.
8. Phil Spector.
9. Caterpillar.

161

1. What does the Blue Peter flag signify?
2. Who succeeded Oliver Cromwell as Lord Protector?
3. In which country is the Legion of Honour the highest civil decoration?
4. Who developed theories of 'sprung rhythm', 'inscape' and 'instress' in his poetry?
5. With whom did Martina Navratilova win the 1982 Wimbledon ladies' doubles?
6. In which film did Lauren Bacall ask Bogey if he knew how to whistle?
7. What does the DIN number denote in photographic film?
8. What is the biggest-selling solo album of all time?
9. What is a *Quercus robur*?

532

1. Gazing into a reflective surface to divine the future is called what?
2. What relation was William of Orange to Charles I?
3. Where do the Walloons live?
4. Who suggested eating poor babies as a solution to preventing them 'becoming a burthen to their parents or country'?
5. How many hat tricks did Jimmy Greaves score in the 1960–61 season?
6. Which long-running TV Western first brought Clint Eastwood to the public's attention?
7. The 'Sage of Monticello' was which US president?
8. Who was the original singer in X-Ray Spex?
9. Lop Nor is the atomic testing-ground of which country?

903

1. In which sauce were baked beans first sold?
2. What was the Bedchamber Crisis of 1839?
3. Three major rivers flow into the Baltic Sea. Name two.
4. Who described Los Angeles as 'a city with all the personality of a paper cup'?
5. Who introduces TV's 'The Big Match'?
6. Who played Rose in TV's 'Upstairs, Downstairs'?
7. Who was Alice Perrers?
8. Who had their first hit with the soul classic 'Hold On! I'm A-Comin''?
9. What wood were canal lock-gates and even waterpipes made from?

161

1. All aboard, I'm putting to sea.
2. His son Richard.
3. France.
4. Gerard Manley Hopkins.
5. Pam Shriver.
6. *To Have and Have Not* (1944).
7. The speed of the film.
8. Michael Jackson's *Thriller*.
9. An oak tree.

532

1. Scrying.
2. Grandson.
3. Belgium.
4. Jonathan Swift.
5. Six.
6. 'Rawhide'.
7. Thomas Jefferson.
8. Poly Styrene.
9. China.

903

1. Molasses.
2. Peel requested that some of Victoria's Whig Ladies of the Household should be removed before he became Prime Minister.
3. Oder, Vistula, Neva.
4. Raymond Chandler.
5. Brian Moore.
6. Jean Marsh, who also helped devise the series.
7. The rapacious mistress of Edward III who controlled his every move at the end of his life and gave him syphilis.
8. Sam and Dave.
9. Elm, as it is resistant to water.

162

1. What are a clove hitch, single sheet bend and a double bowline?
2. At what time did William I's curfew start each night?
3. In which Irish county is the Giant's Causeway?
4. In which book is Captain Cuttle on the run from Mrs MacStinger?
5. What game is played in the World Series?
6. Which film starred Kris Kristofferson and Bob Dylan?
7. When did Castro become Prime Minister of Cuba?
8. Who sang the theme song in the film *The Man With the Golden Gun*?
9. What is the usual name for coryza?

533

1. Who is the 'Queen of the High Fibre Diet'?
2. What were Nivôse, Brumaire, Vendémiaire and Ventôse?
3. In which country is the city of Salamanca?
4. Which is the first book of the Bible?
5. Who won the 1,500 metres gold medal at the 1980 and 1984 Olympics?
6. Tatum, daughter of Ryan O'Neal, won an Oscar for her first film. Name it.
7. Who said in the nineteenth century, 'Buy land, they've stopped making it'?
8. Who was known, variously, as the Sultan of Sob, the Tearleader and the Prince of Wails?
9. John Glenn was the first American to orbit the earth. From which branch of the armed services was he?

904

1. For what does QED stand?
2. In whose reign was the last English possession on the French mainland lost?
3. In which desert do the Bushmen wander?
4. Who recites 'The Walrus and the Carpenter'?
5. Who has won more races over jumps than any other jockey?
6. Chico, Harpo, Groucho – name the fourth Marx brother in films.
7. The Greek hero Oedipus was named after what?
8. Who wrote the opera *A Masked Ball*?
9. Where the ulnar nerve lies over the humerus is a spot generally known as what?

162

1. Knots.
2. 8 o'clock.
3. County Antrim.
4. *Dombey and Son.*
5. Baseball.
6. *Pat Garrett and Billy the Kid.*
7. 1959.
8. Lulu.
9. The common cold.

533

1. Audrey Eyton (of *F-Plan Diet* fame).
2. Months of the French revolutionary calendar.
3. Spain.
4. Genesis.
5. Sebastian Coe.
6. *Paper Moon.*
7. Mark Twain.
8. Johnnie Ray.
9. US Marine Corps.

904

1. *Quod erat demonstrandum.*
2. Mary I's; Calais was lost in 1558.
3. The Kalahari.
4. Tweedledee in *Through the Looking Glass.*
5. John Francome.
6. Zeppo.
7. His swollen feet.
8. Verdi.
9. The funny bone.

163

1. What does Lord Nelson's statue in Trafalgar Square weigh?
2. What did William Pitt the Younger introduce as a temporary wartime financial measure?
3. What is the capital of the state of Tennessee?
4. Who said, 'We must love one another or die'?
5. In which sport do the terms yoi, yame, seremade and hantei occur?
6. What part did John Gielgud play in the 1970 film *Julius Caesar*?
7. From which country does snooker star Eddie Charlton come?
8. How many dance a *pas de deux*?
9. What is the period of the revolution of the earth around the sun?

534

1. How many M Ps are there?
2. In which country was the Neanderthal valley?
3. What was designed by Alfred Gilbert, unveiled in 1893, stands 9 feet high and represents charity?
4. Whose last novel was *Jude the Obscure*?
5. What is considered to be the world's fastest team game?
6. Name a panellist on many popular TV and radio games whose trademark is a pink bow tie.
7. Which Messenger of God was at first believed in only by his wife but within 6 years of his death had followers capturing Jerusalem?
8. Who organized the concert for Bangladesh?
9. The snake-like, legless, harmless lizard, *Anguis fragilis*, is known as what?

905

1. The Romans used seven letters to represent their numbers. One of each put together forms which highest number?
2. What did the entry *Hoc est vasta* mean in the *Domesday Book*?
3. By what name is Stalingrad, defended by Stalin in 1917 against the White Russians, now known?
4. Of which novel is Fanny Price the heroine?
5. Which Wimbledon tennis tournament did Ivan Lendl first win?
6. Who directed the film of *Tommy*?
7. If you go aft on a boat, where do you go?
8. Who composed the score for *Zorba the Greek*?
9. What does a celestial map show?

163

1. 18 tons, excluding the column.
2. Income tax.
3. Nashville.
4. W.H. Auden.
5. Karate.
6. Julius Caesar.
7. Australia.
8. Two.
9. A year.

534

1. 635.
2. Germany.
3. Eros in Piccadilly.
4. Thomas Hardy's.
5. Ice hockey.
6. Frank Muir.
7. Muhammad.
8. George Harrison.
9. The slow-worm.

905

1. 1666 (MDCLXVI).
2. 'Here is laid waste' – a reference to the devastation of the North by William I.
3. Volgograd.
4. *Mansfield Park* by Jane Austen.
5. Junior Wimbledon.
6. Ken Russell.
7. To the stern.
8. Mikis Theodorakis.
9. The positions of the stars.

164

1. From what is black pudding made?
2. Who was the last monarch to wash the feet of the poor on Maundy Thursday?
3. How high is the platform at the top of the Eiffel Tower?
4. Who gave his name to a form of light verse which is generally biographical and consists of four lines?
5. When was ice dancing first contested at the Winter Olympics?
6. *Per un Pugno di Dollari* – what is the English title of this film?
7. What nationality was Rousseau?
8. Who cried a river in the 1950s?
9. If water vapour is cooled below its dew point, what does it form?

535

1. In money terms, what is a 'monkey'?
2. What was the age of consent for marriage before 1929?
3. Where were the Spice Islands of the Middle Ages?
4. Who received a Nobel Prize, declined a peerage from the first Labour government and wrote, 'We learn from history that we learn nothing from history'?
5. In tennis, what have Manuel Orantes, Borg and Lendl got in common?
6. Who 'invented' the topless swimming costume in the 1960s?
7. Who is the American artist who uses soup tins, etc., in his pop art?
8. Where did Tony Bennett leave his heart?
9. How many times does a Bactrian camel get the hump?

906

1. If you eat kosher food what religion would you probably be?
2. Why were coins minted in the shape of a four-leaf clover in 1060?
3. Africa has four great rivers. Name three.
4. How was Clive Bell related to Virginia Woolf?
5. Who coxed the Oxford crew to victory in the 1981 and 1982 boat races?
6. Who played King George IV in the 1972 film *Lady Caroline Lamb*?
7. Who founded the Boy Scout movement?
8. Who wrote 'A Lincoln Portrait'?
9. Which is the only fish able to hold objects in its tail?

164

1. Pig's blood and fat.
2. James II.
3. 985 feet.
4. Edmund *Clerihew* Bentley.
5. 1976.
6. *A Fistful of Dollars.*
7. Swiss.
8. Julie London.
9. Fog.

535

1. £500.
2. Twelve for a girl, fourteen for a boy.
3. The East Indies, especially the Moluccas.
4. G. B. Shaw.
5. They all won Junior Wimbledon.
6. Rudi Gernreich.
7. Andy Warhol.
8. San Francisco.
9. Two.

906

1. Jewish.
2. So that the leaves could be broken off and given as change.
3. Nile, Niger, Congo and Zambezi.
4. Brother-in-law.
5. Susan Brown.
6. Ralph Richardson.
7. Robert Baden-Powell.
8. Aaron Copland.
9. The sea-horse.

165

1. What was Rolls-Royce's first car called?
2. When did women over thirty first get the vote?
3. What was unusual about the towers of the cathedrals of Winchester, Gloucester, Worcester, Lincoln and Ely?
4. In which Sheridan play does Puff appear?
5. Who is the most famous motor-racer that Brazil has ever produced?
6. Whose real name is Pal?
7. Which English art critic was sued by an American and translated into French by Marcel Proust?
8. Who composed 'Get out of Town'?
9. Where is the biggest crop of potatoes to be found?

536

1. What is the Latin for seven?
2. The two kings at the Field of the Cloth of Gold (1520) had a wrestling match. Who won?
3. Which is the highest volcano in Europe?
4. In which Sheridan play does Sir Benjamin Backbite feature?
5. Who was the first holder of the World Drivers Championship?
6. James Cagney once played a Shakespearian character. Which one?
7. What is Margaret Thatcher's middle name?
8. Which jazz musician made a great recording of the *Flight of the Bumble Bee* on the trumpet?
9. What is a group of quails called?

907

1. How old is a poussin?
2. Twenty-three Nazi leaders were tried at Nuremberg. How many were acquitted?
3. Where did apples and pears originate?
4. Who proclaimed, 'Good heavens! I've been talking prose for over forty years without realizing it'?
5. Name the throwing events at the Olympics.
6. Which radio programme does the catch-phrase 'I go, I come back' come from?
7. What are most fishing-rods made of these days?
8. Which composer and lyricist was played by Cary Grant in *Night and Day*?
9. Saffron is more expensive than gold. About how many dried stamens from the plant make up 1 lb of saffron?

165

1. Silver Ghost.
2. 1918.
3. They all collapsed.
4. *The Critic.*
5. Emerson Fittipaldi.
6. Lassie's.
7. John Ruskin.
8. Cole Porter.
9. Russia.

536

1. *Septum.*
2. François I threw Henry VIII.
3. Mount Etna in Sicily.
4. *The School for Scandal.*
5. Giuseppe Farina (1950).
6. Bottom, in a 1935 Hollywood film version of *A Midsummer Night's Dream.*
7. Hilda.
8. Harry James.
9. A bevy.

907

1. 4 to 6 weeks (a baby chicken).
2. Three.
3. Afghanistan.
4. Jourdain, in Molière's *Le Bourgeois Gentilhomme.*
5. Shot put, discus, hammer and javelin.
6. 'ITMA'.
7. Fibreglass.
8. Cole Porter.
9. 200,000.

166

1. What is Davy Jones's locker?
2. Who said, 'The only thing we have to fear is fear itself'?
3. In which British city were the first pavements?
4. To whom does Squire Hardcastle say, 'This is Liberty Hall, gentlemen'?
5. Which sport do FISA and FOCA govern?
6. Who played Mrs Miniver?
7. Who said, 'To cease smoking is the easiest thing I ever did: I ought to know because I've done it a thousand times.'
8. Annie Mae Bullock didn't sound right, so she changed it. To what?
9. One of the world's first computers, Maniac, was set to do which job?

537

1. If you were born on 28 July, what star sign would you have?
2. Who was killed at the pass of Thermopylae in 480 BC?
3. On which island would you find huge ancestral figures carved from volcanic rock?
4. Who wrote *Das Kapital*?
5. Who delivers the ball in baseball?
6. Who plays Benson in 'Soap'?
7. Who re-designed Buckingham Palace?
8. Who was known as 'The giant of the oratorio'?
9. What does a drosometer measure?

908

1. Which car manufacturer's original title was 'Société Industrielle de Mécanique et de Construction Automobile'?
2. According to Toynbee how many civilizations have there been?
3. Where is Arnhem Land?
4. What is Stevenson's sequel to *Kidnapped* called?
5. Which brother and sister rode and trained Three Troikas to victory in the 1979 Prix de L'Arc de Triomphe?
6. Who played the vampire *Nosferatu* in the film of the same name?
7. Who was the last pope to be recognized as a saint?
8. Frank Zappa's daughter, Moon Unit, had a US hit with which record?
9. What is similar to a porpoise but has a beak-like snout and swims further from land?

166

1. The bottom of the sea which is the legendary grave of drowned sailors.
2. F. D. Roosevelt, at his first Inaugural Address on 4 March 1933.
3. Edinburgh, along High Street and Cowgate in 1688.
4. Marlow and Hastings (in *She Stoops to Conquer*).
5. Motor racing.
6. Greer Garson.
7. Mark Twain.
8. Tina Turner.
9. Weather-forecasting.

537

1. Leo.
2. King Leonidas and 300 Spartans.
3. Easter Island.
4. Karl Marx.
5. The pitcher.
6. Robert Guillaume.
7. John Nash.
8. Handel.
9. Dew.

908

1. Simca.
2. Twenty-one.
3. North Australia.
4. *Catriona.*
5. Freddie and Christine Head.
6. Klaus Kinski.
7. Pope Pius X (d. 1914; sanctified in 1954).
8. 'Valley Girl'.
9. A dolphin.

167

1. Which mark of government property was formerly on convicts' clothing?
2. Who were the parents of Elizabeth I?
3. In which American state did the surrender by Cornwallis take place?
4. In the rhyme about magpies, 'One for sorrow, two for joy . . .', what are six magpies for?
5. Who won the 1984 European Cup for football?
6. By what name is Peggy Middleton better known?
7. Of whom did a journalist in 1809 say, 'An unfortunate lunatic whose personal inoffensiveness secures him from confinement'?
8. Who composed the *Golden Sonata*?
9. What type of precious stone is an aquamarine?

538

1. How many originals of the Magna Carta are in existence?
2. In what year did Charles I (the last Habsburg) lose his throne?
3. What is the modern Italian name for the Roman Mediolanum?
4. Who wrote the novel *Sailor Billy Budd*?
5. Which brother and sister played together and won the mixed doubles trophy at Wimbledon in 1980?
6. Who directed *The Last Movie*, even though it wasn't?
7. For what is Patricia Roberts famed?
8. Which highway did Bob Dylan revisit?
9. In 1845 Thomas Scroggy invented a machine for making what useful object?

909

1. What was the difference between 'taverns' and 'inns'?
2. What was the 'lovers' telegraph' exhibited at the Centennial Exhibition, Philadelphia, in 1876?
3. What was the colonial name for Malawi?
4. Who called Johnson 'That great Cham of literature'?
5. Name Rugby League's first £50,000 transfer.
6. Who wrote an autobiography entitled *Will There Really be a Morning*?
7. In which country was Giuseppe Garibaldi born?
8. Who ate cannibals?
9. What is numbered 10 on the Beaufort scale, between a 'strong gale' and a 'storm'?

167

1. A broad arrow.
2. Anne Boleyn and Henry VIII.
3. Virginia (at Yorktown, to Washington).
4. Gold.
5. Liverpool.
6. Yvonne de Carlo.
7. William Blake.
8. Henry Purcell.
9. Beryl.

538

1. Four (two in the British Museum, one each at Salisbury and Lincoln cathedrals).
2. 1918 (of Austria–Hungary).
3. Milano.
4. Herman Melville.
5. John and Tracy Austin.
6. Denis Hopper.
7. Knitting patterns.
8. Highway 61.
9. Porous pipes for draining soil.

909

1. Taverns, unlike inns, could only provide casual refreshment and couldn't entertain or put up guests.
2. The telephone.
3. Nyasaland.
4. Tobias Smollett, writing to John Wilkes on 16 March 1759.
5. George Fairburn.
6. The tragic American screen actress Frances Farmer, the subject of a recent biopic.
7. France (in Nice in 1807).
8. To To Caelo.
9. A 'whole gale'.

168

1. How many faces has a dodecahedron?
2. Who first demonstrated electric telegraphy by sending a message from Washington to Baltimore in 1844?
3. Which was the first country to abolish capital punishment?
4. Which book opens, 'It was a bright cold day in April and the clocks were striking thirteen'?
5. In which sport did Karen Briggs win world and European titles in 1982?
6. Who directed *Aguirre, Wrath of God*?
7. Which famous painter, who was also a sculptor and potter, wrote a play called *Desire Caught by the Tail*?
8. Who sang about Denis?
9. What is a male swan called?

539

1. What is another name for ladies' fingers?
2. Which country held the first secret ballot at a parliamentary election?
3. What is the number of the present French Republic?
4. Whose brothers were Agravain, Gaheris and Gareth?
5. In which sport are the terms 'telemark' and 'stem Christie' used?
6. Natalie Wood and Richard Beymer starred in which memorable musical film?
7. Whom, thanks to Christopher Isherwood, did W. H. Auden marry?
8. What sort of motor-bike was Dylan riding when he crashed in 1966?
9. What is the difference between oily fish and white fish?

910

1. What is a coparcener?
2. To what use was the space around the Albert Memorial in Kensington Gardens put in the Second World War?
3. What, strictly speaking, is a Creole?
4. Who wrote *A History of the English-speaking Peoples*?
5. What is the name of the style of Japanese wrestling where combatants try to become very fat in order to have a low centre of gravity?
6. Which member of the Monkees appeared in 'Coronation Street'?
7. What does *Private Eye* call Margaret Thatcher?
8. Dave Dee and who else?
9. What is a young swan called?

168

1. Twelve.
2. Samuel Morse.
3. Effectively Russia in 1826, when Nicholas I proclaimed that all death-sentences would be commuted to exile to Siberia (except those given for treasonous acts).
4. *1984* by Orwell.
5. Judo.
6. Werner Herzog.
7. Pablo Picasso.
8. Blondie.
9. A cob.

539

1. Okra.
2. Australia, colony of Victoria in 1856.
3. The fifth (it was instituted in 1958).
4. Sir Gawain's.
5. Skiing.
6. *West Side Story*.
7. Erika Mann (daughter of Thomas Mann) to get her a British passport; they first met on their wedding-day.
8. A Triumph.
9. In the former there is oil throughout the fish; in the latter just in the liver.

910

1. A joint heir.
2. Allotments.
3. A person of European blood born in the West Indies or Spanish America.
4. Winston Churchill.
5. Sumo.
6. Davy Jones, as a child actor.
7. Hilda.
8. Dozy, Beaky, Mick and Titch.
9. A cygnet.

169

1. What is the common name for the suspension damper on a car?
2. When was the Greater London Council formed?
3. Which USA state is closest to the USSR?
4. Complete Peter Pan's protestation, 'To die will be an awfully . . .'
5. Which international wicket-keeper and international striker share the same name?
6. Who preceded Linda Thorsen as Emma Peel?
7. In which city does 'St Peter and St Paul' by El Greco hang?
8. Who claimed to be 'Kaiser Bill's Batman'?
9. What is kinetic energy?

540

1. Who said, 'You can have it any colour, so long as it's black'?
2. Who was the first king to wear a kilt?
3. What bizarre accident took place on 28 July 1945 in New York due to fog?
4. Who wrote the poem 'Anthem for Doomed Youth'?
5. In which sport is there a 'York round'?
6. What was unusual about Robert Montgomery's role in the 1946 movie, *The Lady in the Lake*?
7. Who painted the 'Urbino Venus'?
8. Who had a No. 1 hit with 'Silence is Golden'?
9. Which breed of dog was known as a coach dog?

911

1. What heraldic colour is 'vert'?
2. The most destructive British earthquake occurred in 1884. Where?
3. Where is Poets' Corner?
4. Who is the narrator in Anthony Powell's *Dance to the Music of Time*?
5. In which sport do college teams compete for the Sugar, Orange, Cotton and Rose Bowls?
6. What was Max Miller's nickname?
7. On whose grave, by his own directions, is said to have been carved a cylinder enclosing a sphere?
8. Who was the lead singer in The Doors?
9. Which process, now gaining ground, did Dennis Gabor develop in 1947?

169

1. The shock absorber.
2. 1965.
3. Alaska.
4. '... big adventure'.
5. Rodney Marsh.
6. Diana Rigg.
7. Leningrad; in the Hermitage Gallery.
8. Whistling Jack Smith.
9. Energy which bodies have by virtue of their motion.

540

1. Henry Ford.
2. George IV (on his visit to Edinburgh in 1822).
3. A US bomber crashed into the Empire State Building at the 79th floor (the 81st floors and above were in sunshine).
4. Wilfred Owen.
5. Archery.
6. He was never seen directly, only glimpsed in mirrors.
7. Titian.
8. The Tremoloes.
9. Dalmatian.

911

1. Green.
2. Colchester.
3. Westminster Abbey.
4. Nicholas Jenkins.
5. American football.
6. The Cheeky Chappie.
7. Archimedes.
8. Jim Morrison.
9. Holography.

170

1. Of these, which is the least edible: albatross, pigeon, blackbird, sparrow?
2. The UK engaged $5\frac{1}{2}$ million troops in the First World War. How many were killed?
3. Which town lies beneath Ben Nevis at the start of the Caledonian Canal?
4. What, in Greek mythology, was ichor?
5. Which country did Lasse Viren represent?
6. Which part did Nicholas Grace play in the ITV series 'Robin Hood'?
7. Who was the 'Philosopher of Ferney'?
8. Who sang the original version of 'Blue Suede Shoes'?
9. Which is the fastest swimming bird?

541

1. Where would you find the line of Mars and the girdle of Venus?
2. During what event did the first recorded public performance of 'God Save the King' take place?
3. From which country does Petite Suisse cheese come?
4. In which play does the Procession of Protracted Death appear?
5. What have the Emperor Nero, General Patton and Dr Benjamin Spock in common sports-wise?
6. Which was the first James Bond film?
7. In which sport would you 'hang ten'?
8. Who is Belgium's most famous jazz guitarist?
9. The bird species the tits are known in America as what?

912

1. Who are the wholesalers of the Stock Exchange?
2. The last successful invasion of Britain occurred when and by whom?
3. Where are the Hen and Chickens Islands?
4. Which monarch touched Dr Johnson for the King's Evil?
5. Who is the world record holder in motor racing with twenty-seven World Championship victories?
6. Who was the creator of the TV series 'The Man from UNCLE'?
7. Who was the official war artist from 1940 to 1942?
8. Who rabbited?
9. Which planets are bigger than the earth?

170

1. Albatross, by far.
2. 765,399.
3. Fort William.
4. Ethereal fluid flowing in the veins of the gods.
5. Finland.
6. The Sheriff of Nottingham.
7. Voltaire, who spent the last 20 years of his life there.
8. Carl Perkins.
9. The penguin.

541

1. On your palm. They are terms in palmistry.
2. The '45 Jacobite invasion. It was an unannounced addition to the programme at Drury Lane Theatre on 28 September 1745.
3. France.
4. *Hassan* by James Elroy Flecker.
5. They all took part in the Olympics (chariot racing in AD 66, the pentathlon in 1912 and rowing in 1924).
6. *Dr No* (1962).
7. Surfing.
8. Django Reinhardt.
9. Chickadees.

912

1. The jobbers.
2. 1688 by William III.
3. Just off the coast of North Island, New Zealand.
4. Queen Anne in 1712 (no cure was effected).
5. Jackie Stewart.
6. Ian Fleming.
7. Henry Moore.
8. Chas and Dave.
9. Jupiter, Saturn, Uranus, Neptune.

171

1. Which was the first firm to sell internal combustion cars?
2. What was celebrated at Lammastide?
3. When it is noon GMT in London, what time is it in Port Stanley?
4. Who is the hero of Scott's *The Talisman*?
5. The world's first organized cycle race occurred in the year of a famous revolt and in the same city. Where?
6. Who plays John Steed in 'The Avengers'?
7. How tall was Alexander Pope?
8. Who had a hit with 'Video Killed the Radio Star'?
9. Where would you find the pyloric sphincter?

542

1. What were the followers of John Wyclif, the religious reformer, called?
2. How old, within 3 years, was Henry VIII when he ascended the throne?
3. Of where is Valetta the capital?
4. Who said "tain't a fit night out for man nor beast'?
5. What is the highest live attendance of any football match?
6. Which director described actors as cattle?
7. Who invented the game Dungeons and Dragons?
8. What happened on the day the music died?
9. What is the brown bear's main source of animal food in the wild?

913

1. What is the cube root of $\frac{1}{8}$?
2. In which decade was the first British general election held by secret ballot?
3. What was the colonial name for Zambia?
4. What was Scott Fitzgerald's last novel?
5. Barring rain, in which athletics track event do you tend to get wet?
6. Who was George Raft describing when he said, 'She stole everything but the cameras'?
7. Who said, 'I think, therefore I am'?
8. What was Richard Nixon's favourite song?
9. What colour is the flesh of a charentais melon?

171

1. Benz.
2. The wheat harvest. On Lammas day (1 August) loaves would be taken to church as offerings, hence (probably) 'Loaf-mass' or Lammas.
3. 8 a.m.
4. Sir Kenneth or the Knight of the Leopard.
5. Paris (1868); an Englishman won.
6. Patrick MacNee.
7. 4 feet, 6 inches.
8. The Buggles.
9. Between the stomach and the duodenum.

542

1. Lollards.
2. Eighteen.
3. Malta.
4. W. C. Fields in *The Fatal Glass of Beer*.
5. 205,000, at Brazil versus Uruguay in the 1950 World Cup.
6. Alfred Hitchcock.
7. Gary Gygax.
8. Buddy Holly was killed.
9. Salmon.

913

1. $\frac{1}{2}$.
2. 1870s (1874).
3. Northern Rhodesia.
4. *The Last Tycoon* (1941 and unfinished).
5. The steeplechase.
6. Mae West.
7. René Descartes.
8. 'Okie from Muskogee'.
9. Deep orange.

172

1. Whose portraits appeared on the first US postage stamps?
2. Why did Lieutenant Hiroo Onoda hide on the Philippine island of Lubang for over 29 years?
3. Which Ethiopian city's name means 'new flower'?
4. Incunabula are books printed before which year?
5. Who was the first member elected to the USA's Swimming Hall of Fame?
6. Who is Warren Beatty's actress sister?
7. Which colour is worth six points at snooker?
8. Which three brothers originally called themselves the Rattlesnakes?
9. How many teats has a healthy normal cow?

543

1. Which animals are associated with the Stock Exchange?
2. To which organization was the only Nobel Peace Prize given during the First World War?
3. From where did voodoo come?
4. In which village does Miss Jane Marple live?
5. Who was reputedly the only man ever to knock out Jack Dempsey?
6. What part does Norman Painting play in 'The Archers'?
7. How many wives did the Mormon leader Brigham Young marry?
8. For what is a platinum record awarded?
9. As what was Robert Stroud better known?

914

1. What does AD mean?
2. Who wrote his first book *Under the Moon in Mars* in 1911 under the name Norman Bean?
3. What does the name 'Haiti' mean?
4. To court whom did Leander swim across the Hellespont every night?
5. What is Fulham FC's ground called?
6. Who wrote *Chicken Soup with Barley*?
7. Who became the first person to publish a set of rules for whist?
8. Many consider Beethoven's Ninth Symphony to be his greatest work. How many times did he hear it performed?
9. What is parallel to the ulna?

172

1. 5 cents Benjamin Franklin, 10 cents George Washington.
2. Because he did not know that the Second World War was over.
3. Addis Ababa.
4. 1500.
5. Johnny Weissmuller (Tarzan).
6. Shirley MacLaine.
7. Pink.
8. Barry, Robin and Maurice Gibb – the Bee Gees.
9. Four.

543

1. Bulls, bears and stags.
2. The International Red Cross.
3. Haiti.
4. St Mary Mead (Agatha Christie).
5. John Paul Getty, Dempsey's sparring partner in 1923 (later the world's wealthiest man).
6. Phil Archer.
7. Twenty-seven.
8. An LP selling a million.
9. The Birdman of Alcatraz.

914

1. In the year of our Lord (anno Domini).
2. Edgar Rice Burroughs, Tarzan's creator.
3. Mountainous.
4. Hero.
5. Craven Cottage.
6. Arnold Wesker.
7. Edmond Hoyle, in 1742.
8. Never. He was totally deaf when he wrote it.
9. The radius.

173

1. For chopping off which part of the body was the guillotine originally invented?
2. Originally, what were the Mamelukes, who became the ruling class of Egypt?
3. Which people invented bedsprings?
4. Who was the Roman goddess of the moon?
5. In which game does the ball travel fastest?
6. Who runs a flying school for female pilots in *Goldfinger*?
7. What is calligraphy?
8. On which track does the Chattanooga Choo Choo leave Pennsylvania station?
9. What is the difference between fog and mist?

544

1. To which English name does the Italian 'Giovanni' correspond?
2. Who defeated Prince Rupert at Marston Moor?
3. How far is South America moving away from South Africa each year?
4. Which magic words opened the treasure cave in *Ali Baba and the Forty Thieves*?
5. What colour is the lowest rank judo belt?
6. At which hospital did Dr Kildare work?
7. In which country were the earliest recorded works of art – cave paintings – found?
8. On which pipe of the bagpipes is the tune fingered?
9. Which poison was given to Socrates?

915

1. During which season do most burglaries take place?
2. Who did Ramon Mercader kill in Mexico on 20 August 1940?
3. Where does 70 per cent of the world's grapefruit come from?
4. Who was Oberon's wife?
5. Where is the Ebor Handicap run?
6. Which police force was created by Mack Sennett?
7. Who composed this epitaph for himself: 'When I am dead, I hope it may be said – "His sins were scarlet but his books were read"'?
8. In which of Wagner's operas does 'Here Comes the Bride' originate?
9. How have Spanish scientists increased milk production?

173

1. Hands.
2. Circassian slaves.
3. The Greeks.
4. Diana.
5. Jai alai.
6. Pussy Galore.
7. The art of handwriting.
8. Track 29.
9. Distance. If visibility is over 1,100 yards, it's a mist; if under, it's a fog.

544

1. John.
2. Oliver Cromwell.
3. 2 inches (Continental Drift).
4. 'Open Sesame.'
5. White.
6. Blair General Hospital.
7. France.
8. The chanter.
9. Hemlock.

915

1. Summer – holiday time.
2. Leon Trotsky.
3. Florida.
4. Titania.
5. York.
6. The Keystone Kops.
7. Hilaire Belloc.
8. *Lohengrin.*
9. By fitting cows with false teeth to improve their ability to digest grass.

174

1. What colour are British fire engines?
2. How many astronauts died in 1967 when their Apollo capsule caught fire?
3. What is the name of the capital of the Minoan civilization in Crete?
4. Who died in the pass of Roncesvalles?
5. What is fives?
6. Who is Mary Martin's famous son?
7. What nationality was James Whistler?
8. How many horn concertos did Mozart write?
9. What is a pill or medicine called when given solely to appease the patient?

545

1. In Scottish folklore, a kelpie is a ghost. In what form?
2. Which ship left Boston for Genoa in 1872 and was found abandoned four weeks later in the Atlantic?
3. In which country did paper originate?
4. According to the Bible, what 'quencheth the thirst of the jackasses'?
5. Which football club is nicknamed 'The Shakers'?
6. What do dilithium crystals power?
7. By what name was outlaw Harry Longbaugh better known?
8. Who wrote the opera *The Olympians*?
9. What type of animal was Sergeant Tibbs in *101 Dalmatians*?

916

1. Which currency rule was named after an English economist?
2. Who died of a surfeit of peaches and cider?
3. Which North Sea island was a German naval base in the First and Second World Wars?
4. Who created Inspector Maigret?
5. Which countries compete for the Calcutta Cup?
6. Which actress starred in *Never on Sunday*?
7. Three dice are used in backgammon. Two are used for movement; for what is the third used?
8. Which Gilbert and Sullivan opera was completed by Edward German?
9. Approximately how many inches of snow are equal to 1 inch of rain?

174

1. Red.
2. Three.
3. Knossos.
4. Roland – in spite of his enchanted horn.
5. A hand-ball game played by pairs in a three-walled court.
6. Larry Hagman ('J.R.').
7. American.
8. Four.
9. A placebo.

545

1. A horse.
2. The *Mary Celeste*.
3. China.
4. Water.
5. Bury.
6. The Starship *Enterprise*.
7. The Sundance Kid.
8. Sir Arthur Bliss.
9. A cat.

916

1. Gresham's Law.
2. King John.
3. Heligoland.
4. Georges Simenon.
5. England and Scotland.
6. Melina Mercouri.
7. Doubling.
8. *The Emerald Isle*.
9. 10 inches.

Q

175

1. What must all dogs have attached to their collar, by law?
2. Which people founded the cheese-making industry in England?
3. Where is the centre of London's diamond trade?
4. Which poet, born in 1887, whose best-known poem is *The Soldier*, died during the First World War?
5. At which weight did Maurice Hope fight?
6. Which football team does Alf Garnett support?
7. Which biscuit is named after a famous Italian patriot?
8. What was curious about the cast of Puccini's opera *Suor Angelica*?
9. Which breed of dog is called the 'King of the Terriers'?

546

1. What is a sabot?
2. Of whom did Queen Victoria say, 'Such a head! I wish we had her at the War Office'?
3. What is the US military academy called?
4. What are the Synoptic Gospels?
5. With which sport is Penny Chuter associated?
6. Which film made international stars of Paul Muni and George Raft?
7. Which English staymaker supported the American revolutionaries, designed an iron bridge and became an honorary Frenchman?
8. What is the name given to the deepest singing voice?
9. Who built the railway engine called the *Rocket*?

917

1. Who speak Romany?
2. Austerlitz (1805) is known as the Battle of the Three Emperors. Why?
3. In which country would you be if you were at the Lion Gate of Mycenae?
4. What is Mr Toad's full name?
5. Where do they play the wall game?
6. Who shot J.R.?
7. Which politician was killed at the opening of the Liverpool to Manchester railway in 1830?
8. Who played the part of Paganini in *The Magic Bow*?
9. On the Thames, what is the yearly trip for the purpose of marking birds called?

175

1. A disc with the owner's name and address.
2. The Romans.
3. Hatton Garden.
4. Rupert Brooke.
5. Light middleweight.
6. West Ham.
7. Garibaldi.
8. It consisted entirely of women.
9. The Airedale.

546

1. A wooden shoe.
2. Florence Nightingale.
3. West Point.
4. Those of Matthew, Mark and Luke, written along the same lines.
5. Rowing.
6. *Hell's Angels*.
7. Tom Paine.
8. Basso profundo.
9. Robert Stephenson.

917

1. Gypsies.
2. Napoleon (Emperor of France) routed the Emperors of Austria and Russia. All were there in person.
3. Greece.
4. J. Thaddeus Toad.
5. Eton.
6. Kristen.
7. Huskisson.
8. Stewart Granger.
9. Swan-upping.

176

1. Atephobia is a fear of what?
2. What fault caused two Comets to crash in 1954?
3. What is the town Giza known for?
4. Which Poet Laureate rewrote *King Lear* with a happy ending?
5. Which horse won the 1961 English Derby?
6. Which playwright created a 6-foot rabbit called Harvey?
7. Who produced a painting made up of multiple images of Marilyn Monroe?
8. What does *largo* mean?
9. Ruby and sapphire are different forms of which mineral?

547

1. What is the Molink?
2. After what event did the last beheadings (as opposed to hangings) take place?
3. What is the official language of Pakistan?
4. In Egyptian mythology who was the creator of all things?
5. Who first won three TT events in one year?
6. What did Bogart say of the Maltese Falcon in the last line of the film?
7. Where would you find the Empress, the Chariot, the Hermit and the Fool all together?
8. Who had a 1964 hit with 'You've Lost That Lovin' Feeling'?
9. Roughly how many extant species of bird have been recorded?

918

1. What are Grapnel, Bruce, Danforth and Plough?
2. Who was the fourth wife of Henry VIII?
3. Which river separates Stockton from Middlesbrough?
4. Who says, in which play, 'Reading isn't an occupation we encourage among police officers. We try to keep the paperwork down to a minimum'?
5. Which famous newscaster's father invented the googly?
6. Who played Robin Hood in the first British TV series?
7. For what is Barbara Hepworth famous?
8. The last theme of Beethoven's violin concerto features the song of what bird?
9. What are the largest living reptiles?

176

1. Imperfection.
2. Metal fatigue.
3. It contains the Great Sphinx and the largest Pyramid.
4. Nahum Tate.
5. Psidium.
6. Mary Chase.
7. Andy Warhol.
8. Slow.
9. Corundum.

547

1. The hot line between Washington and Moscow.
2. The '45 Rebellion.
3. Urdu.
4. Ptah.
5. Mike Halewood in 1961.
6. He said that it was 'the stuff that dreams are made of'.
7. In a Tarot pack.
8. The Righteous Brothers.
9. 8,600.

918

1. Types of anchor.
2. Anne of Cleves.
3. The Tees.
4. Truscott in *Loot*.
5. Reginald Bosanquet's; which is why the googly is also known as 'the Bosie'.
6. Richard Greene; the series ran for 165 episodes.
7. Sculpture.
8. The blackbird.
9. Crocodiles.

177

1. What is a tutu?
2. Name the vessel which carried Scott's Antarctic expedition in 1910.
3. Which ocean is sometimes referred to as 'the Herring Pond'?
4. Name Shakespeare's Merchant of Venice.
5. Which jockey rode the Derby winner, 'Never Say Die', in 1954?
6. What does MASH stand for?
7. Who was the first president of the Royal Academy?
8. Who composed the Symphonie Fantastique?
9. Pluto is now thought to have a moon. What is it called?

548

1. To which trade were 'tumblers' apprenticed?
2. Where was Nelson's Pillar erected in 1809?
3. Which American state contains the Great Salt Lake?
4. What is the subject of Ariosto's *Orlando Furioso*?
5. In which year did David Hemery win his Olympic gold medal in the 400-metre hurdles?
6. What part did John Gielgud play in the 1953 film, *Julius Caesar*?
7. How many novels did Jane Austen write?
8. Which composer did Richard Chamberlain play in *The Music Lovers*?
9. Lack of which vitamin causes scurvy?

919

1. About how much does the total daily food consumption by people in Britain weigh?
2. In whose reign did English become the official language of the law courts?
3. Where is the 'Confessor's shrine'?
4. Who wrote the best-selling book, *Fear of Flying*?
5. Which famous Olympic gold medallist once finished second in the Grand National?
6. Who played Dr Watson to Basil Rathbone's Sherlock Holmes?
7. Who was the fabricator of the Popish Plot of 1678?
8. Who sang the theme song in the James Bond film, *From Russia With Love*?
9. By what name is the plant *Impatiens* more commonly known?

177

1. A ballet skirt.
2. *Terra Nova*.
3. The Atlantic.
4. Antonio.
5. Lester Piggott.
6. Mobile Army Surgical Hospital.
7. Sir Joshua Reynolds.
8. Hector Berlioz.
9. Charon.

548

1. Window-cleaning.
2. Dublin. It was blown up by Republican extremists in 1966.
3. Utah.
4. Charlemagne's war with the Saracens.
5. 1968.
6. Cassius.
7. Six.
8. Tchaikovsky.
9. Vitamin C.

919

1. 80,000 tonnes.
2. Henry VII's.
3. Westminster Abbey.
4. Erica Jong.
5. Harry Llewellyn.
6. Nigel Bruce.
7. Titus Oates.
8. Matt Monro.
9. Busy lizzie.

178

1. What type of material is guipure?
2. How many Eleanor Crosses were erected by Edward I after his Queen's death?
3. Where has every English Coronation since 1066 been held?
4. Where is Greene's *The Quiet American* set?
5. Who is the only British player to have scored twice in a European Cup Final?
6. What was the first 3-D movie?
7. Which Tuscan painter and architect is far better known as a biographer?
8. What did 'Lovely Rita' do for a living?
9. Which plant is known as the mile-a-minute plant?

549

1. How many faces has an icosahedron?
2. In which decade did the first legal cremation in Britain since the time of the Roman Occupation take place?
3. Which part of England had its own parliaments and courts until 1897?
4. In what form did Zeus visit Leda?
5. Where is the motor racing track Watkins Glen?
6. What is the first name of MASH's Corporal Klinger?
7. What is the New Yorkers' affectionate name for the Museum of Modern Art?
8. Who asked, 'What Have They Done to My Song, Ma?'?
9. What is a sea lemon?

920

1. Finish Lord Acton's phrase: 'Power tends to corrupt . . ."
2. Who founded the first public library in the City of London?
3. In which river valley are the special grapes for port grown?
4. Who are the two Biancas in Shakespeare?
5. Give the surname of showjumping father and son, Harvey and Robert.
6. Who played Tonto in 'The Lone Ranger'?
7. If you pot the following sequence at snooker, what is your score? Red, blue, red, pink.
8. Who sang, 'Oh, Superman' in 1981?
9. A very large dinosaur has been renamed Apatosaurus. What was it previously called?

178

1. Lace.
2. Twelve, at each resting place of her coffin from Hadby in Nottinghamshire to Westminster Abbey.
3. Westminster Abbey.
4. Vietnam, during the war of liberation against the French.
5. Bobby Charlton.
6. *Bwana Devil.*
7. Giorgio Vasari.
8. She was a traffic warden.
9. The Russian vine.

549

1. Twenty.
2. 1880s. It took place in 1885 at Woking in Surrey.
3. Devon and Cornwall (the Stannaries).
4. As a swan.
5. New York state.
6. Maxwell.
7. MOMA.
8. Melanie.
9. A type of sea slug.

920

1. '. . . and absolute power corrupts absolutely.'
2. Dick Whittington.
3. The Douro.
4. Kate's younger sister in *The Taming of the Shrew* and Cassio's mistress in *Othello.*
5. Smith.
6. Jay Silverheels.
7. Thirteen points.
8. Laurie Anderson.
9. Brontosaurus.

179

1. Most of us have collected parking tickets, but what is parkin?
2. What was a cottar?
3. Where was the treaty signed at the end of the American War of Independence?
4. Who lived in the Hundred Acre Wood?
5. Who achieved Britain's only gold medal in the 1978 European Championships?
6. Which dramatist wrote *The Crucible*?
7. Why did Handel compose *The Messiah*?
8. Who sang with Robert Palmer in the 1970s band, Vinegar Joe?
9. What is frost?

550

1. Where would you find zig-zags, ladders, diamonds, rig and fur, steps and prints o' the hoof?
2. Who introduced the place-name endings of '-ton' and '-ham'?
3. Which island off the Cornish coast do some consider to be part of the lost kingdom of Lyonesse?
4. To which king was Jezebel married?
5. Name the first footballer transferred for £100,000 between British clubs?
6. Who played Hoss in TV's 'Bonanza'?
7. By which name is Lancelot Brown better known?
8. Who wrote 'Chirpy Chirpy, Cheep Cheep'?
9. Which is the second planet from the sun?

921

1. The red flag, flown by certain French ships and called the Joli Rouge, was the origin of what?
2. In which year did traffic wardens (male) appear?
3. In which country is the Kwanza the unit of currency?
4. From which Southwark inn did Chaucer's pilgrims set out?
5. What was the best innings ever in a one-day international?
6. How did Maurice Chevalier begin his show business career?
7. What was the collective name for the group of artists whose best-known members were Cotman and Crome?
8. Who was court organist at Weimar and later became blind?
9. What is a palmiped?

179

1. A biscuit or cake made with (among other things) oatmeal and treacle.
2. A villein who occupied a cottage with a holding of land attached.
3. Versailles (1783).
4. Owl. (*Winnie-the-Pooh* by A. A. Milne.)
5. Steve Ovett in the 1500 metres.
6. Arthur Miller.
7. Principally because he needed the money.
8. Elkie Brooks.
9. Frozen dew.

550

1. On guernseys or ganseys. They are knitting patterns.
2. The Saxons. They mean 'settlement'.
3. St Michael's Mount.
4. Ahab.
5. Alan Ball. He was transferred for that sum from Blackpool to Everton in 1966.
6. Dan Blocker.
7. 'Capability' Brown.
8. Middle of the Road.
9. Venus.

921

1. The Jolly Roger.
2. 1960.
3. Angola.
4. The Tabard.
5. 189 not out, scored by Viv Richards.
6. As an acrobat.
7. The Norwich School of Painters.
8. J. S. Bach.
9. A web-footed animal or bird.

180

1. 'In every hierarchy an employee tends to rise to his level of incompetence' is an expression of what law?
2. How many hundreds of 'heretics' were burnt in the reign of Bloody Mary?
3. What is the main island of Japan called?
4. What did William Langland dream on the Malvern Hills?
5. In 1964 more than 300 people were killed during a riot following an Olympic qualifying football match in which country?
6. Who died on the show 'Live at Her Majesty's'?
7. What is Graham Miles's game?
8. By what name is John Henry Deutschendorf better known?
9. Suspecting fraud, George Shaw of the British Museum tried to prise off the bill of one of these. What was it?

551

1. Name the pair who joined forces in 1906 to make a very famous car.
2. Which famous school was founded in 1440?
3. Which is the highest mountain in Europe?
4. Who called patriotism 'the last refuge of a scoundrel'?
5. Which racing driver was killed in a plane crash in 1975?
6. Which Australian actor played a doctor in 'Emergency Ward 10'?
7. Which – sometimes censored – English novelist had an exhibition of paintings closed down by the police?
8. The proprietor said of his famous jazz club, 'Even the mice eat next door'. What is the name of the club?
9. Who is known as 'the father of chemistry'?

922

1. What are croûtons?
2. For how long did Alexander the Great rule?
3. Cape Comorin is the most southerly point of which country?
4. In which play would you find a fly, a fox, three birds, and Sir Politic Would-be, and where was it set?
5. Where would you find Beecher's Brook and Valentine's Brook?
6. Who played Catherine the Great in the 1934 film *The Scarlet Empress*?
7. Who, says Keats, gazed 'Silent, upon a peak in Darien'?
8. Who wrote the hymn, 'God Moves in a Mysterious Way'?
9. Which was the first beast of burden to be domesticated?

180

1. The Peter Principle.
2. Three – i.e. about 300.
3. Honshu.
4. *The Vision of William concerning Piers the Plowman.*
5. Peru.
6. Tommy Cooper.
7. Snooker.
8. John Denver.
9. A duck-billed platypus.

551

1. Charles Rolls and Henry Royce.
2. Eton.
3. Mont Blanc.
4. Samuel Johnson.
5. Graham Hill.
6. Ray Barrett.
7. D. H. Lawrence.
8. Ronnie Scott's.
9. Robert Boyle.

922

1. Small pieces of bread fried or toasted.
2. 12 years.
3. India.
4. *Volpone*, which is set in Venice.
5. Aintree racecourse.
6. Marlene Dietrich.
7. Cortés. In fact it was Vasco Núñez de Balboa who first saw the Pacific in 1513.
8. William Cowper.
9. The ass.

181

1. To the nearest 10 million, how many times does the average car tyre rotate in its lifetime?
2. Which French king was known as 'the Fat'?
3. What is the capital of Monaco?
4. What is known as 'the decalogue' in the Bible?
5. Who won the British Jumping Derby in successive years on Mattie Brown?
6. Who played the harassed employer in the original 'Rag Trade'?
7. A secret communications system for controlling torpedoes was filed in 1942 by which famous actress?
8. Who is called 'the Big O'?
9. How many noughts are there in one British octillion?

552

1. Approximately what percentage of women are colour blind?
2. Which black revolutionary took over the French colony of Haiti, was eventually captured, and died in France in 1803?
3. On which river does the legendary Lorelei lie in wait?
4. Who was the creator of the stylish twenties detective, Philo Vance?
5. Which tennis player bore the nickname 'Muscles'?
6. What is the motto of the BBC?
7. Who owns the Skywalker Ranch?
8. Who wrote 'Kisses Sweeter than Wine'?
9. How many times its own weight can an ant pull?

923

1. How many calories does the gum on a postage stamp contain?
2. Whose face appeared on the famous First World War recruiting poster bearing the legend, 'Your Country Needs You!'?
3. How many stars appear on the flag of New Zealand?
4. In 1596 *The Metamorphosis of Ajax* was published. Which new household system did the book explain?
5. At which weight did Jim Watt win the world boxing title?
6. Who played Peter Sellers's daughter in *I'm All Right, Jack*?
7. Who said, 'We have to make war as we must, not as we like'?
8. What was Mott the Hoople's first hit single?
9. Which comet is depicted in the Bayeux Tapestry?

181

1. The present average is something over 30 million.
2. Charles II.
3. Monte Carlo.
4. The Ten Commandments.
5. Harvey Smith.
6. Peter Jones.
7. Hedy Lamarr.
8. Roy Orbison.
9. Forty-eight.

552

1. Less than 1 per cent.
2. Toussaint L'Ouverture.
3. The Rhine.
4. S.S. Van Dine.
5. Ken Rosewall.
6. 'Nation shall speak peace unto nation'.
7. George Lucas.
8. Pete Seeger.
9. About ten times.

923

1. About $\frac{1}{10}$ of a calorie.
2. Lord Kitchener's.
3. Four.
4. The water closet.
5. Lightweight.
6. Liz Fraser.
7. Lord Kitchener.
8. 'All the Young Dudes'.
9. Halley's.

182

1. Mitre, dovetail, jig and hack are all types of what?
2. How many were killed and wounded in the Peterloo Massacre of 1819?
3. Which country does the wine Bulls' Blood come from?
4. Who taught English in Berlin between the wars and later wrote three plays with W. H. Auden?
5. Who won the Monaco Grand Prix five times in the 1960s?
6. Which 'Archers' character sings Country and Western songs?
7. Which US president was nicknamed 'Old Hickory'?
8. Which Rolling Stone was once an RAF serviceman?
9. What drives the fly wheel, the gear box, the water pump, the fan and the generator in a car?

553

1. Where would you find the Mount of Apollo, the Mount of the Moon and the Girdle of Venus?
2. Who was the last English monarch to be born abroad?
3. How many miles is London from Sydney?
4. Who is the child of Leontes and Hermione, according to Shakespeare?
5. How do you qualify for the Bobby Jones Golf Classic?
6. Who headed the Lord Chamberlain's Company with whom Shakespeare acted?
7. Where does 'Charles I' by Van Dyck hang?
8. Which instrument does Joe Pass play?
9. Which constituent gives vinegar its sharpness?

924

1. New Year's Eve in Scotland celebrates which saint's day?
2. Why did Henry II allow himself to be flogged in public?
3. On which river is the Hoover Dam?
4. Name two authors who wrote of Vanity Fair.
5. Tyrrell tried out a new type of car in the 1976 Spanish Grand Prix. What was unusual about it?
6. Name the film in which Spencer Tracy and Katharine Hepburn first starred together.
7. Albert Schweitzer had a famous cousin. Who?
8. What position did the Beatles' 'Please Please Me' reach in the British charts?
9. With whom are the three Laws of Motion associated?

182

1. Saw.
2. 600.
3. Hungary.
4. Christopher Isherwood.
5. Graham Hill.
6. Eddie Grundy.
7. Andrew Jackson.
8. Bill Wyman.
9. The crankshaft.

553

1. In the palm of the hand.
2. George II, who was born in Hanover in 1683.
3. 10,558 miles.
4. Perdita (*The Winter's Tale*).
5. Your name must be Bobby Jones.
6. The Burbage family.
7. The National Gallery, London.
8. The guitar.
9. Acetic acid.

924

1. Saint Sylvester.
2. He wanted to do penance for Thomas à Becket's death.
3. The Colorado river.
4. There are in fact three: Bunyan, Thackeray and Dornford Yates.
5. It had six wheels.
6. *Woman of the Year* (1942).
7. Jean-Paul Sartre.
8. No. 2.
9. Sir Isaac Newton.

183

1. What is the origin of the word 'antimacassar'?
2. The hottest English summer of 1976 was just hotter than the summer of which other year?
3. Where is Herm Island?
4. Who wrote which book originally entitled *The Romantic Egotist*?
5. Which girl achieved six British Judo titles in the 1970s?
6. Who were the Joker, the Riddler and the Penguin?
7. What have Richard Burton, William Saroyan, Dorothy Parker and Natalie Wood in common, maritally?
8. Which musical instrument did Samuel Pepys play?
9. What did Jethro Tull invent?

554

1. What is the singular of 'dice'?
2. What did William II, Henry VIII, Charles I, George V and George VI have in common?
3. How did the landau carriage get its name?
4. What is the connection between E. J. Thribb and Lord Gnome?
5. Which British boxer was the first to win three Lonsdale Belts outright?
6. Who directed *The Pleasure Garden* – his first feature film?
7. What is a boat's diary called?
8. For which instrument was Beethoven's Grande Sonate Pathétique written?
9. By what name is scorpion grass better known?

925

1. What is an iamb?
2. Jack Ketch was often featured in Punch and Judy shows. Who was he?
3. The Union of Soviet Socialist Republics is a union of how many republics?
4. Who were Shakespeare's Mrs Ford and Mrs Page?
5. Which team lost a World Cup quarter final in spite of scoring five goals?
6. Sch . . . who did the Schweppes voice-overs for nine years?
7. Who sculpted 'The Burghers of Calais'?
8. Who rewrote a Sam Cooke song and made it a massive hit as 'Sweet Soul Music' in 1967?
9. How far away from a 100-kiloton nuclear explosion would you have to be to escape immediate burns?

183

1. Macassar was a proprietary name for a nineteenth-century hair oil. Antimacassars protected upholstery from this oil.
2. 1947.
3. It is one of the Channel Islands.
4. Scott Fitzgerald, *This Side of Paradise.*
5. Christine Child.
6. The arch-enemies of Batman and Robin.
7. They have all married one partner twice.
8. The recorder.
9. The seed-drill (about 1701).

554

1. Die.
2. They were all second sons.
3. It was first made in Landau, Germany, in 1757.
4. They are pseudonyms in the satirical magazine *Private Eye.*
5. Henry Cooper.
6. Alfred Hitchcock.
7. A log.
8. The piano.
9. Forget-me-not.

925

1. A metrical foot, consisting of one short followed by one long syllable.
2. Executioner and hangman, 1663–86.
3. Twenty-nine.
4. The Merry Wives of Windsor.
5. Switzerland, beaten 7–5 by Austria in 1954.
6. William Franklyn.
7. Auguste Rodin.
8. Arthur Conley.
9. About $7\frac{1}{2}$ miles.

184

1. How long is a £5 note?
2. Which award was first given to Lieutenant Charles Lucas in 1854?
3. Which of the Great Lakes is entirely contained within the USA?
4. What emerged from Aladdin's lamp?
5. In what type of racing do just two cars compete at a time?
6. In which radio programme did the catchphrase, 'Left hand down a bit', originate?
7. Who led the Chinese against the Japanese in the Second World War?
8. What was Roxy Music's first hit single?
9. What is the name of the famous gannet breeding ground off North Berwick?

555

1. In humans, what is the effect of ageing on blue eyes?
2. Who was the only English Pope?
3. In which country would you get 100 condors for 1 escudo?
4. Who is Nero Wolfe's assistant in Rex Stout's detective stories?
5. Who rode Flanagan with distinction?
6. Who played Purdey in 'The New Avengers'?
7. Which American president refused to shake hands while in office?
8. Who was the first white woman vocalist to be signed to the Motown record label? (She was British.)
9. What is formed when iron oxidizes?

926

1. In what ratio do male alcoholics outnumber female alcoholics?
2. The first of its kind was called Nekal, produced in Germany in 1917. What was it?
3. How many independent kingdoms united to form the United Arab Emirates?
4. What was the first Penguin book?
5. Who – better known in another racing sphere – is the owner of Towcester racecourse?
6. Who played Lord Peter Wimsey in the BBC series?
7. How many bullets were found in the bodies of Bonnie and Clyde?
8. Iggy Pop and the —?
9. Name a quadruped beginning with N.

184

1. Approximately $5\frac{3}{4}$ inches.
2. The Victoria Cross.
3. Lake Michigan.
4. A genie.
5. Drag racing.
6. 'The Navy Lark'.
7. General Chiang Kai-shek.
8. 'Virginia Plain'.
9. Bass Rock.

555

1. They get lighter as their owners get older.
2. Nicholas Breakspear, Pope Adrian IV (1154–9).
3. Portugal or Chile.
4. Archie Goodwin.
5. Show-jumper Pat Smythe.
6. Joanna Lumley.
7. George Washington – he preferred to bow.
8. Kiki Dee.
9. Rust.

926

1. About 5 to 1.
2. Detergent.
3. Seven.
4. *Ariel* by André Maurois.
5. Lord Hesketh.
6. Ian Carmichael.
7. 104 (54 in Clyde; 50 in Bonnie).
8. Stooges.
9. Nutria, nilgai, newt – there aren't many!

185

1. What is the award for mystery fiction – the equivalent of an 'Oscar' – called?
2. Before John Paul II, who was the last non-Italian Pope?
3. The railway from Bangkok through Kuala Lumpur ends where?
4. Which play ends with the words 'Mon Panache'?
5. Who won the 1,500 metres silver medal at the 1984 Olympics?
6. In one of his films, Humphrey Bogart played a vampire. Name the film.
7. Which US president was nicknamed 'the Rail-Splitter'?
8. Name the 1950s skiffle hit by Nancy Whiskey and Chas McDevitt.
9. In 1796 a physician, Dr Franz Gall, first announced his theory of character. What was it called?

556

1. For how long, on average, does a British coin stay in circulation?
2. A very early set of false teeth has been discovered. Which civilization produced it?
3. Which nation reads the most books per capita?
4. Which was Shakespeare's last play?
5. Who won the English Football League in 1984?
6. By what name was Gladys Smith better known?
7. Who founded the state of Utah and was survived by seventeen widows?
8. With what is tinpan alley associated?
9. What are Norwegian sprats known as?

927

1. What is metoposcopy?
2. Who was murdered by Robert the Bruce in 1306 in a Dumfries churchyard?
3. Which country has a famous national dish called sukiyaki?
4. In Greek mythology, what was the name given to the sea nymphs who lured sailors to their death on the rocks?
5. Which boxer did Paul Newman play in *Somebody Up There Likes Me*?
6. Which school was featured in ITV's 'Please, Sir' series?
7. Which French king befriended Leonardo da Vinci and had his portrait painted by Raphael?
8. Which Gershwin work contains 'I Got Plenty of Nuthin''?
9. Cashmere is the hair of which animal?

185

1. An Edgar.
2. Adrian VI.
3. At Singapore.
4. *Cyrano de Bergerac* by Edmond Rostand.
5. Steve Cram.
6. *The Return of Dr X* (1939).
7. Abraham Lincoln.
8. 'Freight Train'.
9. Phrenology.

556

1. About 25 years.
2. The Phoenician civilization; it was found in a grave at Sidon.
3. The Icelanders.
4. *Henry VIII.*
5. Liverpool.
6. Mary Pickford.
7. Brigham Young, the Mormon.
8. Popular music.
9. Brislings.

927

1. The art of reading character from the forehead.
2. Red Comyn.
3. Japan.
4. The Sirens.
5. Rocky Graziano.
6. Fenn Street.
7. François I.
8. *Porgy and Bess.*
9. The cashmere goat.

186

1. Who were gunned down in the St Valentine's Day Massacre by Al Capone's men?
2. Which Englishman became Charlemagne's teacher and archbishop of Tours?
3. Where is the village of Mucking?
4. By what name was Jane Austen's book *First Impressions* later known?
5. Who was the first Grand Prix driver to use a safety belt, in 1967?
6. On what subject does Peter Seabrook broadcast?
7. For which Sunday paper was Clement Freud a football correspondent?
8. Which composer's first sonatas were published when he was seven years old?
9. Which insect is called the 'steam bug' in Lancashire?

557

1. The range of tides varies with the moon; what name is given to tides occurring at new moon?
2. Who or what was the Sick Man of Europe?
3. What is a cadastral map?
4. Who taught Alice to dance the Lobster Quadrille?
5. Who won the overall gold medal for gymnastics at the 1976 Olympics?
6. Which murderer was the subject of *10 Rillington Place*?
7. What is a catamaran?
8. What was Gonzales?
9. What is an anodyne?

928

1. What is the only wine that can legally be called Champagne?
2. How many months were there in the old Roman year?
3. Where is the dong used as currency?
4. Which Irishman wrote the novels *Molloy*, *Malone Meurt* and *L'Innommable*?
5. What was the collective nickname of Henri Cochet, Jean Borotra, René Lacoste and Jacques Brugnon?
6. What was the name of the film Marilyn Monroe was working on when she died?
7. Who coined the term 'the social contract'?
8. Who lived 'Next Door to an Angel'?
9. For what would you use a hygrometer?

186

1. The Bugs Moran gang.
2. Alcuin of York.
3. In Essex.
4. *Pride and Prejudice.*
5. Jackie Stewart.
6. Gardening.
7. The *Observer.*
8. Mozart's.
9. The cockroach.

557

1. Spring tides.
2. The Turkish Empire (according to Nicholas I of Russia).
3. A large-scale map that shows individual properties.
4. The Mock Turtle.
5. Nadia Comaneci.
6. John Christie.
7. A boat with twin hulls.
8. Speedy (according to Pat Boone and several other artists who recorded versions of the song).
9. A pain-killing drug.

928

1. Wine made by the Champagne method in the region around Reims.
2. Ten.
3. Vietnam.
4. Samuel Beckett.
5. The Four Musketeers. They formed a successful French Davis Cup tennis team from 1922 to 1934.
6. *Something's Got to Give.*
7. Rousseau.
8. Neil Sedaka.
9. Measuring the humidity of the air.

187

1. How many years of marriage does a ruby anniversary celebrate?
2. Which commodity did Nathaniel Canopus (a Cretan) bring to England for the first time in 1641?
3. Where is the Whitney art gallery?
4. Who said in Paris, 'I am dying beyond my means'?
5. How long did the longest recorded rally in tennis last (to the nearest five minutes)?
6. *THX–1138* is a sci-fi cult movie. Who directed it?
7. Who was the first British royal to become a motorist?
8. Which operatic venue celebrated its fiftieth anniversary season in 1984?
9. Ford Prefect came from a star in which constellation?

558

1. Of what is taramasalata made?
2. For how many terms was George Washington President of the USA?
3. Which navigator gave his name to a continent yet didn't go to sea till he was almost fifty?
4. Who wrote, 'To err is human; to forgive divine'?
5. In the 1973 Grand National, who beat Crisp in a course record time?
6. By what name is Julie Elizabeth Edwards better known?
7. The Belgian author of *Pelléas et Mélisande* received the Nobel Prize for Literature in 1911. Who was he?
8. By what name is Steveland Morris better known?
9. Which is the world's fastest animal?

929

1. What is cock-a-leekie?
2. Where was 'Praise the Lord and pass the ammunition' said?
3. Which was the first country to legalize abortion?
4. Who are *The Ragged Trousered Philanthropists*?
5. Which British team first won the Cup Winners' Cup?
6. Who played the lead in Costa-Gavras's political thriller *Z*?
7. What maximum score can be rolled in a single frame of ten-pin bowling?
8. Which band is named after a gang in Woody Guthrie's book *Bound for Glory*?
9. Why do the gases argon, neon and helium form a unique group in chemistry?

187

1. Forty.
2. Coffee.
3. New York.
4. Oscar Wilde.
5. 51½ minutes – an estimated 1,029 strokes.
6. George Lucas.
7. The Prince of Wales, later Edward VII.
8. Glyndebourne.
9. Orion (Betelgeuse).

558

1. Smoked cod's roe.
2. Two (1789–97).
3. Amerigo Vespucci.
4. Pope (*Essay on Criticism*).
5. Red Rum.
6. Julie Andrews.
7. Maurice Maeterlinck (1862–1949).
8. Stevie Wonder.
9. The cheetah, which has been timed at 70 m.p.h.

929

1. A Scottish soup made from chicken and leeks.
2. Pearl Harbor (7 December 1941, by Howell Forgy).
3. The USSR (by decree, in 1920).
4. Painters and decorators in Robert Tressell's book (who 'give' their services to their employers).
5. Tottenham Hotspur (in 1963).
6. Yves Montand.
7. Three hundred.
8. Boomtown Rats.
9. Because no compound has ever been made from them.

188

1. Who, in his will, left a fortune for the establishment of a new phonetic alphabet to assist spelling?
2. Which tax did John Hampden refuse to pay?
3. How long is the Grand Canyon?
4. What was Gulliver's first name?
5. Who play home soccer at the Den?
6. Which legendary American radio DJ is featured in the film *American Graffiti*?
7. After whom is the science fiction award the Hugo named?
8. Which group were '2000 Light Years from Home'?
9. What is Aristotle's Lantern?

559

1. Linnaeus gave the name 'food of the gods' to what drink?
2. Where was Edward the Martyr, sixteen-year-old king of England, murdered?
3. What river runs through York?
4. Who put Daniel in the lions' den?
5. From which country was Jacky Ickx?
6. Who was radio's Man in Black?
7. How old, to the nearest 3 years, was Oliver Cromwell when he became a nationally important politician?
8. Who was runnin' scared?
9. How many times was the Apollo lunar module test-flown before the first moon landing?

930

1. In 1631 Robert Barker's Holy Bible was destroyed and the printer fined £300. Why?
2. Who was made to laugh by John Scogan?
3. Which country's communist party was the first to be run by a general?
4. In which novel do members of the Pontifex family appear?
5. Which sport does the film *North Dallas Forty* feature?
6. Hitchcock appears, fleetingly, in many of his films. How did he crop up in *Rope*?
7. How tall was the poet John Keats?
8. Who had a massive hit in 1965 with 'Here Comes the Night'?
9. What is the fruit of the plantain?

188

1. George Bernard Shaw.
2. Ship-money.
3. 217 miles.
4. Lemuel.
5. Millwall.
6. Wolfman Jack.
7. Hugo Gernsback.
8. The Rolling Stones.
9. The mouth parts of a sea urchin.

559

1. Chocolate.
2. Corfe Castle (by retainers of his stepmother).
3. The Ouse.
4. King Darius.
5. Belgium.
6. Valentine Dyall.
7. Forty-three.
8. Roy Orbison.
9. Twice.

930

1. Because the Seventh Commandment read: 'Thou shalt commit adultery.'
2. Edward IV. (Scogan was the court jester; his japes are recorded in *The Geystes of Skoggan.*)
3. Poland's (Jaruzelski).
4. *The Way of All Flesh* (by Samuel Butler).
5. American football.
6. In outline, on a neon sign.
7. 5 feet ¾ inch.
8. Them.
9. A variety of large banana.

189

1. What is Britain's second highest decoration for bravery?
2. When the Great Wall of China was being built, who were the Romans fighting?
3. The Aberfan disaster was due to what?
4. What is the connection between a garland, an arcade, a thread, and an angular?
5. How many play at one time on a Gaelic football team?
6. Which Cliff Richard musical film featured his song 'Bachelor Boy'?
7. Who formulated the notion of 'body image'?
8. Complete the following group name: Blodwyn —.
9. 1 cheval-vapeur (1 c.v.) is almost equivalent to what in the British system?

560

1. In which year did British women get the vote at the age of twenty-one?
2. What title did Charlemagne receive at his coronation in Rome on 25 December 800?
3. What keeps Norway from being as icebound as Greenland?
4. Which more famous work was written by the author of *Moll Flanders*?
5. How many Olympic gold medals did gymnast Olga Korbut win?
6. Which band was featured in Jean-Luc Godard's English film *One Plus One*?
7. Which doctor practised in London, Newcastle and Paris and was murdered in his bath?
8. Who was Figaro's mother?
9. Which birds are linked with the Tower of London?

931

1. Which of the seven wonders of the world was at Halicarnassus?
2. Who was murdered by a Lord Mayor of London in front of his followers?
3. In which country would you find Inca ruins?
4. How many 'pillars of Islam' are there?
5. Who won the 1972 Badminton horse trials on Great Ovation?
6. In which film did James Cagney make his first appearance for 20 years?
7. Who writes the bridge column in the *Sunday Times*?
8. Name the two legendary rock venues in psychedelic San Francisco.
9. What is cuckoo-spit?

189

1. The George Cross.
2. The Carthaginians (Second Punic War).
3. Collapse of the mining tip above the town.
4. They are all connecting strokes in handwriting.
5. Fifteen.
6. *Summer Holiday.*
7. Wilhelm Reich.
8. Pig.
9. 1 horsepower (1 h.p.).

560

1. 1928.
2. Emperor of the West.
3. The waters of the Gulf Stream.
4. *Robinson Crusoe* (by Daniel Defoe).
5. Four.
6. The Rolling Stones.
7. Jean-Paul Marat.
8. Marcellina.
9. Ravens.

931

1. The mausoleum of King Mausolus of Caria.
2. Wat Tyler (1381).
3. Peru.
4. Five.
5. Mark Phillips.
6. *Ragtime.*
7. Boris Schapiro.
8. The Avalon and the Filmore.
9. White foam surrounding green bugs that feed off plants.

190

1. Which is the only month in which there may not be a full moon?
2. Who was the erstwhile tutor of Nero who killed himself at the emperor's command?
3. Which country once issued a postage stamp in recognition of the world's heaviest smoker?
4. Who broke the little bear's chair?
5. At which rowing venue is the Prince Philip Cup competed for?
6. By what name is Maurice Micklewhite better known?
7. What was Wiley Post's claim to fame in 1933?
8. For whom did Neil Sedaka write 'Oh Carol'?
9. What is Force 11 on the Beaufort scale?

561

1. How do you pronounce the surname Cholmondeley?
2. What accommodation first erected in France in 1916 earned its inventor the DSO?
3. What was the name of the Royal Navy frigate which in 1984, attempting to turn in the River Thames, hit London Bridge?
4. What line follows 'East is East and West is West'?
5. How many times did Red Rum win the Grand National?
6. What is the cartoon version of Kenny Everett called?
7. What is judged at the gurning championships?
8. Which jazz trumpeter had a hit with 'Hello Dolly'?
9. What is a Suffolk punch?

932

1. What is the height of a £1 note?
2. Who, in 1938, said, 'I believe it is peace for our time – peace with honour'?
3. Glogau gold mine in Wales is notable for providing what?
4. Whose shrine were Chaucer's pilgrims on their way to visit?
5. Which tobacco company publishes an annual football yearbook and a rugby yearbook?
6. Until his death, which 'Coronation Street' character was played by Jack Howarth?
7. What nationality was Dame Nellie Melba?
8. Who was lost in France – in 1976?
9. What is the umbilicus?

190

1. February – about once in 20 years.
2. Seneca (in AD 60).
3. Albania.
4. Goldilocks.
5. Henley.
6. Michael Caine.
7. He was the first man to fly solo around the world.
8. Carole King – his girlfriend at the time.
9. A storm.

561

1. Chumley.
2. The Nissen hut (invented by Captain Peter Nissen).
3. HMS *Jupiter*.
4. 'And never the twain shall meet' (Kipling).
5. Three.
6. Captain Kremmen.
7. The ability to pull the ugliest face.
8. Louis Armstrong.
9. A breed of horse.

932

1. Approximately $2\frac{1}{2}$ inches.
2. Neville Chamberlain.
3. Gold for royal wedding rings.
4. Thomas à Becket's.
5. Rothmans.
6. Albert Tatlock.
7. Australian.
8. Bonnie Tyler.
9. The navel.

191

1. What are salopettes?
2. Who founded the Grand National Consolidated Trades Union in 1834?
3. Approximately how many more miles of canals has Birmingham than Venice?
4. What was the middle name of Jerome K. Jerome?
5. Who scored six goals in the 1982 World Cup finals?
6. What is the title of Edward G. Robinson's autobiography?
7. Who betrayed Samson?
8. Who sang the theme song in the James Bond film *Thunderball*?
9. Which animal can defend itself by squirting blood from its eyes?

562

1. What unusual weather condition occurred just before the 1975 drought in the British Isles?
2. What was the date of the killer London pea-souper in which 4,000 more deaths were recorded than average?
3. Where would you find the Casquets?
4. Where did Mr Micawber end up as a magistrate?
5. How many penalties did Gary Bailey save when Manchester United lost to Ipswich in 1980?
6. What part did Linda Blair play in *The Exorcist*?
7. How many children did Queen Victoria have?
8. Who picked pops on radio on Sunday afternoons?
9. Where is the Meteorological Office?

933

1. Which stimulant occurs in tea, coffee and cocoa?
2. What necessitated chairpersons in 1975, but only just?
3. When and where was the world's worst air disaster?
4. How old was the author at the time of writing *The Young Visiters*?
5. Which team did Hungary clobber 10–1 in the 1982 World Cup?
6. Who was presenter of the 'Saturday Club' in the 1960s?
7. What country, looted by a French marshal, rewarded an English general with paintings?
8. What was Tom Robinson glad to be?
9. Which society cared for the plague victims when the physicians left London in 1665?

191

1. Snow-proof, dungaree-type trousers.
2. Robert Owen.
3. Twenty-two.
4. Klapka – after a Hungarian friend of his father's.
5. Paolo Rossi of Italy.
6. *All My Yesterdays.*
7. Delilah.
8. Tom Jones.
9. The horned toad (American).

562

1. Snow in June in many parts.
2. 5–10 December 1952.
3. Off the Channel Islands.
4. In Australia.
5. Three.
6. Regan MacNeil.
7. Nine (four sons and five daughters).
8. Alan Freeman.
9. Bracknell, Berks.

933

1. Caffeine.
2. The Sex Discrimination Act (passed on 29 December 1975).
3. In 1977 at Tenerife airport (two jumbos collided on the ground).
4. Nine (Daisy Ashford).
5. El Salvador.
6. Brian Matthew.
7. Spain (plundered by Soult in the Napoleonic Wars and liberated partly due to the Duke of Wellington).
8. Gay.
9. The Society of Apothecaries.

192

1. By what title is the Parliamentary Commissioner for Administration generally known?
2. Extremists from where murdered the Archduke Franz Ferdinand in 1914?
3. If you were a Croat, of what nationality would you be?
4. In which magazine does Lord Gnome appear?
5. Of what nationality was the winner of the 1983 Safari rally?
6. What was the name of the computer in *2001*?
7. For what were Jean and François Clouet known?
8. Who drove his Chevvy to the levee?
9. Which animal other than human did the lion's share of farm work during the Middle Ages?

563

1. What are the dog days?
2. What single leader was responsible for conquering the largest amount of territory?
3. Honolulu to Moscow is how far in miles?
4. To what was Pepys referring when he wrote in 1660, 'I did send for a cup of—which I had never drank before'?
5. In which sport is the Lance Todd memorial trophy awarded?
6. Who was the first resident cartoonist in *TW3*?
7. What colour is cochineal?
8. Declan McManus is better known as who?
9. From which South American shrub does cocaine come?

934

1. In which publication was the term 'suffragette' first used?
2. Which British borough possesses the earliest recorded royal charter?
3. What was the colonial name of Mali?
4. What is the other title of *Mr Salteena's Plan*?
5. Which dog won the 1984 Greyhound Derby?
6. Which Hitchcock film was based on *The Wheel Spins* by Ethel Lina White?
7. Which English Romantic poet and critic lived in the Lake District and was a great friend of Wordsworth?
8. 'You'll Never Walk Alone' – a hardy perennial – first appeared in which musical?
9. What is albedo?

192

1. The Ombudsman.
2. Serbia.
3. Yugoslavian.
4. *Private Eye.*
5. Finnish (Ari Vatanen in an Opel Ascona).
6. HAL.
7. They were French miniaturists and portrait painters.
8. Don McLean.
9. The ox.

563

1. The period between the rising and setting of Sirius, the dog-star (around 11 August).
2. Genghis Khan (approx. 4,860,000 square miles in 21 years). His empire included northern China, Mongolia, southern Siberia and central Asia.
3. 7,036.
4. Tea.
5. Rugby League.
6. Timothy Birdsall.
7. Red.
8. Elvis Costello.
9. Coca.

934

1. The *Daily Mail* (1906).
2. Barnstaple, Devon (charter granted in 930).
3. The French Sudan.
4. *The Young Visiters.*
5. Whisper Wishes.
6. *The Lady Vanishes.*
7. Samuel Taylor Coleridge.
8. *Carousel.*
9. The percentage of sunlight reflected from an object.

193

1. What is the correct style of address for an archbishop?
2. Where did Napoleon Bonaparte suffer his last defeat?
3. From the language of which country does 'anorak' come?
4. What is the winged horse of Greek mythology called?
5. Who was the only golfer to have his life story made into a film?
6. Who was BBC TV's Mastermind in 1984?
7. Who painted the famous 'Boyhood of Raleigh'?
8. Who played Caruso in the 1951 film *The Great Caruso*?
9. Who was Orville Wright's older brother?

564

1. How long does it take an average crematorium to burn a corpse?
2. What was first used in France in 1792 in the Place de Grève?
3. Which African country has the highest population?
4. In the poem by Kipling, what was Gunga Din's job?
5. How many barriers must be cleared in the 3,000 metres steeplechase?
6. Who is Bilko's colonel?
7. From what did Harry Houdini die?
8. By what name was Alfred Arnold Cocozza better known?
9. Which breed of dog won Crufts in 1984?

935

1. GATT is an acronym for what?
2. Which Roman statesman was assassinated on the Ides of March?
3. Why is the city of La Paz in Bolivia safe from fire?
4. Who was Desdemona's husband?
5. How many players take part in the game on a cricket pitch?
6. Who is Joan Fontaine's actress sister?
7. Gerald Peters was Elvis Presley's chauffeur. To which eminent person had he previously been chauffeur?
8. Which was the first tune that Louis Armstrong learned to play on the trumpet?
9. What happens to the eyes when sneezing?

193

1. The Most Reverend His Grace the Lord Archbishop of —.
2. Waterloo.
3. Greenland.
4. Pegasus.
5. Ben Hogan (*Follow the Sun*).
6. Margaret Harris.
7. Millais.
8. Mario Lanza.
9. Wilbur Wright.

564

1. $1\frac{1}{2}$ hours.
2. The guillotine.
3. Nigeria.
4. Water carrier.
5. Thirty-five (including seven water jumps).
6. John T. Hall.
7. A blow to the stomach.
8. Mario Lanza.
9. The Lhasa Apso.

935

1. General Agreement on Tariffs and Trade.
2. Julius Caesar.
3. Because it is so high above sea level that there is not enough oxygen to support fire.
4. Othello.
5. Thirteen.
6. Olivia de Havilland.
7. Sir Winston Churchill.
8. 'Home Sweet Home'.
9. They close.

194

1. In Britain, which body is known by the initials CRE?
2. What had the code-name Operation Overlord?
3. Which is France's leading university?
4. Who created Noddy?
5. For how many years were the Wimbledon tennis championships held before women were allowed to compete?
6. Who played Rocky Graziano in the 1956 film *Somebody Up There Likes Me*?
7. Eddie D. Slovik was a private in the US army. How did he die?
8. Who had a hit in 1968 with 'Tiptoe Through the Tulips'?
9. What is called the ship of the desert?

565

1. What are the good reporter's six questions?
2. How many slaves did Patrick Henry own when he made his famous speech about freedom?
3. Which country is the second largest consumer of tea in the world?
4. From which Victorian melodrama does the line 'Dead, and never called me mother' come?
5. Which golfer won the Vardon Trophy in 1970, 1971 and 1972?
6. Who's missing – Compo, Foggy, —?
7. What nationality was the artist Titian?
8. What caused Alban Berg's death?
9. Why do murderers like acetylcholine?

936

1. Which famous mystery writer created a mystery by disappearing in 1926?
2. Which British nurse helped 200 soldiers escape to Holland and was executed in 1915 by the Germans?
3. Who is the patron saint of Germany?
4. Who was Robinson Crusoe's native companion?
5. How many strokes under par is a birdie?
6. Who heads UNCLE?
7. Which two suits have one-eyed jacks?
8. What is the official song of the state of Kansas, USA?
9. Which animals attract the most fleas?

194

1. Commission for Racial Equality.
2. The invasion of Normandy.
3. The Sorbonne.
4. Enid Blyton.
5. Seven. They began in 1877 for men only; women were not admitted until 1884.
6. Paul Newman.
7. He was executed in 1945, the only U S soldier to die for desertion since 1864.
8. Tiny Tim.
9. The camel.

565

1. Who, what, when, where, why, how?
2. Sixty-five.
3. The USA.
4. *East Lynne*.
5. Lee Trevino.
6. Clegg ('The Last of the Summer Wine').
7. Italian.
8. Blood poisoning resulting from a bee sting.
9. Because it is a totally untraceable poison.

936

1. Agatha Christie.
2. Edith Cavell.
3. St Boniface.
4. Man Friday.
5. One.
6. Mr Waverley.
7. Hearts and spades.
8. 'Home on the Range'.
9. Red squirrels.

195

1. What are the four c's that denote the value of a diamond?
2. Which king was killed at the Battle of Hastings?
3. Which city's public transport lost property office is the busiest?
4. What is the shortest name in the Bible?
5. In which event did seventeen-year-old Bob Mathias of the USA win a gold medal at the 1948 London Olympics?
6. For which paper does Superman work?
7. Which actress did Reynolds paint as the Tragic Muse?
8. Which smaller instrument of the same type do professional flautists also usually play?
9. For what purpose was Coca-Cola originally sold?

566

1. What fits into a mortise to form a joint?
2. After whom was the state of Georgia in the US named?
3. Which English county possesses the most rats?
4. Vladimir and Estragon feature in which of Beckett's plays?
5. How many players are on each side in volleyball?
6. In which film did Omar Sharif star with Catherine Deneuve?
7. Who was the Wasp of Twickenham?
8. Which famous piece comes from Rimsky-Korsakov's opera *The Tsar Saltan*?
9. How many times greater is the earth's surface gravity than that of the moon?

937

1. What do magicians consider to be the most dangerous trick?
2. Approximately when did the gypsies arrive in Britain?
3. Which British city is sometimes called the Athens of the North?
4. For which skill was Castor famed?
5. Who was the only boxer to win a title without ever having had a manager?
6. Who was termed the First Lady of the Silent Screen?
7. In which Welsh town were Richard Burton and Tom Jones born?
8. When was the song 'Happy Birthday to You' composed?
9. What is atmospheric vapour frozen in crystalline form called?

A

195

1. Cut, carat, clarity, colour.
2. Harold.
3. Tokyo's.
4. Uz.
5. The decathlon.
6. The *Daily Planet.*
7. Sarah Siddons.
8. The piccolo.
9. As a patent medicine.

566

1. A tenon.
2. King George II.
3. Nottinghamshire.
4. *Waiting for Godot.*
5. Six.
6. *Mayerling.*
7. Alexander Pope.
8. 'The Flight of the Bumblebee'.
9. Six.

937

1. Catching a bullet in their teeth.
2. AD 1500.
3. Edinburgh.
4. Horse training.
5. Jake La Motta.
6. Lillian Gish.
7. Pontypridd.
8. 1936.
9. Snow.

196

1. What is ombrophobia?
2. Which race did the Ancient Britons belong to?
3. At 30 miles, Figueroa Street is the longest street in the world. Which city does it run through?
4. Who wrote the novel *QB VII*?
5. Which German football club won the European Cup in 1974, 1975 and 1976?
6. Who played Becket in the 1964 film of the same name?
7. What nationality was the painter Fra Angelico?
8. Who composed the symphony based on Dante's *Divine Comedy*?
9. What does vitamin K assist?

567

1. Approximately how many tons of diamonds are mined annually?
2. In ancient China, titles were conferred on which breed of dog?
3. Which country has three newspapers which each sell ten million copies daily?
4. Who created detective Philip Marlowe?
5. What sporting event is Stoke Mandeville known for?
6. In which novel was the word 'Nadsat' coined?
7. By what name was Cristobal Colin better known?
8. Which composer appears on the French 10-franc note?
9. Which vitamin is produced by the action of ultra-violet light on the skin?

938

1. How many nobles did a monetary pound comprise?
2. Who was Emperor of Austria from 1848 to 1916?
3. In Venezuela, why do lovers use pink envelopes?
4. Who said, 'Life does not cease to be funny when people die, any more than it ceases to be serious when people laugh'?
5. Where do Liverpool FC play home games?
6. With whom is the role of the Cisco Kid most associated?
7. Who succeeded Brian Epstein as manager of the Beatles?
8. What type of dance is a *Ländler*?
9. Approximately how many species of spider are there in the UK?

196

1. Fear of rain.
2. The Celts.
3. Los Angeles.
4. Leon Uris.
5. Bayern Munich.
6. Richard Burton.
7. Italian.
8. Liszt.
9. Blood-clotting.

567

1. Five.
2. The pekinese.
3. Russia.
4. Raymond Chandler.
5. Paraplegic games.
6. *A Clockwork Orange*.
7. Christopher Columbus.
8. Hector Berlioz.
9. Vitamin D.

938

1. Three.
2. Franz Josef.
3. Because they are then charged half the usual postage.
4. George Bernard Shaw.
5. Anfield.
6. Cesar Romero.
7. Alan Klein.
8. A slow waltz.
9. 580.

197

1. Boob Day is the Spanish equivalent of what in Britain?
2. What did the Cree Indians use as currency?
3. Which country is farthest from New Zealand?
4. Who was the beautiful wife of Uriah the Hittite?
5. Where is the St Leger run?
6. Which famous big-game hunter played himself in the 1951 film *Perils of the Jungle*?
7. In 1922 Theresa Vaughn was put on trial. For what crime?
8. How was Berlioz's *Symphonie funèbre et triomphale* to be played?
9. What is the largest number of parson's noses found to date on a single turkey?

568

1. What is chromophobia?
2. Who preached 'communism' at Blackheath during the Peasants' Revolt of 1381?
3. In which war did 'Remember the Alamo' become a US battle slogan?
4. Whose valet is Mervyn Butler?
5. In netball, if you had a bib with WD, what position would you be playing?
6. By what name is James Baumgarner better known?
7. Which numbers flank 16 on a dartboard?
8. Whose last unfinished work was the opera *L'Atlantida*?
9. Which part of the body contains the most gold?

939

1. Which word has come into about 1,200 different languages without changing?
2. What did ENSA stand for in the Second World War?
3. Where is Elizabeth I buried?
4. What was Margaret Mitchell's only book?
5. What is the world record for turns of a hand-held skipping rope in a single skip?
6. Who played Ahmet Bey in *The Mummy* (1932)?
7. Whose girlfriend had a pet snake called Enid?
8. Who wrote the theme music for the film *Limelight*?
9. By what name is the giant kingfisher better known?

197

1. April Fool's Day.
2. Pipes.
3. Spain.
4. Bathsheba.
5. Doncaster.
6. Clyde Beatty.
7. Bigamy, but she turned out to be a polygamist, having married sixty-two men in 5 years!
8. While marching.
9. Three.

568

1. Fear of a colour.
2. John Ball.
3. The Mexican War.
4. Lord Peter Wimsey's.
5. Wing defence.
6. James Garner.
7. 7 and 8.
8. Manuel de Falla's.
9. The toe-nails.

939

1. Amen.
2. Entertainment National Service Association.
3. Westminster Abbey.
4. *Gone with the Wind.*
5. Five.
6. Boris Karloff.
7. Hitler's.
8. Charlie Chaplin.
9. The laughing jackass.

198

1. How did ten-year-old Roy Gadd persuade a leopard to stop clawing his friend's arm in 1969?
2. Whose horse was called Black Nell?
3. What is the Italian town of Parma noted for?
4. Who wrote *The Napoleon of Notting Hill*?
5. Where is the largest bowling alley in the world?
6. What does MGM stand for?
7. Who was the most prolific writer of children's books?
8. What was Elvis Presley's original back-up group called?
9. How long does a lost finger-nail take to grow back?

569

1. What number does the Roman numeral X represent?
2. Charles II was the father of the Duke of St Albans. Who was the Duke's mother?
3. In which country are the Angel Falls?
4. Which Sussex castle is the seat of the Duke of Norfolk?
5. What are the five events in the modern Olympic pentathlon?
6. Who is Mastermind's question-master?
7. By what name was the actress and columnist who was born into the Fluck family and who died in 1984 better known?
8. Campdown racetrack is how long?
9. What is the olfactory sense?

940

1. What is the term *Brassica rapa* used for?
2. By how long did Catherine Parr, Henry VIII's wife, survive him?
3. How did Tibetans dispose of the bodies of their dead relatives, up till about 1940?
4. What are antonyms?
5. What first sports meeting took place in 776 BC?
6. What is tattooed on Popeye's arm?
7. Which numbers flank 17 on a dartboard?
8. Who composed 'Alexander's Ragtime Band'?
9. What is the name given to the belt of low pressure over the equator?

198

1. He punched it on the nose.
2. Wild Bill Hickok's.
3. Ham.
4. G. K. Chesterton.
5. Japan. The Tokyo World Lane Bowling Center has 252 lanes.
6. Metro-Goldwyn-Mayer.
7. Enid Blyton, who wrote over 600, 59 of them in 1955.
8. The Blue Moon Boys.
9. 4 to 5 months.

569

1. 10.
2. Nell Gwyn.
3. Venezuela.
4. Arundel Castle.
5. Horse-riding, fencing, pistol-shooting, swimming and cross-country running.
6. Magnus Magnusson.
7. Diana Dors.
8. 5 miles.
9. The sense of smell.

940

1. Turnips.
2. 1 year.
3. They chopped them up and fed them to the birds.
4. Words of opposite meaning.
5. The first Greek Olympic Games.
6. An anchor.
7. 2 and 3.
8. Irving Berlin.
9. The doldrums.

199

1. What was Blackbeard's pirate ship called?
2. Who was put to death by a firing squad on 17 January 1977, the first person to be executed in the USA for 10 years?
3. From which country did Tunisia and Algeria gain independence?
4. What was the nickname that Anne Frank gave her diary?
5. Who was the first British woman athlete to win an Olympic gold medal?
6. As what was HMS *Jonah* disguised in the 1969 film *The Private Life of Sherlock Holmes*?
7. What poker hand just pips the two aces and two kings?
8. Who wrote the poems for William Walton's *Façade*?
9. What is the correct name for the funny bone?

570

1. In how many categories are Pulitzer Prizes awarded?
2. Who was William's joint sovereign?
3. What is known as the New World?
4. Why was the Globe theatre destroyed by fire?
5. Which plough-horse once won the Grand National?
6. In which 1978 film did Robert Shaw, Harrison Ford and Edward Fox star?
7. Who originally illustrated *Alice in Wonderland*?
8. By what name is Antonio Benedetto better known?
9. What is lycanthropy?

941

1. What is saponification?
2. Who was the first captain to sail his ship all the way round the world?
3. What London palace built by Henry VIII was destroyed by fire in 1698?
4. Who said that Shakespeare had 'small Latin and less Greek'?
5. What are the New York Knickerbockers?
6. Of which English play was the Flemish *Elkerlye* a forerunner?
7. What did Mrs Mary Gillick design?
8. Who wrote 'God Bless America'?
9. What was the largest creature ever to fly?

199

1. *Queen Anne's Revenge.*
2. Gary Gilmore, who was the illegitimate grandson of Harry Houdini.
3. France.
4. Kitty.
5. Mary Rand.
6. The Loch Ness Monster, *Jonah* being an experimental submarine.
7. Three twos.
8. Edith Sitwell.
9. The humerus (naturally!).

570

1. Eighteen.
2. Mary.
3. The Americas.
4. During a performance of *Henry VIII*, a cannon used in the play set fire to the roof.
5. Rubio in 1908 at 60–1.
6. *Force 10 from Navarone.*
7. Sir John Tenniel.
8. Tony Bennett.
9. The supposed ability of a human being to assume the form of a wolf.

941

1. The process by which soap is made.
2. Sir Francis Drake (Magellan died en route).
3. Whitehall.
4. Ben Jonson.
5. A professional American basketball team.
6. *Everyman.*
7. The British coinage for Elizabeth II before decimalization.
8. Irving Berlin.
9. The pterodactyl. Fossilized skeletons have been found with a head 4 feet long and a wingspan of 18 feet.

200

1. On which current British coin does a portcullis feature?
2. Which cavalry regiment was George Armstrong Custer's last command?
3. Which mountains separate Asia from Europe?
4. Name Dora Copperfield's pet spaniel.
5. What are the colours of the five Olympic rings?
6. Who plays the butcher in 'Dad's Army'?
7. What did Thomas Hardy originally study?
8. Which famous singer co-wrote the words to the song 'California, Here I Come'?
9. What is a female sheep called?

571

1. What are the seven virtues?
2. On which East Indies island did Captain William Bligh land after being cast adrift?
3. Which is the largest city in the southern hemisphere?
4. What is detective Philip Marlowe's favourite brand of cigarettes?
5. At the Melbourne Olympics, which set of events had to be held in Sweden and why?
6. Who played Eliza Dolittle in the 1964 film *My Fair Lady*?
7. Who designed the first steamship to make regular Atlantic crossings?
8. Who was the oldest Beatle?
9. How long did Louis Blériot take to cross the English Channel in his historic flight of 1909?

942

1. What is ETAOINSHRDLU?
2. On which day and month in 44 BC was Julius Caesar killed?
3. Which London street is reputedly the world's centre for men's tailoring?
4. Who was Queen to King Arthur?
5. Which Olympic events have a course of 1 mile 427 yards?
6. Who is Fred Flintstone's wife?
7. What is Leighton Rees's game?
8. Who are Alan, Wayne, Merrill, Jay, Donny, Marie and Jimmy?
9. A dirigible is a balloon. But what is special about it?

200

1. On the penny.
2. The Seventh.
3. The Urals.
4. Jip.
5. Black, blue, red, green and yellow.
6. Clive Dunn.
7. Architecture.
8. Al Jolson.
9. A ewe.

571

1. Faith, hope, charity, fortitude, justice, prudence and temperance.
2. Timor Island.
3. Buenos Aires.
4. Camels.
5. The equestrian events, due to Australia's strict horse quarantine laws.
6. Audrey Hepburn.
7. Isambard Kingdom Brunel.
8. Ringo Starr.
9. 40 minutes.

942

1. Twelve letters of the alphabet in the order of frequency with which they are used in English.
2. 15 March.
3. Savile Row.
4. Guinevere.
5. Rowing events.
6. Wilma.
7. Darts.
8. The Osmonds.
9. It can be steered or directed.

201

1. Of what are Old Honiton, Genoese and Mechlin forms?
2. What forerunner of many was opened in London on 25 June 1801?
3. In which year did the first woman climb the summit of Mount Everest?
4. Which American essayist wrote detective stories as Edgar Box?
5. To which country did England lose an international soccer match 7–1 in 1954?
6. Who has presented TV's 'Police Five' since 1962?
7. Which world championships are held annually in September at Egremont, in Cumbria?
8. What is Captain Sensible's real name?
9. Name the first teddy-bear in space.

572

1. In 1912 David Sarnoff received a morse signal in New York carrying bad news. What was its gist?
2. When was the Automobile Association founded?
3. Where is the river Orinoco?
4. Name the gull who assisted the rabbits in *Watership Down.*
5. Which Continental country first defeated England on home ground at soccer?
6. As which duchess did Gemma Jones become famous?
7. Which movie mogul said, 'Don't say yes until I've finished talking'?
8. What was Suzie Quatro's first British hit?
9. By what name is the chaparral cock better known?

943

1. What is *Rauchen verboten* in English?
2. Who was the reigning British monarch during the First World War?
3. Who are known as the *Képis blancs*?
4. Whose pseudonym was a single letter of the alphabet?
5. Which non-league team knocked Liverpool out of the FA Cup?
6. Which DJ hosted the 'Perfumed Garden' show in the late 1960s?
7. Who was Kitty Muggeridge describing when she said, 'He rose without trace'?
8. Who provided the musical interlude on the 'Goon Show'?
9. A climbing orchid with bright green fleshy leaves and fragrant greenish-white flowers is used as a flavouring. What is it?

201

1. Lace.
2. The first massage parlour.
3. 1975.
4. Gore Vidal.
5. Hungary.
6. Shaw Taylor.
7. The World Gurning Championships.
8. Ray Burns.
9. Mishka – the 1980 Olympic mascot.

572

1. That the SS *Titanic* had run into an iceberg and was sinking fast.
2. 1905.
3. Venezuela.
4. Kehaar.
5. Hungary, in 1953.
6. As 'The Duchess of Duke Street'.
7. Darryl F. Zanuck.
8. 'Can the Can'.
9. The roadrunner.

943

1. No smoking.
2. George V.
3. The Foreign Legion.
4. Arthur Quiller-Couch, otherwise known as Q.
5. Worcester City, in 1959.
6. John Peel.
7. David Frost.
8. The Ray Ellington Quartet.
9. The vanilla plant.

202

1. In which language did St Paul write his epistles?
2. Which British gold coin was first struck in 1663 for trading in Africa?
3. Which country did the Pharaohs rule?
4. With whom did Frederick Engels write the *Communist Manifesto*?
5. Who was the oldest Formula 1 driver ever to win the World Grand Prix?
6. What is Dick Grayson's secret identity?
7. Which Ugandan styled himself the Conqueror of the British Empire?
8. Name the National Anthem of France.
9. How many sides has a decagon?

573

1. What time does the clock above the leading article in *The Times* always show?
2. Who was prisoner 40886 at Atlanta Federal Prison?
3. Who were the Thugs?
4. Who was the King of the Fairies in *A Midsummer Night's Dream*?
5. Which F A team has Griffin Park as its home ground?
6. Who was the first person to earn a million pounds by the age of ten?
7. Who designed Nelson's column in Trafalgar Square?
8. What was the Big Bopper's biggest hit?
9. All horses have one official birthday. When is it?

944

1. Which R A F rank is equivalent to the Army's second lieutenant?
2. In which year did Scott's Antarctic expedition take place?
3. Which is the largest city in the U S A in total land area?
4. Who was Queen of the Fairies in *A Midsummer Night's Dream*?
5. Which county cricket side won the 1982 Schweppes County Championship?
6. How long does the Oberammergau Passion Play take to perform?
7. When is a painting classed as ancient?
8. Which instrument of the orchestra usually has forty-seven strings?
9. What is a blue-grey gnatcatcher?

202

1. Greek.
2. The guinea.
3. Egypt.
4. Karl Marx.
5. Juan Manuel Fangio, who was aged forty-six when he won in 1957.
6. Robin, the Boy Wonder.
7. Idi Amin.
8. The 'Marseillaise'.
9. Ten.

573

1. 4.30.
2. Al Capone.
3. Professional robbers and murderers in India.
4. Oberon.
5. Brentford.
6. Shirley Temple.
7. William Railton.
8. 'Chantilly Lace'.
9. 1 January.

944

1. Pilot officer.
2. 1910.
3. Jacksonville, Florida (460 square miles).
4. Titania.
5. Middlesex.
6. $8\frac{1}{2}$ hours.
7. When it dates from before the fifth century.
8. The harp.
9. A bird.

203

1. Approximately what proportion of the world's population customarily eats with chop-sticks?
2. Who was the first American in space?
3. With which island is voodoo particularly associated?
4. Whose first book was *Pebble in the Sky*?
5. Who was Coroibos of Olis?
6. Whom did Vanessa Redgrave portray in the 1979 film *Agatha*?
7. By what name was John Merrick better known?
8. Which orchestral instrument did Denner reputedly invent?
9. Name Britain's first test-tube baby.

574

1. What is sake made from?
2. At the Battle of Crécy in 1346 the French lost about 4,000 men. How many did the English lose?
3. Who wrote many of his novels in his Jamaican retreat 'Goldeneye'?
4. Which Ernest Hemingway novel dealt with bull-fighting?
5. Who was the first woman to break 2 minutes in the 200 yards individual medley?
6. Which 1935 film made Errol Flynn famous?
7. Who is Barbie Doll's boyfriend?
8. Who wrote the song 'Give My Regards to Broadway'?
9. What did Wilhelm Roentgen discover in 1895?

945

1. What title did Harold Macmillan take on his ninetieth birthday?
2. The ships of Britain, France and which other country took part in the Battle of Trafalgar?
3. In which country did Leon Trotsky die?
4. Who created the amateur detective Albert Campion?
5. From which wood are cricket bats traditionally made?
6. Name the Good Witch of the North.
7. Which US president won a Pulitzer Prize?
8. From which musical does the song 'Some Enchanted Evening' come?
9. At what speed does a wind become a hurricane?

203

1. One-third.
2. John Glenn, on 5 May 1961.
3. Haiti.
4. Isaac Asimov's.
5. A cook, the Greek athlete who became the first Olympic champion by winning the only event, the 200-yard dash, at the first Olympics in 776 BC.
6. Agatha Christie.
7. The Elephant Man.
8. The clarinet.
9. Louise Brown.

574

1. Rice.
2. Less than 100.
3. Ian Fleming.
4. *Fiesta.*
5. Tracy Caulkins.
6. *Captain Blood.*
7. Ken.
8. George M. Cohan.
9. X-rays.

945

1. Earl of Stockton.
2. Spain.
3. Mexico.
4. Margery Allingham.
5. Willow.
6. Glinda, in *The Wizard of Oz.*
7. John F. Kennedy.
8. *South Pacific.*
9. 73 m.p.h.

204

1. What is Yom Kippur?
2. Who was Director of the FBI from 1924 until his death?
3. What is the capital of the People's Democratic Republic of Yemen?
4. Who wrote *The Honourable Schoolboy*?
5. Who won the Wimbledon men's singles in 1939?
6. By what name was Alfred Schneider better known?
7. Who declared himself Chancellor of Germany at the Bürgerbräu Keller, a Munich beer house?
8. Which 1972 hit record by the New Seekers was originally heard as a Coca-Cola commercial?
9. Who was awarded the Nobel Prize for Physics in 1921?

575

1. Which three tradesmen were in a tub?
2. Which king of England outlawed cricket in 1477?
3. Which country was once known as Serendib?
4. Which was the only case Perry Mason ever lost in court?
5. Who trained the 1983 Grand National winner?
6. Who played James Herriot in the 1974 film *All Creatures Great and Small*?
7. By what name was Manfred von Richthofen better known?
8. Who portrayed Louis Armstrong in the 1954 film *The Glenn Miller Story*?
9. In the binary system what would 100 represent?

946

1. How many Pope Johns have there been?
2. Who reigned in England from 1558 to 1603?
3. What was the strip of land between the enemy trenches in Flanders and France called in the First World War?
4. What was the motto of the Three Musketeers?
5. At which weight did 'Sugar' Ray Robinson hold the world boxing title between 1946 and 1951?
6. Who assembled Steve Austin as the Bionic Man?
7. With what is luchre played?
8. Whom did Robert Walker portray in the 1947 film *Song of Love*?
9. Where did the first controlled atomic fission reaction take place?

204

1. The Jewish Day of Atonement.
2. John Edgar Hoover.
3. Aden.
4. John Le Carré.
5. Bobby Riggs.
6. Lenny Bruce.
7. Adolf Hitler.
8. 'I'd Like to Teach the World to Sing'.
9. Albert Einstein.

575

1. The butcher, the baker and the candlestick-maker.
2. Edward IV.
3. Sri Lanka (Ceylon).
4. 'The Case of the Terrified Typist'.
5. Jenny Pitman.
6. Simon Ward.
7. The Red Baron.
8. He played himself.
9. 4.

946

1. Twenty-one.
2. Queen Elizabeth I.
3. No Man's Land.
4. 'All for one and one for all.'
5. Welterweight.
6. Dr Rudy Wells.
7. Cards.
8. Brahms.
9. At the University of Chicago.

205

1. Where can the largest bell in the world be found?
2. How many toes did Charles VIII of France have on his right foot?
3. Where is the centre of the English cutlery industry?
4. Who is the Owl of the Remove?
5. Which modern game does the old Aztec game of *ollamalitzli* most closely resemble?
6. In 1926, which film star's funeral in New York was attended by over 100,000 people?
7. How many snooker points are scored from three reds, a black and a pink?
8. Which country does the rumba come from?
9. What was the original zip-fastener called?

576

1. Why are camel-hair brushes so called?
2. Which famous seaman commanded the *Triumph* during the Armada's attack?
3. With which country is the chow-chow particularly associated?
4. Who lived at 7 Savile Row and travelled?
5. Who succeeded Bruce Jenner as Olympic decathlon champion?
6. Who wrote the novel on which the film *Caravan to Vaccares* was based?
7. What did George Nissen invent?
8. Who composed 'Blue Moon'?
9. What is obtained when barley is soaked in water, allowed to sprout and dried in a kiln?

947

1. Of what is 'Liberty Enlightening the World' the official name?
2. Who was the first peer to disclaim his title under the 1963 Peerage Act?
3. What is the national flower of the USA?
4. What do the initials in D. H. Lawrence's name represent?
5. Which professional golfer landed a 1,358-pound marlin off Australia in 1978?
6. Who is Batman's butler?
7. Who was guillotined for killing Marat in his bath?
8. What does *lento* mean?
9. What is the colloquial name for asafoetida, the evil-smelling medicinal gum resin?

205

1. In the Kremlin, Moscow.
2. Six.
3. Sheffield.
4. Billy Bunter.
5. Basketball.
6. Rudolph Valentino's.
7. Sixteen.
8. Cuba.
9. C-Curity.

576

1. *Not* because they are made from camel hair, but from the name of their inventor – Camel.
2. Frobisher.
3. China.
4. Phileas Fogg, in *Around the World in Eighty Days.*
5. Daley Thompson.
6. Alistair Maclean.
7. The trampoline.
8. Richard Rodgers.
9. Malt.

947

1. The Statue of Liberty.
2. Anthony Wedgwood Benn.
3. There is none, Congress never having been able to agree on one.
4. David Herbert.
5. Jack Nicklaus, and this was the biggest fish caught off Australia in that year.
6. Alfred.
7. Charlotte Corday.
8. Slow.
9. Devil's dung.

206

1. When is Gowk's Day?
2. Which famous painting was completed in 1506?
3. In which desert did Mark Thatcher get lost in the fourth Paris to Dakar rally?
4. Which duke married Viola?
5. Which track race is known as the Metric Mile?
6. How tall is Sophia Loren?
7. Who did Marcello Caetano replace as dictator of Portugal in 1968?
8. Which is the largest instrument in a regular string quartet?
9. How long does a new hair take to show up in the follicle of a hair plucked out with tweezers?

577

1. 'Husky' was the code name for what invasion?
2. What did John Wesley Hyatt invent in 1869?
3. What is the national drink of Yugoslavia?
4. Who wrote the novel *Once Over Lightly*?
5. Who delivers the balls in baseball?
6. Whose badge number is 627?
7. Which illustrator, whose name has now entered the English language, became famous for his drawings of absurd inventions?
8. Who was the first singer to sell a million records?
9. Why do corpses nowadays deteriorate less quickly than they used to?

948

1. An assegai is a type of what?
2. What was the population of England and Wales at the 1821 Census to the nearest half a million?
3. Which sea separates Yugoslavia from Italy?
4. Who wrote *1984* and *Animal Farm*?
5. In which country was Arkle bred?
6. On whose life was the film *Rocky* loosely based?
7. Which member of the Royal Family rode Good Prospect and Allibar in steeplechases?
8. Which dance was based on a Bohemian courtship dance and goes 1-2-3 hop?
9. What, on a bird, is the nictitating membrane?

206

1. 1 April.
2. The Mona Lisa.
3. The Sahara.
4. Orsino.
5. The 1,500 metres.
6. 5 feet 8 inches.
7. Salazar, but no one told Salazar and he ended his days thinking he still ruled Portugal (he had had a stroke).
8. The cello.
9. About 56 days.

577

1. The Allied invasion of Sicily in July 1943.
2. Celluloid.
3. Slivovitz.
4. David Niven, in 1951.
5. The pitcher.
6. Theo Kojak.
7. Heath Robinson.
8. Enrico Caruso.
9. Because of the preservatives in food that was eaten while alive.

948

1. Spear.
2. 12 million.
3. The Adriatic.
4. George Orwell.
5. Ireland.
6. Chuck Wepner.
7. Prince Charles.
8. The polka.
9. A sort of third eyelid.

207

1. What is the French for 'to have'?
2. Why did Louis XIV order table knives to have rounded rather than pointed ends?
3. Which country produces the greatest number of varieties of sausage?
4. What is the framework for the *Arabian Nights*?
5. How do you score points in a parachuting competition?
6. Name the film starring Charlotte Rampling and David Birney based on an Alistair Maclean novel.
7. What two special connections did Matthew Arnold have with schools?
8. With which group was Keith Moon the drummer?
9. Which planet did William Herschel discover in 1781?

578

1. What is the motto of the FBI?
2. How many estimated man-hours of labour did the construction of Stonehenge take?
3. Which canal connects two oceans?
4. Recite the shortest verse in the Bible.
5. Where are the headquarters of Warwickshire County Cricket Club?
6. Which actress and singer's fourth husband was Ernest Borgnine?
7. Who had the nickname 'the Rail Splitter'?
8. On which novel by H. G. Wells was the 1963 musical *Half a Sixpence* based?
9. To which family is the sawfish related?

949

1. In his lifetime how many months does the average man spend shaving?
2. The Local Defence Volunteers were renamed what?
3. The US has about one car for every two people. How many cars per mile of paved road does this figure indicate?
4. Who wrote *The Tailor of Gloucester*?
5. How many players of each sex are there in a korfball team?
6. Which was Fay Wray's most famous film?
7. Who succeeded Joseph Smith as head of the Mormon Church?
8. Which great English contralto died of cancer in 1953?
9. What interval separated the first controlled atomic reaction and the first atomic explosion?

207

1. Avoir.
2. So that his quarrelsome dinner guests could not stab each other.
3. Germany, with over 2,000 varieties.
4. The tales were told for 1,001 nights by Scheherazade to her husband to stave off her morning execution.
5. Points are awarded for how close you land to the centre of a target.
6. *Caravan to Vaccares.*
7. His father was Dr Thomas Arnold, a headmaster of Rugby, and he himself was a school inspector.
8. The Who.
9. Uranus.

578

1. Fidelity, Bravery, Integrity.
2. $1\frac{1}{2}$ million.
3. The Panama Canal.
4. Jesus wept (John 11.35).
5. Edgbaston.
6. Ethel Merman.
7. Abraham Lincoln.
8. *Kipps.*
9. The rays.

949

1. 4 months.
2. The Home Guard.
3. Twenty-five per mile (or one every 70 yards).
4. Beatrix Potter.
5. Six men and six women.
6. *King Kong.*
7. Brigham Young.
8. Kathleen Ferrier.
9. 2 years, 7 months (Dec 1942 – July 1945).

208

1. In 1987 and 1990 British Summer Time will start a week earlier to prevent it beginning on which day?
2. In the nineteenth century which country used bamboo as money?
3. From which European country does half the world's cork supply come?
4. Who was betrothed to Edwin Drood as a child?
5. Who was the first English footballer to win 100 caps for his country?
6. What is Hutch's CB handle?
7. What movement were Jean Arp, Marcel Duchamp, Max Ernst and Man Ray involved with?
8. Who was the first black entertainer to win an Emmy award?
9. Which bird can't fly, yet swims?

579

1. Who is the patron saint of shoemakers?
2. In 1685 the Earl of Argyll was the last person in Britain to be executed by which method?
3. In which Indian state is about half of India's tea grown?
4. From what was Cinderella's coach made?
5. Which football club is located at Anfield Road?
6. Anthony Daniels played the robot C-3PO in which 1977 film?
7. In an artist's palette which digit fits into the hole?
8. What was the nickname given to Mozart's Symphony No. 36 in C (K.425)?
9. What were the first hairsprings for watches made from?

950

1. Which girl's name means 'chaste'?
2. What was Christopher Columbus's flagship called?
3. In which county is the market town of Grantham?
4. Who created the detective Mr J. G. Reeder?
5. Who broke Muhammad Ali's jaw?
6. Who portrayed King Faisal in the 1962 film *Lawrence of Arabia*?
7. Who was the USA's first honorary citizen?
8. What is Fats Waller's real first name?
9. Something we think of as a modern material was used as wicks in the lamps of the temple of the Vestal Virgins in Rome. What was it?

208

1. Easter Sunday.
2. China.
3. Portugal.
4. Rosa Bud.
5. Billy Wright.
6. Blond Blintz.
7. Dada.
8. Harry Belafonte.
9. The penguin.

579

1. St Crispin.
2. The guillotine.
3. Assam.
4. A pumpkin.
5. Liverpool.
6. *Star Wars*.
7. The thumb.
8. Linz.
9. Pig's hair.

950

1. Agnes.
2. The *Santa Maria*.
3. Lincolnshire.
4. Edgar Wallace.
5. Ken Norton.
6. Alec Guinness.
7. Winston Churchill.
8. Thomas.
9. Asbestos.

209

1. From which fruit is slivovitz made?
2. Which queen declared that handkerchiefs should always be square?
3. Which river does the Woolwich ferry cross?
4. From which mountain did Moses view the Promised Land?
5. Which British racing driver won the Indianapolis 500 in 1966?
6. Who started out as Mortimer in 1928?
7. Who was the most prolific of all great painters?
8. From which film did the song 'My Kind of Town' come?
9. What is the average capacity of the human stomach in pints?

580

1. Which was the first ship to use the SOS distress signal?
2. Which king adopted the name of Windsor for the house of our Royal Family?
3. Which is Europe's highest volcano?
4. Which is the only play in which Shakespeare mentions America?
5. Which country's team always lead the Olympic procession at the opening ceremonies?
6. Who plays Mr Humphries in 'Are You Being Served'?
7. To whom was Oona O'Neill married?
8. Who killed Cock Robin?
9. In the binary system what would 1,000 represent?

951

1. What are the constituents of the drink Black Velvet?
2. In which cathedral was Thomas à Becket murdered?
3. On which river is Windsor Castle?
4. Name Adam and Eve's three children.
5. How wide is a hockey goal?
6. Whose was the voice of Winston Churchill in the 1956 film *The Man Who Never Was*?
7. Who did Jan Lodvik Hock become?
8. Whom was Eric Clapton's wife Pattie Boyd formerly married to?
9. In the 1860s Napoleon III gave a banquet to the King of Siam served up in dishes made of a metal then more precious than gold. What was it?

209

1. Plums.
2. Marie Antoinette.
3. The Thames.
4. Mount Nebo.
5. Graham Hill.
6. Mickey Mouse.
7. Picasso – 13,500 paintings, 100,000 prints, 34,000 book illustrations and 300 sculptures.
8. *Robin and the Seven Hoods.*
9. 4 pints.

580

1. The *Titanic.*
2. George V.
3. Etna.
4. *The Comedy of Errors* (III, ii).
5. Greece.
6. John Inman.
7. Charlie Chaplin.
8. The sparrow.
9. 8.

951

1. Champagne and stout.
2. Canterbury.
3. The Thames.
4. Cain, Abel and Seth.
5. 12 feet.
6. Peter Sellers's.
7. Robert Maxwell.
8. Ex-Beatle, George Harrison.
9. Aluminium.

210

1. What do kleptomaniacs do?
2. How old is the oldest bikini found in Britain?
3. Of which park are Kensington Gardens a part?
4. Who married Mary Morstan?
5. From whom did the boxer Roberto Duran take the Lightweight Championship of the World in 1972?
6. What was Mae West's pet monkey's name?
7. How many men did John Wesley Hardin kill in shoot outs?
8. For what were the Guarneri family famous?
9. How old was Roy Rogers's horse Trigger when he died?

581

1. What is the American equivalent to Britain's Sandhurst?
2. After whom are Rhodes Scholarships named?
3. What does the name Punjab mean?
4. Who said, '... this night, before the cock crow, thou shalt deny me thrice'?
5. In the first two years of the Schweppes Gold Trophy (1963 and 1964) the same horse and jockey won. Name either of them.
6. How many people can utilize the Starship *Enterprise*'s transporter simultaneously?
7. What is the maximum legal weight of a bowling ball?
8. What nationality was the composer Poulenc?
9. How many ounces in a pound?

952

1. How many biscuits do Associated Biscuits Ltd manufacture every hour?
2. Who was Britain's first PM?
3. How many piastres are there in an Egyptian pound?
4. In which novel does Dandy Dinmont appear – after whom the dogs are named?
5. For which country did Pancho Segura play tennis?
6. Who won an Oscar for playing 'Dragline' in the film *Cool Hand Luke*?
7. What is the capital of Yugoslavia?
8. What was Fritz Kreisler's instrument?
9. Which planet's largest satellite is Titan?

210

1. Steal compulsively.
2. About 1,900 years, found near the Roman temple of Mithras in London.
3. Hyde Park.
4. Dr Watson, Sherlock Holmes's friend.
5. Ken Buchanan.
6. Boogie.
7. Forty.
8. Violin-making.
9. Thirty-three.

581

1. West Point.
2. Cecil Rhodes, the British Colonist.
3. 'Five rivers'.
4. Jesus Christ (to Peter).
5. Rosyth was ridden by Josh Gifford.
6. Six.
7. 16 pounds.
8. French.
9. Sixteen.

952

1. 5 million.
2. Robert Walpole.
3. 100.
4. *Guy Mannering* by Sir Walter Scott.
5. Ecuador.
6. George Kennedy.
7. Belgrade.
8. The violin.
9. Saturn.

211

1. What did the dish run away with?
2. In which year was the Berlin Wall built?
3. What is Paris's main thoroughfare called?
4. From which village did Tom Sawyer of *Huckleberry Finn* hail?
5. In which city was the first Ali–Spinks World Heavyweight Championship fought?
6. Who plays B.J. in 'MASH'?
7. Who attempted to cross the Snake River on Skycycle X-Z?
8. By what name was Eleanor Holliday better known?
9. Which planet is known as the 'Red Planet'?

582

1. What cabinet position includes being Master of the Royal Mint?
2. What was Anna Edson Taylor, in October 1901, the first to do?
3. To what does the expression 'seven seas' refer?
4. Name six of the twelve sons of Jacob.
5. Which game has a playing surface measuring 9 feet by 5 feet?
6. Which film featured the 'Springtime for Hitler' musical sequence?
7. What fashion did Civil War General Ambrose Burnside originate?
8. Which opera centres round a female worker in a cigar factory?
9. What percentage humidity would the air have if it was supersaturated?

953

1. What is the flavour of the liqueur Tia Maria?
2. What was British PM William Gladstone's middle name?
3. Who is the patron saint of France?
4. Who is Miss Marple's writer nephew?
5. In the 1924 Winter Olympics which country's ice hockey team scored 104 goals in their first four games?
6. Who succeeded Mrs Emma Peel?
7. What odds are paid for a single number at roulette?
8. Who was Elvis Presley's manager?
9. Of what did Dr Robert Liston say to fellow doctors: 'This Yankee dodge beats mesmerism to a hollow'?

211

1. The spoon.
2. 1961.
3. The Champs Elysées.
4. St Petersburg.
5. Las Vegas, Nevada.
6. Mike Farrell.
7. Evel Knievel.
8. Billie Holliday.
9. Mars.

582

1. Chancellor of the Exchequer.
2. Go over Niagara Falls in a barrel.
3. To all the waters of the earth.
4. Reuben, Simeon, Levi, Judah, Zebulun, Issachar, Dan, Gad, Asher, Naphthali, Joseph, and Benjamin.
5. Table tennis.
6. Mel Brooks's *The Producers*.
7. Sideburns.
8. *Carmen*.
9. More than 100 per cent.

953

1. Coffee.
2. Ewart.
3. St Denis.
4. Raymond West.
5. Canada's.
6. Tara King ('The Avengers').
7. 35 to 1.
8. Colonel Tom Parker.
9. Ether anaesthetic.

212

1. What do pyromaniacs do?
2. Which American traitor became a brigadier-general in the British Army?
3. Which is Europe's largest fortress?
4. Which Greek hero reputedly killed the Minotaur?
5. Who was the first sportswoman to win $100,000 in one year?
6. What was Sweeney Todd's profession?
7. Unity Mitford was a girlfriend of which dictator?
8. What are Biblical stories called that are performed by soloists, chorus and orchestra without the aid of action or scenery?
9. About how much larger is the sun than the earth?

583

1. Which abbreviation denotes unknown authorship?
2. Where did the Albigensians, against whom there was a Holy Crusade, flourish?
3. Tanzania was made up of two states. What were their names?
4. Who created Dick Tracy?
5. Where in England is the National Water Sports Centre?
6. By what name was Harlean Carpenter better known?
7. Who wrote under the pseudonym Anthony Morton?
8. In 1962 who had a hit record with 'Speedy Gonzales'?
9. What is a sky with clouds in long, white, thin parallel masses called?

954

1. In which direction do the Chinese read?
2. How did the poet Virgil acquire a plot of land without paying the then high Roman taxes on it?
3. Where are the world's largest coins used for currency?
4. In which Orwell book are some 'more equal than others'?
5. How old was Stanley Matthews when he won his first FA Cup Winners medal?
6. Which famous play is based on the real-life incident of a naval cadet being falsely accused of stealing?
7. What colour are the eyebrows on the Mona Lisa?
8. Who composed the Oscar-winning song 'Moon River'?
9. By what name is the Russian wolfhound better known?

212

1. Compulsively set things on fire.
2. Benedict Arnold.
3. The Kremlin in Moscow.
4. Theseus.
5. Billie Jean King.
6. Barber.
7. Hitler.
8. Oratorios.
9. 330,000 times. (Accept within 10 per cent.)

583

1. Anon.
2. Southern France and northern Italy (in the twelfth and thirteenth centuries).
3. Tanganyika and Zanzibar.
4. Chester Gould.
5. Nottingham.
6. Jean Harlow.
7. John Creasey.
8. Pat Boone.
9. A mackerel sky.

954

1. Top to bottom, right to left and 'back to front'.
2. He buried a fly in it and declared it a cemetery as cemeteries were not taxed.
3. On the island of Yap in the Pacific where a coin can be 12 feet across.
4. *Animal Farm.*
5. 38 years old.
6. *The Winslow Boy.*
7. There are no eyebrows on the Mona Lisa.
8. Henry Mancini.
9. Borzoi.

213

1. When was the last 'Blue Moon' seen in Britain?
2. How many people survived the 'Hindenberg' disaster of 1937?
3. Which other Roman road just south of Lincoln does the Fosse Way join?
4. How tall is a hobbit?
5. Which tennis player was sued by his fan club?
6. Who played James Bond in *Casino Royale*?
7. Which famous painter worked as an occasional diplomat for the Netherlands, when it was a Spanish province, and was knighted by Charles I of England?
8. Who did the collage on the Beatles' *Revolver* album cover?
9. In meteorology what does the Torro scale measure?

584

1. What is a painter used to fasten?
2. Who built the first Lotus car in 1948?
3. What does 'Hong Kong' mean?
4. Name the Roman god of love.
5. Where is the Lincolnshire Handicap run?
6. Who hosts the 'Tonight' show in America?
7. What type of art is based on the idea that light and movement can create a work of art?
8. Who was the best-known lead singer with The Dakotas?
9. If the sun was a 2-foot ball, how far, on the same scale, would the planet Jupiter be from it?

955

1. What percentage proof is the strongest possible beer obtainable from yeast fermentation alone?
2. Which were Queen Victoria's two favourite types of biscuits?
3. Where did the biggest meteorite known to have fallen in the British Isles land?
4. Who was Thane of Glamis?
5. At which Olympic Games were eleven Israeli competitors murdered?
6. By what name is Edward Israel Iskowitz better known?
7. A French notable who fought for the Americans in their war of independence also helped put a 'citizen king' on the throne of France in 1830. Who?
8. Who composed the opera *Ruslan and Ludmila*?
9. Which is the world's most widely used vegetable?

213

1. 26 September 1950.
2. Sixty-two.
3. Ermine Street.
4. 2–4 feet high.
5. Jimmy Connors.
6. David Niven.
7. Sir Peter Paul Rubens.
8. Klaus Voorman.
9. Tornadoes.

584

1. A boat.
2. Colin Chapman.
3. Fragrant harbour.
4. Amor.
5. Doncaster, as Lincoln is now closed.
6. Johnny Carson.
7. Kinetic art.
8. Billy J. Kramer.
9. Half a mile.

955

1. $24\frac{1}{2}$% proof.
2. Albert and Osborne.
3. Limerick, Ireland.
4. Macbeth.
5. The 1972 Games at Munich.
6. Eddie Cantor.
7. Lafayette.
8. Glinka.
9. The onion. (Potatoes and tomatoes are produced in greater quantities but are less widely used.)

214

1. The Wolves, Curlews, Bulls and Ravens were the first groups of what?
2. How much was a groat worth?
3. In which country were Tom Sharpe's first novels set?
4. Which Russian novelist wrote *Dead Souls*?
5. What nationality is Ivan Lendl?
6. Who played Tarzan in *Greystoke*?
7. Where can Rembrandt's 'Night Watch' be seen?
8. Who is the lead singer with Thin Lizzy?
9. Which animal is faster than a horse, can go longer without water than a camel and can see behind without moving its head?

585

1. For how many nights does the Jewish festival *Chanukah* last?
2. Which king was beheaded at Whitehall in 1649?
3. From which midwestern US town did Smokey Robinson and the Miracles come?
4. Who was Gulley Jimson?
5. Which golfer won the British Open and Amateur Championships, and the American Open and Amateur Championships, all in the same year?
6. Which human co-starred with Muffin the Mule?
7. Who presided over the 'Bloody Assizes'?
8. Percy Sledge was 25 when he had his first big soul hit in 1966. Name it?
9. A nectarine is a cross of which two fruits?

956

1. How many milligrams of caffeine are there in the average cup of tea?
2. How many English King Edwards have there been?
3. To which penal colony was Alfred Dreyfus sent?
4. Remember *Girl*? Who was 'the greenest girl in the school'?
5. Why were women not permitted to watch the original Olympic Games?
6. Who gave a fine performance as Quentin Crisp in 'The Naked Civil Servant'?
7. Where was Dr Crippen travelling to when he was caught?
8. Which Buffy Sainte-Marie protest song was a hit for Donovan in 1966?
9. What is a Camberwell Beauty?

214

1. Boy Scouts.
2. Fourpence. (First minted in the reign of Edward I.)
3. South Africa.
4. Gogol.
5. Czechoslovakian.
6. Christopher Lambert.
7. The Rijksmuseum, Amsterdam.
8. Phil Lynott.
9. The giraffe.

585

1. Eight.
2. Charles I.
3. Detroit.
4. The outrageous artist hero of Joyce Cary's *The Horse's Mouth*.
5. Bobby Jones.
6. Annette Mills.
7. Judge Jeffreys.
8. 'When a Man Loves a Woman'.
9. A peach and a plum.

956

1. Seventy.
2. Eight.
3. Devil's Island.
4. Lettice Leefe – a cartoon character.
5. Because all the competitors were male – and naked.
6. John Hurt.
7. Canada.
8. 'The Universal Soldier'.
9. A butterfly.

215

1. What are lentigines?
2. When were labour unions first given legal status in Britain?
3. Which city does Dum Dum airport serve?
4. In which of his novels does Kurt Vonnegut tell of the deadly chemical 'ice-nine'?
5. For what feat did Jean-Marc Boivin win the International Award for Valour in Sport in 1980?
6. Who was 'Uncle Mac'?
7. Who was Sandie Shaw's first husband?
8. What instrument does Buddy Miles play?
9. Name the bitter-tasting herb reputed to relieve migraine headaches.

586

1. In 1735 the *Gentleman's Magazine* published a poem about which devoted old couple?
2. Robert the Bruce and how many Scots defeated 20,000 English at the Battle of Bannockburn?
3. Where do Novacastrians live?
4. What is the name of Nicolas Freeling's fictional Dutch detective?
5. Which is the longest golf course to stage the British Open?
6. Which city burned in *Gone with the Wind*?
7. Who hosted TV's 'Zoo Quest'?
8. What wouldn't come back for Charles Drake?
9. How many times per minute does a canary's pulse beat?

957

1. What do Americans call what the British call waistcoats?
2. Dressed as what did Bonnie Prince Charlie escape to Skye?
3. The ferry from Larne goes where?
4. Who does *Private Eye* refer to as Brenda and Yvonne?
5. Where did Alan Minter win his world middleweight title in 1980?
6. Who did Alfie Bass and Bill Fraser play in 'The Army Game'?
7. What was curious about the chess game played between world champions Botwinnik and Smyslov in 1962 at the Moscow Sport Palace?
8. Which soul singer had his first big UK hit with 'In the Midnight Hour'?
9. Name the steam engine designed by Sir Nigel Gresley which established a then world record speed of 126 m.p.h. in 1938.

215

1. Freckles.
2. 1871.
3. Calcutta.
4. *Cat's Cradle.*
5. Climbing K2, the world's second highest mountain, then jumping off the top with his hang-glider.
6. Derek McCulloch – presenter of BBC radio's 'Children's Hour'.
7. The clothes designer Jeff Banks.
8. The drums.
9. Feverfew.

586

1. Darby and Joan – the phrase stayed.
2. About 10,000.
3. Newcastle.
4. Van der Valk.
5. Carnoustie (7,066 yards).
6. Atlanta. In fact it was the old *King Kong* set, which needed to be cleared.
7. David Attenborough.
8. His boomerang.
9. About 1,000.

957

1. Vests.
2. Dressed as a woman, in 1746.
3. To Stranraer, Scotland.
4. The Queen and Princess Margaret.
5. Las Vegas (Caesar's Palace).
6. Bootsie and Snudge.
7. The chess pieces were human. (The game was a draw.)
8. Wilson Pickett.
9. The *Mallard*.

216

1. On a standard roulette wheel, what colour are the even numbers?
2. What relation was Pope Hormisdas (514–23) to Pope Silverius (536–7)?
3. How long is Hadrian's Wall?
4. Which was the first state-subsidized theatre in the English-speaking world?
5. Which county did F. E. Woolley represent at cricket?
6. Which film producer reputedly first said, 'Include me out'?
7. Who said, reputedly, 'The Lord is a shoving leopard'?
8. Who packed her trunk and said goodbye to the circus?
9. Who created the first pair of bifocal lenses?

587

1. Of whom was the Colossus of Rhodes a statue?
2. Why do barristers wear black?
3. In which country are needles still legal currency for giving small change?
4. Which sister is missing? Cordelia, Regan, —?
5. Who is nicknamed 'the Louisville Lip'?
6. Who played Captain Brunel in *Juggernaut*?
7. For how long was Michael Faraday, the chemist, reputedly dead at his club before someone lifted the newspaper from over his face?
8. Who first recorded 'As Time Goes By'?
9. Which organs of the body are affected by Bright's disease?

958

1. What colour were the shirts of Mussolini's fascists?
2. Who was known as Curtmantle?
3. Which is the most populous city south of the equator?
4. In Arthurian legend, why was the Holy Grail in Britain?
5. What do the Dallas Cowboys play?
6. Who organized the Shakespeare Jubilee of 1769 in Stratford-upon-Avon?
7. In what abstract game does the board represent an uninhabited island which the two players must colonize?
8. The pop group Spirogyra took their name from what?
9. What are small fry in the piscine world?

216

1. Black.
2. Father.
3. 73½ miles.
4. The Abbey Theatre, Dublin (1924).
5. Kent.
6. Sam Goldwyn.
7. The Rev. Dr Spooner of New College (famous for his 'spoonerisms').
8. Nellie the Elephant.
9. Benjamin Franklin.

587

1. Apollo.
2. Because they are still in mourning for Queen Mary, who died in 1694.
3. Nigeria.
4. Goneril.
5. Muhammad Ali.
6. Omar Sharif.
7. 2 days.
8. Rudy Vallee.
9. The kidneys.

958

1. Black.
2. King Henry II (because of his shorter, Angevin tunic).
3. São Paulo, Brazil.
4. It was brought by Joseph of Arimathea, being the cup used by Christ at the Last Supper.
5. American football.
6. David Garrick.
7. Go.
8. The commonest type of algae.
9. Recently hatched salmon.

217

1. What is the longest recorded sequence of one colour turning up on a roulette wheel?
2. Who was Nicholas Breakspear?
3. What project was taken over by Waterhouse on the death of Fowke in 1865?
4. What is Bottom's first name in *A Midsummer Night's Dream*?
5. Who played in the 1948 F A Cup final?
6. Who was Kookie?
7. Which London district is associated with two groups of English painters?
8. What is David Bowie's real name?
9. What is tripe?

588

1. How many calories are there in half a pint of milk?
2. When were débutantes last presented at court?
3. In which country is Mont Blanc?
4. In which Dickens novel does the cheerful Mark Tapley appear?
5. Who died trying to break the water speed record on Coniston Water in 1967?
6. What is the title of the Philip K. Dick book on which *Blade Runner* was based?
7. Which chess-playing French painter was photographed in drag by Man Ray?
8. Who are Dave Stewart and Annie Lennox?
9. What is a castrated cock chicken called?

959

1. What did Joseph W. Swan invent in 1879?
2. How many fingers had Anne Boleyn?
3. Of which country is José Olmedo the most famous poet?
4. Hercules was killed by Nessus. What kind of creature was Nessus?
5. What was Eva Shain's claim to fame?
6. Who played the Emperor Franz Josef in the film *Oh, What a Lovely War*?
7. Who was the subject of the controversial portrait painted by Graham Sutherland and later destroyed by the sitter's wife?
8. In which century did Chopin live?
9. What type of animal is the vmi-vmi?

217

1. 29 times.
2. Pope Adrian IV (1154–9), the only English Pope.
3. The design of the Natural History Museum.
4. Nick.
5. Everton and Watford.
6. The hair-combing sidekick in '77 Sunset Strip'.
7. NW1 (home of the 'Camden Town Group' and the 'Euston Road Group').
8. David Jones.
9. The inner lining of the stomach of the ox.

588

1. 180.
2. 1958.
3. France.
4. *Martin Chuzzlewit.*
5. Donald Campbell.
6. *Do Androids Dream of Electric Sheep?*
7. Marcel Duchamp.
8. The Eurhythmics.
9. A capon.

959

1. The electric light bulb.
2. Eleven (six on her left hand).
3. Ecuador.
4. A centaur.
5. She was the first woman to judge a heavyweight boxing championship fight. (She was also one of the judges of the Muhammad Ali–Ernie Shavers fight on 29 September 1977.)
6. Jack Hawkins.
7. Winston Churchill.
8. The nineteenth.
9. A very small pig.

218

1. What is the main ingredient of a Manhattan?
2. What is the origin of F D on British coins?
3. What is the currency of Czechoslovakia?
4. Who wrote, 'What is truth? said jesting Pilate; and would not stay for an answer'?
5. Who was the first footballer to be knighted?
6. What was the film predecessor of 'Dixon of Dock Green'?
7. Which French poet, writing about the Salon of 1846, suggested that 'the best criticism of a picture may be a sonnet or an elegy'?
8. Who was given a guitar because his parents couldn't afford the bike he wanted for his twelfth birthday?
9. What connects the ignition coil to the spark plugs in a car?

589

1. What are Unaone, Soxisix, Novenine?
2. What relation was George I to James I?
3. In which country is the Mekong delta?
4. Which American who met Turgenev, Zola and Flaubert eventually lived and wrote in Rye, Sussex?
5. In which season did the Football League introduce three points for a win?
6. Which US TV series featured Efrem Zimbalist Jnr?
7. The sport of free-fall parachuting in international competition has a 'ceiling' to the jumps. What altitude is it?
8. Who asked Wendy Richard to come outside?
9. What makes sparkling wine sparkling?

960

1. In Hinduism, what consists of 3,110,400,000,000 days?
2. Which of Benjamin Franklin's ideas was first introduced in Britain in 1916?
3. Elat is at the head of which gulf?
4. By what name did Jane Austen's book *Elinor and Marianne* become known?
5. In three-day county cricket matches, what is the maximum number of overs allowed to the opening side?
6. Gene Autry rode Champion. Which horse did Roy Rogers ride?
7. Who wrote *Venice Preserv'd* and died of starvation?
8. What was the Rolling Stones' first single?
9. On which Christmas Day was the moon first orbited by man?

218

1. Whisky of any sort.
2. It stands for Fidei Defensor, a title which the Pope bestowed on Henry VIII for his treatise against Luther.
3. The koruna.
4. Francis Bacon (*Essays*: 'Of Truth').
5. Stanley Matthews.
6. *The Blue Lamp*, in which Dixon was killed.
7. Baudelaire.
8. Elvis Presley.
9. The distributor.

589

1. International communication phonetics for numbers 1, 6, 9.
2. Great-grandson.
3. Vietnam.
4. Henry James.
5. 1981–2.
6. '77 Sunset Strip'.
7. 12,000 feet.
8. Mike Sarne.
9. Carbon dioxide given off during fermentation.

960

1. A single day of Brahma.
2. Daylight saving.
3. The gulf of Aqaba.
4. *Sense and Sensibility*.
5. One hundred.
6. Trigger.
7. Thomas Otway.
8. 'Come on/I want to be Loved.'
9. 25 December 1968.

219

1. Of which religion are Brahmin, Ksatriya, Vaisya and Sudra, the four basic castes?
2. Which king of England was called 'The Lionheart'?
3. Which land did Eric the Red explore and colonize?
4. Who wrote *The Swiss Family Robinson*?
5. Who captained Spurs in 1961, the year of their Cup and League double?
6. What was the name of the Peter Lorre character in *The Maltese Falcon*?
7. What 'brotherhood' was attacked by Dickens and defended by Ruskin?
8. Who walked into the Sun Record Studio in Memphis in 1954 and paid to record two songs?
9. About how many species of living mammals are there?

590

1. If something is 'caseous' what is it like?
2. In what century did cholera first come to Britain?
3. Where was the first lending library in Britain?
4. What is the name of the Duke of Illyria in *Twelfth Night*?
5. Who was the first European footballer of the year, in 1956?
6. Which 'First Lady of the Silent Screen' returned in Altman's *A Wedding*?
7. Which post-impressionist said that the impressionist, Monet, 'is no more than an eye, but what an eye!'?
8. Who said she would cry if she wanted – it was her party?
9. In the year 1918 the brightest nova this century blazed in the equatorial sky. What was it called?

961

1. What does 'cap-à-pie' mean?
2. After how many years was it that Quentin Crisp said that 'You don't notice the dust'?
3. Which country imports the most champagne?
4. Whose first novel was *Chrome Yellow*?
5. What was Westpark Mustard, a phenomenon of the 1970s?
6. What was Tod Browning's most notorious film?
7. What in snooker is doubling?
8. William Herschel was first a musician. What instrument did he play?
9. What does an anemometer measure?

219

1. Hinduism.
2. Richard I.
3. Greenland.
4. J. R. Wyss.
5. Danny Blanchflower.
6. Cairo.
7. The Pre-Raphaelite Brotherhood.
8. Elvis Presley.
9. Four thousand.

590

1. Cheese.
2. The nineteenth (first outbreak from Russia in 1831).
3. Edinburgh (in 1726).
4. Orsino.
5. Stanley Matthews.
6. Lillian Gish.
7. Cézanne.
8. Lesley Gore.
9. Nova Aquilae.

961

1. From head to foot.
2. Four.
3. Britain.
4. Aldous Huxley's.
5. A record-breaking champion greyhound.
6. *Freaks* (1932), which featured a cast of misshapen unfortunates.
7. When an object ball strikes one or more cushions on its way to a pocket.
8. The organ.
9. Wind speed.

220

1. If you were born on 29 October what star sign would you be?
2. What did Mège-Mouries invent in 1870 to win a prize offered by Napoleon III?
3. With what is the town of Redditch particularly associated?
4. Who created Sir Roger de Coverley?
5. Who is the youngest player ever to play in a World Cup?
6. In which film did Salvador Dali, Ingrid Bergman and Alfred Hitchcock join forces?
7. Under what name does Mrs Gower Robinson write?
8. Who was Phyllis Sellick's piano-playing partner?
9. Which animal is pregnant longest?

591

1. Which was the first company to produce petrol-driven motor cars?
2. In which year did traffic wardens (female) appear?
3. What currency is used by Albania?
4. Who is the tinker dressed up as a lord in the Introduction to *The Taming of the Shrew*?
5. Where are the Doherty Gates?
6. By what name is Michael Shalhoub better known?
7. What form of modern sculpture was invented by Calder and christened by Duchamp?
8. With which country is *The Soldier's Song* associated?
9. What is the major ingredient in washing soda?

962

1. The 'Red Flag Act' of 1865 specified that every road locomotive must have three persons in attendance. What were their jobs?
2. What was the largest shipwreck in history?
3. What currency do they use in Bahrain?
4. Who wrote *The Doctor's Dilemma*?
5. Who was the first person, officially, to drive faster than 250 m.p.h.?
6. What was Walt Disney's middle name?
7. Which school did Humphrey Lyttelton and James Goldsmith both attend?
8. Duran Duran nicked his name. Who was he?
9. What is another name for Ursa Major?

220

1. Scorpio.
2. Margarine. The competition involved making something resembling butter that didn't go rancid so quickly.
3. Needles.
4. Richard Steele. (The squire was further used by Addison in the *Spectator*.)
5. Norman Whiteside (17 years 42 days).
6. *Spellbound*: Dali designed the dream sequence; Bergman was the leading lady; Hitchcock directed.
7. Ursula Bloom.
8. Cyril Smith.
9. The elephant (gestation period 645 days).

591

1. Daimler.
2. 1964.
3. The lek.
4. Christopher Sly.
5. Wimbledon.
6. Omar Sharif.
7. The mobile.
8. Ireland (Eire).
9. Sodium carbonate.

962

1. One to stoke, one to steer, and one to walk ahead waving a red flag.
2. That of the oil tanker *Olympic Bravery* in 1976 off the French coast.
3. The dinar.
4. G. B. Shaw.
5. Sir Malcolm Campbell.
6. Elias.
7. Eton.
8. The villain in *Barbarella*.
9. The Great Bear.

221

1. Which naval tradition ceased in 1970?
2. In which year did the *Titanic* sink?
3. Of the two townships on the Falkland Islands, Stanley is one. What is the other?
4. Which book features Topsy who 'growed'?
5. Where did the worst accident in the history of motor racing take place in 1955, when eighty-three spectators were killed?
6. Charles Chaplin and Buster Keaton appeared together in which film?
7. Who invented tramways?
8. What is the name of Bob Seger's backing band?
9. What do you call a castrated horse?

592

1. What are calamares?
2. How did Heinrich Himmler die?
3. Who was Greece's greatest poet?
4. Who injured herself riding, eloped with a poet, and loved her dog Flush?
5. What game would you be playing if you hit the ball on to the 'service penthouse'?
6. In 'MASH', what is Radar's real name?
7. Who first wrote as Walter Ramal and received a civil list pension at thirty-six?
8. As who was Charles Hardin Holley better known?
9. Which was the first of the rare metals to be discovered?

963

1. Which is the world's largest newspaper in sheer bulk?
2. Who was named khan of all the Mongols in 1206?
3. In which country are the Vosges mountains?
4. Whose only novel was entitled *The Cardinal's Mistress*?
5. Jimmy Doyle died during a title fight in 1947. Who was his opponent?
6. Who played Buster Keaton in the 1950 film *Sunset Boulevard*?
7. For which world championship is the Bermuda Bowl the trophy?
8. What is curious about the piece of music by John Cage called *Four Minutes Thirty-three Seconds*?
9. Travelling at the speed of light, how long would it take to reach Pluto?

221

1. The issue of rum.
2. 1912.
3. Port Darwin.
4. *Uncle Tom's Cabin* by Harriet Beecher Stowe.
5. Le Mans.
6. *Limelight.* They tried to give a recital together.
7. James Outram.
8. The Silver Bullet Band.
9. A gelding. (Do *not* accept 'frustrated' as an answer.)

592

1. Squid.
2. He committed suicide.
3. Homer.
4. Elizabeth Barrett Browning.
5. Real tennis.
6. Walter O'Reilly.
7. Walter de la Mare.
8. Buddy Holly.
9. Gold.

963

1. The Sunday edition of *The New York Times.* (The largest, published on 17 October 1965, consisted of 946 pages!)
2. Genghis Khan.
3. France.
4. Benito Mussolini's.
5. Sugar Ray Robinson.
6. He played himself.
7. Contract bridge.
8. It is silent.
9. About 6 hours.

222

1. What does a sextant measure?
2. Prior to 1857, how could a divorce be obtained in England?
3. Of the two islands twenty degrees west of Valparaiso one is called Alexander Selkirk Island. What is the other called?
4. Which Brecht play takes place in the Thirty Years War?
5. If you are a very good skier, what is the ideal colour-graded slope for your standard?
6. Kurosawa's 1960 film *Throne of Blood* was a version of which play?
7. Who wrote about Los and painted Job?
8. Which English composer wrote 'Onward, Christian Soldiers'?
9. What is a sidewinder?

593

1. Whose summer residence is Castel Gandolfo?
2. In which decade was bear-baiting finally prohibited?
3. Name the Channel Islands.
4. Which grandson of a famous biologist wrote a novel about the horrors of controlled reproduction?
5. At which Olympic Games was judo introduced?
6. Ben Lyon and Bebe Daniels had a popular radio programme in the 1950s. What was it called?
7. Count Louis Hamon called himself 'Cheiro' when he practised what art?
8. Short people don't have what, according to Randy Newman?
9. The Arctic tern has a remarkable life cycle, travelling from where to where?

964

1. If you were born on 25 January what star sign would you be?
2. In 1900, with what were Persian soldiers paid?
3. In which London square is the famous church of St Martin-in-the-Fields?
4. In which Dickens novel does Mr Micawber appear?
5. Who were the three West Ham players in the England 1966 World Cup winning team?
6. What is Starsky's CB handle?
7. Who was killed when Senator Edward Kennedy's car went off Dike Bridge, Chappaquiddick, in 1969?
8. Who wrote the opera *The Queen of Spades*?
9. How long does it take a pint of milk to lose half of its vitamin B when left in bright sunlight?

222

1. Angles.
2. By private Act of Parliament only.
3. Robinson Crusoe Island.
4. *Mother Courage*.
5. Black.
6. *Macbeth*.
7. William Blake.
8. Sir Arthur Sullivan.
9. A rattlesnake.

593

1. The Pope's.
2. The 1830s (1836).
3. Jersey, Guernsey, Alderney, Sark.
4. Aldous Huxley (*Brave New World*).
5. Tokyo 1964.
6. 'Life with the Lyons'.
7. Palmistry (cheiromancy).
8. A reason to live.
9. The Arctic to the Antarctic and back.

964

1. Aquarius.
2. Donkeys.
3. Trafalgar.
4. *David Copperfield*.
5. Geoff Hurst, Martin Peters and Bobby Moore.
6. Puce Goose.
7. Mary Jo Kopechne.
8. Tchaikovsky.
9. 2 hours.

223

1. Who said, 'Some newspapers dispose of their garbage by printing it'?
2. Which English king was beheaded in 1649?
3. Which two countries does the Brenner pass link?
4. Whom did the Mad Hatter and the March Hare push into a teapot?
5. Who was the PGA's leading money-winner eight times between 1964 and 1976?
6. By which name is Captain Benjamin Franklin Pierce known in 'MASH'?
7. Rollo, an engineer working for NASA's Apollo project, designed the forerunner for what popular sport?
8. What was Bing Crosby's theme song?
9. What is the largest living creature without a backbone?

594

1. What is the French for 'man'?
2. In which year was the Battle of Mons fought?
3. In which country are dogs not permitted in city streets?
4. Which novel did Dickens set partly in America?
5. In which sport did Willie Shoemaker make his name?
6. Who won an Oscar for his performance as the marshal in *High Noon*?
7. How many skittles are used in table skittles?
8. Which family were famed for composing waltzes and polkas?
9. If the duration of man's evolution, estimated at 1,750,000 years, were compressed into a single year, on what date would the earliest civilization occur?

965

1. Why do you hang meat?
2. How many children did Queen Anne have?
3. Why wasn't Magellan the first circumnavigator of the globe?
4. Who travelled around the country on horseback to prove the hardship of the peasantry and wrote down his findings?
5. Which sport means literally 'easy way'?
6. In which film was the Arabian horse Cass Olé featured?
7. Which historian 'preached the gospel of silence in forty volumes'?
8. Which Beethoven symphony became associated with victory in the Second World War?
9. Which famous chemist and tax-collector was a victim of the guillotine in the French Revolution?

223

1. Spiro T. Agnew.
2. Charles I.
3. Austria and Italy.
4. The Dormouse.
5. Jack Nicklaus.
6. Hawkeye.
7. Hang-gliding.
8. 'Where the Blue of the Night Meets the Gold of the Day'.
9. The giant squid.

594

1. Homme.
2. 1914.
3. China.
4. *Martin Chuzzlewit.*
5. Horse racing.
6. Gary Cooper.
7. Nine.
8. The Strauss family.
9. 30 December after 5 p.m.

965

1. To tenderize and develop flavour.
2. Seventeen.
3. He was killed in the Philippines although his ships returned to Europe.
4. William Cobbett (*Rural Rides*).
5. Judo.
6. *The Black Stallion* (1979).
7. Thomas Carlyle.
8. The Fifth.
9. Lavoisier.

224

1. From what type of establishment did the clubs White's and Boodle's develop?
2. How did Alexander the Great solve the problem posed by the Gordian knot?
3. In which country is Transylvania?
4. In which novel did Sherlock Holmes first appear?
5. Where is the British Grand Prix held?
6. To which club did Phileas Fogg belong?
7. What was art director Cedric Gibbons's best-known design?
8. Which Engelbert Humperdinck opera was based on a fairy tale by the brothers Grimm?
9. Approximately how many calories would you burn if you knitted a jumper for 1 hour?

595

1. Which letters flank the 'G' on the typewriter?
2. Which currency note appeared in 1797, disappeared in 1821, and reappeared in 1928?
3. How much can you be fined for sleeping in Islington's public library in London?
4. Who were Dryden's Absalom and Achitophel?
5. Who was the top tennis junior of 1982?
6. Who plays Timothy in the TV series 'Sorry'?
7. Who won the World Professional Snooker Championship from 1973 to 1976?
8. For what were the Amati family famous?
9. How many more chromosomes has the chimpanzee than man?

966

1. If you were born on Christmas Day what is your star sign?
2. Which battle brought the Wars of the Roses to an end?
3. Which is the world's busiest airport?
4. Which sleepy character appears in the works of Dr Diedrich Knickerbocker?
5. If you were 'bull riding' what would you be involved with?
6. Who starred in *The Italian Job*?
7. For what is Sheila Scott famous?
8. What did Bartolommeo Cristofori invent?
9. At what point in an aeroplane flight (including taxiing, take-off and landing) are the chances of death the highest?

224

1. The coffee house.
2. He cut through it with a sword.
3. Romania.
4. *A Study in Scarlet.*
5. Silverstone.
6. The Reform.
7. The statuette used for the Academy Awards – the Oscar.
8. *Hansel and Gretel.*
9. Seventy-eight.

595

1. F and H.
2. The £1 note.
3. £50.
4. The Duke of Monmouth and Lord Shaftesbury.
5. Pat Cash of Australia.
6. Ronnie Corbett.
7. Ray Reardon.
8. Violin-making.
9. 2 (48 to 46).

966

1. Capricorn.
2. The Battle of Bosworth Field.
3. O'Hare (Chicago, USA).
4. Rip Van Winkle.
5. A rodeo.
6. Michael Caine.
7. Exploits in aviation.
8. The hammer-action piano.
9. Landing approach.

225

1. Name the food formed by boiling oatmeal in water.
2. Which Spanish king and queen financed Christopher Columbus's first voyage to the New World?
3. The belt of forest running from Scandinavia to Japan is known as what?
4. What was Dr Doolittle's two-headed llama styled?
5. Which football twins joined Luton from Chester?
6. Mae West wrote her first play under the pseudonym Jane Mast. Name the play.
7. Who was George Joseph Smith?
8. Of where was St Swithun bishop?
9. What would you buy in a joke or toy shop that contains hydrogen sulphide?

596

1. For what would you use pectin?
2. Augustus II of Poland is said to have sold a regiment of dragoons for Ming porcelain. How many pieces of Ming did he get?
3. Which English seaside resort has a famous tower?
4. What now popular girl's name was coined in *Peter Pan*?
5. By what name is Arnold Cream better known?
6. Which half of a famous comedy team died in May 1984?
7. Where did Bunyan write *Pilgrim's Progress*?
8. For what do the initials ISCM stand?
9. Which is the only bird that can fly all day without once flapping its wings?

967

1. What is a dibber in gardening?
2. In which year were the Manchester United football team involved in the Munich air crash?
3. Which is the largest island in the Balearics?
4. Who was the first and greatest of the metaphysical poets?
5. How many weight divisions are there in Olympic boxing competitions?
6. Which actress was nicknamed 'Queen of the Surf'?
7. For what writings is Joseph Addison noted?
8. In which field was Vaslav Nijinsky a virtuoso?
9. How does a marsupial carry its young?

225

1. Gruel.
2. King Ferdinand and Queen Isabella.
3. The taiga.
4. The Pushmi-Pullyu.
5. Ron and Paul Futcher.
6. *Sex* (1926).
7. The 'Brides in the Bath' murderer.
8. Winchester.
9. Stink bombs.

596

1. For setting jellies and jams.
2. Fifty.
3. Blackpool.
4. Wendy.
5. Jersey Joe Walcott.
6. Eric Morecambe.
7. In Bedford jail.
8. International Society for Contemporary Music.
9. The albatross.

967

1. A pointed instrument used to make a hole in the ground when planting out.
2. 1958.
3. Majorca.
4. John Donne.
5. Eleven.
6. Esther Williams.
7. Essays.
8. Ballet dancing.
9. In a pouch.

226

1. Who said, 'There is no fortress so strong that money cannot take it'?
2. Whom did William of Orange succeed as king of England?
3. Which USSR city is twinned with Nottingham?
4. Which writer was the first recipient of the Carnegie medal?
5. What does the shot weigh in the Olympic men's shot-put?
6. What was the film *The Italian Job* about?
7. From where did Lord Elgin take the Elgin Marbles?
8. Who composed the light operas *The Student Prince* and *The Desert Song*?
9. What is a young deer called?

597

1. What kind of food is devils-on-horseback?
2. What relation was Edward the Confessor to Ethelred the Unready?
3. For what proportion of the year is there daylight at the North Pole?
4. What is the name of the rabbit in *Bambi*?
5. Which horse won the Grand National in 1976?
6. Which film introduced Jean Harlow?
7. Who died in flames after saying, 'That unworthy hand! That unworthy hand!'?
8. Who composed the Abegg variations?
9. Who was the Father of Geometry?

968

1. How much fat would a normal person lose after walking for 24 hours?
2. Who reputedly confessed to having cut down a cherry tree?
3. On which river does Wichita lie?
4. Name the horse with which Velvet Brown won the Grand National.
5. What is Spurs' home ground called?
6. Who is 'His Immenseness' on Ork?
7. On which island was Prince Philip born?
8. From which show does the song 'There is Nothing Like a Dame' come?
9. The appearance of which kind of crab suggests a violinist?

226

1. Cicero.
2. James II.
3. Minsk.
4. Arthur Ransome.
5. 16 pounds.
6. A bullion raid.
7. The Parthenon on the Acropolis in Athens.
8. Sigmund Romberg.
9. A fawn.

597

1. Bacon wrapped around prunes.
2. Son.
3. Half.
4. Thumper.
5. Rag Trade.
6. *Hell's Angels.*
7. Archbishop Cranmer.
8. Schumann.
9. Euclid.

968

1. 1 pound.
2. George Washington.
3. The Arkansas.
4. The Pie.
5. White Hart Lane.
6. Orson.
7. Corfu.
8. *South Pacific.*
9. The fiddler.

227

1. Of which two years of the 1970s are diaries interchangeable?
2. Which race of people started the trend of drilling teeth to insert gold, diamonds, etc.?
3. Which Scottish mountains separate the Highlands from the Lowlands?
4. Who is Hercule Poirot's confidential secretary?
5. In which year did Manchester United win the European Cup?
6. Which Australian body-builder also starred in *Pumping Iron*?
7. Who was the first man to swim the English Channel?
8. Which composer boasted that he could set a laundry list to music?
9. How far can a very active mole burrow in one night?

598

1. What day follows Shrove Tuesday?
2. Who led the siege defenders at Mafeking against the Boers?
3. What is the Irish name for Ireland?
4. What was Alice's pet cat called?
5. What was the nickname of the Indian prince who played cricket for Sussex and England?
6. Which film festival awards the Golden Palm for the best film of the year?
7. Who is Viscount Linley's mother?
8. Who sang about 'The Good Ship Lollipop' in the 1934 film *Bright Eyes*?
9. What is the more common name for nacre, found inside shells?

969

1. For how much did Edward McLean buy the forty-four carat Hope Diamond in 1911?
2. Which harbour did the Japanese attack on 7 December 1941?
3. What is London's equivalent of New York's Wall Street?
4. Who wrote *The Emperor's New Clothes*?
5. What is the distance from the service line to the net in tennis?
6. Which family is the focus of 'Only Fools and Horses'?
7. Who is the cartoonist responsible for Judge Dredd?
8. Who composed the 'Polovtsian Dances'?
9. How many hands had the first mechanical clock?

237

1. 1973 and 1979.
2. The Incas of Peru.
3. The Grampians.
4. Miss Lemon.
5. 1968.
6. Arnold Schwarzenegger.
7. Captain Matthew Webb (in 1875).
8. Rossini.
9. 100 yards.

598

1. Ash Wednesday.
2. Robert Baden Powell.
3. Eire.
4. Dinah.
5. Ranji.
6. Cannes.
7. Princess Margaret.
8. Shirley Temple.
9. Mother of pearl.

969

1. £60,000.
2. Pearl.
3. Lombard Street.
4. Hans Christian Andersen.
5. 21 feet.
6. The Trotters.
7. Brian Bolland.
8. Borodin.
9. None.

228

1. How long was the jail sentence given to David Berkowitz, 'Son of Sam'?
2. What ringing mechanism did James Ritty invent in 1884?
3. What colour was Lincoln cloth?
4. Who wrote *The Rime of the Ancient Mariner*?
5. For what do the initials MCC stand?
6. Name Julia Lockwood's actress mother.
7. What is considered to be the world's most valuable painting?
8. What name is given to Beethoven's fifth piano concerto?
9. Which bird has its nostrils at the end of its beak?

599

1. Which coin was called a tanner?
2. At what age did Mary Stuart become queen of Scotland?
3. What is the level of rainfall at Calama, in the Atacama desert, Chile?
4. Who is Tiny Tim's father?
5. Which football club has its home ground at The Valley?
6. To which monastery does Caine in *Kung Fu* belong?
7. From which country did the Renaissance artist Albrecht Dürer come?
8. Which opera by Mozart is subtitled *The School for Lovers*?
9. Bulls are not excited specifically by the colour red. Why not?

970

1. How many points has the star of David?
2. What was the *Bounty*'s cargo at the time of the mutiny?
3. Who preceded Georges Pompidou as President of France?
4. What happened to everything King Midas touched?
5. Who was the first black heavyweight boxing champion of the world?
6. Who did Dame Anna Neagle portray in the 1942 film *Wings and the Woman*?
7. Who was *Playboy*'s first Playmate of the Month?
8. Who wrote the musical *The Sound of Music*?
9. What is the study of fossils called?

228

1. 547 years.
2. The cash register.
3. Green.
4. Samuel Taylor Coleridge.
5. Marylebone Cricket Club.
6. Margaret Lockwood.
7. The 'Mona Lisa' by Leonardo da Vinci.
8. The Emperor.
9. The kiwi.

599

1. The sixpence (2½ p).
2. At 6 days old.
3. Nil. It has never rained there.
4. Bob Cratchit.
5. Charlton Athletic.
6. Shaolin.
7. Germany.
8. *Così fan tutte.*
9. Because they are colour-blind.

970

1. Six.
2. Breadfruit trees.
3. Charles de Gaulle.
4. It turned to gold.
5. Jack Johnson, who defeated Tommy Burns in 1908.
6. Amy Johnson.
7. Marilyn Monroe.
8. Rodgers and Hammerstein.
9. Palaeontology.

229

1. In what type of Chinese restaurant would you eat chicken and cashews, crispy duck and deep fried beef in chilli?
2. During which century were solid blocks of tea used as money in Siberia?
3. Who discovered Natal on Christmas Day?
4. Who wrote 'I am' between bouts of delusion that he was Napoleon?
5. Which city is home for the Ajax football team?
6. What extraordinary trick could the actor Pierre Messie perform?
7. Who was known as the Desert Fox?
8. Musically, what does 'piano' mean?
9. What is a whale's nostril called?

600

1. What was Carl Magee's invention of 1935 that motorists have cursed ever since?
2. In the eighteenth century, how long did the London to Brighton mail coach journey take?
3. What is Kenya's capital?
4. What was Aesop famous for writing?
5. Which is Amsterdam's best-known soccer club?
6. Who was Jack Watson's comedian father?
7. Who with Braque started the Cubist movement?
8. Who wrote the words to the song 'Drink to me only with thine eyes'?
9. How many drams are there in an ounce?

971

1. What type of angle is less than ninety degrees?
2. How many centuries are covered by entries in the Anglo-Saxon Chronicle?
3. Which are on average the world's tallest people?
4. *The Sea Cook* was the original title of which R. L. Stevenson novel?
5. Who was the last player to defeat Bjorn Borg at Wimbledon before his five consecutive championship wins?
6. Which producer of silent comedy films was nicknamed the King of Comedy?
7. What does 'ludo' mean?
8. What is the musical term for 'from the beginning'?
9. How many pounds are there in a stone?

229

1. Peking.
2. The eighteenth.
3. Vasco da Gama.
4. John Clare.
5. Amsterdam.
6. He could make his hair stand on end without mechanical aid.
7. Erwin Rommel.
8. Soft.
9. A blowhole.

600

1. The parking meter.
2. 2 days.
3. Nairobi.
4. Fables.
5. Ajax.
6. Nosmo King.
7. Pablo Picasso.
8. Ben Jonson.
9. Sixteen.

971

1. Acute.
2. Twelve (from Caesar's invasion to 1154).
3. The Watutsi or Tusi tribe of East Africa.
4. *Treasure Island*.
5. Arthur Ashe, in the 1975 quarter finals.
6. Mack Sennett.
7. I play.
8. Da capo.
9. Fourteen.

230

1. For what is 'half-inch' rhyming slang?
2. Where was the French revolutionary Marat born?
3. Which country with an army of 400,000 has never been to war?
4. Who wrote the 'de Richleau' novels?
5. How long is a tennis court?
6. What is Bruce Wayne's secret identity?
7. In which style of architecture was St Mark's, Venice, built?
8. Who sang the theme song in the 1952 film *High Noon*?
9. Which is the largest and heaviest of all snakes?

601

1. Who wrote, 'Scientists have odious manners, except when you prop up their theory; then you can borrow money from them'?
2. What did Aristotle claim to be the most delicate of all table meats?
3. In which European capital is Wenceslas Square?
4. Who created Psmith?
5. How old was Floyd Patterson when he became the youngest heavyweight champion of the world?
6. Who is the hero of the Oscar-winning cartoon *The Two Mousketeers*?
7. With which wood did Thomas Chippendale mainly work?
8. Who composed 'The Flight of the Bumblebee'?
9. What was the teddy bear Mishka's claim to fame in 1979?

972

1. When is St Andrew's day?
2. Who was the head of Hitler's SS?
3. Which is the only state in the USA over which no foreign flag has ever flown?
4. Who was Wordsworth's 'marvellous boy' to whom Keats dedicated 'Endymion'?
5. What did Ferenc Puskas play?
6. Who played Derek Flint in the 1966 film *Our Man Flint*?
7. Who is credited with formulating the rules to many popular card games?
8. What is a counter-tenor?
9. What is a one-humped Arabian camel called?

230

1. Pinch.
2. Switzerland.
3. Switzerland.
4. Dennis Wheatley.
5. 78 feet.
6. Batman.
7. Byzantine.
8. Tex Ritter.
9. The anaconda of South America.

601

1. Mark Twain.
2. Camel.
3. Prague, Czechoslovakia.
4. P. G. Wodehouse.
5. Twenty-one.
6. Jerry.
7. Mahogany.
8. Rimsky-Korsakov.
9. He was the first teddy to orbit the earth, in Salyut 6.

972

1. 30 November.
2. Heinrich Himmler.
3. Idaho.
4. Thomas Chatterton.
5. Football (for Hungary).
6. James Coburn.
7. Edmond Hoyle (1672–1769).
8. A male alto.
9. A dromedary.

231

1. How do you pronounce the surname Featherstonehaugh?
2. In which year did 'Coronation Street' start?
3. Where is the World Trade Center?
4. Which of Agatha Christie's thrillers was retitled for the American market *And Then There Were None*?
5. Which German ex-paratrooper and PoW became an outstanding goalkeeper for Manchester City in the 1950s?
6. Who played the master of ceremonies in the film *Cabaret*?
7. Which is generally considered to be Rembrandt's greatest painting?
8. They started out as the Detours, then became the High Numbers–then?
9. How many grams are there in a kilogram?

602

1. What was the device for city-dwellers patented in 1972 by Henry Doherty of Wayne, New Jersey?
2. Henry VII made a grant of £10 'to him that found the new isle'. Who was he?
3. In which city is Waverley the main-line station?
4. Which monthly magazine has the world's largest circulation?
5. Which soccer club won the first five European Cup finals?
6. Who sang the weekly calypso on 'TW3'?
7. What was the pseudonym used by the Poet Laureate, C. Day Lewis, when writing detective fiction?
8. In which year were the Beatles awarded their MBEs?
9. What is a camelopard now called?

973

1. Veal comes from what age of calf?
2. Who at the peace conference at Versailles said to his experts, 'Tell me what's right and I'll fight for it'?
3. The Kielder reservoir lies in which group of hills?
4. In which Shakespeare play does Gower the Poet appear?
5. For which country do the Pumas play rugby?
6. Who starred opposite Jane Fonda in *Klute*?
7. Which Russian nicknamed 'the dissolute' was shot by a prince?
8. Where do Kraftwerk hail from?
9. How many muscles are there in the trunk of an elephant?

231

1. Fanshaw.
2. 1960.
3. New York.
4. *Ten Little Niggers.*
5. Bert Trautmann.
6. Joel Grey.
7. 'The Night Watch'.
8. The Who.
9. 1,000.

602

1. The poop-scoop for dog's excrement.
2. John Cabot, the discoverer of Newfoundland.
3. Edinburgh.
4. The *Reader's Digest.*
5. Real Madrid.
6. Lance Percival.
7. Nicholas Blake.
8. 1965.
9. A giraffe.

973

1. Between 2 weeks and 1 year.
2. President Wilson.
3. The Cheviots.
4. *Pericles.*
5. Argentina.
6. Donald Sutherland.
7. Rasputin.
8. Germany.
9. About 40,000.

232

1. What colour is cerulean?
2. What is the name of the tiny island in the North Atlantic annexed to Britain in 1955?
3. Which is the longest strait in the world?
4. Who created Charlie Chan?
5. Name the boxer nicknamed 'the Fighting Barber from Hanley' whose son was famous in another sport.
6. Who played young Bill in 'William Tell', the children's TV series of the 1950s?
7. Who was known as the Coonskin Congressman?
8. Who composed a famous piece for the G string?
9. What is unusual about Wytch Farm, Dorset?

603

1. Who sits on the Woolsack?
2. For how long did the Greeks besiege Troy?
3. Which is the smallest of Northern Ireland's six counties?
4. In *Much Ado About Nothing*, what is Dogberry?
5. Name one of the English team that played Spain at polo in September 1981.
6. What is the name of Callan's sidekick in the TV series of the same name?
7. Whose accurate observations of the moon helped Newton to formulate the laws of gravity?
8. In which forest did Horst Jankowski take a walk?
9. What is the common household name for sodium chloride?

974

1. What were Twinkletoes and Lucky Jim, two stuffed cats, the first to do?
2. Which king in 1377 pioneered the fork as an eating implement?
3. What is the capital of Morocco?
4. In mythology, which gift was given to Cassandra by Apollo?
5. Which Briton won the world middleweight boxing title in 1960?
6. Who is the former miner who plays the holiday camp host Ted Bovis in 'Hi-de-Hi'?
7. Which diarist met George III wandering in Windsor Great Park and was later interned in France?
8. Who wrote and performed 'Mrs Robinson'?
9. What is a cassowary?

232

1. Deep blue.
2. Rockall.
3. The strait of Malacca.
4. Earl D. Biggers.
5. Jack Matthews, father of Sir Stanley Matthews.
6. Conrad Philips.
7. Davy Crockett.
8. Johann Sebastian Bach.
9. It is a producing oil-field.

603

1. The Lord Chancellor.
2. 10 years.
3. Armagh.
4. A constable.
5. John Horswell, Martin Brown, Robert Graham, Prince Charles.
6. Lonely.
7. John Flamsteed's.
8. The Black Forest.
9. Salt.

974

1. Fly across the Atlantic in a plane, accompanying Alcock and Brown.
2. Richard II.
3. Rabat.
4. The gift of prophecy.
5. Terry Downes.
6. Paul Shane.
7. Fanny Burney.
8. Simon and Garfunkel.
9. A large Australian flightless bird.

Q

233

1. What are kreplach?
2. Who tried to arrest five MPs in the House of Commons in 1642?
3. Which US state is called the 'Wonder State'?
4. In which book did the 'Slough of Despond' feature?
5. Who was the first winner of the women's Olympic 1,500 metres?
6. Who were the stars of the radio comedy series 'The Navy Lark'?
7. Name either pretender to the English throne in Henry VII's reign.
8. Who do the Coconuts play with?
9. By what name is the bird *Pica pica* better known?

604

1. What is 3 to the power of 4?
2. During the reign of Elizabeth I, why did only the rich wear beards?
3. What is the name given to the promontory at the eastern end of the South Downs?
4. What is the name of Bill Sykes's dog?
5. How high is the crossbar on an American football goal-post?
6. What was the name of Sir David Low's famous colonel?
7. Where was Snoopy born?
8. Who did Gustav Leonhardt play in the 1969 film *Chronicles of Anna Magdalena*?
9. For what does SCUBA stand?

975

1. How many old pennies were there in a guinea?
2. What was borough-English?
3. The statue of the Little Mermaid is at the entrance to which harbour?
4. What was Esau's payment for his birthright?
5. Whom did Maurice Hope beat to gain his world boxing title?
6. On which book was the film *The Village of the Damned* based?
7. What are the names of Wyatt Earp's brothers?
8. Which record company turned down the Beatles?
9. For approximately how long is a cow pregnant?

233

1. Jewish ravioli – sort of.
2. Charles I.
3. Arkansas.
4. *Pilgrim's Progress.*
5. Ludmilla Bragina (USSR) at the Munich Olympics.
6. Jon Pertwee and Leslie Phillips.
7. Perkin Warbeck, Lambert Simnel.
8. Kid Creole.
9. Magpie.

604

1. 81.
2. Because they were taxed.
3. Beachy Head.
4. Bullseye.
5. 10 feet.
6. Blimp.
7. Daisy Hill Puppy Farm.
8. Johann Sebastian Bach.
9. Self-Contained Underwater Breathing Apparatus.

975

1. 252.
2. A tenure by which land passed to the youngest instead of the eldest son.
3. Copenhagen.
4. A mess of pottage.
5. Rocky Mattioli.
6. *The Midwich Cuckoos.*
7. Virgil and Morgan.
8. Decca.
9. 280 days.

234

1. In which subjects did Prince Charles pass A-levels?
2. How did the Emperor Nero die?
3. Which European country's flag is blue with a yellow cross?
4. According to German legend, who was Lohengrin's father?
5. How many men are seeded in the Wimbledon tennis singles championship?
6. Which of his film biographies did Ken Russell describe as 'a love story between a homosexual and a nymphomaniac'?
7. Who lives at 1 Snoopy Place?
8. What was Glenn Miller's band's theme tune?
9. From where does spinach originate?

605

1. What is an American policeman's truncheon called?
2. To which British king did Robin Hood swear allegiance?
3. In which city is James Joyce's *Ulysses* set?
4. Which bird returned to Noah's ark with an olive branch?
5. How many medals–more than anyone else–has Sixten Jernberg of Sweden won in the Winter Olympics?
6. What is Linda Lee Danvers's other identity?
7. Which painter had a neatly trimmed parted beard named after him?
8. How many blackbirds were baked in the pie?
9. Rank these animals in order of longevity: man, Indian elephant, horse, pig, cat.

976

1. To the nearest 5,000, how many umbrellas are lost each year on London's bus and underground systems?
2. Which king built the Tower of London?
3. On which river is England's highest waterfall, Caldron Snout?
4. Who created Parker Pyne?
5. Which country won the Davis Cup in 1983?
6. In which film did Charles Bronson play the part of the Tunnel King?
7. Who was called 'The Lady with the Lamp'?
8. Who composed the oratorio *Elijah*?
9. In which country does the cow tree grow?

234

1. French and history.
2. He committed suicide.
3. Sweden's.
4. Parsifal.
5. Sixteen.
6. *The Music Lovers*, about Tchaikovsky.
7. Charles Schulz, Snoopy's creator.
8. 'Moonlight Serenade'.
9. Iran.

605

1. A nightstick.
2. Richard the Lionheart.
3. Dublin.
4. The dove.
5. Nine.
6. Supergirl.
7. Van Dyck.
8. Twenty-four.
9. Man, Indian elephant, horse, cat, pig.

976

1. 75,000.
2. William the Conqueror (not personally).
3. The Tees.
4. Agatha Christie.
5. Australia.
6. *The Great Escape.*
7. Florence Nightingale.
8. Mendelssohn.
9. Venezuela. The sap of the cow tree resembles milk in both taste and looks.

Q

235

1. What was the anti-Nazi graffito initiated by a Belgian lawyer, Victor de Levelaye, on 14 January 1941?
2. Between 1600 and 1800 about half the girls in England had one of three names. Give one.
3. Which world championship is held annually at Coxheath, Kent?
4. Who wrote, 'Pastime with good company/I love and shall, until I die/Grudge who list, but none deny'?
5. Which weight world championship did Marvin Hagler win?
6. Name the hecklers in 'The Muppet Show'.
7. What was the name of Elvis Presley's twin brother?
8. What is Paul Jones's real name?
9. When was the first hydrogen bomb exploded?

606

1. What is dwyle-flonking?
2. Which was the second postage stamp issued?
3. Which is the only city to have produced three winners of the Nobel Prize for Literature?
4. Which B. S. Johnson novel consisted of sections which the reader was free to assemble in any order?
5. Which boxer held world titles at three weights simultaneously?
6. Who said on 'Laugh-In', 'Very interesting . . . but stupid'?
7. Which member of a famous comedy team filed two patents for a wrist heart alarm in 1969?
8. Who was 'Walking Back to Happiness' in 1961?
9. What is the female mosquito's favourite food?

977

1. What is Tokay?
2. Of what were sixty-eight million issued from May 1840?
3. Where in Paris is the tomb of the unknown soldier?
4. Who completed a translation of Strauss's *Life of Jesus* and lived with George Lewes, a married man?
5. Which then current women's 1,500 metres world record holder failed to make the 1976 Olympic finals?
6. Who was the star of 'Interpol Calling' in the late 1950s?
7. What were 'volitos', first demonstrated in 1823 in Windmill Street, Soho, London, and later to become a worldwide craze?
8. In 1958, who had the whole world in his hands?
9. What is the lightest known substance?

235

1. V for victory.
2. Mary, Anne, Elizabeth.
3. The World Custard Pie Championship.
4. Henry VIII.
5. Middleweight.
6. Statler and Waldorf.
7. Jesse.
8. Paul Pond.
9. 1952.

606

1. The flinging of wellington boots–or other objects. The furthest throw wins.
2. The Twopenny Blue.
3. Dublin (Beckett, Shaw, Yeats).
4. *The Unfortunates*.
5. Henry Armstrong.
6. Arte Johnson.
7. Zeppo Marx.
8. Helen Shapiro.
9. Blood.

977

1. A Hungarian wine.
2. The first postage stamp–the Penny Black.
3. Beneath the Arc de Triomphe.
4. Mary Ann Evans, alias George Eliot.
5. Grete Waitz.
6. Charles Korvin.
7. Roller skates.
8. Laurie London.
9. Hydrogen.

236

1. What do funambulists do?
2. When was the last invasion of British soil by foreign troops?
3. Which, alphabetically, is the world's last postal place-name?
4. Who created Superintendent Alleyn?
5. How many consecutive Rugby games did Gareth Edwards play for Wales?
6. Who played Georgina in TV's 'Upstairs, Downstairs'?
7. Whose signature appears on Bank of England notes printed in 1984?
8. Who was the drummer in the Jimi Hendrix Experience?
9. What does a giraffe use to wash out its ears?

607

1. How many holes are there in a telephone dial?
2. How does the inscription on Edward I's tomb in Westminster Abbey describe him?
3. In which country is the world's highest post office?
4. Who was the hero of *The Catcher in the Rye*?
5. Of which championship was the centenary celebrated at Wimbledon in 1984?
6. Who did Honor Blackman play in 'The Avengers'?
7. Who was the first man to sail non-stop around the world, single-handed?
8. Who is 'Born to Run'?
9. What is the official British bird?

978

1. How many gallons of water does an average bather use?
2. In which war did the Minutemen fight?
3. Where can the statue of the Vénus de Milo be seen?
4. In which river did John the Baptist baptize Jesus Christ?
5. Who was Muhammad Ali's opponent for the world title in Zaïre in 1974?
6. In which film did Cliff Richard sing his first million-seller 'Living Doll'?
7. Which famous potter was mainly responsible for developing bone porcelain?
8. Which group recorded under the alias 'Wonder Who'?
9. Which part of the body is affected by conjunctivitis?

236

1. Walk tightropes.
2. 1797, when the Irish-American General Tate landed with 1,400 French troops near Fishguard.
3. Zyznow, in Poland.
4. Ngaio Marsh.
5. Fifty-three.
6. Lesley-Anne Down.
7. D. H. F. Somerset's.
8. Mitch Mitchell.
9. Its tongue.

607

1. Ten.
2. As the Hammer of the Scots – 'Malleus Scotorum'.
3. Peru.
4. Holden Caulfield.
5. The ladies' singles.
6. Cathy Gale.
7. Robin Knox-Johnstone.
8. Bruce Springsteen.
9. The robin.

978

1. Thirty to forty.
2. The American War of Independence.
3. In the Louvre, Paris.
4. The Jordan.
5. George Foreman.
6. *Serious Charge* – in 1959.
7. Josiah Spode.
8. The Four Seasons.
9. The eye.

237

1. On which day of the week does Ascension Day always fall?
2. Why is it thought that Custer shot himself at the Battle of Little Big Horn?
3. Which river forms the northern border of Matabeleland?
4. In which tale does Chaucer write of 'The smyler with the knyf under the cloke'?
5. Why were two Zambian footballers who played for the Green Buffaloes banned for life in 1980/81?
6. Who first played the Saint on TV?
7. Which president has his name written on the moon?
8. What was the Kinks' first No. 1 hit in the UK?
9. Of the seven Mercury astronauts chosen, how many flew?

608

1. How do you address a surgeon?
2. Where did Admiral Beatty say, 'There's something wrong with our bloody ships today'?
3. What have the mayors of Birmingham, Leeds and York in common?
4. Who instigated the publication of W. H. Davies's *Autobiography of a Super-Tramp*?
5. From which country did Jaroslav Drobny originate?
6. To whom is Sophia Loren married?
7. For what was the Australian Clement Wragge known?
8. Who replaced Brian Jones in the Rolling Stones?
9. Where do you have to stand to see a rainbow?

979

1. What is the season for pheasant?
2. In which decade was slavery abolished in the British Empire?
3. When was London's last smog?
4. Who loved 'Skittles' and wrote *Esther*?
5. Who captained the British Lions in 1971?
6. Richard Kiel's most memorable film role to date had 'bite'. What was it?
7. Which playwright was an MP, supported the impeachment of Warren Hastings, was friendly with the Prince of Wales and was buried with full honours in Westminster Abbey?
8. Who had a hit with 'Purple People Eater'?
9. What is a knot garden?

237

1. Thursday.
2. Ashamed of his defeat, he was probably spared by the Indians as he was a blood brother of Sitting Bull.
3. The Zambesi.
4. 'The Knight's Tale'.
5. Because they assaulted a linesman.
6. Roger Moore.
7. Richard Nixon.
8. 'You Really Got Me' (1964).
9. Six.

608

1. As 'Mr' rather than 'Doctor'.
2. At the Battle of Jutland (1916).
3. They are Lord Mayors.
4. G. B. Shaw.
5. Czechoslovakia.
6. Carlo Ponti.
7. He was the first person to give hurricanes names, notably those of politicians he disliked.
8. Mick Taylor.
9. With your back to the sun and facing a rain shower.

979

1. 1 October to 31 January.
2. The 1830s (1833).
3. 1962.
4. Wilfrid Scawen Blunt.
5. John Dawes.
6. As Jaws in *The Spy Who Loved Me* and *Moonraker*.
7. R. B. Sheridan.
8. Sheb Wooley.
9. A garden of small hedges, herbs, etc., in complicated geometric patterns or knots.

238

1. What does Zip stand for in the American Zip code?
2. In which year did man first land on the moon?
3. Which town in Lombardy is famous for its cheese?
4. According to the Bible, what 'gladdeneth the heart of man'?
5. Which country were the British team touring in 1924 when they were nicknamed the Lions?
6. In which London street did Sweeney Todd work?
7. Who was assassinated in Box 7 at Ford's Theater?
8. Which Austrian composer wrote over 600 songs in his thirty-one-year life?
9. How does a female goldfish let her mate know that she is ready to lay eggs?

609

1. With which flavour is Cointreau associated?
2. What did Keir Hardie wear on his head when admitted to the Commons?
3. What is Turkey's currency called?
4. Complete the opening of *Pride and Prejudice*: 'It is a truth universally acknowledged, that a single man in possession of a good fortune must . . .'
5. Which horse won the 1983 Grand National?
6. For which film did Jack Nicholson receive his first Oscar?
7. What colour pigment is made from henna?
8. In which orchestra did the piccolo double bass appear?
9. What were the four humours of the ancient doctors?

980

1. What are the three most common causes of death in the 20–30 age group?
2. Who led the forces defeated by Alfred at the Battle of Edington?
3. Elba lies between Italy and where?
4. Who were the Anthropophagi?
5. Who first put the shot over 70 feet?
6. Spock is half earthling, half – what?
7. Who, before being guillotined, said, 'You must show my head to the people. It is worth showing'?
8. Who went 'Doo Wah Diddy Diddy'?
9. In which liquid does deuterium take the place of ordinary hydrogen?

238

1. Zone Improvement Plan.
2. 1969.
3. Gorgonzola.
4. Wine.
5. South Africa.
6. Fleet Street.
7. Abraham Lincoln.
8. Franz Schubert.
9. She blows bubbles.

609

1. Orange.
2. A cloth cap.
3. The lira.
4. '. . . be in want of a wife.'
5. Corbiere.
6. *One Flew Over the Cuckoo's Nest.*
7. Reddish.
8. The Hoffnung Symphony Orchestra.
9. Blood, phlegm, yellow bile, black bile.

980

1. Accident, poisoning and violence.
2. Guthrum the Dane.
3. Corsica.
4. According to Pliny, Scythian cannibals.
5. Randy Matson.
6. Vulcan.
7. Georges Danton.
8. Manfred Mann.
9. Heavy water.

239

1. In Russia, what is the name for a vehicle drawn by three horses abreast?
2. Who ruled China at the time of Marco Polo's visit in 1271?
3. On which river is Aswan?
4. Which book contains 773,692 words?
5. Whom did Jimmy Connors beat in a challenge match in Las Vegas in 1975 to take 500,000 dollars?
6. Who is Rhoda's doorman?
7. What have *The Provok'd Wife* and Blenheim Palace in common?
8. What was the theme song of Count Basie's orchestra?
9. What acid cannot be kept in a glass container?

610

1. What is a tonsorialist?
2. Which racecourse did Charles II make famous by his personal patronage?
3. Which island is joined to Wales by the Menai Bridge?
4. What was the pen name of Mary Ann Evans?
5. The winner of which Olympic event is considered to be the world's greatest athlete?
6. Which character did Arthur Lowe play in 'Dad's Army'?
7. Which poet sold his home, Newstead Abbey, to pay his debts?
8. Who is Tweety Pie's nemesis?
9. What was the original colour of lupins?

981

1. Apart from water, what is the main ingredient of bouillabaisse?
2. Which legendary highwayman rode Black Bess?
3. From where was the Hope Diamond originally stolen?
4. Name the Linton family estate in *Wuthering Heights*.
5. Which Dutchman reached the Wimbledon men's singles semi-finals in 1978?
6. Who asked Cary Grant to 'Come up and see me sometime'?
7. Who was the first airman to circumnavigate the world?
8. Whose theme song is 'It's Not Unusual', recorded in 1967?
9. Which was the first synthetic plastic?

239

1. A troika.
2. Kublai Khan.
3. The Nile.
4. The Bible (King James version).
5. John Newcombe of Australia.
6. Carlton.
7. Their creator, Sir John Vanbrugh.
8. 'One O'Clock Jump'.
9. Hydrofluoric acid – it dissolves glass.

610

1. A barber.
2. Newmarket.
3. Anglesey.
4. George Eliot.
5. The decathlon.
6. Captain Mainwaring.
7. Byron.
8. Sylvester the cat.
9. Blue.

981

1. Fish.
2. Dick Turpin.
3. A Burmese temple.
4. Thrushcross Grange.
5. Tom Okker.
6. Mae West.
7. Sir Charles Kingsford-Smith.
8. Tom Jones's.
9. Celluloid (1865).

240

1. Who or what is Tsar Kolokol?
2. Which country is said to have been ruled by a dog for 3 years in the eleventh century?
3. Which British town is nicknamed Pompey?
4. Which was the first novel by Jackie Collins, sister of Joan?
5. Which were Britain's two finalists in the men's 100 metres breast-stroke at the 1976 Olympics?
6. Which instrumental piece from the film *Deliverance* became a hit?
7. What did Emperor Menelik II of Abyssinia use as his imperial throne?
8. About what sort of heart did Elvis Presley sing?
9. Which planet is called the evening star?

611

1. In Parliament, the Commons vote 'Ay' and 'No'. How do the Lords vote?
2. Which American general, later president, won the Battle of Horseshoe Bend?
3. Where are the Aubrey Holes?
4. Who wrote *The Eye of the Needle*?
5. Which was the first English soccer club to win the European Cup?
6. What was the film follow-up to *Stardust*, also starring David Essex?
7. The name of which priest, doctor and writer has been turned into an adjective for exuberance and coarseness?
8. Name Iggie Pop's backing band.
9. How many surfaces has a cone?

982

1. What, in Greek mythology, is the food of the gods?
2. For what purpose did the British use bronze from Russian guns captured at Sebastopol in 1855?
3. Which Yorkshire town inspired Bram Stoker to write Dracula?
4. Who wrote *The American Way of Death*?
5. Who captained Arsenal in their 'double' year 1970/71?
6. Which children's TV serial, devised by Phil Redmond, provoked controversy when it began in 1980?
7. Who is buried in the chapel of the Invalides in Paris?
8. Who recorded as Dib Cochran and the Earwigs?
9. What is a marsupial?

240

1. A massive bell in the Kremlin in Moscow.
2. Norway.
3. Portsmouth.
4. *The World is Full of Married Men.*
5. David Wilkie and Duncan Goodhew.
6. 'Duelling Banjos'.
7. An electric chair.
8. A wooden one.
9. Venus.

611

1. 'Content' and 'Not content'.
2. Andrew Jackson.
3. Stonehenge.
4. Ken Follett.
5. Manchester United (1968).
6. *That'll Be the Day.*
7. Rabelais.
8. The Stooges.
9. Two.

982

1. Ambrosia.
2. To make Victoria Crosses.
3. Whitby.
4. Jessica Mitford.
5. Frank McLintock.
6. 'Grange Hill'.
7. Napoleon Bonaparte.
8. Marc Bolan and David Bowie.
9. An animal that carries its young in a pouch.

241

1. What does 'soviet' mean?
2. What were the Institutes of Gaius?
3. In which country is Tiahuanaco?
4. Who was Harriet Vane's chief defence counsel?
5. On which racecourse are the Champion Hurdle and Gold Cup run at the National Hunt festival each March?
6. Who wrote the novel on which the film *Love Story* is based?
7. By what name was the Italian painter Jacopo Robusti better known?
8. Where is the ballet 'La Boutique Fantasque' set?
9. What other particles are thought to hold quarks together in the nucleus of an atom?

612

1. What are chitterlings?
2. What was the worst defeat suffered by a modern army at the hands of men with virtually no guns?
3. What are Tiree, Sule Skerry, Bell Rock, Dowsing?
4. What is the name of the duke in *Measure for Measure*?
5. Who was the flat-race champion jockey in 1979?
6. Which film featured the advertising come-on, 'How'd you like to tussle with Russell'?
7. Which schoolmaster got the Queen's Medal for poetry for his plays?
8. Who sang about Sylvia's mother?
9. Which wood is plywood mostly made from?

983

1. What does the term 'avast' mean?
2. What was the nickname of King Edmund who defeated Canute but in turn was defeated by him at Ashingdon?
3. What is the 'Chandler Wobble'?
4. What was the real name of Hardy's Casterbridge?
5. Which county won the Gillette Cup and John Player League in 1979?
6. Who wrote the screenplay for Hitchcock's *Strangers on a Train*?
7. Who said of whom, 'He speaks to me as if I was a public meeting'?
8. What do 'Not Fade Away', 'Oh Boy' and 'Heartbeat' have in common?
9. What is a smew?

241

1. Workers' council.
2. A digest of Roman law of the second century AD.
3. Bolivia.
4. Sir Impey Biggs (in *Strong Poison* by Dorothy L. Sayers).
5. Cheltenham.
6. Eric Segal.
7. Tintoretto.
8. In a toyshop.
9. Gluons.

612

1. The smaller intestines of animals, fried or boiled for food.
2. The British defeat at Isandhlwana (1879).
3. Coastal weather stations.
4. Vincentio.
5. Joe Mercer.
6. *The Outlaw.*
7. Christopher Fry.
8. Dr Hook.
9. Birch.

983

1. Stop. (What you are doing?)
2. Ironside.
3. The 'wobble' of the earth's axis as it spins.
4. Dorchester.
5. Somerset.
6. Raymond Chandler.
7. Queen Victoria of Gladstone.
8. They were all written by Buddy Holly.
9. A species of duck.

242

1. Who places the crown on the new sovereign's head?
2. What was the Allies' code name for Winston Churchill during the Second World War?
3. Where is Britain's unknown soldier buried?
4. Who created Dr Fu Manchu?
5. Where is the headquarters of the Lancashire county cricket club?
6. How old was Shirley Temple when she made her first film appearance?
7. How did multi-millionaire John Jacob Astor die?
8. Which 'Peanuts' character is the Beethoven fanatic?
9. How many gallons of ale are in a pin?

613

1. How many pairs of chromosomes should you have?
2. Parliamentarily, what did the Long turn into?
3. If you drove from Montreux to Berne which cheese region would you pass through?
4. In the Bible, who was David's son?
5. To which English classic does the French Prix de Diane equate?
6. Who was the first host/compère on 'The Generation Game'?
7. Under what name did T. E. Lawrence enlist in the RAF?
8. Which boy did Twinkle sing about?
9. What does a manometer measure?

984

1. How many old shillings were there in a guinea?
2. Who said to his successor, 'Do not imitate my wars and my love of building'?
3. Which country ruled the Ottoman Empire?
4. Who wrote *Little Dorrit*?
5. Which motor-racing driver was the first to win the world championship in his own make of car?
6. Who succeeded Roger Moore as Simon Templar in *Return of the Saint*?
7. What was Aleksei Leonov the first to do?
8. Who was the lead singer in the Cardiff band Amen Corner?
9. What do ichthyologists study?

242

1. The Archbishop of Canterbury.
2. Agent.
3. Westminster Abbey.
4. Sax Rohmer.
5. Old Trafford, Manchester.
6. Three.
7. He went down on the *Titanic*.
8. Schroeder.
9. $4\frac{1}{2}$.

613

1. Twenty-three.
2. The Rump.
3. Gruyère.
4. Solomon.
5. The Oaks.
6. Bruce Forsyth.
7. T. E. Shaw.
8. Terry.
9. The pressure of gases.

984

1. Twenty-one.
2. Louis XIV (le Roi Soleil).
3. Turkey.
4. Charles Dickens.
5. Jack Brabham.
6. Ian Ogilvy.
7. Walk in space (in 1965).
8. Andy Fairweather-Low.
9. Fish.

Q

243

1. Of which bird does the fabulous griffin have the head?
2. What was the name of the third British D-Day beach besides 'Gold' and 'Juno'?
3. Which active volcano is near Naples?
4. Who sent Paddington Bear to England?
5. Which seeker of precious nacre won the 1947 Derby?
6. Who played W. C. Fields in the 1976 film *W. C. Fields and Me*?
7. Of which country was Urho Kekkonen elected president in 1956?
8. What was the tap-dancer Bill Robinson's nickname?
9. How do Tiffany, Josephine, and Beryl differ from Audrey, Ann, and Dotty?

614

1. Where did Anne Frank die?
2. What was the name for a Mesopotamian temple tower?
3. Where must the President of the United States have been born?
4. Which book did fifty-four scholars complete in 1611?
5. Who won a showjumping world championship on Beethoven?
6. Who played the headmaster in 'Whacko' on the BBC in the 1950s?
7. Who led the 1450 uprising of Kentish men?
8. Name any one of three musicians (apart from Jim Morrison) who played in The Doors.
9. For what is Hazchem the warning sign?

985

1. What is Big Ben? (Be accurate.)
2. From which Roman coin did the pre-decimal penny take the letter d?
3. What is the opposite of the orient, the east, where the sun rises?
4. Who was bred an' bawn in a brier patch?
5. In golf, which number wood is the driver?
6. Which actress will be always be associated with the screen portrayal of Agatha Christie's Miss Marple?
7. What is Darryl F. Zanuck's middle name?
8. Which home of the Promenade Concerts was destroyed by air attack in 1941?
9. What is the principal metal in pewter?

243

1. The eagle.
2. 'Sword'.
3. Vesuvius.
4. Aunt Lucy.
5. Pearl Diver.
6. Rod Steiger.
7. Finland.
8. Bojangles.
9. They are oil-fields. The others are gas-fields.

614

1. In Belsen concentration camp.
2. A ziggurat.
3. In the United States.
4. The Authorized Version of the Bible.
5. David Broome.
6. Jimmy Edwards.
7. Jack Cade.
8. Jim Densmore, Robbie Krieger, Ray Manzarek.
9. Dangerous or hazardous chemicals.

985

1. The hour bell in the clock tower of the Houses of Parliament, Westminster.
2. The denarius.
3. The occident, the west, where the sun sets.
4. Brer Rabbit.
5. One.
6. Margaret Rutherford.
7. Francis.
8. The Queen's Hall.
9. Tin.

244

1. For what do the initials VLCC stand, as applied to oil-tankers?
2. Who was Cesare Borgia's father?
3. What comes after Fastnet, Irish Sea, Shannon, . . . ?
4. By what name is Robert Macgregor better known?
5. Who immediately preceded Henry Rono as 3,000 metres world record holder?
6. Under which name did Marjorie Robertson achieve cinema fame?
7. Who preceded Kyprianou as President of Cyprus?
8. Which role in Benjamin Britten's *Midsummer Night's Dream* was created by Owen Brannigan?
9. About how many species of fossil (plant and animal) are known?

615

1. What is a hummum?
2. How many followed Mao Tse-tung on his 6,000-mile 'long march' in 1934–5?
3. Where is the Great Bitter Lake?
4. Who said, 'Who steals my purse steals trash'?
5. When did Shirley Heights win the Derby?
6. Which 'Coronation Street' character was played by Geoffrey Hughes?
7. Who was elected President of the United States in 1952?
8. Who wrote the words of 'Auld Lang Syne'?
9. Which mammal besides the spiny ant-eater (echidna) lays eggs?

986

1. What size is quarto paper?
2. Which prime minister led the last Liberal government?
3. In which city is the Pont Neuf the oldest bridge across the Seine?
4. In the Bible, who are Miriam's two brothers?
5. Which country has won the world championships for curling most often?
6. Bashful, Sleepy, Grumpy, Sneezy, Happy and Doc. Who is the missing dwarf?
7. From what did Milton die?
8. Which is the smallest orchestral woodwind instrument?
9. The Campbell-Stokes recorder measures what with a glass ball?

244

1. Very Large Crude Carrier.
2. Pope Alexander VI (Rodrigo Borgia).
3. Rockall.
4. Rob Roy.
5. Brendan Foster.
6. Anna Neagle.
7. Archbishop Makarios.
8. Bottom.
9. 300,000.

615

1. A Turkish bath.
2. 90,000.
3. In the middle of the Suez Canal.
4. Iago, in *Othello*.
5. 1978.
6. Eddie Yeats.
7. Dwight D. Eisenhower.
8. Robert Burns.
9. The duck-billed platypus.

986

1. 8 by 10 inches.
2. Asquith (1908–15).
3. Paris.
4. Moses and Aaron.
5. Canada.
6. Dopey.
7. Gout.
8. The piccolo.
9. Sunshine.

245

1. How many lives has a cat, according to legend?
2. Which king wrote, 'As the holly groweth green/And never changeth hue/So I am, ever have been/Unto my lady true'?
3. Where is Cape Clear?
4. Who wrote *Dr Finlay's Casebook*?
5. Who rode Crepello to victory in the Derby?
6. Which British comedian played Bud Flanagan in the recent revival of *Underneath the Arches*?
7. Who reputedly said, 'History is bunk'?
8. What are the ridges across guitar fingerboards called?
9. Which part of the body does a cutaneous disease affect?

616

1. Which three letters in the English alphabet are not in the classical Latin alphabet?
2. Of which French king was the Comtesse du Barry the mistress?
3. Of which new county is the old county of Denbighshire a part?
4. In *Measure for Measure*, what is Abhorson?
5. The American triple crown for horse-racing consists of the Belmont Stakes, the Preakness Stakes, and . . .?
6. Name the film based on President Kennedy's naval exploits in the Second World War.
7. John Flamstead was England's first what?
8. What was Gene Vincent's real name?
9. Where was the A-bomb tested for the first time in 1945?

987

1. What is the German for 'no'?
2. Which Egyptian queen was defeated at the Battle of Actium?
3. In Bulgaria, how many stotinki are there in a lev?
4. According to Marlowe, who made a pact with Mephistopheles?
5. Who did Ezzard Charles defeat in 1950 to become world heavyweight boxing champion?
6. What was Rosalind Russell's profession in the film *His Girl Friday*?
7. Which movement was pioneered in Australia by John Gore and Edward Saunders?
8. How many musical keys are there?
9. For approximately how long is an ass pregnant?

245

1. Nine.
2. Henry VIII.
3. Southern Ireland.
4. A. J. Cronin.
5. Lester Piggott.
6. Roy Hudd.
7. Henry Ford.
8. Frets.
9. The skin.

616

1. J, U, W.
2. Louis XV.
3. Clwyd.
4. An executioner.
5. The Kentucky Derby.
6. *PT 109*.
7. Astronomer Royal.
8. Eugene Vincent Craddock.
9. Nevada, USA.

987

1. Nein.
2. Cleopatra.
3. 100.
4. Dr Faustus.
5. Joe Louis.
6. Journalism.
7. The Salvation Army.
8. Twenty-four (twelve major, twelve minor).
9. A year.

246

1. Which part of a woman's body did the Chinese consider it to be too provocative to paint?
2. In ancient China, only the aristocracy were allowed to own a certain breed of dog; which breed?
3. By what name is Tanganyika now known?
4. Name Goethe's goblin who lured children away.
5. Who won the first transatlantic yacht race in 1960?
6. Which actor wrote the book *The Outlaw Trail*?
7. £2,000 was paid in 1975 for a set of 'Taddy's Clowns and Circus Artists'. What were they?
8. What instrument did Myra Hess play?
9. What is the science of celestial bodies called?

617

1. What was the name of the white poodle given to Marilyn Monroe by Frank Sinatra?
2. Name the battle in Ireland at which William of Orange defeated James II.
3. What is the smallest state of the USA?
4. What was Captain Flint's ship called?
5. From which point does the Olympic flame start out?
6. Who plays the Fugitive?
7. What was the surname of the Hungarian brothers who invented the ballpoint pen?
8. Which musical instrument means 'small' in Italian?
9. Which planet did Clyde Tombaugh discover in 1930?

988

1. Which is the world's most widely used seasoning?
2. Which king of England broke with the Roman Catholic Church?
3. In which country is Africa's northernmost point?
4. Who wrote *Utopia* (1516)?
5. Who was the oldest man to win the Wimbledon men's tennis singles championship?
6. Who plays Callan?
7. Which film was Grace Kelly making when she met Prince Rainier?
8. The original title of this Lennon/McCartney composition was 'Daisy Hawkins'. Under what name was it a hit?
9. E. O. Lawrence received a Nobel Prize in 1939 for inventing what?

246

1. The feet.
2. Pekinese.
3. Tanzania.
4. The Erl King.
5. Francis Chichester.
6. Robert Redford.
7. Cigarette cards.
8. The piano.
9. Astronomy.

617

1. Mafia.
2. The Battle of the Boyne (1690).
3. Rhode Island.
4. *Walrus*.
5. From the site of the original games at Olympia, Greece.
6. David Jansen.
7. Biro.
8. Piccolo.
9. Pluto.

988

1. Salt.
2. Henry VIII.
3. Tunisia.
4. Sir Thomas More.
5. Arthur W. Gore, at 41, in 1909.
6. Edward Woodward.
7. *To Catch a Thief*.
8. 'Eleanor Rigby'.
9. The cyclotron.

247

1. When can Halley's comet next be seen?
2. On the Solomon Islands, dogs' teeth were used for money until the middle of which century?
3. By what name is Siam now known?
4. Don Quixote de la —?
5. Name the baseball-like game, played with a larger ball pitched underarm?
6. Which dramatist wrote *The Crucible*?
7. Who built the Rotherhithe tunnel under the Thames?
8. Who composed the song 'Swanee'?
9. Approximately how many years elapsed between the invention of the lens and of the telescope?

618

1. How many is a 'baker's dozen'?
2. Who were the leaders of the two sides at the Battle of Worcester in 1651?
3. What is the unit of currency is the United Arab Emirates?
4. Who wrote: 'If God did not exist it would be necessary to invent Him'?
5. What is a tsukahara?
6. Who directed *The Graduate*?
7. Which American president resigned?
8. Give the names of the Monkees.
9. In the brain, the operation of which parts of the human body take up more space than any other?

989

1. Which country has the highest suicide rate?
2. What were Prince Albert's last words?
3. If you were in the 'Equality State', where would you be?
4. Complete: 'His death which happen'd in his berth,/At forty-odd befell:/They went and told the sexton, and . . .'
5. Which Irish international rugby player also played football for Limerick United?
6. Name Captain Nemo's pet seal in the 1954 film *20,000 Leagues Under the Sea.*
7. Who wrote *An Investigation into the Laws of Thought*?
8. After which conductor was a West End show named?
9. On what date did a man last walk on the moon?

247

1. 1986.
2. The nineteenth century.
3. Thailand.
4. Mancha.
5. Softball.
6. Arthur Miller.
7. Brunel senior (Isambard Kingdom Brunel's father).
8. George Gershwin.
9. 3,000.

618

1. Thirteen.
2. Prince Charles (later Charles II) and Oliver Cromwell.
3. The dirham.
4. Voltaire.
5. A vault in gymnastics.
6. Mike Nichols.
7. Richard M. Nixon.
8. Peter Tork, Mike Nesmith, Micky Dolenz and Little Davy Jones.
9. The lips and the hands.

989

1. Hungary (42·6 per 100,000 in 1977).
2. 'Good little woman.'
3. Wyoming, USA.
4. '. . . The sexton toll'd the bell.' ('Faithless Sally Brown' by Thomas Hood.)
5. Tony Ward.
6. Esmeralda.
7. George Boole.
8. Beecham.
9. 13 December 1972.

248

1. Who awards the Nobel Peace Prize?
2. When was the last time the Thames in London froze sufficiently hard for people to walk across it?
3. Which country uses the tugrik as currency?
4. In which novel does Tony Last get stuck in the Amazonian jungle reading Dickens to his captive?
5. Name one of the three Llanelli players who played throughout in the 1976 Welsh Grand Slam team.
6. Who played the errant ice-hockey player in *Slap Shot*?
7. What were ombre and quadrille?
8. Which Sandie Shaw hit won the Eurovision Song Contest?
9. Of what are mothballs made?

619

1. What is a sheet bend?
2. Joshua Slocum was the first to do what by 1898?
3. Where is the shortest street in England?
4. Complete Chesterton's line from *The Rolling English Road*: 'The night we went to . . . by way of . . .'
5. Who was the first black man to win the US tennis championship?
6. Which American cartoonist won a Pulitzer Prize?
7. Who was the first nude male centrefold in *Cosmopolitan*?
8. Who sang 'The Crying Game'? (Ages ago . . .); he wore black leather gloves.
9. If the sky was full of nimbostratus clouds, what type of weather would you expect?

990

1. Which was the first public building in Britain to be protected by a lightning conductor?
2. The French army at Agincourt numbered approximately 18,000 men. How large was the English army (to the nearest thousand)?
3. In which country is Agadir?
4. Who wrote *The Count of Monte Cristo*?
5. Which county plays home cricket matches at Grace Road?
6. Name the character played by Harrison Ford in *Raiders of the Lost Ark*.
7. Which king is always shown in profile?
8. For what is Rouget de Lisle famous?
9. About how many species of living insects are there?

248

1. A committee of the Norwegian parliament.
2. 1813–14.
3. Mongolia.
4. *A Handful of Dust* (Evelyn Waugh).
5. Phil Bennett, Ray Gravell or J. J. Williams.
6. Young blue-eyes: Paul Newman.
7. Popular card games in the eighteenth century.
8. 'Puppet on a String'.
9. Naphthalene.

619

1. A knot joining two ropes which are usually of unequal thickness.
2. To sail alone around the world.
3. Queen Charlotte Street in Windsor, Berks. It is 51′ 10″ long.
4. '... Birmingham ... Beachy Head'.
5. Arthur Ashe.
6. Gary Trudeau, creator of Doonesbury.
7. Burt Reynolds.
8. Dave Berry.
9. Rain: they are rain clouds.

990

1. St Paul's Cathedral.
2. 6,000 men.
3. Morocco.
4. Alexander Dumas (father).
5. Leicestershire.
6. Indiana Jones.
7. The King of Diamonds in a pack of cards.
8. He composed 'The Marseillaise'.
9. 800,000.

249

1. What do somnambulists do?
2. Who first concocted cold cream?
3. Name two countries that gained independence from Britain in 1947–8.
4. What is the 'U' word for 'wealthy'?
5. In which sport may you not play left-handed?
6. Who played Mr and Mrs Larkin in the 1950s?
7. Who was the intended victim of the assassination attempt in *The Day of the Jackal*?
8. At which horrific Rolling Stones concert was a man murdered in front of the stage?
9. How long does an oyster take to reach maturity?

620

1. What is the principal ingredient of sauerkraut?
2. Why was Abraham Lincoln's coffin opened in 1887 and 1901?
3. In which English county is Château Piddle wine made?
4. What is the 'U' word for 'passed away'?
5. Which tennis player failed a screen test for *Top Hat*?
6. 'Z Cars' began as a single play. What was its title?
7. In the comic strip, what is the name of Blondie's husband?
8. As what were Veronica Bennett, Estelle Bennett and Nedra Talley collectively known?
9. What is a chinook?

991

1. Who could choose to be hanged by a silken rope in preference to one made of hemp?
2. In the mid 1500s, what (approximately) was the population of England?
3. Which cathedral has the tallest spire in England?
4. Which was Norman Mailer's first novel?
5. Who rode Nijinsky to victory in the 1970 Epsom Derby?
6. Which American actor played Adam Cartwright in 'Bonanza'?
7. By what name was Hablot Knight Browne, Dickens's illustrator, known?
8. Who had a hit with 'Lily the Pink' in 1968?
9. How many safety matches have been lit on the moon?

249

1. Sleepwalk.
2. The Greek physician Galen, about AD 150.
3. Choose from Burma, Ceylon, India or Pakistan.
4. Rich.
5. Polo.
6. David Kossoff and Peggy Mount.
7. Charles de Gaulle.
8. Altamont.
9. 3 years.

620

1. Cabbage.
2. To make sure that the body was still there.
3. Worcestershire; it is made and bottled in North Piddle.
4. Died.
5. Fred Perry.
6. *Jacks and Knaves* (1961).
7. Dagwood.
8. The Ronettes.
9. A warm wind which blows in the western states of North America.

991

1. Peers of the realm.
2. 3,000,000.
3. Salisbury (404 feet).
4. *The Naked and the Dead.*
5. Lester Piggott.
6. Pernell Roberts.
7. 'Phiz'.
8. The Scaffold.
9. None – it's impossible to light them on the moon.

250

1. Which cereal was invented at Battle Creek Sanitarium in 1890?
2. What were the Declarations of Indulgence?
3. What was the ancient Greek name for the continent of Africa?
4. Who were the parents of Sir Galahad?
5. In which year did the BBC first televise tennis from Wimbledon?
6. Who chairs 'Pop Quiz' on BBC TV?
7. From which legendary figure is Socrates supposed to have been descended?
8. Which instrument can play the highest note: the violin, the flute, the cornet or the xylophone?
9. Which bird has the country name of 'yaffle'?

621

1. If the icecaps of the earth melted, at which of the Empire State Building's 102 storeys would sea-level be?
2. What is George V reputed to have said on his deathbed?
3. In which country did the Hudson's Bay Company function?
4. Who wrote, 'One half of the world cannot understand the pleasures of the other'?
5. Where was badminton devised?
6. Who wore a sarong on the road?
7. Who designed the stained glass in Coventry Cathedral?
8. Who composed the opera *The Barber of Seville*?
9. What is a bellwether?

992

1. In England, how many degrees proof are whisky and gin?
2. When, to the nearest 5 years, was Nelson's *Victory* built?
3. Where would a khidmutgar wait at table?
4. Who wrote the libretto for Stravinsky's *The Rake's Progress*?
5. Which film star was runner-up in the 1979 Le Mans 24-hour race?
6. What film was the biggest box-office success of all time?
7. If you pot the following sequence at snooker, what is your score: red, pink, red, brown, red, black?
8. What night did the Drifters go to the movies?
9. Within 3 miles of the coast, all catches of this occasional visitor to Britain belong to the Crown. What is it?

250

1. Cornflakes (by Dr Kellogg).
2. Proclamations of Charles II and James II suspending laws against Dissenters and Catholics.
3. Libya.
4. Sir Lancelot and Elaine.
5. 1937.
6. Mike Read.
7. Daedalus.
8. The violin.
9. The woodpecker.

621

1. The twentieth.
2. 'Bugger Bognor' (or maybe 'How is the Empire?').
3. Canada.
4. Jane Austen (in *Emma*).
5. At Badminton Hall.
6. Dorothy Lamour, co-star of numerous 'Road' movies with Crosby and Hope.
7. John Piper.
8. Rossini.
9. The leader of a flock of sheep.

992

1. 70°.
2. 1765.
3. India.
4. W. H. Auden.
5. Paul Newman.
6. *ET*.
7. Twenty.
8. Saturday.
9. The sturgeon.

251

1. What is filigree?
2. In whose reign did Hanover and Britain cease to share a ruler?
3. Where is the Isle of Axholm?
4. What did Moses and the American Joseph Smith have in common?
5. Who won Britain's first orienteering championship in 1967?
6. Who directed *Pretty Baby*?
7. What was the Christian name of the famous English landscape gardener Capability Brown?
8. Nobody knew what it meant, but Procul Harum had a hit with it in 1967. What was it?
9. In a car, what does the alternator do?

622

1. Which 1934 invention of Percy Shaw's has proved a boon to motorists?
2. If you had been standing, just after sunrise, looking east over Maskelyne, what would you have seen on 30 July 1969?
3. Where was the Spanish Main?
4. In which play do Nagg and Nell live in dustbins?
5. How many players are there in a rounders team?
6. Who played the Thin Man?
7. In how many mutinies was Captain Bligh actually involved?
8. Who wore 'short shorts'?
9. Which animal produces its own 'sun-tan lotion'?

993

1. How many passengers does a DC-10 hold?
2. Whose was the sword Joyeuse?
3. Which monks have their home at La Trappe Abbey in France?
4. In which play does the lyric 'Fear no more the heat of the sun' appear?
5. Who won the 1971 Badminton Horse Trials on Great Ovation?
6. Which Elizabethan actor-manager founded a public school?
7. In Paris many of the original Métro entrances were designed in 1900; in which style?
8. Who wrote 'Anyone Who Had a Heart' for Dionne Warwicke?
9. What is the process of development from a caterpillar to a butterfly called?

251

1. Fine, lacy metalwork.
2. Victoria's (because the Salic law preventing female succession applied in Hanover).
3. East of Doncaster and bounded by the Trent.
4. They both received tablets from the Lord (in stone and gold respectively).
5. Gordon Pirie.
6. Louis Malle.
7. Lancelot.
8. 'A Whiter Shade of Pale'.
9. Produces electricity.

622

1. Cats' eyes.
2. The Eagle landing (Apollo II).
3. The northern coast of South America.
4. Beckett's *Endgame*.
5. Nine.
6. William Powell.
7. Three. The mutiny on the *Bounty* was the first.
8. Royal Teens.
9. The hippopotamus.

993

1. 380.
2. Charlemagne's.
3. Trappists.
4. *Cymbeline* by Shakespeare.
5. Mark Phillips.
6. Edward Alleyn.
7. Art Nouveau.
8. Burt Bacharach.
9. Metamorphosis.

252

1. When was flogging abolished in Britain?
2. Who was drowned in drink in 1478?
3. In which country is Marrakesh?
4. Name one of the sisters in *Women in Love*.
5. In which year did Jimmy Connors first win Wimbledon?
6. Who played Fagin in both stage and screen versions of *Oliver*?
7. If you were on the stern of a boat and you were 'pooped', what would happen to you?
8. Who slaughtered Tchaikovsky in the early 1960s?
9. What is the name of a pipe made from a natural block of hydrated magnesium silicate?

623

1. In which industry do the Trade Unions SOGAT and NATSOPA operate?
2. Which monarch wrote 'A Counterblast to Tobacco'?
3. Where is the Limpopo river?
4. Which island's fight for freedom was supported by Boswell?
5. In ice hockey, what is the minimum period for which a player may be sent to the 'sin bin'?
6. In which film did Garbo talk for the first time?
7. Who was the chief representative of France at the Versailles peace conference?
8. Who sang about the little old lady from Pasadena?
9. What is the chemical symbol for tin?

994

1. How many known deaths have occurred in spacecraft?
2. How did Lord Kitchener die?
3. Salisbury, Wiltshire, stands at the junction of two rivers; what are they?
4. What monstrous animal did Shaw conceive out of the Belloc–Chesterton writing team?
5. Which former disc-jockey and TV personality is a regular marathon runner?
6. Who used to be the censor of plays in the British theatre?
7. Which painter was shot by Valerie Solarnis?
8. What is the number of the Pastoral Symphony of Beethoven?
9. What is the more common name for the oesophagus?

252

1. 1948.
2. The Duke of Clarence, in Malmsey wine.
3. Morocco.
4. Ursula or Gudrun Brangwen.
5. 1974.
6. Ron Moody.
7. You would get wet. It is when a wave overtakes a boat from behind and water comes on board.
8. B. Bumble and the Stingers with 'Nut Rocker'.
9. A meerschaum.

623

1. Printing.
2. James I.
3. South Africa.
4. Corsica's.
5. 2 minutes.
6. *Anna Christie* (1930).
7. Georges Clemenceau.
8. Jan and Dean.
9. Sn.

994

1. Seven.
2. He was drowned off the Orkneys in 1916.
3. The Wylye and the Avon.
4. Chesterbelloc.
5. Jimmy Saville.
6. The Lord Chamberlain.
7. Andy Warhol.
8. The sixth.
9. The gullet.

253

1. Who built the massive aircraft called the 'Spruce Goose'?
2. Which tea party precipitated a war?
3. From where do hula-hula girls hail?
4. Who claimed: 'I am a citizen not of Athens or Greece, but of the world'?
5. Which 'throwing' events date back to ancient games?
6. Who directed *Saturday Night and Sunday Morning*?
7. Which woman sailed solo across the Atlantic in 1976 in 29 days, 1 hour and 52 minutes?
8. Whose old man was a dustman?
9. Which famous general wrote a book called *Holism and Evolution*?

624

1. For what is PS the abbreviation?
2. Which English king had the most (legitimate) children?
3. Which river flows through Germany, Austria and Hungary?
4. Where is the first mention of the British lion as the emblem of Great Britain?
5. How many goals did Ted MacDougall score for Bournemouth against Margate in 1971?
6. Who played Hotlips Hoolihan in the film version of *MASH*?
7. What are the three primary colours?
8. Denny Laine toured with McCartney's Wings, but who did he play with first?
9. What is another name for the windhover?

995

1. What was a 'Nuremburg egg'?
2. During which battle did the Charge of the Light Brigade take place?
3. Which was the first peak over 8,000 metres to be climbed?
4. What work begins with the words 'Arma verumque cano'?
5. In golf, where is the US Masters always played?
6. Who played the nymphet Lolita in Kubrick's film?
7. Who did Martin Luther describe as 'a fool who wanted to turn the Universe upside down'?
8. What was Paul Anka's only No. 1 hit in Britain?
9. Newton's dog was said to have caused a fire in Newton's laboratory, destroying some manuscripts. What was its name?

253

1. Howard Hughes.
2. The Boston Tea Party (1773).
3. Hawaii.
4. Socrates, according to Plutarch in *De Exilio*.
5. Javelin and discus.
6. Karel Reisz.
7. Clare Francis.
8. Lonnie Donegan's (in 1960).
9. General Smuts.

624

1. Post scriptum.
2. Edward I. He had eighteen.
3. The Danube.
4. In Dryden's *The Hind and the Panther* (1687).
5. Nine.
6. Sally Kellerman.
7. Red, blue and yellow.
8. The Moody Blues.
9. Kestrel.

995

1. An early watch or pocket clock.
2. Balaclava (1854).
3. Annapurna I.
4. Virgil's *Aeneid*.
5. Augusta, Georgia.
6. Sue Lyon.
7. Copernicus.
8. 'Diana'.
9. Diamond.

254

1. What did W A A F stand for?
2. Who was the last Pope to be a father?
3. Which city does Santa Cruz airport serve?
4. Who, in the Old Testament, was eaten by dogs?
5. In which sport might you perform a stem-christie?
6. Which dance group was the first to appear regularly in 'Top of the Pops'?
7. How does this rhyme end: 'Had you seen but these roads before they were made/You would hold up your hands and bless . . .'?
8. Where is Gilbert and Sullivan's *Gondoliers* set?
9. For how long can porpoises stay under water without breathing?

625

1. Which organization has the words 'Blood and Fire' on its badge?
2. Who said, 'Not by revolutions and majority votes ... but by blood and iron . . .'?
3. Which country once issued a postage stamp shaped like a banana?
4. For what sort of stories was the magazine *Black Mask* known?
5. Who won soccer's 1984 European Championship?
6. Ian McEwan wrote *The Imitation Game*, but can you name his *un*transmitted TV play?
7. By what name was Goldie Mabovitch better known?
8. Which album had the biggest sale in the 1960s?
9. What is the kookaburra's nickname?

996

1. Which number gives you the same answer whether you add 6 to it, or multiply it by 6?
2. How many countries signed the Warsaw Pact on 14 May 1955?
3. In which city would you find St David's main line station?
4. Who wrote: 'A good hanging prevents a bad marriage'?
5. Which tennis player had a cameo role in the Bond film *Octopussy*?
6. Which film featured the song 'Raindrops Keep Fallin' On My Head'?
7. Who created Zuleika Dobson?
8. *The 5,000 Spirits or the Layers of the Onion*: in 1967, the album seemed to be everywhere. Who recorded it?
9. What is the more common name for convallaria?

254

1. Women's Auxiliary Air Force.
2. Rodrigo Borgia, who became Pope Alexander VI in 1492.
3. Bombay.
4. Jezebel.
5. Skiing.
6. Pan's People.
7. 'General Wade'.
8. Venice.
9. About 5 minutes.

625

1. The Salvation Army.
2. Otto von Bismarck.
3. Tonga.
4. Crime – one of its most famous contributors was Raymond Chandler.
5. France.
6. *Solid Geometry* – apparently banned because it featured a male organ pickled in formaldehyde.
7. Golda Meir.
8. *Bridge Over Troubled Water* by Simon and Garfunkel.
9. The laughing jackass.

996

1. $1\frac{1}{5}$ (1·2).
2. Eight.
3. Exeter.
4. Shakespeare, in *Twelfth Night*.
5. Vijay Amritraj.
6. *Butch Cassidy and the Sundance Kid*.
7. Max Beerbohm.
8. The Incredible String Band.
9. Lily of the valley.

255

1. What hallmark is stamped on silver objects from Birmingham?
2. In which decade was electric street-lighting introduced to London?
3. What is a lee shore?
4. Which 'decadent' was the half-brother of an actor-manager and knighted in 1939?
5. What type of car was Graham Hill driving when he won the 1968 World Championship?
6. Who was the Six Million Dollar Man?
7. What is a spinnaker?
8. Tracey Ullman asked Darling to move over. Who sang the original?
9. In computer jargon, what does the acronym ASCII mean?

626

1. From which stationery group did Conran de-merge in 1971?
2. What was the name of Henry VIII's fool?
3. Who is the Queen of Canada?
4. Which son of a miner wrote *A Collier's Friday Night*, illustrative of his teenage at Eastwood?
5. In 1967, Spurs' goalkeeper Pat Jennings scored with a long kick. Who was the opposing goalkeeper?
6. Name Tom Mix's horse.
7. Who, in pidgin English, is 'number one fellah belong missus Queen'?
8. Who doesn't know what is happening?
9. Opaque 2 is a development in the modern 'Green Revolution'. What is it?

997

1. What were Fourier's phalansteries?
2. How many New Deals did Roosevelt inaugurate?
3. What is the Paris underground railway generally called?
4. Complete this sentence from *The Love Song of J. Alfred Prufrock*: 'Let us go then you and I/When the evening is spread out against the sky/ . . .'
5. Who was the first tennis player to achieve the grand slam (Australia, France, Wimbledon and USA Championships)?
6. Which Irish actor played Leopold Bloom in *Ulysses*?
7. What are padmasana, sirsasana and savasana?
8. Who told us to wear flowers in our hair in 1967?
9. What is odd about Golden Queen and Golden King holly?

255

1. An anchor.
2. In the 1870s (1879, on the Thames Embankment).
3. A shore lying off a ship's leeward side.
4. Max Beerbohm.
5. A Lotus.
6. Lee Majors.
7. A large, triangular sail, usually very brightly coloured, used when running before the wind.
8. Doris Day.
9. American Standard Code for Information Interchange.

626

1. Ryman's.
2. Will Somers.
3. Queen Elizabeth II.
4. D. H. Lawrence.
5. Alex Stepney (Manchester United).
6. Tony.
7. The Duke of Edinburgh.
8. Bob Dylan's Mr Jones.
9. A new variety of maize.

997

1. Proposed socialist communities of about 1,800 people, owning no private property and living as one family.
2. Three.
3. The Métro.
4. '. . ./Like a patient etherized upon a table.'
5. Donald Budge.
6. Milo O'Shea.
7. Yoga positions.
8. Scott McKenzie.
9. The Queen is a male and the King a female variety.

256

1. Why is a Tommy gun so called?
2. Who commanded the British Fleet at the Battle of Jutland in the First World War?
3. Where is Broken Hill, the world's largest silver mine?
4. Who wrote a poem on the death of a friend, A. H. Hallam?
5. Which showjumper competed in all the Olympic Games from 1948 to 1976?
6. The band Slade once made a film. What was it called?
7. Name two actors who have played Philip Marlowe.
8. Which American town does Randy Newman sing about?
9. What is an eagle's nest called?

627

1. What does 'nolens volens' mean?
2. Which son of a king was known as the Bloody Butcher?
3. Which country has the highest rainfall?
4. Where does the couplet come from: 'In arguing, too, the parson own'd his skill,/For, e'en though vanquished, he could argue still'?
5. Which colour belt is worn by beginners at karate?
6. What was the naval star of the BBC documentary series 'Sailor'?
7. For what was Watteau famous?
8. What is Alvin Stardust's real name?
9. What do Americans plant on Arbor Day?

998

1. What does 'Stalin' mean?
2. Which British politician, violently opposed to one war, was prime minister in the next?
3. Which country makes the most TV sets?
4. Who is Percy Blakeney?
5. Who won the Wimbledon men's doubles in 1968/9/70?
6. Who played Manuel in 'Fawlty Towers'?
7. Which American Rhodes scholar was teaching English at West Point when he decided to concentrate on a musical career?
8. Which famous calypso was written by Egbert 'Lord Beginner' Moore?
9. What is the common name for *Juglans regia*?

256

1. It was invented by US General Thompson about 1919 and was called the Thompson gun. When the stock was detached it became a favourite with American gangsters and became the Tommy gun.
2. Admiral Sir John Jellicoe.
3. New South Wales, Australia.
4. Tennyson (*In Memoriam*).
5. Raimondo d'Inzeo.
6. *Flame.*
7. Humphrey Bogart (of course!); Robert Montgomery; Elliot Gould; Robert Mitchum and Dick Powell.
8. Baltimore.
9. An eyrie.

627

1. Willy-nilly.
2. The Duke of Cumberland (second son of George II) after his suppression of the '45 Rebellion.
3. Colombia.
4. *The Deserted Village* by Oliver Goldsmith.
5. White.
6. HMS *Ark Royal.*
7. Painting.
8. Bernard Jewry.
9. Trees.

998

1. Steel.
2. Lloyd George.
3. Japan.
4. The Scarlet Pimpernel.
5. John Newcombe and Tony Roche.
6. Andrew Sachs.
7. Kris Kristofferson.
8. 'Victory Calypso, Lords 1950'.
9. The common walnut.

257

1. Who said he made his fortune out of what people left on the side of their plates?
2. What were Charles II's dying words?
3. Where is Benghazi?
4. Which book opens: 'They order, said I, this matter better in France'?
5. Who won Britain's second orienteering championship in 1968?
6. Who played the Jewish Princess in *Goodbye, Columbus*?
7. By what name was Thomas Jonathan Jackson, an American Civil War Confederate general, better known?
8. Which album cover had a zip on it?
9. Haematite is an ore of which metal?

628

1. What was the original meaning of 'antediluvian'?
2. How many emperors ruled in the year following Nero's suicide in AD 68?
3. Which university has a football stadium and a nuclear reactor built across the San Andreas Fault?
4. Where does *Under Milk Wood* take place?
5. Which club was in the First Division of the Football League for the longest period without winning the League Championship?
6. Which film begins with the line: 'Call me Ishmael . . .'?
7. For what would you use battens in board sailing?
8. For what is Tiny Tim best remembered?
9. What is the chemical name for dry ice?

999

1. What are marrons glacés?
2. Who said: 'I would have liked to go to Ireland, but my grandmother would not let me. Perhaps she thought I wanted to take the little place'?
3. What is the Palmdale Pimple?
4. What is the last book of the Old Testament?
5. On which track was the first British Grand Prix held?
6. Which role did Garbo play twice?
7. What was Euripides before he became a playwright?
8. What did Thunderclap Newman see in 1969?
9. Apollo 11 was not alone during the moon landing. What other active craft was there?

257

1. George Colman, the mustard manufacturer.
2. 'Let not poor Nelly starve.'
3. In Libya.
4. *A Sentimental Journey* by Laurence Sterne.
5. Gordon Pirie.
6. Ali MacGraw.
7. Stonewall Jackson.
8. *Sticky Fingers* by the Rolling Stones.
9. Iron.

628

1. Before Noah's flood.
2. Four – Galba, Otho, Vitellius and Vespasian.
3. Berkeley, Oakland.
4. Llaregyb.
5. Bolton (for 60 years).
6. *Moby Dick.*
7. To help the sail retain its correct shape.
8. His bizarre rendering of 'Tiptoe Through the Tulips'.
9. Solid carbon dioxide.

999

1. Sweet chestnuts preserved in syrup.
2. Kaiser Wilhelm II.
3. A gradually rising dome of rock over the San Andreas Fault.
4. Malachi.
5. Silverstone.
6. Anna Karenina; in 1927 (filmed as *Love*), and in 1935.
7. A painter.
8. 'Something in the Air'.
9. The Russian Luna 15.

258

1. What is pargetting?
2. Which queen died of smallpox at the age of thirty-two?
3. Where was the legendary land of Lyonesse?
4. Who says, 'When sorrows come, they come not single spies,/But in battalions'?
5. In which year was the 'white horse' Cup Final?
6. In this acting family there is Peter and Jane, and their father was Henry. What is their surname?
7. Whose was the first large holiday camp?
8. What was Steppenwolf born to be?
9. What is a zonkey?

629

1. Who can be seen in a glass case in University College, London?
2. What were the names of the three ships that sailed to America with Christopher Columbus?
3. From where does a Cretan hail?
4. What is *Spare Rib*?
5. Who won the 1984 Emsley Carr Mile?
6. Which film features the line 'Love means never having to say you're sorry'?
7. From where did the poet Dante hail?
8. Freddie Bulgara is better known as which lead singer?
9. In horses, where would you find the coffin joint?

1000

1. What percentage of carbohydrates can be found in meat?
2. Which ex-miner was the first Labour MP?
3. Which country do Kyushu, Kyoto and Hokkaido form?
4. What was hung round the neck of the Ancient Mariner?
5. After 64 years, which sport will be re-introduced at the 1988 Olympics?
6. In which film did Marilyn Monroe co-star with Laurence Olivier?
7. Who was married to a German, hounded out of Cornwall in 1916 and lived in New Mexico until 1925?
8. Who starred with Cliff in the film *Expresso Bongo*?
9. What is the other name for hydrophobia?

258

1. Ornamental relief work in moulded plaster on the outside of houses – common in East Anglia.
2. Mary II.
3. Between Cornwall and the Scilly Isles.
4. Claudius in *Hamlet*.
5. 1923.
6. Fonda.
7. Billy Butlin's (in 1935 at Skegness).
8. Wild.
9. A cross between a zebra and a donkey.

629

1. Jeremy Bentham, mummified.
2. *Pinta, Nina* and *Santa Maria*.
3. Crete.
4. A feminist magazine.
5. Peter Elliott.
6. *Love Story*.
7. Italy.
8. Freddie Mercury.
9. The foot.

1000

1. None.
2. Keir Hardie.
3. Japan.
4. The albatross.
5. Tennis.
6. *The Prince and the Showgirl*.
7. D. H. Lawrence.
8. Laurence Harvey
9. Rabies.

259

1. What is Tuesday's child?
2. Which Scottish comedian was knighted in 1919?
3. On which island are the ruins of Knossos?
4. In which Dickens novel did Mrs Gamp appear?
5. In 1973, which British athlete broke the world record for the 10,000 metres?
6. Who played the militant shop steward in 'The Rag Trade'?
7. Who hosted both 'Double Your Money' and 'Opportunity Knocks'?
8. The Shadows had a hit with their first single in 1960. What was it?
9. What lives in a holt?

630

1. What is normal human temperature on the Centigrade scale?
2. Which animal's head had the Egyptian god Anubis?
3. Where might you spend a lev?
4. Which other great writer died on the same day as Miguel de Cervantes in 1616?
5. Which professional cricketer turned amateur in order to captain England?
6. Who used to talk to Pussy Cat Willum on children's TV?
7. Which Benedictine monk perfected the 'champagne method'?
8. Which song from *Casablanca* was a hit in 1977?
9. Which metal is used in galvanizing?

1001

1. For what is a Geiger counter used?
2. What was the 'Whip with Six Strings'?
3. In which country was Expo 70 held?
4. What is the 'U' phrase for 'pleased to meet you'?
5. How many World Championship motor-cycle titles did Giacomo Agostini win?
6. Which TV interviewer hit the headlines in 1977 in his confrontation with the Sex Pistols?
7. Who or what was Ally Sloper?
8. Eivets Rednow: who recorded under this alias?
9. On the Beaufort scale, what speed of wind is classed as a 'strong breeze'?

259

1. Full of grace.
2. Harry Lauder.
3. Crete.
4. *Martin Chuzzlewit.*
5. David Bedford.
6. Miriam Karlin.
7. Hughie Green.
8. 'Apache'.
9. An otter.

630

1. 37°.
2. The head of a jackal.
3. Bulgaria or Romania.
4. Shakespeare.
5. W. R. Hammond.
6. Muriel Young.
7. Dom Pérignon.
8. 'As Time Goes By', sung by Dooley Wilson.
9. Zinc (spelter).

1001

1. Measuring radioactivity.
2. The 1539 Act of Six Articles, for Henry VIII's Church of England.
3. Japan.
4. 'How do you do'.
5. Twelve.
6. Bill Grundy.
7. The first British cartoon strip character, in the 1880s.
8. Stevie Wonder (obviously!).
9. 25–31 m.p.h.

260

1. How much was the twelve-sided British coin worth?
2. For which calling did Henry VIII train?
3. Which country invaded Czechoslovakia in 1968?
4. Which underground newspaper was taken to court in 1971?
5. Which well-known jockey first rode in the Derby at the age of forty-six?
6. Ringo starred in it, Terry Southern wrote it. What was it?
7. By what name is the American Rebecca Rolfe, who rescued a captain and met James I, better known?
8. Whose shoes were 'Letting In Water' in 1967?
9. Name the heavily accented husband-and-wife TV naturalist team, famous in the 1950s.

631

1. In computer jargon, what is a VDU?
2. Which empress emerged from voluntary seclusion in 1876, 15 years after being widowed?
3. After death, which water-lily awaited each soul in a Chinese heaven?
4. Who wrote the first James Bond follow-up, *Colonel Sun*, after Ian Fleming's death?
5. In which sport does Franz Klammer excel?
6. Who is the patron saint of dancers and actors?
7. Which English poet drowned while sailing in Italy in 1822?
8. From where does Helen Reddy come?
9. What is the tallest type of grass?

1002

1. What wording can be found on all our decimal coinage, on the other side from the Queen's head?
2. For whom did Napoleon once buy a dress covered in fresh rose-petals?
3. Name two of the original Cinque Ports.
4. Whose fictional detective was Gervase Fen?
5. Name the first Soviet Union soccer team to play in Britain.
6. What is the newspaper proprietor's name in 'Lou Grant'?
7. How old was Nigel Short when he became Britain's youngest chess International Master?
8. Who is the lead singer in Slade?
9. Which dinosaur's name means 'thunder lizard'?

260

1. 3d.
2. The priesthood.
3. Russia.
4. *Oz.*
5. Willie Shoemaker.
6. *The Magic Christian.*
7. Pocahontas.
8. Traffic's.
9. Armand and Michaela Denis.

631

1. A visual display unit.
2. Queen Victoria, Empress of India.
3. The lotus.
4. Kingsley Amis.
5. Skiing.
6. St Vitus.
7. Shelley.
8. Australia.
9. Bamboo.

1002

1. NEW PENCE.
2. Josephine.
3. Choose from Dover, Hastings, Hythe, Romney and Sandwich.
4. Edmund Crispin's.
5. Moscow Dynamo, in 1945.
6. Mrs Pynchon, played by Nancy Marchand.
7. Fourteen.
8. Noddy Holder.
9. Brontosaurus.

261

1. What do the letters GI stand for?
2. After which event did Sir Charles Napier dispatch the message, 'Peccavi'?
3. Which American city was once called New Amsterdam?
4. Who reputedly first said, 'If in doubt, tell the truth'?
5. What is the French Derby called?
6. Which legendary rock and roll pianist sang the title song in the film *High School Confidential*?
7. Who was the only female member of the BMA for nearly 20 years?
8. By what name was John Ritchie better known?
9. What is the difference between the eyes of flesh-eating animals and those of plant-eating animals?

632

1. Which is the second most commonly spoken language in the world?
2. Which queen was brought up as a boy, ruled for 22 years, and then abdicated?
3. By what name is the Thames known as it passes through Oxford?
4. In Greek mythology, who rowed the dead across the river Styx into Hades?
5. What nationality is tennis ace Vitas Gerulaitis?
6. Who was the first to play the role of Doctor Who?
7. By what name is Alfred White better known?
8. Who is the lead singer in Hot Chocolate?
9. Which acid was first prepared from distilled red ants?

1003

1. Where in Europe, besides Britain, are vehicles driven on the left?
2. How did James Bartley emulate Jonah?
3. Where is the International Court of the United Nations?
4. Which animal faded away, leaving only its grin?
5. At which track is the greyhound classic The Laurels run?
6. Which member of the Kinks starred in the 1970 TV play 'The Long Distance Piano Player'?
7. Who devised 'Doctor Who'?
8. Carole King, who usually wrote for other singers at the beginning of her career, in 1962 had a hit in her own right. What was it?
9. By what name is the false plane tree better known?

261

1. Government Issue.
2. His victory at Hyderabad and capture of Sind in 1843. (It is a pun: 'Peccavi' is Latin for 'I have sinned'.)
3. New York.
4. Mark Twain (Samuel Clemens).
5. The Prix du Jockey Club.
6. Jerry Lee Lewis.
7. Elizabeth Garrett Anderson.
8. Sid Vicious.
9. Flesh-eaters have their eyes at the front of their head, plant-eaters one on each side.

632

1. English.
2. Christina, 'king' of Sweden.
3. The Isis.
4. Charon.
5. American.
6. William Hartnell.
7. James Herriot.
8. Errol Brown.
9. Formic acid.

1003

1. Eire.
2. He was swallowed by a whale and came out alive (in 1891).
3. The Hague, Holland.
4. The Cheshire Cat.
5. Wimbledon.
6. Ray Davies.
7. Terry Nation.
8. 'It Might as Well Rain Until September'.
9. The sycamore.

262

1. What was allowed to take place in London's Serpentine for the first time on 16 June 1930?
2. Who was the Protestant 'Lion of the North' killed in a mist without his armour in the Thirty Years War?
3. Which US state is called the Blue Grass state?
4. In *The Taming of the Shrew*, who is Katharina's father?
5. Who was the youngest jockey to win the Derby this century?
6. What is Stewpot's real name?
7. What was suffragette Mrs Pankhurst's first name?
8. What is DJ David Jensen's nickname?
9. What is represented by an orrery?

633

1. What is the profession of an FRCVS?
2. Who surrendered his forces at the Battle of Saratoga in 1777?
3. Where is the Sugar Loaf Mountain?
4. Which French author isolated himself in a cork-lined room when writing?
5. On which golf course did Tony Jacklin win the British Open in 1969?
6. Which role have Charles Boyer, Herbert Lom and Marlon Brando all played in films?
7. Of which country was Vidkun Quisling prime minister?
8. Which group was known by its initials, BTO?
9. Which is the lightest: gold, lead or platinum?

1004

1. Which regiment is known as the Blues?
2. Which city was the Bride of the Sea?
3. What connects the Sea of Marmara with the Black Sea?
4. Which year was Dryden's 'annus mirabilis'?
5. How old was Lester Piggott when he won the Derby in 1954?
6. Who (not Peter Sellers!) played Inspector Clouseau in 1968?
7. Which school did Prince Charles first attend?
8. Who released an album called *Hergest Ridge*?
9. Which soft silvery metal was discovered in Argyllshire?

262

1. Mixed bathing.
2. Gustavus Adolphus of Sweden.
3. Kentucky.
4. Baptista.
5. Lester Piggott.
6. Ed Stewart.
7. Emmeline.
8. 'Kid'.
9. The planets and their movement.

633

1. Veterinary surgery.
2. John Burgoyne.
3. Rio de Janeiro, Brazil.
4. Marcel Proust.
5. Royal Lytham.
6. That of Napoleon.
7. Norway.
8. Bachman Turner Overdrive.
9. Lead.

1004

1. The Royal Horse Guards.
2. Venice (from the ceremony in which the Doge threw a ring into the Adriatic).
3. The Bosporus.
4. 1666 – the year of wonders, memorable for the Great Fire and English successes over the Dutch.
5. Eighteen.
6. Alan Arkin.
7. Cheam.
8. Mike Oldfield.
9. Strontium.

263

1. How many peals of the Lutine bell mean bad news?
2. Which battle was considered to be the turning-point of the English Civil War?
3. Name two of the other three provinces, apart from Slovakia, which comprise Czechoslovakia.
4. Who wrote *Portrait of the Artist as a Young Dog*?
5. Of which sport is Yabusame a Japanese version?
6. Who shared a touch of a class with George Segal?
7. Who is said to have been the father of geography as an academic discipline?
8. Name Eric Idle's spoof Beatles group.
9. How is polyvinyl chloride familiarly known?

634

1. Of which animal does a griffin have the body?
2. How many, to the nearest hundred, rode in the Charge of the Light Brigade?
3. In which country has General Alfredo Stroessner been in power for over 30 years?
4. Which was Dickens's autobiographical novel?
5. Where is the shoot-out for the Queen's Prize held?
6. Who was the first presenter of 'Celebrity Squares'?
7. Who discovered Cuba (apart from its inhabitants)?
8. Who had a hit with 'Tie Me Kangaroo Down Sport'?
9. Of what is dendrolatry the worship?

1005

1. What is the riddle of the Sphinx?
2. What, measuring 18 by 15 feet, did 146 enter and only 23 leave alive?
3. What would you find at Mardalsfossen, Norway, to amaze you?
4. In which John Buchan novel does Princess Saskin appear?
5. Of what nationality was the athlete who won the pole vault in the Moscow Olympics?
6. What is the name of the captain of the men's team in 'Give Us a Clue'?
7. Which novelist had a dog called Hamlet?
8. Which wonderful contralto, who tragically died of cancer, made her Glyndebourne debut in 1946?
9. What is the more colloquial name for the araucaria?

263

1. One.
2. Marston Moor.
3. Moravia, Bohemia, Silesia.
4. Dylan Thomas.
5. Archery.
6. Glenda Jackson.
7. Karl Ritter.
8. The Ruttles.
9. PVC.

634

1. A lion.
2. 700. (673 to be precise.)
3. Paraguay.
4. *David Copperfield.*
5. Bisley.
6. Bob Monkhouse.
7. Christopher Columbus.
8. Rolf Harris.
9. Trees.

1005

1. 'What is it that walks on four legs in the morning, on two at noon, and on three in the evening?'
2. The Black Hole of Calcutta.
3. A waterfall 655 metres high.
4. *Huntingtower.*
5. Polish. His name was Cwladyslaw Kozkiewicz.
6. Lionel Blair.
7. Sir Walter Scott.
8. Kathleen Ferrier.
9. Monkey-puzzle.

264

1. Which Chinese commune near Soochow did Margaret Thatcher visit in 1977?
2. What was Pride's Purge?
3. Where is Pharaoh's Treasury carved into a cliff face?
4. Which poet wrote *A Shropshire Lad*?
5. Who captained the USA in the first six Ryder Cup golf matches?
6. What are the first names of the two comics Little and Large?
7. What happened to Christopher Marlowe in Deptford?
8. Name any two members of the original Small Faces.
9. What kind of wind is number twelve on the Beaufort scale?

635

1. What is the name of the horse badly injured in a bomb outrage in London and retired in June 1984?
2. Which butcher's son became a cardinal?
3. Upon how many hills is Istanbul built?
4. According to Genesis, to what age did Methuselah live?
5. What is the national sport of Finland?
6. Who played the original Liver Birds?
7. What silver substitute did Thomas Bolsover invent round about 1742?
8. Who claimed that two out of three wasn't bad?
9. Rank the creatures in order of longevity: oyster (fresh-water), hippopotamus, camel, whale.

1006

1. What is the answer to the riddle of the Sphinx?
2. Who was Agrippina's most obnoxious son?
3. What was Djibouti known as before 1967?
4. Who is Charlie Brown's short stop?
5. Which Wimbledon singles tennis champion is Bob Lutz's doubles partner?
6. In which city was 'Shoestring' set?
7. When did Eva Perón of Argentina die?
8. Which British composer was once staff bandmaster in a lunatic asylum?
9. Why are butterflies and moths called lepidoptera?

264

1. The Evergreen Commune.
2. The arrest or shutting out by Colonel Pride on 6 December 1648 of MPs who were seeking a compromise with Charles I.
3. Petra, Jordan.
4. A. E. Housman.
5. Walter Hagen.
6. Syd and Eddie.
7. He was stabbed to death in a tavern brawl.
8. Jimmy Winston, Ronnie Lane, Steve Marriott, Ian McLagan.
9. A hurricane.

635

1. Sefton.
2. Thomas Wolsey.
3. Seven.
4. 969.
5. Motor rallying.
6. Polly James and Nerys Hughes.
7. Sheffield plate.
8. Meat Loaf.
9. Oyster, hippopotamus, whale, camel.

1006

1. Man.
2. Nero.
3. French Somaliland.
4. Snoopy.
5. Stan Smith.
6. Bristol.
7. 1952.
8. Sir Edward Elgar.
9. They have scales on their wings (*Gr.* lepis = a scale).

265

1. Which old silver coin was worth fourpence?
2. Which king returned to England in 1660?
3. In which country were fifty-two American hostages held for 444 days?
4. For how many years was Robinson Crusoe a castaway?
5. How many deliveries normally constitute an over at cricket in England?
6. What word is used in 'Mastermind' to signify a right answer?
7. Who invented the machine gun?
8. Who composed the music (lyrics by Lorenz Hart) to 'Blue Moon' and 'My Funny Valentine'?
9. What was Peter Goldmark's circular invention of 1948?

636

1. What is the Boy Scouts' motto?
2. Which French prison was stormed and taken on 14 July 1789?
3. Where is the Hope Diamond kept?
4. How many days and nights did Elijah spend in the wilderness?
5. Who won the soccer World Cup in 1978?
6. Which TV series featured Emma Peel?
7. Which sense did Milton lose?
8. Who sings the theme song in the Bond film *You Only Live Twice*?
9. Of what are camel's-hair brushes made?

1007

1. What are old boys of Charterhouse School called?
2. What did Nell Gwyn sell?
3. Which British monarch has visited New Zealand?
4. Who wrote *Hotel*?
5. In baseball, what is the distance in feet between bases?
6. Which playing card caused Raymond Shaw to go into a hypnotic trance in *The Manchurian Candidate*?
7. How did the great Greek dramatist Aeschylus die?
8. Which Gilbert and Sullivan opera is about the emperor of Japan?
9. How many points of the compass are there?

265

1. The groat.
2. Charles II.
3. Iran.
4. Twenty-eight.
5. Six.
6. Correct.
7. Richard J. Gatling (in 1862).
8. Richard Rodgers.
9. The long-playing record.

636

1. 'Be prepared'.
2. The Bastille.
3. In the Smithsonian Institute in Washington, DC.
4. Forty of each.
5. Argentina.
6. 'The Avengers'.
7. His sight.
8. Nancy Sinatra.
9. Hairs from squirrels' tails.

1007

1. Carthusians.
2. Oranges.
3. Elizabeth II.
4. Arthur Hailey.
5. Ninety.
6. The queen of diamonds.
7. He was killed when a bird dropped a tortoise on his head from a great height.
8. *The Mikado.*
9. Thirty-two.

266

1. Which sense does a dying person tend to lose first?
2. What did William Young invent in 1800?
3. Which two UK cities have stations named Charing Cross?
4. Which lawyer-detective featured in *The Case of the Lucky Legs*?
5. By what name is Walker Smith better known?
6. Who was the model for Tinker Bell in the Walt Disney production?
7. How old was Whistler's mother when she posed for the famous picture?
8. To whom did Stradivarius become an apprentice at eighteen?
9. How many yards are there in a furlong?

637

1. Where does Indian ink come from?
2. Which British liner went down in the North Atlantic in April 1912?
3. What was the previous name of Camp David, the US Presidential retreat?
4. Who killed Smaug?
5. Which country has won the most Olympic medals since the beginning of the modern Olympic Games?
6. Who played Otis B. Driftwood in the 1935 film *A Night at the Opera*?
7. What was the surname of the last tsar of Russia, Nicholas II?
8. What is Van Cliburn's instrument?
9. What metal would you find in gesundheit?

1008

1. What is the name of the royal yacht?
2. Whom did King Edward VIII marry?
3. Which two countries does the Gulf of Bothnia separate?
4. Which Shakespeare play has been described as a study in fear?
5. In which country is the headquarters of the International Ice Hockey Federation?
6. Which film actress did Howard Hughes marry?
7. Who designed the Eiffel Tower?
8. Who, in 1968, recorded an album entitled *John Wesley Harding*?
9. What is the Salk vaccine used to prevent?

266

1. Sight.
2. Different shoes for the right and left foot.
3. Glasgow and London.
4. Perry Mason.
5. Sugar Ray Robinson.
6. Marilyn Monroe.
7. Sixty-five.
8. Niccolo Amati.
9. 220.

637

1. China.
2. The *Titanic*.
3. Shangri La.
4. Bard the Archer (in J. R. R. Tolkien's *The Hobbit*).
5. The United States.
6. Groucho Marx.
7. Romanov.
8. The piano.
9. None; it is German for 'Your good health'!

1008

1. *Britannia*.
2. Mrs Wallis Warfield Simpson.
3. Finland and Sweden.
4. *Macbeth*.
5. England (London).
6. Jean Peters.
7. Gustave Eiffel.
8. Bob Dylan.
9. Poliomyelitis.

267

1. From which London building is the first proclamation of a new monarch read?
2. Which famous ex-Augustinian monk married an ex-Cistercian nun?
3. Where does 1 ngultrum equal 100 chetrums?
4. Who disguised herself as Ganymede?
5. Who captained England in Australia during the bodyline controversy?
6. Which pop star played Tony Lumpkin in *She Stoops to Conquer* at the Old Vic in 1960?
7. Who followed Khruschev into power in Russia?
8. From which country does the mazurka originate?
9. What are penguins covered in?

638

1. What is the most common international crime?
2. What did Florence Nightingale, George Orwell and Adolf Hitler have in common?
3. Where in the USA is the White House?
4. In which Charlotte Brontë novel is Lucy Snowe the central character?
5. Which town has been the headquarters of horse-racing since the seventeenth century?
6. Who is 'Open All Hours'?
7. By what name was Rose Louise Hovick better known?
8. Who asked for the head of John the Baptist as a reward for her dancing?
9. Which part of an aeroplane is the fuselage?

1009

1. Approximately what proportion of the world's population customarily eat with their fingers?
2. Where was the Charter of Grammont granted in 1068?
3. Of which country is Our Lady of Guadalupe the patron saint?
4. Who was the first human created by God?
5. How high is the netball net from the ground?
6. Whose nephews are Huey, Dewey and Louie?
7. Which are the two one-eyed jacks?
8. How did Jim Reeves die?
9. From which flowers is attar chiefly obtained?

267

1. St James's Palace.
2. Martin Luther.
3. Bhutan.
4. Rosalind (in *As You Like It*).
5. Douglas Jardine.
6. Tommy Steele.
7. Brezhnev and Kosygin.
8. Poland.
9. Feathers.

638

1. Narcotics (drug) smuggling.
2. They all suffered from tuberculosis.
3. Washington, DC.
4. *Villette.*
5. Newmarket.
6. Arkwright the grocer (played by Ronnie Barker).
7. Gypsy Rose Lee.
8. Salome.
9. The body.

1009

1. One-third.
2. Grammont.
3. Mexico.
4. Adam.
5. 10 feet.
6. Donald Duck's.
7. Jack of spades and jack of hearts.
8. He was killed in a plane crash.
9. Roses.

268

1. How is 3,000 written in Roman numerals?
2. Who was England's last Anglo-Saxon king?
3. Which royal castle is near Eton?
4. Who escaped from Devil's Island in Henri Charrière's book?
5. Who won the heavyweight boxing gold medal in the 1964 Tokyo Olympics?
6. What is the name of Citizen Kane's Florida mansion?
7. Whom did Bobby Fischer beat to win the World Chess Championship in 1972?
8. By what name is the Gilbert and Sullivan operetta *The King of Barataria* better known?
9. What is the name for an alloy of iron with some chromium and a small amount of nickel?

639

1. Which is the least used letter in the English alphabet?
2. Which legendary king instituted the Knights of the Round Table?
3. After whom were the Virgin Islands named?
4. Who created the New York City detective John Shaft?
5. From whom did James J. Braddock take the world heavyweight boxing title in 1935?
6. On which planet do Abbott and Costello land in the film *Abbott and Costello Go to Mars*?
7. By what name was Asa Yoelson better known?
8. Who had a big hit with 'Hound Dog'?
9. How long do mayfly eggs take to hatch?

1010

1. What is the qualification for being created Prince of Wales?
2. Which famous battle took place in 1415?
3. Which are the hottest months at the equator?
4. Name any of the three wise men.
5. How many strokes under par is an eagle?
6. Name the Lone Ranger's white stallion.
7. Which Chicago resident said, 'Public service is my motto'?
8. Of which singing group were Diana Ross, Mary Wilson and Florence Ballard the original members?
9. What is the patella?

268

1. MMM.
2. Harold.
3. Windsor.
4. Papillon.
5. Joe Frazier.
6. Xanadu.
7. Boris Spassky.
8. *The Gondoliers*.
9. Stainless steel.

639

1. Q.
2. Arthur.
3. Queen Elizabeth I.
4. Ernest Tidyman.
5. Max Baer.
6. Venus.
7. Al Jolson.
8. Elvis Presley.
9. 3 years.

1010

1. Being the eldest son of the reigning monarch.
2. Agincourt.
3. March and September.
4. Gaspar, Melchior, Balthasar.
5. Two.
6. Silver.
7. Al Capone.
8. The Supremes.
9. The kneecap.

269

1. What was Sir Francis Drake's *Golden Hind* originally called?
2. Who introduced inoculation for smallpox to Britain from Constantinople in 1718?
3. To which country does Crete belong?
4. In Greek mythology, to which creature were the eyes of Argus transferred?
5. What is passed on in an athletics relay race?
6. Which theatre, opened in 1959, was the first to be founded in the City of London since the time of Shakespeare?
7. Who founded the college of Christ Church at Oxford in 1525?
8. To which film was 'Mrs Robinson' the theme music?
9. List the following in order of fat content: milk, butter, cheese, yoghurt.

640

1. Who was Marmaduke Gingerbits?
2. In which year were trousers first issued to the British Army?
3. What is the meaning of 'wich' in place names such as Northwich and Droitwich?
4. Which two fictional doctors live at Arden House?
5. Who rode Red Rum to victory in the 1977 Grand National?
6. On which Shakespeare play is Orson Welles's *Chimes at Midnight* based?
7. At which game are Giorgio Belladonna and Benito Garozzo world champions?
8. Which of the Walkers were brothers?
9. What happens to a liquid when the vapour pressure equals the atmospheric pressure?

1011

1. From which ship did the Lutine bell come?
2. Which Holy Roman emperor was known as 'the Bald'?
3. In which ocean does Tristan da Cunha lie?
4. Name the books of the Pentateuch.
5. For which sport is the Stanley Cup awarded?
6. In which film did Twiggy play her first screen role?
7. What are the names of the two basic knitting stitches?
8. In which film did Elvis Presley play a Red Indian?
9. What is the common name for an animal of the family Ranidae, in the Amphibia class, with a backbone and a tongue but without a tail?

269

1. The *Pelican*.
2. Lady Mary Wortley Montagu.
3. Greece.
4. The peacock.
5. A baton.
6. The Mermaid.
7. Cardinal Wolsey.
8. *The Graduate*.
9. Butter, cheese, milk, yoghurt.

640

1. The cat at the centre of a 1984 court case.
2. 1823.
3. A brine well.
4. Dr Finlay and Dr Cameron.
5. Tommy Stack.
6. *Henry IV*.
7. Bridge.
8. None of them. None of them was called Walker, either.
9. It boils.

1011

1. HMS *Lutine*.
2. Charles II (Charles I of France and King of the West Franks).
3. The South Atlantic.
4. Genesis, Exodus, Leviticus, Numbers, Deuteronomy (the first five books of the Old Testament, attributed to Moses).
5. Ice hockey.
6. *The Boyfriend*.
7. Plain and purl.
8. *Stay Away Joe*.
9. A frog.

270

1. Who first rowed around the world?
2. In the Second World War, whose double was the actor M. E. Clifford James?
3. Which country manufactures the most cars?
4. How old was Mary Shelley when she wrote *Frankenstein*?
5. Roughly, how many of the ninety-two Football League clubs have a chaplain?
6. Why is London's Pall Mall so called?
7. By what name is Avrom Goldenborgen better known?
8. Whom did Prince William of Germany allow to shoot the ash from a cigarette held in his mouth?
9. Which insect has the best eyesight?

641

1. For what is 'titfer' the rhyming slang?
2. Who was accorded a nineteen-gun salute at his funeral, the highest given to a commoner to date?
3. Of which country is Durban a port?
4. Who was the *Merchant of Venice*?
5. From which country does judo originate?
6. Which Marx brother never spoke a line in films?
7. Which contemporary artist is noted for his royal portraits?
8. What is the full title of *The Mikado*?
9. Which water-fowl was thought to feed its young with its own blood?

1012

1. Of what is the Taj Mahal built?
2. Which American president fathered the greatest number of children?
3. Which flag has the nickname 'Old Glory'?
4. Who was the Greek goddess of wisdom said to have been born from the head of Zeus?
5. How many medals for speed skating did Eric Heiden win at the 1980 Winter Olympics?
6. Who plays the Fonz?
7. Who was the first American to win a Nobel Prize?
8. At what age did Mozart compose his first symphony?
9. What are the colours of the rainbow?

270

1. No one has yet attempted to do so.
2. General Montgomery's.
3. The USA – reputedly twelve per minute.
4. Nineteen.
5. Thirteen, at the end of the 1983–4 season.
6. Because there was an alley there for pall-mall, or pell-mell, an ancestor of croquet.
7. Mike Todd.
8. Annie Oakley.
9. The dragonfly.

641

1. Hat (tit for tat).
2. Winston Churchill.
3. South Africa.
4. Antonio.
5. Japan.
6. Harpo.
7. Pietro Annigoni.
8. *The Mikado, or the Town of Titipu.*
9. The pelican.

1012

1. Marble.
2. John Tyler (fourteen, by two marriages).
3. The Stars and Stripes (USA).
4. Athene.
5. Five.
6. Henry Winkler.
7. Theodore Roosevelt.
8. Eight.
9. Violet, indigo, blue, green, yellow, orange, red.

271

1. Which number does the Roman numeral D represent?
2. In which part of France did the Allied troops land on D-Day?
3. Of which country are the Kikuyu the main Bantu tribe?
4. In *Hamlet*, who was Ophelia's brother?
5. How old was the Olympic figure skating champion Sonja Henie when she first competed in the Olympics?
6. In the 1969 film *They Shoot Horses, Don't They?*, what was Jane Fonda's number in the marathon dance?
7. Which French artist became famous for his posters?
8. What is the 'wet' nickname of Chopin's Prelude Op. 28 No. 15?
9. Proverbially, what can't you make a silk purse out of?

642

1. Which is the world's largest airline?
2. How long was the reign of Pope John Paul who died on 28 September 1978?
3. What is the official language of Nigeria?
4. What are the first words of Winnie-the-Pooh after he wakes up each morning?
5. How many brothers and sisters did Sonny Liston have?
6. Who is Mia Farrow's mother?
7. Who gave Joseph Keaton his nickname of 'Buster'?
8. Which British king is thought to have composed 'Greensleeves'?
9. What did James Boyle invent in 1896?

1013

1. What did the Victorians call 'servant regulators'?
2. Which people first used fountain pens?
3. Which part of the British Isles gets the most sunshine?
4. What is the name of the nuclear-powered submarine miniaturized to travel through a human in Isaac Asimov's *Fantastic Voyage*?
5. Which QPR player was the captain of England?
6. What is the name of the MGM lion?
7. What was Charles Luciano's nickname?
8. By what name is the 'Londonderry Air' better known when sung?
9. Which is the brightest star always in the northern sky?

271

1. 500.
2. Normandy.
3. Kenya.
4. Laertes.
5. Eleven.
6. Sixty-seven.
7. Toulouse-Lautrec.
8. The Raindrop.
9. A sow's ear.

642

1. Aeroflot of the USSR.
2. 34 days.
3. English.
4. 'What's for breakfast?'
5. Twenty-four.
6. Maureen O'Sullivan.
7. Harry Houdini.
8. Henry VIII.
9. The self-raising hat.

1013

1. Alarm clocks.
2. The ancient Egyptians.
3. The Channel Islands.
4. *Proteus*.
5. Gerry Francis.
6. Leo.
7. Lucky.
8. 'Danny Boy'.
9. Vega.

272

1. Which April was the sunniest in England since records began?
2. Where was the British Empire Exhibition of 1924 held?
3. Of which country is IS the international vehicle registration?
4. Where did Paddington's Aunt Lucy live?
5. Which sport has styles of competition called Kushti, Sambo, Yagli and Graeco-Roman?
6. What surname has actor Lee Jacoby adopted?
7. For what is Elizabeth Fry best remembered?
8. Who wrote the words and music for *Oliver*?
9. How many times bigger than earth is Saturn?

643

1. What is the principal Herald of Scotland called?
2. When did Constantinople become Istanbul?
3. On which river does Balmoral Castle stand?
4. Who founded the *Daily News* in 1846?
5. In which event did British women win the silver medal in three successive Olympics?
6. Which Reading family catapulted into unexpected stardom as a result of their appearance in 'The Family'?
7. Who was the first American to orbit the earth?
8. Whose dogs were Ruby, Ringwood and Ranter?
9. Which birds did Chinese fishermen train to help them catch fish?

1014

1. What did Lloyd George call 'Mr Balfour's poodle'?
2. Who first used rockets for war?
3. Name the famous town in Mali on the south edge of the Sahara.
4. Who was 'La Pucelle' of Voltaire's poem?
5. Why did a group of pioneer American golfers become known as the 'Apple Tree Gang'?
6. Who, in her early days, was known as the 'Sweater Girl'?
7. Who succeeded Vic Feather as General Secretary of the TUC?
8. Who sang 'I'm Telling You Now' in 1965?
9. What is the European Organization for Nuclear Research near Geneva, Switzerland, otherwise known as?

272

1. April 1984.
2. Wembley Stadium.
3. Iceland.
4. Lima, Peru.
5. Wrestling.
6. Cobb (Lee J.).
7. Prison reform.
8. Lionel Bart.
9. 763.

643

1. Lord Lyon King of Arms.
2. In 1930, on the founding of the Turkish Republic.
3. The Dee.
4. Charles Dickens.
5. The high jump (1952, 1956, 1960).
6. The Wilkins.
7. John Glenn.
8. John Peel's.
9. Cormorants.

1014

1. The House of Lords.
2. The Chinese against the Mongols in 1232.
3. Timbuktu.
4. Joan of Arc.
5. Because they laid out a golf course in an orchard.
6. Lana Turner.
7. Len Murray.
8. Freddy and the Dreamers.
9. CERN.

273

1. What is French for twenty?
2. Of the 147 people who escaped the wreck of the *Medusa* on a raft, how many survived to be rescued?
3. To what bizarre danger did the construction of the Hancock Tower in Boston lead?
4. What is the name of the Rupert Brooke sonnet that begins, 'If I should die, think only this of me . . .'?
5. Who captained Britain's Wightman Cup team in 1978?
6. With which 'Coronation Street' role is Doris Speed associated?
7. What is J. B. Priestley's full name?
8. Where does the song ask Bill Bailey to come?
9. What colour are canaries in the wild?

644

1. What is ormolu?
2. What name did the mighty Hildebrand take on becoming Pope in 1073?
3. What are the Sandwich Islands now called?
4. Who or what were the Houyhnhnms in *Gulliver's Travels*?
5. Which jockey won his first English classic (the 1968 Thousand Guineas) on Caergwrle?
6. Who often said, 'There's another fine mess you've gotten me into'?
7. Who first realized the value of fingerprints to criminal investigation?
8. Who wrote 'Me and Bobby McGee'?
9. About how many people could you feed with a single ostrich-egg omelette?

1015

1. What is the nautical name for the upper edge of a ship's side?
2. Which condiment, made fashionable by George I, is said to have been created in the eighteenth century by Mrs Clements, a Durham woman?
3. Where is the Altiplano?
4. In *Gulliver's Travels*, where did the Houyhnhnms live?
5. What is the length of a hockey pitch?
6. Who plays Mike Baldwin in 'Coronation Street'?
7. Who was Jenny von Westphalen's husband?
8. Who secretly married Sara Lowndes in November 1965?
9. Which planet has the lowest density?

273

1. Vingt.
2. Fifteen.
3. The windows kept falling out.
4. 'The Soldier'.
5. Virginia Wade.
6. Annie Walker.
7. John Boynton Priestley.
8. Home.
9. Greenish-brown.

644

1. Gilded bronze used for clocks and furniture; a French invention.
2. Gregory VII.
3. The Hawaiian Islands.
4. Horses.
5. Sandy Barclay.
6. Oliver Hardy.
7. Sir Francis Galton.
8. Kris Kristofferson.
9. Twelve.

1015

1. The gunwale.
2. Mustard.
3. In the Andes (mostly Bolivia).
4. In Houyhnhnmland.
5. 100 yards.
6. Johnny Briggs.
7. Karl Marx.
8. Bob Dylan.
9. Saturn.

274

1. What is the common nickname for folk with the surname Miller?
2. Who were the Beaker people?
3. Which city is closest to Copacabana beach?
4. Who wrote the five short stories collectively called *Mortal Coils*?
5. Which jockey won his first English classic (the 1964 Oaks) on Homeward Bound?
6. What was the name of the legendary Chinese theatre on Hollywood Boulevard?
7. What was President John Kennedy's middle name?
8. Who wrote the film score for *ET*?
9. Which insect is associated with the Royal Exchange?

645

1. What did France give America on its hundredth anniversary of Independence?
2. Who founded the Jacobins and led the worship of the Supreme Being?
3. In Greek legend, what was Pygmalion's kingdom?
4. In *As You Like It*, who fell in love at a wrestling match?
5. Which two races constitute the 'Autumn Double'?
6. What was the name of the house in *Gone with the Wind*?
7. Who originated psychoanalysis?
8. Who recorded the album *Black and Blue*?
9. Which is your main olfactory organ?

1016

1. What does the Statue of Liberty hold in her right hand?
2. Of whom was it written, 'Across the wires the electric message came: /He is no better, he is much the same'?
3. Which was the first penal colony of New South Wales?
4. Of what was Freyr the Scandinavian god?
5. Which English club plays in the Scottish Football League?
6. Which playwright first attracted attention as PC Graham in 'Z Cars'?
7. How many jacks' eyes can be seen in a pack of cards?
8. What, according to the Chelsea Football Club single, is the colour?
9. How do you pronounce sinh?

274

1. Dusty.
2. Early Bronze Age invaders of Britain.
3. Rio de Janeiro.
4. Aldous Huxley.
5. Greville Starkey.
6. Grauman's.
7. Fitzgerald.
8. John Williams.
9. The grasshopper.

645

1. The Statue of Liberty.
2. Robespierre.
3. Cyprus.
4. Rosalind.
5. The Cesarewitch and the Cambridgeshire.
6. Tara.
7. Sigmund Freud.
8. The Rolling Stones.
9. Your nose.

1016

1. A torch.
2. The Prince of Wales, later Edward VII (during his spell of typhoid. The verse is attributed to Alfred Austin.)
3. Botany Bay.
4. Fertility.
5. Berwick Rangers.
6. Colin Welland.
7. Twelve.
8. Blue.
9. Shine.

275

1. Of which country is T A P the national airline?
2. When was the Wall Street crash?
3. Where is Ouagadougou?
4. Which poet and playwright was vice-consul in Beirut and died of TB in Switzerland?
5. At which motor racing track did Ronnie Petersen die?
6. Who played Gambit in 'The New Avengers'?
7. Who was the first Baron Tweedsmuir?
8. What is the title of the famous musical based on *The Taming of the Shrew*?
9. Of what branch of knowledge is the basic law, 'Like poles repel, unlike poles attract'?

646

1. How many noughts has one million?
2. Why was the Holy Maid of Kent hanged?
3. Name any three of the five main wine-producing regions around the city of Bordeaux.
4. In *Hamlet*, who is Ophelia's father?
5. At which game was Willie Mays a celebrated player?
6. Who directed the Oscar-winning film *Mr Deeds Goes to Town*?
7. Who founded Port Sunlight in Cheshire?
8. Who composed Dead Leaves for the piano?
9. In which geological period were the chief deposits of coal laid down?

1017

1. How many bank holidays a year did Sir John Lubbock introduce in 1871?
2. What, sighted on 12 November 1956, was 208 miles long and 60 miles wide?
3. What do the French call Nova Scotia, New Brunswick and Prince Edward Island?
4. Who wrote *Vom Kriege*, about which it was said it 'should be praised less and read more'?
5. Who owned the 1977 St Leger winner Dunfermline?
6. Who was the man with the X-ray eyes?
7. Which British PM started his parliamentary career as M P for Limehouse?
8. Who was 'travellin' light' in 1959?
9. What is a fairy ring?

275

1. Portugal.
2. 1929.
3. Upper Volta, Africa.
4. James Elroy Flecker.
5. Monza.
6. Gareth Hunt.
7. John Buchan, the author.
8. *Kiss Me Kate*.
9. Magnetism.

646

1. Six.
2. She preached resistance to Henry VIII's break with Rome and prophesied his early death.
3. Médoc, Graves, Sauternes, St Emilion, Entre-deux-Mers.
4. Polonius.
5. Baseball.
6. Frank Capra.
7. William Lever (of soap-manufacturing fame).
8. Debussy.
9. The Carboniferous.

1017

1. Four.
2. An iceberg (near Scott Island in Antarctica).
3. Acadie.
4. Karl von Clausewitz.
5. The Queen.
6. Ray Milland, in the film of the same name.
7. Clement Attlee.
8. Cliff Richard.
9. The traces of darker green left in grass by a circle of fungi.

276

1. What is the Stock Exchange term for people who apply for shares in order to sell them immediately at a profit?
2. Which American war ended in 1783?
3. Where is the port of Fray Bentos?
4. In which novel by Dickens does a cricket match take place between All-Muggleton and Dingley Dell?
5. How many take part in a speed skating international competition race?
6. By what name is Dino Crocetti better known?
7. Which British prime minister died in office aged eighty?
8. Name one of Pink Floyd's first two hit singles.
9. How many wings has a bee?

647

1. What does koh-i-noor mean?
2. Name three of the six countries whose independence from Spain was established by Simon Bolivar.
3. Which London street is nicknamed 'Tin Pan Alley'?
4. What is Tiny Tim's surname in *A Christmas Carol*?
5. What nationality is showjumper Eddie Macken?
6. Who played Rembrandt in Korda's 1937 biopic?
7. Who followed Hugh Gaitskell as leader of the Labour Party?
8. Which element do you associate with Arthur Brown and his Crazy World?
9. What is the fastest speed run by man, approximately, in m.p.h.?

1018

1. How many sides has a pentagon?
2. Which English monarch stood for election as Holy Roman Emperor?
3. On which islands are the oldest rock formations in Europe?
4. In *The Merchant of Venice*, who is Jessica's father?
5. Who was the first man to score a century in cricket's John Player League?
6. In *The Wizard of Oz*, which character was looking for courage?
7. Who was party member No. 7 of the National Socialist Workers' Party of Germany?
8. In which series did Linda Evans, a star of 'Dynasty', first appear?
9. What was a mastodon?

276

1. Stags.
2. The War of Independence.
3. Uruguay. (The first meat-packing plant was there.)
4. *The Pickwick Papers*.
5. Two.
6. Dean Martin.
7. Lord Palmerston.
8. 'See Emily Play' and 'Arnold Layne'.
9. Four.

647

1. Mountain of light.
2. Bolivia, Colombia, Ecuador, Panama, Peru, Venezuela.
3. Denmark Street.
4. Cratchit.
5. Irish.
6. Charles Laughton.
7. Harold Wilson.
8. Fire, the title of his only hit.
9. Twenty-seven.

1018

1. Five.
2. Henry VIII.
3. The outer Hebrides.
4. Shylock.
5. Greg Chappell (Somerset).
6. The Lion.
7. Adolf Hitler.
8. 'The Big Valley'.
9. A primitive type of elephant.

277

1. How long did it take to fly the Gossamer Albatross across the Channel in June 1979?
2. What name is given to the handwriting developed in imitation of the style of the papal chancery in 1450?
3. Which country is nearest to the North Pole?
4. Who wrote *The Riddle of the Sands*?
5. Who preceded Lord Killanin as President of the IOC?
6. Hywel Bennett's first stage role was as Ophelia. What was his first film?
7. In which city did Keats die?
8. Which pair starred in the musical *Top Hat*?
9. What instrument originally measured the rise and fall of the Nile and is now used for any river?

648

1. How much did the *Daily Express* cost in 1945?
2. Which kingdom was ruled by Victor Emmanuel before he became the first king of Italy in 1860?
3. Where is Limassol?
4. Who wrote *Tobacco Road*?
5. From which football club did Liverpool acquire Phil Neal?
6. Who played 'Mad Max'?
7. Who wrote a *History of the World* in the Tower, went to South America for gold, and was executed on his return?
8. In which year did the Eurovision Song Contest begin?
9. What is the characteristic smell of hydrogen cyanide?

1019

1. What is the profession of an FRIBA?
2. What was Britain's first colony?
3. Where are the Aleutian Islands?
4. Who wrote *The Rights of Man*?
5. Which is the first big handicap of the flat-racing season?
6. Which TV film brought Trevor Howard and Celia Johnson together again?
7. Which famous painting is housed in the monastery of Santa Maria delle Grazie in Milan?
8. Who was Robert Palmer's partner as lead vocalist in the 1970s band Vinegar Joe?
9. For what is ethylene glycol chiefly used?

277

1. 2 hours 49 minutes (by pedal power).
2. Italic.
3. Greenland.
4. Robert Erskine Childers.
5. Avery Brundage.
6. *The Family Way.*
7. Rome.
8. Fred Astaire and Ginger Rogers.
9. A nilometer.

648

1. One old penny.
2. Sardinia.
3. On the south coast of Cyprus.
4. Erskine Caldwell.
5. Northampton.
6. Mel Gibson, the Australian actor.
7. Sir Walter Raleigh.
8. 1956.
9. Bitter almonds.

1019

1. Architecture.
2. Newfoundland (annexed in 1583).
3. In the Bering Sea, between Alaska and Russia.
4. Thomas Paine.
5. The Lincoln.
6. Paul Scott's *Staying On.*
7. Leonardo's 'Last Supper'.
8. Elkie Brooks.
9. Anti-freeze (and also in the manufacture of polyester materials).

278

1. Which branch of the police are the 'Sweeney'?
2. In which decade was a company first formed to build a Channel tunnel?
3. What is Holland's largest ever flood-control project called?
4. Who were Charles Kingsley's aquatic infants?
5. Which division four Football League club was referred to in the 1983 headline 'Crisis at Preston Park'?
6. In which film based on a Sinclair Lewis novel did Burt Lancaster star?
7. Where does Metsu's painting 'The Duet' hang?
8. From which disability has Stevie Wonder suffered since birth?
9. Why is a meerschaum pipe so called?

649

1. After whom are 'teddy' bears named?
2. How many famous Roman triumvirates were there?
3. What are Sandray, Pabbay, Mingulay and Berneray?
4. Who wrote the play *Krapp's Last Tape*?
5. Where did the game pelota originate?
6. In *The Wizard of Oz*, which character was looking for brains?
7. For which cosmetics company did Elvis Costello program computers?
8. For which event did Benjamin Britten compose his opera *Gloriana*?
9. What is Fred Hoyle's theory of creation called?

1020

1. What type of salad ingredient is a cos?
2. Who was Britain's prime minister in 1971?
3. Jat is a short word, but who or what is it?
4. In which great hall does Odin live and receive heroes fallen in battle?
5. In which event did Percy Hodge win an Olympic track gold medal for Britain in 1920?
6. What is the Fonz's full name?
7. What is the highest score possible with three darts on a standard board?
8. Which famous Manchester orchestra was named after its founder?
9. To which insect family does the ladybird belong?

278

1. The flying squad (in rhyming slang: 'Sweeney Todd').
2. The 1860s (1867).
3. The Delta Plan.
4. The Water Babies.
5. Tranmere Rovers.
6. *Elmer Gantry*.
7. In the National Gallery in London.
8. Blindness.
9. It's made from the stuff: meerschaum is a form of clay.

649

1. President Theodore Roosevelt.
2. Two.
3. The southernmost islands of the outer Hebrides.
4. Samuel Beckett.
5. Spain.
6. The Scarecrow.
7. Elizabeth Arden.
8. The coronation of Queen Elizabeth II.
9. The steady state theory.

1020

1. A lettuce.
2. Edward Heath.
3. A member of a tribe from north-west India.
4. Valhalla.
5. 3,000-metre steeplechase.
6. Arthur Fonzarelli.
7. 180.
8. The Hallé.
9. The beetle family.

279

1. What is the army equivalent to the RAF rank of squadron leader?
2. What was granted by the Edict of Nantes in 1598?
3. Where is Romaic spoken?
4. What have the phrases 'The Greeks had a word for it' and 'A storm in a teacup' in common?
5. What distinguishes the singles from the doubles court in tennis?
6. Who was Napoleon Solo?
7. How did Belgium's Queen Astrid die?
8. What was Britain's first winning song in the Eurovision Song Contest?
9. Who received the Nobel Prize for Medicine in 1904?

650

1. After which Scandinavian god is Thursday named?
2. Why were black servants relieved by Somersett's case in 1772?
3. Where did the worst flood in modern times drown an estimated million people in 1887?
4. Who was the god of death, wisdom and magic due to be swallowed by Fenrir at the end of the world?
5. Who rode Never Say Die to Derby victory in 1954?
6. Who starred as Maigret in the BBC programmes?
7. Of which country was Raymond Poincaré President throughout the First World War?
8. Who wrote 'Love Letters in the Sand' in the 1950s?
9. What is an ICBM?

1021

1. What percentage of British men have no teeth of their own?
2. Where was Joan of Arc born?
3. What is the capital of Nepal?
4. Which writer gave us the English word 'essay'?
5. In 1972, which TV personality took over as linesman when the referee pulled a muscle during the game between Arsenal and Liverpool?
6. With which 'Coronation Street' role is Bernard Youens associated?
7. Who wrote *Coningsby* and became prime minister?
8. Which tune, attributed to Henry VIII, is twice mentioned in *The Merry Wives of Windsor*?
9. On whom did Joseph Lister perform the first operation using antiseptic?

279

1. Major.
2. Certain guarantees and rights of worship to Huguenots.
3. Greece.
4. They are titles of plays (by Zoë Akins and W. B. Bernard respectively).
5. The tramlines.
6. The action-man agent from UNCLE.
7. In a car accident.
8. 'Puppet on a String' (1967, sung by Sandie Shaw).
9. I. P. Pavlov.

650

1. Thor.
2. It effectively stopped them from being slaves.
3. China, along the Huang-Ho.
4. Odin.
5. Lester Piggott.
6. Rupert Davies.
7. France.
8. Pat Boone.
9. An intercontinental ballistic missile.

1021

1. Twenty-four.
2. Domrémy, in Lorraine.
3. Katmandu.
4. Michel de Montaigne.
5. Jimmy Hill.
6. Stan Ogden.
7. Benjamin Disraeli.
8. 'Greensleeves'.
9. His sister in 1867.

280

1. What are the Three Estates of the Realm in England?
2. Who is considered to have arranged the explosion that killed Darnley?
3. What was Britain's last French possession?
4. In which book did Harriet Beecher Stowe expose slave conditions in America?
5. How many times did Harry Vardon win the British Open Golf Championship?
6. Which tennis star took the role of a coach in the film *Players*?
7. Which general who fought in the Indian Mutiny gave his name to a piece of army officer's equipment?
8. What nationality was Béla Bartók?
9. How many visible stars make up the Plough?

651

1. Whose personal expenditure comes out of the privy purse?
2. What battle was fought before Napoleon entered Moscow?
3. Where is the tomb of King John?
4. Who was Dante's muse?
5. Which county won the Benson and Hedges Cup and the Schweppes County Championship in 1979?
6. Who was the 'sock-it-to-me' girl in 'Laugh-In'?
7. Which game includes Four Winds?
8. Who composed the music for *The Threepenny Opera*?
9. Which British moth spins silk?

1022

1. What size is foolscap paper?
2. Which British passport holders were forced to flee from a volcanic eruption which destroyed their homes in 1961?
3. How many countries have a coastline within the Arctic Circle?
4. Of which play by Oliver Goldsmith is *The Mistakes of a Night* the subtitle?
5. Which country has Graham Yallop captained at cricket?
6. Which music-hall comedian became famous as Old Mother Riley?
7. Who preceded Cecil Day Lewis as Poet Laureate?
8. Who was Radio 1's first girl DJ?
9. Approximately how long is the Hercules beetle?

280

1. The Lords Spiritual, the Lords Temporal and the Commons.
2. Bothwell.
3. Calais (lost in 1558).
4. *Uncle Tom's Cabin.*
5. Six.
6. Pancho Gonzales.
7. Sam Browne.
8. Hungarian.
9. Seven.

651

1. The Queen's.
2. Borodino (1812; 74,000 men were killed).
3. Worcester Cathedral.
4. Beatrice.
5. Essex.
6. Judy Carne.
7. Mah-jong.
8. Kurt Weill.
9. The Emperor.

1022

1. 8 by 13 inches (about 200 by 330 millimetres).
2. The inhabitants of Tristan da Cunha.
3. Five (Canada, Greenland, Norway, USA, USSR).
4. *She Stoops to Conquer.*
5. Australia.
6. Arthur Lucan.
7. John Masefield.
8. Anne Nightingale.
9. 5 inches.

281

1. What proportion of British men are colour-blind?
2. Who was the first king of Great Britain?
3. What was Stalingrad (now Volgograd) called until 1925?
4. Who wrote the play *The Barber of Seville*?
5. What are the two main differences between canoeing and kayaking?
6. In which Hitchcock film did Shirley MacLaine make her movie début?
7. Which Russian statesman married Khruschev's sister?
8. On which radio programme did Cliff Michelmore meet his wife, broadcaster Jean Metcalfe?
9. Which Russian spacecraft name means Travelling Companion?

652

1. Which British title is equivalent to the continental 'count'?
2. Which war was ended by the Treaty of Portsmouth (New Hampshire)?
3. Which valley separates the Cotswolds from the Severn estuary?
4. What was Black Beauty's original name?
5. How often is the Curtis Cup contested between American and British women golfers?
6. Which theatre is the headquarters of the National Youth Theatre?
7. Which country did Silvana Suarez represent as Miss World?
8. Billy J. Kramer and the . . . what?
9. At what phases of the moon do neap tides occur?

1023

1. What is the sign of the zodiac of people born on New Year's day?
2. Who was the original Peeping Tom?
3. Which European city besides Pisa has a leaning tower?
4. Who created Bertie Wooster?
5. Which golfer is known as 'Champagne Tony'?
6. Which German Shepherd shot to fame in Hollywood?
7. Which great artist was also a great inventor?
8. From which of Mendelssohn's works does the 'Wedding March' come?
9. Which element is present in all organic compounds?

281

1. One in ten.
2. James I (so proclaimed in 1604).
3. Tsaritsyn.
4. Beaumarchais.
5. Canoeists kneel and use one paddle, kayakists sit and use two.
6. *The Trouble with Harry* (1956).
7. Malenkov.
8. 'Family Favourites'.
9. Sputnik.

652

1. Earl.
2. The Russo–Japanese War (in 1905).
3. The Vale of Berkeley.
4. Darkie.
5. Once every two years.
6. The Shaw Theatre in London.
7. Argentina.
8. Dakotas.
9. The first and last quarters.

1023

1. Capricorn.
2. Tom the tailor, who looked at Lady Godiva riding naked through Coventry.
3. Bologna (which has two).
4. P. G. Wodehouse.
5. Tony Lema.
6. Rin Tin Tin.
7. Leonardo da Vinci.
8. 'A Midsummer Night's Dream'.
9. Carbon.

282

1. What is the first letter of the Russian alphabet?
2. Whose final words were 'Et tu, Brute'?
3. Which Channel Island is nearest to France?
4. What is Professor Moriarty's first name?
5. Which jockey won the 1972 Two Thousand Guineas on High Top?
6. Adam Ant we know. What was 'Adam Adamant'?
7. Who was called the 'Little Brown Saint'?
8. Who collaborated with Tim Rice on the rock opera *Jesus Christ Superstar*?
9. What was the value of the prize established by Henry Kremer and won by the Gossamer Condor for the first human-powered aircraft to complete a mile-long figure-of-eight course?

653

1. What is the naval equivalent to the rank of major in the army?
2. Which Anglo-Saxon king gave his name to a dyke on the Welsh border?
3. Where is Mary Queen of Scots buried?
4. Who gave Eve her name?
5. What nationality is world champion speed skater Ard Schenk?
6. Which Wodehouse character did Dennis Price play in the TV series 'World of Wooster'?
7. How many lions are there on the royal standard?
8. Who sang about *Songs in the Key of Life*?
9. Who made the first American space walk in 1965?

1024

1. What is 0·621371 of a mile in kilometres?
2. Which son of William I wrote Welsh poetry and died at Cardiff?
3. What did women in the Swiss canton of Vaud do for the first time in 1959?
4. Which Russian writer was awarded the Nobel Prize for Literature while in exile?
5. How many Olympic gold medals did the Russian gymnast Lyudmila Tourischeva win?
6. Which 'Z Cars' character was played by Frank Windsor?
7. Which school did Queen Elizabeth II attend?
8. What was the name of Lulu's former backing group?
9. Which moon of Saturn was discovered in 1966?

282

1. A.
2. Julius Caesar's.
3. Alderney.
4. James.
5. Willie Carson.
6. A 1960s television series starring Gerald Harper.
7. Mahatma Gandhi.
8. Andrew Lloyd Webber.
9. £50,000.

653

1. Lieutenant-commander.
2. Offa.
3. Westminster Abbey.
4. Adam.
5. Dutch.
6. Jeeves.
7. Seven.
8. Stevie Wonder.
9. Edward H. White.

1024

1. One.
2. Robert (his eldest son and duke of Normandy).
3. Vote.
4. Ivan Bunin.
5. Three.
6. Sergeant Watt.
7. None. She was educated by governesses and tutors.
8. The Luvvers.
9. Janus.

283

1. What is psephology?
2. What is the name of the last of the tea clippers?
3. Which city is known as the chocolate capital of the world?
4. Which of the four Gospels is not a Synoptic Gospel?
5. From which English game did baseball develop?
6. Who played David Lloyd George in the 1972 film *Young Winston*?
7. Why wouldn't J. Edgar Hoover allow his chauffeur to turn left?
8. Who played the singer Joey Evans in the 1957 film *Pal Joey*?
9. Of which planet are Deimos and Phobos the two moons?

654

1. For what is a.m. the abbreviation?
2. Which king sent the Armada against Britain?
3. How many mountains over 24,000 feet high are unnamed?
4. What is Hercule Poirot's brother's name?
5. For which US team did Franz Beckenbauer play soccer?
6. What is the name of the Flintstone's pet dinosaur?
7. Which Spanish surrealist painter translated natural forms into simple abstract symbols?
8. Which modern instrument did the viola da gamba most resemble?
9. To which family does the hippopotamus belong?

1025

1. How many are there in a score?
2. Who rode Marengo?
3. For how long after the death of a dear friend or relative do Congo tribesmen not sweep out their houses?
4. What is Jan Struther's best-known book?
5. Which basketball team was founded by Abe Saperstein in Chicago in 1927?
6. What were the three tunnels called in *The Great Escape*?
7. Who did Arthur Scargill call 'the plutonium blonde'?
8. In Mozart's opera *The Marriage of Figaro*, who did Figaro marry?
9. What is the collective name for a group of foxes?

283

1. The study of patterns in voting.
2. The *Cutty Sark*.
3. Hershey, Pennsylvania.
4. John's.
5. Rounders.
6. Anthony Hopkins.
7. Because of his strong anti-communist feelings.
8. Frank Sinatra.
9. Mars.

654

1. Ante meridiem (the Latin for 'before noon').
2. Philip II of Spain.
3. Five.
4. Achille.
5. New York Cosmos.
6. Dino.
7. Joan Miró.
8. The cello.
9. The pig family.

1025

1. Twenty.
2. Napoleon at Waterloo.
3. 1 year.
4. *Mrs Miniver*.
5. The Harlem Globetrotters.
6. Tom, Dick and Harry.
7. Margaret Thatcher.
8. Susannah.
9. A skulk.

284

1. What is the second commonest surname (after Smith) in the USA?
2. What did Joseph Gayetty invent in 1857?
3. What is the name of Moscow's chief square?
4. Who created Horatio Hornblower?
5. Who defended his world heavyweight boxing title twice on the same night in 1906?
6. Who was the subject of the biography *Schnozzola*?
7. What is the best-known work of the sculptor Sir Alfred Gilbert?
8. Which group recorded the album *Abbey Road*?
9. What part of an aeroplane is the empennage?

655

1. Which London cabinet-maker gave his name to a method of slimming?
2. Who was the mother of Edward VI?
3. In which bay are the Andaman group of islands found?
4. Who wrote *Little Men*?
5. Which country has won the most medals in the Winter Olympics?
6. Who created Mickey Mouse?
7. What is the surname of the novelist brothers Alec and Evelyn?
8. Who was Master of the Queen's Musick from 1953 to 1975?
9. That is a female fox called?

1026

1. Which people speak the Romany language?
2. Why was Edgar Allan Poe thrown out of West Point in 1831?
3. What is the main claim to fame of the Mbuti pygmies of Africa?
4. Who was the goddess of the rainbow?
5. Who scored every one of England's five goals in their match against Cyprus in 1975?
6. What is Michael Knight's wonder car called?
7. What did Vicenzo Peruggia steal and keep for 2 years?
8. Which soprano was known as 'La Divina'?
9. Which animal can be broken into thousands of pieces, join itself up again, and continue to live?

284

1. Johnson (there are approximately two million Johnsons).
2. Loo rolls.
3. Red Square.
4. C. S. Forester.
5. Tommy Burns. He knocked out Jim O'Brien and Jim Walker, both in the first round.
6. Jimmy Durante.
7. The statue of Eros in Piccadilly Circus.
8. The Beatles.
9. The tail unit.

655

1. Banting.
2. Jane Seymour.
3. The Bay of Bengal.
4. Louisa May Alcott.
5. Norway.
6. Walt Disney.
7. Waugh.
8. Sir Arthur Bliss.
9. A vixen.

1026

1. Gypsies.
2. Because he turned up for inspection naked.
3. They are the world's shortest race.
4. Iris.
5. Malcolm Macdonald.
6. Kitt.
7. The 'Mona Lisa'.
8. Maria Callas.
9. The red sponge.

285

1. What colour are uncooked lobsters?
2. Which famous robbery took place on 8 August 1963?
3. In which country was the Battle of El Alamein fought?
4. Which is Grace Metalious's most famous novel?
5. In which year did Great Britain win an Olympic gold medal for ice hockey?
6. Who was Olive Oyl's boy friend before she met Popeye?
7. Which is the most popular form of gambling for women in Las Vegas?
8. Who married Miss World 1962 (Catherine Lodders)?
9. Who invented the mercury thermometer?

656

1. What does 'per capita' literally mean?
2. How many pilgrims sailed on the *Mayflower* to Massachusetts in 1620?
3. In which Belgian city can you be jailed for not killing furry caterpillars?
4. Who created Little Lord Fauntleroy?
5. Where in London is the Oval cricket ground?
6. Who plays Arkwright the grocer?
7. Who first said, 'You cannot feed the hungry on statistics'?
8. Which composer wrote a song and a piano quintet with a trout in the title?
9. Approximately how far above the earth is the stratosphere?

1027

1. After which god is March named?
2. Which politician became Lord Avon?
3. Where at one time were Americans obliged to pay taxes in tobacco?
4. How many voyages did Sindbad make?
5. Who was the first man to swim 400 metres in less than 5 minutes?
6. Who played Rosemary Woodhouse in the 1968 film *Rosemary's Baby*?
7. Who was Queen Victoria's favourite gillie?
8. Which decade was known as the Jazz Age?
9. Which planet did J. G. Galle discover in 1846?

285

1. Dark blue or green – they only turn red or orange when cooked.
2. The Great Train Robbery (from the Aberdeen express).
3. Egypt.
4. *Peyton Place.*
5. 1936.
6. Ham Gravy.
7. Slot machines.
8. Chubby Checker.
9. Gabriel Fahrenheit.

656

1. Per head.
2. 102.
3. Brussels.
4. Frances Hodgson Burnett.
5. Kennington.
6. Ronnie Barker.
7. David Lloyd George.
8. Franz Schubert.
9. 6 miles.

1027

1. Mars.
2. Anthony Eden.
3. Virginia, USA.
4. Seven.
5. Johnny Weissmuller (of Tarzan fame).
6. Mia Farrow.
7. John Brown.
8. The 1920s.
9. Neptune.

286

1. What is the Soviet Union's highest military honour?
2. When, according to Jehovah's Witnesses, was the world going to end?
3. A law in Siena, Italy, forbids a woman with a certain name to work as a prostitute. What is that name?
4. Who wrote *Journey into Fear*?
5. Which Englishman won the World Motor Racing Drivers' Championship in 1976?
6. For how much did the silent movie star Ben Turpin insure his squint?
7. Which smoking implement was Stalin always seen clutching in public?
8. Who wrote the comic opera *Il Seraglio*?
9. How much would a matchbox weigh if it were filled with material from the centre of the star Sirius B?

657

1. What do the letters MG stand for on cars?
2. Which famous ship was sunk by the German submarine U-20?
3. In which city is the official residence of the President of the USA?
4. For how many years did Sleeping Beauty sleep?
5. Who was the first man to pass the 7,000-point mark in the decathlon?
6. Which film did a California cinema show before erupting in flames?
7. Which portrait painter born in Germany was knighted by Charles II?
8. What was gangster Louie Brook's favourite song in the 1932 film *Dancing in the Dark*?
9. What is a young turkey called?

1028

1. What is the name of the phantom ship said to haunt the Cape of Good Hope?
2. Where will the last great battle be fought between the powers of good and evil?
3. How many steps (to the nearest hundred) has the Leaning Tower of Pisa?
4. Of which race of mythical giants was Polyphemus the chief?
5. In which sport did Dave Starbrook win medals at the 1972 and 1976 Olympics?
6. Who was the first actor to appear on the cover of *Time* magazine?
7. With what crime was Alger Hiss charged in 1949?
8. After whom are the Promenade Concerts named?
9. From which fish does caviare come?

286

1. The Order of Lenin.
2. 1976 (summertime).
3. Maria.
4. Eric Ambler.
5. James Hunt.
6. 500,000 dollars.
7. A pipe.
8. Mozart.
9. About 50 tons.

657

1. Morris Garages.
2. The *Lusitania*.
3. Washington, DC.
4. A hundred.
5. Bob Mathias (in 1948).
6. *The Towering Inferno*.
7. Lely.
8. 'St Louis Blues'.
9. A poult.

1028

1. The *Flying Dutchman*.
2. Armageddon.
3. 300 (296 to be exact).
4. The Cyclops.
5. Judo.
6. Charlie Chaplin.
7. Spying.
8. Henry Wood.
9. The sturgeon.

287

1. To which London hospital did James Barrie bequeath the copyright of his book *Peter Pan*?
2. What have Stoke, Desborough and Burnham to do with MPs' resignations?
3. Which river flows through Rome?
4. In *Oliver Twist*, what post did Bumble hold?
5. In Britain what is the definition of a thoroughbred horse?
6. By what name is Charles Bunchinsky better known?
7. Whose autobiography is called *Where's the Rest of Me*?
8. What is a backgammon board's central division called?
9. How many years separated the first artificial satellite orbit and the first manned space flight?

658

1. What does *nolens volens* mean?
2. Who or what were on trial in 1692 in Salem, Massachusetts?
3. In which ocean is Bligh's Cap?
4. Which word appears 46,227 times in the Bible?
5. What was Winston Churchill's favourite participation sport?
6. On what was the film *Casablanca* based?
7. Who said you only had to start worrying about the washing up when you got to the fish layer?
8. Who composed the 'William Tell' overture?
9. What does a potometer measure?

1029

1. How many chickens does the average person eat in a lifetime?
2. Which game was illegal in Elizabethan times?
3. Which liqueur is distilled from a cherry grown in Dalmatia?
4. What did John Steinbeck win in 1962, Pearl S. Buck in 1938, and T. S. Eliot in 1948?
5. In which city can the oldest tennis court in existence be found?
6. At what age did Rudolph Valentino die?
7. How old was Jesus when he was crucified?
8. Who starred in the 1969 film *The Trouble with Girls*?
9. By how much does the time required for the earth to orbit the sun increase each century?

287

1. Great Ormond Street Hospital (the Hospital for Sick Children).
2. They form the Chiltern Hundreds, stewardship of which, being a Crown office, means that the holder cannot be an MP.
3. The Tiber.
4. Beadle.
5. One who has seven generations of ancestors in the stud-book.
6. Charles Bronson.
7. Ronald Reagan's.
8. The bar.
9. $3\frac{1}{2}$ (from October 1957 to April 1961).

658

1. Willy-nilly.
2. Women accused of witchcraft.
3. The Indian Ocean.
4. And.
5. Polo.
6. A play by Burnett and Alison, *Everybody Comes to Rick's*.
7. Quentin Crisp.
8. Rossini.
9. Water intake.

1029

1. 800.
2. Bowls (so what was Drake up to?).
3. Maraschino.
4. The Nobel Prize for Literature.
5. Paris. It dates from 1496.
6. Thirty-one.
7. Thirty-three.
8. Elvis Presley.
9. 0·04 of a second.

288

1. How many points are there on a Maltese cross?
2. Which famous tapestry depicts the invasion of Britain in 1066?
3. Where is the Executive Committee Mountain Range?
4. According to the Psalms, how many are 'the days of our age'?
5. In which month does the F A Cup Final take place?
6. What nationality was Oddjob?
7. Who was England's most famous marine painter of the nineteenth century?
8. Which group featured in the film *Rock Around the Clock*?
9. What does a pluviometer measure?

659

1. From which country does mulligatawny soup originate?
2. Under which emperor did the long-term Roman occupation of the British Isles begin?
3. Which was the first state of the USA?
4. How was Tristram Shandy circumcised?
5. What are the two cycling events that make up the Autumn Classics?
6. By what name was comedienne Joyce Phipps better known?
7. Who wrote, 'Men seldom make passes/At girls who wear glasses'?
8. Who was the female vocalist with Brian Auger's Trinity?
9. What is the medical name for cancer of the blood?

1030

1. What is a knout?
2. What was the main religion in England during the Middle Ages?
3. What was discovered at Qumram, Jordan, in 1947?
4. How does the Twenty-third Psalm begin?
5. Who was England's caretaker manager between Alf Ramsey and Don Revie?
6. By what name is Emmanuel Goldenberg better known?
7. Whose autobiography is entitled *Farce from my Elbow*?
8. Who took a magic bus?
9. How many square yards are there in an acre?

288

1. Eight.
2. The Bayeux tapestry.
3. Antarctica.
4. 'Three score years and ten' (i.e., seventy years).
5. May.
6. Korean.
7. Turner.
8. Bill Haley and the Comets.
9. Rainfall.

659

1. India. The name means 'pepper-water'.
2. Claudius (A D 43).
3. Delaware.
4. By a sash-window falling on him.
5. Tour de Paris, Tour de Lombardie.
6. Joyce Grenfell.
7. Dorothy Parker.
8. Julie (Jools) Driscoll.
9. Leukaemia.

1030

1. A Russian flogging-whip.
2. Roman Catholicism.
3. The Dead Sea Scrolls.
4. 'The Lord is my shepherd'.
5. Joe Mercer.
6. Edward G. Robinson.
7. Brian Rix's.
8. The Who.
9. 4,840.

289

1. What made a 'virgin flight' in June 1984?
2. When was Lady Chatterley put on trial?
3. Which state was founded by Mohammed Ali Jinnah?
4. Who wrote, 'In the Spring a young man's fancy lightly turns to thoughts of love'?
5. In which city was the first weightlifting world championship held?
6. Who are Dr Evadne and Dame Hilda?
7. Which American author and humorist invented and patented a rudimentary pair of braces?
8. Who did the Muswell Hillbillies become?
9. Which metal is liquid at room temperature?

660

1. Which language has the greatest number of words?
2. When was the British Broadcasting Corporation founded?
3. In which country are the Mountains of the Moon?
4. In which magazine does Alfred E. Neuman appear?
5. Which Wimbledon tennis event did Ann Jones first win?
6. On which early TV 'soap' did John Leyton sing 'Johnny Remember Me' and become an overnight success?
7. What was the name of John Betjeman's much loved programme on London's suburbs?
8. Which band's first hit single, in 1970, was 'In the Summertime'?
9. What is a jumbuck?

1031

1. What do Methuselahs contain?
2. According to legend, at what age did Arthur become king?
3. What used Taiwan to be called?
4. According to the nursery rhyme, who sat on a wall?
5. Which amateur reached the men's singles semi-finals at Wimbledon in 1977?
6. What is the name of Barry Humphries' cultural attaché creation?
7. Whose private company is Amblin' Productions?
8. What is the name of Elton John's own record label?
9. If a human baby grew as fast as a baby whale, how tall would it be by the time it was two?

289

1. Richard Branson's Virgin airline.
2. 1960.
3. Pakistan.
4. Alfred, Lord Tennyson.
5. London (in 1891).
6. Hinge and Bracket.
7. Mark Twain.
8. The Kinks.
9. Mercury.

660

1. English.
2. 1927.
3. Uganda.
4. *MAD.*
5. Junior Wimbledon.
6. 'Harper's West One'.
7. 'Metroland'.
8. Mungo Jerry.
9. A sheep (Aboriginal Australian).

1031

1. Champagne. They are the largest bottles in which it is sold.
2. Fifteen.
3. Formosa.
4. Humpty Dumpty.
5. John McEnroe (aged 18).
6. Les Patterson.
7. Steven Spielberg's.
8. Rocket.
9. Approximately 65 feet.

290

1. What is the birthstone for March?
2. Of whom did Cicero say, 'While we are his slaves, he is the slave of circumstance'?
3. Which town 50 miles from the coast is America's eighth busiest port?
4. Who was Jacob's first wife?
5. What was Marion Mould's maiden name?
6. Which distinguished American film star was once a circus acrobat?
7. What was the Dutch painter Bosch's Christian name?
8. Who sang about an 'Itsy Bitsy Teeny Weeny Yellow Polka Dot Bikini'?
9. What are Claymore, Ninian, Piper and Thistle?

661

1. Which colour tranquillizer pills have the best effect?
2. Who was the first woman to fly a plane solo?
3. Where did turkeys originate?
4. Who invented the name Vanessa?
5. If you were on skis that allowed your ankle to move up and down, what would you be doing?
6. In 'MASH', what is Radar's home town?
7. Who was President of the Royal Academy from 1944 to 1949 and famed for his paintings of horses?
8. From which musical does 'They Call the Wind Maria' come?
9. How does the archer fish capture its prey?

1032

1. How many fluid ounces form an English pint?
2. Who, in 1801, was created Viscount of the British Navy?
3. If you were in the Mountain Time Zone in the USA how many hours behind GMT would you be?
4. By what was the sword of Damocles suspended?
5. Over what distance is the human steeplechase run?
6. In which film did Gregory Peck win the Oscar for best actor?
7. In which period of art was Titian painting in Italy?
8. Who composed *Christ on the Mount of Olives*, his only oratorio?
9. On which Christian feast day is the earth nearest to the sun?

290

1. Aquamarine.
2. Julius Caesar (46 BC).
3. Houston, Texas.
4. Leah.
5. Coates.
6. Burt Lancaster.
7. Hieronymus.
8. Brian Hyland.
9. North Sea oil-fields.

661

1. Yellow.
2. Blanche Scott (1910).
3. In America.
4. Jonathan Swift.
5. Langlaufing.
6. Ottumwa, Iowa.
7. Sir Alfred Munnings.
8. *Paint Your Wagon.*
9. By squirting water at it to shoot it down.

1032

1. Twenty.
2. Horatio Nelson.
3. Seven.
4. A hair.
5. 3,000 metres.
6. *To Kill a Mockingbird.*
7. The Renaissance.
8. Beethoven.
9. Epiphany (6 January).

291

1. What organization was founded in 1905 to warn motorists of police speed traps?
2. What was the longest construction project ever undertaken by man?
3. In which city is the shrine of Muhammad?
4. In *Macbeth*, which witch speaks first?
5. Which England bowler took ten wickets in his test début in Delhi?
6. Who played Margot Wendice in the 1954 film *Dial M for Murder*?
7. How many different coloured balls are used in snooker?
8. In which city did the eight-year-old Mozart compose his first symphony?
9. Which is the only even prime number?

662

1. For what does NB stand?
2. How did Mark Antony die?
3. How many feet has Mexico City sunk since 1900?
4. The narrator and Harris were two of Jerome K. Jerome's *Three Men in a Boat*. Who was the third?
5. How often is the soccer World Cup contested?
6. Who won the 1965 Oscar for best actor in *Cat Ballou*?
7. Which former child actress became US Ambassador to Ghana?
8. Who composed the Enigma Variations?
9. Which disease does the comma bacillus cause?

1033

1. Which fabled monster has a lion's head and a serpent's tail?
2. In the shape of which leaf were coins minted in 1060?
3. Of what nationality are the majority of immigrants into the USA?
4. Who is Simon Templar?
5. Who rode Troy to victory in the 1979 Derby?
6. Which film featured the play *Springtime for Hitler*?
7. How old was George Bernard Shaw when he wrote his last play?
8. For which composer was the Bayreuth Festival Theatre built?
9. After how many days can a bloodhound still detect a scent?

291

1. The Automobile Association.
2. The Great Wall of China (in both senses: it took 1,700 years to build).
3. Mecca.
4. The First Witch.
5. John Lever.
6. Grace Kelly.
7. Eight (including white).
8. London.
9. Two.

662

1. Nota bene.
2. By falling on his sword.
3. Twenty-two – it is sinking even faster than Venice!
4. George.
5. Every 4 years.
6. Lee Marvin.
7. Shirley Temple.
8. Sir Edward Elgar.
9. Cholera.

1033

1. The chimera.
2. A four-leaf clover.
3. Mexican.
4. The Saint.
5. Willie Carson.
6. *The Producers*.
7. Ninety-three.
8. Wagner.
9. Ten.

292

1. To which Royal House does the Queen belong?
2. For what was Al Capone imprisoned in 1931?
3. Where did Venetian blinds originate?
4. In which novel does Sir Reginald Front de Bœuf appear?
5. Who was the youngest player to win the singles championship at Wimbledon?
6. Who was Elizabeth Taylor's first husband?
7. Who at his execution drew his beard aside and said, 'This has not offended the king'?
8. In the song, what follows the line, 'Drink to me only with thine eyes'?
9. Which is the haymaking month?

663

1. What is the ten-yearly official head-count called?
2. Who was on the throne of England when Columbus discovered America?
3. From which town does port take its name?
4. On which book was Ernest Hemingway working when he killed himself?
5. Which classic race did The Minstrel win in 1977?
6. Who is the communications officer on the Starship *Enterprise*?
7. Who was Liza Minnelli's godfather?
8. Which work did Ravel compose for the dancer Ida Rubinstein?
9. From which country does lettuce originate?

1034

1. Who meet at jamborees?
2. Who were the only father and son to be presidents of the USA?
3. By what name is Northern Rhodesia now known?
4. Who is Oscar Zoroaster Phadrig Isaac Norman Henkle Emmanuel Ambroise Diggs?
5. How many different men who have played Tarzan in films have won Olympic gold medals?
6. Who steals the Pink Panther from Princess Dala?
7. On which thoroughfare in London is the Tate Gallery?
8. In the film *Pinocchio*, which character sings 'When You Wish Upon a Star'?
9. How many dimensions has a solid?

292

1. Windsor.
2. Income-tax evasion.
3. Japan.
4. *Ivanhoe.*
5. Charlotte Dod, aged fifteen (in 1887).
6. Nicky Hilton (of the hotel chain).
7. Sir Thomas More.
8. 'And I will pledge with mine'.
9. June.

663

1. The census.
2. Henry VII.
3. Oporto, in Portugal.
4. *Paris Sketchbook.*
5. The Derby.
6. Lieutenant Uhura.
7. Ira Gershwin.
8. The 'Bolero'.
9. Iran.

1034

1. Scouts or Guides.
2. John Adams and John Quincy Adams.
3. Zambia.
4. The Wizard of Oz.
5. Four.
6. The Phantom.
7. Millbank.
8. Jiminy Cricket.
9. Three.

293

1. What is challa?
2. What is said to have been the last word spoken by Napoleon?
3. By what ratio do cattle outnumber people in Argentina?
4. On which mount did Noah's ark land?
5. In the 1966 World Cup Final who scored the most goals for England?
6. What part did Trevor Howard play in *Mutiny on the Bounty*?
7. What is a quadriga?
8. How many works (to the nearest fifty) did Mozart compose?
9. What travels at 186,272 miles per second?

664

1. Which couple raised Elsa the lioness from birth in February 1956?
2. Who invented the flush toilet in 1878?
3. Which country is the largest consumer of tea in the world?
4. Who was Ebenezer Scrooge's last partner?
5. What are the dimensions of a soccer goal area?
6. Whom did Natalie Wood marry in 1957, divorce in 1963, and remarry in 1972?
7. How many pieces are used in backgammon?
8. Who wrote 'Peter and the Wolf'?
9. Which bird lays the world's largest egg?

1035

1. For what did the Russians use the bones of the 40,000 killed at Sebastopol?
2. Which Roman emperor ordered a wall to be built between Newcastle and Carlisle?
3. In which city are the headquarters of Granada TV?
4. Who was Falstaff's 'knight of the burning lamp'?
5. Who was the first Briton to win the World Motor Racing Championship?
6. What colour is Mr Spock's blood?
7. At which game were the Italian Blue Team world champions for many years?
8. Who had a hit with 'Great Balls of Fire'?
9. What is a brickfielder?

293

1. A type of bread, normally plaited.
2. 'Josephine'.
3. Five to two.
4. Ararat.
5. Geoff Hurst (three).
6. Captain Bligh.
7. A chariot with four horses.
8. Six hundred.
9. Light.

664

1. Joy and George Adamson.
2. Thomas Crapper.
3. Great Britain.
4. Jacob Marley.
5. 6 by 20 yards.
6. Robert Wagner.
7. Thirty.
8. Prokofiev.
9. The ostrich.

1035

1. Fertilizer.
2. Hadrian.
3. Manchester.
4. Bardolph.
5. Mike Hawthorn.
6. Green.
7. Bridge.
8. Little Richard.
9. A hot wind of south-east Australia.

294

1. In which language does 'pupik' mean 'belly-button'?
2. Who first made the cakes known as maids of honour?
3. Which American state is called the Pine Tree state?
4. What was the name of the parrot that taught Doctor Dolittle to talk to the animals?
5. Who won the Derby in 1971?
6. In which film did Humphrey Bogart win the Oscar for best actor?
7. What would you use turpentine for in oil painting?
8. Name three of the four colours of the movements of Sir Arthur Bliss's 'Colour Symphony'.
9. How many bee humming-birds (the world's smallest bird) make up one ounce?

665

1. What is the characteristic ingredient of borsch?
2. What was the date – coinciding with that of America's Bicentennial – of the Israeli commando raid that freed the hostages at Entebbe?
3. Into how many states is Australia divided?
4. For which paper was Winston Churchill a war correspondent in South Africa?
5. Which golf club is called a driver?
6. What was Eric Morecambe's real name?
7. Who was the Governor of California from 1966 to 1974?
8. Which musical term is also the French for 'key'?
9. What colour were all the Model T Fords?

1036

1. From which animals does cony fur come?
2. Name the carrier pigeon that helped save the Lost Battalion in 1918?
3. What is the official language of India?
4. Who created John Mannering/The Baron?
5. In which event and for which country did Errol Flynn compete in the 1928 Olympics?
6. Who created the lawyer Rumpole?
7. Whose girl friend was Virginia Hill?
8. Who wrote the overture 'Roman Carnival?
9. What powered the first automobile to travel faster than 2 miles per minute?

294

1. Yiddish.
2. Anne Boleyn, when she was still a maid of honour at Henry VIII's court.
3. Maine.
4. Polynesia.
5. Mill Reef.
6. *The African Queen* (1951).
7. Thinning paint.
8. Purple, red, blue, green.
9. Eighteen.

665

1. Beetroot.
2. 4 July 1976.
3. Six.
4. The *Morning Post.*
5. A No. 1 wood.
6. Eric Bartholomew.
7. Ronald Reagan.
8. Clef.
9. Black.

1036

1. Rabbits.
2. Cher Ami.
3. Hindi – spoken by about thirty-five per cent of the population. (There are 1,652 Indian languages and dialects.)
4. John Creasey – pen-name of Anthony Morton.
5. Boxing for Ireland.
6. John Mortimer.
7. 'Bugsy' Siegel's. He was killed in her Beverly Hills home in 1947.
8. Berlioz.
9. Steam (in 1906).

295

1. What is the oldest known alcoholic beverage?
2. Which Earp brothers were wounded at the OK Corral?
3. Which US state is called the Lone Star state?
4. What is the word repeated by the raven in Edgar Allan Poe's poem 'The Raven'?
5. By how many wickets did England beat Australia in the first ever test match in England?
6. Who was Ben Hur's rival in the great chariot race?
7. Who was the Lone Ranger's faithful Indian companion?
8. Which sense did Beethoven lose?
9. What are tides of minimum rise and fall called?

666

1. What is a jeroboam?
2. Who was the first prime minister of the Union of South Africa?
3. What is the capital of Bermuda?
4. Of what were the houses of the Three Little Pigs made?
5. In yachting, by what name is the Hundred Guineas Cup now known?
6. For which film was the promotional line, 'Just when you thought it was safe to go back in the water . . .'?
7. What relation was Leonard Jerome, the 'father of the American turf', to Sir Winston Churchill?
8. Which instrument did Sherlock Holmes play?
9. What is the average diameter of an ostrich egg?

1037

1. How many hours of daylight has the longest day in London?
2. What was the name of William Tell's son, from off whose head the apple was shot?
3. Who is the patron saint of Norway?
4. What is Lolita's surname in Nabokov's novel?
5. What is the name given to the large bowls used in level green bowling?
6. Who bought the Las Vegas TV station KLAS so that he could watch late-night movies?
7. What number follows 18 clockwise on a dartboard?
8. In which Gilbert and Sullivan opera does Jack Point appear?
9. From which country does the elkhound originate?

295

1. Mead (made from honey).
2. Virgil and Morgan.
3. Texas.
4. Nevermore.
5. Five.
6. Messala.
7. Tonto.
8. His hearing.
9. Neap tides.

666

1. A large wine-bottle.
2. Louis Botha.
3. Hamilton.
4. Straw, sticks, bricks.
5. The Americas Cup.
6. *Jaws 2*.
7. Grandfather (maternal).
8. The violin.
9. 7 inches.

1037

1. 16½.
2. Walter.
3. Olaf.
4. Haze.
5. Woods.
6. Howard Hughes.
7. 4.
8. *The Yeomen of the Guard*.
9. Norway.

296

1. What do the Chinese call 'electricity talk'?
2. What name was given to the so-called 'Invisible College' in 1662?
3. At what age was King Alfonso XIII of Spain crowned?
4. Who wrote the play *The Corn is Green*?
5. How much does a lacrosse ball weigh?
6. Who played Regan MacNeil in the 1973 film *The Exorcist*?
7. What was the surname of the Russian-born brothers Albert, Harry, Jack and Samuel who founded a motion picture studio in 1923?
8. What is Duke Ellington's real first name?
9. What is the common denominator of places joined on a map by an isohel?

667

1. What is the name for the Sunday before Easter?
2. Which war began on 25 June 1950?
3. Which city gave the name regatta to boat races?
4. Who was murdered where in T. S. Eliot's play *Murder in the Cathedral*?
5. Who was Courtney Jones's ice dance partner?
6. Who created 'Star Trek'?
7. Who is called the father of western philosophy?
8. In which Wagner opera does Beckmesser appear?
9. Who flew in Friendship 7?

1038

1. For what is Cressida a byword?
2. Who was America's most decorated hero of the Second World War?
3. How far below sea level is the Caspian Sea?
4. Which mythological character went down to Hades in search of his wife?
5. Who was the first woman tennis-player to win the grand slam?
6. Who is the star of the film *Deep Throat*?
7. Who designed the Brighton Pavilion in the early nineteenth century?
8. For what does B. Mus. stand?
9. What was the name of the first dog in space?

296

1. The telephone.
2. The Royal Society of London.
3. 1 month.
4. Emlyn Williams.
5. 5 ounces.
6. Linda Blair.
7. Warner.
8. Edmund.
9. Equal sunshine.

667

1. Palm Sunday.
2. The Korean War.
3. Venice.
4. Thomas à Becket in Canterbury Cathedral.
5. Doreen Denny.
6. Gene Roddenberry.
7. Plato.
8. *The Mastersingers*.
9. Lieutenant-Colonel John Glenn (USA).

1038

1. Infidelity.
2. Audie Murphy, songwriter and film star.
3. 92 feet.
4. Orpheus.
5. Maureen Connolly (Little Mo), at the age of nineteen.
6. Linda Lovelace.
7. John Nash.
8. Bachelor of Music.
9. Laika.

297

1. What is the Greek name for the Roman goddess Aurora?
2. Who discovered Christmas Island in the Pacific Ocean in 1777?
3. Of which country is the markka the currency?
4. Who told André Gide that he had put his genius into his life and only his talent into his works?
5. What is a double axel?
6. Who directed *Zabriskie Point*?
7. Who is considered to be the founder of the Post-Impressionists?
8. In which film did Sting spread a little happiness?
9. To which space mission did 'Snoopy' and 'Charlie Brown' belong?

668

1. What makes red wine red?
2. Where was Florence Nightingale's Crimean hospital?
3. In which country is the Matterhorn?
4. How many cheers for democracy did E. M. Forster raise?
5. What was the job of Govind, for whom a testimonial cricket match was played at the end of the 1981–2 Indian tour?
6. What was the subtitle of *Dr Strangelove*?
7. Who said of his own career, 'I started at the top and worked down'?
8. Who wore short shorts?
9. Who was the pilot of the first space shuttle, a man who had been in space more times than anyone else?

1039

1. Where would you find a bick, a throat, a half-swage and a punching-hole?
2. Who was the victor at the Battle of Prestonpans?
3. In which country is K2, the second highest mountain in the world?
4. What is the title of John Lennon's second book?
5. Of what was Britain's Frankie Wainman world champion in 1979?
6. Which of his films did Otto Preminger describe as his most distinguished flop?
7. In a photography dark room what colour is the safe light?
8. With which other famous stars did Buddy Holly die?
9. What is the Latin name for the beech tree?

297

1. Eos.
2. Captain Cook.
3. Finland.
4. Oscar Wilde.
5. A jump of $2\frac{1}{2}$ turns in ice skating.
6. Antonioni.
7. Paul Cézanne (1839–1906).
8. *Brimstone and Treacle.*
9. Apollo 10.

668

1. The fermentation of the skins of red grapes.
2. Scutari.
3. Switzerland.
4. Two (title of a collection of essays).
5. Baggage man (with twenty-five years' service).
6. *How I Learned to Stop Worrying and Love the Bomb.*
7. Orson Welles.
8. The Purple People Eater.
9. John Young.

1039

1. On an anvil (they are all parts of it).
2. Prince Charles Edward, the Young Pretender.
3. Pakistan.
4. *A Spaniard in the Works.*
5. Stock-car racing.
6. *Saint Joan.*
7. Red.
8. The Big Bopper and Richie Valens.
9. Fagus.

298

1. What is the highest allowable percentage of alcohol in table wine?
2. What was on offer at mop fairs?
3. In which part of England did the Danes chiefly settle?
4. Which play was described by its author as 'a trivial comedy for serious people'?
5. Who was Frew McMillan's partner when he won the Wimbledon men's doubles in 1967, 1972 and 1978?
6. Who was the female co-presenter of 'Ready Steady Go'?
7. Who coined the revolutionary cry, 'Liberty, equality, fraternity'?
8. Who sang about the werewolves of London?
9. Which insect is responsible for spreading sleeping sickness?

669

1. Where is the fissure of Sylvius?
2. Who or what was the 'little gentleman in black velvet' responsible for William III's death?
3. From which country does soave wine come?
4. Who said, 'If the law supposes that, the law is an ass – an idiot'?
5. With whom has John McEnroe won the men's doubles at Wimbledon?
6. Who hosts the Camden Palace in London?
7. What was the name of Wellington's dog?
8. What was the Bonzo Dog Dooda Band's first album?
9. Who travelled in Sputnik II in 1967?

1040

1. A knowledge of William Reid's law of storms of 1847 helps one to do what?
2. Which event of 1836 does the Snow Drop Inn, Lewes, Sussex, commemorate?
3. Which country, according to E. Munster (1766–1839), was governed on a system of absolutism tempered by assassination?
4. Who was sent down from Oxford for his atheist beliefs and is now commemorated by a memorial in University College there?
5. Which horse won the 1981 Grand National?
6. Who was the 'It' girl?
7. From what is the dye cochineal made?
8. Who took the last train to Clarksville?
9. If you have chlorosis what colour does your skin go?

298

1. Fourteen.
2. The services of farm-hands and servants.
3. The east, particularly Lincolnshire and Yorkshire.
4. *The Importance of Being Earnest* (by Oscar Wilde).
5. Bob Hewitt.
6. Cathy McGowan.
7. Jean-Jacques Rousseau.
8. Warren Zevon.
9. The tsetse fly.

669

1. In the brain.
2. A mole. The King's horse stumbled over a molehill and threw him.
3. Italy.
4. Mr Bumble in *Oliver Twist.*
5. Peter Fleming.
6. Steve Strange.
7. Boot.
8. *Gorilla* (1967).
9. Laika, the dog.

1040

1. Sail out of an approaching hurricane.
2. A disastrous avalanche that killed eight.
3. Russia.
4. Shelley.
5. Aldaniti.
6. Clara Bow.
7. The dried bodies of female insects reared on cactus.
8. The Monkees.
9. Green.

299

1. For what month is the diamond the birthstone?
2. What was Antipater of Sidon the first to list in the second century AD?
3. Which town, 54 miles from the sea, is England's third busiest port?
4. Which 'poet of the plough' was an excise officer and father (among other children) of two sets of twins?
5. Who starred in *The Greatest*, the film biography of Muhammad Ali?
6. Who was it – later to become a famous film star – who played the lab assistant/android in 'A for Andromeda' on BBC TV in the 1960s?
7. What did the people Lowry painted resemble?
8. Who composed 'Stardust'?
9. How many major moons has the planet Jupiter?

670

1. What are the seven deadly sins?
2. Who is said to have been the greatest of the gladiators?
3. Between which two counties does the river Tamar run?
4. On which Alistair MacLean novel was Howard Hughes's favourite film based?
5. Why did Anders Haugen have to wait until 1974 to receive a bronze medal for skiing in the 1924 Olympics?
6. What do the French say to request an encore?
7. Who was Israel's first prime minister?
8. What is Dizzy Gillespie's real first name?
9. If your eyes were 100 feet above sea level, how far would the horizon be?

1041

1. Which fruit/vegetable was originally called a love-apple?
2. Who was King Solomon's mother?
3. Who was the first US president to visit Moscow?
4. Who was the magician at the court of King Arthur?
5. Which was the first team to win the FA Cup?
6. What was the name of the first Cinemascope film starring Richard Burton?
7. What is the more familiar name for Mohammed Ahmed, who led the revolt in the Sudan in the 1880s?
8. To which music did Torvill and Dean skate their free dance programme in the 1984 Olympics?
9. What is curious about the tail of the Manx cat?

299

1. April.
2. The seven wonders of the world.
3. Manchester.
4. Robert Burns.
5. Muhammad Ali himself.
6. Julie Christie.
7. Matchstick figures.
8. Hoagy Carmichael.
9. Twelve.

670

1. Pride, avarice, wrath, envy, gluttony, sloth, lust.
2. Theogenes, who faced and killed 1,425 men.
3. Devon and Cornwall.
4. *Ice Station Zebra.*
5. Because an error in scoring was not discovered until then!
6. Bis.
7. David Ben-Gurion.
8. John.
9. About 14 miles.

1041

1. The tomato.
2. Queen Bathsheba.
3. Richard Nixon.
4. Merlin.
5. The Wanderers.
6. *The Robe.*
7. The Mahdi.
8. Ravel's 'Bolero'.
9. It doesn't have a tail.

300

1. How many times must the pancake be tossed during the famous pancake race at Olney?
2. By how much did wholesale prices rise during the runaway inflation in Germany between 1918 and 1925?
3. How many thousands of years ago did Britain become an island?
4. Who wrote the poems of Currer, Ellis and Acton Bell?
5. At which football ground were sixty-six people killed when a stand collapsed in 1971?
6. What was Polanski's first feature film?
7. In fishing, what are Limerick, Round Bend, Aberdeen and Octopus?
8. Who was the Monkees' drummer?
9. What are Karakul, Texel and Romney Marsh types of?

671

1. Which magazine folded in June 1984 after 103 years?
2. Which queen ordered Thomas Cranmer to be burnt as a heretic?
3. What merchandise did the Hudson's Bay Company handle?
4. Who wrote, 'I like work, it fascinates me. I can sit and look at it for hours'?
5. Over what distances do men compete in the hurdles?
6. Whose music provided the doom-laden background for *Death in Venice*?
7. Which son of a duke, executed at thirty, has been described as the first classical English poet?
8. What was the title of Norman Greenbaum's rather depressing hit?
9. Which space mission comprised lunar module Aquarius and command module Odyssey?

1042

1. What is the name given to a boat or float used to support a temporary bridge?
2. How did Tyrrell put paid to Rufus?
3. On average, on how many days a week does it rain in Brussels and Amsterdam, the wettest European capitals?
4. Which detective did Donald Hamilton's novel *Death of a Citizen* introduce?
5. For what are the Golden Gloves awarded?
6. What is J.R.'s full name?
7. Which general said of war, 'It is all hell'?
8. Who was known as the prince of polyphony?
9. How many times its own height can an athletic flea jump?

300

1. Three.
2. Approximately a million million times.
3. Eight.
4. The Brontë sisters.
5. Ibrox Park (Glasgow Rangers).
6. *Knife in the Water*.
7. Types of hook.
8. Micky Dolenz.
9. Sheep.

671

1. *Tit Bits*.
2. Mary I.
3. Pelts (furs and skins).
4. Jerome K. Jerome (in *Three Men in a Boat*).
5. 110 and 400 metres.
6. Mahler's.
7. Henry Howard, Earl of Surrey.
8. 'Spirit in the Sky'.
9. Apollo 13.

1042

1. A pontoon.
2. He shot William II (Rufus) as he was hunting in the New Forest – whether accidentally or not is not known.
3. Four.
4. Matt Helm.
5. Winning the premier USA amateur boxing match.
6. John Ross Ewing II.
7. William Sherman (1820–91).
8. J. S. Bach.
9. A hundred.

301

1. Webb's, Cos and Iceberg are types of what?
2. Which English king was born in 1600 at Dunfermline Palace?
3. Why is the Transvaal so named?
4. Who in *Treasure Island* admits, 'Many's the long night I've dreamed of cheese – toasted, mostly'?
5. What is the optimum weight, within 5 kilograms, for a world-class male shot-putter?
6. Who was the original 'man you love to hate'?
7. Who was the defeated finalist in the 1983 World Professional Darts Championship?
8. Where was Eddie Cochran killed?
9. Where would you find Cassini's division?

672

1. What is biltong?
2. Whom did Alfred succeed as king of the West Saxons?
3. Where are the Summer Isles?
4. Who is wooed and won by Touchstone?
5. In which year was the first motor-racing Grand Prix held?
6. Who played Lucille Ball's husband in 'I Love Lucy'?
7. Who walked to Balmoral to give his poems to Queen Victoria and was turned away?
8. Who first recorded the R and B classic 'Smokestack Lightnin''?
9. What are the other two rather whimsically named types of quark besides up, down, top and bottom?

1043

1. In ship's time-keeping, how long is eight bells?
2. 'Corporal Violet' was the French nickname for whom?
3. At what age are people allowed to marry in Japan?
4. What fluid ran through the veins of the Greek gods instead of blood?
5. How many times was Graham Hill world motor-racing champion?
6. Who was Mia Farrow's mother in 'Peyton Place'?
7. Who deciphered the Rosetta Stone?
8. It might as well rain until when?
9. What is Scomber scombrus?

301

1. Lettuce.
2. Charles I.
3. Because it lies over the Vaal river from Natal and the Orange Free State.
4. Ben Gunn.
5. 120–125.
6. Erich von Stroheim.
7. Eric Bristow.
8. Near Chippenham in Wiltshire.
9. Between the rings of Saturn.

672

1. Strips of dried meat.
2. Ethelred I, his elder brother.
3. Off the west coast of Scotland.
4. Audrey (in *As You Like It*).
5. 1906.
6. Desi Arnaz, her real husband.
7. William McGonagall.
8. Howlin' Wolf (Chester Burnett).
9. Strange, charm.

1043

1. Four hours.
2. Napoleon.
3. Eighteen.
4. Ichor.
5. Twice.
6. Dorothy Malone.
7. Jean-François Champollion, a French Egyptologist.
8. September.
9. Mackerel.

302

1. In which year did Concorde first fly the Atlantic?
2. By what name was Mustapha Kemal better known?
3. What is the chief mining product of Kimberley, South Africa?
4. Who wrote about *Five Children and It*?
5. What is the maximum number of feet of bandage a professional boxer may use on each hand?
6. What was the name of the inspector played by Stratford Johns in 'Z Cars'?
7. Who said that a house is 'a machine for living in'?
8. Which country did the Bay City Rollers come from?
9. How many times heavier is an elephant's brain than a man's?

673

1. Which day is named after the Roman god of farming?
2. Which famous London building did the architect John Nash rebuild in 1825?
3. Who led his army on the retreat from Moscow in 1812?
4. Who was under a haycock, fast asleep?
5. Where were the 1984 Summer Olympics held?
6. What was the very first British TV soap opera produced by the BBC?
7. Which member of the royal family took part in an episode of 'The Archers' in June 1984?
8. What sort of emotion had the Righteous Brothers lost in 1964?
9. Which bird is the symbol of peace?

1044

1. Who fell down and broke his crown?
2. What happened at St Peter's Field, Manchester, on 16 August 1819?
3. In which mountain range is Annapurna?
4. Which little book was prosecuted as an obscene publication in 1971?
5. In which year did an English test team include eleven left-handers?
6. Which North American created the Muppets?
7. What was Fats Domino's real first name?
8. Roses, roses everywhere – what colour were Bobby Vinton's blooms?
9. Approximately what percentage of her adult weight is a nine-year-old girl?

302

1. 1977.
2. Ataturk ('father of the Turks').
3. Diamonds.
4. E. Nesbit.
5. Eighteen.
6. Barlow.
7. Le Corbusier.
8. Scotland – they wore bits of tartan to prove it.
9. Five (approximately).

673

1. Saturday (Saturn).
2. Buckingham Palace.
3. Napoleon.
4. Little Boy Blue.
5. Los Angeles.
6. 'The Grove Family' (1953–6).
7. Princess Margaret.
8. 'That Loving Feeling'.
9. The dove.

1044

1. Jack.
2. The Peterloo Massacre, in which the military killed eleven supporters of parliamentary reform.
3. The Himalayas.
4. *The Little Red Schoolbook.*
5. It has never happened.
6. Jim Henson.
7. Antoine.
8. Red.
9. Fifty.

303

1. What are brick, fontina, port salut, quargel?
2. Whose is the oldest surviving British royal signature?
3. How far, to the nearest 100 miles, is London from Reykjavik?
4. Where does the phrase 'Read, mark, learn and inwardly digest' originate?
5. In which Olympic throwing event do women not compete?
6. In which Ealing comedy does Alec Guinness play eight members of the D'Ascoyne family?
7. Which cousin of Stanley Baldwin is best known for his Indian connections and wrote of the jungle?
8. Who sang about the 'Games People Play'?
9. What was the name of the three-man space capsule that the Russians produced before the Americans?

674

1. What originally was a tycoon?
2. Who was the Cape Colony minister who authorized the Jameson raid on the Transvaal?
3. Where does the river Eden flow in England?
4. Who were the parents of Jacob and Esau?
5. Who are the Wallabies?
6. What was the name of the character played by James Arness in 'Gunsmoke'?
7. Who sought anonymity in the RAF under the name of Shaw and died in a motor-cycle accident?
8. Who wrote the blues classic 'Dust My Broom'?
9. Which event prompted Richard Nixon to say, 'This is the greatest week in the history of the world since the creation'?

1045

1. At what temperature should champagne be served?
2. For what is Alaric I, King of the Goths, most famous?
3. From which port did the *Mary Celeste* sail?
4. Who wrote, 'It was roses, roses all the way'?
5. What type of car was James Hunt driving when he won the World Championship in 1976?
6. What was the name of the character played by Olivier in *The Entertainer*?
7. Who was killed and subsequently deified by Hawaiians?
8. Brian Poole and the – who?
9. How is the Bacille Calmette Guérin vaccine for tuberculosis commonly referred to?

303

1. Cheeses.
2. Richard II's (dated 26 July 1386).
3. 1,170.
4. The Book of Common Prayer (collect for the second Sunday in Advent).
5. The hammer.
6. *Kind Hearts and Coronets.*
7. Rudyard Kipling.
8. Joe South.
9. Voskhod (Vostok).

674

1. A Japanese hereditary commander-in-chief.
2. Cecil Rhodes.
3. One flows through Carlisle in Cumbria to the Solway Firth, the other through Edenbridge in Kent to the Medway at Penshurst.
4. Isaac and Rebecca.
5. The Australian Rugby Union team.
6. Marshal Dillon.
7. T. E. Lawrence.
8. Robert Johnson.
9. Man's first landing on the moon.

1045

1. 41–45°F (5–7°C).
2. The sack of Rome in AD 410.
3. New York.
4. Robert Browing (in 'The Patriot').
5. A McLaren Ford.
6. Archie Rice.
7. Captain Cook.
8. Tremoloes.
9. As BCG vaccine.

304

1. What does the name Peter mean?
2. How many ships were involved in the famous mass collision off Newfoundland on 27 May 1945?
3. Where was Prince Charles invested as Prince of Wales?
4. Who is Flash Gordon's girl friend?
5. Which Australian bowler took six for fourteen against England in the 1975 Prudential World Cup?
6. Who is the uncle of Peepeye, Pipeye, Poopeye and Pupeye?
7. Who has carved on his tombstone, 'Workers of all lands, unite'?
8. What does ARCO stand for?
9. In which part of a sheep is haggis boiled?

675

1. Of which generation are your first, second and third cousins?
2. Who was Nazi Germany's minister of propaganda who committed suicide in Hitler's bunker in 1945?
3. On which river does Balmoral Castle stand?
4. Who lives at 23g Gresham Terrace, W1?
5. From whom did George Foreman capture the world heavyweight boxing title in 1973?
6. Who said, 'When I'm good, I'm very good, but when I'm bad I'm better'?
7. What do P. G. Wodehouse's initials stand for?
8. Who wrote 'I Dream of Jeannie'?
9. At what temperature is the international standard yard defined?

1046

1. How many sit on an English jury?
2. To whose shrine were Chaucer's pilgrims going?
3. Which hill leads up to St Paul's Cathedral in London?
4. What is Satan's capital in John Milton's *Paradise Lost*?
5. To which game was the phrase 'hat trick' first applied?
6. In which book and film does North Manual Trades School feature?
7. Who lived in a cottage at Shottery which is now visited by thousands?
8. Why don't any of Mozart's piano pieces contain particularly high or low notes?
9. How would you turn a goldfish white?

304

1. Rock.
2. Twenty-two – yet no lives were lost.
3. Caernarvon Castle.
4. Dale Arden.
5. Gary Gilmour.
6. Popeye the Sailor.
7. Karl Marx.
8. Associate of the Royal College of Organists.
9. The stomach.

675

1. Your own.
2. Joseph Goebbels.
3. The Dee.
4. John Creasey's the Toff (the Honourable Richard Rollison).
5. Joe Frazier.
6. Mae West.
7. Pelham Grenville.
8. Stephen Foster.
9. 62°F (15°C).

1046

1. Twelve.
2. St Thomas à Becket's.
3. Ludgate Hill.
4. Pandemonium.
5. Cricket.
6. *Blackboard Jungle.*
7. Anne Hathaway.
8. Because he wrote for the piano of the day, which had only five octaves.
9. Apart from painting it, by keeping it in a dark room.

305

1. What is the highest army rank?
2. How old was Julius Caesar when he was killed?
3. Which borough lies between the Borough of Kensington and Chelsea and the City of London?
4. What is P. R. Reid's best-known book?
5. Which country won the most medals at the Summer Olympics in Montreal?
6. Which New York precinct is the setting of the TV series 'Naked City'?
7. Of whom did his mother say that her ugly boy, Arthur, was fit food for powder and nothing else?
8. Which well-known band leader and jazz pianist died in April 1984?
9. How many wings has a dragonfly?

676

1. How many heads has the dog Cerberus?
2. In which battle did Nelson lose his arm?
3. In which ocean is the Sargasso Sea?
4. Who was gentleman's personal gentleman to Bertie Wooster?
5. At the 1960 Olympic Games, how many others besides the winner, Herb Elliott, broke the previous Olympic record for the 1,500 metres?
6. Which film producer discovered Jean Harlow and Jane Russell?
7. Which famous Dutch artist painted over sixty self-portraits?
8. Who composed 'Land of Hope and Glory'?
9. What frightened Miss Muppet away?

1047

1. For what does GMT stand?
2. Which historical event is depicted on the Bayeux tapestry?
3. What is the capital of Asia?
4. In the novels of Arnold Bennett, what was the chief industry of the five towns?
5. What nationality is tennis-player Mats Wilander?
6. In 'MASH', what is Major Hoolihan's nickname?
7. Which poet was known as the Bristol boy?
8. When the old man played two, on what did he play nick-nack?
9. To which bird family does the siskin belong?

305

1. Field Marshal.
2. Fifty-eight.
3. The City of Westminster.
4. *The Colditz Story*.
5. The Soviet Union (125).
6. The 65th.
7. The first Duke of Wellington.
8. Count Basie.
9. Four.

676

1. Three.
2. Santa Cruz.
3. The Atlantic.
4. Jeeves.
5. Six.
6. Howard Hughes.
7. Rembrandt.
8. Sir Edward Elgar.
9. A spider.

1047

1. Greenwich Mean Time.
2. The Norman Conquest of England.
3. Asia has no capital, being a continent and not a country.
4. Pottery.
5. Swedish.
6. Hot Lips.
7. Thomas Chatterton.
8. My shoe.
9. Finch.

306

1. William Huskisson was the first person to be run over by what?
2. Who, with Walter the Penniless, preached on the first crusade and entered Jerusalem victorious?
3. Which is Switzerland's smallest canton?
4. Who wrote the play *Trelawny of the Wells*?
5. Who won the European table-tennis championships in 1980?
6. What was Peter Sellers's famous inept detective role?
7. What was Edward Teach's nickname?
8. Which member of the Pink Floyd races vintage Maseratis for fun?
9. In which country did the turnip originate?

677

1. How many in a gross?
2. Which of Henry VIII's wives survived him?
3. In which country is Gothenburg?
4. Who lies next to Swift in St Patrick's Cathedral, Dublin?
5. In which Olympic Games held between 1912 and 1952 did the USSR/Russia not win any gold medals?
6. Who played Beau Brummell in the 1954 film?
7. What is the highest total before going bust at blackjack?
8. Of which disease did Tchaikovsky die?
9. Which is the nearest star to the earth?

1048

1. Which letter begins English words most often?
2. From what were bombs dropped on Venice in 1849?
3. Which Australian state bears the name of a British queen?
4. On which mountain did Moses receive the Ten Commandments?
5. In motor racing, what does a yellow flag signify?
6. Which actor wore the same pair of cuff-links on stage for over 20 years?
7. What is Margaret Thatcher's middle name?
8. What was the theme song of the 1940 film *The Grapes of Wrath*?
9. What colour is a live ermine in summer?

306

1. A railway train (in 1830).
2. Peter the Hermit.
3. Zug.
4. Arthur Pinero.
5. John Hilton.
6. Inspector Clouseau.
7. Blackbeard (the pirate of the West Indies).
8. Nick Mason.
9. Greece.

677

1. 144.
2. Catherine Parr.
3. Sweden.
4. 'Stella' (Esther Johnson).
5. All of them. They did not compete between 1912 and 1952.
6. Stewart Granger.
7. Twenty-one.
8. Cholera.
9. The sun.

1048

1. S.
2. Hot-air balloons.
3. Victoria.
4. Sinai.
5. Slow down and hold your position.
6. Bob Hope.
7. Hilda.
8. 'Red River Valley'.
9. Brown.

307

1. What colour light is shown on the starboard side of a ship?
2. How did Henry H. Bliss meet his death in New York City in 1899 – the first of many to perish from this cause?
3. Under which pass does the Simplon tunnel run?
4. Who created Jemima Puddleduck?
5. Who was the youngest man ever to win the World Grand Prix for motor racing?
6. Who played General Gordon in the 1966 film *Khartoum*?
7. Whose autobiography is entitled *With a Little Bit of Luck*?
8. Who composed the music to *West Side Story*?
9. How many degrees are there in a right angle?

678

1. When is Remembrance Day?
2. Which organization stipulated in the 1930s, 'If you are about to be confined, the corporation reserves the right to terminate your contract'?
3. Which European country has four national languages?
4. Who created Mike Hammer?
5. Which two jockeys have won the English grand slam?
6. Who wrote *Roots*?
7. What is the inscription on Thomas Fuller's tomb?
8. What is Benny Goodman's instrument?
9. From what are pencil leads made?

1049

1. What is travel said to broaden?
2. Whose mob carried out the massacre on 14 February 1929?
3. Why do most Maltese churches have two clocks, one right and one wrong?
4. What is Fanny's surname in *Fanny by Gaslight*?
5. What happened to the Russian Boris Onitshenko in the fencing discipline of the 1976 Olympic modern pentathlon?
6. What was Citizen Kane's dying word?
7. Which signalling system, invented by Edgeworth in 1767, was first adapted for use in 1794 by Claude Chappe?
8. Who was the best-known lead singer with the Supremes?
9. What is the only food of vampire bats?

307

1. Green.
2. He was hit by a car.
3. The Simplon.
4. Beatrix Potter.
5. Emerson Fittipaldi (at the age of twenty-five).
6. Charlton Heston.
7. Stanley Holloway's.
8. Leonard Bernstein.
9. Ninety.

678

1. 11 November.
2. The BBC.
3. Switzerland.
4. Mickey Spillane.
5. Fred Archer and Lester Piggott.
6. Alex Hailey.
7. 'Fuller's earth.'
8. The clarinet.
9. A mixture of graphite and clay – not lead!

1049

1. The mind.
2. Al Capone's (the St Valentine's Day Massacre).
3. To confuse the devil about the times of services.
4. Hooper.
5. He was disqualified for cheating.
6. Rosebud.
7. Semaphore.
8. Diana Ross.
9. Blood.

308

1. What is Sam Barraclough's claim to fame?
2. What happened in England between 3 and 13 September 1752?
3. What is one hundredth of a rial in Iran?
4. Who was captured and kept in a cage by Stromboli?
5. Why was it considered miraculous that Wilma Rudolph won three sprint gold medals at the 1960 Olympics?
6. Who was kidnapped from the Harlem night club 'Fillet of Soul' in the 1973 film *Live and Let Die*?
7. Who shot Martin Luther King Junior?
8. What was the name of George Gershwin's lyricist brother?
9. Where is turpentine found naturally?

679

1. Whose law states that 'Work expands so as to fill the time available for its completion'?
2. How were the bodies of dead crusaders brought home for Christian burial?
3. How are corpses disposed of in New Orleans?
4. Which of Charles Dickens's novels features Wackford Squeers?
5. Which country won soccer's World Cup in 1970?
6. In which TV series do Waldorf and Statler appear?
7. Who was Dora Block?
8. What was the theme song of the 1955 film *The Blackboard Jungle*?
9. How many million blood cells are destroyed per minute in a human body?

1050

1. What date begins the astrological year?
2. What did the Corrupt Practices Act of 1883 make efficient?
3. After which river was India named?
4. What was the prophet Amos's occupation?
5. In which sport is the Leonard Trophy contested?
6. Whose house at 117 Pine Street burnt down?
7. Which famous writer shot himself in 1961?
8. Which was the first LP by a solo singer to sell a million copies?
9. What were the four elements of the ancients?

308

1. He was the first owner of Lassie, the dog.
2. Nothing. In that year the Gregorian calendar replaced the Julian calendar (which was eleven days behind), so 14 September followed 2 September.
3. A dinar.
4. Pinocchio.
5. Because she was crippled by polio as a child.
6. James Bond (played by Roger Moore).
7. James Earl Ray.
8. Ira.
9. In the fresh resin of a conifer.

679

1. Parkinson's.
2. They were chopped up and boiled.
3. They are placed in mausoleums, as the ground is too wet for conventional burials.
4. *Nicholas Nickleby*.
5. Brazil.
6. 'The Muppet Show'. They are the two old hecklers.
7. The seventy-five-year-old Israeli woman not rescued in the raid on Entebbe airport because she was in a Ugandan hospital. She was never seen again.
8. 'Rock Around the Clock'.
9. Fifteen, but they are replaced by fifteen million new ones.

1050

1. 21 March.
2. The secret ballot.
3. The Indus.
4. He was a shepherd.
5. Bowls.
6. Olive Oyl's.
7. Ernest Hemingway.
8. 'Calypso' by Harry Belafonte.
9. Fire, air, earth and water.

309

1. Who or what may proverbially look at a king?
2. Which posting inn was the first stop for travellers leaving London for the north?
3. Which Roman road does the A5 follow for the greater part of its course?
4. What line precedes, 'Makes a man healthy, wealthy and wise'?
5. To the nearest ounce, what does a tennis-ball weigh?
6. In which film did Glynis Johns play a mermaid?
7. Which poet named Rome the Eternal City?
8. Who sang the title song to *Goldfinger*?
9. In the horse world what is the feminine of sire?

680

1. What is the heraldic term for blue?
2. Which Spartan king was married to Helen?
3. What is the seaward extension of the Severn estuary called?
4. What was Shakespeare's Juliet's family name?
5. At what age did Sonja Henie first win the World Figure Skating Championship?
6. Who played Elizabeth Barrett Browning in the 1934 film *The Barretts of Wimpole Street*?
7. Which American general led his troops into the massacre at Little Big Horn?
8. In which land does Puff the Magic Dragon live?
9. Who said in 1969, 'That's one small step for a man, a great leap for mankind'?

1051

1. Why have boots with pockets been invented and patented?
2. Before which Roman governor was Jesus Christ tried?
3. In which country are the Trossachs?
4. Which Dickens character was married to Fanny and had children named Florence and Paul?
5. What is the lowest score ever recorded for an eighteen-hole round on a 5,000-yard-plus golf course?
6. Which revolutionary was portrayed by Marlon Brando in *Viva Zapata*?
7. Where was Francesca da Rimini assassinated?
8. Who composed *Der Freischütz*?
9. Which animals can live the longest without water?

309

1. A cat.
2. The Angel, Islington.
3. Watling Street.
4. 'Early to bed and early to rise.'
5. 2 ounces.
6. *Miranda.*
7. Virgil.
8. Shirley Bassey.
9. Dam.

680

1. Azure.
2. Menelaus.
3. The Bristol Channel.
4. Capulet.
5. Thirteen.
6. Norma Shearer.
7. George Custer.
8. Honalee.
9. Neil Armstrong, the first man to set foot on the moon.

1051

1. For the use of nudists.
2. Pontius Pilate.
3. Scotland.
4. Paul Dombey (in *Dombey and Son*).
5. Fifty-five (by Homero Blancas in Texas in 1962).
6. Emiliano Zapata.
7. Rimini.
8. Weber.
9. Rats.

310

1. Which star sign follows Sagittarius?
2. Who first circumnavigated Australia and New Guinea, discovering New Zealand too?
3. Where is Spurn Head?
4. Who created the fictional detective Lemmy Caution?
5. What was the score when Preston North End beat Hyde by the biggest margin ever in an F A Cup match in 1887?
6. In which TV Western did Steve McQueen star before transferring successfully to the big screen?
7. Where was Nancy Astor, the first woman to sit as an MP, born?
8. With which band is Robert Fripp usually associated?
9. To which country is the emu native?

681

1. Which dictionary word is an anagram of indicatory?
2. What was John Wilkes's fate for describing the King's Speech of 1763 as false?
3. In which UK city is the University of Aston?
4. Where did J. P. Donleavy set *The Ginger Man*?
5. On which two circuits is the British Grand Prix held alternately?
6. Who turned in a memorable performance as the Prince of Wales in 'Edward and Mrs Simpson'?
7. What does David Shilling design?
8. For which 1960s duo was the phrase 'blue-eyed soul' coined?
9. How many noughts are there in a British billion?

1052

1. How many words on average does the normal adult speak in the course of 24 hours?
2. How many English kings have been known by the name James?
3. Which country has the most hospitals?
4. Who created Ripley?
5. Which country won the world team championship for karate in 1975?
6. In which films did Bert Kwouk play a karate-mad houseboy?
7. Who used to shout 'Wakey, wa-a-k-ey!'?
8. For what omission was the Finnish entry in the 1982 Eurovision Song Contest notable?
9. What are devil's darning-needles?

310

1. Capricorn.
2. Abel Tasman.
3. At the mouth of the Humber.
4. Peter Cheyney.
5. 26–0.
6. 'Wanted Dead or Alive'.
7. Mirador, Virginia, USA.
8. King Crimson.
9. Australia.

681

1. Dictionary.
2. He was incarcerated in the Tower of London.
3. Birmingham.
4. Dublin.
5. Brands Hatch and Silverstone.
6. Edward Fox.
7. Hats.
8. The Righteous Brothers.
9. Twelve.

1052

1. Five thousand.
2. Two.
3. The USA.
4. Patricia Highsmith.
5. Britain.
6. The Pink Panther series.
7. Billy Cotton.
8. Failure to score a single point – a distinction shared by two of Norway's entries.
9. Dragonflies.

311

1. Which rank in the police force is immediately above chief inspector?
2. Which was the first US state to require car licences in 1901?
3. Of which country is Asunción the capital?
4. Round which city did Joshua and his armies march for 7 days?
5. Who set a world record in 1980, then lost it to Guido Kratschmer a few weeks later?
6. What is 'The Grand Ole Opry'?
7. Who founded Virgin Records?
8. What name do Cliff Richard and Gary Numan have in common?
9. From what is vodka distilled?

682

1. If contained in an advert, which word attracts the most attention?
2. Who, in 1793, apologized for accidentally stepping on her executioner's foot?
3. Which country was formed by the British North America Act?
4. Who wrote *Zen and the Art of Motorcycle Maintenance*?
5. Who was Ramadhin's famous bowling partner?
6. Who created the TV series 'Dixon of Dock Green'?
7. Who left the editor's chair at the *Spectator* in 1984?
8. Which of the Allman brothers died in a motorbike accident?
9. Bright's disease affects which part of the body?

1053

1. Two dots over the second of two vowels indicate that it is to be pronounced separately (as in Zoë). What are they called?
2. With whom did Major William Careless stay in an oak tree in Boscobel Wood?
3. What do Americans usually call 1-cent coins?
4. Who created the fictional detective Sir John Appleby?
5. How many goals did Bobby Charlton score for England?
6. Who composed the *Chariots of Fire* theme music?
7. Who painted 'The Death of Actaeon'?
8. What was Jimmy Young's biggest hit?
9. Name the two planets in our solar system without moons.

311

1. Superintendent.
2. New York.
3. Paraguay.
4. Jericho.
5. Daley Thompson.
6. An American Country and Western variety show.
7. Richard Branson.
8. Their real surname – Webb.
9. Rye; sometimes potatoes.

682

1. 'Free'.
2. Marie Antoinette.
3. Canada.
4. Robert Pirsig.
5. Valentine – immortalized in the calypso.
6. Ted Willis – now Lord Willis of Chislehurst.
7. Alexander Chancellor.
8. Duane.
9. The kidneys.

1053

1. A diaeresis.
2. Charles II.
3. Pennies.
4. Michael Innes.
5. Forty-nine.
6. Vangelis.
7. Titian.
8. 'Too Young'.
9. Mercury and Venus.

312

1. How many £1,000,000 Bank of England notes are there in existence?
2. Who discovered the West Indies?
3. In which country might drunken drivers face a firing squad?
4. Who wrote the classic children's novel, *The Weirdstone of Brisingamen*?
5. Who died the day before her record of nineteen Wimbledon titles was broken?
6. Who sang the 'Rawhide' theme?
7. Where was Oscar Wilde imprisoned?
8. What was the name of the band with whom George Melly played in the 1950s, immortalized in 'Owning Up'?
9. Why are you safe from bee-stings when it's raining?

683

1. On 27 May 1979, the world's first rally for these was held at Longleat House. What were they?
2. Who was the last Viceroy of India?
3. How many time zones does Canada have?
4. Who wrote *The Women's Room*?
5. Who was the first woman to win an Olympic gold medal?
6. Ian La Frenais usually works with which other scriptwriter?
7. How many pieces form a tangram?
8. Which American record producer played maracas on the first Rolling Stones album?
9. How much longer is a newborn crocodile than the egg from which it hatches?

1054

1. What is the motto of the SAS?
2. What first was achieved by the *Comet* which carried passengers up the Clyde in 1812?
3. Which great American university is at New Haven, Connecticut?
4. Who is Josephine Tey's novel, *The Daughter of Time*, about?
5. Name the famous son of Irish former jockey, Michael 'Mouse' Morris.
6. Which character did Antonio Fargas play in 'Starsky and Hutch'?
7. Niccolò Paganini was a virtuoso player of which instrument?
8. Who sang about a 'swell party'?
9. What is the speed of sound at sea level?

312

1. Two.
2. Christopher Columbus.
3. San Salvador.
4. Alan Garner.
5. Elizabeth Ryan.
6. Frankie Laine.
7. Reading.
8. Mick Mulligan's Magnolia Jazz Band.
9. Because bees cannot fly in the rain.

683

1. Teddy bears.
2. Lord Mountbatten.
3. Six.
4. Marilyn French.
5. Charlotte Cooper of Great Britain. She won the women's tennis singles title in 1900.
6. Dick Clement.
7. Seven, cut from a square.
8. Phil Spector.
9. Three times.

1054

1. 'Who dares wins'.
2. It was the first paddle steamer in Britain.
3. Yale.
4. Richard III. An investigation into the murder of the young princes is conducted by Inspector Grant of Scotland Yard.
5. Lord Killanin (formerly President of the International Olympic Committee).
6. Huggy Bear.
7. The violin.
8. Bing Crosby and Frank Sinatra.
9. 1,100 feet per second.

313

1. How many languages (to the nearest ten) are spoken by at least 1,000,000 people?
2. Of which British king was Henri IV of France the father-in-law?
3. Of which country is Quito the capital?
4. Name the fairy in *Peter Pan*.
5. Who was known as 'the Brockton Bomber'?
6. Who was Dr Kildare's senior and mentor?
7. Which card in a pack is copyright?
8. Who recorded 'True Love' with Bing Crosby in 1956?
9. Which mythological animal resembles a horse and has a single horn growing from the centre of its forehead?

684

1. Who wrote *The Common Sense Book of Baby and Child Care*?
2. What did Walter Hunt invent in 1849?
3. In which country did the Maori wars take place?
4. For whom did Scott Fitzgerald write *College of One*, his book of self-education?
5. In boxing, what do the letters TKO stand for?
6. What is Joe Mannix's profession?
7. Who was Helen Keller's teacher?
8. How many Enigma Variations are there?
9. Who said, after having had a price of 30,000 marks placed on his head, 'I did not know it was worth so much'?

1055

1. What are galligaskins?
2. Who was Marian Fitzwalter?
3. In which island group is Tenerife?
4. Who was the Roman god of the sun?
5. Which is 'the Sport of Kings'?
6. Who lives at 3 Stable Mews?
7. Who painted 'Arnolfini and His Wife'?
8. Which fish gives its name to a Schubert song?
9. Which pigment mainly determines skin colour?

313

1. 156.
2. Charles I.
3. Ecuador.
4. Tinkerbell.
5. Rocky Marciano.
6. Dr Leonard Gillespie.
7. The Ace of Spades.
8. Grace Kelly.
9. The unicorn.

684

1. Dr Benjamin Spock.
2. The safety pin.
3. New Zealand.
4. Sheila Graham.
5. Technical knock-out.
6. Private detective.
7. Anne Sullivan.
8. Fourteen.
9. Einstein.

1055

1. Breeches.
2. Maid Marian, of Robin Hood fame.
3. The Canaries.
4. Apollo.
5. Horse racing.
6. John Steed of 'The Avengers'.
7. Jan Van Eyck.
8. The trout.
9. Melanin.

314

1. What other title does the Bishop of Rome hold?
2. Which is the oldest university in the USA?
3. Where is Tabasco?
4. Whose pupils were 'la crème de la crème'?
5. Lydia Skoblikova won a gold medal in all four women's speed skating races at the Winter Olympics of which year?
6. Who appears 'in persons'?
7. Who invented the game Quizwrangle?
8. Who was the first musician to be knighted in 1842?
9. What is the treatment of eye defects such as squints called?

685

1. What void did Captain Hanson Gregory Crockett create in 1847?
2. Who was the cult leader of the People's Temple who persuaded his 900 followers to commit suicide by poison in Jonestown, Guyana, on 18 November 1978?
3. Where is the International Court of Justice?
4. Name the hotel featured in Arthur Hailey's novel *Hotel.*
5. How many times was Kevin Keegan capped for England?
6. What was Jean Harlow's last film?
7. What is the Prince of Wales's naval rank?
8. Which composer does Schroeder idolize?
9. What is a mandrill?

1056

1. What is the international word sent out as a distress signal?
2. Which city was the first to be bombed, in 1849?
3. The old region of Macedonia now belongs to which countries?
4. Who gave the Black Spot to Bill Bones?
5. Who rode The Pie to victory in the Grand National?
6. 'Wait a minute; wait a minute. You ain't heard nothing yet!' Who said that?
7. A copy of what did Henri Sanson sell to Madame Tussaud's?
8. Which singer was nicknamed 'the Forces' Sweetheart' in the Second World War?
9. What was the most stupid creature ever to inhabit the earth?

314

1. The Pope.
2. Harvard.
3. Southern Mexico.
4. Miss Jean Brodie's.
5. 1964.
6. Mike Yarwood.
7. Maureen Hiron.
8. John Howard Payne, composer of 'Home Sweet Home'.
9. Orthoptics.

685

1. The hole in doughnuts.
2. Jim Jones.
3. The Hague in Holland.
4. St Gregory.
5. Sixty-four times.
6. *Saratoga* (1937). She died while filming it.
7. Commander.
8. Beethoven.
9. A type of baboon.

1056

1. Mayday.
2. Venice.
3. Yugoslavia and Greece.
4. Pew, the blind beggar, in *Treasure Island*.
5. Velvet Brown in *National Velvet*.
6. Al Jolson. It is the first line of spoken dialogue in the first 'talkie', *The Jazz Singer* (1927).
7. His guillotine.
8. Vera Lynn.
9. The stegosaurus. It weighed $6\frac{1}{2}$ tons but its brain weighed only $2\frac{1}{2}$ oz.

315

1. What is fear of noise called?
2. Whom did Clarissa Churchill marry in 1952?
3. From which airport did Israelis free 103 hostages in 1976?
4. Which van Pelt uses a security blanket?
5. In American football how high from the ground is the crossbar of the goalpost?
6. Hattie McDaniel was the first Negress to win an Oscar. In which film?
7. Why did Lady Godiva ride naked through the streets of Coventry?
8. Which singer did Mark David Chapman shoot and kill?
9. *Kaka* means 'parrot' in which language?

686

1. In which year was the two-tier system introduced for inland letters?
2. What did Levi Hutchins invent in 1787 – to the delight of many employers?
3. On which day of the week are General Elections invariably held in the UK?
4. Which book made Nicholas Monsarrat famous?
5. Name the 1968 Olympic heavyweight boxing gold medal winner who became world heavyweight champion in 1973.
6. Who wrote a book, *Nibbles and Me*, about her pet chipmunk?
7. Which US president was the first to travel in a car, in a plane and in a submarine?
8. How many men on the dead man's chest?
9. Why is the bloodhound so called?

1057

1. How many corners has a spinnaker?
2. Which plague reached England in 1349?
3. Before 1939, what was the capital of Germany?
4. What was curious about the Pobble's feet?
5. Name the three Lloyd brothers; all of them have played at Wimbledon.
6. Which sex symbol made her screen debut as an extra in *The Egg and I* (1947)?
7. In which play does Shakespeare refer to billiards?
8. Which band had a hit with 'Pennsylvania 6-5000'?
9. Edward White was the first American to walk where?

315

1. Phonophobia.
2. Anthony Eden, who succeeded Winston Churchill as Prime Minister in 1955.
3. Entebbe.
4. Linus.
5. 10 feet.
6. *Gone with the Wind.*
7. As a protest against the steep taxes imposed by her husband Leofric, Lord of Coventry.
8. John Lennon.
9. Maori.

686

1. 1968.
2. The alarm clock.
3. Thursdays.
4. *The Cruel Sea.*
5. George Foreman.
6. Elizabeth Taylor.
7. Theodore Roosevelt.
8. Fifteen.
9. *Not* for its tracking ability, but because it was the first pedigree or 'pure-blooded' breed of dog.

1057

1. Three – it's a large sail.
2. The Black Death.
3. Berlin.
4. They had no toes, according to Edward Lear.
5. David, John and Tony.
6. Marilyn Monroe.
7. *Antony and Cleopatra.*
8. Glenn Miller's.
9. In space.

316

1. When is St George's Day?
2. Palestine belonged to which empire up to the end of the First World War?
3. Which large American city was named after St Francis of Assisi?
4. How many dwarfs escorted Bilbo Baggins from the Shire to the Lonely Mountain?
5. What does the badge of Northants CCC depict?
6. How old was Rick Blaine in *Casablanca*?
7. How many pieces are on a draught board at the start of a game?
8. In which opera do the Polovtsian Dances feature?
9. Wood is to charcoal as coal is to . . . what?

687

1. Who said, 'What is wrong with the world today is greed, immorality and depravity'?
2. Name the German pocket battleship scuttled by her own crew in December 1939.
3. What is the official language of Andorra?
4. Who wrote *God's Little Acre*?
5. Who was the sole female jockey in the 1981 Grand National?
6. Where was the TV series 'The Prisoner' filmed?
7. Who assumed the name Sebastian Melmoth?
8. Which country does the song 'Cockles and Mussels' come from?
9. Where is your deltoid muscle?

1058

1. Proverbially, what is mightier than the sword?
2. The Romans planned (but failed in AD 9) to extend their empire to the banks of which river?
3. Which nation has the lowest infant mortality rate?
4. Who is the heroine of Shakespeare's *Othello*?
5. In motor racing, what does a red flag mean?
6. Who played Douglas Bader in *Reach for the Sky* (1956)?
7. Who said, 'When a man is tired of London he is tired of life'?
8. Janet Craxton, who died in 1981, was a virtuoso player of which instrument?
9. What breed of dog is Snoopy?

316

1. 23 April.
2. The Ottoman Empire.
3. San Francisco.
4. Thirteen.
5. The Tudor Rose.
6. Thirty-seven.
7. Twenty-four.
8. Borodin's *Prince Igor*.
9. Coke.

687

1. Peter Sutcliffe, the Yorkshire Ripper.
2. The *Graf Spee*.
3. Catalan.
4. Erskine Caldwell.
5. Linda Sheedy.
6. In north Wales.
7. Oscar Wilde.
8. Ireland.
9. In your shoulder.

1058

1. The pen.
2. The Elbe.
3. Sweden.
4. Desdemona.
5. Stop.
6. Kenneth More.
7. Dr Johnson.
8. The oboe.
9. A beagle.

317

1. What was the profession of the father of the outlaws Frank and Jesse James?
2. Who was portrayed in the film *Anne of the Thousand Days*?
3. Which sovereign knighted Isaac Newton?
4. Whom did Stamford introduce to whom?
5. Who was the only player to have won the United States Singles Tennis Championships at Forest Hills seven times?
6. What is the car of Bo and Luke Duke called?
7. Who lived to the age of 969?
8. In which Gilbert and Sullivan operetta do Yum-Yum, Peep-Bo and Pitti-Sing appear?
9. Which group of insects contains the most varieties?

688

1. THE CLASSROOM is a well-known anagram of what word?
2. What unpleasant invention of C. C. Magee's was first used in 1935?
3. Which country has the most cars per mile of road?
4. Who wrote *The Godfather*?
5. Who was the lightest world heavyweight boxing champion?
6. Who wrote the play and film *The Glass Menagerie*?
7. What was Typhoid Mary's profession?
8. 'Ding, dong, bell' – where's pussy?
9. There are 31,622,400 seconds in what period of time?

1059

1. Who said, 'Money is like a sixth sense – and you can't make use of the other five without it'?
2. Name the battle of 1415 in which Henry V defeated the French.
3. What record does Lake Baykal in the Soviet Union hold?
4. Who wrote *Travels with a Donkey*?
5. How many Winter Olympics have been held at Lake Placid?
6. *Chu Chin Chow* is based on which story?
7. What are the oldest gaming implements known to man?
8. Who wrote the play on which Verdi's opera *Don Carlos* is based?
9. Why was the moth-collecting small boy disappointed when he bought a book?

317

1. A minister in the church.
2. Anne Boleyn.
3. Queen Anne.
4. Dr John Watson to Sherlock Holmes.
5. Bill Tilden.
6. The General Lee.
7. Methuselah.
8. *The Mikado.*
9. Beetles.

688

1. Schoolmaster.
2. The parking meter (in the USA).
3. England.
4. Mario Puzo.
5. James Fitzsimmons. He weighed 167 lb when he knocked out James Corbett in 1897.
6. Tennessee Williams.
7. Cook.
8. In the well.
9. A leap year.

1059

1. Somerset Maugham.
2. Agincourt.
3. It's the world's deepest lake – at some points more than a mile deep.
4. R. L. Stevenson.
5. Two.
6. 'Ali Baba and the Forty Thieves'.
7. Dice.
8. Schiller.
9. It was entitled *Hints to Young Mothers*.

318

1. What was known as Old Tom?
2. Which pagan custom, to frighten away evil spirits, survives today at military funerals?
3. How many prisoners can the Isle of Sark prison hold?
4. Who founded the magazine *Playboy*?
5. Which English cricketer shares his name with a Welsh peninsula?
6. Who played the Jackal in the film *The Day of the Jackal*?
7. Which numbers flank 11 on a dartboard?
8. Which march features in *Bridge on the River Kwai*?
9. Which fruit has the greatest protein content?

689

1. Where is the bow of a ship?
2. Who landed in Britain in 55 BC?
3. In which year does Britain's lease of Hong Kong expire?
4. What is the subject of Hemingway's book *Death in the Afternoon*?
5. Which Welsh club was the only non-English team to win the FA Cup? (It won in 1927.)
6. Which is Quincy's favourite restaurant?
7. By what name is Sarah Jane Fulks better known?
8. Name the group formed by the Wilson brothers in 1961.
9. Which is the best form of cloud for gliding?

1060

1. What signal on the bell does a bus conductor give to the driver for an emergency stop?
2. What was Charles Darwin's survey ship called?
3. Who was called 'the Liberator of South America'?
4. Who wrote *A Town Like Alice*?
5. Who was known as 'the Clown Prince of Basketball'?
6. In which century is 'Star Trek' set?
7. What do the initials F.W. stand for in F.W. Woolworth?
8. What was Irving Berlin's first hit song?
9. How many people could sit on the longest bicycle ever constructed?

318

1. Gin.
2. Making a noise – the firing of guns.
3. Two.
4. Hugh Hefner.
5. Gower.
6. Edward Fox.
7. 8 and 14.
8. The 'Colonel Bogey March'.
9. The avocado.

689

1. At the front (the sharp end).
2. Julius Caesar.
3. 1997.
4. Bullfighting.
5. Cardiff City.
6. Danny's.
7. Jane Wyman.
8. The Beach Boys.
9. Cumulus, which is caused by the rising air currents that keep gliders aloft.

1060

1. Three rings.
2. *The Beagle*.
3. Simon Bolivar.
4. Nevil Shute.
5. Meadowlark Lemon of the Harlem Globetrotters.
6. The twenty-third.
7. Frank Winfield.
8. 'Alexander's Ragtime Band'.
9. Ten.

319

1. Who wore a coat of many colours?
2. How many guns of Navarone were there?
3. Which is the world's highest city?
4. In which Dickens novel does Alfred Jingle appear?
5. Which game is similar to the ancient Roman game of paganica?
6. Which film was released in Mexico under the name *Vaselina* and in Italy as *Brilliantino*?
7. Which two *Washington Post* reporters exposed the Watergate cover-up?
8. Who wrote the music to the film *The Odessa File*?
9. Who was the first person to die of radiation poisoning?

690

1. What was the first flush lavatory trade-marked?
2. What was introduced in Britain on 15 February 1971?
3. Which hills end in the Cheddar Gorge?
4. In what field is Professor Henry Higgins an expert?
5. Which ex-Gloucestershire cricketer once scored six centuries in consecutive innings for Rhodesia?
6. Charlie Chaplin ate a boot in the silent film *The Gold Rush*. What was it actually made of?
7. What is the commonest way of cheating at cards?
8. Which brass instrument is considered to be the most difficult to play well?
9. Where do swallows spend the winter?

1061

1. Who wrote two comedies featuring Figaro?
2. How many British sovereigns were there in the nineteenth century?
3. Which town now stands in place of Thebes?
4. What is Captain Hook's pirate ship called?
5. James B. Connolly was the first athlete to win a gold medal at the modern Olympic Games in 1896. For which event?
6. Who was Vera Jane Palmer, with a figure of 40–21–35?
7. Who sculptured 'The Gate of Hell', commissioned as a door?
8. Who wrote the Sinfonia Antarctica?
9. Approximately how many times the weight of an African elephant is a Boeing 747 jumbo jet?

319

1. Joseph.
2. Two.
3. Lhasa in Tibet.
4. *The Pickwick Papers*.
5. Golf.
6. *Grease*.
7. Bob Woodward and Carl Bernstein.
8. Andrew Lloyd Webber.
9. Marie Curie.

690

1. Ajax.
2. Decimal currency.
3. The Mendip Hills.
4. Phonetics.
5. Mike Proctor.
6. Liquorice.
7. Marking them with thumb nails.
8. The French horn.
9. South Africa.

1061

1. Beaumarchais.
2. 4: George III, George IV, William IV, Victoria.
3. Luxor.
4. The *Jolly Roger*.
5. Triple jump (then known as the hop, skip and jump).
6. Jayne Mansfield.
7. Rodin.
8. Ralph Vaughan Williams.
9. Approximately 55 times.

320

1. How much was the family allowance when it was first introduced?
2. The word 'cabal' is an acronym for Charles II's group of ministers of 1667–73. Name two.
3. What was known as the Dark Continent?
4. In Greek mythology, how many eyes did Argus have?
5. Which Rugby League club has the nickname 'the Loiners'?
6. Who plays the transvestite Corporal Klinger in 'MASH'?
7. Who met Stalin and Roosevelt and said of his novels, 'I am a journalist all the time'?
8. Which item of headgear did Procul Harum sing about?
9. Which two gases are the main constituents of coal gas?

691

1. What is meant when a member of the House of Lords talks about 'the Other Place'?
2. For how long, to the nearest 50 years, did the Byzantine Empire last?
3. Name four of the six old counties of Northern Ireland.
4. Which poet was called 'the Ettrick Shepherd'?
5. Which Scot was world side-car champion in 1980?
6. Which of 'The Professionals' started life as a ladies' hairdresser?
7. Who made the first pair of bi-focal specs?
8. Jonathan King had his first hit while still a Cambridge undergraduate. What was it?
9. Some 5,000 satellites orbit the earth. Which is the largest?

1062

1. Who in fact was the Akhund of Swat?
2. In 1958, Life Peers were created by what?
3. Where is Rotten Row?
4. Which clown's memoirs were edited by Charles Dickens?
5. How many gold medals did Ingemar Stenmark win at the 1980 Winter Olympics for skiing?
6. Who was the Galloping Gourmet?
7. In flat green bowls what distance must the jack travel from the mat?
8. Which pop star literally broke through to the 'Big Time' via Esther Rantzen's programme of that name?
9. Which is the heaviest: lead, gold, mercury or platinum?

320

1. 5*s*. (25p) for each child after the first.
2. Clifford, Ashley, Buckingham, Arlington and Lauderdale.
3. Africa.
4. 100.
5. Leeds.
6. Jamie Farr.
7. H. G. Wells.
8. The homburg.
9. Hydrogen and methane.

691

1. The House of Commons.
2. 1,058 years (from the separation of the Roman Empire in 395 to the capture of Constantinople in 1453).
3. Fermanagh, Tyrone, Armagh, Down, Londonderry and Antrim.
4. James Hogg.
5. Jock Taylor.
6. Lewis Collins.
7. Benjamin Franklin.
8. 'Everyone's Gone to the Moon'.
9. The Moon. The others are man-made.

1062

1. The king and high-priest of the north-western provinces of India.
2. The Life Peerage Act.
3. Hyde Park.
4. Joseph Grimaldi's.
5. Two.
6. TV cook Graham Kerr.
7. 25 yards.
8. Sheena Easton.
9. Platinum.

321

1. Which country innovated Father's Day?
2. When did Robert Peel found the Metropolitan Police?
3. Wigtown, Kirkcudbright and Dumfries now come under which new county of Scotland?
4. Who was the 'onlie begetter'?
5. How many swimming gold medals did Sharon Davies win in the 1978 Commonwealth Games?
6. Who starred and sang in the film *The Ugly Duckling*?
7. From 1548, who spent 10 years teaching the art of navigation in England?
8. How many fiddlers had Old King Cole?
9. Where in the body are Betz cells?

692

1. Who lives at No. 11 Downing Street?
2. David Rizzio, an Italian musician, was secretary to who?
3. Flotta, Nigg Bay, Cruden Bay and Dalmeny are all what?
4. Who is the *Standard*'s well-known political cartoonist?
5. Which world champion boxer was nicknamed 'Homicide Hank'?
6. Which TV series launched Arthur Negus as a personality?
7. Which British mountaineer was the only man to survive the first successful attempt on the Matterhorn – his three companions and two of their three guides perishing during the descent?
8. Who wrote that only mad dogs and Englishmen go out in the midday sun?
9. How does the baby kangaroo first get into the mother's pouch?

1063

1. To which country would a car with the letters SF belong?
2. Who was Catherine of Aragon's first husband?
3. James Grant and John Speke discovered the source of which river in 1862?
4. In *Twelfth Night*, what is Feste?
5. Who coxed the Cambridge crew to victory in the 1950 Boat Race?
6. Which actor took over from William Hartnell as Doctor Who?
7. Who said about the Falklands: 'The utmost exertion of right is always invidious; and where claims are not easily determinable, is always dangerous'?
8. What was the title of Lulu's Eurovision Song Contest entry?
9. Who flew in Friendship 7 in 1962?

321

1. The USA.
2. 1829.
3. Dumfries and Galloway.
4. Mr W. H. (of Shakespeare's Sonnets).
5. Two.
6. Danny Kaye.
7. Sebastian Cabot.
8. Three.
9. The brain.

692

1. The Chancellor of the Exchequer.
2. To Mary, Queen of Scots.
3. Terminals for North Sea oil.
4. Jak.
5. Henry Armstrong.
6. 'Going for a Song'.
7. Edward Whymper, in 1865.
8. Noël Coward.
9. The mother licks a wet strip in her fur and the baby crawls up it.

1063

1. Finland.
2. Prince Arthur, Henry VIII's brother who died.
3. The White Nile.
4. A jester.
5. Anthony Armstrong Jones (Lord Snowdon).
6. Patrick Troughton.
7. Dr Johnson, in 1771.
8. 'Boom Bang-A-Bang'.
9. John Glenn.

322

1. Where is 'The Mother of Parliaments'?
2. Which king was born at Monmouth?
3. The six old counties of Northern Ireland have been split up into how many districts?
4. Who wrote: 'Unto the pure all things are pure'?
5. In which sport is the Lancome Trophy one of the main European competitions?
6. Who played Ronnie Barker's cell mate in 'Porridge'?
7. Who flew, by pedal power, the Gossamer Albatross across the Channel?
8. When did Paul Weller's band, Jam, split up?
9. The metal known as columbium in the USA is called what in the UK?

693

1. If all were alive, how many great-great-grandparents could you have at most?
2. Who was the first American to orbit the earth?
3. What position was held by the first man caught in Oslo's new radar speed assessor?
4. Who wrote *Toomai of the Elephants*?
5. Which wicket keeper has played most often for England?
6. Who was Marilyn Monroe's last husband?
7. Whose last words were: 'I want to wash my feet'?
8. Which group had a hit with 'Puff the Magic Dragon'?
9. What aid to farmers did William Murchland invent in 1889?

1064

1. What is the main ingredient of taramasalata?
2. When did Viscount Grey of Fallodon say: 'The lamps are going out all over Europe; we shall not see them lit in our lifetime'?
3. What are the natives of Caledonia nowadays more commonly called?
4. In *Love's Labour's Lost*, what is Holofernes?
5. Who rode Arkle to victory in the 1964 Cheltenham Gold Cup?
6. Anne Kirkbride plays which 'Coronation Street' character?
7. By what name was Phoebe Anne Mozee better known?
8. What colour were Fats Domino's 'Sails in the Sunset'?
9. The name of which Russian spacecraft means 'salute'?

322

1. Westminster.
2. Henry V.
3. Twenty-six.
4. St Paul.
5. Golf.
6. Richard Beckinsale.
7. Brian Allen.
8. 1982.
9. Niobium.

693

1. Sixteen.
2. Colonel John Glenn.
3. Oslo's police chief.
4. Rudyard Kipling.
5. Alan Knott.
6. Arthur Miller.
7. Henri Désiré Landru (the French mass woman murderer).
8. Peter, Paul and Mary.
9. The milking machine.

1064

1. Cod's roe.
2. 1914, on the eve of war.
3. Scots.
4. A schoolmaster.
5. Pat Taafe.
6. Deirdre.
7. Annie Oakley.
8. Red.
9. Salyut.

323

1. Which is the tenth letter of the Greek alphabet?
2. Where did the battleship *Royal Oak* go down in the Second World War?
3. Where is the Jasper National Park?
4. In *Twelfth Night* who was Sebastian's twin?
5. Which two jockeys each rode two Epsom Derby winners in the 1960s?
6. Who played the brummie Monica in BBC radio's 'Educating Archie'?
7. Of where was Colonel William Farquar the first British Resident Governor, in 1819?
8. On which H. G. Wells story was *Half a Sixpence* based?
9. In which country were the first golden hamsters found in 1930?

694

1. If you are misocapnic, what do you abhor?
2. To mark which occasion was a statue of Raffles unveiled on 27 June 1887, in Singapore?
3. Where do Muscovites live?
4. Who wrote *Waverley*?
5. Who did Pat Taafe ride to victory in the 1966 Cheltenham Gold Cup?
6. Who wrote *The Hitch-Hiker's Guide to the Galaxy*?
7. Who was the 'Washington of South America'?
8. Who is 'sweet baby James'?
9. Leman Bank, Indefatigable, Viking and Frigg are all what?

1065

1. What was built as the centrepiece of the British Empire exhibition of 1924?
2. For what percentage of his lifetime was Louis XIV King of France?
3. Where is London's only horse market?
4. Who wrote *An Enemy of the People*?
5. On which British golf course is the renowned 'Postage Stamp' hole?
6. Which gospel did Pasolini film?
7. Who built a model village at New Lanark?
8. Under what alias have Linda and Paul McCartney and their group Wings also performed?
9. Who landed on the moon in Apollo 14?

323

1. Kappa.
2. Scapa Flow.
3. Alberta, Canada.
4. Viola.
5. Lester Piggott and Scobie Breasley.
6. The inimitable Beryl Reid.
7. Singapore.
8. *Kipps.*
9. Syria.

694

1. Tobacco smoke.
2. Queen Victoria's Golden Jubilee.
3. Moscow.
4. Sir Walter Scott.
5. Arkle.
6. Douglas Adams.
7. Simon Bolivar.
8. Singer/songwriter James Taylor.
9. Offshore gas wells in the North Sea.

1065

1. Wembley Stadium.
2. 95 per cent (he reigned for 72 out of his 76 years).
3. Southall.
4. Henrik Ibsen.
5. Troon.
6. The Gospel According to St Matthew.
7. Robert Owen.
8. Suzy and the Red Stripes.
9. Alan Shepard.

324

1. In sailing-ship days which member of the crew acted as 'ship's doctor'?
2. How, in 1517, did Luther publicize his protests against papal indulgences?
3. On which Riviera is Menton?
4. Who is the Scandinavian god of thunder?
5. On which course are golf's World Match Play Championships staged annually?
6. Who is Ray Galton's usual co-writer?
7. Which Egyptian king abdicated in 1952?
8. What are 'choir', 'great', 'swell', 'solo', and 'echo'?
9. How many moons has Saturn?

695

1. About how many acres do the Houses of Parliament in Westminster cover?
2. Which king called the 'Model Parliament' into being in 1295?
3. Which Roman Road connected London and Chichester?
4. In which Shakespeare play does Launcelot Gobbo appear?
5. The use of which cricket fielding position indicates lack of faith in the wicket keeper?
6. In *The Wizard of Oz*, which character was looking for a heart?
7. For what were Holbein the Elder and Younger famous?
8. Who was San Francisco's 'Captain Trips'?
9. An isoneph is a line on a map joining what?

1066

1. Which queen rode in an open carriage at Queen Elizabeth II's coronation – when it was bucketing down?
2. After which war did cigarette smoking become popular?
3. Which is the Diamond state?
4. *Sir Quixote of the Moors* was whose first novel?
5. Where are the Coventry Stakes run?
6. Which rag and bone men had a horse called Hercules?
7. What was 'Bumper Harris's' job on the London underground?
8. Bach's two sets of twenty-four preludes and fugues in all twenty-four keys are known by what name?
9. For blind people there is type apart from braille; what is it?

324

1. The cook.
2. By nailing them to the door of the castle church in Wittenberg.
3. The French Riviera.
4. Thor.
5. Wentworth.
6. Alan Simpson.
7. King Farouk.
8. The manual keyboards of an organ.
9. Ten.

695

1. Eight.
2. Edward I.
3. Stane Street.
4. *The Merchant of Venice.*
5. Long stop.
6. The Tin Man.
7. Portraits.
8. The Grateful Dead's Jerry Garcia.
9. Places having equal average cloud coverage.

1066

1. Queen Salote of Tonga.
2. The Crimean War (1854–6); the Russian habit was first picked up by fashionable officers.
3. Delaware, USA.
4. John Buchan's.
5. Ascot.
6. Steptoe and Son.
7. He was employed to ride up and down the first escalators installed at Earl's Court station, to give the public confidence as he had a wooden leg.
8. *The Well-Tempered Clavier.*
9. Moon type.

325

1. Pinchbeck is often confused with which precious metal?
2. Name Sir Ernest Shackleton's ship, trapped by polar ice in 1915.
3. What comes after Viking, Forties, Cromarty, Forth . . . ?
4. Who were the two sons of Mars and Rhea Silva, a vestal virgin, who were left to die?
5. Which Test Match ground is owned by Prince Charles?
6. Where was Ursula Andress born?
7. What was Lieut. C.D. Lucas, RN, the first to win?
8. At which instrument is Emil Gilels a virtuoso?
9. What did Whitworth do in 1841?

696

1. The American helicopter the 'Chinook' was named after what?
2. Which English city and American president share a name?
3. As a philanthropic experiment to give debtors from English prisons a chance, General Oglethorpe founded what in 1733?
4. Who wrote the words of the 'Jubilee Hymn'?
5. What was the venue of the 1984 Royal International Horse Show?
6. Who won a BAFTA award for her portrayal of 'Edna the Inebriate Woman'?
7. Who did Charles II make First Duke of Albemarle?
8. On which instrument is Rostropovitch a virtuoso?
9. Sandstone found in chalky soil is given what name?

1067

1. 'Order, Order!': from where were these the first words ever broadcast?
2. Which movement held its first camp in Hampstead in 1910?
3. Rank these British isles in descending order of size: Anglesey, Orkney Mainland, Mull, Jura.
4. Who is Ivanhoe's wife?
5. Which former winner of golf's British Open was tried for attempted murder in 1970?
6. Who portrays Reginald Perrin?
7. Name one of Britain's two PMs of 1963.
8. Who composed the opera *The Turn of the Screw*?
9. What is the main cause of the tides?

325

1. Gold.
2. *Endurance.*
3. Tyne.
4. Romulus and Remus.
5. The Oval.
6. Switzerland.
7. The VC.
8. The piano.
9. He standardized British screw threads.

696

1. A wind (in the Rockies).
2. Lincoln.
3. The state of Georgia, USA.
4. Sir John Betjeman.
5. The National Exhibition Centre, Birmingham (for the first time).
6. Patricia Hayes.
7. George Monck.
8. The cello.
9. Sarsen.

1067

1. The House of Commons.
2. The Girl Guides.
3. Mull, Anglesey, Orkney Mainland, Jura.
4. Rowena.
5. Bobby Locke.
6. Leonard Rossiter.
7. Harold Macmillan; Sir Alec Douglas-Home.
8. Benjamin Britten.
9. The moon.

326

1. To which dog was a statue erected in Edinburgh?
2. Who did Queen Catherine marry, after Henry V died?
3. Which island was awarded the George Cross?
4. Who wrote *The Midwich Cuckoos*?
5. Who won Britain's first ever gold medal for fencing at the 1956 Olympics?
6. Which comedian was originally a maths and music teacher?
7. Which American revolutionary tested the electrical charge of a thunderstorm?
8. In which song do the Beatles 'take a sad song and make it better'?
9. What is the more common name for the 'Lent Lily'?

697

1. What colour is a Catholic cardinal's skull cap?
2. Who was the 'Warming Pan Baby'?
3. Which republic was formerly French Sudan?
4. Who wrote the play *The Passing of the Third Floor Back*?
5. What is the minimum distance for an international bobsled run?
6. Who was the subject of the biopic *Star!*?
7. What does Ken Livingstone keep as pets?
8. Where do Prince Buster, Dave and Ansil Collins, and Desmond Dekker come from?
9. If the fastest man was a wind, what would he be classed as (on the Beaufort scale)?

1068

1. White Burgundy wine must be made from only which type of grape?
2. Which French king was known as 'the Simple'?
3. Where is the Ligurian Sea?
4. What is the sequel to the poem that starts: 'Of Man's First Disobedience, and the Fruit/Of that Forbidd'n Tree, . . .'?
5. Which British girl won the women's modern pentathlon world title in 1978?
6. Which husband and wife team star in 'A Fine Romance'?
7. Which US president completed the Louisiana purchase of 1803?
8. Which contralto made her Glyndebourne début in Benjamin Britten's *The Rape of Lucretia*?
9. The name of which Russian spacecraft means 'union'?

326

1. Greyfriars Bobby.
2. Owen Tudor.
3. Malta.
4. John Wyndham.
5. Gillian Sheen.
6. Tom O'Connor.
7. Benjamin Franklin.
8. 'Hey Jude'.
9. The daffodil.

697

1. Red.
2. The Old Pretender (son of James II who, it was claimed by the Whigs, was swapped for the Queen's still-born baby by the ruse of a warming pan).
3. Mali.
4. Jerome K. Jerome.
5. 1,500 metres.
6. Gertrude Lawrence.
7. Salamanders.
8. Jamaica.
9. A strong breeze.

1068

1. Chardonnay.
2. Charles III.
3. Between Corsica and the Italian Riviera.
4. Milton's *Paradise Regained.*
5. Wendy Norman.
6. Michael Williams and Judi Dench.
7. Thomas Jefferson.
8. Kathleen Ferrier.
9. Soyuz.

327

1. Anosmia is the loss of which sense?
2. With whom did the USA go to war in 1898?
3. In the creation of the new counties, Rutland was lost to which county?
4. Who is father to Goneril, Regan and Cordelia?
5. Who won the men's singles in the first World Badminton Championships (1977)?
6. Who plays Mavis in 'Coronation Street'?
7. Who was born first: P. B. Shelley, Jane Austen, John Constable or Gioacchino Rossini?
8. What would you be if you were a coryphée?
9. Which country's flag was first on the moon?

698

1. Which famous London store has as its motto 'Omnia Omnis Ubique'?
2. What was the occupation of William the Conqueror's father?
3. If you were climbing with Sherpas, in which country would you probably be?
4. Whose first detective novel was *A Man Lay Dead*?
5. Who won the Stella Artois tennis singles in 1979, 1980 and 1981?
6. Which drink does Leonard Rossiter regularly pour over Joan Collins?
7. Who received the Nobel Prize for Literature in 1925?
8. How many pieces made up Mendelssohn's *Songs Without Words*?
9. Which chemical element has a name containing just three letters?

1069

1. What did the name 'Avon' originally mean?
2. Who died saying: 'Crito, I owe a cock to Asclepius'?
3. The ferry from Holyhead goes where?
4. Which Scots poet wrote: 'London, thou art the flower of cities all!'?
5. What does the Puissance event test in showjumping?
6. Which former Goodie is a keen birdwatcher?
7. Which synthetic fibre did J. R. Whinfield discover?
8. On which TV programme was singer Mary Hopkin 'discovered'?
9. Which inflammable gas is produced by the action of water on calcium carbide?

327

1. Smell.
2. Spain (over Cuba).
3. Leicestershire.
4. King Lear.
5. Flemming Delfs of Denmark.
6. Thelma Barlow.
7. Jane Austen (1775).
8. A ballet dancer.
9. The Soviet Union's – miniature flags were dropped there from Luna 2 in 1959, 10 years before the first landing, when the USA flag was erected.

698

1. Harrods.
2. He was a tanner.
3. Nepal.
4. Ngaio Marsh.
5. John McEnroe.
6. Cinzano.
7. George Bernard Shaw.
8. Forty-eight.
9. Tin.

1069

1. Stream or river.
2. Socrates.
3. Dún Laoghaire, Ireland.
4. William Dunbar.
5. The horse's ability to jump heights.
6. Bill Oddie.
7. Terylene.
8. 'Opportunity Knocks'.
9. Acetylene.

328

1. What ceased on 12 June 1921?
2. What were the Roman equivalent of the Greek satyrs?
3. The flooding of the Nile before the Aswan Dam was built used to be due to seasonal rainfall in which lake?
4. Which actor's autobiography was called *Happy Go Lucky*?
5. Which place, now an airport, once staged the Grand National?
6. Which film begins 'Last night I dreamt I went to Manderley again . . .'?
7. Who was called the Apostle of the Indies?
8. What do campanologists do?
9. Which method of healing involves needles being inserted into the body?

699

1. What does the word *Panzer* mean?
2. At which abbey did the 'Hell Fire Club' mainly meet?
3. Which city in England must the sovereign ask permission to enter?
4. In which of Dickens's novels do Dick Swiveller and Mr Quilp appear?
5. Where is the Rally of a Thousand Lakes held?
6. Which former prime minister presided over two editions of the short-lived 'Friday Night . . . Saturday Morning'?
7. What did Sir Henry Landseer specialize in painting?
8. Which group sang about 'Baggy Trousers'?
9. What is the heaviest known substance?

1070

1. What was a 'bawbee'?
2. The King of Thailand presented Singapore with a bronze statue of which animal to mark his visit in 1871?
3. Which islands are separated by the Windward Passage?
4. Who wrote *One Day in the Life of Ivan Denisovich*?
5. Who owned Dunfermline, the 1977 St Leger winner?
6. Who portrayed the rugby-playing miner in *This Sporting Life*?
7. Under what pseudonym does David John Moore Cornwell write spy thrillers?
8. Who composed the music of the 'Jubilee Hymn'?
9. Alligator-type animals are known in Africa and America. Where else?

328

1. Sunday postal deliveries.
2. Fauns.
3. Lake Tana.
4. Kenneth More's.
5. Gatwick.
6. *Rebecca.*
7. St Francis Xavier.
8. Ring bells.
9. Acupuncture.

699

1. Armour.
2. Medmenham.
3. The City of London.
4. *The Old Curiosity Shop.*
5. Finland.
6. Harold Wilson.
7. Animals.
8. Madness.
9. Osmium.

1070

1. A pre-decimal ½d.
2. An elephant.
3. Cuba and Haiti.
4. Alexander Solzhenitsyn.
5. The Queen.
6. Richard Harris.
7. John Le Carré.
8. Malcolm Williamson.
9. China and India.

329

1. Why, on certain Thursdays, might you think that you can catch a train from Polling anywhere in the country?
2. Which movement held its first camp on Brownsea Island in 1908?
3. Which is France's longest river?
4. Who wrote the novel *Rob Roy*?
5. Where did the Olympic Games take place in 1912?
6. Name the 'Punch and Judy' dog.
7. Whose famous war horse was named Traveller?
8. Who composed *Let's Make an Opera*?
9. A Tamworth is a type of what?

700

1. What was said in legend to be the result of a tree bearing barnacles as fruit which then dropped into the sea?
2. Name two leading clerics of the Oxford Movement.
3. In which county are the Langdale Pikes?
4. In Greek mythology who slew the monstrous Argus?
5. Why were the first eighty-eight drivers of the 1981 Safari Rally booked for speeding?
6. Who plays the title role in 'Bergerac'?
7. What are nicknamed 'Devil's picture books'?
8. What did the jolly swag-man camp by?
9. Which marsupial is native to America?

1071

1. How many clangs on the Lutine bell mean good news?
2. What secret organization did Hasan-i-Sabah found in 1090, members of which he rewarded with hashish?
3. What was Gwent, prior to the new county re-organization?
4. Edward Lear, perhaps surprisingly, wrote out his limericks in how many lines?
5. Which racecourse is referred to as Knavesmire?
6. What was the first of Crosby and Hope's 'Road' movies?
7. By what name is Marie Gresholtz better known?
8. Who chaired 'Juke Box Jury'?
9. Which flowers does the Fleur-de-Lys depict?

329

1. Because British elections are always held on Thursdays and the legend Polling Station springs up everywhere.
2. The Boy Scouts.
3. The Loire.
4. Sir Walter Scott.
5. Stockholm.
6. Toby.
7. General Robert E. Lee's.
8. Benjamin Britten.
9. Pig.

700

1. The barnacle goose.
2. John Keble, J. H. Newman, R. H. Froude, E. B. Pusey or Isaac Williams.
3. Cumbria.
4. Hermes.
5. Because the organizers forgot to inform the police that it was on!
6. John Nettles.
7. Playing cards.
8. A billabong.
9. The opossum.

1071

1. Two.
2. The Assassins.
3. Monmouthshire.
4. Three lines.
5. York.
6. *Road to Singapore*.
7. Madame Tussaud.
8. David Jacobs.
9. Three lilies (but accept one iris!).

330

1. In which month is the Munich beer festival held?
2. What does the prefix 'geo-' mean?
3. Going from west to east around Africa, place the following coasts in order: Slave Coast, Ivory Coast, Gold Coast, Grain Coast.
4. How was *Nicholas Nickleby* first published?
5. Which Austrian first won the World Racing Drivers Championship?
6. Peter Yates directed *Bullitt* – but name his first feature film.
7. Where did Byron die?
8. Where do Musical Youth come from?
9. Which chemical element has the symbol Zn?

701

1. What was the filling of the very first sandwich made by the Fourth Earl of Sandwich?
2. Sir Joseph Banks discovered it in 1772 and gave it the name of a hero who turned out to be a fake. What was it?
3. In Africa, what is an *erg*?
4. In *The Winter's Tale* who is Perdita's father?
5. Who won the 1984 Stella Artois tennis singles championships?
6. Who invented the Diddymen?
7. Who became leader of the Labour Party in 1935?
8. Which composer introduced the dodecaphonic scale?
9. What metal has the symbol Fe?

1072

1. Which animal represents the US Republican Party?
2. Where did King John reputedly lose his treasure and baggage?
3. Machapuchare, a peak in the Annapurna Massif, means what?
4. For whom is the *Adi Granth* a holy book?
5. Brother and sister Andreas and Hanni Wenzel both won World Cup titles in 1980. In which sport?
6. Who left Luton airport to try her hand at acting?
7. What were the names of the Rev. Patrick Brontë's children?
8. Which unlikely pair had an unexpected hit with a cover version of 'You're the One That I Want'?
9. Entomology is the study of what?

330

1. October.
2. Earth.
3. Grain Coast; Ivory Coast; Gold Coast; Slave Coast. (The coasts of modern-day: Liberia; Ivory Coast; Ghana; and Togo, Benin and western Nigeria.)
4. As a serial.
5. Jochen Rindt.
6. Cliff Richard's *Summer Holiday*.
7. Missolonghi, in Greece.
8. Birmingham.
9. Zinc.

701

1. Roast beef.
2. Fingal's cave.
3. A desert region of shifting sand.
4. Leontes.
5. John McEnroe.
6. Ken Dodd.
7. Clement Attlee.
8. Arnold Schönberg.
9. Iron.

1072

1. The elephant.
2. In the Wash.
3. Fishtail.
4. The Sikhs.
5. Skiing.
6. Lorraine Chase.
7. Charlotte, Emily, Anne and Branwell.
8. Arthur Mullard and Hylda Baker.
9. Insects.

331

1. What first did Jacques Garnerin achieve in 1797?
2. What did the navy introduce in 1795 to combat scurvy?
3. Place these ports in order going from east to west: Dunkerque, Boulogne, Calais, Le Touquet, Le Havre, Dieppe.
4. In *Hamlet*, how did Ophelia die?
5. Which country won the first four Olympic ice hockey gold medals?
6. Who won an Oscar for his part in the film *Mister Roberts*?
7. Who was the first western explorer and navigator to reach India by sea from Europe?
8. Who was Birmingham University's most famous professor of music?
9. Which plant did Mendel use in working out the laws of heredity?

702

1. Which Canadian political scientist became known for his 'swing-o-meter' on election-night broadcasts?
2. What nationality were the kamikaze pilots of the Second World War?
3. The ferry from Fishguard goes where?
4. Who owned the hammer Mjolnir?
5. Where did softball originate?
6. Which Shakespeare character did James Cagney once play in a film?
7. Cornelius Vermuyden was employed by the Earl of Bedford in the seventeenth century to do what?
8. How close to destruction did Barry McGuire get?
9. Achievement, Streamline and Enorma are types of what?

1073

1. What does the Hindu word *puttees* mean?
2. What did Henry IV think Paris was worth?
3. In which country did Alexander Dubcek try to bring about reforms?
4. Of what was Freya the Scandinavian goddess?
5. Who won the 3,000-metre steeplechase gold medal at the Mexico Olympics, running in his first steeplechase?
6. Who is *supposed* to have said, 'Let's bring it up to date with some snappy nineteenth-century dialogue'?
7. Who exposed conditions in Soviet prison camps and was exiled in 1974?
8. Clive Dunn has had only one hit. What was it?
9. How many species of tits are native to Great Britain?

331

1. He made the first parachute jump from the air.
2. Rations of limejuice.
3. Dunkerque, Calais, Boulogne, Le Touquet, Dieppe, Le Havre.
4. She drowned.
5. Canada.
6. Jack Lemmon.
7. Vasco da Gama.
8. Sir Edward Elgar.
9. The garden pea.

702

1. Robert McKenzie.
2. Japanese.
3. To Rosslare, Ireland.
4. Thor.
5. The USA.
6. Bottom.
7. Drain the Fens.
8. The eve . . .
9. Runner bean.

1073

1. Bandages.
2. A mass.
3. Czechoslovakia.
4. Love.
5. Amos Biwott (Kenya).
6. Sam Goldwyn.
7. Alexander Solzhenitsyn.
8. 'Grandad'.
9. Eight.

332

1. What was a blunderbuss?
2. The pirate Henry Morgan was appointed acting governor of which island in 1680?
3. What was Istanbul called before it was Constantinople?
4. In the hymn, which line precedes 'All things wise and wonderful'?
5. What term is used for nil in tennis?
6. What was Noelle Gordon's role in 'Crossroads'?
7. What physical handicap did the painter Toulouse-Lautrec have?
8. In Walt Disney's *Music Land*, what lies between the Isle of Jazz and the Land of Symphony?
9. What is the commonest cause of accidents to jet planes?

703

1. In Britain, how many boys are born to each 100 girls?
2. In which century were spectacles invented?
3. Between which two countries does the Solway Firth run?
4. Across which stretch of water did Leander swim nightly to court Hero?
5. Who is the only player to have played in three soccer World Cup Championship teams?
6. Which famous film director has made a cameo appearance in over half of his films?
7. With which game is the Blackwood Convention associated?
8. Which instrument usually gives an orchestra its note for tuning-up?
9. What is the fertilizing powder produced by plants called?

1074

1. Which public school did Winston Churchill attend?
2. Who was Britain's prime minister in 1965?
3. Name the Post Office satellite tracking station in Cornwall.
4. Who wrote the novel *The Arrow of Gold*?
5. For how many seconds must a cowboy stay on a bucking bronco?
6. Of where is Professor Kokintz the leading scientist?
7. Who was the village of Grasmere's most famous poet?
8. For what type of composition is Sigmund Romberg best known?
9. How many hulls has a catamaran?

332

1. A type of gun.
2. Jamaica.
3. Byzantium.
4. 'All creatures great and small'.
5. Love.
6. Meg Mortimer.
7. Under-developed legs.
8. The Sea of Discord.
9. Birds being sucked into the jets.

703

1. 106.
2. The thirteenth century.
3. England and Scotland.
4. The Hellespont.
5. Pelé of Brazil in 1958, 1962 and 1970.
6. Alfred Hitchcock.
7. Contract bridge.
8. The oboe.
9. Pollen.

1074

1. Harrow.
2. Harold Wilson.
3. Goonhilly.
4. Joseph Conrad.
5. Eight.
6. Grand Fenwick in the film *The Mouse on the Moon* (1963).
7. William Wordsworth.
8. Operettas.
9. Two.

333

1. What is the most frequent single cause of business errors?
2. Which Australian school did Prince Charles attend in 1966 for 7 months?
3. From which port did the *Mayflower* leave for America?
4. Which magic city is located in 'the Valley of the Blue Moon'?
5. For which county did W. G. Grace play cricket?
6. John Adams, discovered on Pitcairn Island in 1812, was the only survivor from which group of mutineers?
7. Who was called 'the Hero of Trafalgar'?
8. Who wrote 'My Old Kentucky Home'?
9. Of which insect are there some 3,700 different species in England alone?

704

1. What is the total of the degrees of the three angles of a triangle?
2. Who ordered the execution of John the Baptist?
3. In which European city is the Arch of Titus?
4. Where was John Cleland when he wrote his book *Fanny Hill*?
5. In 1978 the US Open Tennis Championships moved from Forest Hills to where?
6. Who produces the voice of Miss Piggy in 'The Muppet Show'?
7. What hand in poker is known as 'the dead man's hand'?
8. Who was shot and killed in front of Dakota, his New York home, on 8 December 1980?
9. How many feet are there in a fathom?

1075

1. Which is the largest note in general circulation in the USA?
2. Who circumnavigated the globe between 1577 and 1580 in the *Golden Hind*?
3. Which American state is nicknamed 'the Sunshine state'?
4. Who wrote 'The Pit and the Pendulum'?
5. What sport did Jim Clark (killed in 1968) compete in?
6. Who played Philip Marlowe in the first film of *The Big Sleep*?
7. With which game is Ceri Morgan associated?
8. What is Louis Armstrong's nickname 'Satchmo' short for?
9. Sleet is a mixture of what?

333

1. Illegible handwriting.
2. Timbertop, or Geelong School.
3. Plymouth.
4. Shangri-La in James Hilton's *Lost Horizon.*
5. Gloucestershire.
6. Those from HMS *Bounty.*
7. Admiral Horatio Nelson.
8. Stephen Foster.
9. Beetles.

704

1. 180.
2. King Herod.
3. Rome.
4. Newgate Prison.
5. Flushing Meadows.
6. Frank Oz.
7. A pair of aces with a pair of eights.
8. John Lennon.
9. Six.

1075

1. The $100 note.
2. Sir Francis Drake.
3. Florida.
4. Edgar Allan Poe.
5. Motor racing.
6. Humphrey Bogart.
7. Darts.
8. 'Satchel mouth'.
9. Snow and rain.

334

1. What do the letters RSVP stand for?
2. Which newspaper sent Henry Morton Stanley to find Dr David Livingstone in Africa in 1871?
3. Between which two cities did the *Flying Scotsman* run?
4. Who was the wife of Odysseus?
5. Which game do Lions, Wallabies and Springboks play?
6. Who said, 'Here's looking at you, kid'?
7. By what name is Lesley Hornby better known?
8. Who had a hit in 1970 with 'Bridge over Troubled Water'?
9. By what name is magnesium sulphate better known?

705

1. Which ship did Christopher Jones captain?
2. Whose last words reputedly were, 'My neck is very slender'?
3. What US purchase was known as 'Sewald's Folly'?
4. In Dickens's *A Christmas Carol*, what is Scrooge's first name?
5. Which female swimmer won the 100-metre freestyle at three consecutive Olympics?
6. What was Walt Disney's first original cartoon character?
7. Which brothers lost a fortune trying to control the silver market in 1980?
8. Name the first group founded in 1955 by John Lennon and Paul McCartney.
9. How many pints are in a quart?

1076

1. Which two figures are generally depicted holding tridents?
2. Between where and where did Watling Street run?
3. Which famous colonel is buried in the rock of Lookout Mountains, Colorado?
4. Which book did Robert Louis Stevenson write while on his honeymoon?
5. How long between rounds in boxing?
6. For how much was Schnozzle Durante's nose insured?
7. In which city is the Walker Art Gallery?
8. Who had a big hit with 'See ya later, Alligator'?
9. Although Alexander Fleming discovered penicillin in 1928, it was not introduced into medicine until when?

334

1. *Répondez s'il vous plaît*: please reply.
2. The *New York Herald*.
3. London and Edinburgh.
4. Penelope.
5. Rugby football.
6. Humphrey Bogart.
7. Twiggy.
8. Simon and Garfunkel.
9. Epsom salts.

705

1. The *Mayflower*.
2. Anne Boleyn's (before losing her head).
3. The purchase of Alaska from Russia in 1867, for $7,200,000.
4. Ebenezer.
5. Dawn Fraser of Australia in 1956, 1960 and 1964.
6. Oswald the Rabbit.
7. Bunker and Nelson Hunt.
8. The Quarrymen.
9. Two.

1076

1. Britannia and Neptune.
2. Dover and Chester.
3. Buffalo Bill (Colonel William Cody).
4. *Travels with a Donkey*.
5. 1 minute.
6. £70,000.
7. Liverpool.
8. Bill Haley and the Comets.
9. 1940.

335

1. Name the ship in which Sir Francis Drake sailed round the world.
2. Which American revolutionary hero's last words were, 'I only regret that I have but one life to lose for my country'?
3. What is Count Dracula's home country?
4. Who wrote *Beau Geste*?
5. How many rounds are there in an Olympic boxing match?
6. Where does Yogi Bear live?
7. What is Professor Rubik's first name?
8. Who was the youngest Beatle?
9. What is the colour of yak's milk?

706

1. With what did the sparrow kill Cock Robin?
2. What was the first stage of the Bolshevik uprising in Russia called?
3. Where is Britain's smallest prison?
4. Name the old fisherman in Hemingway's *The Old Man and the Sea.*
5. Which horse won both the Oaks and the St Leger in 1977?
6. Name Mr Spock's home planet.
7. Which sculptor created 'The Kiss'?
8. Who composed the opera *La Clemenza di Tito*?
9. Travelling at the speed of light, about how long would it take you to reach the farthest star in our own galaxy?

1077

1. In about 1750, brick dust mixed with olive oil was a popular remedy. What was it supposed to cure?
2. What did St Bernard do to the swarm of flies that interrupted his preaching?
3. By what name is Mesopotamia now known?
4. With what did Saladin cure Richard the Lionheart's illness?
5. What is the clump of grass dislodged by golfers called?
6. What nickname did Bing Crosby confer on Bob Hope?
7. Who invented the Manhattan cocktail?
8. Who was the first drummer to perform in Elvis Presley's band?
9. What is the laughing jackass also known as?

335

1. The *Golden Hind*.
2. Nathan Hale.
3. Transylvania.
4. P.C. Wren.
5. Three.
6. Jellystone National Park.
7. Erno.
8. George Harrison.
9. Pink.

706

1. His bow and arrow.
2. The October Revolution.
3. On the Isle of Sark.
4. Santiago.
5. Dunfermline.
6. Vulcan.
7. Rodin.
8. Mozart.
9. About 75,000 years.

1077

1. Gout.
2. He excommunicated them.
3. Iraq.
4. The Talisman.
5. A divot.
6. 'Ski Nose'.
7. Lady Randolph Churchill (Winston Churchill's mother).
8. D.J. Fontana.
9. The kookaburra.

336

1. On which date does the Trooping the Colour ceremony take place?
2. For which French king was the Palace of Versailles built?
3. Which country produces the most coffee?
4. Who wrote the short story, 'The Secret Life of Walter Mitty'?
5. Which pair of Argentinian World Cup footballers were bought by Spurs?
6. What does Popeye eat for strength?
7. By what name was author Eric Blair better known?
8. Who composed *A Ceremony of Carols*?
9. In a primary rainbow, which colour is on the inside of the curve?

707

1. To whose band did Will Scarlet belong?
2. What first did George Samuelson and Frank Harpo achieve in 1896?
3. What happened to Niagara Falls during the winter of 1925?
4. Who was the daughter of the chief of the Piccaninnies rescued by Peter Pan?
5. What is the upper weight limit of a professional senior middleweight boxer?
6. Name Jonathan and Jennifer Hart's dog.
7. Who is Snoopy's brother?
8. 'Playing with each note detached' – what is the musical term?
9. Which animal stands on its feet for the longest period?

1078

1. Which public school did Prince Philip, Duke of Edinburgh, attend?
2. What was the *Olympic*'s sister ship?
3. In which country did the word 'plonk' (meaning wine) originate?
4. Who is Tiny Tim's father?
5. Who won the 1984 London Marathon?
6. In how many different categories are Oscars awarded?
7. Captain James Cook was born in Yorkshire. Where did he die?
8. What is the name of the theme song of 'MASH'?
9. What was Edwin H. Land's snappy invention in 1947?

336

1. 10 June.
2. Louis XIV.
3. Brazil.
4. James Thurber.
5. Ardiles and Villa.
6. Spinach.
7. George Orwell.
8. Benjamin Britten.
9. Violet.

707

1. Robin Hood's.
2. They were the first men to row across the Atlantic. It took them 56 days.
3. It froze completely.
4. Tiger Lily.
5. 160 lb.
6. Freeway.
7. Spike.
8. Staccato.
9. The African elephant, which sleeps standing up and often lives for more than 50 years.

1078

1. Gordonstoun.
2. The *Titanic*.
3. Australia.
4. Bob Cratchit.
5. Charlie Spedding.
6. Twenty-three.
7. Hawaii.
8. 'Suicide Is Painless'.
9. The polaroid camera.

337

1. It was prophesied that Chalcus the Greek would die on a certain day. He did. Of what?
2. Which Italian went to China and became a diplomat for Kublai Khan?
3. By what name is Peiping now known?
4. Who is Aladdin's father?
5. What do the initials W.G. stand for in W. G. Grace?
6. Who played King George III in the 1954 film *Beau Brummell*?
7. Which Liberal MP wrote light verse and biographies of Robespierre and Cromwell?
8. Who composed the opera *Mozart and Salieri*?
9. Which flower did Tennyson call 'February fair-maid'?

708

1. Alfred Packer was the only man in the USA to be convicted of one particular crime. Which crime?
2. Who lost her head on 8 February 1587?
3. Which American state is the Badger state?
4. What is Captain Nemo's submarine called?
5. What is the Cresta Run?
6. What is the other identity of Dr Robert Bruce Banner?
7. Who named Greenland?
8. Who sang about Samantha?
9. Where did the leek originate?

1079

1. With which colour is Robin Hood associated?
2. In which century did Attila the Hun operate?
3. Which is the oldest unchanged national flag in existence?
4. What is Beatrix Potter's Puddleduck's first name?
5. Why was Fred Lorz disqualified after ostensibly winning the 1904 Olympic marathon?
6. Name Liz Fraser's basset hound, often seen with her on TV.
7. Which colours 'advance' a picture towards a viewer?
8. How many form an octet?
9. Where in the body is the retina?

337

1. Laughing too heartily because he wasn't dead.
2. Marco Polo.
3. Peking.
4. Mustafa the tailor.
5. William Gilbert.
6. Robert Morley.
7. Hilaire Belloc.
8. Rimsky-Korsakov.
9. The snowdrop.

708

1. Cannibalism.
2. Mary, Queen of Scots.
3. Wisconsin.
4. *Nautilus*.
5. A toboggan track.
6. The Incredible Hulk.
7. Eric the Red, the Norwegian explorer.
8. Bing Crosby in *High Society*.
9. Asia.

1079

1. Lincoln green.
2. The fifth century.
3. Denmark's, which dates back to the thirteenth century.
4. Jemima.
5. He hitched a lift for part of the way in a car!
6. Banjo.
7. Reds and oranges.
8. Eight.
9. The eye.

338

1. Which bird is the symbol of peace?
2. Who made George Washington's false teeth?
3. By what name is Persia now known?
4. Who wrote *Gulliver's Travels*?
5. Which golf course was used for the British Open for the first time in 1977?
6. What did TV's first cookery demonstration teach viewers to make?
7. Where in London is the National Gallery?
8. What was the hymn played by the band on the *Titanic* as it sank?
9. Which disease is spread by mosquitoes?

709

1. If you were an ancient apothecary, how many pennyweights would there be to a lb weight?
2. In which century was the spoked wheel thought to have been introduced?
3. By what name is the Belgian Congo now known?
4. Name the island where Captain Flint buried his treasure, which Ben Gunn dug up.
5. Where did squash originate?
6. Who is the assistant of Arkwright, the grocer?
7. What is Denis Healey's middle name?
8. Who composed a symphony nicknamed 'the Hen'?
9. In the solar system there are two Mount Olympuses. Where are they?

1080

1. What was J. F. Glidden's ripping invention of 1874?
2. Which war was called 'the War to End All Wars'?
3. In China, what colour does a bride wear at her wedding?
4. Who fought at the Reichenback Falls?
5. Where was the first World Surfing Championship held?
6. Who played the Mahdi in the 1966 film *Khartoum*?
7. Who did Albert Alexandre Louis Pierre Grimaldi marry on 19 April 1956?
8. In the song, how many trombones were there?
9. Which breed of dog was Best in Show at Crufts in 1984?

338

1. The dove.
2. Paul Revere.
3. Iran.
4. Jonathan Swift.
5. Turnberry.
6. An omelette.
7. Trafalgar Square.
8. 'Nearer My God to Thee'.
9. Malaria.

709

1. 240.
2. 1900 BC.
3. Zaïre.
4. Skeleton Island, just south of Treasure Island.
5. Harrow School.
6. Granville.
7. Winston.
8. Joseph Haydn.
9. Greece and Mars.

1080

1. Barbed wire.
2. The First World War.
3. Red.
4. Sherlock Holmes and Professor Moriarty.
5. Sydney, Australia, in 1964.
6. Laurence Olivier.
7. Grace Kelly (Mr Grimaldi is Prince Rainier III).
8. Seventy-six.
9. Lhasa apso.

339

1. What is Monday's child?
2. During the Stone Age, from what kind of stone were tools and weapons usually made?
3. On which canal is the town of Colon situated?
4. In which Richard Sheridan comedy did Mrs Malaprop feature?
5. Who is the patron saint of skaters?
6. Whom is Miss Piggy in love with?
7. Who was attacked and murdered in Africa on 4 January 1980?
8. How old was 'the Naughty Lady of Shady Lane'?
9. What is a group of peacocks called?

710

1. What is a caret?
2. Who was the thirty-fifth president of the USA?
3. From which language did the word 'tycoon' come?
4. In which Dickens novel does the Artful Dodger appear?
5. Who was the first woman to win four consecutive US Open Tennis Championships?
6. Who is Donald Duck's girlfriend?
7. Which artist painted a poster which advertised the can-can and had the name Jane Avril on it?
8. In which of Puccini's operas does Scarpia appear?
9. On whom was the first successful heart transplant performed by Dr Christian Barnard?

1081

1. Which is the lowest title handed down from father to son?
2. What type of plane was the Second World War Hurricane?
3. On which river is Runnymede situated?
4. Who was Little Black Sambo's father?
5. Who won the World Grand Prix Racing Championship in 1978?
6. Who plays Barney Miller?
7. Which Venetian painter was responsible for the work 'The Assumption of the Virgin'?
8. This song featured in *The Birth of the Blues* and *The Jolson Story*; words by Edward Madden, music by Gus Edwards. Name the song.
9. What type of rock forms the white cliffs of Dover?

339

1. Fair of face.
2. Flint.
3. The Panama Canal.
4. *The Rivals.*
5. St Lidwina.
6. Kermit the Frog.
7. Joy Adamson.
8. 9 days.
9. A muster.

710

1. A printer's insertion mark.
2. John F. Kennedy.
3. Chinese (but accept Japanese).
4. *Oliver Twist.*
5. Chris Evert (Lloyd).
6. Daisy Duck.
7. Toulouse-Lautrec.
8. *Tosca.*
9. Louis Washkansky, who lived for 18 days.

1081

1. Baronet.
2. A fighter.
3. The Thames.
4. Black Jumbo.
5. Mario Andretti.
6. Hal Linden.
7. Titian.
8. 'By the Light of the Silvery Moon'.
9. Chalk.

340

1. Bohea is a type of what?
2. Who were the first people to use antibiotics to cure diseases?
3. With which place is 'the Stone of Destiny' associated?
4. Who wrote the comedy *Worm's Eye View*?
5. Which German once held the world heavyweight boxing title?
6. Name the secretary of M (James Bond's boss).
7. Who was *Time* magazine's 'Man of the Year' for 1938?
8. Which singer wrote the book *Twixt Twelve and Twenty* in 1958?
9. What is the most poisonous fish in the world?

711

1. Which traffic light colour precedes amber alone?
2. In which year was London's first airport, at Hounslow, opened?
3. Which textile is mainly associated with Lancashire?
4. Which Harriet Beecher Stowe novel is subtitled 'Life Among the Lowly'?
5. Who preceded Sonny Liston as world heavyweight boxing champion?
6. Who starred in *Private Benjamin*?
7. At which part of the body were Siamese twins, Chang and Eng Bunker, joined?
8. Which American city is called Music City?
9. Which is the largest British land carnivore?

1082

1. Since the invention of Coca-Cola, how many men have ever known the formula?
2. When was V E Day?
3. Which English city's hallmark is a Tudor rose?
4. Who is Snoopy's sister?
5. At which ground was the first ever Test Match in England played?
6. What was John Wayne's nickname?
7. What is Cecil B. DeMille's middle name?
8. How old was Mozart when he composed his first minuet?
9. Which famous quintuplets did Dr Alan Roy Dafoe deliver?

340

1. Tea.
2. The Ancient Egyptians, who used mouldy bread.
3. Scone (the Stone of Scone).
4. R. F. Delderfield.
5. Max Schmelling.
6. Miss Moneypenny.
7. Adolf Hitler.
8. Pat Boone.
9. The stonefish.

711

1. Green.
2. 1919.
3. Cotton.
4. *Uncle Tom's Cabin*.
5. Floyd Patterson.
6. Goldie Hawn.
7. The chest.
8. Nashville, Tennessee.
9. The badger.

1082

1. Seven (no women).
2. 8 May 1945.
3. Sheffield.
4. Belle.
5. The Oval.
6. Duke.
7. Blount.
8. Five.
9. The Dionne quintuplets.

341

1. 'Mardi' is French for which day of the week?
2. Who succeeded Winston Churchill as Prime Minister in 1955?
3. Of which country is Moravia a province?
4. Who wrote the series of books entitled *Strangers and Brothers*?
5. How many times did Joe Louis successfully defend his world heavyweight title?
6. Who does Perry Mason's private investigating?
7. By what name was the painter Kyriakos Theotokopoulos better known?
8. Which of Schubert's symphonies is known as 'the Tragic'?
9. Gutta-percha, once used for insulating submarine telegraph cables, is a form of which naturally occurring substance?

712

1. By what name is 1600 Pennsylvania Avenue, Washington, DC, better known?
2. To which Indian tribe did Chief Crazy Horse belong?
3. In which bay is Alcatraz sited?
4. How many were there in 'The Charge of the Light Brigade'?
5. Which country's badminton championship is universally regarded as the sport's world championship?
6. Who did John Travolta play in the film *Saturday Night Fever*?
7. Henri Rousseau was an exponent of what type of art?
8. How did Madame Butterfly die?
9. How many sides has a snow crystal?

1083

1. What is the minimum school-leaving age in this country?
2. In 1603 James VI of Scotland also became James I of England. Who was his mother?
3. Where in Massachusetts did the Pilgrim Fathers land?
4. Which dwarf could spin straw into gold?
5. Which golfer is nicknamed 'the Walrus'?
6. Who plays B.J. in 'MASH'?
7. Who, in 1964, was the youngest man to win the Nobel Peace Prize?
8. Who wrote the Savoy Operas?
9. What are Portland vases made of?

341

1. Tuesday.
2. Anthony Eden.
3. Czechoslovakia.
4. C.P. (Lord) Snow.
5. Twenty-five – scoring twenty knockouts.
6. Paul Drake.
7. El Greco.
8. The Fourth.
9. Rubber.

712

1. The White House.
2. The Sioux.
3. San Francisco Bay.
4. 600.
5. England's.
6. Tony Mareno.
7. Primitive art.
8. She killed herself with her father's sword.
9. Six.

1083

1. Sixteen.
2. Mary, Queen of Scots.
3. New Plymouth.
4. Rumpelstiltskin.
5. Craig Stadler.
6. Mike Farrell.
7. Martin Luther King, Jr, aged thirty-five.
8. Gilbert and Sullivan.
9. Glass.

342

1. Who is Wednesday named after?
2. Name Buffalo Bill's horse.
3. Where is Mount Andrew Jackson?
4. Who wrote the collection of short stories called *Dubliners*?
5. How wide is a soccer goal?
6. Who is the doctor on the Starship *Enterprise*?
7. Gauguin, Van Gogh and Cézanne were the chief figures in which artistic movement?
8. Which song is always played as the horses parade for the Kentucky Derby?
9. Which planet in our solar system has the shortest day?

713

1. How many in a score?
2. After whom was the Caesarean operation named, as he was reputedly brought into the world by this method?
3. Which region of Africa is partly submerged beneath Lake Nasser?
4. Who wrote *For Whom the Bell Tolls*?
5. How many dimples has a golf ball?
6. Who starred in the Broadway play *Buck White*?
7. Where was St Bernadette born?
8. In which film was the song 'New York, New York' introduced?
9. What does a pluviometer measure?

1084

1. What is German for 'please'?
2. Which ship was captained by Hans Langsdorff?
3. To which country does Robinson Crusoe Island belong?
4. Which legendary king of Crete was the son of Zeus and the father of Ariadne?
5. In basketball what is the distance from the free throw line to the basket?
6. Which country makes the most films per year?
7. Who had the nickname 'The Lone Eagle'?
8. Who sings the theme song in the Bond film *Diamonds are Forever*?
9. Where did the orange originate?

342

1. Woden.
2. Brigham.
3. Antarctica.
4. James Joyce.
5. 24 feet.
6. Leonard McKoy, played by DeForest Kelley.
7. Post-impressionist.
8. 'My Old Kentucky Home'.
9. Jupiter, which completes a rotation on its axis in less than 10 earth hours.

713

1. Twenty.
2. Julius Caesar.
3. Nubia.
4. Ernest Hemingway.
5. 336.
6. Muhammad Ali.
7. Lourdes.
8. *New York, New York.*
9. Rainfall.

1084

1. Bitte.
2. The *Graf Spee.*
3. Chile.
4. Minos.
5. 19 feet.
6. India.
7. Charles Lindbergh.
8. Shirley Bassey.
9. In China.

343

1. When does the wine harvest usually begin?
2. What was the gun called that Sir Walter Scott arranged to be removed from the Tower and returned to Scotland in 1829?
3. Which lake was created by the Hoover Dam?
4. William Ireland claimed to have 'discovered' two plays by Shakespeare. Name one.
5. Who is the only Wimbledon men's tennis singles champion to be left handed and double fisted?
6. Who said: 'Fasten your seat belts, it's going to be a bumpy night'?
7. Who was Bluebeard's last wife?
8. Who was the first black performer to have a No. 1 hit in the UK?
9. When was the first kidney transplant performed?

714

1. Paddy, after harvest and with the husks removed, becomes what?
2. Who, dying, said: 'Monks! Monks! Monks!'
3. Where is Inchŏn?
4. Who did Aeneas fall in love with in Carthage?
5. In which year did a man first run the 100 metres in under 10 seconds?
6. Who was the 'Oomph Girl'?
7. Who said: 'Scratch an actor – and you'll find an actress'?
8. Which piano concerto was featured in *Elvira Madigan*?
9. The motions of the seven planets were music to which Greek mathematician?

1085

1. Whose ship was represented on the old ½d?
2. Who was the legendary founder of Carthage?
3. Which town became the centre of Calvin's movement?
4. Who is married to Regan in *King Lear*?
5. What game played on ice equates to flat green bowls, more or less?
6. Who directed the recently reconstructed French epic *Napoléon*?
7. By what title is Karol Wojtyla better known?
8. Who wrote and played the theme tune in *Genevieve*?
9. Of what are Dorothy Perkins, Grandpa Dickson and Iceberg all varieties?

343

1. Mid-September.
2. Mons Meg (in Edinburgh Castle).
3. Lake Mead.
4. *Henry II* or *Vortigern and Rowena.*
5. Jimmy Connors.
6. Bette Davis, in *All About Eve.*
7. Fatima.
8. Winifred Atwell.
9. 1961.

714

1. Rice.
2. Henry VIII.
3. South Korea.
4. Dido.
5. 1968.
6. Ann Sheridan.
7. Dorothy Parker.
8. Mozart's piano concerto No. 21 in C Major.
9. Pythagoras.

1085

1. Sir Francis Drake's.
2. Dido.
3. Geneva.
4. The Duke of Cornwall.
5. Curling.
6. Abel Gance.
7. Pope John Paul II.
8. Larry Adler.
9. Roses.

344

1. The English system of five vowels has to represent how many vowels sounds?
2. Which queen of England married her brother-in-law?
3. Which country uses kips as currency?
4. Who are the 'Makaris' that William Dunbar laments?
5. Which game was originally called 'Gossima'?
6. What was the name of the charlady in 'ITMA'?
7. Who was born at Burnham Thorpe rectory and was made the Duke of Bronte, in Sicily, by the King of Naples?
8. How old was Brian Jones when he died?
9. What is hydroponics?

715

1. Which was the first British company to arrange tourist excursions?
2. Name one husband of Mary, Queen of Scots.
3. In which country is the Meru National Park?
4. In what language did Sir Thomas More write *Utopia*?
5. Which club won soccer's 1982 European Cup?
6. Who was ITV's first compère of 'Sunday Night at the London Palladium'?
7. Which artist lived by, painted and is buried in Hampstead Heath?
8. What is Sting's real name?
9. What is a collection of ravens?

1086

1. What type of road is a corduroy road?
2. Who was captured landing from a German submarine in Ireland on 21 April 1916?
3. There are four different time zones in the USA. Name three of them.
4. Who (principally) does Sir Percy Blakeney outwit?
5. How many players are there in a water polo team?
6. Who played Soames in BBC TV's 'The Forsyte Saga'?
7. Who said: 'I myself have become a Gaullist only little by little'?
8. Which pseudonyms did Mick Jagger and Keith Richard use in their early songwriting days?
9. Where does a nightjar lay its eggs?

344

1. Twelve (and eight diphthongs).
2. Catherine of Aragon, Henry VIII's first wife. She was previously his elder brother Arthur's wife.
3. Laos.
4. The makers, that is, the poets.
5. Table tennis.
6. Mrs Mopp.
7. Horatio Nelson.
8. Twenty-six.
9. The soil-less cultivation of plants.

715

1. Thomas Cook.
2. Choose from Francis II of France, Lord Darnley and the Earl of Bothwell.
3. Kenya.
4. Latin.
5. Aston Villa.
6. Tommy Trinder.
7. John Constable.
8. Gordon Sumner.
9. An unkindness.

1086

1. A road of logs laid side by side across swampy ground.
2. Sir Roger Casement.
3. Eastern, Central, Mountain and Pacific.
4. Chauvelin (Sir Percy is the Scarlet Pimpernel).
5. Seven (and four reserves).
6. Eric Porter.
7. General de Gaulle.
8. Nanker and Phelge.
9. On the ground.

345

1. What do strikers call those who refuse to strike?
2. How many kills are credited to the 'Red Baron'?
3. Where was the O K Corral?
4. In Charles Kingsley's *The Water Babies* who made Tom sweep chimneys?
5. Which horse won the Cheltenham Gold Cup in three successive years?
6. Who won the Best Actress Oscar for *The Country Girl* in 1954?
7. What is gold-leaf made from?
8. According to the song, who is it 'what gets the blame'?
9. From which kind of goat does mohair come?

716

1. What is a kukri?
2. The Germans built a cargo version of one of these which travelled to Baltimore in the First World War. What was it?
3. Which country uses the ringgit as currency?
4. Who founded Zap Comix in the late 1960s?
5. Who was the captain of England's Grand Slam winning rugby union team of 1980?
6. The sci-fi film nonentity *The Blob* featured which (later to be famous) film star? (Hint: he 'escaped' to better things.)
7. Who deciphered Linear B?
8. What does rust never do, according to Neil Young?
9. Wild marjoram is also known as what?

1087

1. Which is the lee side of a boat?
2. Who crowned Napoleon Bonaparte Emperor of France?
3. Which ship first reached the North Pole?
4. Which writer was Lord Chancellor and imprisoned for corruption?
5. When did Dick Fosbury first use his 'flop' technique to win an Olympic high jump gold medal?
6. Which British actress was painted gold in *Goldfinger*?
7. Benjamin Disraeli bought up all the shares owned by an Egyptian Khedive, in 1875, to gain a 44 per cent control in which enterprise?
8. Who claimed that 'England swings'?
9. Where is the giant salamander found?

345

1. Scabs or black-legs.
2. Eighty.
3. Tombstone, Arizona.
4. Mr Grimes.
5. Arkle.
6. Grace Kelly.
7. Gold.
8. The poor.
9. The Angora.

716

1. A Gurkha knife.
2. A submarine.
3. Malaysia.
4. Robert Crumb.
5. Bill Beaumont.
6. Steve McQueen.
7. Michael Ventris.
8. It never sleeps.
9. Oregano.

1087

1. The side away from the wind.
2. He crowned himself.
3. The American submarine *Nautilus*, in 1958.
4. Francis Bacon.
5. 1968.
6. Shirley Eaton.
7. The Suez Canal.
8. Roger Miller.
9. Japan.

346

1. What does 'gnomic' mean?
2. Off which island did Sir Richard Grenville fight the Spaniards?
3. Of which West Indian island is Scarborough now the capital?
4. Who created Nero Wolfe?
5. In which colours do Brazil play football?
6. What do Marlene Dietrich and Joan Crawford have in common (a toothy question...)?
7. Name Picasso's famous picture depicting the bombing of a Spanish town?
8. Colin Blunstone had a hit twice over – once with the Zombies and once under a pseudonym – with which song?
9. Which are the two types of brakes used by cars?

717

1. If a 20-metre-thick layer of peat were buried under 3 kilometres of sediment how thick would the resultant seam of coal be?
2. Which is the odd year out: 1808, 1900, 1952, 1984?
3. Where is the Bridge of Sighs?
4. Who wrote *Tales from Shakespeare* with his sister?
5. What are traditionally eaten at Wimbledon?
6. Who said: 'Didn't he do well?'?
7. For what is George III's retainer William Forsyth remembered?
8. Who took off his hat to Larry?
9. What are the two types of non-migratory trout found in England?

1088

1. What is the Royal Yacht called?
2. What to the nearest 5 years was the date of the first English-printed book?
3. Of which country is Lisbon the capital?
4. Which was Shakespeare's first play?
5. Who won the FA Cup in 1984?
6. Who plays Lily Munster?
7. Which poet enlisted as Silas Tomkyn Comberback in the 15th Dragoons?
8. Who composed the Ghost Trio?
9. About how far out in space is the so-called geo-stationary orbit where telecommunication satellites are placed?

346

1. Pithy or epigrammatic.
2. Flores, the westernmost of the Azores.
3. Tobago.
4. Rex Stout.
5. Yellow shirts, blue shorts.
6. They both had their molars out to enhance the height of their cheek-bones.
7. 'Guernica'.
8. 'She's Not There'.
9. Disc brakes and drum brakes.

717

1. 2 metres thick.
2. 1900 – it was not a leap year.
3. Venice.
4. Charles Lamb.
5. Strawberries and cream.
6. Bruce Forsyth.
7. Forsythia.
8. Del Shannon.
9. Rainbow trout and brown trout.

1088

1. *Britannia.*
2. 11 November 1477.
3. Portugal.
4. *The Comedy of Errors.*
5. Everton.
6. Yvonne de Carlo.
7. Coleridge.
8. Beethoven.
9. 22,300 miles.

347

1. What industry did El Niño virtually destroy in 1972–3?
2. Which British PM held that office for a record five times?
3. Where is Gibraltar Point?
4. Who, at Yeats's suggestion, visited the Aran Islands and wrote a play that caused riots in Dublin and America?
5. In which decade did pole vaulters start using fibre glass poles?
6. In the film *Guess Who's Coming to Dinner*, which actor was?
7. Which writer, son of a weaver, became a baronet and sponsored Scott of the Antarctic?
8. Van Morrison began life with a Belfast band. What was their name?
9. Who was the second Russian astronaut to orbit the earth?

718

1. When was the automobile ignition key introduced?
2. Which queen introduced the Act of Supremacy?
3. Where does the Mekong river rise?
4. Which one-time ship's surgeon translated *Gil Blas* and wrote a celebrated epistolary novel?
5. What are the Western Roll and Eastern Cutoff?
6. Who is noted for his 'odd odes'?
7. At what did the Brewers' Shades win the 1978 World Championship?
8. Who did the Banshees play with?
9. Hydrocyanic acid is often referred to in detective stories as what?

1089

1. When is Sheer Thursday?
2. Who was the father of Alexander the Great?
3. The world's greatest snow falls have all occurred where?
4. Who was 'thine handmaid', Abigail?
5. Who was world 500cc motor cycle champion in 1956, and from 1958 to 1962?
6. What was Sidney Greenstreet's first film role?
7. Which USA president referred to his radio broadcasts to the nation as 'fireside chats'?
8. Who said he'd rather have a nice cup of tea?
9. In which month would you expect to see delphiniums, foxgloves, petunias and nasturtiums blooming?

347

1. The Peruvian anchovy industry (it was a warm current).
2. Stanley Baldwin (1923–4, 1924–9, 1935–6 and for two brief periods around the Abdication).
3. In Lincolnshire, south of Skegness.
4. J. M. Synge (*Playboy of the Western World*).
5. The 1960s.
6. Sidney Poitier.
7. J. M. Barrie.
8. Them.
9. Herman Titov.

718

1. 1949.
2. Elizabeth I (which made her head of the Church).
3. Tibet.
4. Tobias Smollett (*The Expedition of Humphry Clinker*).
5. Techniques for high jumping.
6. Cyril Fletcher.
7. Marbles.
8. Siouxsie.
9. Prussic acid.

1089

1. The Thursday in Holy Week, Maundy Thursday. ('Sheer' comes from a Shakespearian word meaning 'to purify'.)
2. Philip II of Macedon.
3. The Rockies, North America.
4. The wife of Nabal and subsequently David (I Samuel 25).
5. John Surtees.
6. The 'fat man' in the legendary *Maltese Falcon*.
7. President F. D. Roosevelt.
8. Boy George – he preferred it to sex.
9. July.

348

1. England's first census occurred when?
2. For which service did the press gangs of the early nineteenth century recruit?
3. What do the rivers Wey and Trent do that is extremely unusual for British rivers?
4. Which breed of dog did Bill Sykes have?
5. Who won the women's javelin at the Montreal and Munich Olympics?
6. What was Shirley MacLaine's first film?
7. Who is Colonel-in-Chief of the Royal Highland Fusiliers?
8. Who sang 'Wimoweh' in 1962?
9. The Italian Chianina is recognized as being what?

719

1. What are the octane values of 2-star and 3-star petrol?
2. For which single military action were eleven Victoria Crosses given?
3. What was the name of the longest lived hurricane in the North Atlantic?
4. Who first wrote: 'If Winter comes, can Spring be far behind?'?
5. In which country does the soccer club Setubal play?
6. Which film was advertised as 'the motion picture with something to offend everybody'?
7. Who painted 'The Hay Wain'?
8. Who got his mojo working?
9. What are secateurs?

1090

1. The brass ornaments traditionally carried by draught horses were originally used for what purpose?
2. Which social reformer said to a partner: 'All the world is queer save thee and me and even thou art a little queer.'
3. Which country produces Camembert cheese?
4. Which famous diarist wrote *Fumifugiu*, on air-pollution in London?
5. In which Italian town do Juventus play?
6. By what name is Douglas Elton Ullman better known?
7. What was W. R. Morris's title?
8. By what name is Robert Cassotto better known?
9. Chlorine is one of the five elements known as halogens – name another.

348

1. 1086 (Domesday Book).
2. The navy.
3. They flow from south to north.
4. A bull terrier.
5. Ruth Fuchs.
6. *The Trouble with Harry.*
7. Princess Margaret.
8. Karl Denver. (Group rendition allowed here . . .)
9. The oldest breed of cattle.

719

1. 92 and 94 respectively.
2. The defence of Rorke's Drift in the Zulu Wars (1879).
3. Ginger.
4. Percy Bysshe Shelley.
5. Portugal.
6. *The Loved One.*
7. John Constable.
8. Muddy Waters – composer of the R and B standard.
9. Pruning shears.

1090

1. To ward off magic and the evil eye.
2. Robert Owen.
3. France.
4. John Evelyn.
5. Turin.
6. Douglas Fairbanks, Sr.
7. Lord Nuffield.
8. Bobby Darrin.
9. Fluorine, bromine, iodine and astatine.

349

1. About how many calories does half a pint of beer contain?
2. In which decade was a regulation naval uniform first introduced?
3. Princess Eugénie of France opened what in 1869?
4. Who was Henry Irving's secretary who wrote of a legendary Hungarian count?
5. What are the two types of technique generally used in the high jump these days?
6. Of what did Alfred Hitchcock admit to being terrified?
7. How many woods has each singles player in flat green bowling?
8. Who sang 'How Much Is that Doggie in the Window'?
9. About how many species of living flowering plants are known?

720

1. What ham results from pigs fed on peaches and nuts, the meat being smoked over hickory fires?
2. Who was the last English monarch to be buried abroad?
3. What is the capital of Tasmania?
4. Who was the medical student who fell in love with Fanny Brawne and wrote 'La Belle Dame Sans Merci'?
5. Name one of Irina Rodnina's two great ice-skating pairs partners.
6. Who was famous for the 'peek-a-boo' hair style she sported in the 1940s?
7. Who coined the epithet 'Sloane Ranger'?
8. Who is known as the King of the High Cs?
9. The Russians have left behind a number of robot lunar crawlers on the moon. What was the first one called?

1091

1. What are mimolette, samosoe, banon and monterey jack?
2. The Great Chartist Petition of 1848 had 5,706,000 signatures. What percentage were declared invalid?
3. In 1519 Tenochtitlan was the capital of where?
4. Gerrit Gerritzoon was better known by what name?
5. Who was Bernard Ford's ice dance partner?
6. Who was 'The Man of a Thousand Faces'?
7. Which famous poet and short-story writer wrote a novel called *The Light That Failed*?
8. Who owned the legendary Sun record label in Memphis?
9. Who first analysed pendulums by watching lamps during Mass?

349

1. 150.
2. The 1850s (1857).
3. The Suez Canal.
4. Bram Stoker (*Dracula*).
5. The Fosbury flop and the straddle.
6. Policemen.
7. Four.
8. Lita Roza, in 1953.
9. 286,000.

720

1. American Virginia.
2. George I (at Leine Schloss, Hanover – his bones were transferred to Herrenhausen after the Second World War).
3. Hobart.
4. Keats.
5. Alexander Zaitsev or Alexai Ulanov.
6. Veronica Lake.
7. Peter York, in *Harpers and Queen*.
8. Luciano Pavarotti.
9. Lunokhod I.

1091

1. They are all cheeses.
2. 65 per cent.
3. The Aztec Empire.
4. Erasmus.
5. Diane Towler.
6. Lon Chaney.
7. Rudyard Kipling.
8. Sam Phillips.
9. Galileo.

350

1. About what percentage of fat children grow up to be fat adults?
2. In 1726, how old was the chief executioner of Paris?
3. How many hills of Rome are there?
4. Who was Russell Thorndike's smuggling parson?
5. Which horse has won the Derby in consecutive years?
6. What was the name of the womanless planet on which Bob Hope and Bing Crosby found themselves in *The Road to Hong Kong*?
7. What colours would a scraperboard drawing be?
8. Which great dancer was born Margaret Hookham?
9. How was lead shot invented?

721

1. Who said, 'Elementary, my dear Watson'?
2. To whose band did Little John belong?
3. Which river marks the northern boundary of the Transvaal?
4. What was Sancho Panza's donkey named?
5. How many sleds may each country enter in the two-man Olympic bobsled event?
6. Name two of the three Gabor sisters.
7. What does a kibitzer do in bridge?
8. Of which group were Brian Jones and Bill Wyman members?
9. Which was the first satellite in orbit?

1092

1. Which is the word most often used in English conversation?
2. To whom did the sword Colada belong?
3. Which is the largest island in the Mediterranean?
4. What was Cinderella's slipper made from?
5. Who was the first goalkeeper to win the Footballer of the Year Award?
6. Who was the first member of the Royal Family to be interviewed on TV?
7. Who won snooker's Professional World Championship in 1972 and 1982?
8. Name Manchester's greatest orchestra.
9. What breed are Eskimo dogs?

350

1. 80 per cent. (Accept 75–85 per cent.)
2. Seven years old. (The post went from father to son.)
3. Seven.
4. Dr Syn.
5. No horse can do this, as the Derby is for three-year-olds *only*.
6. Plutonium.
7. Black and white.
8. Dame Margot Fonteyn.
9. By a man climbing to the top of a Bristol church in 1782 and pouring molten lead into cold water on the ground.

721

1. *Not* Sherlock Holmes. This line does not occur in any of the Conan Doyle stories.
2. Robin Hood's.
3. The Limpopo.
4. Dapple.
5. Two.
6. Zsa Zsa, Magda, Eva.
7. Watch the play.
8. The Rolling Stones.
9. Sputnik I.

1092

1. 'I'.
2. El Cid.
3. Sicily.
4. Glass.
5. Bert Trautmann, in 1956.
6. Prince Philip, on 'Panorama' in 1961.
7. Alex Higgins.
8. The Hallé Orchestra.
9. Huskies.

351

1. What is steganography?
2. Who said when dying: 'All my possessions for a moment of time'?
3. Which country does the wine Mosel come from?
4. Who 'is willin'' in *David Copperfield*?
5. What is the basic school figure in ice skating?
6. Who played Bronco?
7. What did Victoria say on hearing she had become Queen?
8. Simon and Garfunkel started their working life as . . .?
9. Who was the first man to be totally alone and out of sight of earth?

722

1. In the USA, how many pounds make up a hundredweight?
2. When did Britain go off the gold standard?
3. Into which sea does the Danube flow?
4. How old was Lolita when she first appears in the book?
5. Which ex-England goalkeeper played for Fort Lauderdale Strikers?
6. Who starred in the film *Lenny*?
7. In which era was Raphael painting?
8. Which Beethoven opera is subtitled *Wedded Love*?
9. Of the 163 recognized breeds of dog, how many originated in the British Isles?

1093

1. As applied to wine, what does 'brut' mean?
2. Which English playwright died on 23 April 1616?
3. Why was Venice's Bridge of Sighs so named?
4. Who wrote *The Ugly Duckling*?
5. On whose life was the film *The Great White Hope* based?
6. What is Peter Parker's other identity?
7. How old was Jane Austen when she wrote *Pride and Prejudice*?
8. As what was Brian Epstein best known?
9. Name the baby monkey that rode with Thor Heyerdahl on *Ra I*.

351

1. The writing of messages with invisible ink.
2. Elizabeth I.
3. Germany.
4. Barkis.
5. Eight.
6. Ty Hardin, born Orson Whipple Hungerford II.
7. 'I will be good.'
8. Tom and Jerry.
9. Michael Collins.

722

1. 100 lb.
2. 1932.
3. The Black Sea.
4. Twelve.
5. Gordon Banks.
6. Dustin Hoffman.
7. During the Renaissance.
8. *Fidelio.*
9. Forty-seven (accept a variation of three either way).

1093

1. Dry.
2. William Shakespeare.
3. Because prisoners crossed it, rarely to return.
4. Hans Christian Andersen.
5. Jack Johnson, the first black heavyweight boxing champion of the world.
6. Spiderman.
7. Twenty-one.
8. As manager of the Beatles.
9. Safi.

352

1. To what was an Albert chain usually attached?
2. Which fleet tried to invade England in 1588?
3. Which language is most widely spoken in Belgium?
4. Who said, 'Off with their heads!' in Wonderland?
5. Who held the world heavyweight boxing title longest?
6. Who was the oldest actress to have played the part of Shakespeare's Juliet?
7. Who was exchanged for the Russian spy Colonel Rudolf Abel?
8. What was Elvis Presley's middle name?
9. A human being sheds skin continuously. How long does it take to replace the complete outer layer?

723

1. What number does the Roman numeral L represent?
2. Name Julius Caesar's third wife.
3. Which countries constitute Great Britain?
4. Who was Professor Moriarty's greatest enemy?
5. Which country took every gold medal for boxing in the 1904 St Louis Olympics?
6. Who said to whom: 'There's another fine mess you've gotten me into'?
7. Who was the only British monarch to write his autobiography?
8. Who was the lead guitarist of the Beatles?
9. In what does a fellmonger deal?

1094

1. How many lawful wives may a Muslim husband have?
2. Which Indian tribe was victorious at the Battle of Little Big Horn?
3. On which river is Rome built?
4. Who wrote *Around the World in Eighty Days*?
5. Which country won soccer's last ever Home Internationals?
6. Who played Rudolph Valentino in the 1977 film *Valentino*?
7. By what name was Jean François Grandet better known?
8. At what time was Little Susie woken by the Everly Brothers singing?
9. Which animal is the symbol of the World Wildlife Fund?

352

1. A watch.
2. The Spanish Armada.
3. French.
4. The Queen of Hearts.
5. Joe Louis, from 1937 until his retirement in 1949.
6. Sarah Bernhardt, at the age of seventy.
7. The U-2 pilot Gary Powers.
8. Aaron.
9. 28 days.

723

1. Fifty.
2. Calpurnia.
3. England, Scotland and Wales.
4. Sherlock Holmes.
5. USA.
6. Oliver Hardy to Stan Laurel.
7. Edward VIII.
8. George Harrison.
9. Animal skins.

1094

1. Four.
2. The Sioux.
3. The Tiber.
4. Jules Verne.
5. Northern Ireland.
6. Rudolf Nureyev.
7. Blondin, the tightrope walker.
8. 4 a.m.
9. The giant panda.

353

1. What colour is the habit of a Franciscan monk?
2. How were Queen Victoria and Prince Albert related, other than by marriage?
3. What is the capital of Hungary?
4. What is Charles Duff's macabre handbook called?
5. Who won all three alpine skiing events in the 1968 Winter Olympics?
6. What good luck charm has Robert Morley carried with him since he first entered show business?
7. From which country did the painter and engraver David Jones originate?
8. To which note do the players in an orchestra tune their instruments?
9. Where would you find your gluteus maximus?

724

1. Which fashion designer created the mini-skirt in the 1960s?
2. Who was the oldest and wisest Greek general who fought at Troy?
3. In which house did the Brontë sisters live for nearly all their lives?
4. Who is the central male character in *Lorna Doone*?
5. What position does Snoopy play in Charlie Brown's baseball team?
6. What was Patrick McGoohan's number in 'The Prisoner'?
7. Which people were the inventors of the lacrosse?
8. From which musical does the song 'Ol' Man River' come?
9. Which metal has the atomic number of 30?

1095

1. What is the longest English word that does not repeat a letter?
2. Which king of England was crowned King of France in 1431?
3. What is the length of a French president's term of office?
4. Who was King Lear's favourite daughter?
5. The Winter Olympics of 1964 and 1976 were held in the same place. Where?
6. Who is Hazard County's sheriff?
7. Whose first victim was Mary Anne Nicholls?
8. What is a hecklephone?
9. What type of creature can focus its eyes most quickly?

353

1. Grey.
2. They were cousins.
3. Budapest.
4. *Handbook of Hanging.*
5. Jean Claude Killy of France.
6. A teddy bear.
7. Wales.
8. A.
9. In your buttocks – it is the body's largest muscle.

724

1. Mary Quant.
2. Nestor.
3. Haworth Parsonage, West Yorkshire.
4. John Ridd.
5. Short stop.
6. Six.
7. The North American Indians.
8. *Showboat.*
9. Zinc.

1095

1. Uncopyrightables.
2. King Henry VI.
3. 7 years.
4. Cordelia.
5. Innsbruck, Austria.
6. Roscoe P. Coltrane.
7. Jack the Ripper.
8. A woodwind instrument.
9. A bird.

354

1. What do mnemonics assist?
2. Who was nicknamed 'The Desert Fox'?
3. Which Italian region's language was adopted as standard Italian?
4. In which Jules Verne novel does the submarine *Nautilus* feature?
5. What is tennis player Mariana Simionescu's married name?
6. Who played Diamond Lil?
7. For what type of painting is Sir Peter Lely famous?
8. Which composer was known as the 'Napoleon of Music, Signor Crescendo'?
9. How much water can an elephant that has been travelling on a hot day drink in 24 hours?

725

1. On which day of the week was President Kennedy assassinated?
2. By what name was Henry IV known before his accession?
3. In which British city is Adolf Hitler said to have studied art?
4. Who asked for more?
5. How wide is a tennis singles court?
6. Name one of the two films in which Cary Grant played a submarine skipper.
7. After his death, how many notches were discovered on Pretty Boy Floyd's pocket watch, representing the number of people he had killed?
8. What is the theme song of the Harlem Globetrotters?
9. Which acid has the chemical formula HNO_3?

1096

1. What are the Roaring Forties?
2. On which British ship did President Roosevelt and Churchill sign the Atlantic Charter on 14 August 1941?
3. Which country's airline is Olympic Airways?
4. How did Judas Iscariot die?
5. Who was the first heavyweight boxer to win back his championship after he had lost it?
6. What is the name of Micky Mouse's dog?
7. Who owned the middle names 'Fingal O'Flahertie Wills'?
8. Who wrote the opera *War and Peace*?
9. Which Mexican drink is obtained from the agave plant?

354

1. Memory.
2. Erwin Rommel.
3. Tuscany.
4. *20,000 Leagues Under the Sea.*
5. Mariana Borg.
6. Mae West.
7. Portraits.
8. Rossini.
9. 50 gallons.

725

1. Friday.
2. Bolingbroke.
3. Liverpool.
4. Oliver Twist.
5. 27 feet.
6. *Operation Petticoat* or *Destination Tokyo.*
7. Ten.
8. 'Sweet Georgia Brown'.
9. Nitric acid.

1096

1. Winds.
2. HMS *Prince of Wales.*
3. Greece.
4. He hanged himself.
5. Floyd Patterson (from Ingemar Johansson in 1960, after losing it in 1959).
6. Pluto.
7. Oscar Wilde.
8. Prokofiev.
9. Tequila.

355

1. Nencn-Kona was the first US consumer product for sale in the USSR. What is it?
2. Who was Britain's prime minister in 1956?
3. From which London station do Paris-bound trains leave?
4. What weapon did David use to kill Goliath?
5. Which football league club is nicknamed 'The Pilgrims'?
6. How many times did Humphrey Bogart speak the line, 'Here's looking at you, kid' in *Casablanca*?
7. Who was Germany's most notorious First World War spy?
8. What was Louis Armstrong's instrument?
9. Who is recognized as being the father of medicine?

726

1. How tall is Nelson's Column in Trafalgar Square?
2. Who was the last monarch to refuse the Royal Assent to an Act of Parliament?
3. Which city does Dyce airport service?
4. Who wrote *Fanny's First Play*?
5. In which year were the Winter Olympic Games introduced?
6. Which Marx brother didn't appear in the Marx brothers' films?
7. Of which Indian tribe was Sitting Bull the chief?
8. Who composed the hit song 'Help Me Make It Through the Night'?
9. The Irish mathematician William Hamilton was appointed to what chair at Trinity College, Dublin, when still an undergraduate and just 22 years old?

1097

1. What grows in paddy fields?
2. To whom was Bathsheba married?
3. Which is France's largest port?
4. Who wrote *England Made Me*?
5. What is the minimum weight of a professional heavyweight boxer?
6. Which perfume did Marilyn Monroe claim was the only thing she wore in bed?
7. Who preceded Georgi Malenkov?
8. How many drummers were drumming?
9. What was the original profession of Richard Arkwright, the inventor of the Spinning Jenny?

355

1. Pepsi Cola.
2. Anthony Eden.
3. Victoria.
4. Sling and stone.
5. Plymouth Argyle.
6. Four.
7. Mata Hari.
8. The trumpet.
9. Hippocrates.

726

1. 172 feet 2 inches.
2. Queen Anne.
3. Aberdeen.
4. G. B. Shaw.
5. 1924.
6. Gummo.
7. The Sioux.
8. Kris Kristofferson.
9. Astronomy.

1097

1. Rice.
2. King David.
3. Marseilles.
4. Graham Greene.
5. 175 lb.
6. Chanel No. 5.
7. Joseph Stalin.
8. Twelve.
9. He was a barber.

356

1. How many £1,000,000 notes have been printed?
2. Who was the first king of the Israelites?
3. Which continent has the greatest number of countries?
4. Who is the Toff's valet?
5. What is the maximum and minimum distance covered by Grand Prix races?
6. What number is on the door of the General Lee, the Dukes of Hazard's car?
7. Who was called 'the world's greatest lover'?
8. Which song did Judy Garland sing to Mickey Rooney's photograph in the film *Babes in Arms*?
9. If an object reflected no light, what colour would it be?

727

1. Of which alphabet is omega the final letter?
2. Who is reputed to have said, 'Let them eat cake'?
3. What were moidores?
4. Who in *The Tempest* did Prospero call 'a freckled whelp hag-born'?
5. Which ball game uses the largest field?
6. Who led the Sharks in *West Side Story*?
7. Which school of painting produced Bellini, Tintoretto and Veronese?
8. 'O mistress mine, where are you roving': from which play does this song come?
9. Taking the sun as a starting point and working outwards, which is the sixth planet in our solar system?

1098

1. Of what are half hitches and sheepshanks forms?
2. During which war did Joan of Arc lead the French against the English?
3. In which castle is the Blarney Stone?
4. For refusing to worship which king was Daniel thrown to the lions?
5. Who partnered Ilie Nastase to victory in the 1970 and 1972 Wimbledon mixed doubles championships?
6. Who is the chaplain at the 4077th MASH?
7. Who died on his birthday in 1616?
8. What line precedes: 'Our shelter from the stormy blast'?
9. By which nickname was the Model T Ford known?

356

1. Two.
2. King Saul.
3. Africa.
4. Jolly.
5. 150–250 miles.
6. 01.
7. Casanova.
8. 'I Cried for You'.
9. Black.

727

1. Greek.
2. Queen Marie Antoinette.
3. Portuguese gold coins.
4. Caliban.
5. Polo.
6. Bernardo.
7. Venetian.
8. Shakespeare's *Twelfth Night*.
9. Saturn.

1098

1. Knots.
2. The Hundred Years War.
3. Blarney Castle.
4. King Darius.
5. Rosie Casals.
6. Father Francis Mulcahy.
7. William Shakespeare.
8. 'Our hope for years to come'.
9. Tin Lizzie.

357

1. Of which university is the Slade School of Fine Art a department?
2. Who was killed by an assassin in Sarajevo, Bosnia, on 28 June 1914?
3. What is the tenth letter of the Greek alphabet?
4. Who is Hugh Lofting's best-known creation?
5. A husband and wife won gold medals for athletics in the 1952 Olympics; who were they?
6. Which country tried to steal Chitty-Chitty Bang-Bang?
7. What number is opposite 20 on a darts board?
8. Who wrote the Carnival of the Animals?
9. Which is the fastest dog in the world?

728

1. September, by virtue of its name, should be the seventh month. Why is it the ninth?
2. Against which English king did Hereward the Wake fight?
3. Which is the largest town in Northumberland?
4. Of which book is *The Memoirs of a Woman of Pleasure* the subtitle?
5. What was the name of the bear mascot of the Russian 1980 Olympics?
6. How many Marx brothers played in the film *Animal Crackers*?
7. Who beat Alex Higgins in the final of the 1976 World Professional Snooker Championships?
8. Who composed, with Frederick Loewe, 'Almost Like Being in Love'?
9. Which lightly smoked fish are bloaters?

1099

1. Which is the world's largest office building?
2. Name the first battle in the Civil War between Parliament and Charles I.
3. Which city is home to Trajan's Column?
4. Who was the elder brother of Moses who became the first High Priest of Israel?
5. Roger Uttley captained England; in which game?
6. In which town was Superboy raised by Mr and Mrs Kent?
7. Who was the original illustrator of *Alice in Wonderland*?
8. Which song opens the film *The Graduate*?
9. What is the plural of mongoose?

357

1. University College, London.
2. The Archduke Franz Ferdinand and his wife.
3. Kappa.
4. Doctor Dolittle.
5. Emil Zatopek (marathon) and Dana Zatopek (javelin).
6. Vulgaria.
7. 3.
8. Saint-Saëns.
9. Either saluki or greyhound can be accepted as an answer.

728

1. Because the year used to begin in March, when it would have been correct.
2. William I.
3. Newcastle-upon-Tyne.
4. *Fanny Hill.*
5. Misha.
6. Four.
7. Ray Reardon.
8. Alan Jay Lerner.
9. Herrings.

1099

1. The Pentagon.
2. Edgehill.
3. Rome.
4. Aaron.
5. Rugby.
6. Smallville, Illinois.
7. Tenniel.
8. 'The Sounds of Silence'.
9. Mongooses.

358

1. Which army rank comes above captain?
2. What did Marshal James Wilson discover at Sutter's Mill, California, in 1848?
3. Which ancient city was also called Ilium?
4. Who wrote *Les Misérables* and *Notre Dame de Paris*?
5. Which Derby winner bore the name of a historic Welshman?
6. Who plays Callan?
7. What is the total most frequently rolled with two dice?
8. By which name was Ferdinand Morton better known?
9. As dogs are canine, what are crows?

729

1. Which is the highest rank in the navy?
2. For how many years did the Hundred Years War last?
3. At which ski resort is the Cresta Run?
4. Who hid in a house in Amsterdam for 2 years and wrote a diary which was published?
5. Who is the only man to win tennis's grand slam twice?
6. Who played Isaac Newton in the 1957 film *The Story of Mankind*?
7. Which Nobel Prize winner in physics was offered, but turned down, the presidency of Israel?
8. Who composed the opera *Love for Three Oranges*?
9. Which bird is often called the fish hawk?

1100

1. What follows a gibbous moon?
2. What carried 34,753 pieces of mail between St Joseph, Missouri and Sacramento, California in 1860 and 1861?
3. In which city is the Trevi Fountain?
4. Who eventually married Lord Peter Wimsey?
5. Who won the 1984 British Superstars Championship?
6. Who played Ned Kelly in the 1970 film of that name?
7. Which combination of two cards makes pinocle?
8. Which part of Glasgow was the setting for a ballet by Robert Helpmann?
9. When did Britain's first jet-propelled aircraft fly?

358

1. Major.
2. Gold.
3. Troy.
4. Victor Hugo.
5. Owen Tudor.
6. Edward Woodward.
7. Seven.
8. Jelly Roll Morton.
9. Corvine.

729

1. Admiral of the Fleet.
2. 116 years (1337–1453).
3. St Moritz.
4. Anne Frank.
5. Rod Laver.
6. Harpo Marx.
7. Albert Einstein.
8. Prokofiev.
9. The osprey.

1100

1. A full moon.
2. The Pony Express.
3. Rome.
4. Harriet Vane (in the detective novels of Dorothy Sayers).
5. Gary Cook.
6. Mick Jagger.
7. Jack of Diamonds and Queen of Spades.
8. The Gorbals.
9. In 1941.

359

1. What is a meerschaum?
2. Who was Britain's Foreign Secretary from 1945 to 1951?
3. Which two countries does the Rio Grande separate?
4. How many eyes had Cyclops?
5. Which country didn't lose a match during the final stages of the 1974 World Cup?
6. What is Princess Dala's (the owner of the Pink Panther) pet poodle's name?
7. What is a hand containing cards of one suit only called?
8. Which group had a big hit with 'Wild Side of Life'?
9. Artificial fibres are generally thought to be made from oil, but from what is rayon made?

730

1. Which anti-whaling organization operates the ship *Rainbow Warrior*?
2. What shut out the light between 1691 and 1851?
3. What is the national flower of Australia?
4. Name the jester in *Hamlet.*
5. Which county and country did Peter May captain at cricket?
6. What part does Robert Mandan play in 'Soap'?
7. Who beat Alex Higgins in the final of the 1980 World Professional Snooker Championships?
8. Who was known as 'The Poet of the Piano'?
9. What is the least radiation-sensitive part of the body?

1101

1. Which letter appears in all sixty-six different alphabets?
2. When was eating chocolate invented?
3. What does the name 'Bharat' mean?
4. Whose fiancée is Prudence Pimpleton?
5. Which F A team have the nickname 'The Cobblers'?
6. What is Bugs Bunny's favourite expression?
7. If you were a French polisher, what would you be dealing with?
8. Stravinsky was born in Russia. Of which country did he become a citizen in 1945?
9. Which is the only creature capable of rotating its head in an almost complete circle?

359

1. A pipe.
2. Ernest Bevin.
3. Mexico and the USA.
4. One.
5. Scotland.
6. Amber.
7. A flush.
8. Status Quo.
9. Wood pulp.

730

1. The Greenpeace Foundation.
2. The window tax.
3. The wattle.
4. Yorick.
5. Surrey and England.
6. Chester Tate.
7. Cliff Thorburn.
8. Chopin.
9. The brain.

1101

1. O.
2. 1847.
3. The Republic of India.
4. Fearless Fosdick's.
5. Northampton.
6. 'What's up, Doc?'
7. Furniture.
8. The USA.
9. The owl.

360

1. What ingredient must French ice cream contain, by law?
2. What was the nickname of Davy Crockett's rifle?
3. Between which two cities does the Trans-Siberian railway run?
4. In which Shakespeare play does Sir Toby Belch appear?
5. Sir Eyre Massey Shaw had a particular claim to Olympic fame. What was it?
6. Which great actress continued her career after losing a leg?
7. Who was nicknamed 'The Little Tramp'?
8. Whose theme song is 'I'll Be Seeing You'?
9. How many men have walked on the moon?

731

1. Who saw Cock Robin die?
2. Which officer was with Nelson as he lay dying?
3. Which is the world's third largest island?
4. What was to be the Pied Piper's fee for freeing Hamelin of rats?
5. How many rounds are in an Olympic boxing match?
6. Who is the master sergeant of corporals Henshaw and Barbella?
7. Where in London would you find Rodin's 'The Burghers of Calais'?
8. Who portrayed Louis Armstrong in the 1959 film, *The Five Pennies*?
9. What is the collective name for a group of kittens?

1102

1. What prize was jointly won in 1978 by Menachem Begin and Anwar Sadat?
2. Which king was responsible for the building of Deal Castle?
3. Where can the Kon-Tiki raft now be seen?
4. Name Shakespeare's shrew.
5. Until 1867, what did professional boxers wear on their fists?
6. Who lives at 345 Stone Cave Road?
7. What is the highest bid in bridge?
8. Who was known as 'The First Lady of Jazz'?
9. What was 'oil of vitriol' to the early chemists?

360

1. Eggs.
2. 'Old Betsy'.
3. Moscow and Vladivostok.
4. *Twelfth Night.*
5. At seventy he was the oldest man ever to win an Olympic gold medal. (In 1900, for yachting – and the record still stands.)
6. Sarah Bernhardt.
7. Charlie Chaplin.
8. Liberace's.
9. Twelve.

731

1. The fly (with his little eye).
2. Hardy.
3. Borneo.
4. 1,000 guilders.
5. Three.
6. Ernie Bilko.
7. Next to the Houses of Parliament.
8. He played himself.
9. A kindle of kittens.

1102

1. The Nobel Peace Prize.
2. Henry VIII.
3. Oslo.
4. Katharina.
5. Nothing.
6. Barney Rubble and family.
7. 7 No trumps.
8. Ella Fitzgerald.
9. Sulphuric acid.

361

1. What is the commonest symbol on the flags of the world?
2. What did Guy Fawkes and friends attempt to blow up in 1605?
3. Which country is alphabetically last?
4. Which French writer, while exiled in Britain, wrote of the wrongful conviction of Alfred Dreyfus?
5. How wide is a tennis doubles court?
6. What is the name of the dog in Punch and Judy?
7. How did Ernest Hemingway die?
8. Who wrote 'O Susanna'?
9. What was the vital commodity that five special ships were built to import from Sweden during the Second World War?

732

1. What is the British term for a thumbtack?
2. In which century was the rococo style of art and interior design popular?
3. What is Greece's most popular alcoholic drink?
4. Who refused five proposals of marriage from Perry Mason?
5. What is the upper weight limit of a professional flyweight boxer?
6. What is the name of the bulldog in the Tom and Jerry cartoons?
7. Of what is the Parthenon in Athens built?
8. To what did the group known as The Quarrymen change their name?
9. What is the anatomical name for the shinbone?

1103

1. What does a polyandrous person have several of?
2. What disrupted traffic on the M40 in Buckinghamshire on 21 May 1983?
3. How many red stripes has the United States flag?
4. Who is the chief of Spectre?
5. Over what distance is the Greyhound Derby run?
6. How many angry men were there in the Henry Fonda film?
7. By what other name was T. E. Lawrence known?
8. Who composed the 'Tragic Overture'?
9. 'Electricity' derives from the Greek word for what substance?

361

1. A star.
2. The Houses of Parliament.
3. Zimbabwe.
4. Émile Zola.
5. 36 feet.
6. Toby.
7. He shot himself.
8. Stephen Foster.
9. Ball-bearings.

732

1. A drawing-pin.
2. The eighteenth.
3. Ouzo.
4. Della Street, his secretary.
5. 112 lb.
6. Butch.
7. Marble.
8. The Beatles.
9. The tibia.

1103

1. Husbands.
2. 3 inches of snow.
3. Seven.
4. Ernst Stavro Blofeld.
5. 500 metres.
6. Twelve.
7. Lawrence of Arabia. (But accept Shaw.)
8. Brahms.
9. Amber.

362

1. What did Smith's Bon-Bons become known as after the 1840s?
2. Who was the king of Munster who defeated the Danes in 1014?
3. In which Italian city did Mussolini found his Fascist party?
4. In which Thomas Hardy play do the Spirit of the Years, Nelson and Napoleon appear?
5. After how many games are the balls *first* changed at Wimbledon?
6. Who chaired 'The Good Old Days' for nearly 30 years?
7. Name two of the founders of the SDP, the 'Gang of Four'.
8. For which group did John Bonham, Jimmy Page and John Paul Jones all play before they formed Led Zeppelin?
9. On which planet is the highest known mountain in our solar system?

733

1. At least how old is three-star brandy?
2. What is the Russian name for the council of state set up by Tsar Nicholas II?
3. In which country is the Gran Chaco?
4. Who created Babbitt?
5. Who was the first Briton to win the 'King of the Mountains' title in the Tour de France?
6. In *My Fair Lady*, which character asked why a woman couldn't be more like a man?
7. Of what is Minerva the goddess?
8. Who wrote the theme music to 'Man Alive'?
9. Approximately what proportion of the air is oxygen?

1104

1. What is the Shanghai gesture?
2. Who first referred to the English as a nation of shopkeepers?
3. In which country is the Sierra Madre mountain range?
4. Who wrote *Braided Lives*?
5. Who won the 1984 single-handed transatlantic yacht race?
6. Which nuclear disaster greatly increased the relevance of *The China Syndrome*?
7. Which Motown star was fatally shot by his father in 1984?
8. Which former member of the Q-Tips became successful in his own right in 1983?
9. How long does it take light from the sun to reach the earth?

362

1. Christmas crackers.
2. Brian Boru.
3. Milan.
4. *The Dynasts.*
5. Seven – and subsequently after every nine games.
6. Leonard Sachs.
7. Shirley Williams, Bill Rodgers, David Owen, Roy Jenkins.
8. The Yardbirds.
9. Mars (Mons Olympus).

733

1. 5 years.
2. The duma.
3. Paraguay.
4. Sinclair Lewis.
5. Robert Millar (1984).
6. Professor Higgins.
7. Wisdom.
8. Tony Hatch.
9. One-fifth.

1104

1. Thumbing one's nose (cocking a snook).
2. Napoleon Bonaparte.
3. Mexico.
4. Marge Piercy.
5. Yvon Fauconnier.
6. The one on Three Mile Island.
7. Marvin Gaye.
8. Paul Young.
9. About 8 minutes.

363

1. What was banned on London underground trains from 9 July 1984?
2. To what were the Stoics indifferent?
3. How much more energy does Western Europe consume than it produces?
4. 'The Last Time I Saw Paris' is a well-known song. Who wrote the book of that name?
5. In which sport do members of the PGA engage?
6. Who plays Private Lurk in 'Up the Front'?
7. Who created Andy Capp?
8. Who was the Mick Jagger look-alike lead singer in the New York Dolls?
9. What is a jennet?

734

1. Which cathedral was badly damaged by fire in July 1984?
2. To whom was Louis XVI married?
3. For which country is N the international aircraft registration mark?
4. What is the name of the story that ends, 'Which came out of the open door – the lady or the tiger?'?
5. How many games did Jimmy Connors take in the 1984 Wimbledon men's singles final?
6. Which is the world's longest-running TV pop show?
7. Which sense did the poet Milton lack?
8. Who wrote the theme tune to 'Emmerdale Farm'?
9. Deficiency of which vitamin causes beri-beri?

1105

1. What does 'Führer' mean?
2. In which country was the Volstead Act passed in 1919?
3. Which two implements are depicted on the Russian flag?
4. Who wrote *Last Exit to Brooklyn*, which was the subject of legal action when published in Britain?
5. How many points are scored for a touchdown in American football?
6. Which gunfighter left a calling card in 'Have Gun Will Travel'?
7. At which English public school was Raymond Chandler educated?
8. Which instrument does jazzman John Coltrane play?
9. What type of fruit is a Blenheim Orange?

363

1. Smoking.
2. Pain or pleasure.
3. More than twice as much.
4. Elliot Paul.
5. Golf. (Professional Golfers' Association.)
6. Frankie Howerd.
7. Reg Smythe.
8. David Johansson.
9. A small Spanish horse.

734

1. York Minster.
2. Marie Antoinette.
3. USA.
4. *The Lady or the Tiger?* by Frank R. Stockton (1884) – and no one ever found out the answer . . .
5. Four.
6. BBC's 'Top of the Pops'.
7. Sight.
8. Tony Hatch.
9. Vitamin B.

1105

1. Leader, guide.
2. The USA. (Better known as Prohibition.)
3. Hammer and sickle.
4. Hubert Selby Jr.
5. Six (plus one further point if it is converted).
6. Paladin (played by Richard Boone).
7. Dulwich College.
8. The saxophone (tenor and soprano).
9. An apple.

364

1. If you were crapulous what would you be?
2. Who said, 'England is the mother of Parliaments'?
3. Nowadays, where is St Petersburg?
4. What is referred to in *Twelfth Night* and Farquhar's *The Recruiting Officer* and is now in the Victoria and Albert Museum?
5. Who succeeded Allan Brown as manager of Nottingham Forest?
6. Which was the first of the Ealing comedies?
7. How many times has the Rembrandt been stolen from the Dulwich College Art Gallery?
8. What type of instrument is a cor anglais?
9. Besides being a parasite, dodder is an example of a plant without what?

735

1. What is the army rank next below sergeant?
2. Of whom, and where, was it said by Edward III, 'Let the boy win his spurs'?
3. Under the flag of which country do the three biggest oil tankers operate?
4. What is the name of Launce's dog in *The Two Gentlemen of Verona*?
5. Who rode Cut Above to victory in the 1981 St Leger?
6. Who played the priest in *On the Waterfront*?
7. Which prime minister was instrumental in having Queen Victoria proclaimed Empress of India?
8. To what did John Lennon change his middle name, Winston?
9. What is kieselguhr, provided by a 150-foot-thick bed of fossilized plankton in Germany?

1106

1. To the nearest million, how many Jews were killed in the Holocaust?
2. What was the main contest of medieval tournaments?
3. Between which two territories is the Bering Sea?
4. What is the name of the donkey in *Travels with a Donkey*?
5. Of the five major Wimbledon tennis titles, how many were retained in 1984 by the 1983 winners?
6. What are Hollywood 'extras' now called?
7. What are the three secondary colours?
8. In which country is *Billboard* a leading pop magazine?
9. What sort of bird is an egress?

364

1. Drunk.
2. John Bright (in a speech at Birmingham in 1865).
3. The USA (one in Florida, one in Pennsylvania).
4. The Great Bed of Ware.
5. Brian Clough.
6. *Passport to Pimlico.*
7. Four.
8. A woodwind instrument rather like an oboe.
9. Chlorophyll.

735

1. Corporal.
2. The Black Prince at Crécy (1345).
3. France.
4. Crab.
5. Joe Mercer.
6. Karl Malden.
7. Disraeli.
8. Ono.
9. Polishing powder.

1106

1. Six.
2. Jousting.
3. Alaska and Siberia.
4. Modestine.
5. All five.
6. Atmosphere people.
7. Green, orange, purple.
8. The USA.
9. It isn't a bird, it's an exit.

365

1. What is a parlour boarder?
2. What were the followers of the philosopher Zeno called?
3. Of which country is CH the international vehicle identity mark?
4. Who continued Anthony Trollope's Barsetshire series long after his death?
5. Where were the first world athletic championships held?
6. Who played Irene in 'The Forsyte Saga'?
7. Who claimed to be the first man to skate in Africa? (Lucky if you've drawn this question, Maureen Hiron!)
8. From which book was the musical *Camelot* adapted?
9. To which country is the koala bear native?

736

1. Fulvous looks like a Lewis Carroll word, but it isn't. What does it mean?
2. At what percentage of alcohol did it become illegal to manufacture or sell drink during Prohibition in the USA?
3. Roughly how many times more energy does the Middle East produce than it consumes?
4. Whom did Emma Woodhouse marry?
5. Where would you wedel?
6. Who wrote the series *A Dance to the Music of Time*?
7. Who was Jean-Paul Sartre's constant companion?
8. Which group's first record was 'Come On'?
9. What are young otters called?

1107

1. Apart from Frenchmen in 1792, what do Septembrists shoot?
2. Who was appointed Poet Laureate in 1972?
3. Is there anything significantly peculiar about the river Mole?
4. Where was Oscar Wilde when he wrote 'The Ballad of Reading Gaol'?
5. Where was golf's British Open held for its first 11 years?
6. What appropriate misdemeanour merits instant dismissal from the BBC?
7. Who said that anybody who hates children and dogs can't be all bad?
8. Who composed the 'Moonlight Sonata'?
9. What is the chameleon's special characteristic?

365

1. A pupil at a boarding school who enjoys special privileges.
2. Stoics.
3. Switzerland.
4. Father Ronald Knox.
5. Helsinki, Finland (1983).
6. Nyree Dawn Porter.
7. The father of one of your editors, H. W. M. Hiron, who opened an ice-rink in Johannesburg around the turn of the century.
8. *The Once and Future King* by T. H. White.
9. Australia.

736

1. Dull yellow – tawny.
2. 0.5.
3. Ten.
4. Mr Knightley.
5. On a ski slope.
6. Anthony Powell.
7. Simone de Beauvoir.
8. The Rolling Stones.
9. Kittens.

1107

1. Partridges.
2. John Betjeman.
3. No, not as far as the editors know, but fire away . . .
4. Reading Gaol.
5. Prestwick, Scotland.
6. Having a TV without a licence.
7. W. C. Fields.
8. Beethoven.
9. Its ability to change colour to match its background.

366

1. What is the name of the Lord Mayor of London's official home?
2. Where did the Royal Military College move to from Great Marlow in 1812?
3. What are the grasslands of Russia called?
4. Who used the pen-name Michelangelo Titmarsh?
5. Which tennis doubles specialist is nicknamed 'Jumping Jack Flash'?
6. Who was successively a mill-boy, miner, amateur vocalist, and a major hit at the London Pavilion?
7. What did Sir William Mills invent that bears his name?
8. By what name is legendary bluesman McKinley Morganfield otherwise known?
9. What do frugivores eat?

737

1. What is contained in a tantalus?
2. In English history, who had a well-documented wart on his face?
3. What is the furthest destination by underground from Richmond without changing?
4. Who wrote *The Balkan Trilogy*?
5. What was Georgina Clarke's sporting claim to fame?
6. Where does the rhyming couplet 'But Englishmen detest a/Siesta' come from?
7. Who became President of Cyprus in 1960?
8. Which instrument did David play in the Bible?
9. How much does a gallon of water weigh?

1108

1. What is mal de mer?
2. What was 'safeguarding' in Great Britain in the 1920s?
3. To which island did USA immigrants go to be examined?
4. Who said, 'Out, damned spot, out, I say'?
5. What colour jersey does the overall race leader in the Tour de France cycle race wear?
6. In which 1967 spy film do Yul Brynner and Britt Ekland star?
7. For what does the N stand in C. N. Parkinson (the author of Parkinson's Law)?
8. Name any two members of Scaffold.
9. What kind of creature is a barbastelle?

366

1. The Mansion House.
2. Sandhurst.
3. The steppes.
4. Thackeray.
5. Paul McNamee.
6. Sir Harry Maclennan Lauder.
7. The 'Mills bomb' – a hand-grenade.
8. Muddy Waters.
9. Fruit.

737

1. Drink in decanters.
2. Oliver Cromwell.
3. Upminster.
4. Olivia Manning.
5. She was the first woman to umpire a main event singles final at Wimbledon.
6. Noël Coward's 'Mad Dogs and Englishmen'.
7. Archbishop Makarios.
8. The harp.
9. 10 lb.

1108

1. Seasickness.
2. Preventing 'unfair' foreign competition by means of an import tax, first levied in 1921.
3. Ellis Island.
4. Lady Macbeth.
5. Yellow.
6. *The Double Man.*
7. Northcote.
8. John Gorman, Roger McGough, Mike McGear.
9. A bat.

367

1. 900 can be written in Roman numerals as DCCCC. What is the alternative?
2. In the thirteenth and fourteenth centuries, which was regarded as the richest city in Europe?
3. In which country is the Black Forest?
4. In which town are Colin Watson's crime novels set?
5. In which sport do you have a tie-break?
6. Who plays the Resident Magistrate in Channel Four's 'The Irish RM'?
7. What nationality was the poet Longfellow?
8. How many semiquavers are there in a semibreve?
9. What variety of fruit is a cantaloup?

738

1. Where does the nightly ceremony of the keys take place?
2. What was the name of the British battleship, completed in 1906, whose design rendered all existing warships obsolete?
3. Which country forms the easternmost boundary of Indonesia?
4. Who wrote the *Gormenghast* trilogy?
5. Of which game is dakyu the Japanese form?
6. On which Bizet opera is *Carmen Jones* based?
7. After whom is Bolivia named?
8. In what subject did Paul Robeson, the singer, have a degree?
9. By what name is the purple fruit of the egg-plant known?

1109

1. By what name is the first day of Lent known?
2. Why was Leonidas famous?
3. What is Norway's parliament called?
4. Who wrote *Sesame and Lilies*?
5. Which young athlete left South Africa in 1984 to compete for Britain?
6. In which film, nominated for four Oscars, did Paul Newman make his directing début?
7. Who was the father of Admiral of the Fleet Sir Caspar John (who died in July 1984)?
8. What is the name of the pop opera composed and performed by The Who?
9. What colour is the gemstone peridot?

367

1. CM.
2. Lisbon, mainly because of treasures brought back by famous explorers such as Vasco da Gama.
3. Germany.
4. Flaxborough.
5. Tennis.
6. Peter Bowles.
7. American.
8. Sixteen.
9. Melon.

738

1. The Tower of London.
2. HMS *Dreadnought.*
3. Papua New Guinea.
4. Mervyn Peake.
5. Polo.
6. *Carmen.*
7. Simon Bolivar.
8. Law.
9. Aubergine.

1109

1. Ash Wednesday.
2. For his (unsuccessful) defence of the pass at Thermopylae in 480 BC.
3. The Storthing.
4. John Ruskin.
5. Zola Budd.
6. *Rachel, Rachel* (1968).
7. Augustus John, the painter.
8. *Tommy.*
9. Green.

368

1. For what product are the Smith & Wesson company famous?
2. How has the Royal Society (Edinburgh) changed since it was founded in 1783?
3. How many bridges across the Tiber were there in ancient Rome?
4. Name five of the six main Romance languages.
5. Which game is featured in *Tom Brown's Schooldays*?
6. Who wrote 'Don't Let's Be Beastly to the Germans'?
7. How many people can sit down to eat round a standard snooker table?
8. Where was Mrs Worthington advised not to put her daughter?
9. How many pounds of lettuce make up one thousand calories?

739

1. What won't a rolling stone gather?
2. Which American gunsmith was famous for his small, single-shot, muzzle-loading pistols?
3. Which is reputed to be the finest street on the American continent?
4. What is the Rig Veda? (Nothing to do with North Sea oil!)
5. Approximately how many tennis balls are used per year, worldwide?
6. Name the entertainments manager in 'Hi-de-Hi!'.
7. What was Hiram Maxim's best-known invention?
8. Who wrote the two-act opera *L'Elisir d'amore*?
9. How many calories does a large poached or boiled egg contain?

1110

1. Who meet in chapter houses?
2. Who is the muse of history in Greek mythology?
3. In which country is Dubrovnik?
4. Who is Apollyon?
5. Which Scottish international footballer was killed by lightning on a London golf course in 1964?
6. What is Top Cat's nickname in the cartoon series of that name?
7. What is special about a chess clock?
8. What happens (mechanically) when you press the soft pedal on a piano?
9. What is a pollywog?

368

1. Revolvers.
2. Its activities no longer include literature; it is now confined to science.
3. Eight or nine (no one seems to know for sure). Three are still standing.
4. French, Italian, Portuguese, Provençal, Romanian, Spanish.
5. Rugby.
6. Noël Coward (1943).
7. Twenty-four.
8. On the stage (by Noël Coward).
9. $12\frac{1}{2}$.

739

1. Moss.
2. Henry Derringer (1786–1868).
3. Avenida Rio Branco (ex-Central) in Rio de Janeiro.
4. It is the oldest of the four existing collections of Hindu scriptures (*c.* 1000 BC).
5. 25 million.
6. Jeffrey Fairbrother.
7. The first true modern machine-gun.
8. Donizetti.
9. Ninety.

1110

1. Clergy of a collegiate or cathedral church.
2. Clio.
3. Yugoslavia.
4. The Devil.
5. John White. (He played for Tottenham.)
6. T.C.
7. It is two clocks side by side within one construction.
8. The hammers strike one string instead of the usual three.
9. A tadpole.

369

1. How many acres are there in a square mile?
2. What are runes?
3. In which country is the Gobi desert?
4. Who wrote *The Light That Failed* and *Rewards and Fairies*? (Be warned, they are not his best-known books!)
5. What is used as the ball in the Afghan game of buzkashi?
6. What is the title of the last film in which Jane Russell appeared?
7. What was made at Nailsea?
8. Which group did Steve Marriott go on to form when he left the Small Faces?
9. Where are guavas grown?

740

1. Sanskrit is an old language. What does the word mean?
2. How long did Lent last in the second century?
3. Where is the Queen's Norfolk residence?
4. Who wrote *White Fang*?
5. All other things being equal, how high could the world high-jump record-holder jump if he were on the moon?
6. Who sits in judgement in Channel Four's 'Case on Camera'?
7. Who was the first barrister ever to be appointed a QC?
8. Who had a hit with 'Long Haired Lover from Liverpool'?
9. By what name is quicksilver otherwise known?

1111

1. Toc H is a comradely society. From where does the odd name come?
2. Where was Kilburn Wells?
3. Leningrad was partly built on rubble brought from where?
4. Who wrote *A Minstrel in France* and *Wee Drappies*?
5. In which country do they play holani, a form of hockey?
6. Who chairs BBC TV's 'Ask the Family'?
7. The eldest son at Knebworth House is Viscount Knebworth. What is his father's title?
8. Which was the first Gilbert and Sullivan opera?
9. How many square yards are there in a rood?

369

1. 640.
2. Letters of the alphabet of the ancient Teutonic peoples of north-western Europe.
3. China.
4. Rudyard Kipling.
5. The skin of a ritually slaughtered goat, filled with sand.
6. *Darker than Amber* (1970).
7. Decorative glass.
8. Humble Pie.
9. The West Indies.

740

1. Put together, perfected.
2. 40 hours. It had extended to about 40 days by the fourth century and was defined as beginning on Ash Wednesday (exactly 40 days before Easter) by the eighth or ninth century.
3. Sandringham.
4. Jack London.
5. $48\frac{1}{2}$ feet.
6. Alan King-Hamilton.
7. Sir Francis Bacon, in 1604.
8. Little Jimmy Osmond.
9. Mercury.

1111

1. The initials of Talbot House (toc is the signallers' former name for T).
2. Oddly enough, it was an eighteenth-century spa in Kilburn, north-west London.
3. London – after the Great Fire.
4. Sir Harry Lauder.
5. Turkey.
6. Robert Robinson.
7. The Earl of Lytton.
8. *Thespis* (1871).
9. $30\frac{1}{4}$ is one possibility but it varies locally up to 1,210 – the figure now generally accepted. (Accept anything in between.)

370

1. What does the name Tabitha mean?
2. Which soft-nosed rifle bullet was banned from use in war by the Hague Convention of 1899?
3. Which town replaced Riobamba, Ecuador, destroyed by an earthquake in 1797?
4. Who wrote the sci-fi classic *Tiger! Tiger!*?
5. Who was world speedway champion in 1981 and 1982?
6. Who plays Blake Carrington in 'Dynasty'?
7. After whom was the notorious Tammany Hall named?
8. In which Gilbert and Sullivan opera does Sir Roderic Murgatroyd's portrait come alive?
9. How many times its own weight can an average ant lift?

741

1. What utensils should be used for eating asparagus?
2. Name two of the three kings who ruled England in 1066.
3. For what is California's Napa Valley famed?
4. Which Betjeman poem featured Miss J. Hunter Dunn?
5. It is not an Olympic event, but roughly what is the record for throwing a cricket ball?
6. Which countryman presents the series 'One Man and His Dog'?
7. What were the poet H. W. Longfellow's Christian names?
8. Who was the lead singer in the Irish group Them who went on to greater success as a solo artist?
9. By what name is the Arabian gazelle-hound better known?

1112

1. Which is the holy day of the week for Muslims?
2. What is the link between the village of Eyam, Derbyshire, and 1665?
3. In which country are women prevented from ruling by the Salic Law?
4. In the Bible, who was visited by three 'comforters'?
5. Which Wimbledon tennis title did Pat Cash win in 1982?
6. Who created Reginald Perrin?
7. Who or what is or was a talma?
8. With which San Francisco five-piece band did Janis Joplin begin her short career?
9. How many legs has a fly?

370

1. Gazelle.
2. The dumdum.
3. Riobamba, but 3 miles away.
4. Alfred Bester.
5. Bruce Penhall.
6. John Forsythe.
7. Tammanend, an Indian Chief.
8. *Ruddigore.*
9. Fifty.

741

1. Fingers.
2. Edward the Confessor, Harold Godwin, William the Conqueror.
3. Wine.
4. 'The Subaltern's Love-Song'.
5. 422 feet.
6. Phil Drabble.
7. Henry Wadsworth.
8. Van Morrison.
9. The saluki.

1112

1. Friday.
2. The Plague arrived (via a trunk of clothes sent from London) and was successfully isolated at the cost of many lives.
3. France.
4. Job.
5. Junior Wimbledon.
6. David Nobbs.
7. A loose cloak named after the French actor J. F. Talma.
8. Big Brother and the Holding Company.
9. Six.

371

1. What are the two most vital ingredients of a Bloody Mary?
2. What occupied the site of St Paul's Cathedral before the Great Fire of 1666?
3. What now stands on the site of the Pantheon on the south side of London's Oxford Street?
4. Who was the skipper in *Moby Dick*?
5. What nationality is tennis-player Hanna Mandlikova?
6. Which programme gave birth to 'The Avengers'?
7. In fishing, what are otter boards?
8. Who was the first lead singer with the Drifters?
9. Approximately what proportion of the air is nitrogen?

742

1. Describe a pawnbroker's sign.
2. Which English king had a wife known as the She-wolf of Anjou?
3. Which river is also called the Sorrow of China?
4. How did the phrase 'Doubting Thomas' originate?
5. What was 'plunging', an event included in the 1904 Olympics?
6. Who became famous at the Oxford music hall and later in pantomime at Drury Lane?
7. With what is spangy played?
8. What was Scaffold's hit novelty record of 1967 with which the group is always closely associated?
9. What is a lactometer?

1113

1. What have amnesia sufferers lost?
2. Who was Fair Rosamond?
3. How long is the Suez Canal?
4. Whom did Pharaoh's daughter discover in the bulrushes?
5. How many games must a player be the first to take in order to win the tie-break at tennis?
6. Who always shouted 'Charge' as he rushed upstairs?
7. What is the link between Sloane Square (Chelsea) and the British Museum?
8. With whom did Peter Asher sing 'World Without Love' in the mid 1960s?
9. Which animal is traditionally associated with Lapland?

371

1. Vodka and tomato juice.
2. Old St Paul's.
3. Marks and Spencer.
4. Captain Ahab.
5. Czechoslovakian.
6. 'Police Surgeon'.
7. Wood or steel panels that keep the trawl net open.
8. Clyde McPhatter.
9. Four-fifths.

742

1. Three gold balls, hanging.
2. Henry VI.
3. The Yellow River (Hwang-Ho).
4. From Thomas, the disciple, who would not believe that Jesus had risen from the dead until he had actually seen him.
5. Attempting to float the greatest distance in 60 seconds from a standing dive at the side of a swimming pool.
6. Marie Lloyd (1870–1922).
7. Marbles.
8. 'Thank U Very Much'.
9. An instrument for testing density of milk.

1113

1. Their memories.
2. The mistress of Henry II. The jealous Queen Eleanor is said to have sought her with dagger and poison.
3. 100 miles.
4. Moses.
5. Seven (or by a margin of two clear points if six all is reached).
6. The eccentric brother in *Arsenic and Old Lace*.
7. Sir Hans Sloane: he founded the museum and the square was named after him.
8. Gordon Waller (as Peter and Gordon).
9. The reindeer – especially those of Santa Claus.